THE UNITED STATES AND CANADA

THE UNITED STATES AND CANADA

G. H. DURY
Professor of Geography and Geology
University of Wisconsin

and

R. S. MATHIESON
Senior Lecturer in Geography
University of Sydney

HEINEMANN EDUCATIONAL
BOOKS LTD · LONDON

Heinemann Educational Books Ltd

LONDON EDINBURGH MELBOURNE TORONTO
AUCKLAND SINGAPORE JOHANNESBURG IBADAN
HONG KONG NAIROBI NEW DELHI

ISBN 0 435 34270 3

First published 1970
Reprinted 1971

Published by Heinemann Educational Books Ltd
48 Charles Street, London W1X 8AH
Printed in Great Britain by
Fletcher & Son Ltd, Norwich

PREFACE

This book forms part of a comprehensive series designed for advanced secondary and general tertiary study. But quite apart from this consideration, we believe that there is ample room for a new overview of the geography of the North American continent. The theme is one which must continue to excite and to fascinate geographers.

The complexity of our subject is such that, despite all our determined efforts, we may not have avoided every potential error. We should be most grateful for comments and information directed to us in care of our publishers, and will undertake to add them to our running files of revision data.

G. H. DURY
The University of Wisconsin

R. S. MATHIESON
The University of Sydney

1 September 1969

ACKNOWLEDGEMENTS

In preparing the text and illustrations for this book, we have been aided principally by the statistical publications of the U.S.A. and Canadian governments, and by the research facilities of a number of institutions, including the University of Sydney, the State University of Florida at Tallahassee, and the Royal Geographical Society. We gratefully record the research assistance provided by our respective wives, Muriel Dury and Elli Mathieson.

The U.S. Information Service supplied the originals of Plates 3, 5, 8–10, 13–15, 17, 19–29, 34–41, 44–46, 49–57, 61–63, 66–71, 73, 75, 77–80, and 82; and, in addition, those of Plates 31 (courtesy Gordon Co.), 47–48 (courtesy Florida News Bureau), and 64 (courtesy National Geographic). The Canadian High Commission supplied the originals of Plates 12 and 19; of Plates 4, 7, 11, 32, 58, and 74 (National Film Board photographs), 16 and 18 (courtesy Photographic Surveys), 30 (courtesy Canadian Dept of Fisheries), 33 (courtesy Canadian Dept of Transport), 42 (courtesy Canadian Travel Bureau), 43 (courtesy MALAK), 60, 76, and 81 (courtesy George Hunter), and of Plate 72 (courtesy Canadian Pacific). We thank the agencies and individuals concerned, with whom the copyrights remain, for permission to reproduce the photographs here.

G. H. Dury
R. S. Mathieson

CONTENTS

PART ONE

PART TWO

LIST OF PLATES

LIST OF FIGURES

PART ONE

CHAPTER ONE

PERSPECTIVE AND PURPOSE

By people who live in other continents, the term *North America* is often used as though it were synonymous with the U.S.A. Indeed, it is so employed within the States themselves, for there is no unique name, corresponding to Mexicans or Canadians, for the inhabitants of the U.S.A. These commonly refer to themselves as North Americans, Americans, and American citizens, using one of these names from time to time in contradistinction to Canadian or Mexican. In actuality, the U.S.A. occupy less than half of the North American landmass. Mexico extends over three-quarters of a million square miles; the conterminous States measure three million square miles, with something over half a million additional square miles in Alaska; and Canada amounts to nearly four million square miles.

Mexico, being by common usage included in Latin America, falls outside the scope of this book. Latin America takes in the countries between Cape Horn and the Rio Grande, with territories in the South American continent, the great isthmus of Central America, some of the West Indian islands, and Mexico itself. All these countries have inherited Spanish or Portuguese language and traditions. By way of distinction from Latin America, the U.S.A. and Canada are not infrequently called Anglo-America. The implication of this term is presumably that the language of the peoples is English, and that social and political institutions are Anglo-Saxon in origin. But the implication will not bear detailed scrutiny: it certainly cannot be construed to mean that the peoples of the U.S.A. and Canada are exclusively English, or even British, by descent. Spanish influences – particularly on speech and on styles of building – are not lacking in the south-west of the U.S.A. Noticeable fractions of the population of that country have dominantly Irish or Italian ancestors, while a considerable minority is coloured. Canada, in its province of Quebec, has a determinedly French-speaking minority, of dominantly French descent. And whereas English is the one official language in the U.S.A., French shares official status in Canada. Again, although the political institutions of the two countries can be claimed to derive ultimately from British practice, and in particular from British parliamentary government, they involve marked and highly important distinctive elements of their own. Each of the two countries is a federation. The U.S.A., with a written constitution of great significance in its day-to-day political life, is a republic; and Canada, although acknowledging the British monarch as the titular head of state, acts in many practical contexts as if it were a republic also. At the same time, strong political contrasts distinguish Canada and the U.S.A. from one another. The greatest and at the same time the most obvious of these is that the two are separate nations. As will eventually be seen, their separate political identity is responsible with varying directness for certain geographical differences. These differences are all the more striking, because the U.S.–Canadian boundary cuts at right-angles across the major trend of physical distributions. Thus the two nation-states constitute our basic units. Even on the continental scale, however, political distributions need not be wholly tidy. Since the mid-Pacific archipelago of Hawaii constitutes a state of the American Union, it will be dealt with in subsequent chapters.

One of our tasks will be to trace the geographic and economic development of Canada and of the U.S.A., and to summarize, even if we do not fully explain, the way in which the U.S.A. has become enormously powerful in domestic production and in world economy and politics. The impact of this country on world affairs is not to be gainsaid. In terms of European history, however, the exertion of its several influences is recent. That exploration and settlement of North America by Europeans which set up new colonies, and which eventually led to the establishment of two new nations, began close to the year 1500, when some European peoples could already look back on two thousand years of tradition. These circumstances, allied with the initial colonial status both of Canada and of the U.S.A., have made it difficult for some Europeans – and perhaps for some British in particular – to take either North American country altogether seriously. If this statement is correct, it represents a grave error both of judgement and of justice. But it remains true that the full and massive entry of the U.S.A. on the world scene was delayed until well into the twentieth century.

Up to World War I (1914–18), and into the opening years of that war, the U.S.A. pursued a reasonably consistent policy of isolation from the politics of Europe. From the other side of the Atlantic, Europe appeared like the Balkans as seen from the rest of Europe – a collection of small countries adhering to outmoded political systems, and with explosive interrelationships. During the period of isolation, no friction at common boundaries, and for a long time no easy and rapid cultural exchanges, forced the existence of the U.S.A. on the attention of Europeans in general.

Engaging in the later stages of World War I, the U.S.A. rapidly disentangled itself from European politics after fighting ceased in 1918, refraining for instance from taking a place in the League of Nations. It was entirely possible for the peoples of Europe, deeply concerned with their severe economic troubles in the post-war years, and bitterly conscious of appalling losses of troops on the static battlefields of the trenches, to regard the brief intervention of American troops, and their comparatively brief tally of casualties, as little more than incidentals. Canada's entry into the war at its very beginning could be taken, and in general probably was taken, as the inevitable duty, however loyally observed, of a member of an imperial association. In addition, the comparative size of European and of Canadian populations allowed Canada's effort to be regarded as minor. During and after the four murderous years of war, few Europeans were inclined to think in terms of proportions.

Well before World War I, however, economic ties between Europe and North America had already become powerful and close – far more powerful, and far closer, than was generally realized. The brief political involvement of the U.S.A. with Europe in wartime was succeeded, about a decade later, by an event which rudely demonstrated the strength and complexity of economic ties – the slump of 1929. Beginning with disastrous losses on the New York Stock Exchange, this economic collapse spread throughout the occidental world, laying every national economy in ruins.

In World War II (1939–45) the U.S.A. was once more not immediately committed, although from the outset willing to display sympathy towards, and eventually to supply material help to, the U.K. It is pointless to speculate what might have happened, had not the American fleet been attacked by the Japanese airborne force at Pearl Harbor, Hawaii, in December 1941. The fact is that the attack took place. One may however conclude that, whatever views were entertained at the time about the intentions of the U.S.A. in the Atlantic area, the ruling Japanese politicians had no doubt about the weight of the force available in the Pacific. At one stroke the U.S.A. was committed on two enormously extensive fronts. In the Pacific, war with Japan meant alliance with Japanese-invaded China. On the Atlantic side, it meant war with Japan's ally Germany, and in consequence alliance with Russia, already invaded by German forces in the previous mid-year. The isolationism which had so long proved attractive, and which still in 1939 seemed possible to many, had in little more than two years been swept aside.

Because all but the neutral countries of mainland Europe were under German occupation or control, the principal invasion was planned in, and in 1944 launched from, Britain. On this occasion the forces of the U.S.A. assumed a major part, including provision of the supreme commander. After the war had ended, the U.S.A. undertook to help with, or even completely to effect, the restoration of shattered economies and social structures, and the establishment of political systems where former tyrannies had been destroyed. Nothing on the scale of the Marshall Plan, the comprehensive project of American aid in rebuilding, has ever before been conceived or executed. But neither help nor generosity proved sufficient: twenty years and more after the end of the war, the U.S.A. still maintains forces in Europe, in furtherance of political aims which are long in term and far-reaching in distance.

On the Pacific front, the technical power of the U.S.A. was unforgettably demonstrated by the detonation on the Japanese homeland of two atomic bombs. The second explosion brought the Pacific war to a sudden end. As in Europe, so in Japan, the U.S.A. assumed the task of reconstruction.

Subsequent events in China, in Germany, in Korea, and in Southeast Asia have meant continuing involvement, and have provided the U.S.A. with what are, in effect, common boundaries with nations of opposed policies. We are not here concerned to discuss the political questions involved: nor, for that matter, do we propose to examine the interconnections of economy, politics, and warfare. At the same time, it is pertinent to direct attention to the fact that the course which the U.S.A. has followed since 1941 would have been impossible, had the country not possessed the economic strength which, as one of our proper tasks, we shall describe. The extent to which military action supports political ends depends on the decisions of men. Similarly, the extent to which a country's resources are directed to military ends or to military potential is again a matter of human decision. Once again, the act of providing massive foreign loans, grants, credits, or gifts of foodstuffs is a political act. The development and exploitation of natural resources also constitute matters of decision, at levels ranging from the national down to the personal. But the existence and the nature of resources is outside human control. With the historical, technical, and economic processes which have enabled the U.S.A. to become industrially great, and which have enabled Canada to partake fully in the economic benefits of North American life, we shall be closely concerned.

One inevitable result of awareness of a particular country on the political level seems to be the establishment of national stereotypes, with which go generalizations about national character and national behaviour. It has long been common to define what are supposed to be national characteristics. European writers, particularly perhaps in the seventeenth and eighteenth centuries, when nation-states were becoming truly self-conscious, did not hesitate to ascribe vices to foreigners in the mass, and virtues to their own countrymen, also in the mass. Despite the manifest absurdity of such a practice, much the same kind of thing goes on today – as, for instance, when the inhabitants of the U.S.A. are categorized as friendly, effusive, loud-mouthed, naïve, arrogant, hospitable, or whatever it may be. We regret for the sake of our many friends in Canada and the U.S.A. that most mass descriptions of this kind are apt to be unflattering. And we deplore, as geographers, the fact that such descriptions implicitly deny the internal geographical variety which, in respect of both countries, we shall need to specify. Neither the North American land, nor North American society, is at all uniform.

It seems likely that the mistaken assumption of uniformity in this instance is based partly on the results of certain technical inventions, which exert their influence at the social level, and which reinforce the monolithic impression derived from a unitary political impact. We have in mind here not so much the mechanical inventiveness of North Americans as a group, but specific inventions which tend to present to the outside world quite narrowly selected aspects of North American life. In approximate order of impact, these are the gramophone, the silent film, the motor-car, the talking film, radio, television, and air travel. All these, making familiar chosen facets – and not always the most admirable facets – of present-day North American society, contribute to the production of a North American stereotype. We repeat that such a stereotype is misleading.

Canada and the U.S.A., apparently so simple in their external relationships, are vastly complex within. On any scale of economic measurement they are, as nations, vastly rich. But their wealth is unevenly spread: individual poverty can exist, of an extent dismaying to the central governments and incomprehensible to the generality of the people. Spatially, the size of the continent guarantees marked variations from place to place in anything that can be classed as a geographical characteristic – all aspects of the environment, all modes of grappling with this environment, and all potentialities of economic and social success.

In dealing with the internal variety of the two countries, we necessarily encounter one of the incompletely solved, and perhaps incompletely soluble, problems of geographical description – that of fixing regional boundaries, and indeed of the nature of such boundaries. Alternatively, the problem is one of defining combinations of geographical characteristics for particular areas. It is one thing to adopt the principle of regional treatment, and another to supply criteria of regional differentiation which would produce the same array of regions if they were also applied by others. The problem of regional division is particularly acute in North America, where dissatisfaction with the regional method is very strong in some quarters, while other geographers are seeking to reduce regional partition or regional identity to numbers and formulae.

It is true that the terms employed in many regional accounts of North America were for a long time mainly those of a simple – far too simple – breakdown into agricultural regions: Cotton Belt, Corn Belt, Spring Wheat Belt, and the like. Whatever the original intention of this scheme, the names came to carry harmful implications of monoculture, and of very direct and elementary interrelationships among relief, soils, climate, natural vegetation, and land use. For all that, they presumably have some kind of practical value: they are still widely current outside the literature of geography.

Again, we do not think that the existence of quite strong regional consciousness among the inhabitants of North America can fairly be disputed. Just as some Canadians are aware of living inside or outside of French Canada, or upon the Prairies, so many of the inhabitants of the U.S.A. will frequently refer to themselves as Southerners, Midwesterners, or New Englanders. But regional consciousness of this kind may well be a political matter, rather than a direct and explicit response to a geographical setting. Sectionalism has long been powerful in the internal politics of North America, where it is continuously reflected in the daily press. It operates at the state or province level, or still more frequently at the level of groups of provinces and states. Any regional subdivision obtained by reference to regional consciousness would then prove to have political boundaries. Furthermore, it is hard to judge whether sectional economic and political interests bring regional consciousness into the open, or whether it is regional consciousness that determines politics.

It might be thought that the great towns of North America could provide the basis for regional subdivision, a region being taken as the catchment or service area of a given town. The town–country symbiosis is certainly a theme which until recently has had far less attention than it deserves. However, there is no such thing as an individual catchment area, service area, area of influence, tributary area, or hinterland, exclusively belonging to a single town. In general, the larger the town, the larger the area serving and served by it, and the more complex the range of urban functions. Very large towns extend their influences over areas which include numbers of smaller towns: hence the concept of an urban hierarchy. It would certainly be possible, were the information available, to draw up a regional classification founded on the activities and influence of towns ranking higher than a selected hierarchical grade; and something of the kind seems likely to emerge from the researches into urban geography now being determinedly pursued in North America. For our present purposes, however, such a classification would be unduly limited, as making insufficient allowance for the spatial variation of the physical landscape.

The central part of the problem of regional description is perhaps that regional differences are subjectively observed, but that regional analysis and synthesis ought to be objective. Our extensive travels in North America convince us, as many others before us have been convinced, that regional differences do exist. While we do not favour the mystical concept of regional personality, we concede the case for regional character. Each of us in respect of research interests is a systematic geographer, but we find it useful in many contexts to deal with North America in terms of areal cohesion and areal contrast. The difficulties lie in the definition of regional character, and in identifying and explaining the forces which have created it.

With these various ideas in mind, we have adopted a regional classification which allows the North American continent to be discussed in the broad terms appropriate to the aims of the series to which this book belongs. Being limited in our scope of regional subdivision by the allowable extent of text, we have adopted a grouping into seven large areas (excluding Offshore America, which constitutes an eighth composite area). These units could perhaps be called mega-regions: for we regard the thirty lesser divisions into which these areas are broken down as macro-regions. Thus, the chapter on the Northeast area deals with five macro-regions, of which one, the Industrial Northeast, is itself susceptible of partition into eight regions with an average extent of about 20,000 square miles. It is these least subdivisions which correspond approximately to the regional breakdown made by one of us for the British Isles, where the average regional area is about 10,000 square miles, smaller but of the same order. In dealing with North America, we necessarily work on a large and distinctly coarse scale. The potential degree of regional subdivision on smaller and finer scales is illustrated by a contemporary account of Canada, for which no fewer than sixty-eight regions are distinguished.

Our classification in part reflects the exigencies of textbook design, separate chapters being allocated to each of the large areas. Within the area treated in a given chapter, however, the division into regions is either physiographic or economic. We make use in part of a well-known and carefully thought out physiographic scheme, which is widely used both in and outside geography. The practical advantages of physiographic subdivisions are that their boundaries are defined with reference to visible changes in the form and texture of the landscape. We are of course aware of the difficulties which arise where no rapid change occurs – as for instance where the Southern Plains merge imperceptibly into the Interior Lowlands, or where, in the same general part of the continent, changes in land use fail to coincide with change in terrain. However, a physiographic classification provides a general basis for areal and locational description: and the overt use of a single set of criteria frees us from seeming to imply that all geographical characteristics change with equal speed across a single set of boundaries. Despite the remarkable recent and current progress of thematic studies, we consider that geography has a standing need for areal and locational treatment. One central purpose of the regional chapters in Part Two is to show what the country is like; and we see no objection to treating different parts in different ways.

We mean to offer generalizations. Many of these should desirably be tested, and modified as appropriate, by computer analysis of massive data. There can be no doubt that data-processing will transform the analysis of geographical information of almost every kind; but pending the prosecution of the necessary researches, we have not hesitated to make summary statements about North American geography, either in the regional section where the areal units are large, or in the systematic chapters where we are concerned more to identify trends than to describe the geographical situation at an instant of time. Main responsibility for the systematic section rests with one of us (GHD), that for the regional section with the other (RSM); but the task of writing has been joint. Throughout the book we have relied heavily on original data, and particularly upon analysis of statistics published by agencies of the two national governments. On the chosen scale of working, regional statistics are based principally on returns for entire states or provinces; in consequence, the interregional contrasts which make themselves evident are likely to be less marked in our account than they are on the ground. The systematic section can be regarded either as introductory to the regional accounts, or as consolidated reviews of the total effects produced by selected activities in the various regions. Whatever the sequence followed, we urge that reading be at all times accompanied by the use of an atlas.

For the sake of ease in reading we have refrained from inserting references either in the running text or as footnotes. Where other authors have been drawn upon, they are however named in the text and listed in the chapter bibliographies. These bibliographies, which include additional material also, have intentionally been kept within very strict limits and scope, in accordance with the purpose of the whole book.

Finally, we should like to stress that a geographical text can never be fully up to date. By the time that statistics have been collected, processed, published, drawn upon as source material, and reassembled, a year or two at least must pass. There is a subsequent time-lag in writing and in the mechanics of book-production, and a still further delay between the publication of one edition and revising for the next. Swift events can easily outrun the printed text. We recommend our readers to refresh their acquaintance with North American geography with the aid of current periodical literature, which gives more room for extended treatment of single topics than is available to us here.

CHAPTER TWO

LIVELIHOOD AND LAND USE

With their combined area of some $7\frac{1}{2}$ million square miles, Canada and the continental U.S.A. are more than sixty times as extensive as Great Britain, and almost nine-tenths as extensive as the U.S.S.R. Their combined population total is closely similar to the total population of the U.S.S.R., but is less than four times the total of the much smaller British Isles. This means that the average population-density in North America, about 23 p.s.m., is much less than the average for the British Isles of about 440. But averages of this kind are not very helpful. They conceal for example the difference between Canada, larger than the U.S.A. but with only about a tenth of the combined population, and the U.S.A. itself. The respective average densities are less than 3, and about 50, per square mile. National averages in their turn conceal the contrasts between huge expanses of land which, if they are peopled at all, are peopled very thinly, and great clusters of towns where the inhabitants are numbered by the million. Between the wastes and the towns come areas of intermediate density, also greatly variable among themselves.

In contrast with the British Isles, Canada and the U.S.A. have farmland sufficiently extensive and sufficiently productive to yield national surpluses of certain foodstuffs. As will be seen in a later chapter, the actual level of production is subject to regulation – amounting at times and in some respects to close control – by the two national governments. But both countries have great potential surpluses of basic foodstuffs. Canada's role as a wheat exporter is well known; but it is too seldom realized that the U.S.A. produces more than twice the amount of wheat that the country needs for its own use. The total extent of farmland in North America is about two million square miles – about sixty-five acres per head of population, and more than sixty-five times as much per head as in the British Isles. Whereas the essential task in Great Britain is to sell enough exported goods abroad to pay for imports of food, both Canada and the U.S.A. must deal with their surplus production, either by finding overseas markets or by restricting output.

The matter is far more complex than may immediately appear.

It is not merely a question of producing for export, for external sales imply that customers can pay. A number of possible purchasing countries, however, cannot afford to pay. Again, much of the North American interior was settled by farmers, on the initial assumption that the farms would be to a considerable extent self-reliant, and then later on the modified assumption that markets would be available for surplus products. For a long time markets were indeed available. But a whole complex of changes, including enormously increased productivity on the best land, means that part of the surplus production is, in effect, unwanted.

The extent of North American success in agriculture can be readily indicated in general terms. Although the proportionate contributions to world production, which are about to be cited, depend partly on the size of the North American landmass, it is still true that *per capita* agricultural output there is high. Some portions of Canada, and considerable portions of the U.S.A., are highly favoured agriculturally. The two countries produce about 15 per cent of the world's wheat crop – 9 per cent in the U.S.A. and 6 per cent in Canada. The U.S.A. alone grows 45 per cent of the world's maize. Its output of all the main food grains, and that of potatoes, exceeds domestic consumption. Its meat production amounts to one-fifth of the world total. It feeds more than 10 per cent of the world's cattle and pigs, and both produces and consumes a fifth of the world's meat. It cuts nearly a fifth of the world's annual total of timber, and grows more than a quarter of the world's cotton.

Not only in some leading categories of farm produce, and in lumber, but also in respect of minerals, North America is a major primary producer and exporter. This range of functions again points up the geographical contrasts between North America and Great Britain, where the former external market for the one great primary product, coal, has largely been destroyed. It is true that North American coal exports are not of great economic significance; but, at the same time, the U.S.A. is a leading producer, with a fifth of world output to its record. The two countries combined account for about a third of the world's total extraction of crude oil, with the U.S.A. raising about ten times as much as Canada. The difference narrows considerably in respect of iron ore, measured by iron content – the U.S.A. 16 per cent, Canada 6 per cent of the world total, with Canada's share increasing fast. In the exploitation of certain non-ferrous metal ores, Canada comes to the fore. Whereas the U.S.A. raises about a quarter of the world's annual production of copper ore, against Canada's 10 per cent, and 13 per cent of the lead against less than 10 per cent, Canada is alone responsible for the extraction of two-thirds of the world's nickel ore, and takes a larger share than does the U.S.A. in the combined production of 35 per cent of the zinc ore. As with iron, all these proportions are stated in terms of metal content. A distinctive item among the non-metallic minerals is asbestos, in the mining of which Canada is as prominent as in the extraction of nickel ore.

Pre-eminence in leading divisions of agriculture and mining is matched in North America by equal pre-eminence in manufacturing. Among the available indices of manufacturing strength, it will be enough to select a few of the most obvious. Under this head, the U.S.A. far surpasses Canada in terms of bulk output, although once again, if allowance is made for *per capita* production, Canada too appears in a position of great manufacturing strength.

The U.S.A. consumes about a third of the world's total output of energy. It produces about a third of the world's total of sulphuric acid – a useful rough-and-ready index of industrial activity: a second such index is the output of crude steel, of which the U.S.A. makes about a quarter of the world total. On levels of greater complexity come the manufacture and export of road vehicles and of aircraft: the U.S.A. makes, and operates, something like half the road vehicles in the whole world.

Despite their surpluses, actual or potential, of many primary products, the two North American countries are heavily involved, on account of their elaborate industrial and economic activities, with foreign trade. It is not surprising that the U.S.A. has become a major seafaring nation. The difficulty here is to explain why the main development of its shipbuilding yards, and the expansion of its merchant marine, were so long delayed – to be precise, up to World War II – unless by reference to the policy of isolation discussed in the previous chapter.

LABOUR FORCE AND NATIONAL PRODUCT

As Fig. 2:1 shows, about 2 in 5 people in North America are in paid employment (including self-employment). The largest single occupational class is that of employment in manufacture, which absorbs about a quarter of the total labour force – this, despite the fact that some manufacturing tasks are highly automated. Employment in manufacture, in mining (plus, in Canada, other forms of primary production except agriculture), in transport and public utilities, and in wholesale and retail distribution combines to account for half the total workforce. Strict comparison between Canada and the U.S.A. in respect of the remaining half is made difficult by the forms in which statistics of employment are published. However, as the diagram indicates, service occupations and employment in government agencies require a large fraction – about 20 per cent – of the total of workers. Numbers employed in agriculture are of the same order as numbers unemployed; each of these classes amounts to about 7 per cent of the total workforce of 80 million. The proportion in agriculture is higher than the 4·5 per cent recorded for the U.K., but is of the same order. In North America, as in the U.K., agriculture makes a modest demand upon the work strength.

Generally similar proportions appear in Fig. 2:2, which shows the percentage origin of national pro-

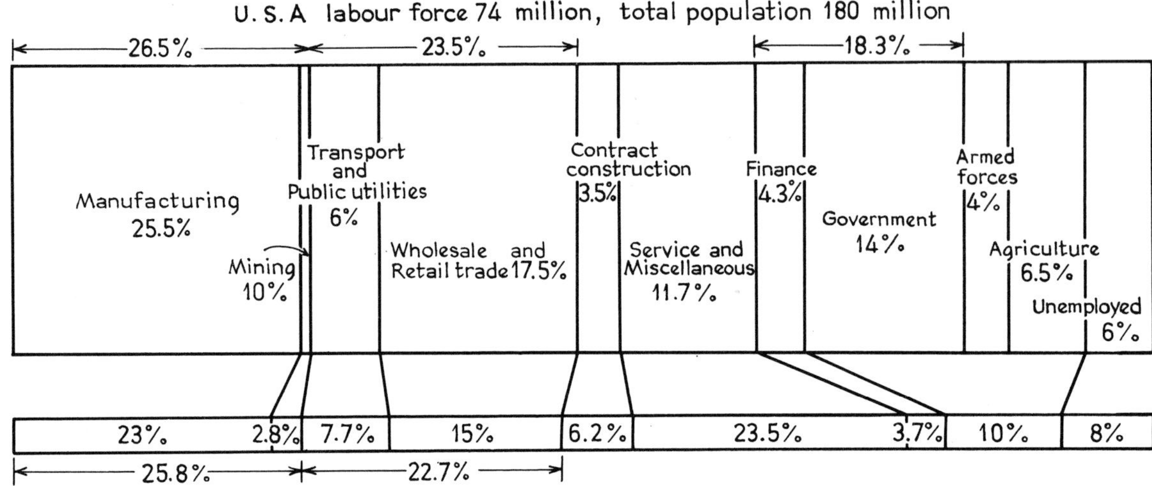

FIG. 2:1 Labour forces

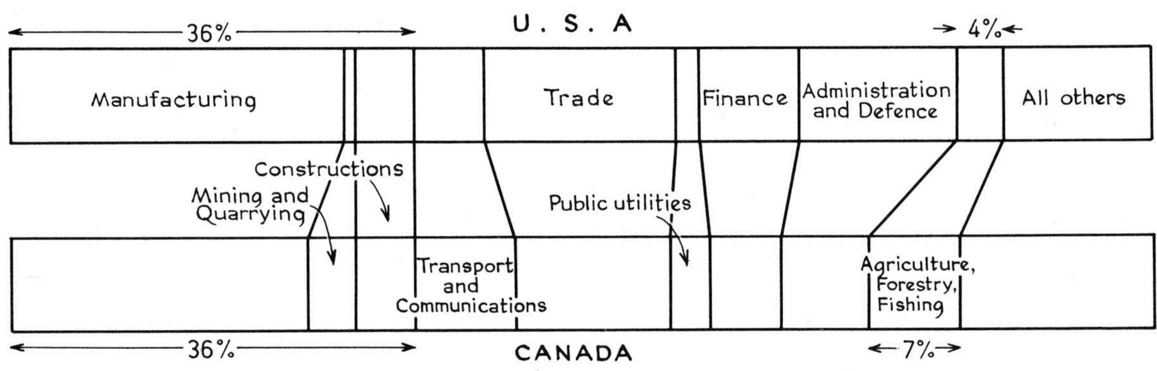

FIG. 2:2 Percentage origin of national products.

duct for the two North American countries. Manufacturing, trading, and finance combined account for 55 per cent of the national product of the U.S.A. and for 45 per cent of that of Canada. The U.S.A. displays a greater proportional concern with defence than does Canada, while the latter relies the more heavily on the exploitation of mines, quarries, farms, and forests. In both countries, agriculture's contribution to the national product is less than its demand on the workforce: in these terms, manufacture is about half as productive again as agriculture.

EXTERNAL TRADE

The U.S.A. in the mid-1960s imported goods at the rate of some $110 a year per head of population, and exported at the rate of about $135 per head. The total value of trade per head was about half the corresponding value for the U.K. Finished manufactures account for nearly 60 per cent of all export trade, while finished and semimanufactures supply nearly 75 per cent. The greatest single class of exports is machinery and vehicles, amounting to nearly one-third of all export trade by value (Fig. 2:3). At the same time, the U.S.A. depends on external markets to take about a third of its tobacco and cotton-farm products, and about two-fifths of its cash grains: in these respects it is a notable primary producer.

Finished manufactures are also prominent in the

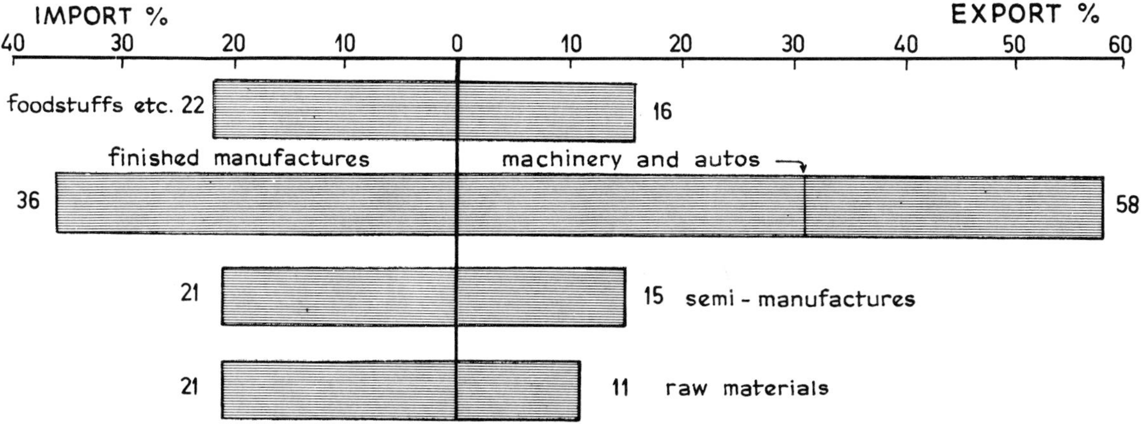

FIG. 2:3 Comparison of import and export trades of the U.S.A.

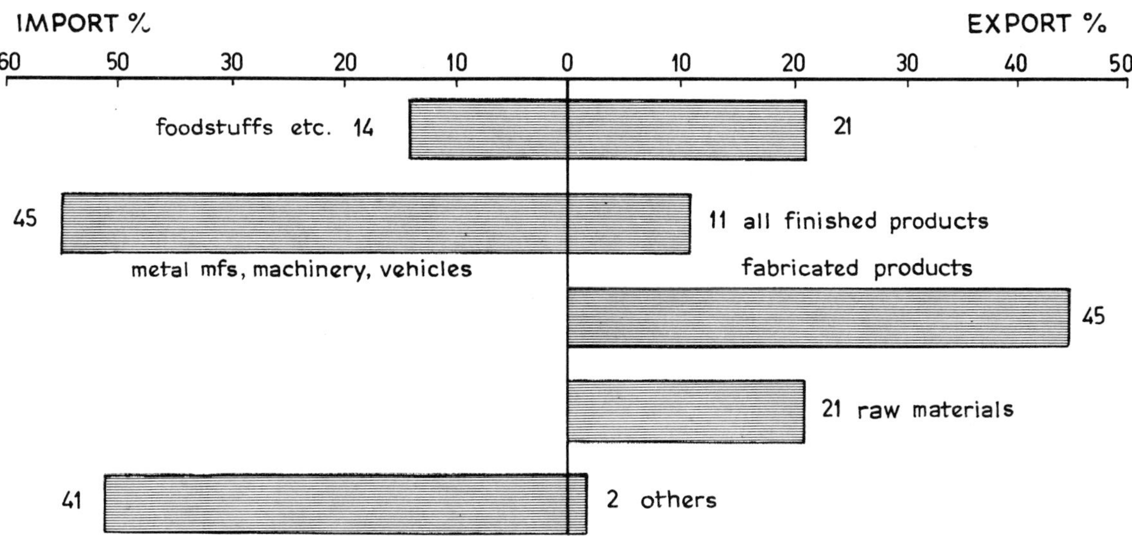

FIG. 2:4 Comparison of import and export trades of Canada.

import trade, of which they take more than a third share. But the import trade is more nearly balanced than the trade in exports, with foodstuffs, semi-manufactures, and raw materials all accounting for at least a fifth of the total import value.

Canada in the early and middle 1960s recorded a very high, and rising, level of external trading, with imports and exports alike running in the mid-1960s at about $425 per head per year. That is, Canada was buying and selling about twice as much *per capita* as the U.K. The form in which the records for Canada are presented makes it difficult both to effect a direct comparison with the U.S.A., and to analyse the import trade in much detail. However, the summary diagram (Fig. 2:4) shows that Canada is, on balance, an exporter of foodstuffs, a supplier of fabricated products and raw materials – timber, pulp, newsprint, and metallic minerals – and a customer for manufactured goods, among which, for instance, textiles contribute part of the unspecified 41 per cent of import value.

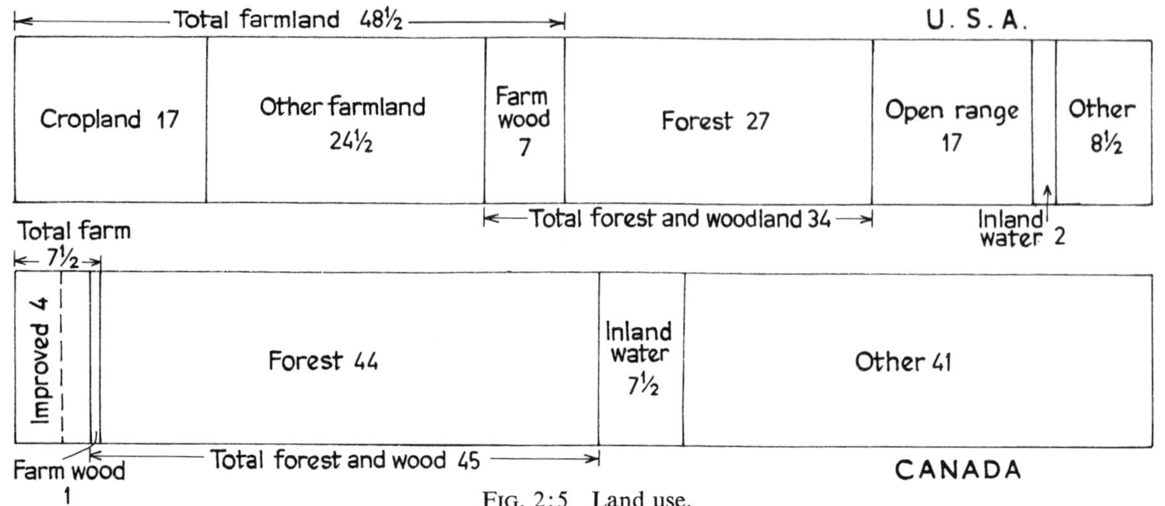

FIG. 2:5 Land use.

LAND USE

About half the total area of the U.S.A. is in farmland, and another 14 per cent is used for grazing under open-range conditions (Fig. 2:5). Rather more than a quarter is in forest other than farm woodland, while forest and farm woodland combined take more than a third of the whole. The percentage of improved farmland is distinctly less than that recorded for England, but is of the same order as the percentage for the Irish Republic. Cropland, amounting to 17 per cent of the total area, is proportionately only half as extensive in the U.S.A. as in England.

Canada is very different. Nearly half the total area is forested. That is to say, forest in Canada is as extensive as farmland in the U.S.A. Less than 8 per cent of the country is in farms (Fig. 2:5), and not much more than half the farmland is classed as improved. Inland water is as extensive as farmland. About two-fifths of the country belongs either to the tundra of the north or to unusable and unproductive mountain in the west.

CONCLUSION

Certain contrasts between Canada and the U.S.A. are already making themselves apparent. But data for whole countries are bound to obscure internal contrasts, such as those outlined later in the book. This chapter has attempted neither detailed description nor explanation: it is meant merely to present in very general terms some leading facts about the present geographical condition of North America.

This short account is both the starting-point and the objective of the chapters which follow, where selected aspects of the physical and historical backgrounds, selected leading aspects of present-day geography, and regional characteristics are discussed in turn. There has been nothing inevitable in the developments which have brought North America to its present geographical state, even though this state reflects, in part, decisions taken on the national level. Different decisions could have produced different circumstances. But only by taking into account the potential and the problems of the environment, and the ways in which North Americans have actually chosen to exploit the potential and to counter the problems, can one hope to understand the geography of North America today.

CHAPTER THREE

PHYSIQUE

North America is built upon a grand, clearly defined plan. The core of the continent is the Laurentian Shield in the north reaching 1200 miles from the Arctic coast to the Great Lakes, and 1800 miles from Labrador almost to the mouth of the Mackenzie. In the west, the Cordillera, more than 1000 miles wide in places, runs 4500 miles from the Mexican border to the extremities of Alaska. In the east of the U.S.A. rise the Appalachians, linking with the mountainous country of New England and the easternmost Canadian border in a system measuring 1600 miles from end to end. The interior of the continent includes high plains next to the Cordillera, and lowlands reaching from Lake Winnipeg to the Gulf. The High Plains extend from near the Arctic coast to the Rio Grande, a distance of 3000 miles, and attain widths of 500 miles. The Interior Lowlands, broken in a few places by upland blocks, merge southward into the still lower ground of the Gulf coast; this, sweeping round the southern end of the Appalachians, is extended by the Atlantic Coastal Plain.

These major elements in the physique of North America cannot be comprehended as wholes except on a map. Nevertheless, indigenous peoples and settlers were alike compelled to respond to their total qualities. The Appalachians for a long time constituted a barrier between the Atlantic coast and the inland; modern traffic is still concentrated on a dozen routes across the Cordillera; and the multitudinous lakes and drainage-ways of the Southern Shield led first the Indians and then the explorers and trappers to move about in summer by canoe. This sample of responses could be very greatly extended, although it would soon come to include references not simply to the form of the ground but also to climate – indeed, climate has already appeared in the mention of travel on the Southern Shield. On the grasslands of the High Plains, migratory herds of bison were incorporated in migratory systems of Indian hunting; in the dry Southwest, fixed Indian settlements depended chiefly on water-supply and on the growing of corn; in the cold north, the Eskimo practised winter fishing and sealing, and summer hunting of the caribou.

Whether immigrants or American-born, settlers soon came to recognize, and to name, physical divisions of a smaller kind – the Blue Ridge in the Appalachians, the Adirondacks in New England, the Mississippi Delta, the Great Valley of California, the Canadian Prairies. These are divisions of the physical landscape which, although far too large to take in by a sweep of the eye, are nevertheless small enough for their unity to be recognized in the field: many of them, recognized as units by the Indians, had their Indian place-names taken over by the pioneers.

Later took place the deliberate assessment of the form of the ground by geologists and geomorphologists. That assessment was in part fostered by the compulsory interest in landform and land quality which pioneering settlement entailed. But it was in part also an expression of the modern spirit of scientific inquiry, which underwent its main first development in the nineteenth century – precisely when the interior of North America was being turned to farmland, and when the West was being opened. Some of the scientific accounts of western explorations are classics of their kind. The joint outcome of judgement by settlers on the one hand, and scientific investigation on the other, is a complete system of physical subdivision (Fig. 3:1). This is widely accepted by geographers, and proves readily acceptable to others.

The Laurentian Shield

The Laurentian Shield is an ancient crustal block, its contorted, altered, heavily-injected and highly-

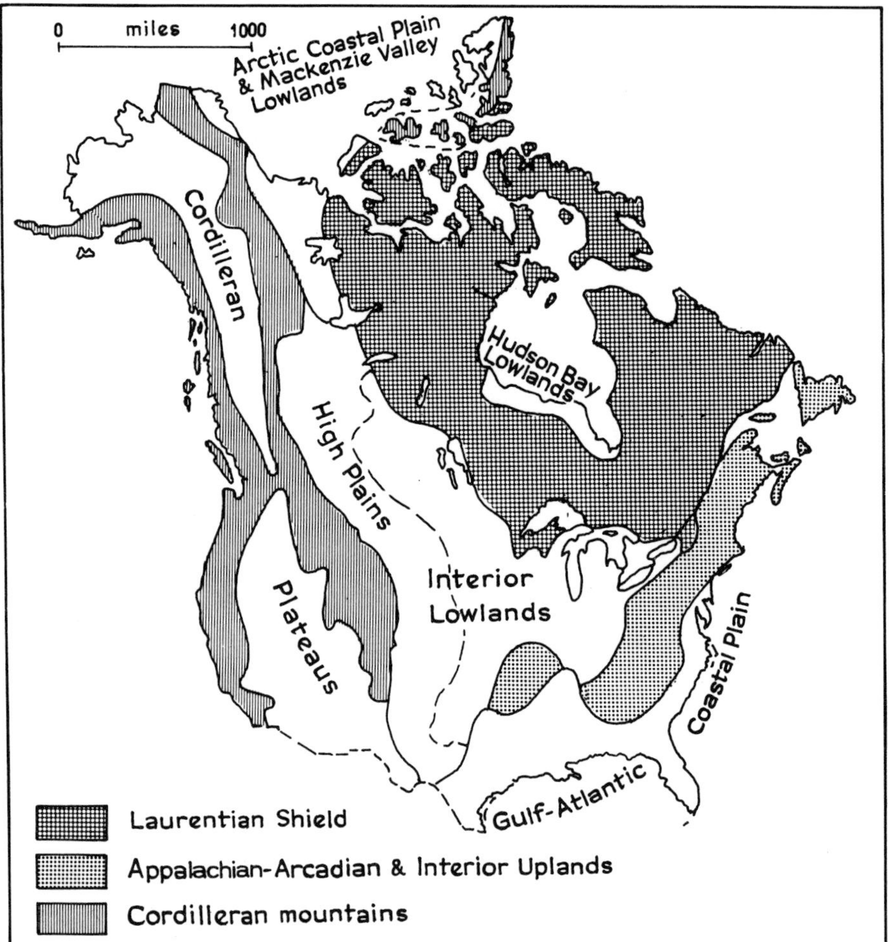

FIG. 3:1 Major physical divisions.

mineralized Precambrian rocks recording the history of more than one episode of mountain-building. Its counterpart in Europe is the Baltic Shield. In all probability, these two shields were once united with the Arctic Archipelago of Canada, with Greenland, and with the Siberian Shield in a super-continent, Laurasia. This super-continent appears to have sundered apart, its colossal fragments drifting slowly away from one another.

Five or six hundred million years ago, the Shield was already reduced to extremely feeble relief. Its former mountains had all been destroyed; their planated roots, truncated by an extensive erosional plain, displayed the results of alteration at great depths underground. Then, sinking beneath the sea, the great block was covered with the sediments which now form rocks of Palaeozoic age (Table 1:1). When uplift brought these rocks above sea-level, they cannot fail to have protected the crystalline basement so long as they resisted erosion. When, eventually, they were largely stripped away, the basement remained so low in elevation, and proved so resistant, that it has undergone no more than a modest lowering. Strong relief occurs only where uplift has been greatest, or where the Shield terminates in an abrupt rim. It rises sharply as much as 2000 ft above the St Lawrence Lowlands, attains heights of 5000 ft in the Adirondacks and the Torngak Mountains of Labrador, and exceeds 10,000 ft in Ellesmere Island. Elsewhere, little of it rises above 1500 ft and much is below 1000. Northwards towards the Arctic coast, and throughout most of the great arc of its southern limit, the Shield slopes gently away underground, passing gradually

TABLE 3:1
The Geological Time-Scale

Era	System	Approximate age (in millions of years)
	Recent* Pleistocene*	2
Tertiary	Pliocene Miocene Oligocene Eocene Palaeocene	70
Secondary	Cretaceous	135
	Jurassic	180
	Triassic	225
Primary	Permian	270
	Pennsylvanian	310
	Mississippian	350
	Devonian	400
	Silurian	440
	Ordovician	500
	Cambrian	600
	Pre-Cambrian	

*The recent and Pleistocene systems can be grouped together as the Quaternary.

beneath what remains of the complete former cover.

A series of lakes studs the southern rim. The chief are the Great Bear and Great Slave Lakes, Lakes Athabaska and Winnipeg, and the members of the Great Lakes system – Superior, Michigan, Huron, Erie, and Ontario. The lakes owe part at least of their existence, and much of the detail of their form, to the glaciation of the last Ice Age. During this last million years or so of geological time, the Shield underwent its only severe erosion since the Precambrian.

A continental ice-sheet, probably coming into being on the high ground east of Hudson's Bay and the islands to the north, thickened and spread, merging with growing local accumulations in a mass which attained a thickness of 10,000 ft and an area of five million square miles. Ice spread far beyond the limits of the Shield: it traversed the plains on the west, as far as the foot of the Canadian Rockies; on the south, it reached a line roughly defined by the present Mississippi and Ohio Rivers; on the southeast, it reached the present coastline at Long Island.

Over the whole of the Shield its main effect was erosive. Four major episodes of ice-accumulation, advance, and decay have left the subdued plain intricately roughened in detail, its drainage complex and disorganized, and a large fraction of its extent bare of soil. Erosion continued even when the ice had stagnated and was melting back; for meltwater flowing in tunnels through and under the ice was able to cut thousands of minor channels. In its glaciated character, the Laurentian again resembles the Baltic Shield of Europe.

Under the weight of the ice-caps, much or all of the Shield was depressed – as Greenland still is to-day. The maximum depression is likely to have been some 3000 ft, compensating for the loading of ice 10,000 ft thick. But the southern and south-eastern parts of the Shield, which have been best studied, were less severely affected. Recovery is not yet complete (Fig. 3:2); in the north of the Superior Basin and along the St Lawrence, the land is still rising at a rate of 15 or 16 inches a century.

Fluctuations of the ice-margins, glacial damming of drainage, and warping of the crust combined in the Great Lakes–St Lawrence area to produce a complex sequence of change. As late as 8000 or 7500 years ago, ice still occupied the northern parts of the existing lake basins, forcing drainage to pass southwards to the Mississippi, or through the Mohawk gap and the Champlain–Hudson Trench (Fig. 3:3). When the melting ice uncovered the valley of the Ottawa River, this stood low enough to act as an outlet for water spilling from Lake Huron across the site of Lake Nipissing. But the rebound of the land which followed further melting raised the Ottawa spillway, and finally brought into use the Great Lakes–St Lawrence system as it now exists.

New England to Newfoundland

Like the Laurentian Shield, the high ground of Newfoundland, parts of the Maritime Provinces, New England, and the Appalachians, has its counterpart in Europe. Here again appear signs that the European and North American continents were once joined together.

In the British Isles, two mountain systems converge. One, represented in Norway, Scotland,

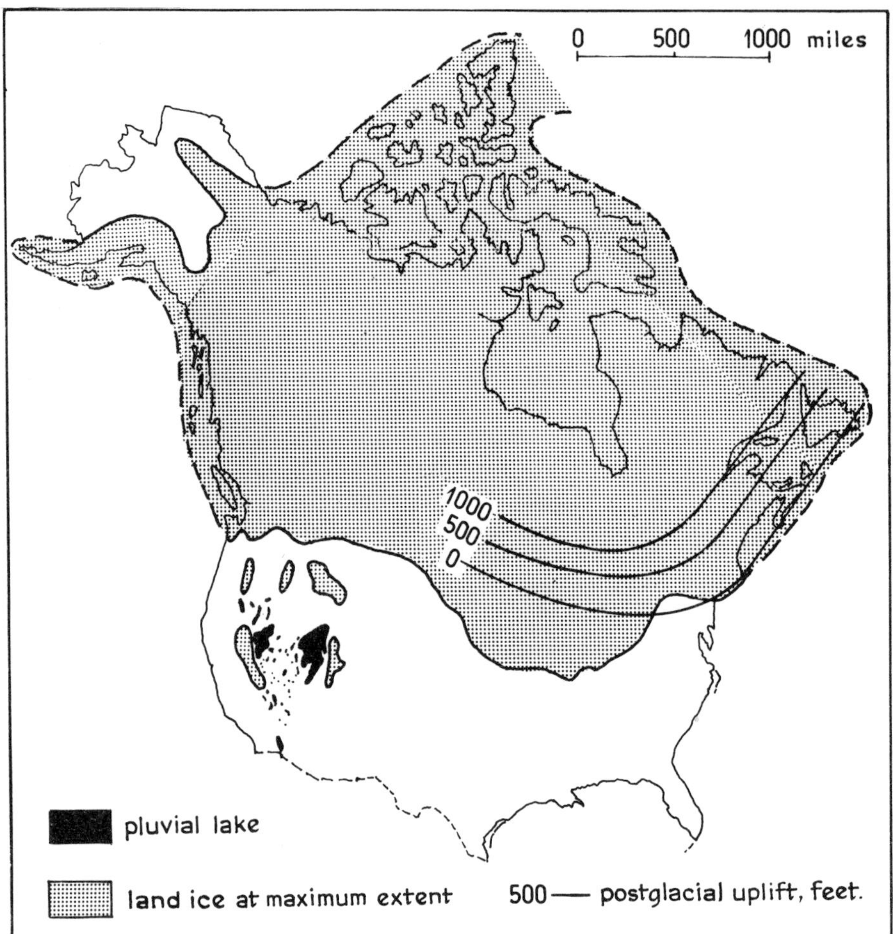

FIG. 3:2
Extent of ice at last glacial maximum; amount of uplift since last glacial maximum; pluvial lakes in the Cordillera, at last maximum extent.

northwest Ireland, and north and central Wales, is the system of the Caledonides. Its grain in the British area runs N.E.–S.W. The second, the system of the Altaides, is represented in the Massif Central of France, in Brittany, in southwest England, South Wales, and the south of Ireland. Its structures, abutting on or even overwhelming the structures of the older Caledonides in Wales and Ireland, point westwards into the Atlantic. On the American side of that ocean, the two systems complete their crossing.

In New England, Newfoundland, and the higher parts of the Maritime Provinces, rock formations of ages greater than Carboniferous are incorporated in the remnants of ancient mountains. Some of the rocks are Precambrian; others are granitic, emplaced not later than Devonian times when the last main episode of crustal deformation occurred. In the usual way, mountain-building was accompanied by alteration of rocks at depth. Prolonged erosion has caused these rocks to appear widely at the surface from the Hudson Valley to Newfoundland. They help to compose the remains of what, in North America, correspond to the Caledonides of Europe. The Altaides are represented only in the lower eastern parts of the Maritime Provinces, where certain of the rocks are coal-bearing.

During Triassic times, considerable faulting took place in New England, mainly on north–south lines. Long strips of crust foundered; the trenches were filled with sediment and received extruded basaltic lava. In consequence, the larger south–north valleys contrast strongly in their geological quality with the enclosing high ground. But most of

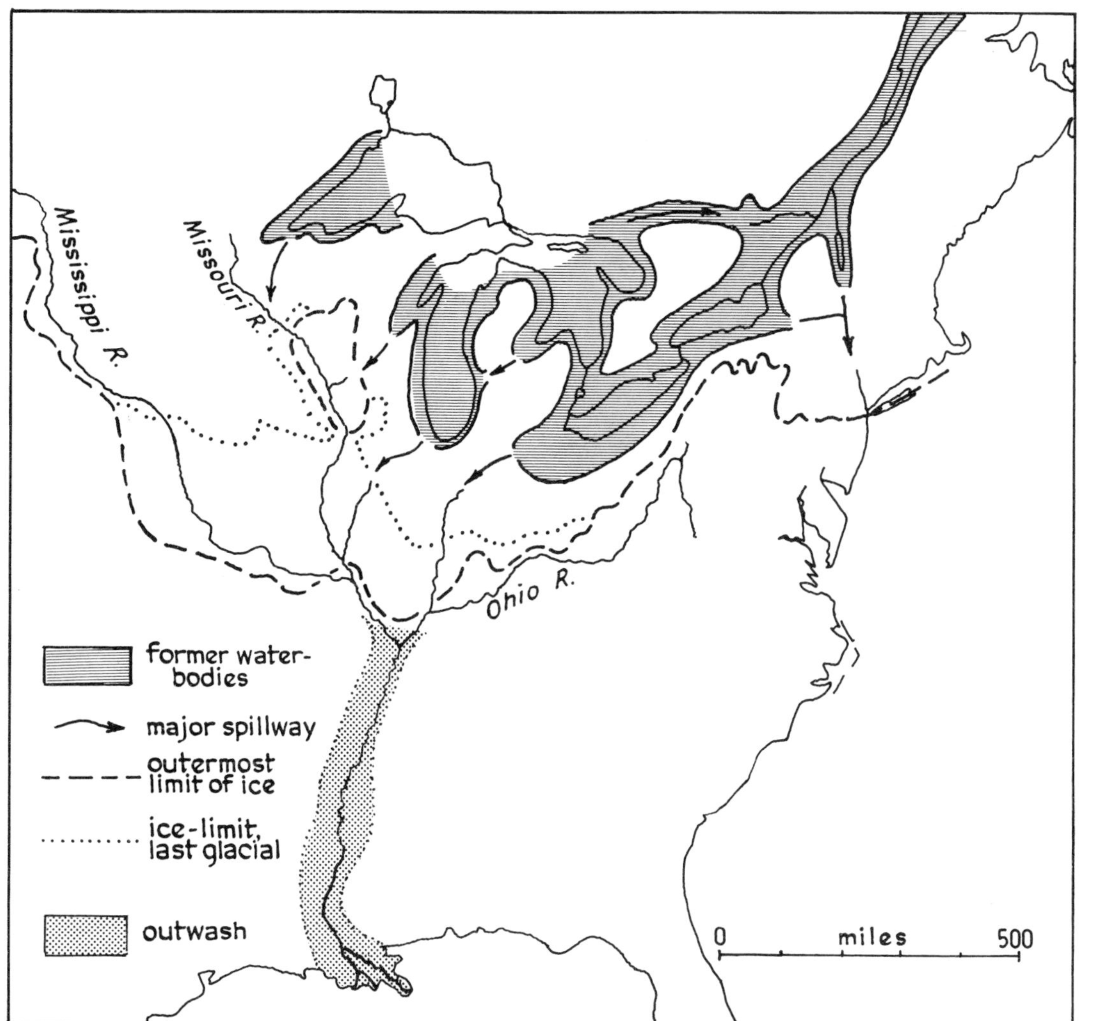

FIG. 3:3 Glacial limits; water-bodies in the Great Lakes area during last glacial recession. Not all lakes were contemporaneous; the St Lawrence–Lake Ontario area was at times submerged by the sea.

the existing relief dates either from Tertiary or from Pleistocene times. During the Tertiary the old massifs were re-elevated, undergoing renewed erosion which has left them with generally subdued and in some parts extensive summits, but has caused them to be dissected by systems of deep valleys. The summit platforms vary in altitude between about 1000 and 2000 ft with residuals rising to 4000 ft or more. The valleys have been considerably modified by Pleistocene ice, some of it accumulated locally but some spreading southeastwards from the Laurentian Shield. Glacial deposits and outwash deposits, where they occur, are mainly coarse, and in consequence do not everywhere increase the agricultural possibilities of the land; indeed, some of the early settlers were compelled to clear away glacially-deposited boulders before they could attempt to plough. Some of the deposits form terraces of sandy outwash, or of sediment laid down alongside the melting ice, in the south-trending valleys (Plate 1). The terrace surfaces are pitted by kettle-holes, where detached masses of ice were once buried, and where the sand collapsed when the ice melted. In the Connecticut Valley, a large ice-mass for a time blocked the outlet through the basaltic Holyoke Range, damming up Glacier

1. Kame terrace in the Connecticut Valley: gravelly outwash with kettle-holes, supporting mainly grass and scattered juniper. Holyoke Mountains in the background, forested.

Lake Hitchcock; the former lake-floor now provides a spread of flat land of an unusual size for New England.

Glaciation may have influenced the form of the sea-bed off New England, Nova Scotia, and Newfoundland. Here occur the Grand and other Banks, providing feeding-grounds for fish, and directly relevant to the early history of exploration and exploitation. The Banks are possibly, at least to some extent, glacially deposited. Alternatively, they may represent the underwater extension of the Atlantic Coastal Plain.

The Appalachians

Southwest of the Hudson Valley, crystalline rocks of Precambrian age and of greatly altered character continue to the far extremity of the Appalachians. Their principal extent, although not their most striking expression, belongs to the Piedmont, a low dissected plateau which reaches tide-water at the mouth of the Hudson and at the heads of Delaware and Chesapeake Bays, but which is then separated from the sea by the Atlantic Coastal Plain (Fig. 3:4). The Piedmont, 50 to 100 miles wide, reaches heights of about 1000 ft on the western (inland) side, where it abuts sharply throughout most of its length on a prominent and almost continuous belt of mountain. This belt, also composed mainly of Precambrian materials, includes the Blue Ridge and the Great Smoky Mountains, in which its summits overtop 6000 ft.

The break between the Piedmont and the Blue Ridge is partly erosional and partly structural: in some parts, the Blue Ridge and its continuations have been thrust higher than the Piedmont. The latter, constituting a distinctive crustal block, reflects in its subdued general appearance the result of planation, in its waste-mantle the result of prolonged weathering, and in its shallowly dissected condition the combined result of uplift and resistance. For uplift has been sufficient to promote renewed downcutting by streams, but the bedrock is at the same time strong enough to make incision slow, wherever downcutting streams encounter it. Thus, along the southeastern edge of the Piedmont in its broadest part occur the knickpoints of the Fall Zone, where rivers are working directly on the crystalline materials.

Next west of the Blue Ridge, and extending beyond it at both ends, comes the ridge-and-valley division of the Appalachians; next west again come the Appalachian plateaus. The Piedmont and the Blue Ridge between them make up the Older Appalachians; the ridge-and-valley division and the plateaus form the Newer Appalachians, which continue the Altaides of Europe.

The Newer Appalachians are composed mainly of rocks ranging in age from Cambrian to Carboniferous, strongly deformed in Permian times in the ridge-and-valley division and deeply eroded since then. But they are nowhere so deeply eroded as to expose mountain roots, and rarely metamorphosed. Alteration by pressure is displayed in the northeast, where compression was greatest: it was able to con-

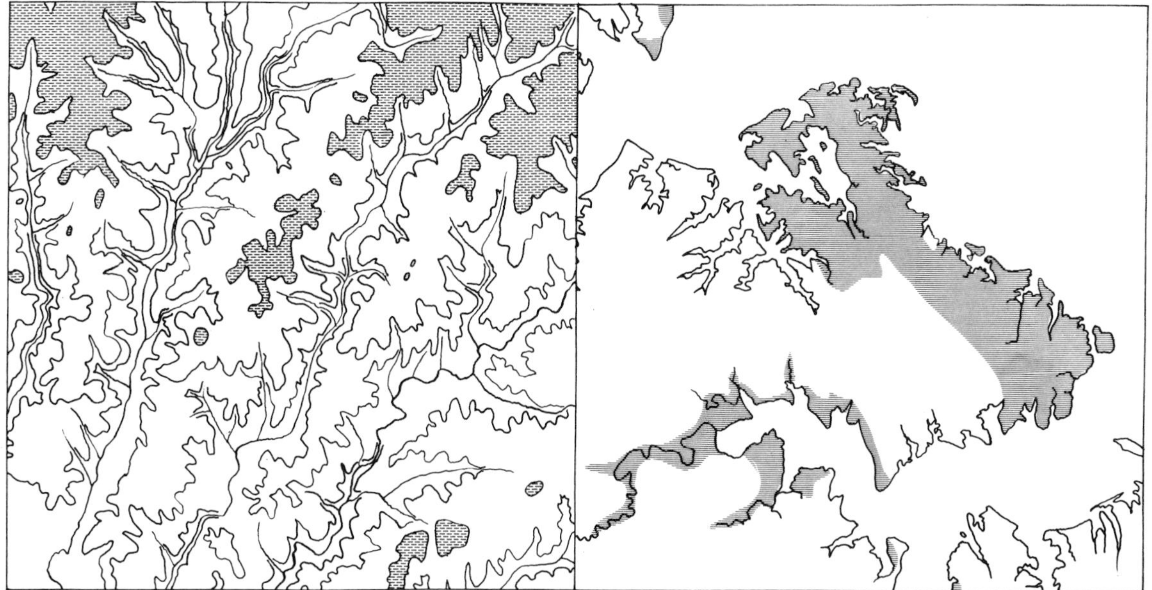

FIG. 3:4 Piedmont and Coastal Plain topography: each frame represents about 50 square miles. Left, part of the Piedmont near Charlotte, N.C.; contour interval 50 ft; areas above 700 ft tinted. Right, part of the coast of Chesapeake Bay: the highest point in the area is only 12 ft above sea-level; tinting represents swamp and salt-marsh.

vert shales into slates and coal into anthracite, just as anthracite was produced by tight folding in the west of South Wales. Elsewhere in the Appalachians, as elsewhere in Britain, the coals of Carboniferous age are bituminous. For all that, compression throughout the ridge-and-valley division was severe, producing sharp folds which plunge away at their ends. Erosion, beginning simultaneously with the Permian deformation and uplift, and promoted spasmodically by later uplifts, has removed a depth of perhaps 40,000 ft of rock. Dissection of the folds has produced a zigzag pattern of ridges (Fig. 3:5).

Immediately next to the Blue Ridge, the ridge-and-valley division includes a wide vale – the Great Appalachian Valley. In the early days of penetration and occupance, this was a line of movement; and it still serves to guide present-day traffic. Among the routes of access to it was, and is, the Susquehanna Valley, where the Blue Ridge dies out and the ridge-and-valley country lies adjacent to the Piedmont. Not far northeast of the Susquehanna, the ridge-and-valley narrows rapidly in part of the Delaware Valley, and continues without much increase in width into the valley of the Hudson.

Seen in a general view, as for instance from the Blue Ridge, the ridges of the Newer Appalachians look remarkably even-topped. At lower levels, many of the valleys – including the Great Appalachian Valley – possess broad and seemingly accordant floors. These characteristics are due to episodes of planation and partial planation, occurring from Triassic times onwards, and separated by episodes of uplift. With each interval of erosion was associated deposition of sediment offshore to the southeast. As the Appalachian area was eroded, lightened, and uplifted, so the earth's crust to the southeast was weighted by sediment and depressed. The reconstructed levels of planation in the mountains converge towards the sea, cross somewhere near the edge of the continent, and are continued farther seaward by the splaying unconformities between sedimentary systems.

Etching into relief of the zigzag folds has been accompanied by the development of subsequent streams. These run along the strike of weak outcrops, whereas the ridges are composed everywhere of the stronger materials. Extension of subsequents, aided by a certain amount of river capture, has gone far to replace drainage directly to the southeast by

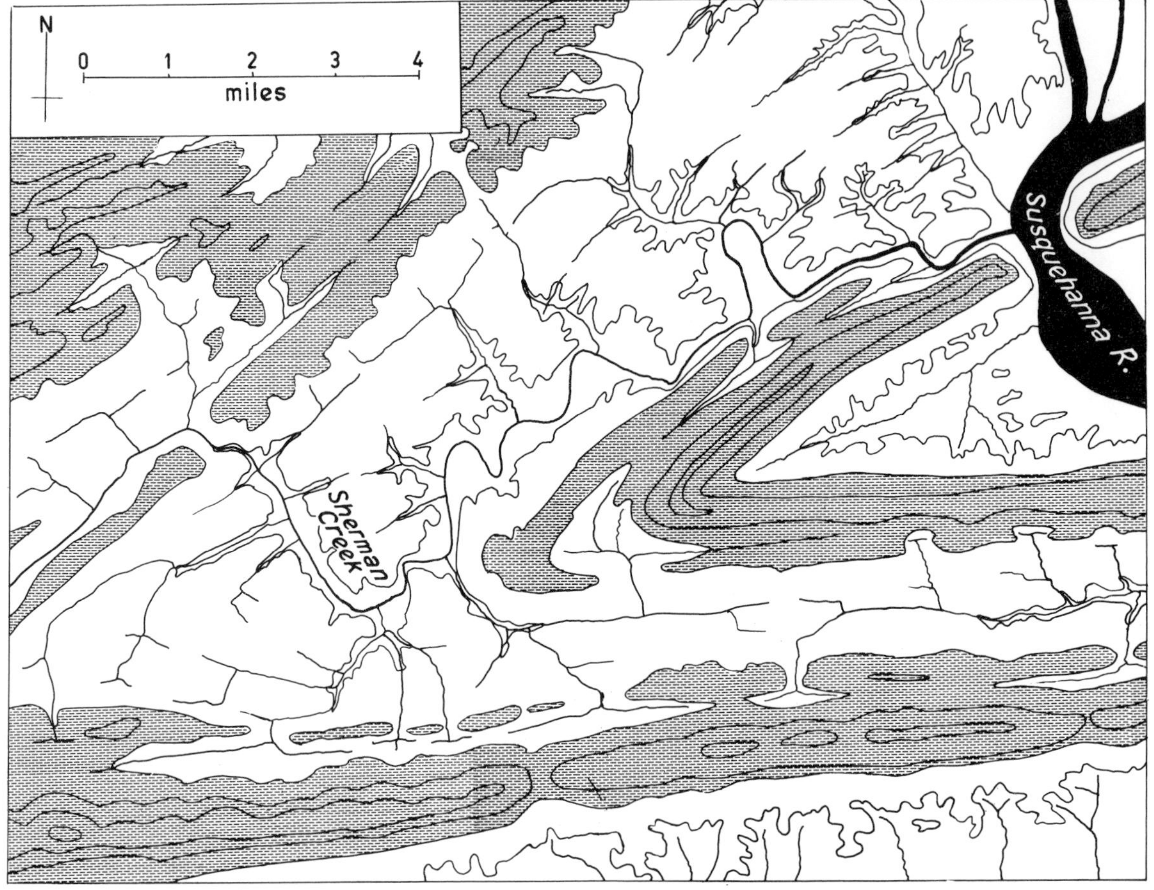

FIG. 3:5 Nose of a plunging anticline: part of the Folded Appalachians in Pennsylvania.

trellis-like networks in which the majority of elements are aligned N.E.–S.W. or S.W.–N.E. Gentle large-scale doming of the rising planated surfaces is also likely to have produced its effect on drainage, although this effect is difficult to extricate from the dominant trellised pattern. The doming is partly responsible for the variation in ridge-top height along the length of the ridge-and-valley division, from as low as 1000 to as high as 6000 ft.

The Appalachian plateaus are similar in age, and broadly similar in rock type, to the ridge-and-valley division: but they have undergone much less marked deformation. Their strong rocks appear as cappings on plateaus. However, the plateau surfaces are not solely due to resistant caps: they record episodes of planation similar to those identified in the Older Appalachians, except that here the general slope is to the northwest. At the northern and the southern ends, respectively in the Allegheny Front and in the Cumberland Scarp, high plateau edges facing southeast dominate the ridge-and-valley country.

Pleistocene ice overrode parts of the plateau country in the extreme north and northwest, forming the Finger Lakes of upper New York State where it poured through a series of cols. Mainly, however, the plateaus escaped glaciation. Their preglacial nets of drainage, unaffected either by invading ice or by strong folding, have remained dendritic. The chief collecting stream is the Ohio.

Unglaciated plateau country at somewhat lower elevations – up to about 1000 ft above sea-level – occupies the triangle bounded by the southern Appalachian plateaus, the Tennessee River, and the Ohio. Much of the rock at the surface is Mississippian limestone. Corresponding broadly in age to the Carboniferous limestone of Britain, this rock is also similar in developing karstic features. The chief assembly of such features is, of course, the Mammoth Caves of Kentucky.

Gentle structural doming has taken place both in the low plateaus and in the plateau division of the Appalachians. In the low plateaus, erosion of the Lexington and Nashville domes has led to inversion of relief. In the Appalachian plateaus, doming is significant chiefly for bringing coal seams near the surface in the Pennsylvania, West Virginia, and Alabama fields.

The Cordillera

Despite its great length, this mountain system of North America is no more than a fraction of a very much larger system. It belongs to a belt of crustal deformation which extends from Cape Horn along the Andes, through Central America, Mexico, and the Caribbean, and which in the far north is continued from Alaska by way of the Aleutian and Kurile Islands to Japan. Beyond Japan it incorporates a whole series of archipelagoes in the west Pacific, running thence by way of New Zealand to the Antarctic.

The whole of this circumPacific belt of disturbance is liable to earthquake shock, although the frequency and severity of earthquakes varies considerably from place to place. It is also liable to volcanic outbreaks, although active volcanoes are unevenly distributed along it. Many areas which have no active volcanoes today were however the scene of eruptions not many thousand years ago; and some of them possess fields of geysers and fumaroles, indicating that the earth's internal heat is escaping at an unusual rate. In parts of the North American sector, deformation of the crust is occurring so fast that movement along lines of faulting can be measured.

In this sector, the immediate cause of crustal compression is thought to be the spreading of the floor of the Pacific Ocean. A convection current in the earth's outer body, rising in mid-Pacific, appears to be promoting an eastward drift of the suboceanic crust towards the North American continent. At the continental edge this current sinks, wedging down beneath the land and promoting buckling. Chemical changes at depth produce melts, which invade the mountain roots and help to buoy them up.

Rocks involved in the Cordillera range in age from Precambrian onwards: some of the youngest deposits, no more than a few thousand years old, are those of volcanoes. A long and enormously complicated sequence of folding, faulting, elevation, subsidence, volcanic activity, erosion, and deposition has produced a threefold Cordilleran system. On the east come the Rockies, on the west the mountains of the Pacific border where most deformation is occurring today. Between these two elements, along the axis of the Cordillera, lies a chain of plateaus broken by mountain knots.

It is scarcely possible to discuss the Cordillera without reference to glacial and to present-day climates. At glacial maximum a Cordilleran ice-sheet extended slightly south of 49° N latitude: today, the plateaus south of that line are arid or semi-arid. On both counts it is convenient to treat the Cordillera in the conterminous U.S.A. separately from that in Canada–Alaska.

Mountain-building in the American Rockies began at least as early as the Cretaceous, when the intermont plateaus were also much uplifted. Volcanic outbursts continued well into the Tertiary, renewed growth of mountains into the Pleistocene. From the High Plains the Rockies look like a wall. In views from the air, much of the highest ground is tabular with a general slope towards the east. This slope, continuing across residual summits on the plains, shows that the existing distinction between plains and mountains is due partly to differential erosion.

The Southern Rockies lie mainly in Colorado, their topmost peaks exceeding 14,000 ft above sea-level. Beyond the structural and topographic sag of the Wyoming Basin, the Northern Rockies at first closely approach 14,000 ft but fall below 9000 about the head of the Yellowstone. Geysers and terraced springs in Yellowstone National Park add to the attractions of highland country that is strongly glaciated; near the Canadian border small remnantal glaciers still persist, whereas the Southern Rockies were but moderately glaciated at high levels.

There are three plateau groups in the conterminous U.S.A. – the Colorado Plateau, the basin-and-range country, and the Snake–Columbia Plateau. The Colorado Plateau, roughly equal in area to the British Isles, has undergone some faulting and warping, but its rocks are mainly flat-lying. General uplift, far outpacing erosion, is responsible for elevations of 5–9000 ft. But the effects of erosion are

2. Residual hills in Oak Creek Canyon, Arizona; sparse scrub vegetation in the valley bottom and on the lower hillsides. Haziness of the middle and far distance is produced by desert dust.

nevertheless impressive, including, as they do, the dissection of extinct volcanoes in the south into whole fields of volcanic necks and the cutting of canyons in the remainder. The Grand Canyon of the Colorado, best known of all, trenches more than a mile downwards into the Precambrian basement.

Canyons owe their existence to incision, their form to geology and climate. Generally resistant, vertically-jointed, and little-disturbed rocks favour the cutting of steep valley-walls, which the dry climate helps to preserve without inhibiting the development of spectacular weathering features (Plate 2). Dryness also means an open net of drainage, with canyons widely separated by expanses of plateau: the only perennial streams are those fed from the Rockies. Flat plateau surfaces correspond both to flat-lying rocks and to pediplanation – that is, the cutting of gently-sloping, concave-upward pediments which merge together in pediplains.*

In the basin-and-range country, faulted crustal blocks have been uplifted, depressed, or tilted. Elevated blocks now form elongated ranges of mountain, glacially sculptured in the north and fringed by pediments throughout. Depressions have been thickly alluviated. Some ranges attain 10,000 ft above sea-level, the floor of the Great Basin of Nevada stands at about 5000 ft; and Death Valley, California, descends to nearly 300 ft below sea-level. South of the Colorado Plateau, the basin-and-range country is drained externally by the Gila and the Rio Grande. Rivers elsewhere, if they exist, fail to reach the sea. The climate is arid or semi-arid throughout: the Humboldt ends in Carson Sink, and many smaller streams do no more than nourish salt-pans or playa lakes. At times of glacial maximum, however, climate was cooler and more humid. Two lake complexes formed – Lahontan, 5000 square miles in area and more than 500 ft deep, and Bonneville, 10,000 square miles in area and 1000 ft deep (Fig. 3:2). They were accompanied by many smaller lakes, also contained in topographic basins. Their last high stands were attained as late as 12,000 years ago: but Bonneville is now represented only by abandoned high beaches, by shrunken water-bodies of which the Great Salt Lake is the chief, and by the salt-flats of its bottom sediments.

On the U.S.–Canadian border, the Rockies swing into contact in the Okanagan Mountains with the mountains of the Pacific border, enclosing the northern side of the Snake–Columbia Plateau. Tertiary basaltic lavas here have largely covered an earlier landscape. The earth's crust repeatedly opened in fissures, extruding repeated floods of molten rock. Individual floods were tens of feet deep: the maximum total depth exceeds 5000 ft. Some undrowned mountains and groups of later volcanic cones overtop the plains of solidified

* The making of pediments and pediplains involves back-wearing of hill-slopes, whereas peneplanation is supposed to involve downwearing of high ground. This whole matter is controversial. Nothing said in the present text is meant to imply that pediments are restricted to areas of dry climate, even though they are most easily recognizable there.

3. View across the Hood River valley, Oregon, with the snow-capped Mount Hood, a peak of the Cascades, in the distance. The lower ground is mainly under orchards.

basalt; and earth-movements have ensured that the lava surface now ranges from sea-level to over 6000 ft. In bulk the basalt is highly permeable, simulating limestone country with dominantly underground drainage. Vertical jointing enables many valley-walls to rise sheer. Like the Colorado Plateau, this is canyon country, with the Columbia River incised to a depth of half a mile and the Snake twice as deeply.

In the angle of the two rivers occur great abandoned channels, called coulées, broken by waterfalls and grossly pitted by scour-holes. Associated with the coulées are networks of shallower channels, much encumbered by coarse sediment, typifying areas called scablands. Coulées and scablands alike are the products of glacial events. The former were cut by lake-water which, impounded against high ground by ice, was suddenly released during phases of glacier decay and concentrated into single channels. Scablands occur where the released waters flowed in braided fashion.

In the Pacific border, mountains to landward and seaward enclose a discontinuous series of long structural depressions. Mountain-building occurred here in late Jurassic to early Cretaceous, and again in late Tertiary to Pleistocene times. In the earlier episode, masses of crystalline rock were emplaced at depth. One of these, now exposed at the surface, forms the westward-tilted block of the Sierra Nevada, 25,000 square miles in area. Its steep eastern rim marks a crustal break where movement is still in progress. The Sierra belongs to the landward system of mountains in the Pacific border, continued northward by the Cascades where volcanic cones are numerous. Among these, Mount Baker was active in the last century and Mount Lassen in the present century, while Crater Lake occupies a collapse crater formed during the Pleistocene.

All the highest summits in this portion of the Pacific border lie in the range 14,000–14,500 ft above sea-level; fourteen in number, they include the extinct volcanoes of Mounts Whitney, Shasta, and Rainier. An identical height-range has already been noticed for the Southern Rockies: the American section of the Cordillera as a whole possesses no fewer than seventy peaks of this altitude (Plate 3).

In the extreme south of the Pacific border, the Salton depression is separated by the Colorado Delta from the depressed Gulf of California to which it belongs. Between the Sierra Nevada and the Coast Ranges intervenes the Great Valley of California, 400 miles long and heavily alluviated in the floor. Part of the Puget Sound–Willamette Valley Lowland, farther north, is drowned on account of subsidence: more extreme cases of drowning will appear later.

Mountains on the California coast are partly composed of Precambrian rocks, and are widely affected by faulting; the San Andreas Fault – responsible for the San Francisco earthquake of 1906 – is still moving (Fig. 3:6). Summits in this portion range from 5000 to 6000 ft, overtopping raised shore-platforms which again testify to crustal instability.

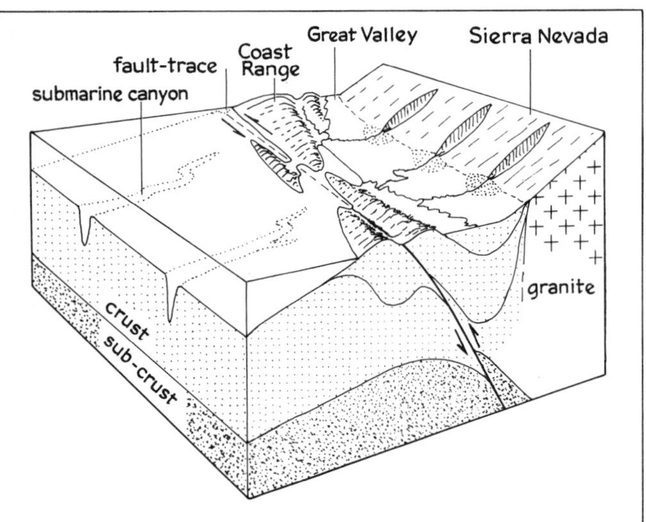

FIG. 3:6 Gross structural relationships in central California. The fault is the San Andreas.

The single major break in the line of mountains occurs at the Golden Gate. In Washington and Oregon the Coast Ranges include highly disturbed rocks of Tertiary age, with some volcanic materials, and attain heights of 3000–8000 ft. Continuing uplift has caused streams to incise themselves in canyons, the main breach in the mountains being that of the Columbia River.

All the really high parts of the Pacific border, well placed to receive moist Pacific winds, were glaciated during the Pleistocene. The Sierra Nevada still records heavy snow in winter, while its Yosemite district is scenically famous on account of glacially-eroded forms. Valley glaciers survive in the Cascades, being especially well known on Mount Rainier, and much-shrunken relics of similar glaciers exist in the northern Coast Ranges.

Since the history of earth-movement north of the Canadian border resembles that to the south, it need not be repeated. In Canada, the term Rocky Mountains is limited by custom to a strip about thirty miles in width, bordered on the northeast by foothills, and on the southwest by the Rocky Mountain Trench which in places is but a mile wide (Fig. 3:7). The Canadian Rockies and the extensions which take them into the Brooks Range of Alaska consists largely of Palaeozoic sedimentary rocks in which deformation varies from slight tilting to strong folding. Peaks attain heights of 10,000 to nearly 13,000 ft in the Canadian part, and of 8–9000 ft in the Brooks Range.

In the southeast of British Columbia, the Columbia Mountains continue the Okanagan Mountains northward. The Columbia Mountains, with peaks exceeding 10,000 ft, are so deeply grooved on north–south structural lines that they form an array of mountain chains: their rocks are chiefly metamorphic or deep-emplaced crystalline. Next northwestwards lies the Interior Plateau of British Columbia, most of it draining to the Fraser River, underlain by lava or by gently-dipping Cretaceous or younger sediments; little of this Plateau exceeds 5000 ft except for Tertiary or later volcanoes. A large complex of plateau and mountain, roughly equal in area to the Interior Plateau, terminates the latter on the northwest, eventually giving way to the Yukon Plateau which ranges across Precambrian from about 6000 ft in the upper Yukon Basin to a few hundred feet above sea-level near the Arctic coast.

On this northern side of the international border, the Coast Ranges correspond to the Cascades of the U.S.A. They resemble the Sierra Nevada in being composed largely of coarsely crystalline rock, emplaced probably in Jurassic times. Summit heights range from 13,000 to 8000 ft, being least opposite the gap between Vancouver Island and the Queen Charlotte Islands. Despite dissection – including glacial dissection – the Coast Ranges display a marked summit-plane, which testifies to former levelling followed by uplift. In the Alaska Range, which extends the Coast Ranges towards the mountain arcs of Asia, is located Mount McKinley, the highest point in North America at 20,320 ft above sea-level. Farther beyond again, peaks decline in the Aleutian Range to 8–9000 ft. All these parts of the landward belt of the Pacific border record vulcanism, whether by extinct volcanoes of Tertiary or later age, or by intermittent present-day activity, including the fumaroles in the Valley of Ten Thousand Smokes.

The axial depressions of this section of the Pacific Border lie chiefly beneath the sea – Puget Sound, the strait between Vancouver Island and the mainland, and the complex of passages in the Alaskan Panhandle. The seaward mountains form peninsulas or chains of islands. Only in the St Elias and

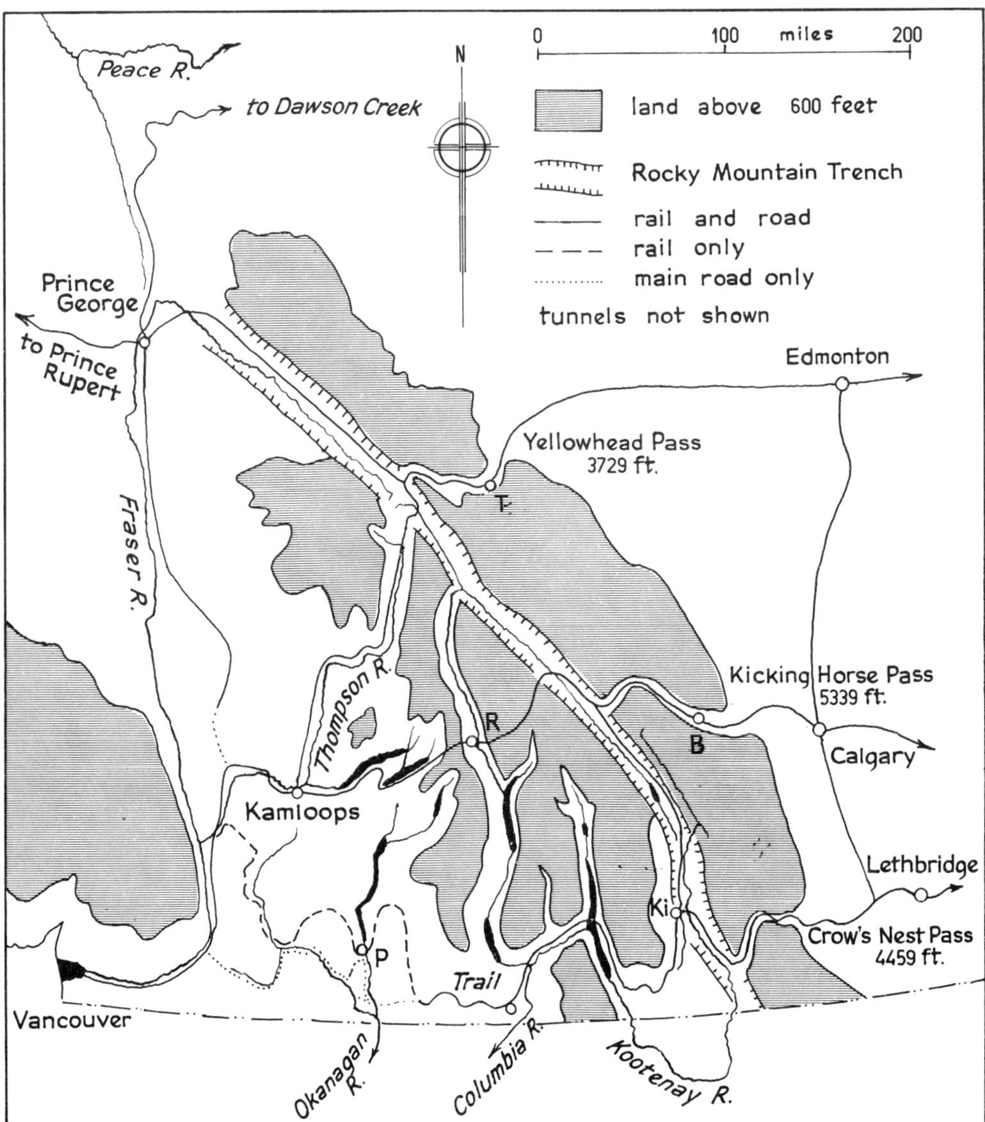

FIG. 3:7 Gross relief of the southern Canadian Rockies and the country next west. Major lines of movement run east–west, leaving the Rocky Mountain Trench only partly used by routes.

Wrangell Mountains, where Mount Logan approaches 20,000 ft and the active volcano Mount Wrangell reaches 14,000, does the floor of the depressed strip re-emerge, or the seaward mountain belt rejoin the continent.

At the most intense cold of the last Ice Age, the Yukon Plateau escaped glaciation because it was dry – hemmed in by mountains and overspread by cold arctic air. Elsewhere in the Canadian–Alaskan part of the Cordillera, signs of glaciation are intense, although their lowest limit, like the present snowline, rises markedly away from the Pacific. Valley glaciers still survive both in the Canadian Rockies and in the mountains of the Pacific border, being associated in this latter division with local ice-caps on high, gently sloping ground, and reaching the sea in the Alaskan section. During the Pleistocene, ice covered a great deal of the whole

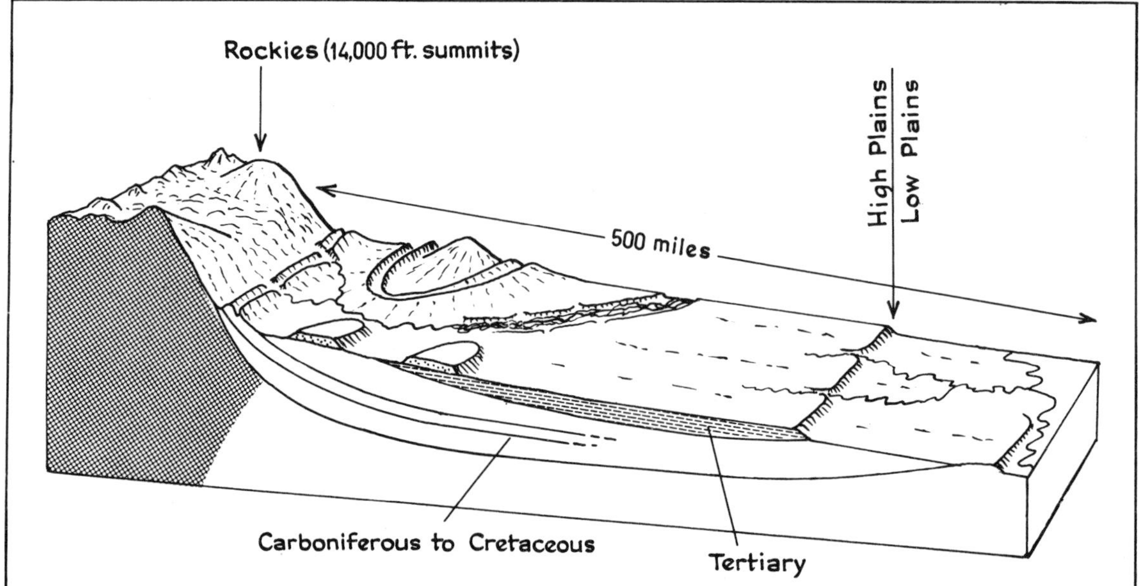

FIG. 3:8 Relief and structure of part of the Great Plains, partly adapted from Atwood: the two low tabular hills in the foreground symbolize remnants of dissected pediments.

Cordillera from the Okanagan Mountains to the mountains of Alaska, savagely grooving the lines of structural weakness – already selected by rivers – in the Columbia Mountains and in the Coast Ranges. At the highest levels the rocks were split by frost, summits were gnawed by cirques, and mountain flanks were troughed by streams of moving ice. Along the coast of the time, glaciers were able to erode below sea-level before their ends floated and broke off as icebergs; and although the land is now rebounding after losing most of its heavy load of ice, recovery has by no means dried out the fjords in which glacier troughs enter the sea.

The Interior and the South

For purposes of human geography, the High Plains bordering the Cordillera on its eastern side are styled the Great Plains. This title refers both to landform and to the extensive short-grass prairie which confronted the early explorers and pioneers: the Great Plains looked far more open than did equally subdued country farther east. Ever since the name was accepted, geographers have been investigating the nature of the eastern limit – with somewhat inconclusive results: all one can say is that, on the Great Plains proper, a change in soil character is broadly associated with a change in the former natural vegetation. Such physical breaks as occur between the Great Plains and the Interior Lowlands are facts of convenience rather than factors of discrimination.

Structurally, much of the Great Plains division is underlain by a major system of gentle downfolding (Fig. 3:8); but its rocks are widely truncated by pediplain surfaces, across which spread alluvial deposits of varying coarseness derived from the Rockies. From the foot of the Rockies at about 5000 ft, the Plains fall slowly eastwards to about 1000 ft above sea-level at the conventional margins of the Interior Lowlands. In the Canadian portion, and in the U.S.A. as far south as the Missouri River, the details of relief are due to deposition by the great continental ice-sheet. South of the former limit of continental ice, loess is almost continuous to about the southern border of Kansas, except where in Nebraska it is massively interrupted by sandhills, or where in South Dakota the updomed Black Hills form an outpost of the Rockies. From Kansas southwards, the eastern edge of the High Plains is reasonably well defined by east-facing scarps.

Rivers crossing the Great Plains are, as a group,

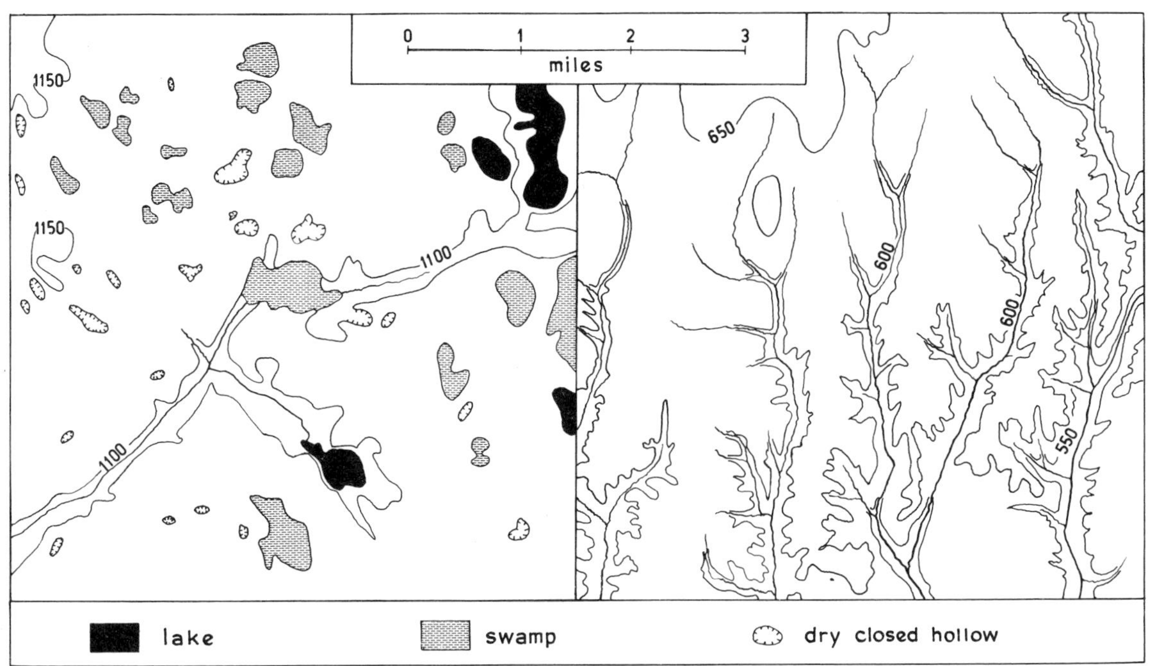

FIG. 3:9 Topographical contrast between young and older tills. Left, the latest till sheet in western Minnesota: drainage still unorganized. Right, an older till sheet in southern Illinois, completely dissected in detail by a highly-organized drainage net.

incised. Many of them, supplied with abundant bedload from glacial deposits in the Rockies and from the erodible sandy rocks which they traverse, and provided moreover with incohesive banks, are also braided. They are highly sensitive to environmental changes: for numbers are known to have undergone a rapid widening and shallowing of their channels, shortly after the first pioneers arrived – probably in association with the swift increase in river-loading which exploitation of farmland brought about. The most recent development, however, is a tendency for them to revert to channels of the earlier, narrower, form.

In the Interior Lowlands, rocks of Palaeozoic age – including Carboniferous coals – are gently warped into low structural domes and shallow structural basins. Little of the ground exceeds 1000 ft above sea-level, and much is less than half that height. From Lake Winnipeg to about the line of the Missouri and Ohio, this division was formerly covered by continental ice. Its unglaciated southwestward extension is an area of subdued relief typified by wide vales and low cuestas, somewhat resembling the low plateau country between the lower Ohio and the Appalachians. Beyond the limit of the last ice advance, the earlier glaciated portion consists of till plains shallowly dissected by a dense net of streams, whereas within that limit the forms of glacial deposition are strikingly fresh (Fig. 3:9). They comprise the shoreline and bottom deposits of Glacier Lake Agassiz, the ancestor of Lake Winnipeg; huge complexes of lobate moraines which repeat the curved southern outlines of Lakes Michigan, Huron, and Erie; sheets of outwash and till between successive moraines; drumlin fields, especially in Wisconsin, and pitted outwash plains, riddled by kettle-holes, especially in Minnesota. Spillways which formerly discharged the water of ice-dammed lakes now contain rivers, among them the Wabash, Illinois, Mississippi, and Missouri. Only in the Driftless Area of Wisconsin, where gently-dipping Palaeozoic rocks form low dissected plateaus, was the ground high enough to escape glaciation, either at the last or at earlier advances.

In general appearance, the Interior Highlands

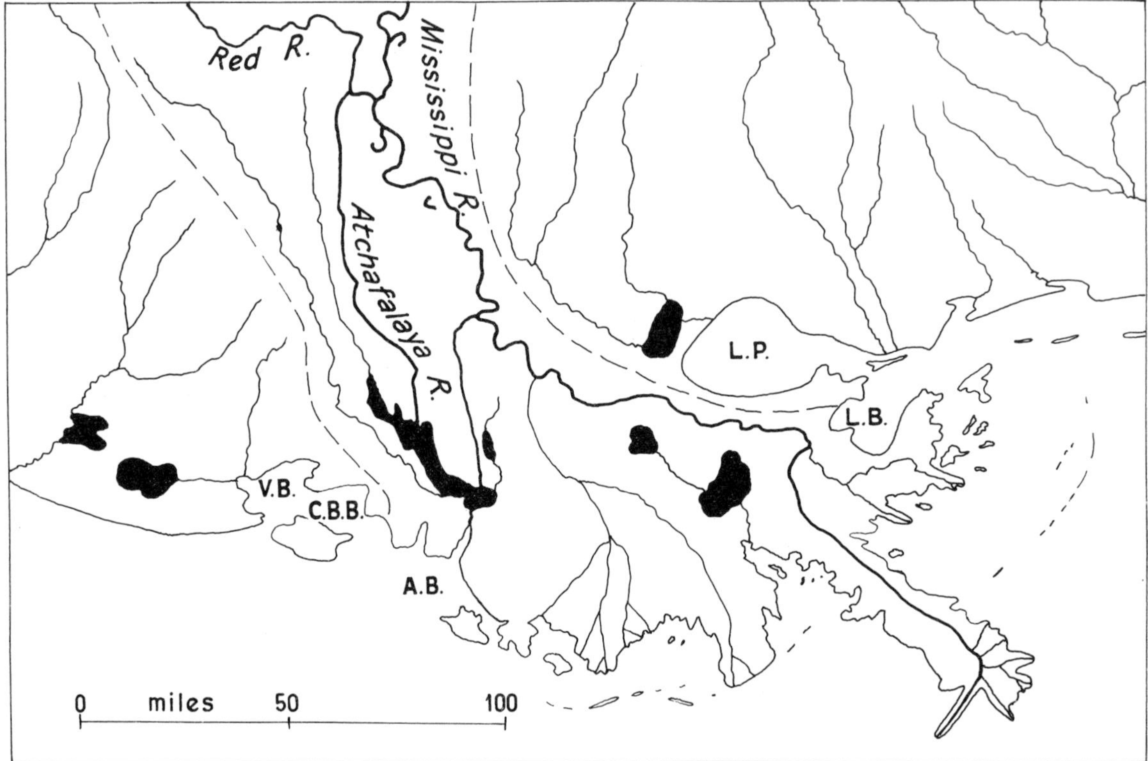

FIG. 3:10 The Mississippi Delta. Pecked lines mark the bounds of drainage to and by the Mississippi. A.B. Atchafalaya Bay; C.B.B., Cote Blanche Bay; V.B., Vermilion Bay; L.B., Lake Borgne; L.P., Lake Pontchartrain.

resemble the Driftless Area: they consist mainly of tabular divides between which streams have cut valleys a few hundred feet deep. But whereas the Driftless Area is mantled with loess and underlain by little-disturbed rocks, the Interior Highlands are loess-free and structurally complex in places. Gentle doming in the Ozarks brings the Precambrian basement to the surface, while the Ouachitas, south of the Arkansas River, comprise zigzag ridges like those of the Appalachian ridge-and-valley division.

Towards the Gulf and Atlantic coasts, the sedimentary rocks of the coastal plains dip gently seaward. Cretaceous beds appear on the inner margin, but large areas are underlain by unconsolidated Tertiary sands and gravels. Some relatively strong formations in the Atlantic Coastal Plain have been etched into low inward-facing cuestas, while Florida is built of flat-lying limestone abundantly pocked by sinks and swamps. The net outcome of movements both of the crust and of sea-level is a drowned shoreline, with large branching inlets in Delaware and Chesapeake Bays; but long stretches of shore possess fringing barriers, which either enclose estuarine swamps and lagoons, or – as on the east of Florida – rest directly against the land.

Occupying an alluvial trough 50 or more miles wide and 600 miles long from the Ohio confluence to the sea, the lower Mississippi divides the Gulf Coastal Plain into two. When the Pleistocene icecaps were at their maxima, they locked up so much water that sea-level was brought far below its present mark – possibly, at one time, 450 ft below. Swollen by waters melted from the continental ice of North America, the Mississippi excavated a great trench, which became filled with alluvium whenever deglaciation took place and sea-level rose once more. This means that the alluvium of the Mississippi constitutes valley fill, the present floodplain being only a surface veneer. Since the river is a levee-builder, breaches of its banks are potentially disastrous in floodtime; and since it tends constantly to shift its meandering course, flood protection and channel maintenance are all the more difficult. The Mississippi Delta, protruding a hundred miles out to sea, records a history of sedimentation going back many millions of years. Subsidence, keeping close pace with deposition, has ensured a close approach to equipoise; but, affecting the surroundings in addition to the delta itself, it has helped to form the Blanche Bay system of inlets on the west and the Lake Pontchartrain system on the east.

CHAPTER FOUR

THE NATURAL COVER: ASSESSMENTS OF CLIMATE

One signal difficulty in describing the physical environment is that this environment is perceived as a whole, whereas discussions of it are usually analytical: that is, particular aspects of the environment are selected for treatment in serial form, one after the other. A well-established order is geology–relief–climate–soils–vegetation, or some variation thereon. Two objections to analytical treatment are that some parts of the total environment interact on others, and that serial discussion tends to carry implications of geographical determinism.

In the very broad view, correspondences exist between the gross distribution of vegetation-types in North America and the distribution of major elements of relief. Locally and in detail vegetation varies with detail of relief – with aspect, slope and with site drainage. Vegetation is also affected by climate, both on the macro- and on the micro-scale. Climate in turn affects soil, both through the limitations which it imposes on vegetation cover and also through the profile drainage characteristics which it promotes. Soil both affects vegetation and is affected by it, while its mechanical properties are determined in the first instance by parent material – i.e., by geology. Thus, distributional maps of soil and of vegetation represent the outcome of whole complexes of interaction.

However, our language is not well adapted to develop simultaneously a whole array of interwoven themes. It is linear rather than concentric or interlocking. In consequence, the arrangement of environmental topics in a serial order is a matter of practical convenience, and indeed to a considerable extent a matter of practical necessity. There can, naturally, be no dispute that geology – the formation and deformation of rocks – determines, with the aid of erosional and depositional processes, the landforms which constitute the surface of the ground. Already, however, considerable allowance needs to be made for the action of climate, whether that of the present or of the late geological past, for climate exerts considerable control on the quality and power of erosion. Climate in turn is powerfully modified by variation in relief, and by distributions of land and sea. Some of the complex determinants of the character of soil have already been mentioned; and climate can only be said to determine vegetation, after full allowance has been made for the influences of soil and site characteristics, and for the actual history of floristic development and succession. In discussing the physical environment of North America, we are concerned with what this environment is like, and with how it in fact has been produced. We should be reluctant to introduce ideas of inevitability, particularly if these appeared to imply something inevitable in the human response to the environment. This would be geographical determinism in its crudest form – an approach which, unfortunately, the traditional treatment in the order geology–relief–climate–soils–vegetation seems to encourage.

For this reason, we propose to follow the preceding account of rocks and land-forms with a summary description of soils and wild vegetation, continuing to deal with visible objects throughout. It was the visible environment which the first explorers and the first settlers could observe directly. The first settlers were involved with land as land, many being led in simply by the fact that land was open to them. The climatic part of the environment was something to which they adapted themselves, perforce, on pain of ruin or even of death. Its measurement, and its classification, were in general deferred until well after settlement had taken place.

THE NATURAL COVER

When Indians and Eskimo lived in North America in pre-contact days, they looked on vegetation little changed by man. When the first European explorers touched on the coast, and when the first settlers arrived, they, too, saw a plant cover in its natural state. Every acre of farmland cleared and cultivated, every bit of ground taken for building, has involved a drastic vegetational change: and even where the land is not enclosed, grazing on the open range and lumbering in the most accessible forests have profoundly altered the character of the vegetation, even if they have not everywhere modified its general appearance.

Nevertheless, it is still possible to define and to reconstruct the former pattern (Fig. 4:1). Inevitably, the major shapes in this pattern bear a marked relationship to the distribution of climates. In the north of the continent, low-growing tundra plants characterize areas too cold for forest. Southwards, the tundra merges through cold parkland into the boreal forest of largely needleleaf and largely evergreen trees. Along its own southern edge in the Great Lakes area, this forest changes in character with the admixture of broadleaf deciduous trees which become dominant in a large block of the eastern U.S.A. Farther southwards still, broadleaf deciduous forest yields to oak–pine forest in which oaks thin away towards the southeast, while needleleaf forest both evergreen and deciduous appears in Florida.

The main climatic change from Hudson's Bay to the Gulf is an increase in temperature. Westwards across the Interior Lowlands on to the Great Plains, decrease of precipitation is more important. West of the latitude of Lake Michigan, broadleaf deciduous forest passes into deciduous woodland interspersed with tall grassland, this into dominant tall grassland, and this again into short grassland. In the Cordillera, precipitation is greatest on the higher ground, while temperature falls both with increasing height and with increasing latitude. The enclosed plateaus in the U.S.A. are too dry for anything but scrub or short grassland, while needleleaf evergreen forest, mantling the tops of the southern Cordillera, descends northward to link eventually with the boreal forests of Canada.

Roughly speaking, the forest lands are lands of water surplus – those where annual precipitation is greater than potential annual losses to evapotranspiration (= evaporation + transpiration). In the grassland and scrub country, annual precipitation is less than potential evapotranspiration: these are lands of water need.

Tundra

A sweep of the far north of the continent which, straddling Hudson's Bay, also includes most of the Yukon and of Alaska and juts extensions southwards along the Cordillera, is clad by tundra (Plate 4). On the Shield and in the lower Mackenzie Valley, tundra is dominated by mosses, lichens, and other herbaceous plants than grass, supporting also lowly frost-resistant shrubs. Muskeg (peat) forms in enclosed shallow depressions. The climate is too severe for trees. Winter's first frost blasts any plants which have failed to complete their annual growth-cycle, or, at the least, arrests their development for another year. The growing season is measured in weeks. Lack of trees and the generally subdued terrain make the landscape look as bleak as the climate feels. Although conditions are no less severe in the mountains, the specialized Alpine flora includes some natural grassland. Along the southern frontier of the tundra, the frost-free period averages no more than sixty days and in mid-continent is as short as forty: mean January temperatures range from −12° F down to −30° F (−25° C to −35° C), while mean July temperatures are about 55° F (13° C).

North of the Arctic Circle the subsoil is perennially frozen. This is the land of permafrost, where ground-ice persists beneath a thin layer of seasonally-melting topsoil. Frost-stirring of the ground produces networks of stones or tussocks on flat surfaces, while melting in the brief season of least cold enables the topsoil to shift slowly downhill on every slope. South of the Arctic Circle, discontinuous permafrost – in which some patches of ground lack perennially frozen subsoil – occupies the southern tundra and overlaps into the adjacent cold parklands. Spruce, hardiest of conifers, appears here in small patches and then later in larger stands amid the expanses of low plants and muskeg. As in the tundra, evaporation in the cold parkland is so

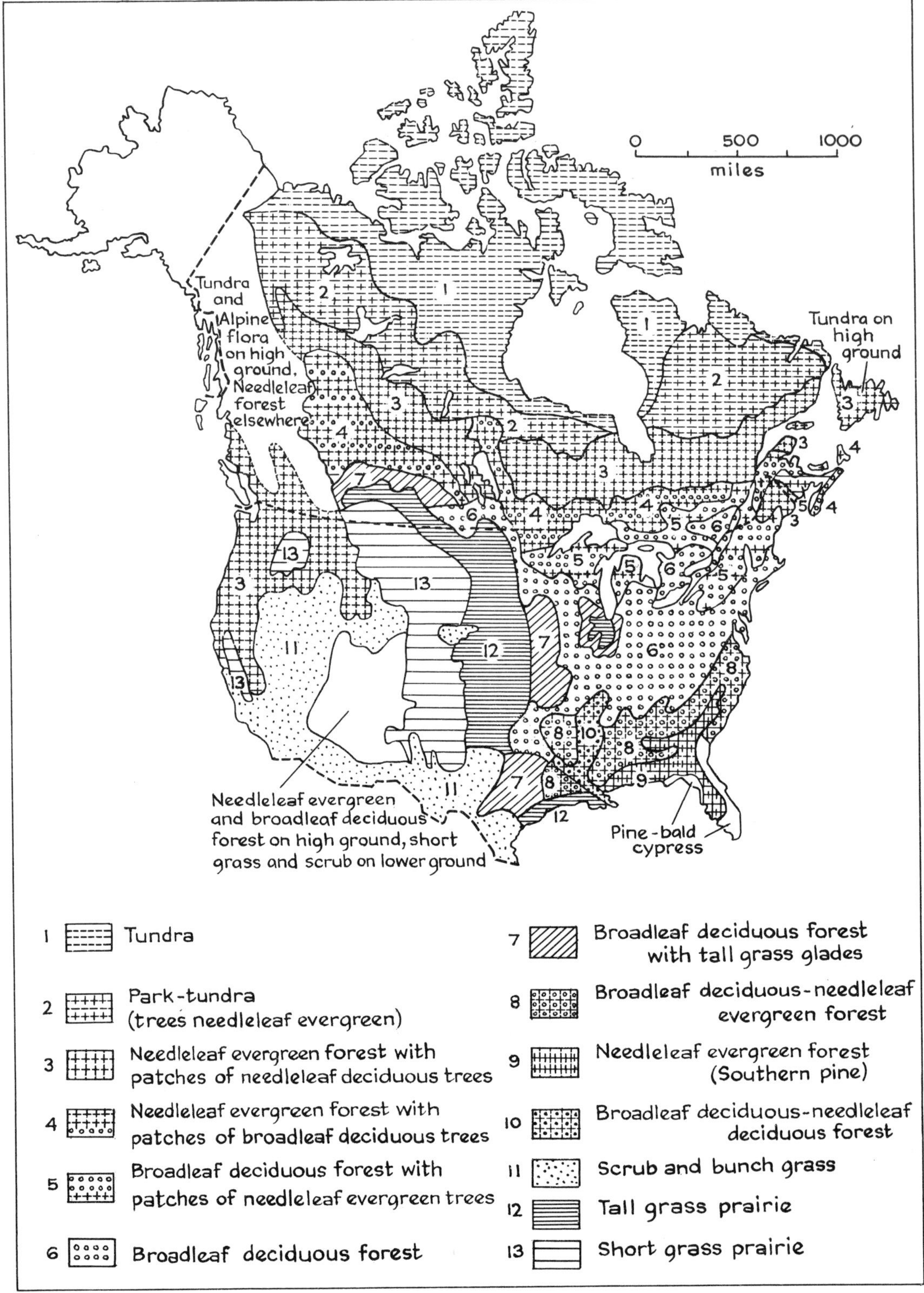

FIG. 4:1 Wild vegetation.

4. The Mackenzie Delta at Aklavik (centre). Swamp vegetation is tending to fill enclosed hollows, some of which have been produced by permafrost. Nearness to the ocean sufficiently mitigates the tundra climate here to permit limited growth of trees.

slight that even a low winter snowfall will cause the ground to remain moist throughout the poor approach to summer. Representative mean temperatures at the southern edge of parkland are −15° F to −10° F (−26° C to −23° C) in January, and 55° F to 60° F (13° C to 15° C) in July, while the frost-free season averages about eighty days.

Frost stirs the parkland soils both in areas of permafrost and outside them, but as a whole these soils are best grouped as lithosols – shallow, poorly-developed (= skeletal) soils formed on the coarse materials left by decaying ice or spread by meltwater. In respect of gross distributions, the transition from tundra to cold parkland on the Shield corresponds approximately to the northern boundary of lithosols (Figs. 4:1, 4:2). In the tundra, continuous permafrost and seasonal thaw to depths of but a few inches emphasize the atmospheric savagery of the winters: even if trees could withstand the cold air, they could not root. In the parkland, however, tree-roots can form and spread: seasonal melting here reaches depths of a few feet over the permafrost, and the patchy mantle of coarse rock-waste allows trees to take hold. Neither the tundra nor the parkland has agricultural potential: the soils are as poor as the climate is rigorous.

Boreal Forests

Needleleaf evergreen trees make up a great deal of the boreal forests, although deciduous trees both needleleaf and broadleaf also occur. East of the Cordillera these forests are roughly delimited along their southern edge by the January and July mean temperatures of 0° F and 65° F (−18° C and +18° C), and by the ninety-day average for the frost-free season. Ground temperatures are somewhat higher than would be expected for permafrost, but patchy permafrost nevertheless occurs up to the southern forest edge east of the Cordillera, and is also known as far south as the Northern Rockies. On the lower ground, permafrost is partly relict: formed when the land was laid bare by melting continental ice, it has not yet disappeared.

The boreal forests are noteworthy for extensive pure stands, in which one type of tree covers large areas: alternatively, two or three species appear as co-dominants. Around the head of James Bay, and again on the western side of Lake Winnipeg, the evergreen spruce and the deciduous larch – both needleleaf – are associated, while pine–spruce–larch comes in along the northwestward swing of the Shield boundary. From the Gulf of St Lawrence almost to Lake Winnipeg, evergreen needleleaf forest of spruce–fir is typical. Next on the south, where patches of broadleaf deciduous trees variegate the spread of needleleaf – westward from the upper Ottawa River along the head of Lake Superior to the eastern shore of Lake Winnipeg – the forest cover includes spruce–birch, or spruce–aspen. This last association renews itself further, reaching

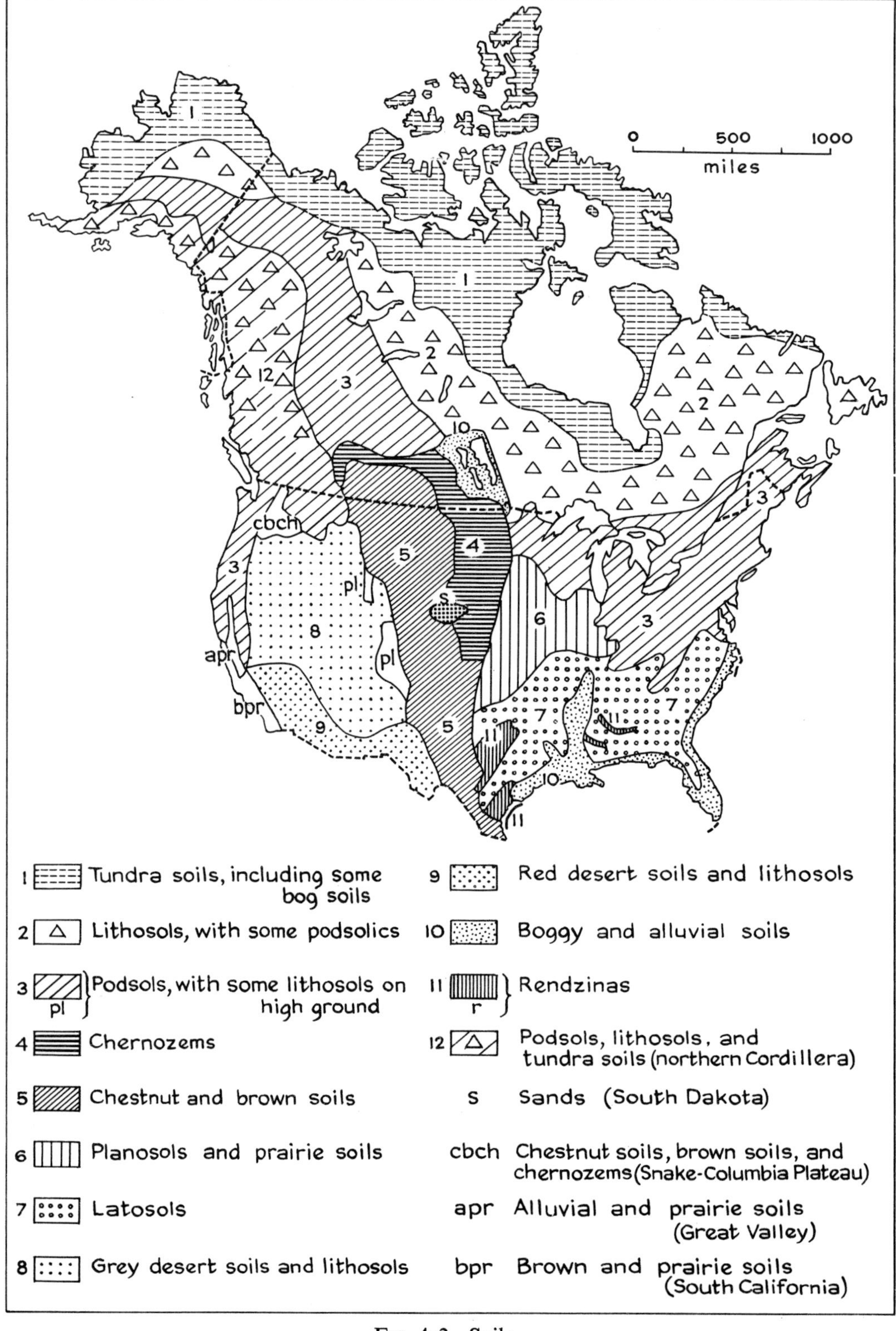
0 500 1000
miles
1
2
3
4
5
6
7
8
9
10
11
12
s
pl
cbch
apr
bpr
1 Tundra soils, including some bog soils
2 Lithosols, with some podsolics
3 pl Podsols, with some lithosols on high ground
4 Chernozems
5 Chestnut and brown soils
6 Planosols and prairie soils
7 Latosols
8 Grey desert soils and lithosols
9 Red desert soils and lithosols
10 Boggy and alluvial soils
11 r Rendzinas
12 Podsols, lithosols, and tundra soils (northern Cordillera)
s Sands (South Dakota)
cbch Chestnut soils, brown soils, and chernozems (Snake-Columbia Plateau)
apr Alluvial and prairie soils (Great Valley)
bpr Brown and prairie soils (South California)

FIG. 4:2 Soils.

almost to the foot of the Cordillera. In the mountains, pine, spruce, and fir occur in various combinations.

Although the southern limit of boreal forest on the Shield resembles the southern limit of lithosols, the resemblance is accidental. Wherever the soil is thick enough and sufficiently well drained through the profile, it is podsolized. The topmost layer is darkened by the acid humus which leaf-fall supplies; the grey layer beneath is strongly leached by downward-percolating water; and below this, humic materials and iron compounds block the soil pores and tend to form an impermeable cement. Soils which are distinctly boggy, or which possess very poor site drainage and profile drainage, occur around the head of James Bay, and in the Lake Winnipeg area where Glacier Lake Agassiz formerly stood: these are the districts dominated by spruce–larch. In the Cordillera, the soils under needleleaf forest are podsolized where they reach any depth, and consist of lithosols elsewhere.

Very little of the boreal forest country has been brought into agricultural use. Neither the strongly leached and acid podsols nor the climate favour agriculture, quite apart from question of competition with warmer and better-placed areas. The few exceptional sites are located between James Bay and the Great Lakes and in the southern catchment of Lake Winnipeg, where the clays of former ice-dammed lakes have proved worth draining. Some of the difficulties which confront cultivation are indicated by the wide distribution of needleleaf trees: these are adapted to withstand drought – not the climatic drought of low rainfall and high temperatures, but the physiological drought of brief growing - seasons between long winters when soil moisture is frozen.

In the angle between Lakes Superior and Michigan, between Lake Huron and the head of the Gulf of St Lawrence, in parts of the upland country of New England, and in the northeast Appalachians, the forest scene changes with the incoming of maple. The combinations maple–yellow birch–hemlock–pine and maple–beech–hemlock are both widespread. This forest division is renowned for its autumn colours – yellows, golds, bronzes, reds – for which the maple is chiefly responsible. From the air, wherever the forest cover is reasonably intact, the autumn scene is unforgettable: and the display of seasonal colour attracts tourists who, if they will, can move southward with the colour-change. The southern limit of this forest type corresponds approximately with an annual frost-free season of 120 days, and with January and July mean temperatures of 25° F and 70° F (−4° C and 22° C).

Water surplus and downward leaching ensure that the soils of this division are also podsolic, wherever they are deep enough for profile development: lithosols occur on high ground and on steep slopes. But increasing geniality of climate, and decreasing acidity of soil, have allowed this division to be encroached on considerably by farming.

Broadleaf Deciduous Forest

The main block of natural broadleaf deciduous forest lies chiefly in the U.S.A., east of the Mississippi and north of the latitude of the southern end of the Appalachians (Plate 5). It spreads from the Interior Lowlands southwards on to the low plateaus of Kentucky and Tennessee, sends a projection past Lakes Erie and Ontario to the mouth of the Ottawa River, and, ascending the Appalachians from the west, crosses them in a second projection which reaches Boston. Maple is again prominent in this division, introducing brilliant displays of autumn colour into the combinations beech–maple and oak–ash–maple, while oak–tulip tree dominates the southern of the two eastward prongs. Along the southern edge, the average frost-free season rises to about 150 days, while January and July mean temperatures are about 35° F and 75° F (2° C and 25° C). That is to say, no month has a mean temperature below freezing.

In this forest division also, soils are mainly of podsolic kinds except in the southwest. But although in the natural state these podsolics are acid in reaction, they constitute better agricultural propositions than do the podsols of the boreal forest. Capable of responding well to fertilizers, they have been brought widely into cultivation except on high or steeply-sloping ground.

Broadleaf deciduous forest overlaps from the belt of podsolic soils towards the southwest, encroaching on the adjoining latosols both in the low unglaciated plateau country of Tennessee, and in the equally unglaciated but somewhat higher Ozarks. Latosols possess affinities with the laterites of parts of the tropics, and may indeed be mainly relict –

5. Broadleaf deciduous forest around East Corinth, Vermont. Village layout and style of building are typical of upstate New England.

i.e., formed in alternating hot–wet and warm–dry seasons in a former climate warmer than that of today. The rocks on which the latosols occur are deeply weathered. As a group, these soils display no great profile development: strongly leached, they are naturally poor in plant nutrients but respond to fertilizers. Their distinctive reddish and yellowish hues are due to iron compounds which have survived leaching.

Forests and Swamplands of the South

In addition to the areas already named, latosols occupy much of the U.S. South, wrapping round the southern end of the Appalachians and reaching along the Piedmont and the Coastal Plain almost to Chesapeake Bay. Their natural cover here is oak–pine forest, in which pine rises to dominance where the frost-free season averages 220 days or more, and where January and July mean temperatures reach 45°F and 80°F (8°C and 27°C). However, the principal expanses of pine forest reflect soil quality rather than local (as opposed to regional) climate: they correspond to outcrops of permeable sands which are very strongly leached indeed. Strips of natural grassland curving concentrically to the southern end of the Appalachians correspond to outcrops of limestone, where rendzinas have developed – lime-rich soils with alkaline humus blackening their uppermost horizon. Large additional patches of rendzina, also naturally in grass, adjoin the latosols west of the Mississippi.

Estuarine swamps along the south Atlantic and Gulf coasts, and swamps inland in Florida, possess boggy soils on which cypress is associated chiefly with pine in partly deciduous and partly evergreen needleleaf forest (Plate 6). Trees here are adapted to moist soils but also to high air temperatures. On the alluvial lowlands of the Mississippi, cypress joins with bay, tupelo, and gum in deciduous forest which is part needleleaf and part broadleaf.

Wooded Prairies and Grass Prairies

West of the Mississippi – or, more accurately, west of a line from Lake Michigan to the head of the alluvial trough of the Mississippi and thence to the Delta – a general westward change in soils and in vegetation makes itself evident. It is heralded round the southern end of Lake Michigan, in the angle between the Wabash and Mississippi Rivers, by an irregular but noticeable development of tall grassland, surrounded by deciduous woodland and tall-grass glades: the distributions marked in Fig. 4:1 are highly generalized. Broadleaf deciduous forest renews itself along the upper Mississippi and in the valleys of the main tributaries, linking southwards with the forests of the Interior Highlands where oak–hickory dominates, and northwestwards with the deciduous fringe of the Canadian forests where the association is aspen–oak. Westward again, the forest thins into woodland as dryness increases, and tall-grass glades reappear, until trees become confined chiefly to ribbons of hardwood along valley-bottoms and the grass cover – in which bluegrass is generally dominant – occupies the low flattish interfluves.

It is clear from what has already been said that site characteristics – especially site drainage – profoundly influence the detailed pattern of woodland–grass combinations. Nevertheless, the relevant gross distributions of plant cover are reasonably well related to distributions of climate. Little of the broadleaf deciduous forest occupies land where the climate is drier than humid.* The woodland with tall-grass glades belongs with a moist subhumid climate, while climate in the dominantly tall-grass country ranges from moist subhumid to dry subhumid, most falling in the latter category and experiencing on the year's balance a distinct water need. The still drier short-grass country next on the west is semi-arid (cf. Fig. 4:13).

A general southward increase in temperature ensures that the change from dominant natural forest or woodland to dominant natural grassland, or the change from subhumidity of the tall grassland to the semi-aridity of the short grassland, does not occur at a fixed isohyet. On the Gulf coast, the passage from moist to dry subhumidity takes place at about the 30-inch isohyet, whereas on the Canadian border it comes at about 20 inches.

The complex entanglement of forest with woodland, and of woodland with grassland, means difficulty in relating plant cover to generality of climate. However, the main area in which broadleaf trees grow in forest or in woodland, along and on either side of the upper Mississippi corresponds fairly well with the area in which the frost-free season averages 120 to 160 days, where January mean temperatures are 10° F to 30° F (−12° C to 1° C), July means are 70° F to 80° F (21° C to 27° C), and mean annual precipitation runs at 25 to 30 inches. In this same area, prairie soils and planosols are widespread. The prairie soils are darkened by humus in their upper part, but are sufficiently leached in the natural state to be slightly acid and to lack accumulations of lime. Planosols, formed on flat ground with poor site drainage, possess well-defined clay layers in the lower part of the profile: their chief development has occurred on the southernmost, oldest, and most-weathered sheets of glacial deposit between the lower Ohio and the lower Missouri. Planosols vary widely in potential, according to parent mater-

* The climatic categories used here are drawn from Thornthwaite's classification.

6. Cypress growing in a flooded sinkhole in the Florida Panhandle.

ial and possibilities of drainage, but the prairie soils include some of the best in the continent.

Projection of the hardwood forest, southeastward on to latosols in the Interior Highlands, has been noticed above. The northwestward projection which carries a strip of this forest into Canada brings it on to the belt of chernozems. These are very dark to wholly black soils, roughly co-extensive in distribution with natural tall grassland and with dry subhumid climate, occupying a boundary strip of the Interior Lowlands in the U.S.A., but in Canada swinging away westward across the Great Plains from the lakefloor flats of Glacier Lake Agassiz, and recurving south at the foot of the Rockies. Chernozems owe their blackness and their high humus content to the organic additions made by tall grass – mainly, by decay of root-mat. Their distinctive lime content below the surface indicates absence of downward leaching, and the failure of soil moisture to make contact with the ground-water table. At their northern boundary in Canada, the chernozems have become degraded in response to a slight worsening of climate since they were formed: this same shift is responsible for driving the strip of deciduous forest southward on to the grassland soils.

Chestnut and brown soils on the Great Plains also developed under grassland: but this was the short grassland of semi-arid climates, dominated by grama grass, buffalo grass, or needle grass. The chestnut and brown soils are less highly humified than the chernozems, but are more greatly enriched by lime below the surface. Problems of cultivation are largely climatic, concerned with rainfall and water-supply, except that the Nebraskan sandhills which lie athwart the chernozem–chestnut soil boundary possess mineral soils unadapted to farming and incompletely clad by specialized grass and scrub.

The Cordillera

Great diversity of relief in the Cordillera entails equal diversity of local climate and of vegetation. Similar diversity characterizes Cordilleran soils. Nevertheless, generalization in respect of gross distributions can be attempted. Podsolic soils and lithosols accompany the southward extension of needleleaf evergreen forest across the 49th parallel – forest in which pine and firs are prominent, with juniper increasingly numerous on the Colorado Plateau. Above the needleleaf forest, lithosols support the Alpine vegetation of the summits, while oakwood fringes the lower edge of needleleaf in the Southern Rockies, on the Colorado Plateau, and in the Great Valley of California. Oak–fir forest with podsolic soils occupies the lowest and most rain-shadowed part of the Puget Sound–Willamette Valley Lowland, while short grassland occurs on the chernozems and chestnut and brown soils of the rain-shadowed Snake–Columbia Plateau where mean annual precipitation is about 10 inches. Similar grassland under a somewhat higher precipitation but with higher temperatures recurs on alluvial and prairie soils in the Great Valley of California.

In the Great Basin and in the Wyoming Basin, climate is arid, the limit of aridity being fairly well defined by the 10-inch isohyet. Vegetation is dominated by broadleaf evergreen shrubs, closely adapted to long spells of drought: its most prominent constituent varies southward from sagebrush to shadscale. Soils are the shallow lithosols of pediments, the equally shallow lithosols of block-faulted mountains, or the grey desert soils formed on basin fills. Being very little leached, grey desert soils are rich in mineral nutrients: but the vegetation under which they form is so sparse that their humic content is negligible. On account of climate, they cannot be cultivated except under irrigation; and where they pass into saline soils, cultivation becomes impossible.

The higher parts of the Colorado Plateau have already been noticed as supporting tree cover. The lower parts, generally pedimented, carry sagebrush scrub or short grama grassland on the lithosols of an arid to semi-arid climate. South of the Great Basin, the remainder of the basin-and-range country sustains broadleaf evergreen shrubs – especially creosote-bush associations – and cactus. Except in colour, the red desert soils here resemble the grey desert soils farther north. Shrubland extends eastward along the Mexican border past the end of the Southern Rockies; it occupies the southern end of the Great Plains, encroaching on the chestnut soils in an area where these, nearing their southern limit, are distinctly reddened, and passes even farther on to the Gulf Coastal Plain almost to the sea. In these districts, mesquite shrub is associated with mesquite grass in a climate where the frost-free season exceeds 200 days, and where January mean temperatures of 40°F to 60°F (4°C to 16°C) and July means of above 80°F (27°C) imply warmth more than sufficient to offset an annual precipitation ranging from 10 to 40 inches.

ASSESSMENTS OF CLIMATE

This section deals with the classification of North American climates, with certain aspects of climatic variation, and with leading climatic controls. Among the latter come air-masses and air-streams, ocean currents, land-and-sea distribution, and major distributions of relief.

Climatic Controls: Air-masses and Air-streams

An air-mass is a large body of air, hundreds or thousands of miles across, varying little in its physical properties across its width. The air-masses which will be specified here as affecting North American climates are all low-level bodies, which reach near-equilibrium with underlying surfaces of land or sea. Heat, and frequently moisture also, are exchanged between the air and the underlying surface. In order for the exchange to take place, the air must remain more or less stationary for periods of upwards of a few days, over the *source region* where it acquires its distinctive qualities. When the

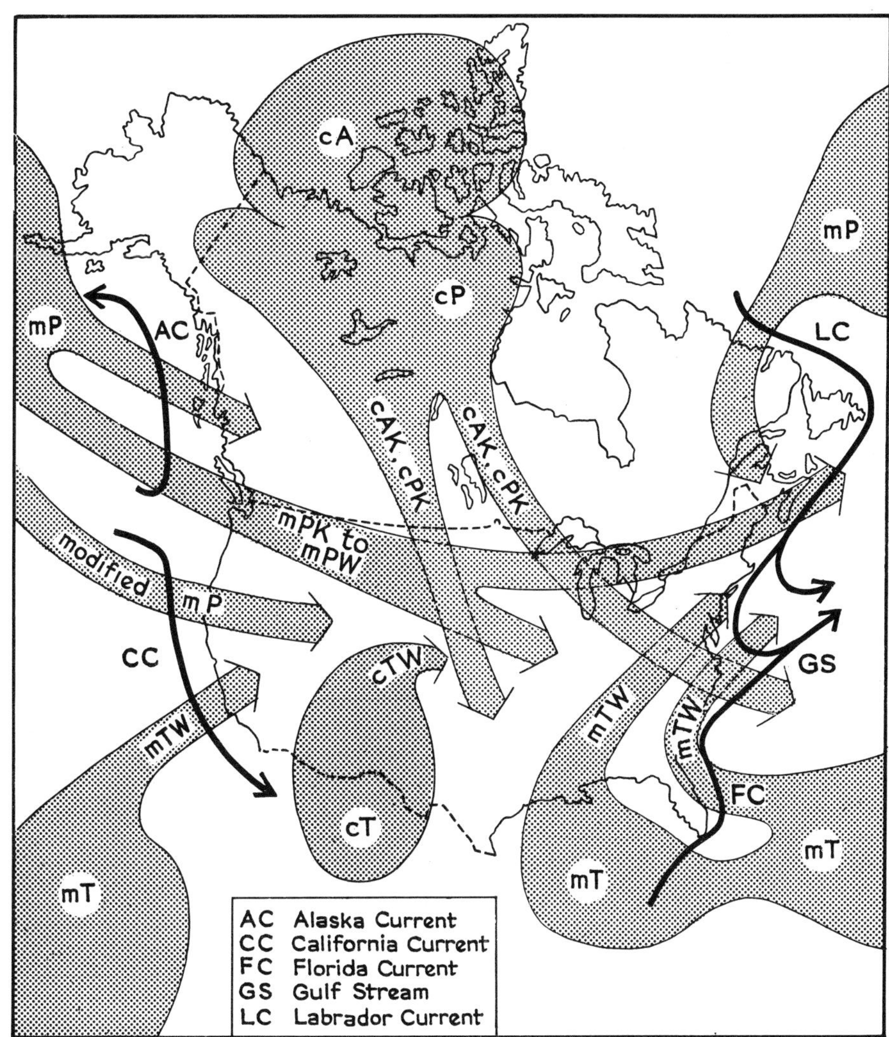

FIG. 4:3
Air-mass source regions, directions of air outflow, ocean currents.

air moves out of the source region it becomes an *air-stream*. Areas over which the air-stream flows will receive winds ranging from warm to cold and from wet to dry, according to the characteristics of the air-stream compared to those of the invaded area.

Air-masses, and the air-streams which they produce, are classified in a number of ways simultaneously. For present purposes, it is enough to classify by nature of source region – whether land or sea – by position of the air-mass within the scheme of the general circulation, and by relative warmth or coldness.

Air-masses which form over the sea are labelled *m*, for maritime; those which form over the land, or over the frozen polar sea, are given the symbol *c*, for continental. Air-masses belonging initially to the low-latitude circulation – in the main, to the low-latitude belt of high-pressure cells – are called *T*, for tropical. Air-masses originating in the high north are either *P*, polar, or *A*, arctic. Where the polar and arctic fronts exist, *P* air lies between them and *A* air on the poleward side of the arctic front.

Maritime tropical, *mT*, air-masses can develop, for instance, over the Gulf of Mexico. If *mT* air-streams reach the Southern States in winter, they are invariably warmer than the land over which they blow: hence the use of the further symbol *W*, giving *mTW*, for maritime tropical warm. Continental polar and arctic air frequently moves southward in winter across the interior of the continent, bringing increased cold to areas which it crosses: here the notation is *cPK* or *cAK*, for continental polar, or continental arctic, cold air.

The dominance of certain source regions, the kinds of air produced, and the preferred paths of air-streams go far to account for the seasonal and spatial variation of North American climates. The principal source regions are arranged in two distinct belts (Fig. 4:3). Off the western extremities of Alaska, and again off southern Greenland, occurs a source region of mP air, corresponding roughly in each case to the winter lows of the average map of pressure. The air-streams moving out from these source regions are moist, in terms of relative humidity, but the absolute humidity of the Atlantic streams is kept down by low temperatures. In addition, these streams do not always penetrate the North American continent, being often diverted into the west-to-east zonal circulation. The mP air-streams from the Pacific, in strong contrast, affect the western coastlands from Alaska to about the Golden Gate. Whereas in summer the more northerly of them may arrive as mPK air, the more southerly have been modified during their long passage across the ocean, and in winter invariably come in as mPW. Wherever these streams ascend the west-facing slopes of the Cordillera, they are inevitably cooled, condensing their moisture content into additional cloud and yielding abundant precipitation. Their depth of penetration varies both with season and with latitude. In winter, they are normally excluded from all but the immediate coastlands of Alaska and much of British Columbia by high pressures developed over the seasonally chilled land. On the central Californian coast, mP air arrives only during the winter when the major belts of wind and pressure have been displaced to the south. In between the two areas, the incoming mP air can cross the Cordillera fairly readily; and here are found the main paths of entry for lows travelling from the west.

Development of cP and cA air in the northern interior during winter is, in the first instance, a function of cooling above a frozen and snow-covered surface. But the air-streams which the two source regions discharge contribute importantly to the general circulation. The transport of air by the zonal westerlies has a poleward component, both at low levels and at high. The tendency for air to be fed into the polar area is compensated from time to time by outbursts towards the south. The waves of cPK and cAK air spreading across the North American interior in winter constitute precisely such outbursts: they return air from high latitudes into the circulation of the tropics.

The southern array of source regions includes three which are maritime and one which is continental. Coinciding with a cell of tropical high pressure, the Pacific source delivers streams of mTW air, which are however mainly stable, and in consequence not great rain-bringers. The other two source regions of mT air, one over the Gulf and one over the Atlantic, also deliver mTW air, but air which is frequently very moist and highly unstable. It is moisture transported, and delivered, by these southerly or southeasterly mTW streams which accounts for most of the precipitation of the interior.

Continental tropical air forms in a source region straddling the U.S.–Mexican border. This air is always dry, and in summer is very hot. Although the high summer temperatures might be expected to result in low pressures, and these in the invasion of air-streams from outside, the cT air belongs essentially to the belt of subtropical highs, and is in consequence not easily displaced. The source regions emit streams of cTW air, particularly to the northeast and east; recurrent drought in southern portions of the Great Plains corresponds to increases in their frequency and strength.

Ocean Currents

Ocean currents modify the qualities of air-streams which pass over them. The one fundamental fact is that warm currents, tending to make the overlying air unstable, tend in consequence to encourage convective uprising, the upward transport of moisture, the increase of atmosphere humidity, and the the increase in capacity to precipitate. Cold currents act in precisely the reverse way, limiting the supply of moisture from sea to air, increasing atmospheric stability, and keeping precipitation down.

Warm currents off North America are northward-moving; cold currents flow towards the equator, bringing low sea-surface temperatures into low latitudes. Off the west coast, the Alaskan Current (Fig. 4:3) produces its main effect on terrestrial climate in southern Alaska, when it has already moved northward through a considerable distance but has not had time to give up much heat. It delivers heat and moisture alike to the onshore streams of mP air, making them warmer, more unstable, and moister than they would otherwise be, and helping to account for the heavy rainfall and snowfall of the northwestern coastland. The opposing Californian Current is cold. Its effect is mainly negative, for transfer of heat and moisture from air to sea is slow and difficult. Nevertheless, there can be no doubt that the eastward-moving mP air from the Pacific, greatly modified already by its long passage from the source region, would bring far more rain to California than it does bring, were the current a warm one. The obvious contrast to be drawn is that between offshore conditions of the west coast and offshore conditions of the east coast. The difference is most pronounced in late summer, when sea-surface temperatures reach their maximum values. At this time, the sea surface offshore of the Golden Gate is about 20°F cooler than the corresponding water off Cape Hatteras, in the same latitude on the eastern side of the continent.

Oceanic circulation on the eastern side includes part of the Gulf Stream system. Conventionally, this system is taken to originate with the Florida Current, which flows eastward through the Straits of Florida. In actuality, of course, no particular current can be fully dealt with, unless the supply and the subsequent disposal of its waters are accounted for. A full treatment would mean a summary of the general oceanic circulation. Suffice it to say that the Florida Current is maintained by the input of water under the stress of the Trade Winds – both the Northeast Trades of the Northern Hemisphere, and the Southeast Trades of the Southern Hemisphere, for part of the southern stream of the Atlantic Equatorial Current is diverted into the Northern Hemisphere by the projecting shoulder of Brazil. In consequence, water fed into the Gulf of Mexico is unusually copious, and unusually warm. It escapes through the Straits of Florida, at the remarkably high rate of some 50,000 cubic miles a year, to constitute the Florida Current. High surface temperatures typical of the Gulf are extended far to the northeast. The Florida Current keeps fairly close inshore to about the latitude of Cape Hatteras, where it then strikes out across the Atlantic as the Gulf Stream.

Throughout the winter season, the surface waters of the Gulf of Mexico and of the Florida Current are much warmer than the near-by land. Air from the two mT source regions can, if it is sufficiently unstable, or if it becomes incorporated in travelling lows, yield large amounts of precipitation. In summer, when the land is also warm, delivery of additional heat to incoming mT air also aids precipitation, this time of the convectional type.

Northward from Cape Hatteras, the Gulf Stream is separated from the coast by colder water lying above the continental shelf and slope. A principal origin of this water is in the Labrador Current. This element of the oceanic circulation emerges from the Polar Sea between Greenland and Labrador, swinging round the eastern side of Newfoundland, and moving southwestwards until it swirls into the Gulf

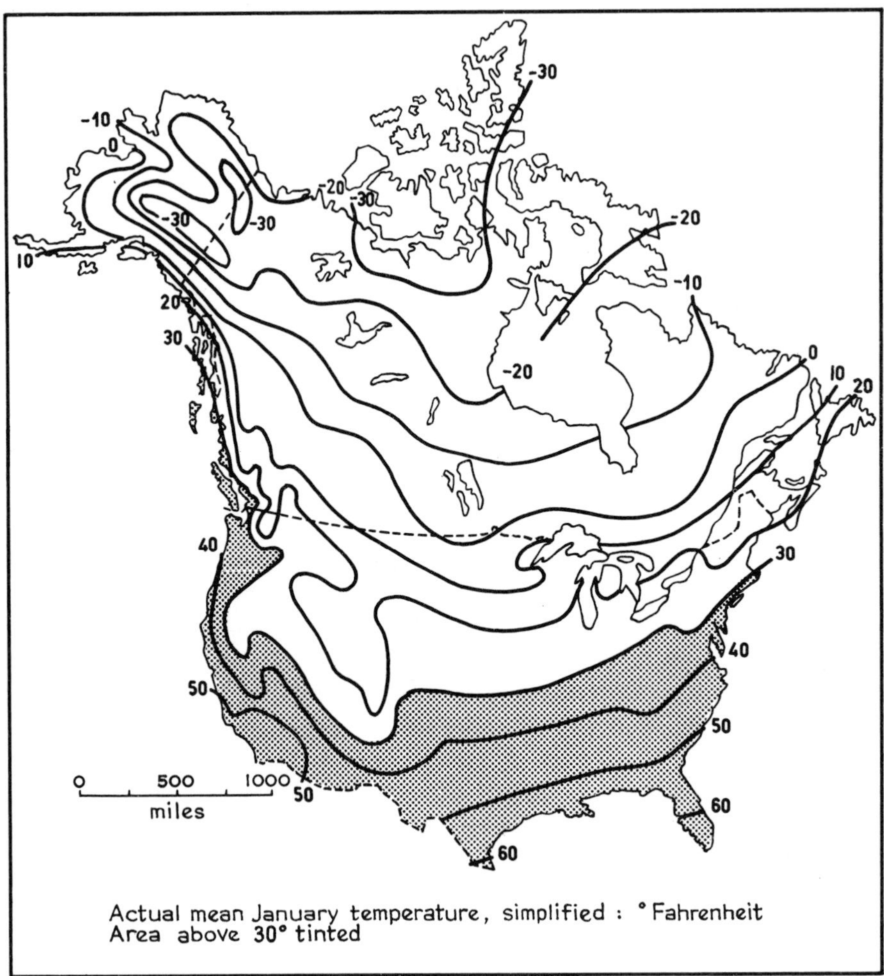

FIG. 4:4.

Stream system or sinks beneath it. Sea-surface temperatures fall off rapidly towards the north over this water-body, which contributes signally to the unpleasantness of winter climates in the northeast, and which also helps to transport icebergs southward, into the Laurentian shipping lanes, during the calving season.

Land-and-sea Distributions

In a general way, range of mean temperatures in North America increases with distance from the oceans, while precipitation decreases with increasing distance inland. Complications arise from the influence of relief, and in particular from the obstructive influence of the Cordillera.

Fig. 4:4 shows that the actual mean January isotherms loop boldly southward in the west of the continent. The 20°F isotherm, crossing on to the land from the Pacific at the north end of the Alaska Panhandle, runs eventually near Denver, Colorado, about 1700 miles farther south. The 40°F isotherm, not very far from the Canadian border on the Pacific coast, closely approaches the Mexican border at the extremity of its southward sweep. The lowest temperature values in January, in comparison with latitude, are reached in three kinds of setting: in the eastern Cordillera, where altitudes measured in thousands of feet above sea-level intensify the seasonal cold of inland areas; in a belt which includes the upper Mississippi Valley and Lake Winnipeg where, in the centre of the continent, January means are kept down by chill air-streams from the north; and in the far north and northwest, either in the source regions of cP and cA air, or in

FIG. 4:5.

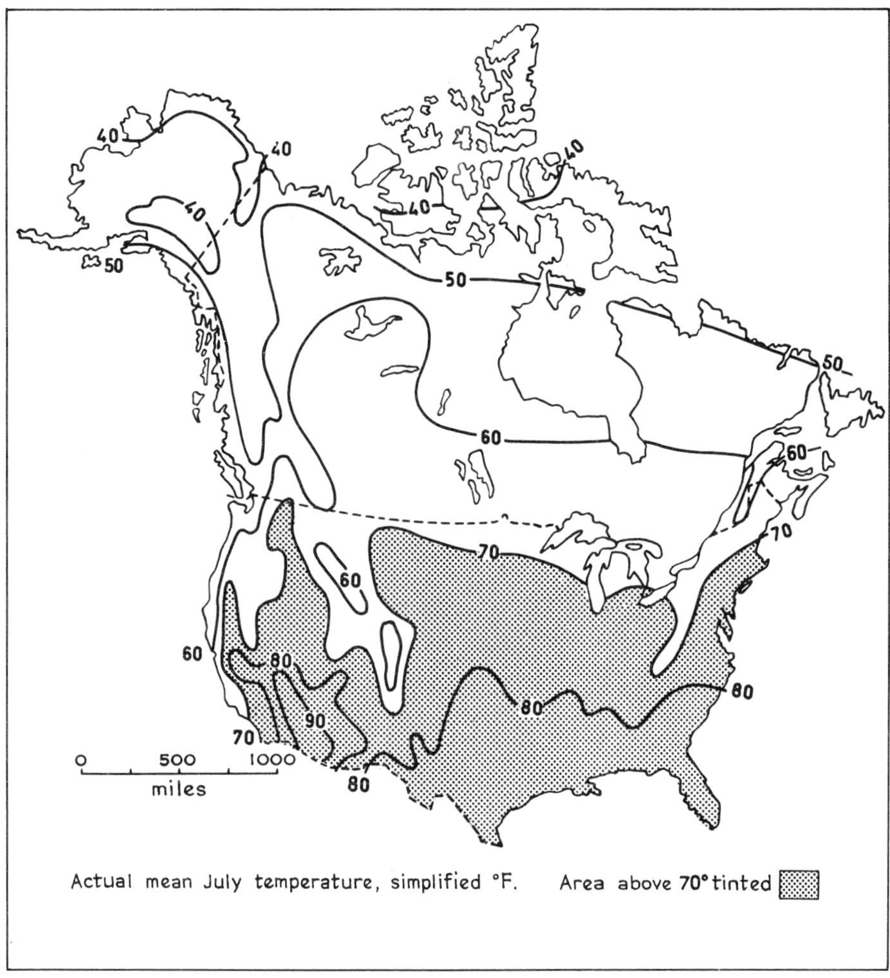

interior Alaska, where means far below zero are recorded both on the mountains and in the basins where cold dense air collects.

On the eastern side of the continent, the January isotherms run but slightly northward with the approach to the coast. The average westerly circulation ensures that, in the winter season, invasion of the east by maritime air is uncommon.

July isotherms swing north over the interior, at least as markedly in places as July isotherms bend to the south (Fig. 4:5). However, the July pattern is complicated by the establishment in the southwest of a closed 90° F isotherm, in the source region of cTW air, and also by the pronounced southward inflection of all relevant isotherms in mountainous areas. The presence of the Appalachians is clearly indicated by the projecting tongue in the 70° F line, which also encloses the Southern Rockies and a massive block of the western Cordillera, mainly in Oregon. About half of the interior of British Columbia records a July mean of less than 50° F, whereas the month is equally warm a thousand miles farther north, between Hudson's Bay and the Yukon.

These two temperature maps help to emphasize the huge extent of North America, showing as they do that the difference in mean temperature between, say, the delta of the Mackenzie and the delta of the Mississippi is about 40° F in July and more than 70° F in January.

Land-and-sea distributions also influence precipitation, although in the west of the continent the effect of distributions proper is highly accentuated by distributions of relief. The source of precipita-

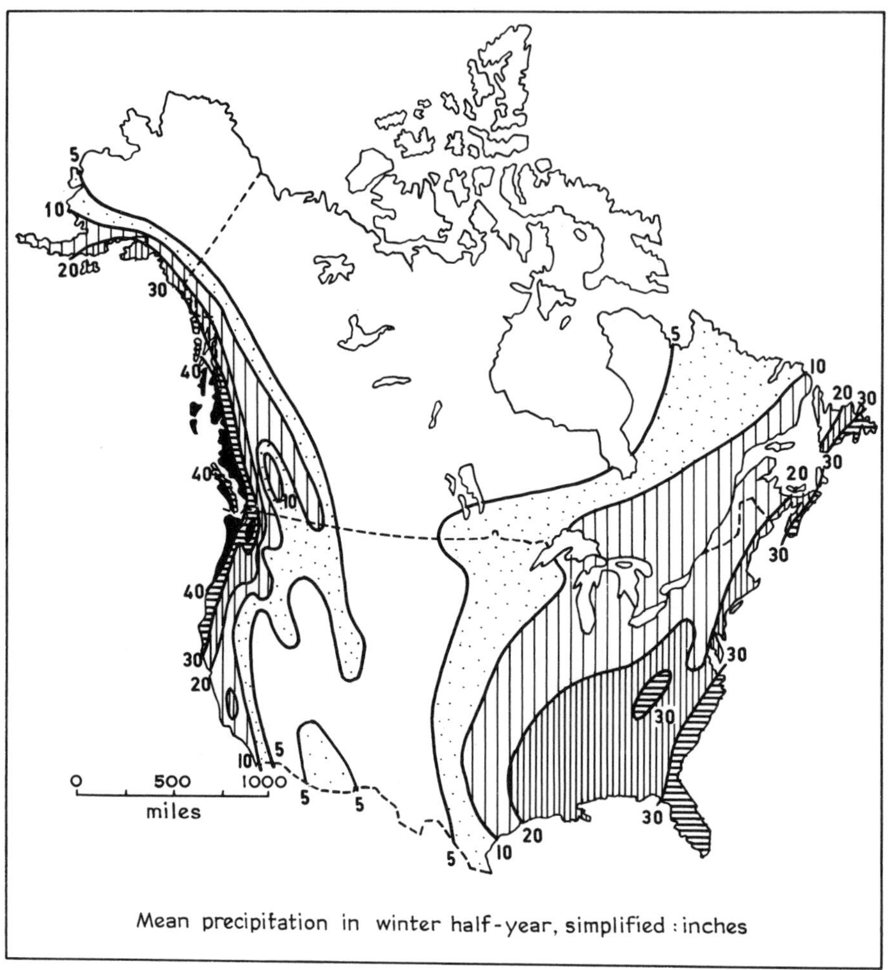

Mean precipitation in winter half-year, simplified : inches

FIG. 4:6.

tion on the west is the Pacific: the transporting agents are the streams of mP and mT air already noticed.

Totals for the winter half-year decrease rapidly towards the east (Fig. 4:6), from more than 40 inches in the wettest parts of the coastlands to less than 5 inches. They also decrease both towards the north and towards the south from the areas of greatest winter rain – northwards on account of increasing cold, which reduces the moisture-carrying powers of the incoming winds, and southwards because the arrival of westerlies is frequently interrupted by temporary high pressures. The eastern part of the continent, far lower in general, and far less varied in relief than the west, displays very clearly the effect of distance from the sea. The 30-inch isohyet keeps close to the coastline, except for reappearing in the Appalachians, and winter precipitation declines fairly steadily along any line drawn at right-angles to the coastal trend, down to the 5-inch mark.

Similarly in the summer half-year (Fig. 4:7), the source of precipitable moisture off to the east and south is obvious from the map. In this season, however, when heating over the land reduces air pressure, when the warmed seasonal air can hold, and deliver, more moisture than the air of winter, and when also the winter highs over the interior no longer exist to fend off potential inflows, precipitation in a great fraction of the continent is as heavy as, or heavier than, that of winter. The course of the 10-inch isohyet in summer, from Hudson's Bay past Lake Winnipeg and south along the Western Plains through Texas, runs in fact farther west than

FIG. 4:7.

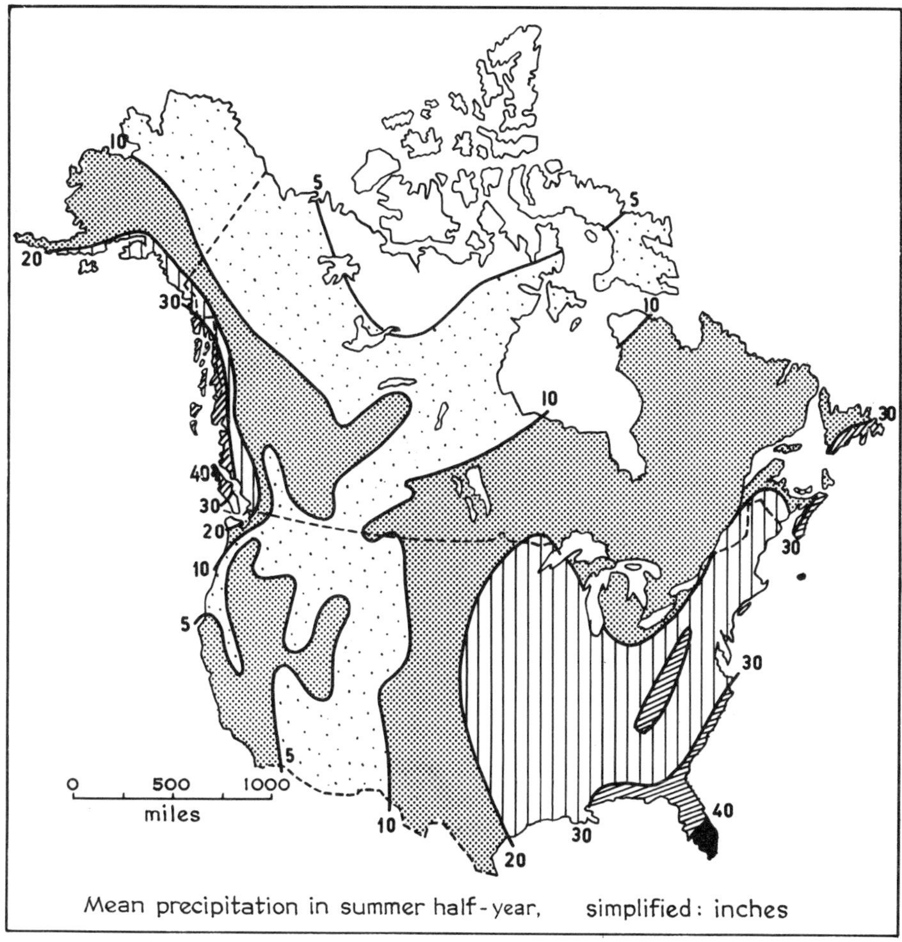

the course of the 5-inch isohyet – generally similar as this is in trend – in winter.

On the western side, the contrast takes an opposite form. The western coastlands and the western hinterlands are in the main drier in summer than they are in winter. In the far southwest they are much drier. But some parts of the Cordillera and most of Canada west of Hudson's Bay are wetter in summer than in winter, not because they receive air from the Gulf or from the Atlantic, but because they are accessible to maritime air from the Pacific. Summer heating over the land extinguishes the high pressures of winter. Frontal rain falls in travelling lows, and convectional rain results from local thermal updrafts.

A spatially restricted but economically important effect, not strictly of land-and-sea distribution but nevertheless of land-and-water distribution, is produced in the Great Lakes area. Until the winter freeze sets in, the Lakes act as reservoirs of heat and moisture. Surface water, cooling as the winter season comes on, sinks downwards: its replacing warmer water, typically at higher-than-air temperatures in the late autumn and early winter, warms and moistens the air above. Since the dominant circulation of air is from west to east, the lands to the east of the Lakes – and especially to the east of Michigan and Huron – receive greater precipitation, and also record a tardier onset of winter, than the lands immediately to the west. Both because of its extreme southerly position in Canada, and on account of this climatic amelioration, the Lake Peninsula is agriculturally special. It raises crops – notably, fruit and tobacco – which are uneconomic or impossible to grow in many other parts of the country.

Influence of Major Relief Distributions

Inevitably, repeated reference has already been made to the influence on climate of the Cordilleran Mountains and the Appalachians, for the effect of high ground both on precipitation and on actual temperatures is obvious on the distribution maps. The Cordillera, being far longer and higher than the Appalachians, and lying athwart the incoming air-streams from the Pacific, constitutes by far the more effective climatic divide. As already stated, it experiences a strong general decline in precipitation from west to east, and displays pronounced differences between western and eastern sides, respectively, in individual ranges.

The Cordillera heavily reinforces the seasonal effect of winter high-pressure systems. These form in the chilled air over the northern interior, being prevented by the Cordillera from draining in any westerly direction, and being protected by the Cordillera from encroachment by any but the most intense of travelling lows. There is no comparable situation anywhere else in the world – one in which low-lying plainland, reaching at one end into the source regions of cP and cA air, leads at the other almost to the tropic where this crosses the ocean.

On a grand scale, the Cordillera produces the effect of rain-shadow. Air-streams crossing it from the west are progressively drained of their moisture as they ascend the mountain barriers. Each ascent, each episode of condensation and precipitation, means that latent heat is released. In consequence, the cooling of the air during its ascent it slow. On the eastern descending side, on the other hand, the air warms up rapidly. It is for this reason that westerlies which succeed in crossing the central parts of the Cordillera in winter or spring arrive on the adjacent Plains as unusually warm and very dry winds. They constitute the Chinook, the eater of snow, capable of evaporating the snow-cover almost directly into the atmosphere, without first producing a soil-soaking intermediary of meltwater.

Seasonal Variation of Climate and Related Considerations

Fig. 4:8 presents temperature graphs for selected stations: these are located in Fig. 4:13. The upper limits of the temperature – bands in the graphs are mean monthly maxima, the lower are the mean monthly minima. Thus, the vertical depth of the bands corresponds to the mean monthly range of temperature.

Juneau, Portland, and Sacramento are all Cordilleran stations. They illustrate the general southward increase in temperatures, the corresponding increase in the length of frost-free season, and the modest annual ranges of temperature which characterize maritime air. Indeed, differences between monthly maxima and monthly minima are also modest, except in summer at Sacramento, where in that season stable mT air or local high-pressure systems produce clear skies: heating occurs freely by day, but radiational cooling is equally free by night. By contrast with these three stations – and, in particular, by contrast with Portland – Spokane experiences an inland climate. Its summer temperatures are wider-ranging than those of Portland, its winter temperatures about 15°F lower; and its frost-free season is almost identical in length with that of Juneau.

Phoenix exhibits the widest separation between monthly maxima and monthly minima, of all the stations illustrated. Here is the influence of clear skies throughout the year – skies kept free of cloud, for a great deal of the time, in the cT air of the southwest.

Winnipeg, Omaha, Montreal, and Memphis record the very large seasonal ranges of temperature which characterize the whole continental interior. Winter cold is most severe at Winnipeg, which is readily accessible to cAK air at that season. But Omaha also, with the average date of the last winter frost in April, can expect May frosts in some years. The reduction of seasonal range of temperature towards the south, and the rapid southward increase in length of frost-free season are alike evident in a comparison of the diagrams for Omaha and Memphis. This latter station is within reach of mT air, which in winter arrives as mTW, whenever the temporary high-pressure systems drain or fall back. Miami, in direct contrast to these inland stations, has a remarkably low annual range of temperature.

Fig. 4:9 indicates that the principal control on the length of the frost-free season – the average interval between the last frost of spring and the first frost of the next oncoming winter – is affected by the influence already noted. The 200-day limit runs from the southern end of the Alaska Panhandle southwards at little distance from the Pacific coast,

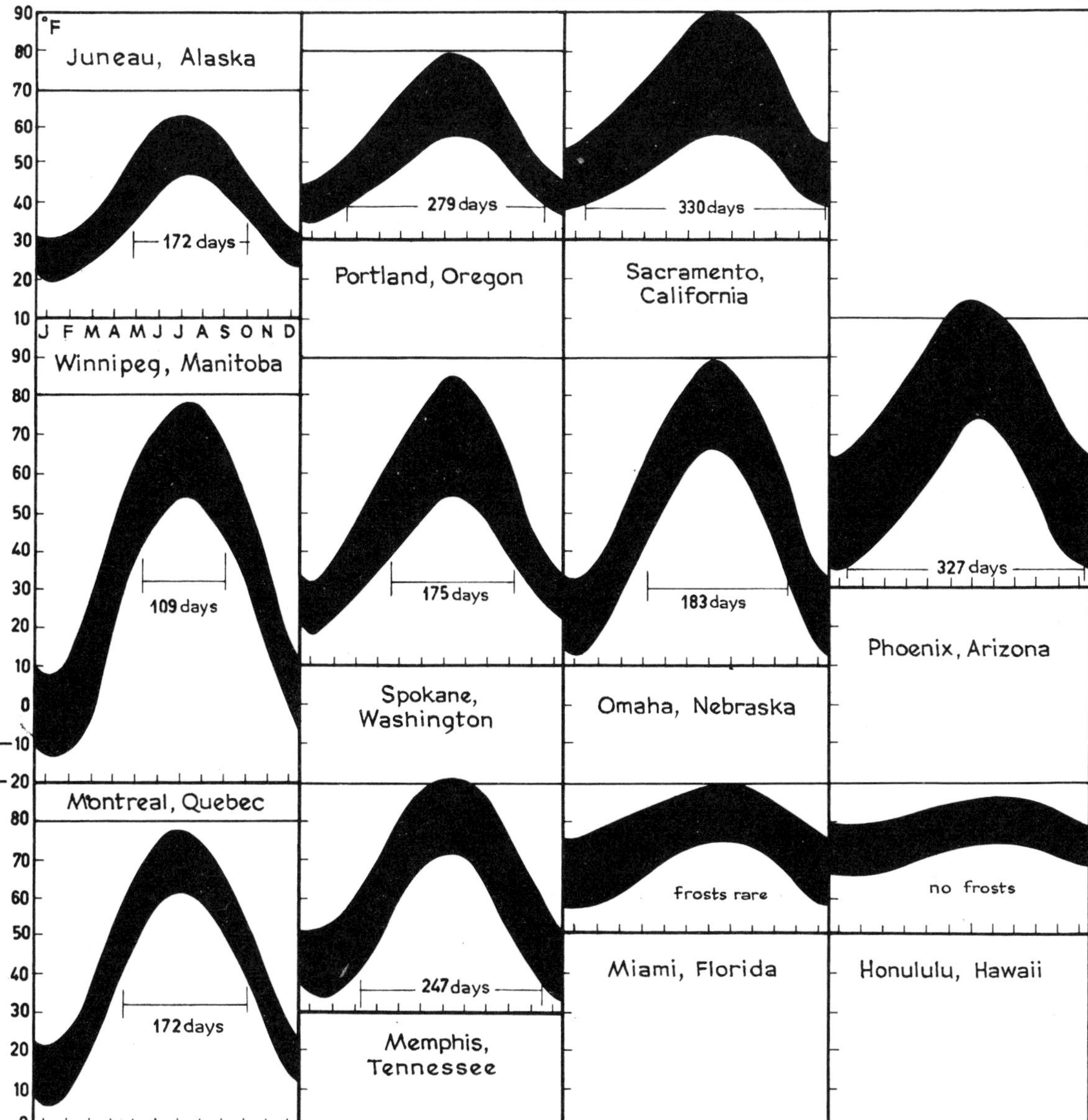

FIG. 4:8 Temperature regimes for selected stations: the bands are defined by mean maximum and mean minimum monthly temperatures.

winds across the Cordillera, and emerges on the Atlantic coast at Chesapeake Bay. The 100-day line follows a somewhat similar but more northerly course, looping round the Southern Rockies and emerging at Newfoundland. Latitude for latitude, the Cordillera is far more liable to frost than is the Pacific coastland, while a broad belt on the eastern side of the continent has a longer frost-free season than that of areas next inland. In the latitude of New York, for instance, the difference is about fifty days. Here again the effect of land-and-sea distribution makes itself apparent.

Length of frost-free season is crucially important in agriculture. Very little commercial cultivation is practised north of the 100-day line. The 200-day line serves as a rough guide, between Virginia and California, to areas in which commercial growing of cotton is possible. The 300-day line is a still rougher guide to areas where a very long frost-free season is favourable to the production of market-

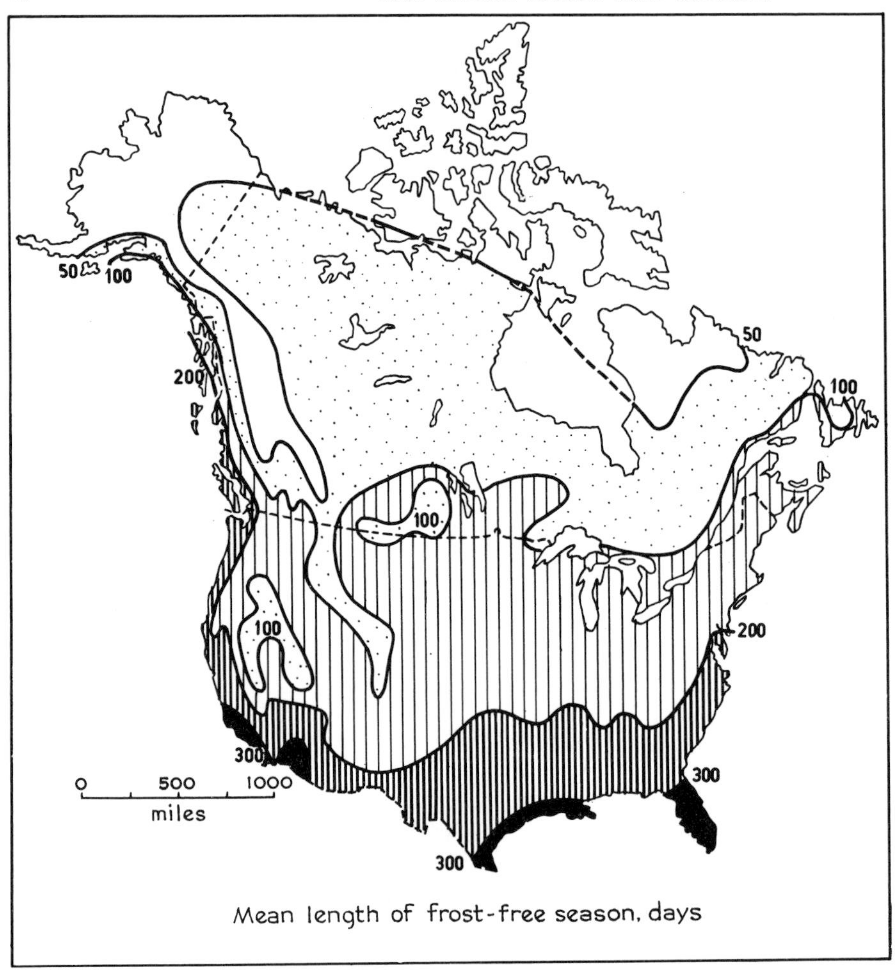

FIG. 4:9.

garden crops and citrus fruits: a somewhat lower mark, perhaps 275 days, would be more fitting here.

The mean length of growing season (Fig. 4:10) is determined differently from the mean length of frost-free season. The latter depends on night minimum temperatures, while the former depends on daily maxima. A common practice is to take 42° F or 43° F as the limit of growth, in accordance with observations that, at lower temperatures, many plants halt their activity. Since it is easily possible for day maxima of more than 42° F or 43° F to be combined with night minima of 32° F or less, growing seasons are usually reckoned as being longer than frost-free seasons: in any event, a frost need not always be a killing frost.

Mean length of growing season decreases on both sides of the continent, latitude for latitude, from the coasts towards the inland. In the extreme north it is but fifty days on the average: one year in two, in the long run, brings a growing season less than seven weeks long. Even on the U.S.–Canadian border, throughout most of its length, the average growing season is only about 175 days in length. It increases progressively, and with increasing speed, towards the south, being 365 days along the whole southern limit of the U.S.A. That is to say, in this southernmost strip, plant growth is possible all the year round.

Another measure of climatic effectiveness is the mean annual sunshine total (Fig. 4:11). Despite the fact that Florida (about 2750 hrs/yr) and South Dakota (about 2800 hyrs/yr) each publicizes itself as the Sunshine State, the maximal area of sunshine is firmly concentrated in the southwest of the U.S.A., where average duration ranges up from more than 3000 hours to more than 4000 hours –

FIG. 4:10.

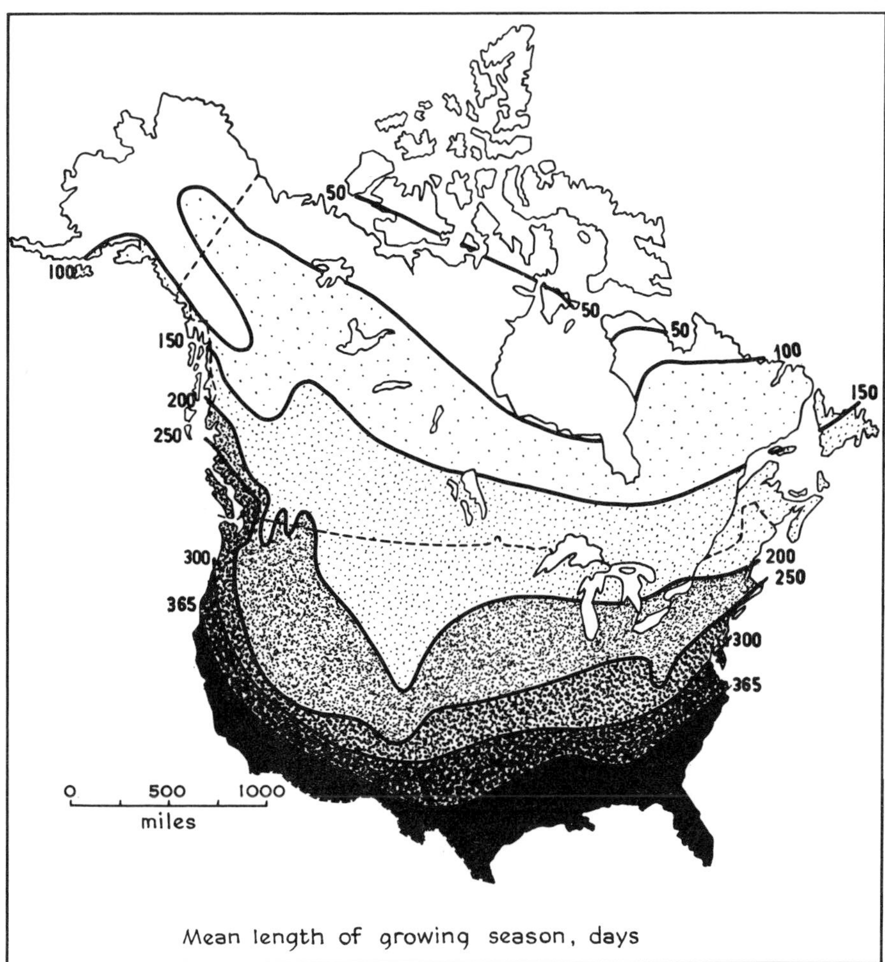

Mean length of growing season, days

that is, to more than ten hours per day. Given sufficient water, this southwestern part, with its very long potential growing season, could be enormously productive of crops. But its lack of rainfall, allied to its remarkably high rate of evaporation, means that commercial cropping is possible only where irrigation water is to be had.

Fig. 4:12 compares the seasonal regime of precipitation with seasonal water need. Its graphs are drawn according to the principles developed by the climatologist Thornthwaite: they relate actual precipitation to computed potential demands on soil moisture by air and plants combined – that is, to evapotranspiration. The diagram for Winnipeg will assist explanation.

During about four winter months, evapotranspiration at Winnipeg is nil. In March–April, even though temperatures are rising, precipitation exceeds demand: a water surplus results, indicated in the Figure by vertical hatching. From May onwards, rising temperatures and stirring plants rapidly increase their intake of water; and although precipitation increases in the mid-year, it cannot match demand. Accordingly, moisture is depleted from the soil. But the reserve of soil moisture is not infinite: it is usually taken as the equivalent of 4 inches of rainfall. After the period of depletion (oblique hatching in the diagram) comes a spell of deficiency, when potential demand still exceeds supply (open circles). At Winnipeg the total deficiency is equal to 5 inches of rainfall. When demand falls swiftly away in the subsequent hasty autumn, the first 4 inches excess precipitation goes to recharge the depleted soil-moisture reserve (oblique hatching). Only after recharge has been effected can the next surplus be counted.

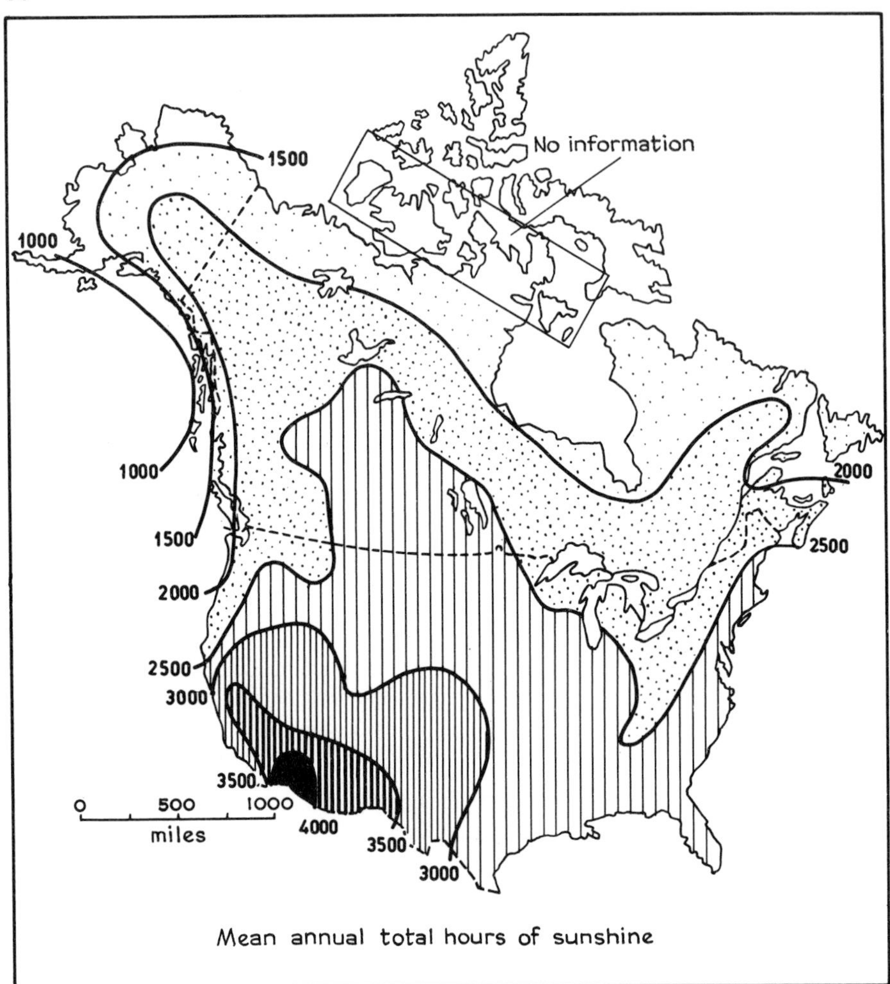

FIG. 4:11.

Analysis in these terms of supply and demand, surplus–depletion–deficiency–recharge, reveals that enormous extents of the North American continent could make use of more precipitation than they experience, were the addition to come in the late mid-year. The extent of deficiency is a measure of the rainfall-equivalent which irrigation would need to supply. Seasonal deficiencies obtain not only in the drier climates of the western interior and the southwest, but also in a large fraction of the natural forest land. On close inspection, that is to say, the earlier classing of the forests as areas of water surplus needs to be qualified.

Vancouver, although having a cold-season surplus of nearly 35 inches, still records a deficiency of nearly 5½ inches in late summer–autumn. At San Francisco, the deficiency is more than 12 inches: at inland stations in the Great Valley it is still more. Precipitation at Phoenix is not even sufficient to charge the soil moisture reservoir with its 4-inch equivalent, while the average annual deficiency is nearly 40 inches. Here, if it were needed, is a convincing demonstration of the impossibility of irrigating all dry lands, unless with the use of water from the sea.

Montreal, however, is different. Not only is its precipitation regime remarkably even – a characteristic found throughout much of the east of the continent, from the St Lawrence to the southern Atlantic coastland – but its protracted winter and brief hurried summer fail to demand the full 4-inch reserve. Soil moisture is an infrequent problem for cultivators in this area, and streamflow, not greatly affected by evaporation, by transpiration, or by recharge, persists strongly throughout the year. It was on this count that the early industrialists in the

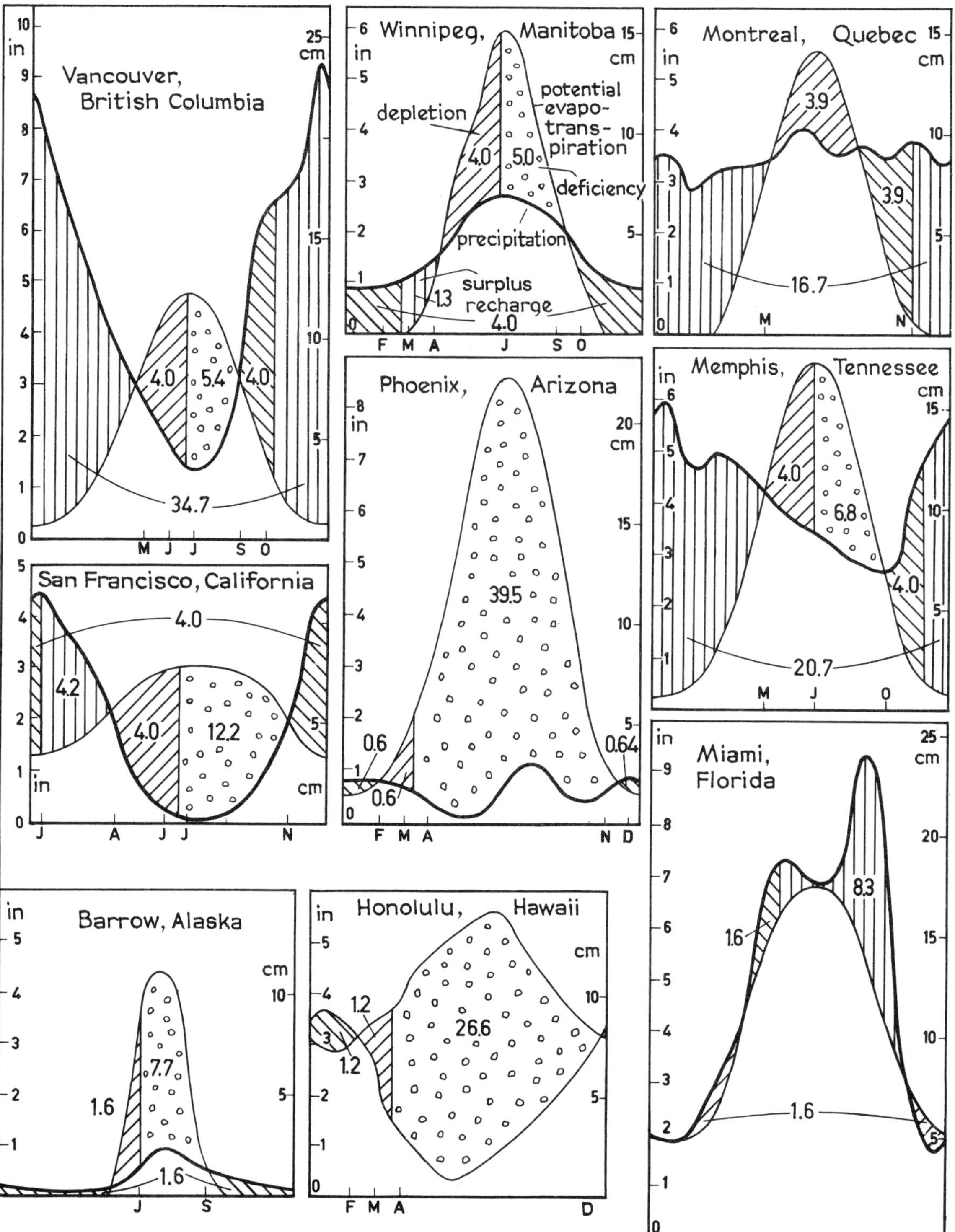

FIG. 4:12 Soil-moisture regimes for selected stations.

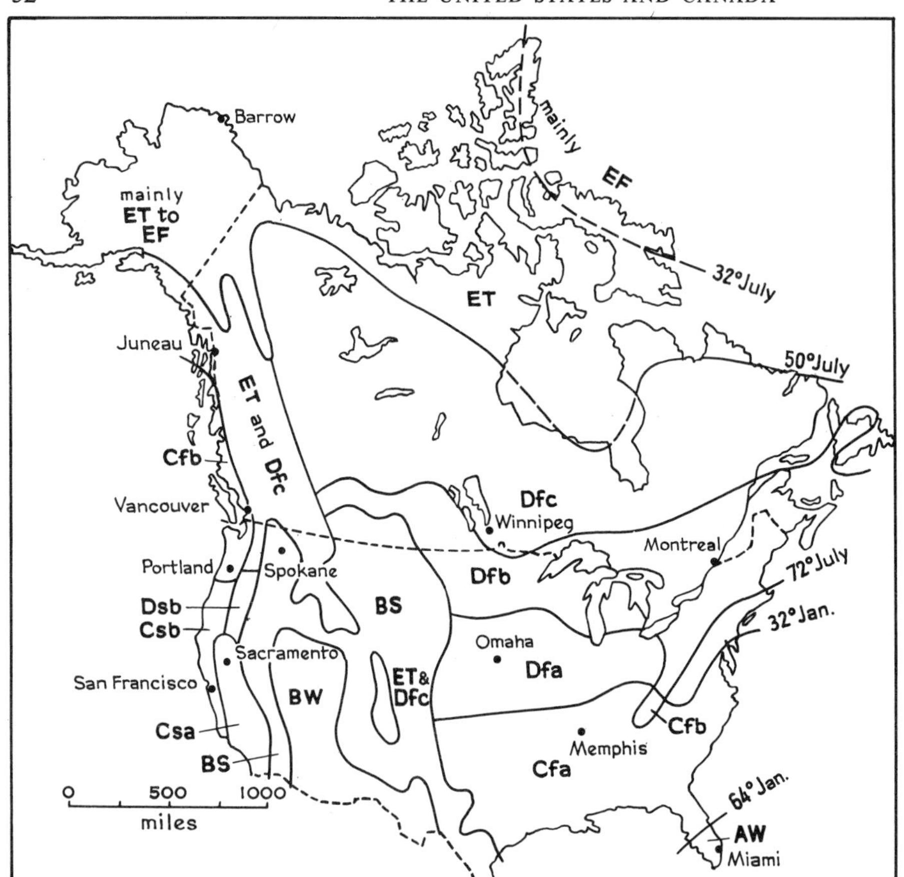

FIG. 4:13 Generalized distribution of climatic types in the Köppen classification.

northeast, and especially in New England, could rely on their mill-streams to flow at all times.

Farther south, and farther inland, Memphis once again exemplifies the manner in which summer-season demand for water can outpace supply, even though summers are quite rainy. At Miami, on the other hand, the concentration of rainfall in the summer months enables supply of moisture to keep pace with demand almost throughout the year. The average condition of water surplus in August–November is an exceptional one.

At Barrow, in Alaska, precipitation is so low that the soil moisture reservoir is theoretically exhausted by the mid-year; however, the thermal environment is such that considerations of soil moisture have little relevance.

Climatic Types

Numbers of schemes of classification have been applied to the climates of North America, and particularly to those of the U.S.A. A frequent disadvantage is that climates are named after particular areas, so that the significance of an areal name has to be understood before the classification is meaningful. An alternative is to employ a symbolic classification, like the one adopted here, where the symbols connote limiting values. The following scheme is taken, with slight modifications, from that developed by the climatologist Köppen. The principal modifications are that temperature values are expressed in round degrees Fahrenheit, as opposed to the strict fractional equivalents of the Centigrade values which Köppen employed, and that the 32° F isotherm is used as one climatic boundary, in place of the approximate 27° F selected by Köppen himself.

In this scheme, climates are grouped under the headings *A*, *B*, *C*, *D*, and *E*. The *B* climates, defined in terms of dryness, lie apart from the remainder. In the range *A*, *C*, *D*, *E*, the primary division depends on temperature.

In the A climates, the monthly mean temperature

never falls below 64° F. In the present context, the January mean of 64° F provides the limit. In turn, the C climates are separated from the D climates by the January isotherm of 32° F: although the C climates experience a winter season, no month records an average below freezing. In high northern latitudes, however, what matters is not the severity of winter, which is anyway great, but the occurrence of summer, if any: the cold E climates are separated from the D climates at the 50° F July isotherm.

Fig. 4:13 gives the distribution of climatic types in Canada and the U.S.A. Discrepancies between the boundaries there drawn, and the boundaries corresponding precisely to the isotherms in Figs. 4:4, 4:5, are due to the generalized presentation of these isotherms.

The A climates have no winter: the notation Aw for Southern Florida (exemplified by Miami: Figs. 4:8, 4:12) stands for a winterless climate with a dry season in the colder months. The mT air which dominates this region is distinctly less stable in the mid-year than at the year's turn.

The occurrence and timing, or the absence, of a dry season is important throughout the range of the C and D climates, which prevail in most of the inhabited and farmed parts of the two countries. The lower-case letter *w* stands in the classification for winter-dry; *s* indicates summer-dry, and *f*, lack of a dry season. Seasonal dryness is defined in practice with the aid of a formula. In North America, the most extensive area of C climates lies in the southeastern States, where the symbol *f* shows that a true dry season is lacking. In addition, throughout the whole vast main spread of D climates, there is also no dry season, judged in terms of precipitation, although there can be periods of soil-moisture shortage.

A further breakdown of the C and D climates relates to length and warmth of summer. The notation *a* indicates that the July mean rises above 72° F. Where it fails to do this, the symbol *b* is used where more than four summer months average over 50° F, and the symbol *c* where fewer than four months do so. In descriptive terms, *a* means a hot summer, *b* a warm summer, and *c* a short, cool summer. But these descriptive terms are relative, while the symbols are precisely defined.

Thus, the full symbol *Cfa* for the southeastern States connotes a climate with a winter season, but with January temperature averaging more than 32° F; no real dry season; and a July mean above 72° F. Memphis experiences climate of the Cfa type. Mean winter temperatures are brought down, and some individual winter readings are brought well down, by incursions of cPK and even of modified cAK air, but the region of Cfa climate is also repeatedly traversed throughout the year by mT air. Interaction of maritime and continental air along the fronts of travelling lows, plus summer convection in unstable mTW air from the south or southeast, ensures precipitation throughout the year. High summer temperatures are guaranteed by heating over the land.

In the southern Appalachians, high altitudes bring July means below the critical mark of 72° F, resulting in a restricted development of Cfb climate.

On the Pacific side of the continent, the Great Valley of California and the southern coastlands of the same State are classified climatically as Csa. They experience a winter season, record hot summers, and have summer dryness or even drought: The distinctive dry season extends north beyond the 72° F July isotherm, in response to the seasonal penetration of stable mTW air of local high pressures, producing Csb climate in parts of the Pacific Northwest. Farther north still, where the dry summer air-streams no longer come in, year-round raininess resumes, and the climate of the British Columbian coast is classified as Cfb. This in turn gives way in the Alaska Panhandle to a narrow strip of Cfc climate – too small to be indicated in Fig. 4:13 – among the complex of islands and inlets where winter cold is mitigated by the adjacent ocean, but where the high latitude prevents summers from being in any way warm. Among the stations used in Figs. 4:8 and 4:12, Sacramento experiences Csa climate. San Francisco and Portland, distinctly more maritime, belong to the Csb region, while Vancouver falls squarely within the Cfb type.

An exceptional development of D climate occurs in the eastern parts of Washington and Oregon, where incoming stable air or the rain-shadow effect act in summer to keep rainfall low. The leading difference from the coastland is that winters are more severe. For the rest, the D climates, as already stated, include no real dry season. They range northward from Dfa, illustrated by Omaha, through Dfb, illustrated by Montreal, to Dfc, illustrated by Winnipeg. All have quite severe winters in the average year, the severity naturally increasing towards the north and towards the deepest interior; and length of summer, and summer warmth, also fall off as latitude increases. The winter at Winnipeg is so severe and so long, and the contrast between winter and summer is so great, that there is scarcely any room in the climatic year either for spring or for autumn.

The regions of Dfa, Dfb, and Dfc climate are susceptible throughout the year to invasion by cPK and cAK air. However, the source regions of cP and cA air-masses are most active in winter, whereas in summer it is readily possible for westerly airstreams to enter. Both the blocking action of winter highs, and the low moisture-holding capacity of frigid winter air, favour summer maxima of precipitation in large parts of the interior. Even in summer, however, the possibility of invasion by originally maritime air decreases signally towards the north. The boundary between Dfb climate, with warm summers, and Dfc climate, with short cool summers, quite closely resembles the mean July position of the polar front. North of this position, cP air dominates even the summer climate.

Beyond the July isotherm of 50° F the E climates begin. These are dominated by arctic air. In the ET (tundra) climate, at least one month rises above freezing: there is a seasonal thaw. In the EF (frost, ice-cap) climate, no such relaxation is known. ET climate degenerates into EF amid the plateau glaciers of the outermost archipelago. In the Alaskan and Canadian parts of the Cordillera, apart from the coasts, Dfc climate at low levels grades into ET with increasing height, and that in turn into EF on glacier-bearing mountains. Details of distribution are far too complex to be given in Fig. 4:13, even in the most summary fashion. Among the stations for which graphs have been drawn, Juneau lies close to the Dfc/ET boundary, while Barrow is deep inside the tundra region.

Climates of the B type are subdivided into BS, steppe climate, and BW, desert climate. Qualities of dryness are determined in relation to temperature by means of a formula. Fig. 4:13 indicates how the eastern limit of BS climate cuts across the east–west spreads of the Cfa, Dfa, and Dfb types: precipitation declines as distance from the main source of supply, the Gulf, increases, and the BS limit occurs roughly on the moister fringe of natural short-grass prairie. In part, then, the development of B climates is a rain-shadow effect. Maritime tropical air from the south is drained of moisture during its passage overland, while Pacific mT air is even more rapidly drained, should it succeed in traversing the Cordillera. Both within the Cordilleran basins, and in a huge belt in the lee of the Rockies, climate is less than humid. But in addition, the most intense expression of B climate, where the BW type is registered in the American Southwest, corresponds in part to the source region of cT air. The two graphs for Phoenix summarize conditions here.

SYNTHESIS

By way of conclusion, selected combinations of vegetation, soils, and climate will now be examined. In Fig. 4:14, distributions are given for what might be taken as distinctive major types of vegetation, rooted in distinctive major types of soil, growing in distinctive types of climate. It is at once clear that only about half the country – outside the Cordillera, which is omitted as too complex for treatment in these terms – is accounted for. Tundra vegetation, tundra soils, and ET (plus EF) climate combine in a broad northern band. But the combination of boreal forest, podsols, and Dfc climate fails to account for a huge belt of country next south of the tundra: the blank area contains great spreads of park-tundra, where tree stands are intermixed with extents of lowly vegetation. Southwards again, the combination of broadleaf deciduous forest with some needleleaf evergreen, again on podsols, with Dfb climate, once more leaves a gap. And the combination of broadleaf deciduous forest proper, still on podsols, with Dfa climate produces a discontinuous array of patches. There is, it is true, a fair correspondence among the distributions of forests of the southern type, latosols, and Cfa climate, particularly if (as in the map) alluvial lands and swamplands are counted in. But even here the correspondence may be in part illusory, for some at least of the latosols may well be relict, unrelated to

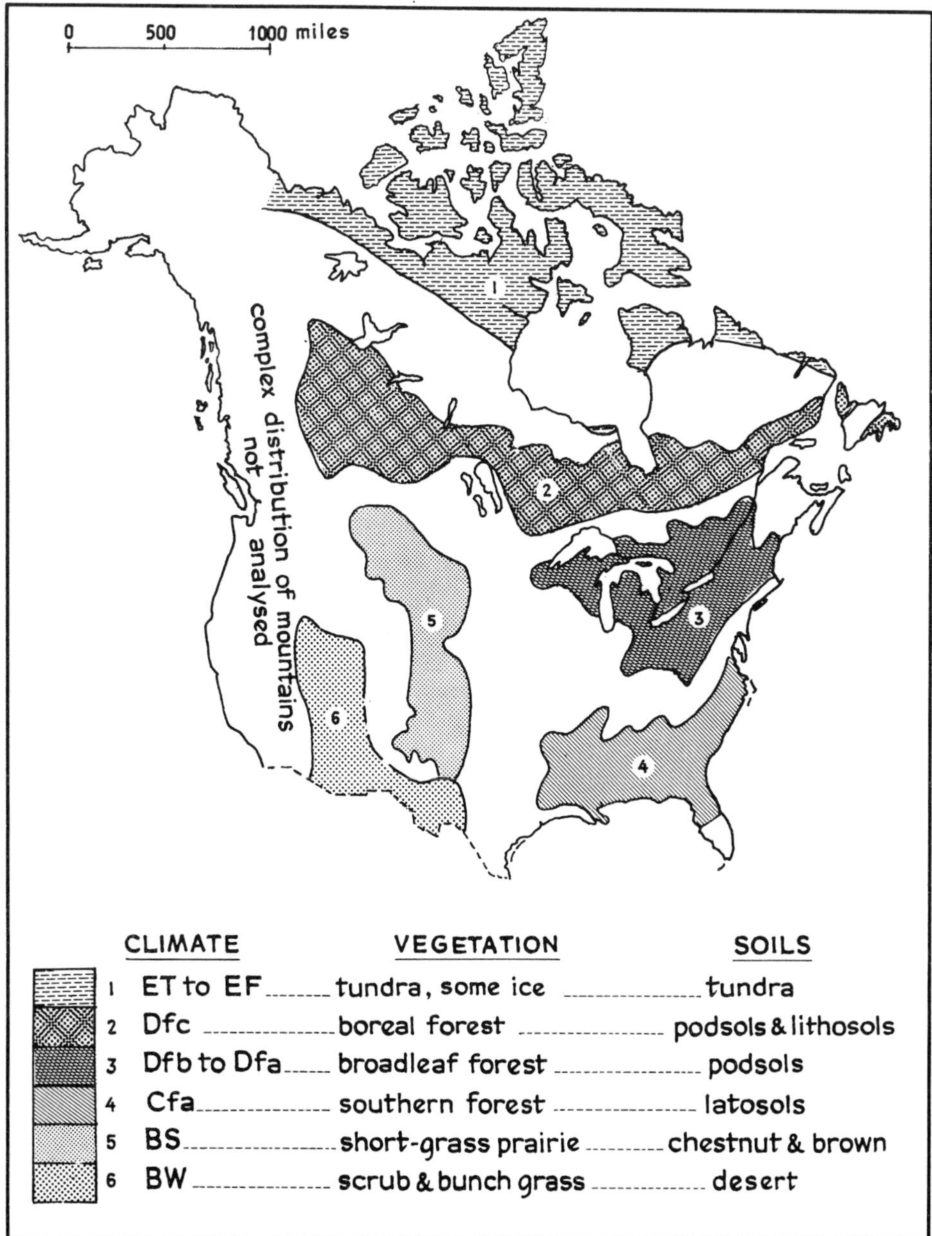

FIG. 4:14 Selected coincidental distributions of climate, vegetation, and soil.

the present climate. Again, a distinct block emerges, in the southwest, where scrub and bunch grass subsist on the desert soils and lithosols under a BSh climate, while the short-grass prairie coincides reasonably closely to the area of chestnut and brown soils and to part of the region of BSk climate. On the other hand, the most productive soils of all, the chernozems, and the former long-grass prairie with which they partly coincide, cut broadly across the limits of climatic regions, in response to latitudinal changes in temperature and in demands on soil moisture. There is no fixed or simple means of equating major distributions of recognizable climates with major distributions either of vegetation or of soil. The concept of natural regions will not bear comparison with reality, on any scale of detail.

CHAPTER FIVE

PEOPLING, POLITICS, AND SEPARATION

A thousand years have passed since Europeans first saw North America; and the series of landings which were to transform the continent's history and its appearance began nearly five hundred years ago. Norsemen sailing from Iceland by way of Greenland in the 900s made the first sightings. But, understandably enough, little is known either of the expeditions or of what precise coasts they saw or touched on. Settlement occurred, but was eventually extinguished. Not until the Renaissance made it possible to believe in a spherical earth – as opposed to a flat circular earth centred on Jerusalem – did European shipmen begin once more to point themselves westward across the Atlantic.

For the purpose in hand, it is less important to scrutinize the respective claims to renown of Columbus, Vespucci, and Verazzano, than to observe that by the year 1500 the existence of Central America and Newfoundland was known. Cabot made landfall in Newfoundland in 1497. By about 1520 Magellan had learned that South America continued unbroken to 55° S latitude, and Mexico had fallen to Cortéz. Spaniards landed in Florida before 1530, reached the Grand Canyon overland from Mexico by 1540, and the Oregon coast by sea shortly afterwards. Frenchmen had by this time explored the St Lawrence. French and Spanish clashed on the south Atlantic coast in the 1560s, while Englishmen in the 1580s attempted both to annex Newfoundland and to colonize Virginia.

Europeans had learned in the course of a century not to mistake the Americas for the East Indies, nor to regard the Americas wholly as obstructions to Far Eastern sea-lanes. Instead, the new-found continents became lands of conquest, exploitation, and self-aggrandizement for some, lands of potential refuge for others. The practice of colonization and the concept of colonialism were understood by 1600. An eventual extension into North America of the shifting power-struggle of Europe was already in preparation.

Early Discoveries: Settlement up to 1700

The first voyages were made in hope and ignorance – hope of discovering westward routes across the globe to the Far East, ignorance that two whole continents intervened. Simple calculations of longitude could have shown that the Americas were not the Indies: but Columbus in 1492 worked with too small a value of the earth's circumference, and ocean captains in his day fixed the positions of their tiny craft partly by dead-reckonings of so many days on a given compass direction. Long-distance navigation was at best approximate. Although the new discoveries were accompanied by remarkable advances in map-making, the initial error persisted: not even Magellan's entry to the Pacific and his voyages there prevented the West Indies and the indigenous American peoples from retaining their mistaken titles. Impetus to westward exploration has a well-known base. The low-volume high-cost trade between Europe and the East had for centuries been controlled in the Mediterranean, where city-states, dukedoms, and small kingdoms rose and flourished. Venice was the greatest of these. But Venice declined with the silting of its harbour and with the depletion of the Adriatic forests which supplied its ships' timber. The Turkish capture of Constantinople in 1453 did not close the overland ways; but it did nothing to relieve the uncertainty of access and the repeated local levies to which the overland spice trade was liable. As Venice was declining, Portugal and Spain were emerging as mercantile and exploring countries. As always, it is easy to recount but difficult to explain the rise of a nation to greatness and power. The basic fact is that both Portugal and Spain in the 1400s and 1500s had enough energy and resourcefulness to explore, expand their trade, send out missions, and engage in foreign conquest. The eyes of both were on the Far East.

Portugal, concerned to open an eastward way around Africa, reacted strongly and at once to the discoveries of Columbus in the service of Spain. The potential dispute between the two countries went in 1493 to the arbitration of the Pope, who awarded the eastern part of the discoverable world to Portugal, the western to Spain. Although the line of demarcation was so drawn that Portugal could, and later did, occupy coastal Brazil, the Portuguese Diaz had already rounded the Cape of Good Hope in 1486, and the Portuguese da Gama reached India by sea in 1498. Portugal turned eastward in earnest, Spain no less earnestly towards the west.

One of the most striking episodes which now followed was the conquest of central Mexico by Cortéz in 1519. This adventuring Spaniard commanded fewer than 600 Europeans. In supply, transport, and artillery he had but 250 Indians, fifteen horses, and ten cannon. But the Aztec hold on its city-based empire was already weak: it relaxed at a blow. Whatever the horrors of their ritual sacrificing, the Aztecs paid in full. If they were not killed in combat or in suppressions of revolt, and if they survived the newly introduced European diseases, the Aztecs and their former subjects passed alike into slavery.

Colonizing Spaniards in Central and South America shared the European view, commonly held in the 1500s and 1600s, that colonies were meant to be exploited. They looked foremost to precious metals for wealth, and to enslaved Indians for labour. Plunder of personal ornaments and of ritual and votary treasures led rapidly to the mining of silver and gold in mineralized areas of the Cordillera, both in the Caribbean area and in the Andes. Predators were however soon in action.

Hawkins's slave carriage from Africa in the 1560s was destroyed by a Spanish attack. Among the survivors was Hawkins's nephew Drake, who in the 1570s began his piratical reprisals. Others, encouraged and financed – as was Drake – by Elizabeth I or her councillors, also fell on the Spanish treasure-ships at sea and on the bullion-trains on shore. These activities helped worsen the relations between England and Spain, between whom a war broke out in which the most noteworthy single event was the defeat of the Armada in 1588. Spain still held Mexico and possessions to the south, continued to develop California and to retain the dry Southwest, and occupied portions of an undemarcated Florida: but Spanish protests failed to uproot the English colony in Virginia, which after Raleigh's unsuccessful earlier attempts made its shaky beginnings at Jamestown in 1607.

Part of the English quarrel with Spain was religious – Protestants against Rome. Within the Protestant realm, dissenting creeds gained strength. The first main split occurred in the early 1600s, when the Separatist forerunners of the New England Puritans migrated from England to Holland. A new migration, designed to preserve the community in its own identity and its chosen ways, aimed in 1620 at Virginia. The ship *Mayflower* made landfall at Cape Cod. Deciding to abandon further voyaging, the migrants formed themselves into a civil organization and fixed on the site of Plymouth for habitation. Thus within less than two decades began the colonization of both those portions of North America which later opposed one another in civil war.

Any summary history of colonization must do less than justice to staunch resolve and to multiple setbacks. All histories except the fullest omit much that is relevant in the European background. So it is with the tale of early French penetration. France in the 1500s was riven internally by the Catholic–Protestant struggle, and externally was usually at odds, and intermittently at war, with Spain. But France nevertheless dispatched the Florentine Verrazano in 1524, who reconnoitred the northeast of the continent, and Cartier, who in 1534, 1535, and 1541 explored the St Lawrence as far as the sites of Quebec and Montreal. Abortive attempts at French colonization in Brazil and Florida were beaten off, but Champlain secured the Northeast when he founded Quebec in 1608. Although twenty of the first twenty-eight settlers died in the first winter, France now had a toehold, established precisely at the time when the first permanent English settlements were fixed on the eastern seaboard. By 1615 Champlain had reached Lake Huron, and by 1634 his emissary Nicolet was on Lake Michigan.

Champlain sought for a passage through America to the Orient, as the Englishmen Frobisher, Gilbert, and Davis had vainly sought round the north of the continent in the later 1500s, and as the tragic Hudson and his successors, contemporaries of Champlain, continued to seek. But the French explorers and the French settlers and woodsmen introduced new elements into the economic and political geography of North America – well-organized trade in furs, and alliances with groups of Indians.

The fur trade had a bioclimatic basis. Fur-bearing animals with their rich winter pelts were as well-adapted to the seasonal cold as the early colonists were ill-adapted by their experience. Indian alliances, obviously helpful to the trade in furs, went far beyond the friendly connections established in Virginia. On the converse side, the French struggle with the hostile Iroquois was something far greater than the sporadic attacks and punitive raids which took place elsewhere. The Iroquois exercised long control over the easiest land routes from the St Lawrence to the Atlantic coast – namely, routes by way of Lake Champlain and the Mohawk into the Hudson Valley. Southward probings by the French in this area were repeatedly checked, especially when the New Englanders gained Iroquois co-operation. French settlements along the St Lawrence remained cut off from the nearest Atlantic.

There was, it is true, a scatter of French forts and missions on the Bay of Fundy, but most of the early settlers occupied land alongside the St Lawrence. Low terraces of estuarine and marine sediments, raised above sea-level when the crust recovered from ice-loading, there offered potential farmland. Despite attempts directed from France to organize great estates, the pioneers built single dwellings near the river, and arranged their farms in long strips at right-angles to the bank. The pattern of holdings survives today.

Direction of colonial affairs by home governments affected all settling groups. It applied, or was at least intended to apply, at all levels. Location and extent of colonies, structure and personnel of colonial government, social organization, economic purpose and administration, were all at one time or other prescribed. No home government was willing to give any colony more than minor responsibility in self-management. Nevertheless, the practical difficulties of governing from a distance permitted many expressions of independence and numerous acts of disobedience. The New Englanders in particular worked out social structures for themselves which involved all in local administration and which provided the foundation for independence.

Grants of land and of rights in the 1600s were as reckless as they were generous, and as inconsistent as they were reckless. Selected examples are mapped in Fig. 5:1. These grants could eventually seem to give legal justification to any party in the long series of territorial disputes, whether between colonies or between nations. Boundary problems multiplied with the multiplication of colonies, which in turn was a response to mounting immigration – and, in New England, to social structure. Political and religious persecution drove to New England so many Puritans that by 1640 the northeastern colonies, already however assisted by natural increase, reached a population of 25,000. New England was itself fragmenting into separate States, and settlement within these States was becoming parcelled in and around numerous towns. Stern local rule by church elders joined with religious schisms in promoting the repeated founding of new settlements – a process which is in part responsible for the thick scatter of towns in New England today.

Differences of religious principle became less serious as religious toleration increased, but some disputes over State boundaries were not resolved until well into the 1700s and even the 1800s. For all that, the practice of demarcating the land in advance of occupation was later, in a developed form, to be of great significance in the settlement of the interior. In the meantime, the English civil war of the 1640s brought the first sign that colonies could combine among themselves – avowedly, for defence against Indians, French, and Dutch.

The Indian danger was chronic, the French menace at first spasmodic, Dutch penetration immediate. A Dutch fort was built near the site of Albany in 1614. Dutch colonization about the mouth of the Hudson began in 1623, and Dutchmen bought Manhattan Island from the Indians in 1626 as a base for their fur trade. So strong did the New Netherlands become, that they were able in 1655 to absorb the colonies which Sweden had been planting on the Delaware for the previous seventeen years. But the New Netherlands were themselves absorbed into the colonial domain of England when in 1644 their capital, New Amsterdam, surrendered without

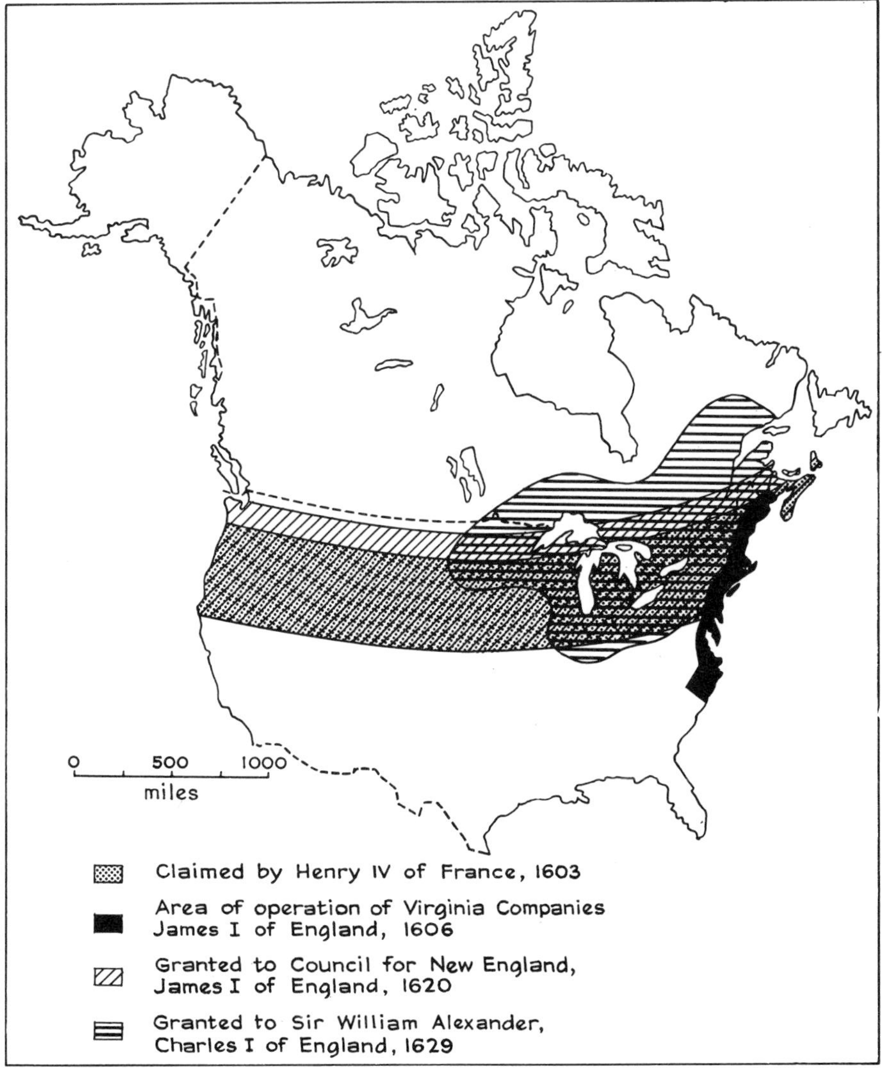

FIG. 5:1
Claims and grants of the early 1600s.

fighting. This town, then with 1500 people, was renamed New York, and its hinterland New York colony. New Jersey and Delaware were shaped from the remainder of the former Dutch possessions.

Next to the south, Penn founded the Quaker colony of Pennsylvania in 1682. This alone of all the colonies was ruled in a temperate manner, free of social oppression and long free of Indian wars. Farther south still, colonization of Maryland and of Carolina had begun respectively in 1634 and 1663. Thus during the seventeenth century the political and habitational patterns of the coastland were founded, and English power there became supreme.

Conditions in 1700

Social and economic structures along the Atlantic coastal strip differed at the end of the century as strongly as did climate. Small New England farms, laboriously cleared from the forest, and many of them established with difficulty on the stony irregular surface of glacial deposits, were designed for subsistence. Of themselves they could not yield a profit. Craft industry was also arranged to meet family needs. And since the New England colonies were not at first fully committed to a cash economy, neither manufacture nor trade was encouraged. Indeed, manufacture was actively discouraged from

London, while trade was deliberately controlled from the homeland. But New England's forests and its access to the fishing grounds of the Banks supplied commodities of trade and fostered the growth of shipbuilding. By the end of the seventeenth century the northeastern colonies were engaged largely with the sea, and were active in the West Indian trade.

Climate on and near the Hudson was somewhat more genial than in New England; the growing season was longer, and farms accordingly more prosperous. Farmhouses built hereabouts on the plan introduced by Swedish settlers were far better adapted to local conditions than were the structures of New England. The Swedes brought the log-cabin which later became standard throughout the North American frontier, and which today makes so strong an emotional appeal to North American feelings. Philadelphia in Pennsylvania had grown by 1700 to a manufacturing town of sorts, with mills for timber and flour, tanneries and potteries, and a vigorous trade with England and the West Indies.

The southernmost colonies depended on planting. They had from the outset possessed elements of an aristocratic social structure. Some of the early migrants were Catholics, ill-disposed to partake in democratic and theocratic experiments like those of New England. Numbers of Cavaliers arrived after the English royalists had lost the civil war; and and although many of these were replaced by adherents of the other side after the monarchy was restored, the incomers to the south were, as a group, richer than those to the northeast. Sons of rich merchants came to make their own fortunes and to invest their fathers' money. These could not be called aristocratic by birth: but they set out to construct what they considered an aristocratic way of life. Twentieth-century English settlement of tropical planters offers many a parallel to their chosen attitude and their aspirations.

Virginia, wrestling with its swampy coastland, soon found in tobacco a staple product. But tobacco-growing needed labour, and labour could only be supplied cheaply by sale of work-time for periods of years. In the beginning, whites were used who at this price could hope to lodge themselves in the New World. Later came white transportees from England, exchanging prison sentences for terms of colonial labour. The most prophetic single happening, however, was the landing of twenty Negroes in 1619. These were committed to a term of service identical with that applied to whites, but indentured employment of Negroes was soon replaced by overt slavery.

In the northern part of Carolina, forest products – naval stores of pitch, turpentine, and tar from the southern pine – were the chief export goods, although the cultivation of indigo and rice in the southern part of this colony developed rapidly. Rice-growing, like the growing of tobacco, demanded labour: but this demand was exclusively for Negroes, since whites died off in the rice-planted coastal swamplands of Carolina. Slavery of Negroes was introduced here also.

As the Atlantic colonies were slowly pushing inland, French soldiers, missionaries, fur-traders, and woodsmen were being led from the Great Lakes over low portages to the Mississippi system. By the end of the seventeenth century the St Lawrence Valley was still unsettled upstream of the rapids at Montreal, but French forts studded the forest trails and the waterways of the upper Lakes and of the Mississippi and its eastern feeders (Fig. 5:2). Montreal had been founded in 1642, Quebec by 1670 had grown to a population of 6000. Three years later, the Joliet–Marquette expedition proved that the Mississippi led southward; in 1682 La Salle reached the mouth of the river, claiming the whole valley for France under the name Louisiana, and attempting in 1685 to fix a French settlement on the Spanish-held coast of Texas.

Although this particular attempt failed, seventeenth-century France under the stimulus of its king, Louis XIV, and his minister, Colbert, linked Canada with the Gulf, and so with French settlements in the West Indies. The mouth of the Mississippi was controlled by settlements founded at Biloxi, Mobile, and New Orleans in the period 1699–1718. Additional forts rose in the trunk valley. The English seaboard colonies were encircled. But whereas these had a quarter of a million inhabitants in 1700 with towns of 10,000 at Philadelphia, 7000 at Boston, and 5000 at New York, and reached a total of a million people by 1750, the vast French territories in this latter year were manned by no more than 80,000.

One reason, and probably the main reason, for the disparity was that French colonial policy re-

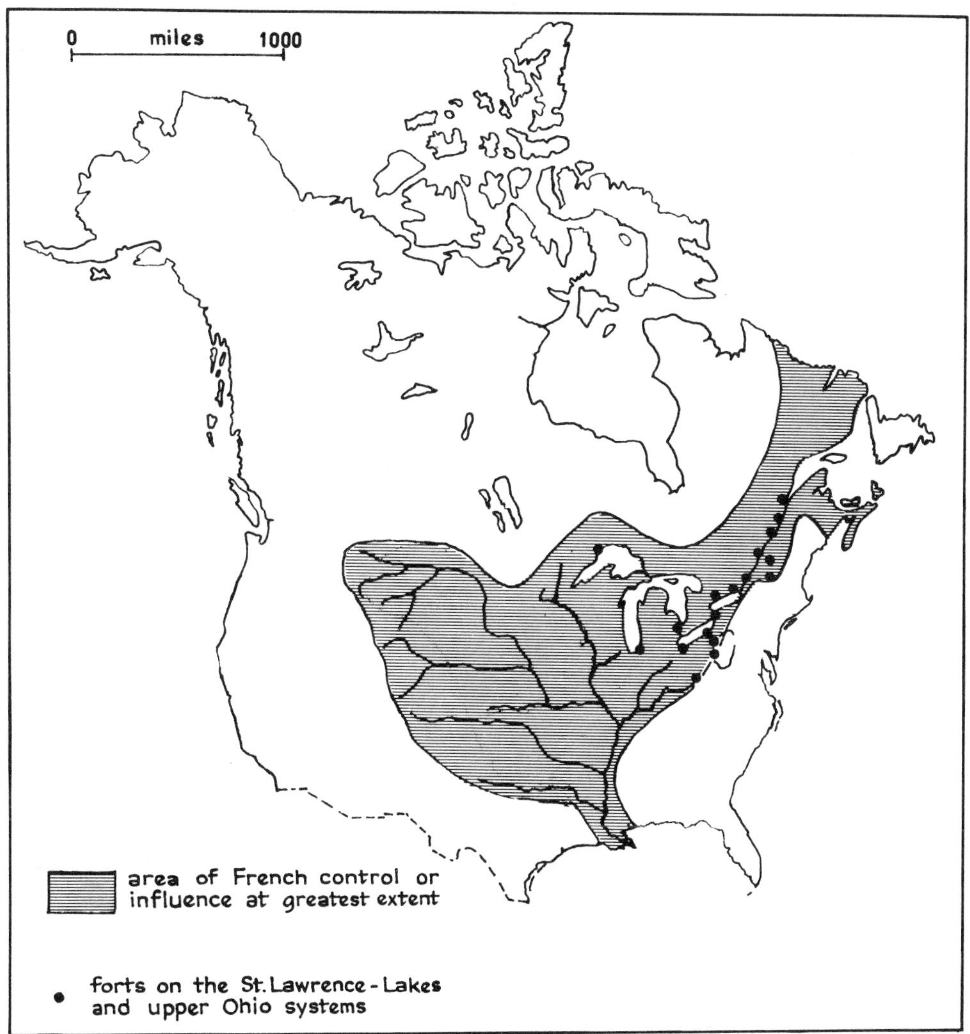

FIG. 5:2 Elements in penetration by the French, about 1700.

mained exploitative. Except in the St Lawrence Valley, no farming settlement followed exploration. Dreams of a waterway to the western seas, or of gold to be had for the taking, faded; but the lucrative fur trade developed strongly, finding an outlet by the Mississippi when the line of French strongholds was driven between the Spanish of Florida and those of Texas. This trade required few operators – not more than 5000 in the whole interior between the Lakes and the Gulf. It was also true that the farming settlement of the St Lawrence exerted no particular pressure towards the west. The French frontier of exploration and fur-trading was a hollow frontier, whereas consolidation followed behind the slow westward shift of the frontier of the seaboard colonies.

Dislodgement of France

Spain was in decline as a European power by 1700, France and England simultaneously in ascent. Spain, France, England, Austria, and the Netherlands were frequently at war, in alliances which aimed either to establish or to prevent dominance of Europe. Close relations between France and the Stuart monarchs had held off combat during parts of the seventeenth century, until the War of the English Succession (1689–97) followed the breaking of the Stuart line. The parallel campaign in North America, there called King William's War, gave colonists practice in border attacks on the fringes of New England and New York, where some English settlements were destroyed and the French menace

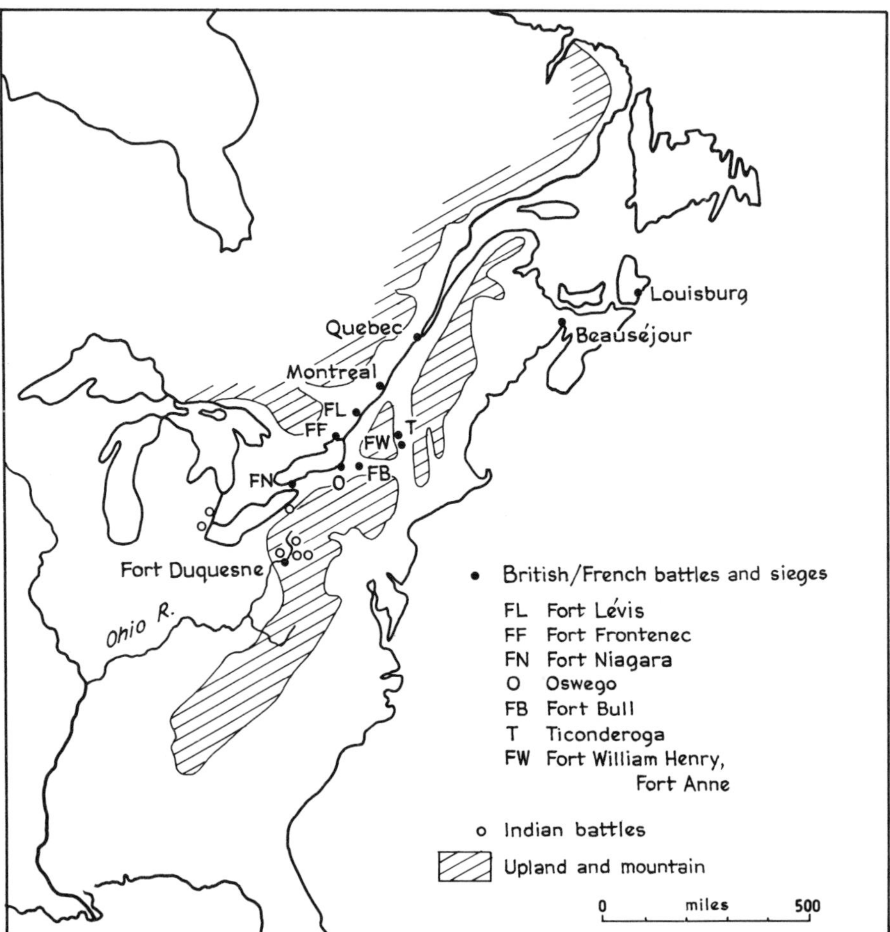

FIG. 5:3 Sites of armed conflict in the French and Indian Wars, 1755–60.

became explicit and real. Neither the war nor the concluding treaty, however, involved permanent change. Border fighting was still more restricted during the War of the Spanish Succession (1702–13), in which England and France were opposed anew; but Queen Anne's War, as it is known in North America, included English invasion of the Nova Scotian peninsula, which with Newfoundland was ceded by France at the war's end. The War of the Austrian Succession (1744–48), the King George's War of America, was wholly inconclusive. Very different results followed from the Seven Years War of 1756–63. England under its prime minister Pitt launched a deliberate campaign to extend English power in North America, and to displace the French entirely. In the French and Indian Wars, to use their North American name, the capture of Louisburg closed the St Lawrence, those of Fort Duquesne on the site of Pittsburg and of Niagara closed the Ohio Valley (Fig. 5:3). Wolfe took Quebec in 1759; Montreal also fell. The whole of the French empire in North America was now in English hands, except for the two small islands of St Pierre and Miquelon which were allowed as bases for the Newfoundland fisheries.

In this war the fading Spain had been allied with France. England gained Florida from Spain in exchange for Cuba. The colony of Georgia having been founded in 1733, England now held the whole of North America east of the Mississippi. The lands of Louisiana west of the Mississippi passed by private royal arrangement to Spain, in compensation for losses suffered elsewhere.

The Colonial Breakaway

The English parliament in 1774 passed the Quebec

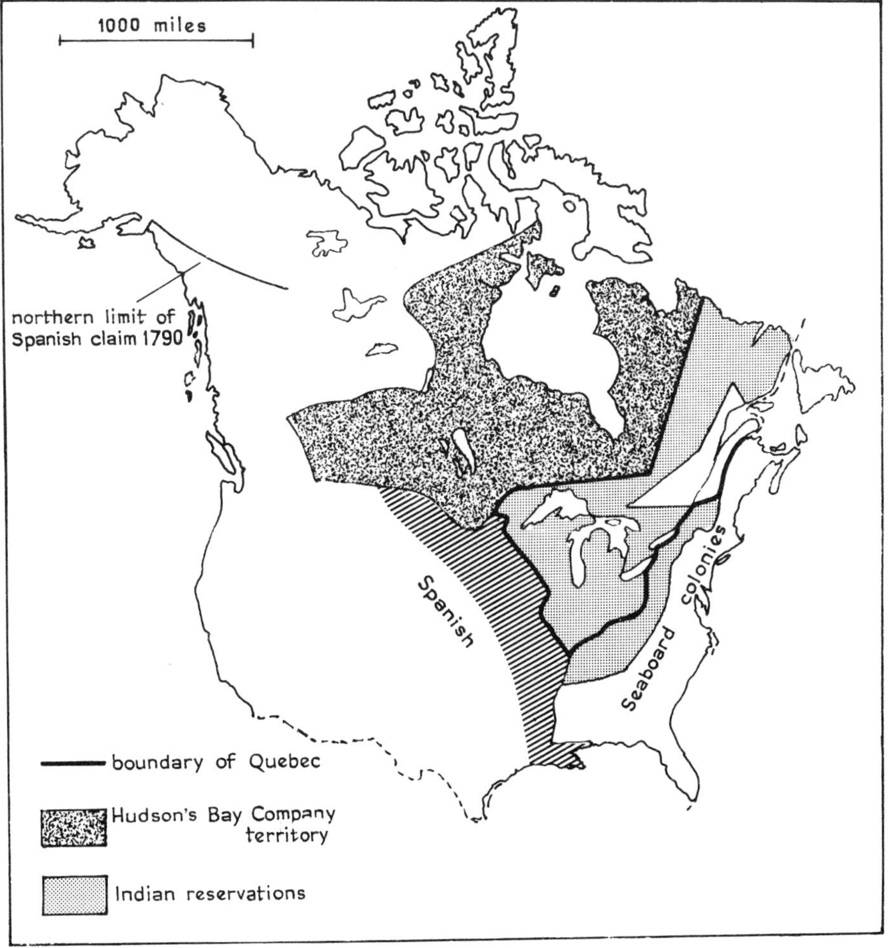

FIG. 5:4 Subdivision of the east, according to the Treaty of Paris (1763) and the Quebec Act (1774).

Act, designed to regulate the territory newly acquired from France. In the north lay the lands tapped by the Hudson's Bay Company, whose fur trade need no longer pass exclusively through ports on the Bay itself. Quebec was defined as extending from the Gulf of St Lawrence to the Mississippi, and northwards from the Ohio to the Company's area (Fig. 5:4). Between the interior and the Atlantic seaboard, the Appalachian and adjoining low plateaus were placed in Indian reserve. Unlike other measures of the time, the Quebec Act was not aimed directly at controlling the colonies on the Atlantic coast; but it strongly inflamed feelings there, since the inherited early land-grants, extending westward to the Mississippi, made no provision for Indian reserve on the Appalachian flanks; Massachusetts, Connecticut, the Carolinas, and Georgia all had titles of a sort to latitudinal strips. New York could make out a case for a vast block between the Tennessee River and the Illinois, Virginia a case for a still larger block which included the present Kentucky and reached the present Illinois (Fig. 5:5). Whereas conflicting claims among States were resolved peaceably, most of them by 1802 or earlier, the eastern Canadian boundary was adjusted by force of arms. No more than thirteen years after the passage of the Quebec Act, the coastal colonies were in revolt.

The British Isles in 1776 had fewer than ten million people. The Atlantic colonies already had two million, with numbers rising fast. This was a new situation – colonies populous enough to weigh as a whole country, and colonies used for a century or more to scrutinize the conduct of their affairs. Government at the local level was far more highly developed than in England, where local authorities

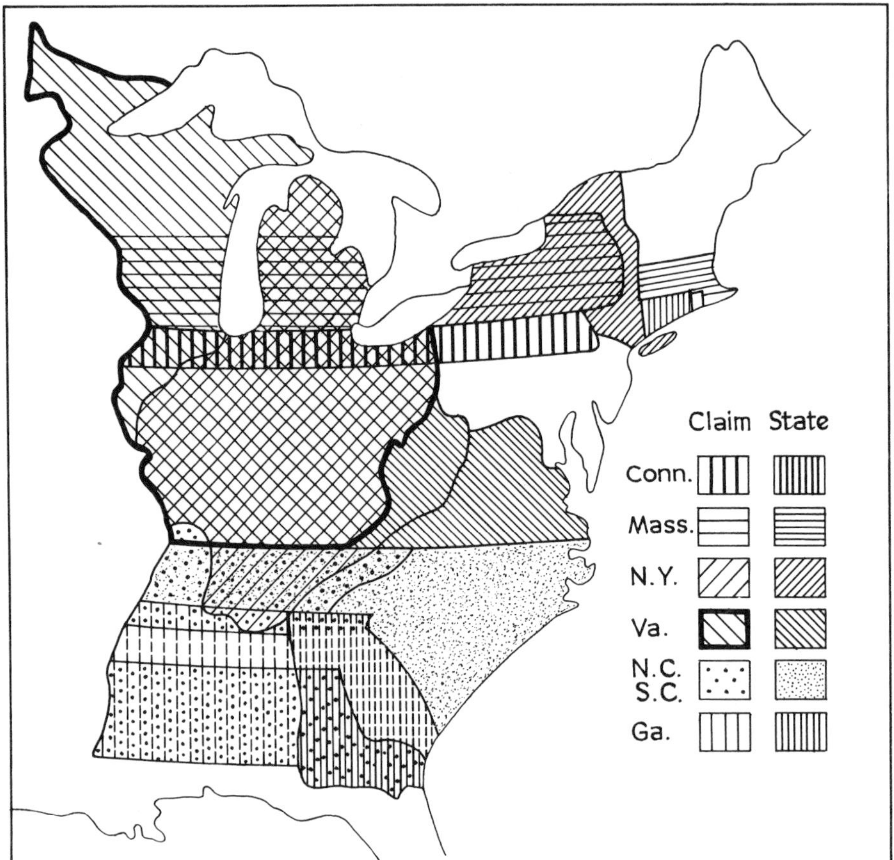

FIG. 5:5
Conflicting claims by individual States in the late eighteenth century.

scarcely existed, and where, furthermore, representation in parliament was an affair of jobbery and bore little relation to the distribution of people. In New England especially, the colonists were deeply involved, and knew themselves involved, in government. Again, all colonists had to be self-reliant: the weak, the stupid, and the feckless starved or froze. The danger implicit in all this was little heeded in England, where high policy was directed towards surpassing European rivals and to expanding trade.

Now although the seaboard colonies are here styled English, the term applied only in the political sense. Ethnically, the population was considerably mixed. In addition to the Dutch and Swedish already mentioned, groups of migrants from south-west Germany had been arriving since the early 1700s. Landing at Philadelphia, they had spread in Pennsylvania along the Susquehanna and in Virginia along the Shenandoah, occupying considerable portions of the Great Appalachian Valley. Dissenting Scotch–Irish came, particularly in the early 1700s, mainly to the middle and southern colonies, occupying the southern Piedmont up to the Appalachian wall.

Nor were penetration and settlement any longer limited wholly to the seaboard. Outrunners were already going far beyond. The Indians in the Ohio Valley were broken in 1768. The trunk river, not the plateau edges farther east, became the effective line of division between land held by Indians and land which could be settled. The areas of Kentucky and Tennessee were reached the next year, Boone passing through the Cumberland Gap into the blue-grass country. Flatboats were on the Ohio in the very year of the Quebec Act, heralding a down-stream carriage of westward-driving pioneers. Population west of the Appalachians at this time has been estimated at 20,000. Some colonists at least knew that settlement could be pushed inland, to and beyond all visible bounds: the reserves laid down by the Quebec Act were already outmoded.

None of these circumstances encouraged obedience to London.

Colonial opposition to the Quebec Act cannot be understood, except in the context of other measures which accompanied it. And these measures make no kind of political sense, unless allowance is made for the influence of economic theory. The theory in question is that of mercantilism, which holds that a country grows rich by trade – specifically, by export trade in processed and manufactured goods which ensures a net import of coin and bullion. On this view, colonies function as suppliers of raw materials and as markets for finished produce. England adopted mercantilism under Elizabeth I, systematized and considerably extended it under Cromwell and the later Stuarts, and embodied it in regulatory measures as late as 1774. Its effect on the North American colonies was to stultify manufacture.

In the earliest days, neglect of or opposition to manufacture were irrelevant. They were not especially serious in 1700. The colonists were looking for land – land which they could themselves own, free from the traditional restrictions of Europe. Not every home government, nor every colonial government, sympathized with the idea of numerous independent farmers. France, as stated, tried to construct large estates in Canada, but the settlers in practice disregarded the prescription. In Spanish America, great estates did come into being; and while the Dutch held the lands on the Hudson, enormous holdings existed there also. In the southern Atlantic colonies, large plantations replaced original settlement in small farms, but in the middle and northern colonies immigrants were able to secure land and to retain it, either by buying cheaply on arrival, or by saving from their wages in a labour-scarce area.

To be an independent landowner was a great thing for a migrant who in his native country had known landowning to be impossible. The colonies offered social and economic opportunities far beyond the range of anything available in Europe, but opportunities chiefly in terms of farming. Both for this reason, and on account of mercantilist restrictions it is not surprising that the seaboard in 1776 was essentially rural, except for the main ports.

Maryland, Virginia, and part of North Carolina relied on tobacco, with lesser exports of farm produce and lumber. Under tobacco the latosols soon lost what productivity they had, and a kind of shifting cultivation developed in which poor second-growth timber or scrub spread on to exhausted and abandoned fields. Rice, chiefly from the marshlands of South Carolina, combined with indigo and naval stores to supply the principal exports of the farthest south. Charleston functioned as the main commercial centre and chief port, reaching a population of about 10,000. Half of these were Negroes.

The middle colonies from Maryland to New York had intensified their farming, building up an export trade in animal products and grain. Their forests, still reasonably accessible from tidewater, yielded lumber. Ships were built for sale abroad, both at Philadelphia and at New York. These ports had increased by 1776 to respective populations of 17,000 and 20,000.

New England, still unable to provide an agricultural surplus, still depended on lumbering, shipbuilding, and fishing for its economic success. Manufacturing of coarse fabrics had admittedly begun, and ironworking had also started. But the chief means of increasing capital, in New England as in all the colonies, was commerce, centred there on Boston with a population equal to that of New York. A system had developed in which lumber, fish, and rum from New England, lumber, grain, and meat from the middle colonies, tobacco, rice, indigo, and naval stores from the southern colonies, sugar and molasses from the West Indies, and slaves from West Africa, were all interchanged. England was deeply involved, supplying trade goods to Africa and shipping slaves to North America. England lay at one terminus of the great-circle route to the West Indies, which touched on all the seaboard colonies. And England, resolutely adhering to mercantilism, was resolute in attempts to control colonial trade.

Mercantilism entailed various forms of discrimination against rival trading nations. In the last resort, there was always war. But measures short of war were usual. England's Navigation and other Acts, from 1650 onwards, directed traffic with English colonies through English ports, and in time attempted to enforce its carriage in English vessels. Colonial nerves had been roughened for generations as the policy developed, and colonists had come to resent with great bitterness the levies of customs and excise. In these unpromising circumstances,

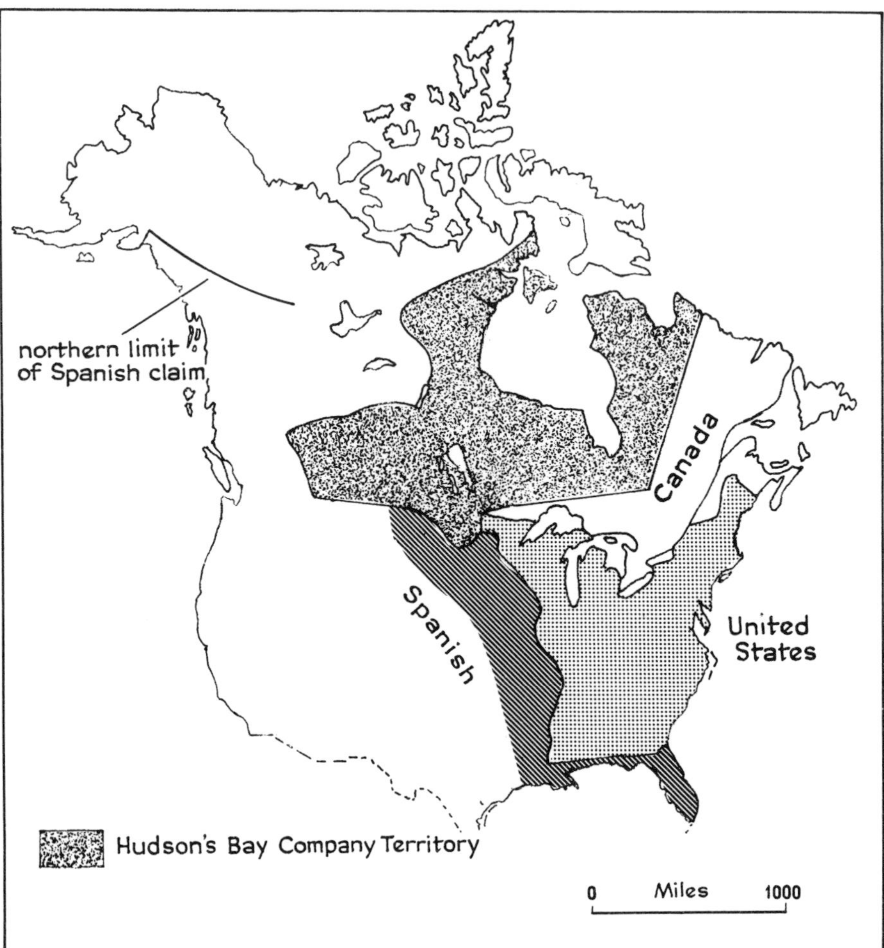

Fig. 5:6 Territorial distribution of 1783.

Parliament set out to make the colonies bear part of the cost of dislodging the French, passing the Stamp Act of 1765. Stamp duty on legal and published documents is nowadays an accepted, even if distrusted, means of taxation: but the 1765 Act aroused so much rage in the colonies that it could not be enforced. In repealing it the next year, Parliament chose to reassert its right to govern and to tax. Tightening and extension of customs practice evoked in retaliation a boycott of English goods, which halved export trade to the colonies within twelve months. The offending duties were repealed in 1770 – all but that on tea. This was retained on the personal instruction of George III, who selected this one duty as an issue of principle.

In 1773 George III gave the flagging East India Company freedom from tea duty in England, enabling it to sell in North America more cheaply than could duty-evading smugglers, even after customs dues were paid. But boycott was again applied, and part of the Boston cargo was thrown into the harbour. This was the culminating deed in a long series of independent gestures, characteristic of Massachusetts for well over a century. That least controllable of colonies George III and his foreign minister Lord North now determined to subdue.

The Quebec Act of 1774 has already been remarked on, as resented by the colonies and as outpaced by events. The four accompanying Acts of the same year precipitated revolt. They provided for the penal closure of Boston port, the government of Massachusetts direct from England, trial in England of capital causes arising in Massachusetts, and what amounted to military occupation of the colony.

All the seaboard but Georgia sent delegates to a

congress at Philadelphia, where the possibilities of union became clear. This is not to say that colonial opinion was wholly anti-English, any more than that the colonies now lacked sympathizers in England. But colonial militia were already under training. Fighting at Lexington, Concord, and Bunker Hill revealed the devastating fire-power of New England musketry; Virginia was also openly rebellious. The second Philadelphia congress appointed George Washington commander-in-chief. He took command of the untrained volunteer army at Boston early in 1776, outfacing the local English commander General Howe and causing him to withdraw to Nova Scotia. In the mid-year, representatives of the thirteen States issued the Declaration of Independence.

Although the war was now joined, it was at first prosecuted with no particular enthusiasm on either side, even though New York and Philadelphia fell to the British forces in 1776 and 1777. But General Burgoyne lost a whole army to the colonials at Saratoga in 1778. The States, already recognized by and militarily allied to France, would not negotiate when far-reaching concessions were offered. A French fleet relieved Philadelphia, and a Franco-American army cleared the south by its victory at Yorktown in 1780.

Spain, entering the war on the American side in 1779, regained Florida in 1781 and checked English attempts to secure control of the Mississippi. England's attempted blockade of the Americans had worsened the country's European relations, particularly with the Dutch on whom war opened in 1780. But the revolution was by that time effectively over and effectively successful. Congress had already begun to consider terms of a settlement. The treaty of 1783 recognized the independence of the U.S.A., extended American territory to the Mississippi, and returned Florida to Spain (Fig. 5:6). The last British warships sailed out of New York. Loyalists, subjected during the revolution and subsequently to widespread persecution, emigrated to England or the West Indies, or – in the main – to Canada.

Set battles and guerrilla campaigns of the revolutionary struggle on the seaboard were accompanied along the inland frontier by smaller-scale but still important onsets. These involved British forces operating chiefly from Detroit and Niagara, Indians who were mainly pro-British, remaining Frenchmen who adhered to the revolutionaries, groups of highly mobile American frontiersmen, and, in the end, punitive brigades of the U.S. army. The detailed story is confused. The simple outcome is that, by 1793, forts as far west as the Mississippi were in American hands, and frontiersmen were already casting their eyes on lands north of the Ohio.

CHAPTER SIX

THE DRIVE TO THE WEST

Whereas in 1775 the frontier of settlement still rested somewhere near the Appalachian divide between coastal and interior drainage, twenty-five years later it touched on the Lakes in the northeast, enclosed much of the low plateau country in the southwest, and had passed broadly across the western Appalachian flanks (Fig. 6:1). In the last decade of the eighteenth century the settled area of the U.S.A. increased by half, and some 500,000 people were installed in the interior. Here was the dramatic beginning of a westward shift which has not yet ceased.

The First Quarter Century

Three million settlers were in the interior by 1825. The frontier had in places crossed the Mississippi, and the way beyond was already open. By the Louisiana Purchase of 1803 the U.S.A. had secured the port of New Orleans and almost the whole Mississippi system. The Lewis and Clark expeditions of 1804–6 ascended the Missouri and crossed the Cordillera to the mouth of the Columbia River. Fur-trading posts were placed on the Columbia from 1809 onwards, and ten years later Oregon Territory was transferred by Spain to the U.S.A., in a settlement which also included the transfer to the U.S.A. of Florida.

The intention of the Louisiana Purchase was to safeguard trade through New Orleans. Spain had secretly returned Louisiana to France in 1800, but continued to administer New Orleans. In 1802 the port was declared closed to traffic originating in the interior. Closure meant ruin, not only to trade in furs, but also to the fast developing export of farm produce. Settlers in the valleys of the Ohio system, the most densely settled part of the interior, were especially alarmed and especially violent in protest.

The background of the Purchase was the Napoleonic Wars. Napoleon, no longer able to sustain an earlier plan of colonizing Louisiana, could at least, by outright sale, supply his treasury and obstruct possible English expansion from Canada. President Jefferson's representatives were instructed to secure passage of trade through New Orleans, and if possible to buy the whole port. They returned with the entire province. A week's negotiation had fixed a price – fifteen million dollars, about three cents an acre. This acquisition doubled the area of the U.S.A.: it was enough to satisfy many of the frontier settlers for another hundred years.

The Florida settlement constituted a recognition of hard facts. The western Gulf coastland was already being pioneered from the States, and Spain, under considerable pressure, yielded the peninsula also. Almost simultaneously, the westward extension of the Canadian boundary was agreed. A few years earlier it might have been fixed by war, for the U.S.A. and Britain were again at odds; but in the event it was settled by negotiation in 1818, Britain surrendering claims to the upper Red River Basin south of the 49th parallel, and the U.S.A. relinquishing land north of that parallel beyond what is now the State of Idaho (Fig. 6:2). The U.S.A. now had unchallenged title to lands running northwestwards as far as the Rockies.

The armed dispute mentioned above was the U.S.–British War of 1812. This, like the Louisiana Purchase, had its background in the Napoleonic Wars. The immediate cause of the war of 1812 was the search of American vessels for deserting British seamen; acts of impressment which recalled colonial times also contributed. In addition, the U.S.A. suffered keenly from the blockade and counter-blockade proclaimed in Europe, losing 1500 vessels in nine years: the new nation reacted in the same way that neutrals had reacted in the War of Independence. The 1812 war produced few noteworthy land actions, except for the burning of public build-

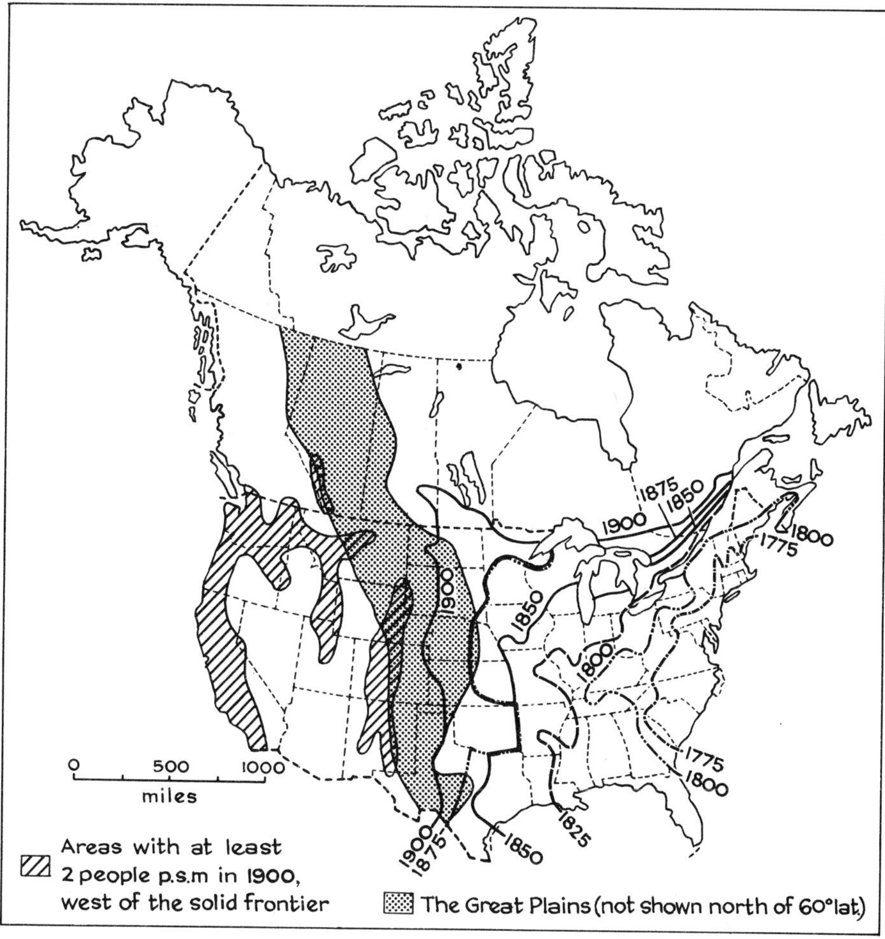

FIG. 6:1 Movement of the frontier: unsettled enclaves, and settled exclaves except for 1900, not shown.

ings in Washington, and for the successful American defence of New Orleans at the war's very end in 1814. Fewer than 4000 American troops were committed in any battle, fewer than 4000 wounded and 2000 killed in the whole war. Fighting along the Canadian border proved inconclusive. The psychological effect, however, was great. The U.S.A. came at last in 1814 into full possession of international rights and of commercial freedom. The latter, as will be seen later, was overdue.

The first quarter of the nineteenth century also brought political changes to the Cordilleran country. While some of these did not immediately affect either the U.S.A. or Canada, others were to prove highly significant before long. Brazil detached itself from Portugal in 1822; what are now Ecuador, Colombia, Venezuela, and Panama became independent of Spain in 1819. The colonial empires were sundering wholesale. The most directly relevant happening was the Mexican war of independence which, after eleven years' fighting, broke Mexico's colonial link in 1821. A concerted European move to subdue the new republics was forestalled when, at the end of 1822, the U.S. President announced the Monroe Doctrine. In summary, this was a policy of American non-intervention in European politics, and of opposition both to European intervention in American politics and to new European colonization in either of the Americas.

1821, then, saw the U.S.A. adjoining an independent Mexico which included Texas and the whole southern part of the Cordillera – nearly a million square miles which are today included in the U.S.A. The same year brought the opening of a territorial conflict with Russia. The Atlantic colo-

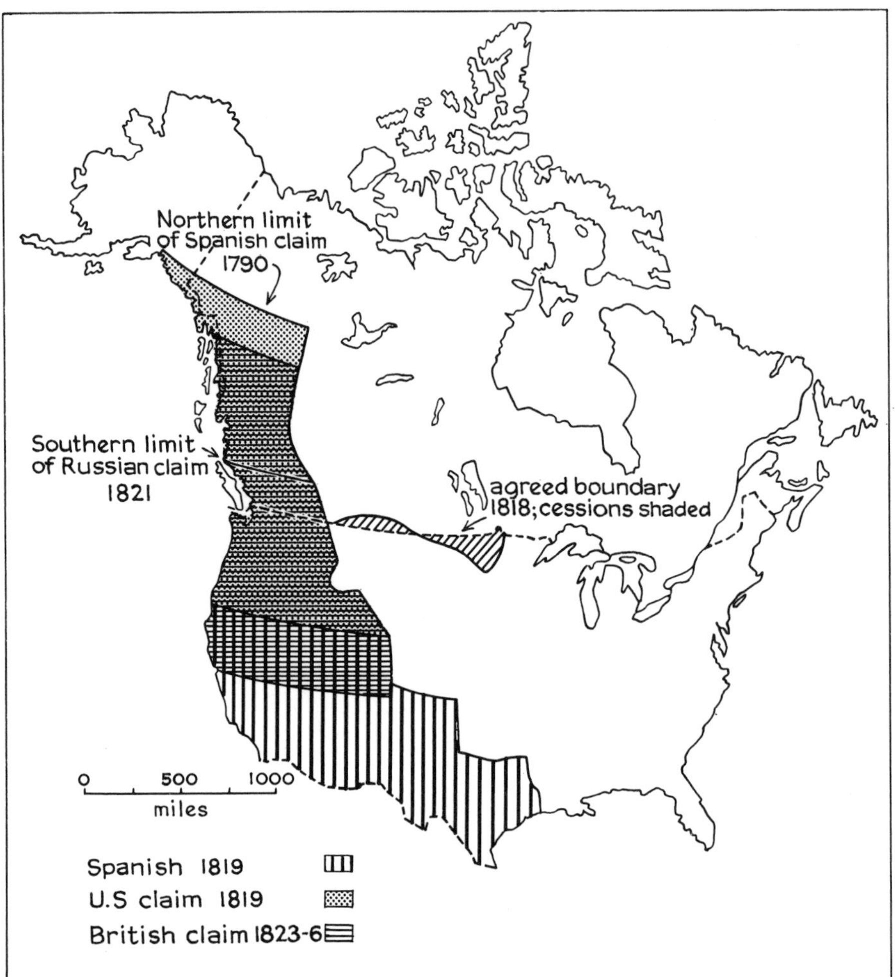

FIG. 6:2
Conflicting claims in the late eighteenth and early nineteenth centuries.

nies in the early 1700s were encircled by the French; during the War of Independence the States were menaced with encirclement by the British; and now, at about the turn of the century, came a threat of enclosure by Spain from the south and by Russia from the north.

Spanish and Russian claims would indeed have overlapped widely, but for a time-gap of two years. Spain in 1790 was claiming Cordilleran territory beyond the north end of the Alaskan panhandle (Fig. 6:2). By the 1819 treaty, the U.S.A. recognized 42°N as the Spanish–American boundary on the south, but itself adopted Spain's line of 1790 in the north. Russian sealers and fur-traders, long established in Alaska, had however already worked their way along the coast, constructing a fort in California in 1812. In 1821 the Czar decreed that lands as far south as 51°N latitude belonged to Russia. Matters were already as confused on the Pacific coast as they had been on the Atlantic coast in the 1600s. Furthermore, Britain in the 1820s was claiming lands between 59°N and 38°N latitude, from the base of the Alaskan panhandle to the Golden Gate. For the time being, however, discord between the U.S.A. and the British claims was hushed, joint occupation of part of the Cordillera having been agreed in 1818. Both nations protested against the Russian decree of 1821, and Russia reduced its Pacific coastal claims to what is now Alaska. North Americans, whether from the U.S.A. or from Canada, had gained access to the Pacific on a front of a thousand miles.

While the U.S.A. was revising its external relationships and adjusting its outer boundaries in

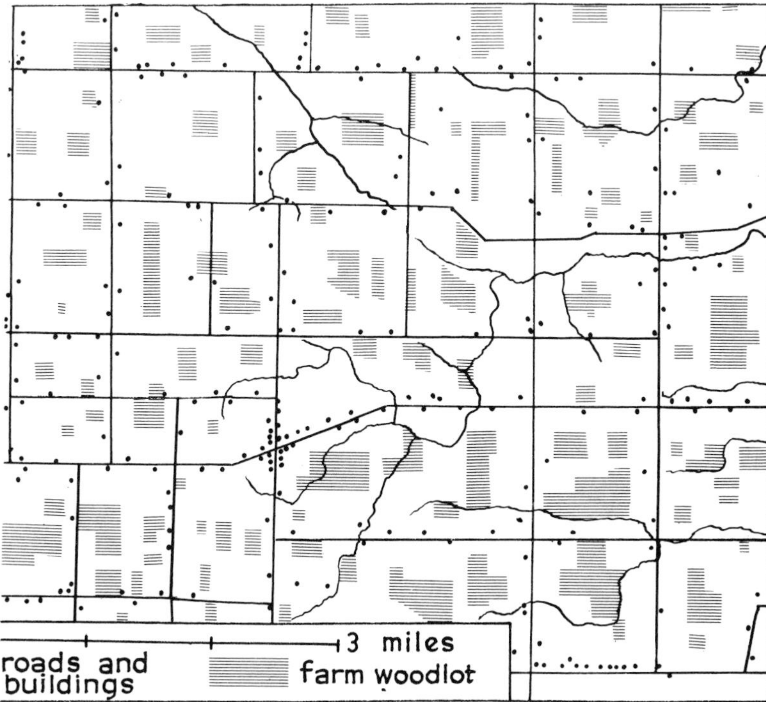

FIG. 6:3 Sample of the landscape-pattern resulting from rectangular subdivision and allocation of farmland in the Midwest.

these various ways, the government formulated an internal policy of land settlement. Under the Land Act of 1786, land from 1800 onwards was offered for sale in blocks of 320 acres at $2 an acre. In 1820 the price came down to $1·25 an acre and the minimum holding to eighty acres. A settler in 1820 could buy a small farm for a hundred dollars,* either cash down, on instalments, or on mortgage. In 1810 the government had enough land for sale, east of the Mississippi alone, to accommodate a million 160-acre farms – that is, to support a million families, and to yield $200 million in sales.

If the climate west of the Mississippi had been as moist as that on the east, the Louisiana Purchase would have provided for another 3½ million 160-acre farms, the sale of which would have brought in $700 million. The problems of the western interior, however, had not yet declared themselves. Not until about 1850 did the settlement frontier pass westwards out of humid into moist subhumid climates. Settlers in the first half of the century occupied lands where drought was rarely a problem, and where most of the natural cover was forest (Figs. 4:1, 6:1).

The 320-acre, 160-acre, and 80-acre lots are, of course, factors of the 640 acres which make up a square mile. When Congress took control of land settlement, it adopted not merely the square mile, but the mile square, as the fundamental unit of subdivision. Both in the U.S. interior and in the interior of Canada, demarcation of province boundaries owes something to the practice followed in early colonial grants; and the subdivision of land open to settlement, in advance of the settlement itself, is reminiscent of the same practice. The use of a mile-square grid ensured that, by contrast with the strip-like or irregularly shaped farms of the seaboard and the lower St Lawrence, farms in the U.S. interior were rectangular from the outset. The quarter-section farm of 160 acres, becoming standard throughout large areas, still powerfully affects the geographical pattern today (Fig. 6:3).

Although the interior farmlands relied on the Mississippi system for goods transport, the settlers entered by routes through the Appalachians. In the U.S.A., as in Britain, turnpike roads were con-

* By 1960 the average value per acre of farms in Indiana and Illinois was about $300. Although the purchasing power of the 1960 dollar was considerably less than that of the 1820 dollar, and although the 1960 values include farm buildings on improved farmland, whereas the 1820 prices relate to land still uncleared, the actual contrast is still sharp.

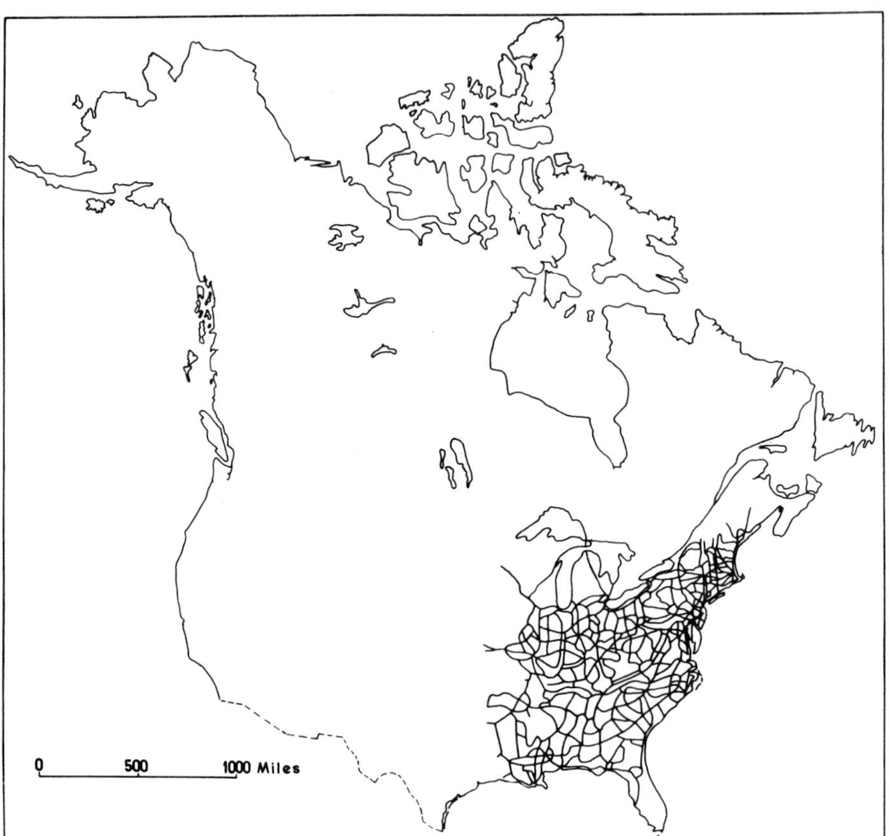

FIG. 6:4 Commercial road net of the mid-nineteenth century (U.S.A. only).

structed. These led inland from Albany on the navigable Mohawk, and from Philadelphia and Baltimore on the coast (Fig. 6:4). The Genesee Turnpike linked Albany with Buffalo on Lake Erie. From Philadelphia the Forbes Road led across the Susquehanna River at Harrisburg, and wound through the Alleghany Mountains to Pittsburg on the Ohio: thenceforward, travel was by flatboat. But already before 1825, the federal government had built the National Turnpike from Cumberland, where the Potomac breaks through the Alleghenies, to Wheeling on the Ohio downstream of Pittsburg. This road was linked to Philadelphia by way of Hagerstown, and to Baltimore by an existing turnpike. Farther south, a road taking off from Hagerstown ran along the Great Appalachian Valley, emerging through the Cumberland Gap* on to the low plateaus of Kentucky. And in the year 1825 itself, the Erie Canal was opened, connecting Albany to Buffalo by water. From the outset it was hugely successful. Within a year it recorded some 40,000 passages, and reduced transport costs between Buffalo and New York by four-fifths. Railway transport was to follow within five years.

Steamboats appeared at the same time. Fulton's *Clermont*, successfully run on the Hudson in 1807, introduced a line of craft which began operating on the interior rivers within a very few years, and which by 1825 were accustomed sights. All these various developments were at once responses to, and promoters of, the westward drive.

The Mid-Century

Most of the pioneers in the first half of the nineteenth century, as in the first quarter, were American-born. The full tide of immigration did not start to flow until the 1840s. In the thirty-seven years between the end of the War of Independence and the year 1820, about a quarter of a million immi-

* Cumberland on the National Turnpike is in Maryland; the Cumberland Gap near the head of the Cumberland River is about 350 miles away to the southwest.

grants arrived – an average of some 70,000 per decade. The rate of inflow doubled in 1820–30, rose fourfold again in 1830–40, and threefold again in 1840–50 (Fig. 6:5). But total immigration of one million between 1673 and 1840, and of nearly three million between 1783 and 1850, accounted for but part of the astonishingly rapid increase of population in the interior. As was said above, this population numbered three million in 1825. Only about a tenth of these could have been immigrants, even if all immigrants had passed through the seaboard States. Since numbers remained near the Atlantic, it follows that more than 90 per cent of the interior settlers of 1825 were American-born.

By 1850 the settlement-frontier was well across the Mississippi still driving vigorously westward and northwestward (Fig. 6:1). The lines marked on this map show the approximate limits of occupance at a density of two per square mile or more – i.e., the western boundary of land, at least one-quarter of which had been taken up. Behind the frontier, settlement consolidated itself; between the Mississippi and the frontier of 1850, in fact, about half the occupied area was already 50 per cent distributed. In advance of the frontier, penetration had leapt across the Cordillera: California, admitted as a State in 1850, was approaching a population of 10,000.

At the mid-century, the U.S.A. had a population of some twenty-three million. About thirteen million of these lived in the seaboard States, ten million in the interior and the South. Several lines of development were now clear. Indians were fast being displaced as the frontier advanced. Back on the Atlantic coast, cotton textile and other industries were absorbing increasing numbers of workers, including many immigrants. Pioneers now came not only from overseas and New England, but also from the whole Atlantic seaboard and from the earlier settled parts of the interior. Town workers in times of depression, those in debt, the discontented, all if they wished could move west. And there developed also a kind of committed frontiersman – the pioneer who, once he found himself with neighbours, would again move on. A second new social element was formed by prospectors, who caused settlement in outlying places to leap ahead of the solid agricultural frontier. On the agricultural side, the corn-growing Interior Lowlands contrasted with the cotton-planting South. On the political side, the U.S.A. in mid-century adjusted its Mexican and Canadian boundaries, in the process achieving a fourfold increase of area in a fifty-year period. In 1854, Perry's fleet opened Japan to American trade: the U.S.A. henceforth was a power in the Pacific.

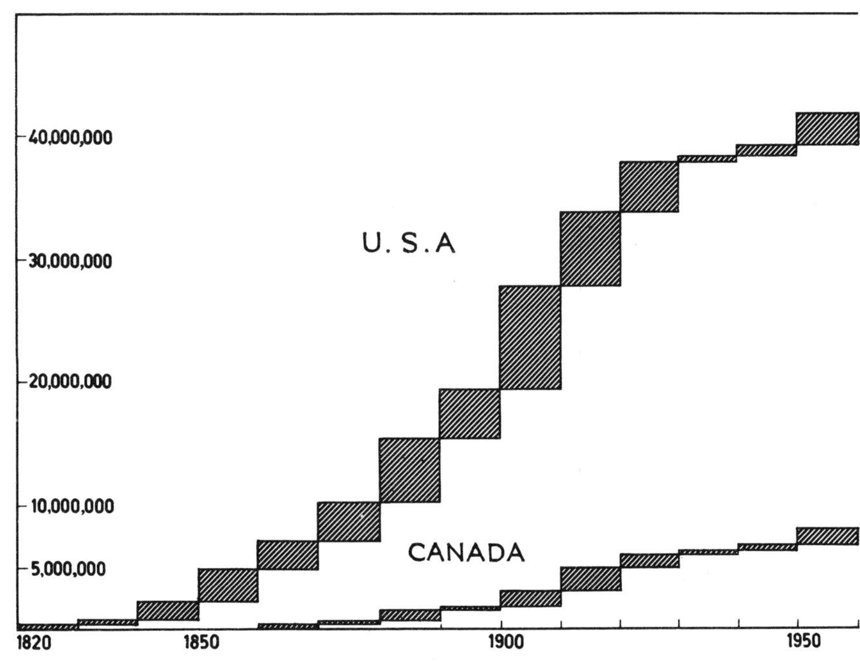

FIG. 6:5
Cumulative totals of migration.

Popular legend and popular myth, grown and nourished on films and on demotic literature, associate the clash between pioneers and Indians with the prairie West. In actuality, an armed struggle prolonged itself from the early 1500s to the end of the 1800s, shifting its location as settlement spread. In the first half of the nineteenth century, most Indian battles occurred either in the southeast, or in what was then the northwest – the country between the Ohio and the Mississippi. Under the presidencies of Monroe and Jackson, 1816–36, a resettlement policy was implemented whereby Indians both from the southeast and from the northwest were relocated beyond the Mississippi. Although the policy of resettlement did not at once halt the savage attacks or savage resistance by either side, it did eventually pacify the eastern interior and the southeast: the Indians were consistently handicapped by being technically outmoded in weapons, tactically and strategically outmoded in organization, and socially ill-fitted to withstand the westward pressure of the frontier. In the end they were forced to make the bitter choice between death and removal.

Deliberate relocation of Indians was perhaps more relevant to the affairs of the South than to those of the interior. The Interior Lowlands east of the Mississippi were taken partly by force, whereas Indian lands in the South were acquired mainly by treaty. In addition, the contrasted ways in which agriculture was developing in the two parts of the country meant that demand for vacant land in the South was especially urgent.

Settlement of the Interior Lowlands made it possible to produce surpluses of pigmeat, milk products, and grain. Podsolic soils cleared of hardwood forest proved by no means unproductive: on the contrary, many of them were distinctly superior to the soils of European farmlands, which after centuries of common-field cultivation had by no means yet recovered, under improved systems of management. From the outset, grain-and-livestock combinations on the podsolic soils helped to maintain fertility. By contrast, the latosols of the South were readily exhaustible, even if tobacco and then cotton had not been exhausting crops. The tobacco-cultivation of the southern Atlantic States was largely replaced or supplanted, in the first half of the nineteenth century, by cotton-planting. This too, except on the crescents of rendzina soils, required a kind of shifting cultivation, in which planting either moved round the extent of existing holdings, or advanced westwards taking the frontier with it. Agriculturally, the northern interior and the South were complementary: by the mid-century, the South was buying from the farms of the interior foodstuffs and livestock equal in total value to the whole export trade of the U.S.A.

Like the growing of tobacco and of rice, the planting of cotton – and the planting of sugar-cane along the Gulf Coast – called for cheap labour. As before, this was supplied by Negroes. Importation of slaves was forbidden in 1808, but Negroes in great number were already present. The South by 1850 had ten million people, of whom about one-third were slaves. Fewer than 10 per cent of the Negroes in the South were free. Slave-holding whites numbered about one-third of a million, about 1 in 20 of the white population; but the majority of slaves belonged to an élite group of about 10,000 planters, about 1 in 600 of the white population.

Despite the unpaid slave workforce, cotton-growing could not have been economic but for a mechanical invention – the cotton gin designed by Whitney in 1793 to separate the raw cotton from the cotton-seed. This was the first of a series of inventions stimulated either by the overt needs of westward-moving cultivation, or by the general nineteenth-century interest in machinery. The iron plough developed by Jethro Wood was, by 1850, in widespread use; it made cultivation, and especially the breaking of virgin land, far easier than hitherto. McCormick's reaper, built in the factory erected at Chicago in 1847, joined with the threshing-machine perfected about 1850 to raise farm productivity. The U.S.A. soon commanded an export trade both in farm machinery and in grain. Reapers and threshers benefited the interior even more than the cotton gin did the South.

Internal policy continued to encourage settlers. By the Pre-emption Act of 1841 a settler could, by occupying his 160 acres, gain first right of purchase from the government, normally at \$1·25 an acre. There were still 250 million acres of public land available, enough for 1½ million new farms.

Mid-century political events included the extension of the U.S.–Canadian boundary to the Pacific,

7. Eastward view along the Canadian–U.S.A. border: this is one of the few undefended international borders in the world.

and the southward shift of the U.S.–Mexican boundary in the Cordillera by more than 600 miles. The possession of Oregon was hotly disputed between Britain and the U.S.A. for about ten years, but negotiations in 1846 arrived at the compromise already adopted farther east – namely, the parallel of 49° N, except that on reaching the Pacific the boundary was made to bend southwards and leave Vancouver Island wholly in Canada (Plate 7). Feelings about Oregon had been running so high that the arrangement would certainly have caused a public outcry, had not the U.S.A. been distracted internally by the rising tension between North and South over the question of slavery, and externally by the Mexican question.

The 1819 treaty with Spain, already noticed in connection with Florida and Oregon, also validated grants of Texan lands to Americans. Colonists continued to enter Texas after Mexico became independent, and by 1830 outnumbered Mexicans four to one. It is true that the total population of Texas was but 15,000 at the time. Nevertheless, the Texan cause roused great sympathy in the States, and volunteers from the U.S.A. assisted the successful revolt of 1836. Texas became an independent country in the following year, and was willingly annexed to the U.S.A. in 1845.

California might at one stage have been bought; but two successive governments in the politically disturbed Mexico were unable to still, or to resist, the hostile clamour which the offer provoked. President Polk in 1846 seized on the excuse of small-scale fighting on the disputed Texas boundary to ask Congress to declare war. This it did: the province of California – the existing State of that name, the whole of Nevada and Utah, much of Arizona, parts of Wyoming, Colorado, and New Mexico – fell without a fight. Battles were pitched south of the Rio Grande, where Monterey fell in 1846 and Vera Cruz and Mexico City in 1847. Loud and determined reproaches by Polk's opponents came too late. In 1848, Mexico ceded more than half a million square miles of Cordilleran territory, receiving in compensation $15 million. This, as it immediately turned out, was a bargain price. In the same year, prospectors struck abundant gold in the Sacramento Valley. In two years California multiplied its population by ten, reaching a total of 100,000 in 1850 and being admitted to the Union.

One last adjustment of the Mexican boundary remained outstanding – the Gadsden Purchase of 1854 (Fig. 6:6). This strip of about 30,000 square miles between the Gila River and the existing boundary was desired, not for any expansionist reason, but for railway-building: it offered a far easier route westward than did the country north of the Gila. Lines from the east coast reached Buffalo in 1850, Pittsburg, Wheeling, and Chattanooga by 1854, and St Louis by 1855. Engineers, entrepreneurs, and politicians were however already aiming at the Pacific.

Improvements in transport, on the sea and on the

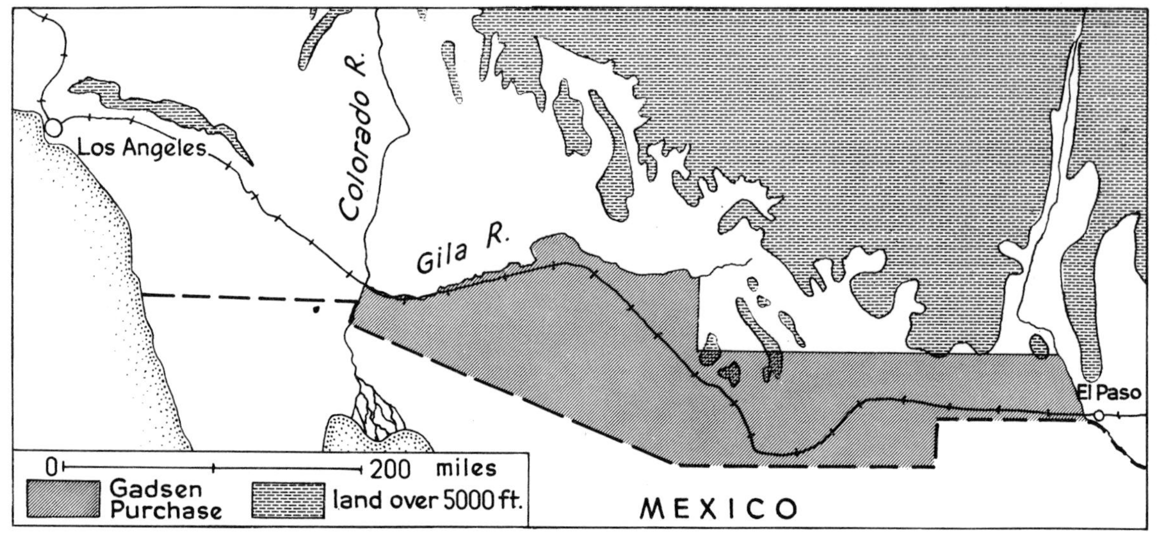

FIG. 6:6 The Gadsden Purchase.

land alike, greatly aided the inflow of migrants and the westward press of settlers. Transatlantic passages by steamship, initiated by the *Savannah's* voyage in 1810, were becoming increasingly usual. Post roads formed an effective network in 1835 from the Atlantic to the Mississippi, and from the eastern Gulf to the southern shores of the Great Lakes. Canals by the mid-century supplemented natural waterways in connecting New York, Philadelphia, Baltimore, and Richmond with the Lakes or the Ohio, and the Lakes with the Ohio and the Mississippi (Fig. 6:7). One direct stimulus to canal-building was the war of 1812, which revealed the defects of transport routes in the northern U.S.A. A more generalized, but perhaps more effective, stimulus was the growing bulk traffic between the interior farms and the industrializing East. Just as the Interior and the South were complementary in the agricultural sense, so were the Interior, the South, and the East self-contained in a tripartite economic system. The Interior produced the food, the South the cotton, and the East the factory goods – except that factories were already arising in some interior towns. Increasing population, increasing farm production, and increasing factory production all demanded improved transport. The first passenger train in North America ran in 1831. Track mileage reached 10,000 in 1850, welding links between neighbouring towns into the beginnings of trunk routes. Within ten years mileage had tripled; western railheads stood on, and in places beyond, the Mississippi. Lines were now coming fast behind the frontier, and were soon to reach beyond it. Beyond the railheads, beyond the waterways of the western feeders of the Mississippi, trails took off for the Cordillera and the Pacific coast (Fig. 6:8).

Ocean-going ships brought migrants to the east coast: road, water, and rail took some of them onwards. The $2\frac{1}{4}$ million who arrived in 1830–50 were mainly Irish and German. The Irish, who formed the majority, came in their greatest numbers hitherto, after the potato blight of 1845–46 during which an estimated three-quarters of a million starved to death. Many of the Irish lodged in the east, where their descendants still strengthen anti-British feeling. The Germans, on the other hand, made for the interior. Leaving their politically upheaved and socially unstable homeland, they did what their forebears had done in the Dark Ages – entered the unknown forest, felled it, and converted it to farmland. At the mid-century, a quarter of the pioneers on the northwestern frontier were foreign-born, and most of this group were German.

By about 1850, certain patterns of distribution were becoming evident; some of them foreshadow the patterns of today. The industrial belt of the northeast was already recognizable (Fig. 6:9). The main area of corn-growing included southern Ohio and central Indiana and Illinois. However, Fig. 6:9 is emphatically not meant to suggest that this

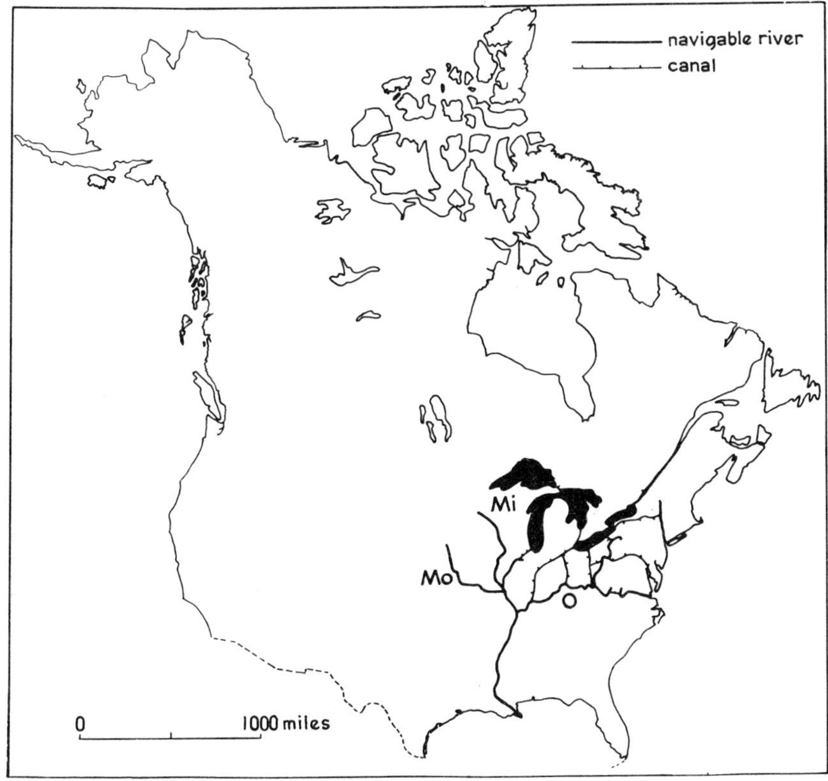

FIG. 6:7
Navigable waterways of the Great Lakes and Mississippi systems in the mid-nineteenth century; main links with the east coast included.
Mi, Mississippi R; Mo, Missouri R; O, Ohio R.

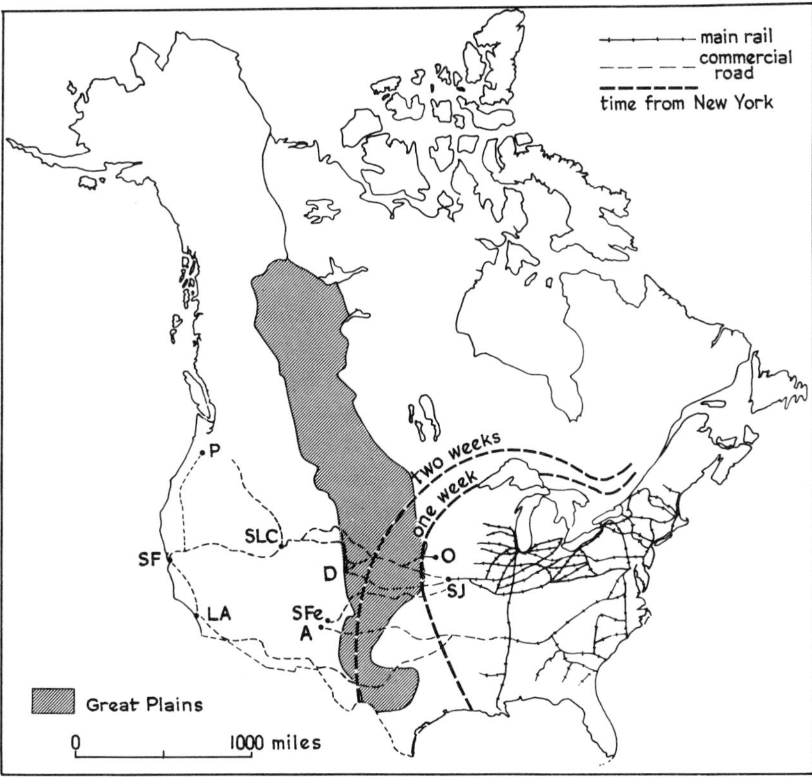

FIG. 6:8
Selected main rail lines about 1850: commercial roads west of the rail net.
O, Omaha; SJ, St Joseph; D, Denver; SFe, Santa Fe; A, Albuquerque; SLC, Salt Lake City; LA, Los Angeles; SF, San Francisco; P, Portland (Ore.).

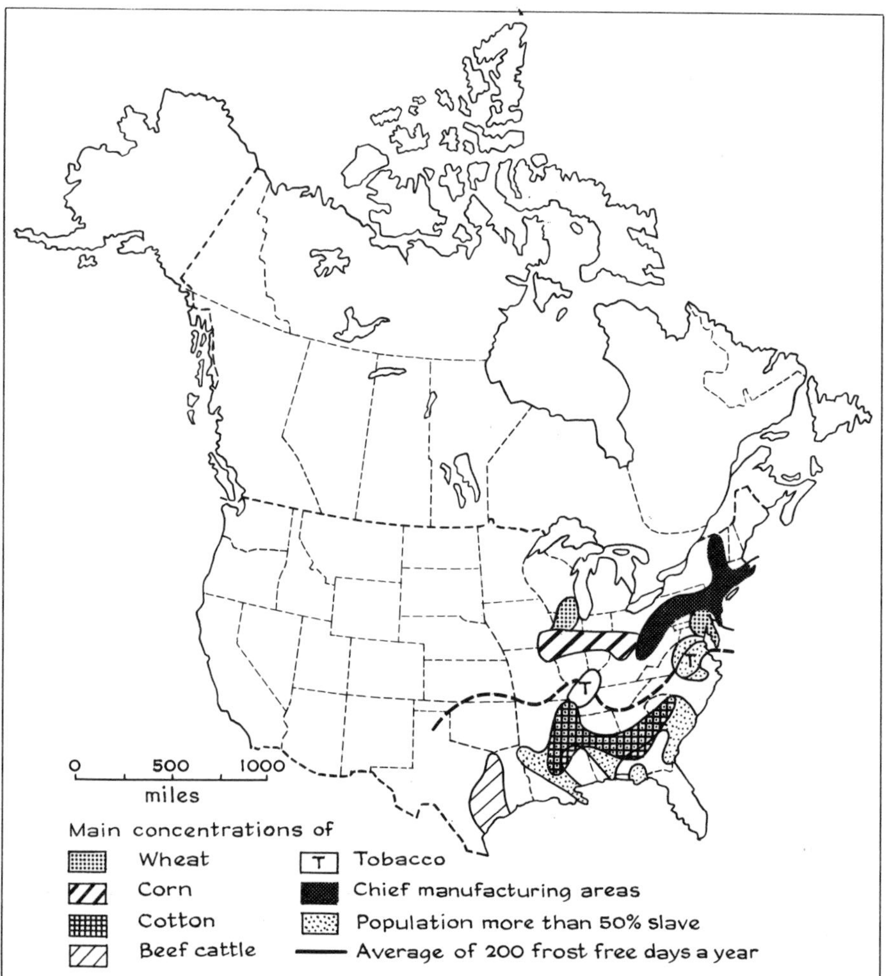

FIG. 6:9
Some elements of the geography of 1850.

was the only corngrowing area – on the contrary, corn was widely cultivated throughout the settled farmlands, except along the swampy coastlands of the Gulf and in Florida. Similarly, wheat was grown in all parts north of the main cotton-producing districts, cotton was well distributed throughout the South, except in Florida, and beef cattle were numerous everywhere except in the southern half of Florida. Tobacco, alone among the elements represented, was almost entirely confined to the area marked.

The two districts of tobacco-planting are crossed by the isopleth of 200 frost-free days. The district which lay mainly in Virginia had a population more than half composed of slaves, resembling in this respect the chief cotton-growing districts which lay everywhere south of the 200-day line. West of the cotton plantation in the settled parts of Texas was the greatest concentration of beef cattle, a portent of the changes which during the next half-century were to come to the West.

The Third Quarter of the Nineteenth Century

In 1850–75 the U.S.A. received about 6½ million immigrants; the settlement-frontier approached the edge of the Great Plains; the Atlantic and Pacific coasts were linked by rail; oil was first struck; Alaska was bought from Russia; and the conflict of interest between North and South led to civil war.

Ireland and Germany still supplied the majority of incomers, although England and Scandinavia now also became prominent. It was the Scandinavians in particular who would open up Wisconsin and Minnesota. Few immigrants went to the South,

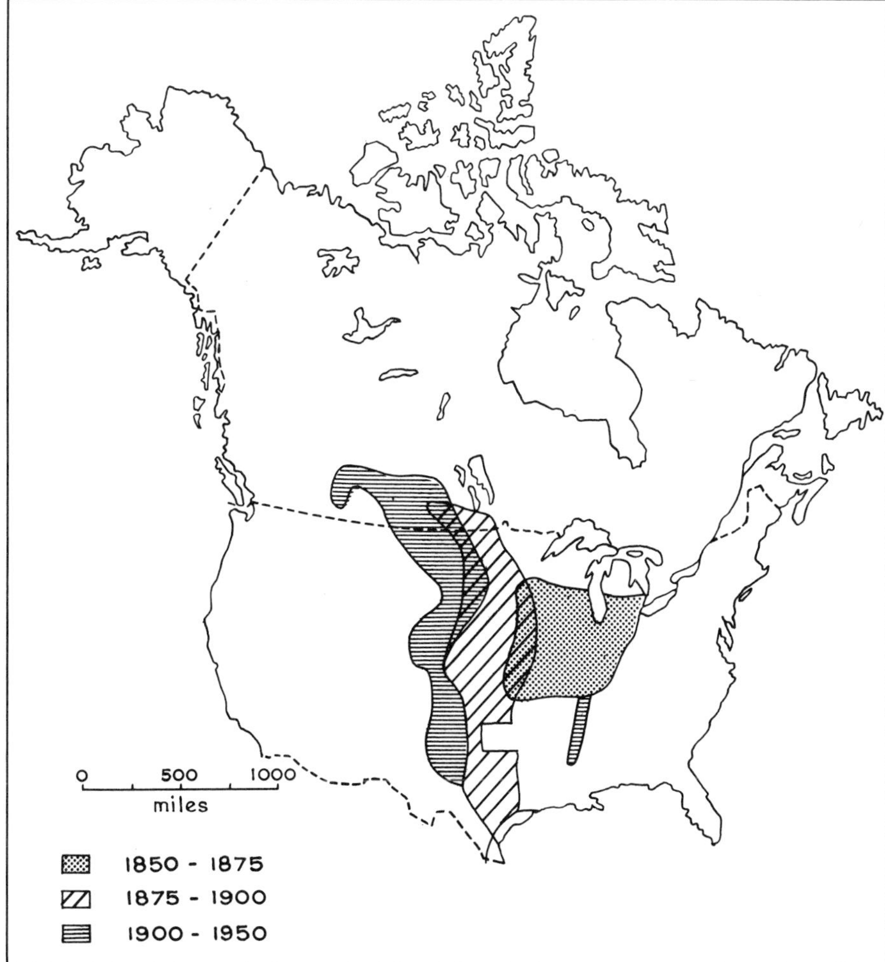

FIG. 6:10
Location of the chief areas of land improvement, 1850–1950.

most of which throughout this twenty-five-year span recorded less than 1 per cent of its population as foreign-born. The northwestern interior, by contrast, had some 30 per cent in this category. Frontier settlement and consolidation behind the frontier were still more strongly encouraged than before, when the Homestead Act of 1862 gave a farmer the right to buy 80 or 160 acres at a very low price, after he had lived on and cultivated the land for five years. There was ample room for consolidation: the main increase in acreage of improved land in the period 1850–75 occurred in the heart of the Midwest (Fig. 6:10), much of it on the prairie soils and planosols, and where the natural cover was mixed woodland and tall grass, or tall grass alone (Fig. 4:1). Invasion of the grasslands was new: at first it required courage, for most pioneer farmers believed that natural grassland was unfit for farmland. The Iowa prairies were taken first. Beyond them to the northwest, a narrowing belt of hardwood forest led clearance on, between the mixed forest on the Shield about the head of Lake Superior on one side and tall grasslands of the main prairies on the other. Pressure of numbers was so great that settlement perforce burst into the grass country.

It was encouraged, and in some areas introduced, by prospecting. Gold strikes in both divisions of the Rockies brought fortune-hunters into what are now Colorado, Idaho, and Montana. At the same time, the enormously rich Comstock lode of silver was located in Nevada in 1859. Mormon settlement at Salt Lake City in 1847 completed the penetration of all parts of the Cordillera. In advance of the solid frontier of 1875, ribbons of settlement stretched along the foot of the Southern Rockies, along the foot of the Wasatch Mountains overlooking the Salt Lake Basin, along the coast of California and along the Great Valley. Smaller patches occurred elsewhere in the mountains. The fact of occupance, the progressive admission of the western States to the Union, and the huge outputs of precious metal, all demanded improved links with the east. The first came in 1861, when New York and San Francisco were joined by telegraph. The second came eight years later, when the same two cities were joined by rail.

Whereas the advance of the frontier between 1800 and 1850 depended on waterways and roads, the land beyond the Mississippi was poor in navigable rivers, and in the natural state largely trackless. It was also occupied by mobile Indians, who rode ponies descended from stock introduced originally by the Spanish. Indian battles in 1850–75 were concentrated on the Great Plains: the earlier story of the lands eastward was repeated, even though the present Oklahoma was reserved as Indian Territory: its status explains the angular kink of the 1875 frontier line marked in Fig. 6:1. Pioneers entering Indian country, if they proposed to settle, grouped themselves to travel by prairie schooner – the large covered wagon which, manned by riflemen, could function at need as an armoured car.

The Civil War of 1861–65 can be used as an argument of geographical determinism. The South, with its thousand-acre plantations, use of slave labour, aristocratic social structure, dominant cotton production, and fundamentally agrarian population had evolved a close adjustment to its geographical environment. The northeastern States, increasingly populous, increasingly industrial and commercial, were less directly adjusted to their settings, but were economically far more successful than the South. The agricultural interior, as yet far less urbanized than the Northeast, was socially democratic, its farmholders inheriting the frontier spirit and not ranging greatly in wealth. Dependence of the South on agricultural produce of the interior and on northeastern cotton markets, dependence of the interior on the demand for farm produce from the South and from the towns of the Northeast, and dependence of the Northeast on both other areas for supplies of primary produce and for markets for its industrial goods, did not prevent strife. Sectional interests became vocal, as soon as sections of the country became self-conscious.

There was, however, far more to the North–South split than this. Political power at the Congressional level was held, in the early days of independence, largely by educated men from the aristocratic South: the first four presidents came from Virginia. Increases in northern population, increasing populations inland, and the possibility of political co-operation between the Northeast and the Northwest threatened the South with minority status. Progressive admissions of new States to the Union repeatedly reopened the slavery question. The nineteenth-century humanitarian movement in the North produced abolitionists, while the South moved progressively towards the view that slavery was not only necessary but also completely justifiable on moral grounds. The whole matter was still further confused by the type of dispute that affects many a federation – the quarrel over states' rights. Two-tier organization seems to lead inevitably to discord between the central government, which formulates and must hope to enforce a national policy, and state or provincial governments which, understandably enough, regard their own interests as paramount.

Internal politics of the U.S.A. by the mid-century were beginning to settle into the pattern, customary in many Western countries, of two major parties who alternate between government and opposition. The Presidential elections of 1860 went to the Republicans, and Lincoln was inaugurated. The Republican policy included protective tariffs, welcome to the Northeast; a Pacific railway and an increased generous land-settlement programme, both highly acceptable in the Interior; and easier naturalization which, like the projected revisions to land-settlement, favoured immigrants.* For the South, somewhat negative measures were proposed – retention of slavery where it existed, but no further extension; and maintenance of the Union. Lincoln's election could be taken in the South as a sign that states' rights would be eroded, and that the slave States would never form a majority in government. South Carolina declared its secession from the Union within a month, followed quickly by the

* As previously observed, the new Homestead law was enacted in 1862, and the Pacific railway finished in 1869.

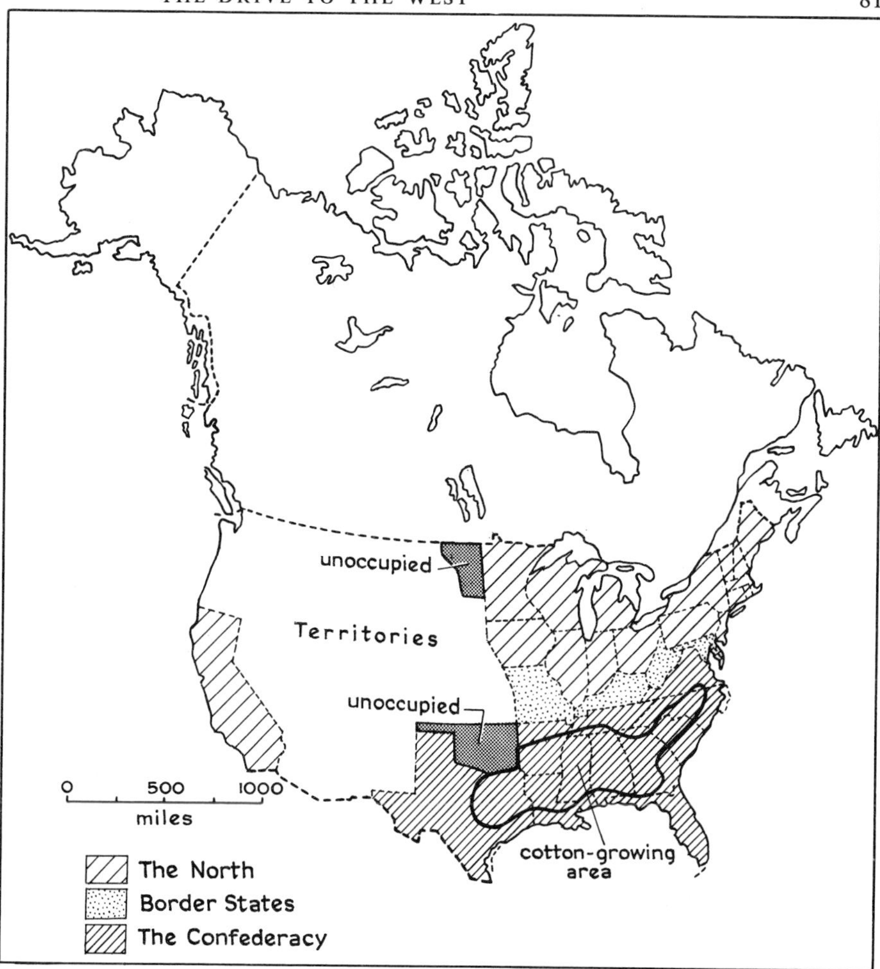

FIG. 6:11
Some distributional aspects of the Civil War.

remainder of the Deep South from Florida to Texas (Fig. 6:11). The Confederacy drew up a constitution, elected Jefferson Davis as President and began to raise an army of 100,000 men. In April 1861, Southern forces took the Federal Fort Sumter in Charleston Harbour. Lincoln called for 75,000 militia to serve three months in suppressing rebellion, and instituted a blockade of southern ports. The wavering border States now had to make their choices. Arkansas, Tennessee, North Carolina, and Virginia joined the Confederacy, Missouri, Kentucky, Maryland, and Delaware the North (Fig. 6:11). All eight were slave States, and only in Delaware was allegiance undivided. Indeed, Virginia was clearly divided between east and west: its upland-dwellers refused to secede, broke away from the easterners, and formed a new State which in 1863 joined the Union as West Virginia.

At the end of 1861, the front between North and South ran through the border States, and between the rival capitals of Washington and Richmond. By the end of 1862, the Northern forces had cleared the plateaus in Kentucky and Tennessee and were pressing down the Mississippi at the approaches to Vicksburg. A year later again, the Union forces had broken through to the Gulf, were pushing back the Confederate armies almost everywhere, and had inflicted his first defeat upon the brilliant Robert E. Lee in the battle of Gettysburg. In 1864, the Northern commander Ulysses S. Grant used Sheridan to lay waste the Shenandoah Valley, and Sherman to conduct the march from Chattanooga to Atlanta and thence to Savannah: between Atlanta and Savannah the Union forces left a fifty-mile-wide belt of destruction. Grant's campaign of attrition dislodged Lee from Richmond early in 1865, and the remains of the Southern forces surrendered at Appomattox.

This brief retrospective summary is not meant to imply that the Union forces were everywhere and at all times successful: on the contrary, many victories went to both sides; and numbers of the most murderous battles were inconclusive. Half a million, possibly three-quarters of a million men, were killed in battle or died on active service. Nonetheless, it is not easy to understand how the almost entirely rural South held out for so long against the industrializing North. Blockade-running and smuggling maintained little more than a token Southern trade; rapidly-diversified agriculture supplied food, but means of transport were deficient; neither time nor technique permitted heavy industrialization, and the South relied mainly upon domestic craft production. The largest town in the South was New Orleans, with a population of some 200,000; the North included Baltimore and Boston, each approaching a quarter of a million; Philadelphia, with half a million; and Greater New York, which had reached the million mark. And the North could feed its people: the frontier continued to shift, and production to rise on the farms behind it.

The year 1865 found the Northern economy more highly developed than ever, that of the South in ruins. Lincoln proclaimed the emancipation of slaves at the beginning of 1863, apparently hoping to disrupt Southern agriculture. No such effect followed: but at the war's end, the freed Negroes found themselves thrown abruptly on the labour market. After the confused early years of reconstruction, a new agricultural system swiftly emerged – one dominated by share-cropping, with tenant-farming as a supplement. Plantations were neither confiscated, nor broken up: but they were subdivided, mainly into forty-acre lots, among which the former concentrated settlement was dispersed. Tenant farmers received tools, land, and draught animals in return for labour, share-croppers received part of the crop instead of wages. Although the share-cropping system lay open to much abuse, it had the practical advantage to Negro croppers of ensuring control of mules, the one means of mobility and a great social asset. The system spread very widely.

Economic recovery in the South was swifter than might have been expected. The average production of cotton for the years immediately preceding the outbreak of war was surpassed in the early 1870s, while the average for the late 1870s was 25 per cent greater than the immediate pre-war average. But social and political bitterness remained, lasting up to the present day. By 1875 the South had hardened almost solidly against the Republicans, the party of Lincoln, turning anti-Democrat only in 1964 when the Republican presidential candidate appeared to commit himself to uphold states' rights – a commitment construed, in the South, as opposing Negro interests.

The year 1867 brought four contrasted but significant political events. Political pressure exerted by the U.S.A. removed from Mexico the Emperor Maximilian, whom Napoleon III of France had installed in 1861; the Monroe Doctrine was upheld. Russia sold Alaska to the U.S.A. for little more than $7 million. American forces took over the unoccupied Midway Island, half-way across the Pacific and close to the 180th meridian, beginning that entry to the oceanic archipelagoes which eventually brought in Hawaii as a State. Canada, of which nothing has been said for some time, was subdivided into the two provinces of Ontario and Quebec, and these confederated with New Brunswick and Nova Scotia into a British Dominion. When in 1869 the Hudson's Bay Company surrendered the rights it had enjoyed for two hundred years, the new Dominion took in the Yukon, Manitoba, and British Columbia. As in the U.S.A., political organization overleapt the western interior to the Pacific coast. But the most immediate geographical significance was the organizing of Manitoba: this move introduced the press of the agricultural frontier on to the Interior Lowlands of Canada.

The Last Quarter of the Nineteenth Century

The division of the time-scale into quarter-centuries is convenient but arbitrary; and if it is construed as rigid, it loses something of its convenience. Some of the developments now to be noticed were already under way before 1875, some ceased before 1900. On the other hand, this quarter-century possesses a distinctive character in historical geography. It saw immigration reach new peaks, with $10\frac{1}{4}$ million entering the U.S.A. in the twenty-five years; it brought the settlement-frontier on to the High Plains of the U.S.A. and moved it westwards across the Prairies of Canada. It witnessed that swift expansion of ranching which, contributing so much

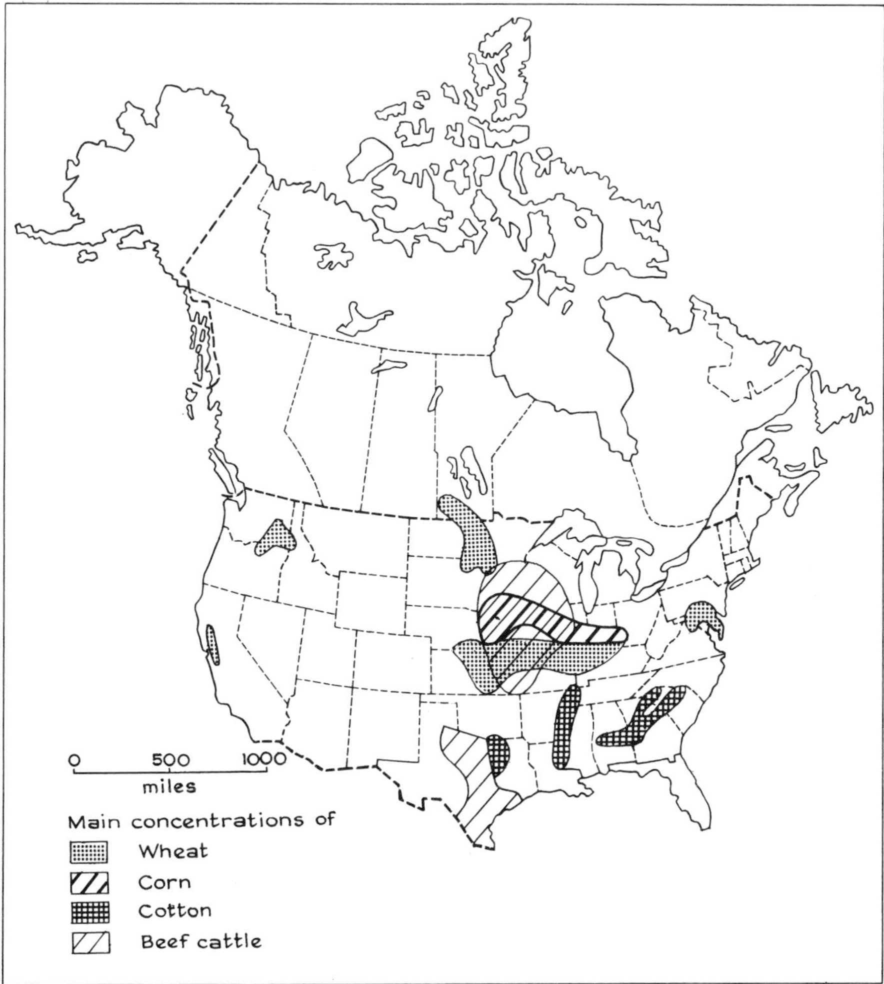

FIG. 6:12
Some elements of the geography of 1900.

to American myth and legend, involved the near-extermination of bison and changed radically with the collapse of the cattle empires. In addition, this period included the disintegration in the U.S.A. of the frontier as it had been understood for more than a century.

In the ten years after the end of the Civil War, 1865–75, the U.S.A. doubled its agricultural production. Much of the increase was contributed by farms in the Northwest. Between 1875 and 1900, the chief expansion of improved farmland occurred either in the western portion of the Midwest, or in country actually settled during the period (Figs. 6:10, 6:12). As in previous years, by no means all the immigrants reached the interior: but those who did were numbered in millions. Preceded or reinforced by some of the one million veterans of the Civil War, the new frontier farmers worked along the wooded valleys and spilled on to the long-grass prairie. When they put their ploughs to the grasslands which had been so long distrusted, they found the land not only arable but also highly productive: the soils were those of the chernozem belt (cf. Figs. 4:1, 4:2), highly suited to wheat in the north and to corn in the south. By 1900 the chernozems were largely occupied. The frontier had reached the western limit of moist subhumid climates and, in places, aided by wet seasons, had penetrated the area of dry subhumidity.

Immigration was deliberately encouraged by the Union during the Civil War: incomers were exempted from military service. The Homestead Act of 1862 aided the westward shift of those who took to farming. Among the source countries,

Germany, Ireland, Great Britain, and Scandinavia continued their massive contribution, but after about 1880 series of new flows began from Italy, Austria-Hungary, Poland, and Russia – countries which hitherto had provided few or no migrants.

Indian battles continued, along or in advance of the frontier, during the early part of this period; they took place chiefly on the Northern Plains and the northern Cordillera. In 1887 the U.S. government took measures to settle Indians as citizens, or to place them in reservations if they wished to maintain their tribal life. Two years later five million acres of Indian Territory were bought, and 60,000 settlers entered what is now Oklahoma in six months: the admission of Oklahoma as a State, however, was deferred until 1907. With nearly all land that was obviously cultivable taken over from the Indians, and with the settlement-frontier on the border of the dry country, the U.S. Bureau of Census in 1890 declared that the frontier line no longer had any meaning. The westward drive of consolidated settlement in the U.S.A. was, in the main, completed.

Railways, running ahead of the settlers, provoked some of the Indian battles: but their extension was not to be resisted. By 1883, the line to San Francisco by way of Omaha and Cheyenne was rivalled by others from New Orleans to Los Angeles, Kansas City to Los Angeles, and Chicago by way of Duluth to Portland, Oregon. In the ten years 1875–85, the trackage of the U.S.A. extended itself enormously, particularly west of the Mississippi. A line built in 1878 entered Canada from the south, bringing American settlers into the Canadian part of the Red River Valley. By 1885 the Canadian Pacific completed its transcontinental line, greatly facilitating direct migration into the Prairies from eastern Canada, and promoting the continued shift of the Canadian portion of the settlement-frontier.

The opening of the Canadian Prairies is largely a matter of the last quarter of the nineteenth century, although settlement of a kind was established in the early 1800s. Numbers of French-Canadians discharged by the Hudson's Bay Company occupied land in the Red River Valley, where also a Scottish colony was placed by the Earl of Selkirk in 1825. But the total population of the Canadian Prairies in 1870 was not much over 10,000 of whom some 90 per cent were of mixed descent. The Land Act of 1872 produced homestead grants from 1873 onwards, on the American pattern of rectangular subdivision in 160-acre lots, for an office fee of $10. Not all settlement, however, was directly controlled by the government; as in the U.S.A., railway companies were granted land as inducement to extend their lines, and the Hudson's Bay Company secured 5 per cent of the whole in the form of scattered lots. In the early years of Canadian Prairie settlement, about half the homesteaders cancelled their claims: but the late 1870s were boom years in which high grain prices coincided with wet seasons, and settlement expanded accordingly. As in the U.S.A., the first settlers – here, mainly those from eastern Canada – kept at first to the woodlands: but pressure of numbers and the lead of the railway took them soon on to the grasslands and the grassland soils.

Despite the subdivision of land in quarter-sections – a practice which assumes the building of single farmsteads – some immigrant groups contrived to make nucleated villages. Prominent among these were the Mennonites, an Anabaptist sect who, originating in Germany, migrated to Canada from Russia. Securing two large blocks of land, overlapping partly with the floor of Glacier Lake Agassiz, the Mennonites pooled their quarter-sections and built street-villages, allotting their arable land in strips and holding other land in common. Here was a wholesale transplantation of European peasant practice – a temporary transplantation, in the event, for the growing reliance on commercial wheat-growing in the Prairies disrupted the village-tenure system by 1920 – that is, within two generations of its inception.

Considerable areas of the Cordillera had considerably increased their population density by 1900 (Fig. 6:1). The Pacific coast, the Snake–Columbia Plateau, the piedmont belts of the Wasatch Mountains on either side of Salt Lake City, and the piedmont of the Southern Rockies – all were more or less continuously occupied. Between the Rockies and the farmlands lay the Great Plains, semi-arid in climate, largely under short natural grass, and so unattractive in their southern parts as to be called the Great American Desert. For the brief spell of twenty years, these were the lands of the cattle baron and the cowboy.

Ranching on the large scale developed first in

Texas, which at the end of the Civil War had five million longhorn cattle. These, developed by selective breeding from descendants of Spanish-introduced stock, could be marketed in the east if they could be transported. The first solution was droving, which began in the first year of peace: cattle went by overland trails to railheads, thence to stockyards and abattoirs in Chicago and Omaha. Large-scale ranching was necessary to much of Texas, on account of high summer temperatures, climates ranging from dry subhumid to semi-arid, and a vegetation cover which included much dry scrub; and Texas, in its days as an independent republic, adopted a land policy which allowed for holdings of 5000 acres or more and supplementation by grazing leases on public lands.

Ranching spread northward from Texas along the short-grass belt of the Great Plains. Hitherto the Plains had supported nothing but bison and Indians, for prospectors had gone on to the Cordillera and farming pioneers to the Pacific coastland. In 1870 the Plains carried an estimated fifteen million bison, on which the Plains Indians were heavily dependent for meat, skins, and sinews. Deliberate slaughter, of which hides were the main by-product, left very few bison alive by 1885; it also deprived the Plains Indians of their means of subsistence, breaking their grip on the short grassland. The joint removal of bison and Indians permitted ranching to spread fast.

In the mid-1870s, however, the Plains were declared open to homesteading: wheat-farming encroached upon them from the east. A three-way conflict developed. Sheepmen and cattlemen were alike hostile to homesteaders, while cattlemen detested sheepmen because sheep eat forage so closely as to starve cattle. Within the ranching area much hinged on control of water. The wind-pump brought underground water to the aid of the scarce and unreliable surface water, while barbed-wire, invented in 1873, enabled ranchers to enclose their holdings and to protect the water which they controlled.

The first main westward encroachment of wheat-farming took place in the late 1870s, which were unusually rainy: homesteaders moved on to the chestnut and brown soils of the short-grass country, both to the south and to the north of the Nebraskan sandhills and the South Dakotan badlands. But although three million people migrated to the Plains in twenty years, in no sequence of wetter-than-average seasons was the whole area divided into 160-acre farms, or even into the larger 640-acre farms permitted in some parts. Nor did all the incomers remain. Drought years between about 1880 and 1890 drove the farmers back, both in Canada and the U.S.A. Although additional advances were to come subsequently, the solid agricultural frontier in the U.S.A. had reached its fluctuating limit: only in Canada was there still much room for the pioneer. In neither country would settlement in this particular phase have gone so far, or have gone on so fast, had it not been for the promotions of land companies and the grant-holding railways. Neither kind of organization took account of climatic limitations.

Ranching, continuing to occupy the Western Plains, became steadily more profitable as railways spread, and as longhorns were replaced by the whitefaces developed from longhorn–Hereford crosses. It became more profitable than ever when refrigerator cars were brought into railway service in the 1870s. Despite the land-settlement policy constructed in the east and applied in the interior, ranchers in considerable areas of the Plains north of Texas succeeded in establishing reasonably large holdings which, given access to public rangeland in addition, could support extensive grazing. West of the Plains, ranching by 1900 spread throughout the Cordillera, except for the most arid southern portions; but the greatest concentration of ranch cattle was on the Plains themselves.

In the industrialized east, the latter part of the nineteenth century produced industrial magnates: and the last quarter of the century produced the cattle empires of the Plains. One single happening, however, overturned many of the greatest ranchers: the Great Blizzard of 1886–87. An especially violent and prolonged outburst of cold air swept southwards over the Plains. When it ceased, half the cattle lay dead. Ranching on the grand scale failed subsequently to recover.

The Final Phases

Drought held the wheat-farmers in check until about 1900, when there occurred a sudden rise in British interest in the Prairie settlement of Canada. In the twenty-five years up to 1915, the Canadian

Prairies increased their population fivefold, from ¼ to 1¼ million. Farmland here reached a total of twenty million acres, rather less than half of which was improved, a third of the improved extent being in wheat. Soil belts and vegetation-patterns loop westward across the Canadian Prairie country (Figs. 4:1, 4:2); and settlement, spreading from the flats of Glacier Lake Agassiz in the Red River Valley, moved more solidly along the best soils than along the C.P.R, directly towards the west. The black-earth belt contained the best soils of all, but the brown prairie soils next to the south proved little inferior as agricultural material. The years 1900–10 on the Canadian Prairies, and 1905–16 on the northern High Plains, brought sequences of wetter-than-average seasons, which coincided with high market prices for wheat. Spring-wheat cultivation moved westward on both sides of the international boundary.

When World War I ended in 1918, the Canadian government instituted a policy of soldier settlement which established 11,500 farms on the Prairies between 1919 and 1924; and between 1924 and 1930, 300,000 migrants entered Alberta, Saskatchewan, or Manitoba. Not all were farmers; but the population of the Canadian Prairies, totalling 2¼ million in 1930, was still nearly two-thirds rural. By 1930 also, very little of the occupied Prairie farmland lay more than ten miles from a railway: the Prairies were heavily committed to the production of cash grain, which occupied 40 per cent of the improved farm acreage and depended wholly on rail for transport.

Among the immigrants to Canada, Ukrainians, Dutch, and Scandinavians were prominent: at least a quarter of the Prairie farmers in the mid-1920s were those born on the European mainland. The majority, however – about half the total – were of British origin, and Canada as a whole received half a million British between 1918 and 1930. Immigration into Canada has been regulated since 1919, that into the U.S.A since 1921 – in part, on account of government suspicion of the possible effects of uncontrolled flow. Canada admitted British migrants freely, and specified the nations of northwestern continental Europe as preferred source countries. The American problem was different. More than 14¼ million immigrants arrived in 1901–20, the bulk of them coming from Italy, Austria-Hungary, Poland, and Russia. The 1921 Act of the U.S.A. imposed annual quotas amounting for each source country of 3 per cent of natives residing in the U.S.A. at the 1910 census. Certain countries, Canada among them, are excepted from this control, and various revisions and the admission of refugees raise the present annual admissions above the total quota of about 155,000 per annum to some 300,000. At the maximum, however, this means 3 million in a decade, as opposed to the more than 8½ million entrants in 1901–10; and even in 1921–30, the U.S.A. actually admitted more than 4 million, bringing its total immigration in the first three decades of this century to nearly 18½ million (Table 6 : 1).

Increasing numbers of immigrants lodged in rapidly growing towns. After about 1900 the rural population of the U.S.A. increased rather slowly, so that, whereas the some 60 per cent of the national total was rural in 1900, the corresponding figure in 1930 was 45 per cent. But enough new farmers, including a high fraction of migrants, arrived in the farmlands to infill the lands behind the frontier of 1900, and to carry improvement still farther to the west on to the eastern portions of the Great Plains: here, and in the Canadian Prairies, occurred the most marked increase in the extent of improved farmland during the first half of this century (Fig. 6:10).

A notable check both to immigration and to extension of farming came in the disastrous early 1930s. The Great Slump, spreading waves of economic destruction outward from the New York Stock Exchange, brought immigration down to

TABLE 6:1
Immigration (thousands)

Into the U.S.A.		Into Canada	
Before 1830	152		
1831–40	599		
1841–50	1,713		
1851–60	2,598		
1861–70	2,315	Before 1870	46
1871–80	2,812	1871–80	367
1881–90	5,247	1881–90	886
1891–1900	3,687	1891–1900	277
1901–10	8,796	1901–10	1,435
1911–20	5,736	1911–20	1,712
1921–30	4,107	1921–30	1,213
1931–40	528	1931–40	156
1941–50	1,035	1941–50	491
1951–60	2,516	1951–60	1,575

50,000 a year and reduced wheat prices to ruinous levels. Seasons which on the whole were dry had afflicted the U.S. Plains since the end of World War I: the early 1930s brought killing droughts to the wheatlands both of Canada and of the U.S.A. – not only to the spring-wheat farms of the Prairies, Montana, and the Dakotas, but also to the winter-wheat farms of Oklahoma and Kansas. In these two states wind erosion was especially severe: farmland soil vanished in the air. The combination of drought with low prices proved crushing: farm settlement was widely reversed into farm abandonment. Both national governments entered still more deeply into agricultural affairs, the Canadian government passing the Prairie Farm Rehabilitation Act in 1935, and the U.S.A. adopting the Agricultural Adjustment Act of 1938 to fix national marketing quotas for specified crops.

Developments subsequent to the late 1930s will be taken up later, when the present condition of agriculture is discussed. This account is concerned primarily with the agricultural frontier. A few last episodes remain to notice. The wetness of the World War II years on the U.S. Plains coincided with high grain prices and high demand – a combination of factors which again drove wheat-growing westwards, especially in Oklahoma–Kansas. Droughts in the 1950s, coinciding with overproduction, brought a renewed retraction of farming. The varying combined effects of fluctuations in demand and in price, and of spells of good or bad years, have not yet been fully accommodated by the agricultural system. Political developments have also continued. Puerto Rico, ceded to the U.S.A. by Spain in 1898, became in 1952 a Commonwealth, with terms of citizenship which allow its nationals free entry into the U.S.A. Canada's Dominion status, established in 1867, left that country without rights to declare war or peace, or to appoint international diplomats. The automatic entry into World War I was partially responsible for the change effected in 1926 by the Statute of Westminster, which made Canada a fully sovereign country.

The reference at the outset of this chapter to the continuance of the westward shift relates not to the movement of the frontier but to movement of people, and in particular to internal migration. This again constitutes a theme resumed in a later chapter. But it seems pertinent at this juncture to suggest that the personal mobility of frontier settlement may have become so inbuilt into North American society that it is mainly responsible for the impressive personal mobility of today. Not only do California, and on a lesser scale British Columbia, receive noteworthy totals of internal migrants: half the population of the U.S.A. moved house between 1955 and 1960, nearly 20 per cent of them moving over some distance. Despite the persistent southward move of people in Great Britain, this latter country can show nothing to correspond with the restless movement of North Americans.

CHAPTER SEVEN

AIMS AND ACHIEVEMENTS OF AGRICULTURE

In so far as they were consciously designed, the processes of rural settlement in North America were in part designed to produce subsistence farmers. Colonial arrangements in French Canada admittedly had some inbuilt commercial purposes, while much of the pioneer settlement of the Canadian Prairies relied from the outset on external, not to say oversea, markets. Again, the primary aim of planting in the U.S. South was commercial production, especially of cotton and tobacco. But the dramatic spread of 160-acre farms across the U.S. interior during the nineteenth century was quite different.

Traditions of peasant cultivation in European homelands, or those of self-sufficiency in early New England, were but two of the factors controlling attitudes towards the new farmers. Another was the conscious association in many minds of political independence at the national level with land-ownership and self-reliance at the personal level. In addition, the first-generation pioneers, pushing into the fringes of the wilds, were inevitably out-running physical linkages with the urban markets behind them to the east. They expected to be as far as possible self-supporting, at least in the beginning. And the progressively liberalized policy of land distribution was meant, specifically, to produce owner-occupiers.

For these reasons among others the concept of the independent family farmer has grown strong in North America, particularly so in the U.S.A. During the nineteenth century this partly mythical figure was held in great social and political esteem – esteem which continued well into the twentieth century, and was still exerting considerable force in the 1950s. In actuality, independence of commercial production swiftly disappeared. However desirable self-sufficiency may seem in the emotional sense, it is economically wasteful. Naturally enough, the pioneer farmers were in no way disposed to object when newly opened routes to expansive markets enabled them not merely to make a living, but to make a profit.

Independence of paid labour was also quickly eroded. Although full information is not available before 1880 (Fig. 7:1), it is scarcely conceivable that in, say, 1850, the unpaid farm workforce of the U.S.A. was more than half as large as the paid workforce. Already in the mid-nineteenth century the farms of the country as a whole were relying far more heavily on paid labour than on unpaid labour. During the next fifty or sixty years the paid workforce continued to increase, while the unpaid workforce remained steady. The proportionate disparity became greater, until at the peak of agricultural employment the paid hands were six times as numerous as the unpaid workers.

A distinction becomes necessary here, between paid hands on the one side and hired hands on the other. The category of hired hands includes wage-workers who are not members of the operating farm-families. The category of paid hands includes all hired hands, plus members of operating families (mainly, farmers' sons working on their fathers' farms) who receive regular wages. Hired hands amount to about a quarter of all farm workers, distinctly below that of the ratio of paid to unpaid workers. But a farmer's son undertaking wage-work for his father is, in an important sense, detached from the original scheme of family-farm operation. He is in the labour market, whether he chooses to market himself or not. In principle, therefore, even if by no means always in practice, the distinction between paid and unpaid workforce

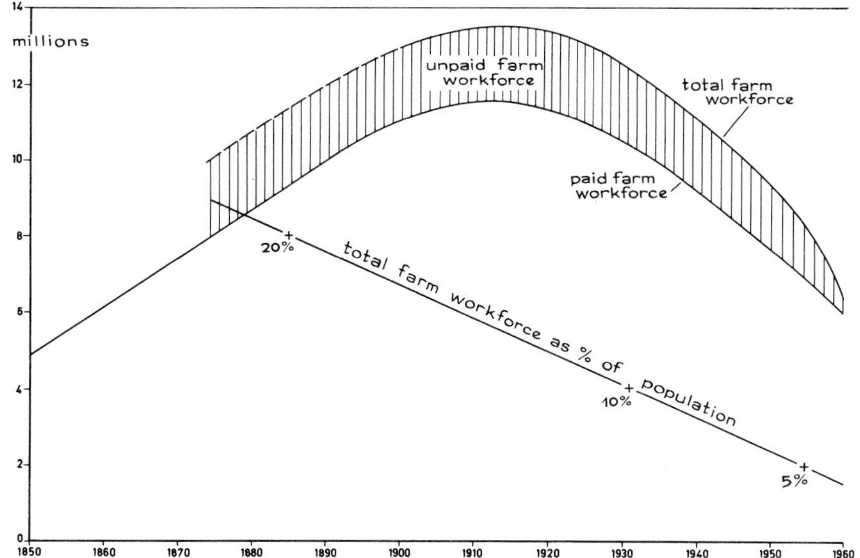

Fig. 7:1
Trends in the U.S. farm workforce.

corresponds to a distinction between family farming and alternative systems.

Since about 1915 the total of farm workers in the U.S.A. has been falling, rather more rapidly than it formerly increased. The proportionate decline in numbers of unpaid workers became very swift in the 1950s: this group promises to become virtually extinct. Moreover, as Fig. 7:1 indicates, the total farm workforce constitutes a progressively smaller fraction of total population. Its absolute increase to a crest failed to match the absolute increase of people of all kinds, while the later relative decline is accelerated by the continued increase in the total number of inhabitants. Whereas towards the end of the nineteenth century the farm workforce amounted to no less than 20 per cent of the whole population, by 1930 it was down to 10 per cent, and by the mid-century to 5 per cent, and still falling at a fairly steady rate of 1 per cent in five years. Should the decline continue, there would be no farm workforce left by 1980.

The reduction in number of farming families and in the demand for paid farm help did not affect all parts of the country in equal measure; nor was it synchronous throughout. But its net effect is undeniable. Even in the interior of the U.S.A., the family farm is reduced largely to the state of myth.

The aim of establishing financially independent farmers has been also diverted by events. Two convenient measures are available here – the extent of farm mortgage debts, and the extent of farm tenancy. The latter will be discussed (Fig. 7:2). The degree of tenancy is low throughout eastern Canada – in and near the Lake Peninsula, in the St Lawrence Valley, and in the Maritime Provinces. It is equally low in the New England states. All these areas underwent early settlement. All have a long history of low capitalization, and a partial history of subsistence production. Tenant farming is also rare in portions of Florida and in the Great Basin. These parts of the country are still to some extent in the pioneering stage. It is still possible in Florida for new farms to be cleared in the forested swampland. Many of the irregularly scattered farm holdings of the Great Basin are also fairly recent; some for instance are owned and operated by Basques, refugees from the Spanish Civil War of the late 1930s. It could be guessed that neither Florida nor the Great Basin has yet had time to experience the intense capitalization which, in the Midwest, has driven many farmers into mortgage transactions or into outright sales. In addition, a shorter history of farming means shorter exposure to climatic or economic disaster: farms established from 1940 onwards escaped the Great Depression.

Much of the interior of the U.S.A. records 20 per

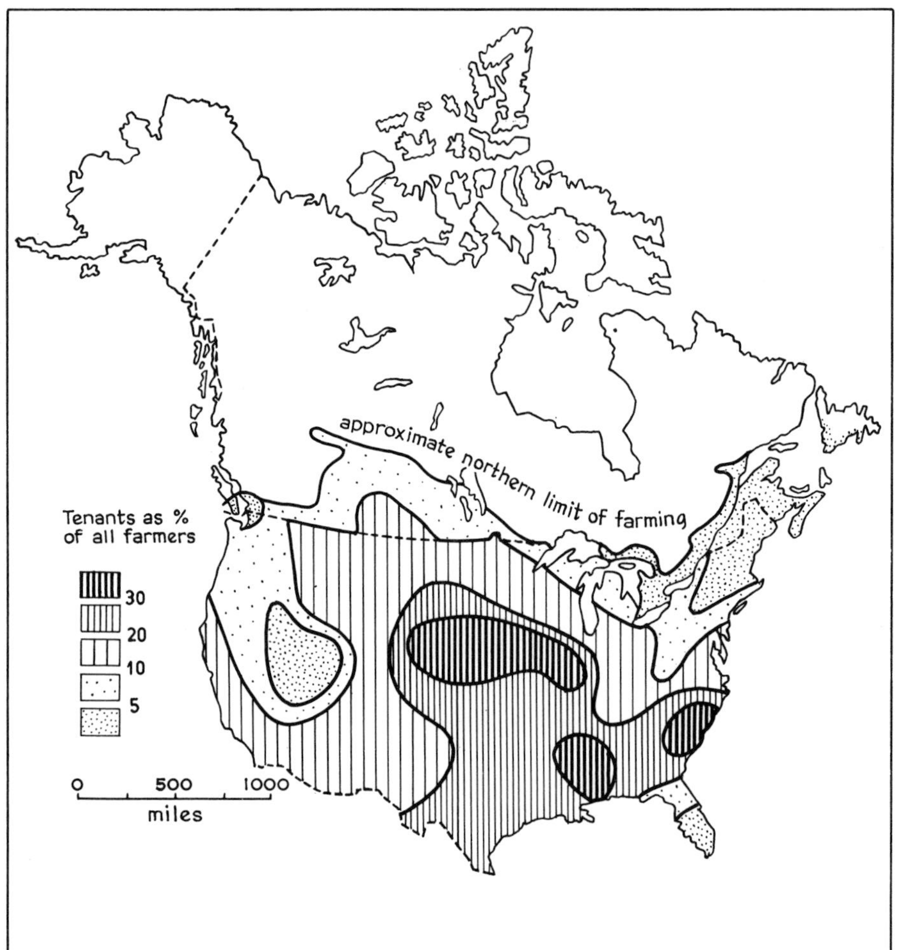

FIG. 7:2
Percentage tenancy, mid-1960s: highly generalized.

cent tenancy or more; the incidence rises above 30 per cent in a district roughly coincident with what used to be called the Corn Belt – that is, with one of the most favoured agricultural areas of the whole world. Attitudes and practice have greatly changed since the pioneering days.

The obvious contrast in Fig. 7:2 between the two sides of the U.S.–Canadian border, with the incidence of tenancy running lower on the Canadian side, suggests that high capitalization and high operating costs of the interior farmlands do not wholly explain the observed developments of tenure in the Midwest. Even more certainly, this contrast cannot be entirely laid to the account of economic or climatic stress, for the farms of the Canadian Prairies are more vulnerable, both climatically and economically, than the farms south of the border in the U.S.A. They rely on a limited range of crops, and depend heavily on an export market. In the 1930s they were very hard hit indeed. It is clear that a political factor is also at work. The free-enterprise economy so widely advocated in the U.S.A. – although by no means so widely practised as commended – seems to include heavy financial risks for the Midwest farmers, and to militate strongly against owner-occupance.

Florida apart, the whole south of the U.S.A. also records a high incidence of tenancy. But whereas in the northern interior farm managers and part-owners are not unknown, the essential distinction is that between owners and tenants. In the South, on the other hand, a more elaborate range of operating practice has evolved. The percentage incidence of tenancy in the South does not represent the whole difference between farm ownership and the lack of it.

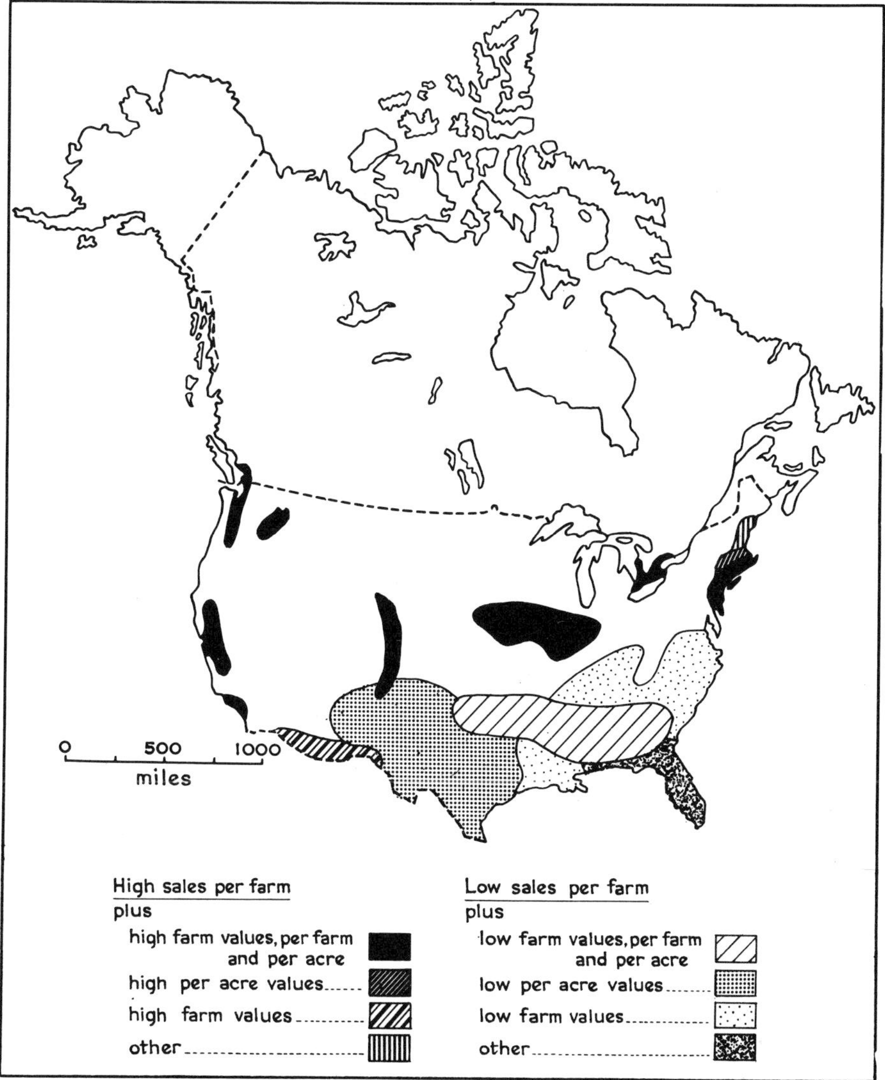

FIG. 7:3 Selected combinations of levels of farm sales and farm values, mid-1960s.

From the early 1600s up to the Civil War, Southern agriculture was, as stated previously, dominated by planting. In its operation by slave-owning families, in its production of elegant plantation houses, and in its generation of personal or family fortunes, the plantation system was fundamentally aristocratic. Had it not been for the intervention of the Civil War, the U.S. South might well have developed a society resembling in many ways that of eighteenth-century England. Two additional aspects of the system are also directly relevant at this juncture. Planting was from the outset a commercial undertaking: in this, it belonged entirely to the Elizabethan concept of colonialism – indeed, Francis Bacon, that great expositor of Elizabethan political concepts, dealt with colonization in an essay entitled *Of Plantations.* But the strongly leached and highly erodible latosols of the South, in conjunction with the heavy demands which cotton makes on soil nutrients, also ensured that planting would take on some of the characteristics of shifting cultivation, such as is practised today by many of the indigenous peoples of the tropical forest lands.

Whatever the practical weaknesses of the plantation system, its overthrow was political and military, as has been summarized in the previous chapter. There, too, reference has been made to the system of share-cropping, in which the standing crop is pledged against working capital. Share-cropping, an alternative to tenancy, reduces the incidence of outright farm ownership in the South below the level which Fig. 7:2 might initially suggest. Ownership has probably also fallen below the level intended. It seems unlikely that the partial break-up of plantations, in the reconstruction days after the Civil War, was deliberately meant to establish classes of share-croppers and tenants. If this is so, then both the pre-Civil War practice and the post-Civil War policy have failed to accomplish their aims of producing land operators who are primarily land-owners.

But although the initial intentions of farming settlement were abandoned, both in the interior and in the South, agriculture in North America has in other ways proved an outstandingly successful experiment. On balance, and taking each country as a whole or the two countries together, it can produce food for the people and surpluses for export. So much has been stated in Chapter Two. But here again, pronounced differences between area and area make themselves apparent.

Fig. 7:3 generalizes farm values and farm income, in terms of farm sales, farm values, and per-acre values. The distinction between farm values and per-acre values allows for the contrast between intensive and extensive working. A small, intensively worked and highly productive farm can record high per-acre values, which can more than offset the low per-acre values of a less heavily yielding but larger property.

High sales value per farm mean a high level of commercial operation. Accordingly, the primary grouping has been made in terms of sales. Where a high sales value is combined with high farm values and high per-acre values, individual farms command high prices on the farm market, and the land yields well. Concentrations of high sales values combined with high farm values and high per-acre values appear in the Lake Peninsula of Canada, between Cape Cod and Delaware Bay, in the core of the Midwest, along the piedmont of the Southern Rockies, in the Snake–Columbia district, in the Cordilleran trough which includes Puget Sound, in the Great Valley, and in Southern California. Systems of cropping and of livestock management vary widely among these districts. All however have developed agricultural specialisms, and all except the North Atlantic coastland, where the pressure of demand comes from near-by towns, have outstanding climatic advantages.

High sales values per farm along parts of the U.S.–Mexican border combine with high farm values but not with high per-acre values. In part, this condition results from the use of irrigation water along the riverine margins of individual holdings, where the remoter land is dry and poor. Sales values are also high along the coastland of New England, but the small extent of many farms allows farm values to remain low although per-acre values remain high.

The South is different. Florida, with a mixture of highly successful specialized farms and modest, small, and poor general farms, is somewhat exceptional. But the remainder of the South is characterized throughout by low sales value per farm: that is, farm income is well below the national average. West of the Mississippi, the low farm incomes in Texas and New Mexico combine with low per-acre values to reflect the influence of the westerly increase in aridity, although the increase in the same direction of farm size prevents per-farm values from descending very low. Along and east of the lower Mississippi Valley, sales per farm and values per farm are alike low. And in much of the Old South, low sales values and low per-farm values combine with low per-acre values, to characterize the least commercially productive and the least saleable farm properties in North America. The main concentration of this agriculturally lagging area projects across the Mississippi to include parts of Oklahoma, where recurrent drought is a leading cause of difficulty.

The use of per-acre values in the foregoing discussion directs attention to productivity. This can be measured not merely in the gross terms of national under-supply or surplus, or in the strictly commercial terms of farm-acre prices which serve to indicate judgements of likely profit, but also in the quite simple, and quite obvious, terms of yield per acre. Under this head, it becomes necessary to signalize revolutionary developments as great in their productive effects as the Agricultural Revolution of Britain.

Corn production in the U.S.A. (Fig. 7:4) illustrates the fundamental sequence. The graph of acreage harvested is closely similar in form and

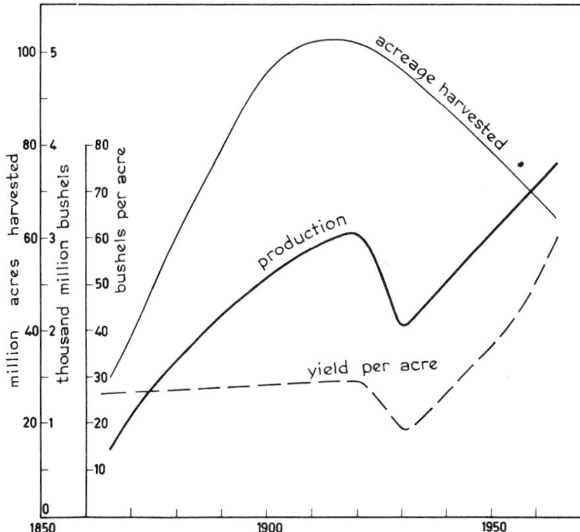

FIG. 7:4 Corn in the U.S.A.: generalized trends.

phase to the graph in Fig. 7:1 of number of farm workers. Its steep ascent through the later nineteenth century to a crest in about 1915 has been succeeded by a steep and still-continuing decline. The acreage harvested in the mid-1960s was but three-fifths the peak figure. But reduction in acreage has not meant a reduction in total yield. Total production rose up to the 1920s in company with acreage, with yield per acre showing a slight but persistent increase. In the depression years, the already noticeable movement towards a reduction of acreage was little affected, but yield per acre fell sharply: the collapse of markets paralysed farming less completely than it did industry, but nevertheless cut activity on the farms far below earlier levels. In the later 1930s, however, production of corn began once more to rise, and to rise faster than it had ever done before. This rise was made possible, in the face of falling acreage, by spectacular increases in yield per acre. Maintained into the 1950s, the rates of yield then underwent a further increase, making per-acre production double what it had been before the depression. The means whereby corn yields were so effectively increased were deliberately sought.

When the east-coast settlers established themselves on the Atlantic coast, they learned the existence of corn – Indian corn, maize to Europeans – from the local Indians. They had no means of knowing that the Indians had, by trial and error over the centuries, selected varieties of corn which were well adapted to the contrasting environments of the country as a whole. The seed grain taken by pioneers into the interior was, in consequence, of eastern varieties. Nevertheless corn succeeded well as a food grain, a fodder grain, and a cash crop, throughout much of the interior and a large fraction of the South. Selection improved the strains, making possible the high grain yields of the corn-growing areas in the later nineteenth and early twentieth centuries, but agricultural scientists set out consciously to develop new strains by the process of crossing existing strains – that is, to perform directed experiments in evolution. The outcome, hybrid corn, was developed and stabilized between 1925 and 1935. This high-yielding grain is one of the greatest agricultural achievements on record. It contributes notably to the increase in yield per acre and in total production. But other factors have also been at work, both on corn-growing farms and elsewhere: they include application of chemical fertilizers, irrigation, improved livestock management, continuing mechanization, and control of diseases, pests, and weeds.

Among three other great field crops of the U.S.A., namely cotton, soybeans, and wheat, the last-named most closely resembles corn in its history of acreage, production, and yield. But, as a comparison of Figs. 7:4 and 7:5 makes clear, maximum wheat acreage was achieved rather later than maximum corn acreage. Neither total production nor yield per acre of wheat was so severely depressed during the slump as were those of corn. The rises in yield per acre and in total production of wheat lag behind the corresponding developments in corn-

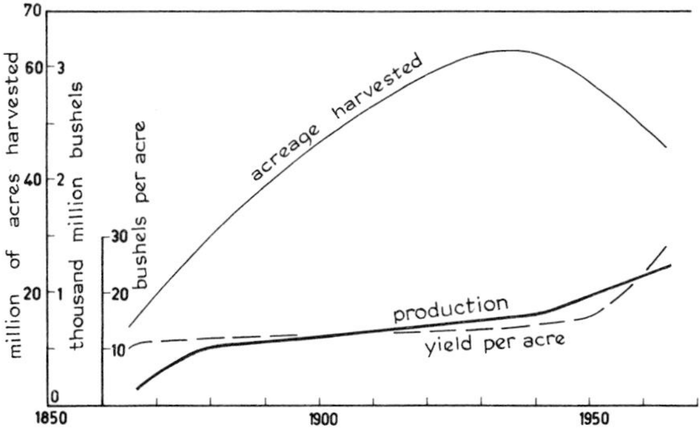

FIG. 7:5 Wheat in the U.S.A.: generalized trends.

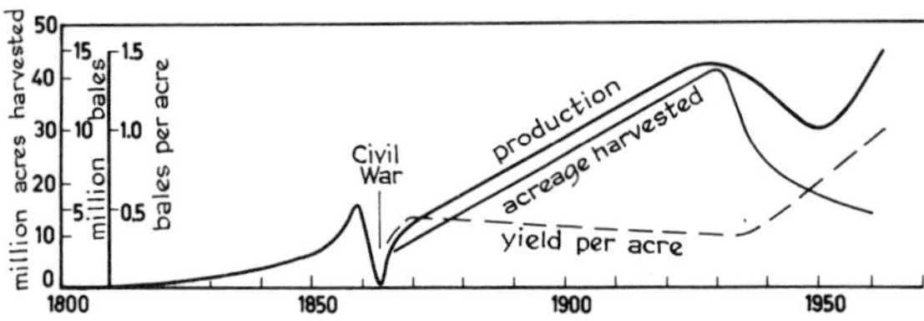

FIG. 7:6 Cotton in the U.S.A.: generalized trends.

growing. But grain farms where wheat is the primary interest are now able, like corn-growing farms, to outpace the decline in acreage with the aid of progressively greater productivity. It would perhaps be more pertinent to say that increased productivity permits the continued decline of acreage.

Cotton in the U.S.A. presents a variant picture (Fig. 7:6). In the decade before the Civil War, production rose increasingly fast. It was not until some few years after the end of the war that the pre-war peak of output was matched; but production by then had already begun a fairly steady rise which continued up to the time of the depression. Acreage harvested tended somewhat to outrun production, on account of the progressive exhaustion of the Southern soils and the increasingly extensive working which the westward shift of cotton-growing involved. In addition, the ever-widening attacks of the boll weevil were increasing the risk of crop damage or crop failure. Between the onset of the Great Depression and the years immediately following World War II, acreage and total output alike declined; but output declined less rapidly than acreage, by virtue of increasing yields. Here again, improved strains and improved techniques come into play. Acreage has continued to decline, but increasing yield per acre has pushed total production up to an all-time peak.

Soybeans, a late addition to the list of leading commercial crops in the U.S.A., have hitherto recorded a simpler history than have corn, wheat, and cotton. The principal increase in per-acre yield was achieved between about 1935 and 1955, since when this measure has remained fairly steady. On the other hand, the crop has proved profitable. Acreage harvested, and total output, began in about 1940 a rapid rise which is still continuing (Fig. 7:7).

Comparative shortness of record for wheat-

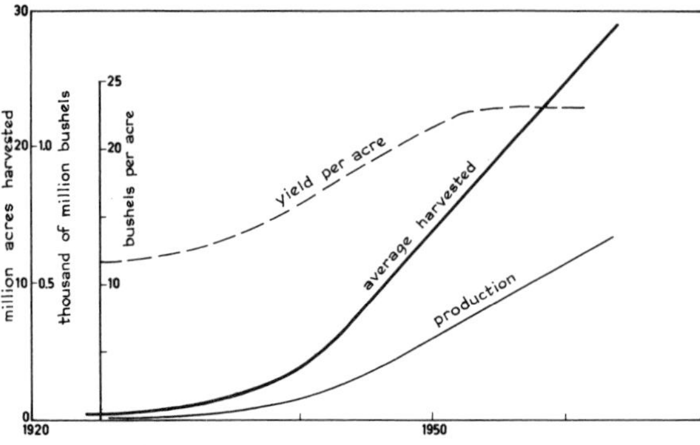

FIG. 7:7 Soybeans in the U.S.A.: generalized trends.

growing in Canada makes it convenient to present this record in full (Fig. 7:8). As the graphs show, the expansion of Canadian wheat acreage took place from about 1910 (or 1900) to 1930, since which time there have been considerable fluctuations but no strong trend either of decrease or of increase. Calculations of running means would certainly show an increase in total production up to 1930, as is clear on sight from the diagram. But subsequent trends are not at all clear. Yield per acre has fluctuated even more violently than acreage or production, but in the total run seems not to have improved. The one potential exception to all these statements relates to the 1960s, where possible signs appear of rises in all three measures.

The wildest fluctuations in the operating of Canadian Prairie farms took place in the 1930s, under the combined conditions of depression and drought which were outlined in the previous chapter. In Saskatchewan especially, the results were to drive farm incomes below operating expenses, and to keep them there through a series of painful years (Fig. 7:9). But since the mid-1930s in Alberta and Manitoba, and since the late 1930s in Saskatchewan, incomes have been drawing encouragingly away

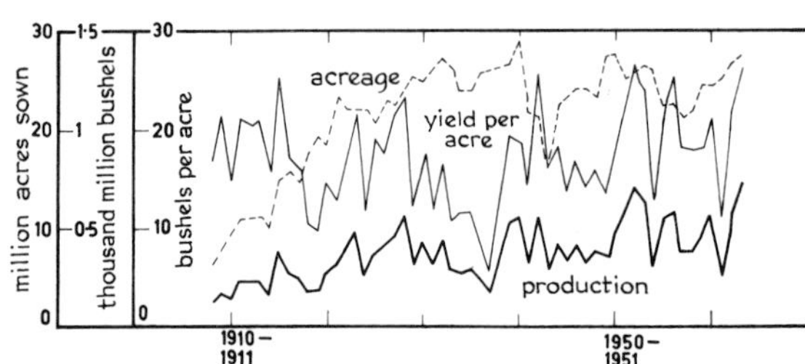

FIG. 7:8 Acreage, production, and yield of wheat in Canada.

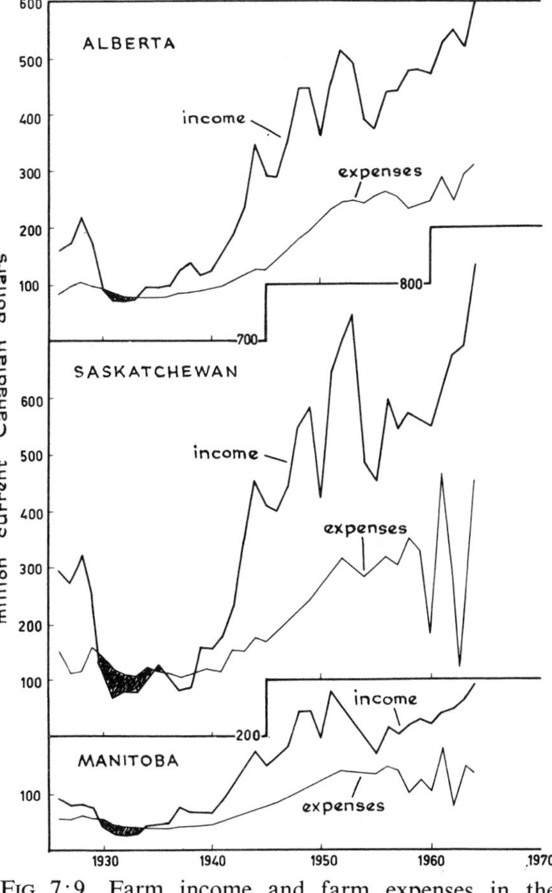

FIG. 7:9 Farm income and farm expenses in the Prairie Provinces.

from expenses. The financial vulnerability of Prairie farmers has passed, at least for the time being.

Part of the move to prosperity results from government programmes of stabilization, but part is due to increased productivity. In about thirty years, between the 1930s and the 1960s, Canada in company with the U.S.A. recorded a dramatic increase in yields, and for the same three basic reasons – improved management, selectively chosen and selectively bred strains, and increased mechanization. Agricultural productivity over the period rose by 75 per cent.

Total farm acreage in the U.S.A. seems to have reached its peak (Fig. 7:10). It rose swiftly through the later half of the nineteenth century, and steadily except for interruption by the Civil War. Its expansion in the first half of the nineteenth century was somewhat less swift, but even steadier. Since the decline in the farm workforce began well before peak acreage was attained, it follows that the acreage/worker ratio has risen. A farm worker of 1960 could deal with two-and-a-half times as much land as his counterpart of 1950, and could cope with enormously improved yields and outputs per farm.

The effect is that of progressive mechanization. Ever since the nineteenth-century introduction of harvesting machines to the grainfields of the Plains, farms in the U.S.A. have been depending more and more heavily on machinery. The most versatile of all farm machines is the tractor, which tows and powers the implements proper. Now the increasingly widespread use of tractors has not only reduced the demand for manpower – it has also eliminated draught animals from many farms. When horses and mules are gone, no land need be set aside to produce their feed.

C. D. Harris has analysed the factors which allowed the U.S.A. to double its agricultural production between 1900 and 1950. He finds that improved yields per acre, such as have been discussed, constitute the major factors, explaining about two-fifths of the total rise in output. The cropping of new land explains about a quarter. The release of land formerly needed to feed draught animals accounts for nearly a third – a very marked contribution indeed.

Total farm acreage in Canada underwent its main expansion between about 1910 and 1930. It too may now be slightly on the decline (Fig. 7:10). The peak of farm employment has also passed, numbers falling away since World War II, more rapidly than they previously rose. The Canadian graph of acres per farm employee shows how the spread of extensive cultivation across the Prairies pushed the ratio upwards, until the depression called a halt to investment in machines. But from about 1940 onwards the acreage/employee ratio has again been climbing, more steeply than ever before.

National totals of farm acreage take no account of land use within farms. The increase in total acreage in the U.S.A. up to about 1950 conceals the fact that the country reached its peak of *harvested* acreage some twenty years earlier – as could be inferred from the acreage graphs for corn, wheat, and cotton. The continued expansion of farm acreage after 1930, combined with a decrease in harvested acreage, shows that cropland accounts for

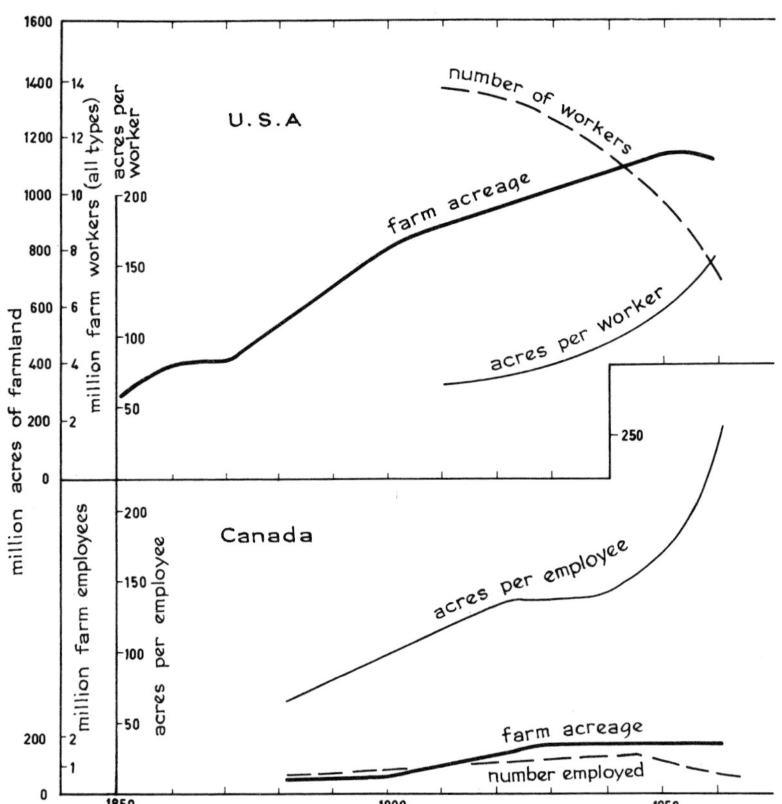

FIG. 7:10
Farm acreage and farm employment: generalized.

a decreasing fraction of land in farms. This circumstance might be thought to make for increased flexibility: on a given farm, the choice of how much land to sow, and which parts of the farm to seed, appears to be less restrained than it formerly was, particularly if land has been released from the demands of draught animals. However, as will shortly be seen, the choice is not as simple as this.

National totals also conceal many individual fluctuations, and many trials which have ended in error. Some of the hard-won farms in upstate New England have been abandoned to second-growth forest. Similar forest has overtaken other farms, also abandoned, in the northern interior, for example in North Michigan. The western and northern edges of the wheatlands, intermittently ravaged by the undependable climate, expand or contract in response to the fall of useful rain.

Again, commercial farming is completely without protection against the vagaries of its markets, so long as it remains organized on the single-farm basis. Co-operatives fare better; but even these cannot withstand every challenge. Both in Canada and in the U.S.A., government agencies intervene strongly in agriculture. One result is at first surprising – the deliberate policy of restricting production.

The Soil Conservation Act of the U.S.A., passed in 1936, was originally designed to combat soil erosion and to encourage the types of land use best suited to particular environments. During World War II, when demand for farm products rose sharply, stress was still laid on conservation but also on intensive cropping. Intensified working was so successful that the post-war years brought problems of surplus. These are by no means easy to solve. It is true that a large fraction of the world's population is underfed, and that it might seem easy to dispose of surpluses by giving them away. On the other hand, farming in North America is a commercial undertaking. Someone is expected to pay for its products. If the buyer is the federal government, then in effect farmers pay taxes to help the nation buy their own products. There is a further argument – that to unload huge amounts of free grain on needy countries would wreck the world's grain market, inflicting serious damage on exporting countries such as Canada and Australia who vitally need their sales abroad.

In these circumstances, the U.S. government instituted a number of measures. As an emergency, it bought and stockpiled as much of the surpluses as possible. In 1956 it authorized the Soil Bank programme, designed to reduce for a number of years the acreage planted to six basic crops – corn, rice, and wheat among the food grains; cotton; peanuts; and tobacco. Up to designated limits, farmers were paid *not* to grow these crops. By the later 1960s the design took effect. Not only had it cut down surplus production – it had withdrawn from cropping some of the best farmland, which could easily be returned to cultivation in time of urgent need.

Market quotas formed the basis of allotting acreages for seeding five of the crops involved. Price supports were offered to farmers observing the limitations decided, while those planting above the limitations were penalized. The sixth, exceptional, crop is corn, to which marketing quotas were not applied. But even here, price-support has either been lessened or has been withdrawn from those planting to excess.

Comparable measures have been brought into force in Canada. The Canadian Prairie Farm Rehabilitation Act of 1935, later extended to British Columbia and to reclamation schemes in the tidal marshlands of the Maritime Provinces, was originally aimed at conservation and reclamation. The Prairie Farm Assistance Act of 1939 provided for support payments in areas of low crop yields: it was designed as a buttress against climatic adversity. The Agricultural Stabilization Act of 1958, and the federal crop insurance scheme instituted in 1959, broaden the basis of safeguard against the physical and economic fluctuations to which agriculture is notoriously open. The measures named for the two countries are, moreover, merely a sample of those taken.

Government intervention in the farming practices of North America extends throughout the administrative structure, from the national down to the lowest local level. It seems important to lay stress on this intervention, in order to forestall the mistaken assumption that the use of land results merely from free competition in a *laissez-faire* economy. This assumption applies to no nation which is currently significant in commercial farming. For all that, it is still possible roughly to identify the major belts of land use in North America with leading aspects of the physical environment – terrain, soils, climate, and productive capability as indicated by natural vegetation.

The next map (Fig. 7:11) presents a generalized distribution of land-use types. In the farming context there is no need to discuss the tundra, the ungrazed boreal forest, the mixed habitats of the northern Cordillera, or the dominantly forested highlands of the Appalachians and their northeastward extension. In all these areas farmland is absent or negligible. In the remainder of the two countries east of the Mississippi occurs a cropland–pasture–woodland combination, with a sizeable extension west of the Mississippi in the U.S. South, and with a second arcuate extension running deeply into Canada on the north. Patchily along the Gulf coast, in Florida, and in the southern Atlantic coast, this type of land use gives way to swampland. In a gross kind of way it resembles the sum distribution of broadleaf evergreen forest with patches of needleleaf evergreen, the main block of natural broadleaf deciduous forest, and the Southern forests of dominant needleleaf evergreen or of co-dominant needleleaf evergreen and broadleaf deciduous. Its northwestern arc is roughly coincident with the natural spread of broadleaf deciduous forest plus tall-grass glades, and with the southern edge of needleleaf evergreen plus patches of broadleaf forest.

In an equally rough manner, the distribution of cropland plus pasture resembles the distribution of tall-grass prairie plus broadleaf deciduous forests with tall-grass glades. Similarly, it is possible to make out a resemblance between the respective distributions of grassland grazing on the one hand, and natural short-grass prairie on the other. And when these two combined distributions of land-use types are compared with the combined distributions of vegetation-types, the correspondence is even closer. In the Southwest there is good correlation of forest-and-woodland grazing on the plateaus with the forest–grass–scrubland combination of natural plant cover, and also of shrubland grazing with the shrub-and-bunch-grass cover; but these correlations are to be expected, from the fact that little improvement of the land or of the plants which it naturally supports has been undertaken in the

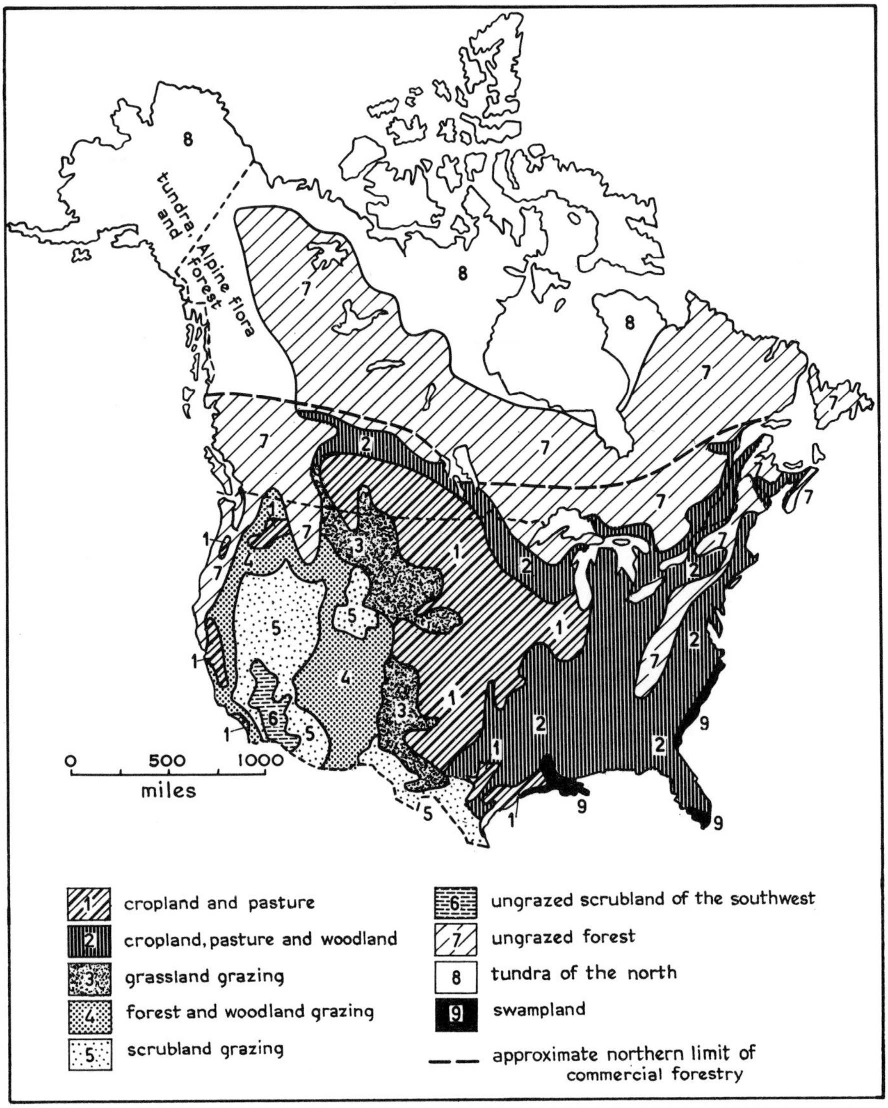

FIG. 7:11
Land-use types.

relevant areas, On a more restricted areal scale, the natural cover of the western Cordillera is also well matched by cultivational types of land use.

Land-use types can be expected to exhibit general correspondences to the natural plant cover, on the grounds that both are strongly influenced by the climatic environment. But, even when full allowance has been made for the effect of government intervention, neither vegetational maps nor land-use maps portray the distribution of farming systems.

In the 1920s it was customary to speak of the Cotton Belt, the Wheat and Cotton Belt, the Winter Wheat Belt, the Corn Belt, the Spring Wheat Belt, and the Hay and Dairy Belt as if these were monocultural – or at best bicultural – agricultural regions. The names have stuck. They carry the same kind of force as the function-names applied to towns. A textile-manufacturing town, so called, may well have no more than 10 per cent of its workers employed in textile trades. In agricultural assessments, a commodity name can mean anything from 40 per cent down to 10 per cent of farmland applied to a particular use.

Consider, for instance, the so-called Spring and Winter Wheat Belts and the Cotton Belt – alike,

FIG. 7:12
Allocation of land on selected typical farms.

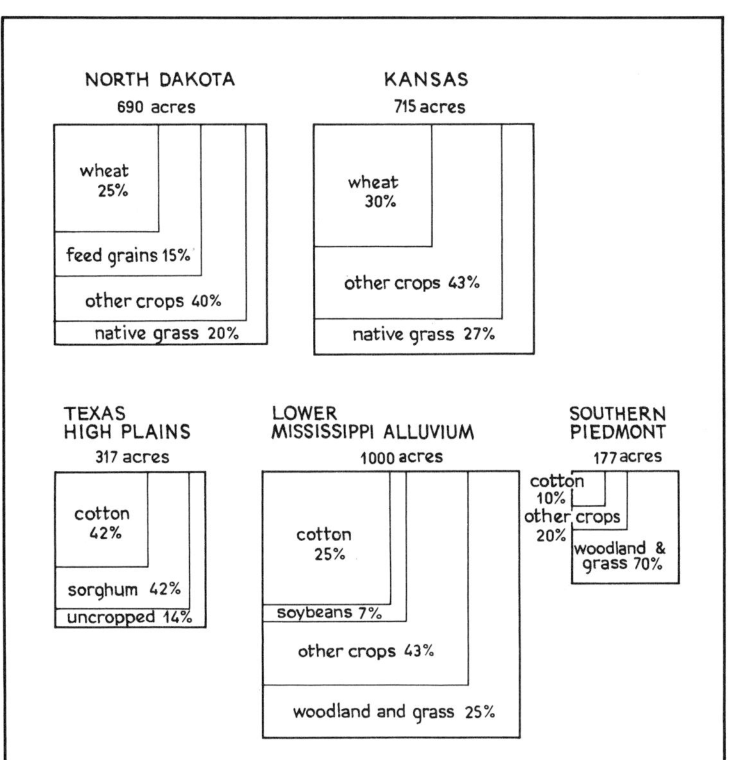

areas of quite specialized cropping. A representative farm in North Dakota, specializing in spring wheat, will have only about a quarter of its area actually sown to wheat, out of 80 per cent of its area under crops. Among crops other than wheat, feed grains are prominent. In Kansas, where many farms specialize in winter wheat, a representative farm still has only 30 per cent of its acreage in wheat (Fig. 7:12), against 43 per cent under other crops. Among these others, sorghum leads. The two diagrams for farms specializing in cotton draw a contrast between the southern Piedmont and the lower Mississippi Valley. The type farm for the Piedmont has no more than 10 per cent of its area in cotton, against 20 per cent in other crops and 70 per cent in pasture and woodland. The much larger farm on the Mississippi alluvium is more highly specialized, with a quarter of its acreage in cotton, but here again the cotton acreage is only one-third of the total cropland. An unusually high degree of specialization, outside the range of fruit farming or market gardening, appears in the representative farm for the Texas High Plains, where most of the total acreage is cropped, being equally divided between cotton and sorghum. Cotton still takes less than half the farm.

Similar effects are obtained with diagrams showing the proportionate use of land for selected States or groups of States (Fig. 7:13). These diagrams contain two items which are unfamiliar in Britain – farm woodland used for pasture, and other farm woodland. In New England, for instance, farm woodland occupies more than half the total farm acreage, with a quarter of it used for pasture; and in Mississippi, where it is also prominent, it occupies about a fifth of all farmland, some 15 per cent of it being used for pasture.

All but a small fraction of Iowa, North Dakota, and Kansas is in farmland, with harvested cropland ranging from two-thirds to half the farm acreage. Grass pasture is significant in all three States. The unassigned farmland, labelled *other* in the diagrams, is land in fallow or land where crops have failed. Fallow is quite extensive in North Dakota and Kansas. The diagram for Mississippi resembles the plot for the Piedmont cotton-growing farm. That for Nevada expectably shows a high proportion of the State in other than farm use – mountain forest

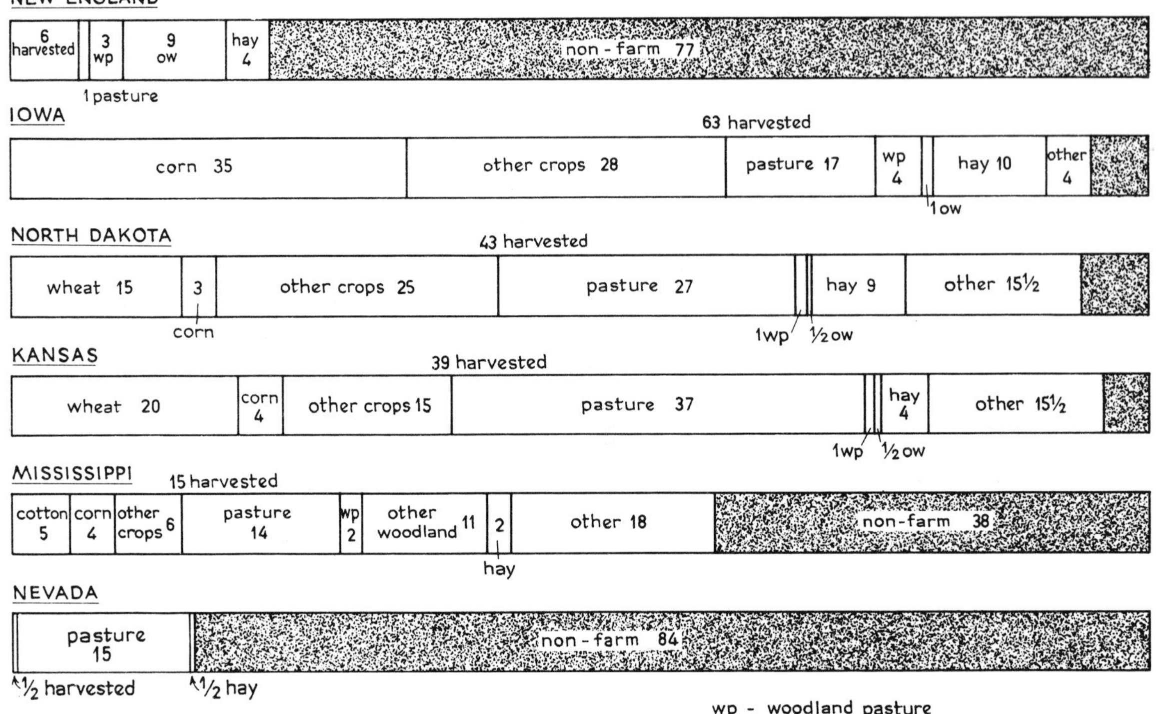

FIG. 7:13 Analysis of land use in selected areas, mid-1960s.

and open range – while the farmland itself is almost entirely pasture.

These examples have been chosen to illustrate land use where farming characteristics are highly distinctive. In some other areas, the relative distributions would be far more evenly balanced. Thus, although concentrations of individual crops or of livestock types appear on individual distribution maps, the realities of farming are best described in terms of combinations. There is more than one way of identifying combinations, however. Either book values or sales values may be used. Hay, for instance, ranks high in book value throughout very large areas, but low in sales value because nearly all of it is consumed on the farms which grow it.

Fig. 7:14 generalizes the distributions of crop-combinations, in which the first and second leading crops by book value are indicated. Cotton and tobacco share the primacy in their respective portions of the South. Hay leads in much of the west, and also around most of the Lake borders with extensions both to northwest and to northeast. Corn is securely in the lead in the Midwest, wheat just as securely on the Northern and Southern Plains. The detailed breakdown for New England is partly a function of the smallness of reporting States, but also reflects the specialized production of apples, maple syrup, tobacco, and sweet corn.

Other combinations appear when attention is limited to commodities – that is, to actual farm sales (Fig. 7:15). Once again, only the two leading items are considered. Cattle – for rearing, fattening, or slaughter – bring in more than any other market product throughout most of the west, much of the Plains, and the whole of the Midwest except where they are less remunerative than corn or hogs. In an area which includes the Southern Rockies, sheep come next in value after cattle. The cattle–dairying combination in much of the remaining southern Cordillera, southeast of Lake Winnipeg, and in a belt running across the Appalachians to Chesapeake Bay, joins with the hog–cattle combination in part of the Midwest, and with the dairying–cattle combination in the north, to bring out the significance of livestock farming in the agriculture of North America. Even where wheat, corn, or cotton lead in sales value, cattle or dairy products typically come second. Areas specializing heavily on the

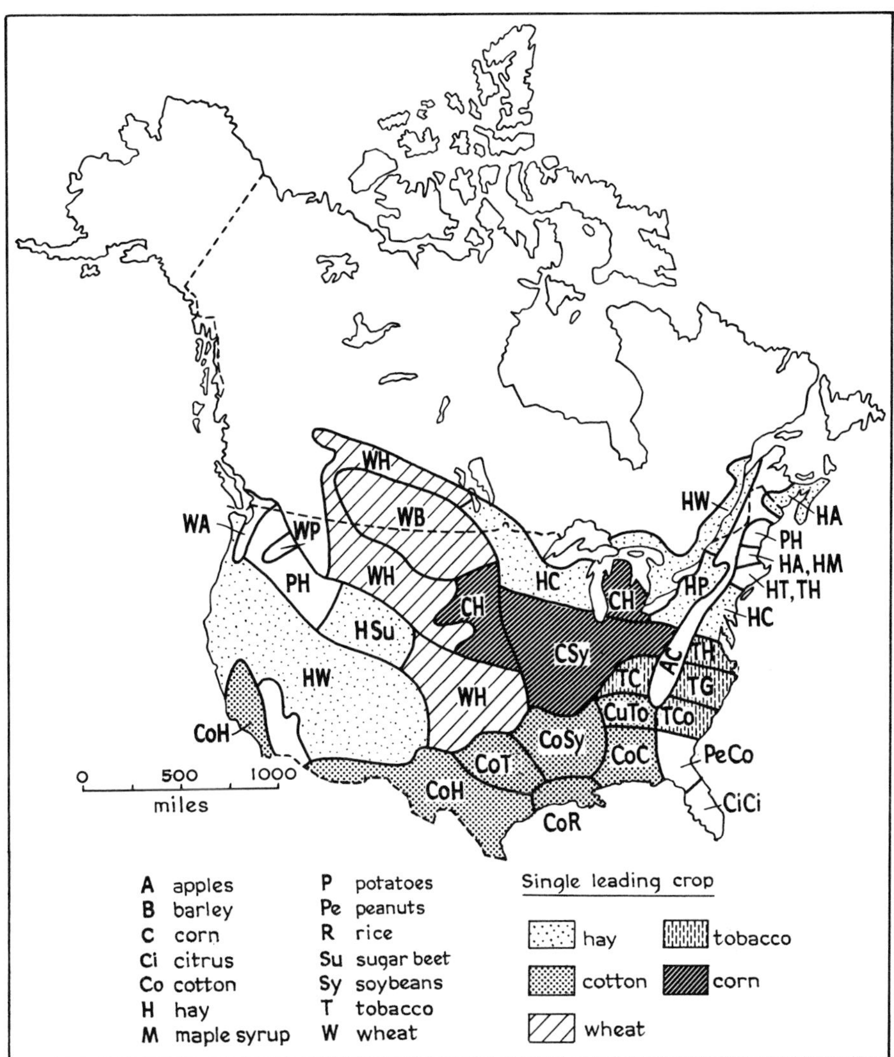

FIG. 7:14 Crop-combinations: two leading crops, by value, mid-1960s.

commercial poultry and tobacco farming are outlined in Fig. 7.15.

A third means of classifying farming combinations depends on types of farming practice. While crop-combinations illustrate one aspect of deliberate use of land, and while commodity-combinations exemplify economic responses, farming combinations classify farms in terms of management, without necessarily identifying specific products. Either wheat or corn, for instance, can be a cash grain. Fig. 7:16 gives, once more in a highly generalized way, the distribution of farming combinations, in which up to three kinds of practice are allowed for.

Dairy and livestock farms, where the sale of milk, butter, and cheese takes precedence over breeding, rearing, and fattening, dominate the St Lawrence Valley, upstate New York, much of the environs of the Great Lakes, and a wide northwestern tongue of country extending through Wisconsin and Minnesota. A variant combination appears east of Lake Michigan, where cash grain replaces livestock as the second interest, while specialized farming takes over the southern Lake Peninsula on the lee side of Lake Huron. Livestock and dairy farms are in the majority in the Maritime Provinces, while New England and the seaboard farther south contain numerous dairy and poultry farms.

Most of the areas so far named as having dairy farming as the leading interest record a climate of the Dfc type (compare Fig. 4:13). Year-round

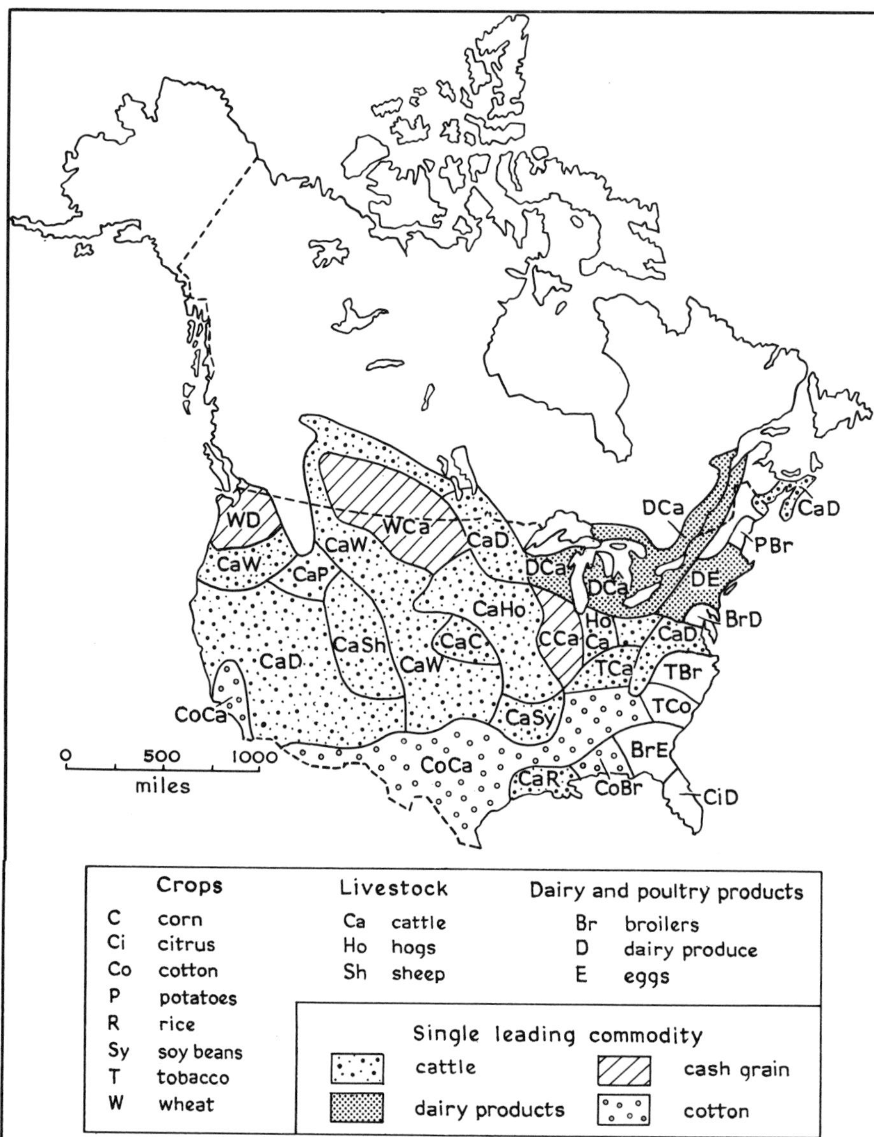

FIG. 7:15 Crop–livestock combinations: two leading farm commodities, by value, mid-1960s.

precipitation is capable in some parts of maintaining the soil-moisture charge throughout the late summer. Grazing grass and hay alike do well in many years; but winters are typically severe, so that cattle are wintered in huge barns where the haylofts beneath the roofs serve both to store feed and to insulate the buildings. On the negative side, grain-growing here could not compete on a large scale with farms to the south and west, although Maine has successfully developed the specialized production and canning of sweet corn. Types of dairy produce vary with costs of marketing, liquid milk production leading near the big eastern towns but the making of butter and cheese in the remoter areas. The Maritime Provinces are too far from consumers of dairy produce for dairying to prevail over stock-raising. In their relation to their urban markets, the dairy and poultry farms of the north-eastern U.S. seaboard recall the production of eggs and milk on farms near the edges of large British towns.

Poultry farming in various combinations is in

actuality widespread throughout the seaboard from New England to Georgia. The dairy, livestock, and poultry combination succeeds the dairy and poultry combination towards the south, and, after an interruption by cotton and livestock farming, is itself replaced by a cotton–poultry combination. The chief object of poultry farming varies: from Connecticut to Delaware Bay it is egg production, but elsewhere it is the production of broilers. This in turn ranges from the breeding and range-feeding of hens to the operation of broiler factories where the birds live, in effect, on conveyor belts.

The western plateaus of the Appalachians carry numerous livestock and dairy farms, where distance from markets raises dairying costs as effectively as high relief brings air temperatures down. The southern part of this district includes specialized tobacco farms. Farther west, where altitudes are less, the Midwest includes a horseshoe of dominantly livestock and cash-grain farming, wrapped round a concentration of the cash grain and livestock combination. The leading cash grain is corn; the principal livestock types are cattle and hogs, in that order except in Iowa where hogs lead. Both types of animal are corn-fed and corn-fattened. Climate throughout is of the Dfa type.

Changes occur in the southwestern and northwestern extensions of the cash grain and livestock combination on to the Plains. In the southwestern extension into Kansas and parts of adjacent States the chief cash grain is wheat, and the lead of cattle over hogs rises sharply. Here is the so-called Winter Wheat Belt, where Dfa climate is degenerating towards the BS type. Preference for winter wheat over spring wheat used to depend on the higher-yielding qualities of the former; but nowadays the persistence of winter wheat in the face of unpredictable spring rains and heavy demands on soil moisture is differently based. If the autumn-sown wheat fails, then a catch crop of sorghum can always be tried.

Towards the northwest, the extension of cash grain and livestock farming runs through the Dakotas into the Prairie Provinces of Canada. It overlaps from the area of Dfb climate into the BS of the Plains. On its cooler northern margin, reaching into the belt of Dfc climate, and on the drier western margin, it is bordered by livestock and cash-grain farming. Except in its southeastern portions, where hogs lead, the chief livestock type throughout this extension is cattle; and the principal grain is everywhere spring wheat. The growing season is far too short, and the winters are far too severe, for winter wheat to be a possibility. But despite the well-known interest of this whole area in the growing of hard wheats for milling, spring wheat remains something of a compromise crop. In the prevailing circumstances of climate – low and unpredictable precipitation, liability to hail in summer – spring wheat is the crop least likely to fail, or to fail to yield a profit.

Farming in the U.S. South is largely characterized by the cotton and livestock combination, with cattle the main livestock types. Specialized farms appear in the swamplands and swampland margins of the southern Atlantic coast, coastal Florida, and the coastlands of the Gulf, taking advantage of long growing seasons and of high water-tables to produce fruits, nuts, and vegetables. Roughly speaking, the combinations now under discussion occupy the belt of Cfa climate. A more accurate northern limit to successful cotton-growing is the line where there is an 80 per cent chance of 200 consecutive frost-free days a year.

Market gardening in North America is called truck farming, from the practice of carrying market garden produce by road. The consumers of Southern truck-farm produce live mainly in the northeastern and lower Lakeside States: the success of the producers relies both on climate and on efficient transport. One signal aspect of the climatic setting is that temperature-gradients along the Atlantic coast are high, particularly northwest of Cape Hatteras where the Florida Current–Gulf Stream sets into the open ocean. In consequence, the populous northeastern towns with their long trying winters, and the rural surroundings of these towns with their pronounced halting season in the farming year, are physically close to farmlands where high temperatures and high humidities are the rule for months on end. A smaller-scale demonstration of a similar effect is given by the lower Lake Peninsula, in its relationship to the great towns of eastern Canada.

The summary combinations so far listed indicate the agricultural characteristics of North America east of the Cordillera, except for the southern parts of the Great Plains. Here, with great summer heat

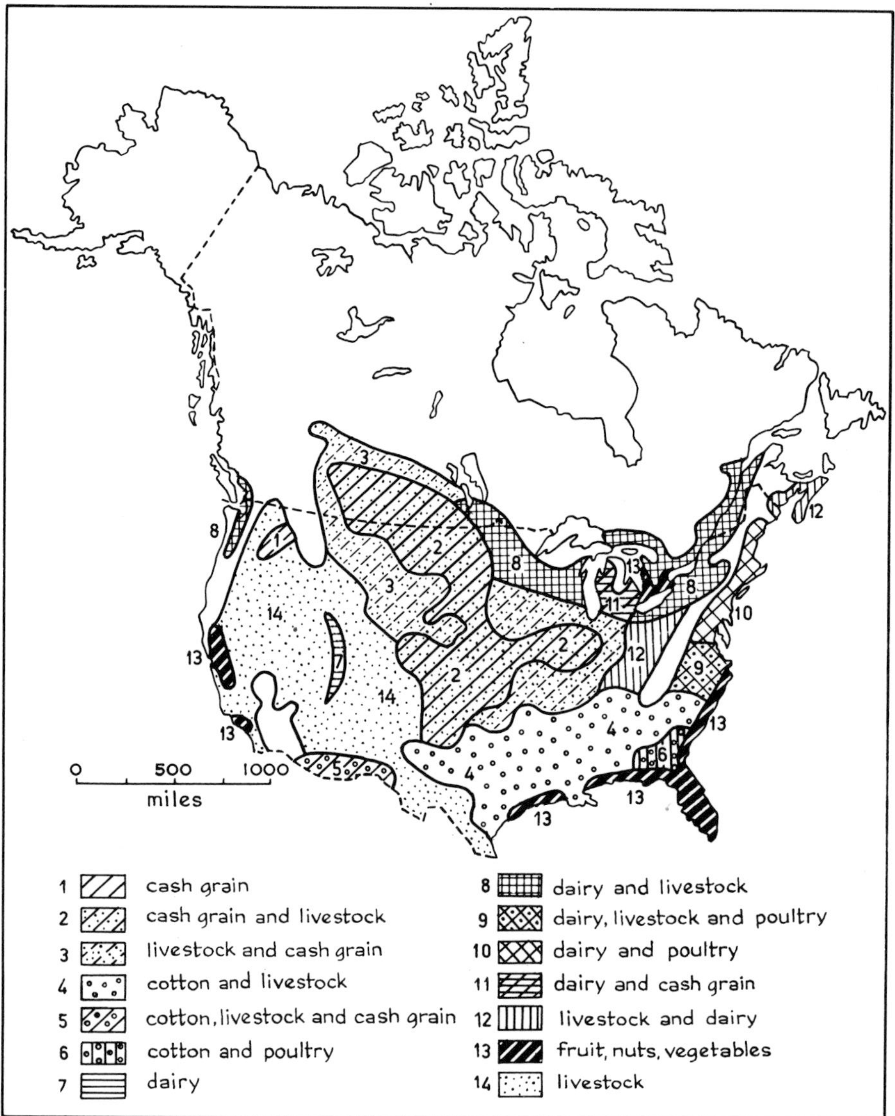

FIG. 7:16
Leading commercial farming combinations, mid-1960s.

discouraging crop farming, livestock management takes over. Concentrations of sheep and goats appear in the distributions of stock.

Farming in and marginal to the Cordillera generally relies heavily on range feeding, including the seasonal movement of cattle and sheep on to high summer pastures. Exceptions to this generalization occur in six main areas. Irrigation along the Piedmont of the Southern Rockies serves a long narrow district of dominantly dairy farms. Irrigation along the Mexican border sustains farms in the cotton, livestock, and cash-grain combination. The outstanding approach to monoculture in the Pacific Northwest of the U.S.A. is located on the basalt soils of the Snake–Columbia Plateau, where the cash-grain wheat is easily the leading product. The dairy–livestock combination reappears about Puget Sound, while a concentration of orchard working, too small to be marked in Fig. 7:16, exists on the terraces of the Okanagan Valley deep in the Canadian part of the Cordillera. Farms in the Great Valley of California tend to be specialized, especially on citrus fruit and on grapes. Irrigation is needed in both cases. A second district of generally similar farming occurs in Southern California. In addition, irrigated cotton – which does not appear among the combinations shown – is an important crop for the State as a whole.

Stress has already been laid on the use of irrigation in some Cordilleran districts. It modifies, but does not wholly offset, the connection between farming practice and climatic setting. Dairying on the Rocky Mountain Piedmont is made possible by irrigation, despite the background characteristics of the local BS climate. Wheat-growing on the Snake–Columbia Plateau is aided by the powerful water-absorbing and water-retaining properties of basalt soils, in a climatic environment which borders on the BS type. Livestock and dairy farming around Puget Sound is suited by Cfb climate. Fruit growing in California benefits from the long sunny summers of the Csa climate, but, since citrus fruits are originally natives of Cfa climates, the advantage of prolonged sun for ripening can only be gained at the cost of irrigation. Similarly, the cotton and grain cropping along the Mexican border relies on heavy watering in a climate indicative, by itself, of desert or near-desert conditions.

A further factor, or rather group of factors, relates to market conditions and market demands. Commercial cultivation tends in a general manner to produce the most profitable combination of products, in given conditions of climate, soil, technique, and market situations. Climate is relatively inflexible, but even it can be countered to some extent – as, for instance, by the use of smoke-pots on fruit farms in a cold wave. The soil resource can be exhausted, or even lost altogether, by ill-advised management; more slowly, and with greater difficulty, it can be deliberately improved. Market demand can be to some extent influenced by sales campaigns, while marketing costs may be liable to reduction in various ways. When these considerations are taken into account, and when further allowance is made for government intervention in agriculture, it is easy to see that the farming combinations outlined here result from an infinity of personal decisions. Distributions represent something far beyond a straightforward response to a set physical environment.

TABLE 7:1

Land in Farms (million acres)

U.S.A.		Canada	
1850	293		
1860	407		
1870	408		
1880	536	1881	45
1890	623	1891	60
1900	839	1901	63
1910	879	1911	109
1920	955	1921	141
1930	987	1931	163
1940	1061	1941	174
1950	1159	1951	175
1960	1158	1961	173
1964	1159		
1967	1140		

TABLE 7:2

Selected Cropping Statistics for the U.S.A.

	Corn		Cotton		Wheat		Soybeans	
	Million acres	Million bushels	Million acres	Million bales	Million acres	Million bushels	Million acres	Million bushels
1866	30·0	731	7·6	2·1	15·4	170		
1870	38·4	1125	9·2	4·4	20·9	254		
1880	62·5	1707	15·9	6·6	38·1	502		
1890	78·4	1650	20·9	8·7	36·7	449		
1900	94·9	2662	24·9	10·1	49·2	599		
1910	102·3	2853	31·5	11·6	45·8	625		
1920	101·4	3070	34.4	13·4	62·3	843	0·4*	5*
1930	101·5	2080	42·4	13·9	62·6	887	1·1	14
1940	86·4	2457	23·9	12·6	53·2	815	4·8	78
1950	81·8	3075	17·8	10·0	61·6	1019	13·8	299
1960	71·6	3422	14·7	13·9	51·9	1356	23·7	555
1964	57·1	3548	13·9	14·7	49·2	1290	30·7	700

*1924 figures.

TABLE 7:3

Livestock (millions)

	U.S.A.				Canada			
	All cattle	(Dairy cattle)	Hogs	Sheep	All cattle	(Dairy cattle)	Hogs	Sheep
1890	60	(15)	57	41				
1900	60	(17)	63	40				
1910	59	(21)	35	40				
1920	67	(20)	59	35				
1930	54	(21)	38	42	5	(4)	4	4
1940	61	(22)	34	40	5	(4)	6	3
1950	77	(21)	56	31	5	(4)	5	2
1960	96	(20)	59	29	5	(3)	5	2
1965	107	(18)	53	23	8		5	1
1967	108	(15)	51	24				

CHAPTER EIGHT

EXPLOITATION AND CONSERVATION

No geographical account of North America can omit the exploitation of natural resources. None should omit resource conservation, if only because conservation involves the explicit definition of certain relationships between man and his environment. The scale and results of resource exploitation in this continent have been, and continue to be, spectacular; and some of its results have proved spectacularly disastrous. At the same time, conservation policies are at least as highly developed and as sympathetically received in Canada and the U.S.A. as in any other countries.

It could of course be argued that the imperative need for conservation arises directly from mistakes, and not exclusively from mistakes in the past. However, there is more to the matter than this. Some connection can certainly be made out between the principle of conservation and the current American policy of maintaining stockpiles of strategic materials; this policy, in turn, has promoted a deliberate assessment of resources and the reckoning-up of reserves. More generally, conservation can be regarded as illustrating a typically North American optimism about the possibilities of bringing parts of the environment under control, and of manipulating it deliberately.

It was this same kind of attitude which helped to promote wasteful exploitation in the first place. It is very doubtful if the early fur trappers imagined that they might destroy their means of livelihood, simply by engaging in it. It is certain that the bison-hunters of the Plains and the sealers of the Pribiloff Islands cared nothing that they were on the way to extinguishing whole species. Lumbermen could see forests stretching ever outward – far enough at least to last their own lifetimes. Trees and animals alike were taken as if they were minerals. In parts of the continent, soil was treated in the same manner. Shifting cultivation of cotton in the U.S. South left the soil exhausted: it also left no protective cover, so that, in the many areas where gullying began, the soil itself disappeared.

Destructive exploitation of this variety blurs the distinction between renewable and non-renewable resources, and consequently between conservation and exploitation. Vegetation and wildlife are in fact potentially renewable, but also potentially destructible. Surface water is renewable in terms of quantity but destructible in terms of quality, while groundwater in some areas is most properly regarded as an exhaustible mineral. Mineral fuels and mineral ores cannot ultimately be conserved; but they can be exploited with degrees of wastefulness which the conservationist would deplore. The ore-miners of pioneering and immediately following times were seeking the maximum rapid profit. Accordingly, they customarily took only the richest ores from fields where quality varied. Some mines on the remoter parts of the Shield work on the same principle today. Now if a field is abandoned after its richest ores have been extracted, it may remain abandoned for a very long time, or for ever. Some of the ore resource has been destroyed, without even being used.

Parallels can be drawn from Western Europe to the reckless North American working of minerals, the needless killing of forests, the extinction of wildlife, and – albeit on a modest scale – to man-activated soil erosion. North American miners, trappers, hunters, fishermen, lumbermen, and farmers were not necessarily more reckless and destructive than those of other parts of the world. But they possessed tools, implements, and weapons, and eventually machines, which enabled them to attack the continent's resources with a speed never before witnessed.

Somewhat ironically, the practice of reckless exploitation can be traced directly back to policies of colonial management developed in Europe, and especially in Britain. After the War of Independence, resource exploitation continued to be encouraged by the apparently inexhaustible stocks of natural wealth, and also, in the U.S.A., by the application of the prevailing economic theory of the time. Perhaps *non-application* would be a better expression: for the theory, in respect of the internal economy of a country, was that private enterprise should be left as far as possible unregulated, producing its results in conditions of free competition. In due course the U.S.A. produced industrial tycoons, whose vast personal fortunes could be regarded as justifying the economic system and the methods of resource exploitation which it entailed.

In what now follows, the uses of and attitudes to selected natural resources will be briefly outlined, the mode of treatment necessarily varying from case to case.

Mineral Fuels: Coal in the U.S.A.

Like Britain, the U.S.A. effected its first great burst of industrial expansion with the aid of thermal power raised by the burning of coal. For a number of reasons, however, the coal-mining industry of the U.S.A. developed later than that of Britain. Fuel wood was still supplying half the energy generated in the U.S.A. as late as 1885, when coal output was equivalent to less than 20 per cent of its later peak. The nearest coalfield to the mid-Atlantic coast is the anthracite field of eastern Pennsylvania, where tight Appalachian folding has raised the coals to a rank unsuitable for industry. Bituminous coal was first worked in quantity on the western flank of the mountains in west Pennsylvania. Here, as is well known, physical conditions are highly favourable to mining. Some of the coals have excellent coking qualities, while the coal-bearing rocks were also found to contain iron ores of the type which, in rather modest quantities, not infrequently accompany coal. The industries which developed in the Pittsburgh district provide classically simple instances of industrial location. To the southwest, in West Virginia, lies a second coalfield, in an area where gentle doming again brings the seams close to the surface; but here, in contrast to western Pennsylvania, the chief aim of mining was to supply coal to the great towns of the eastern seaboard. Southwest again is a third area of doming, that of the Alabama coalfield, where the heavy metal industries of the Birmingham district correspond to those

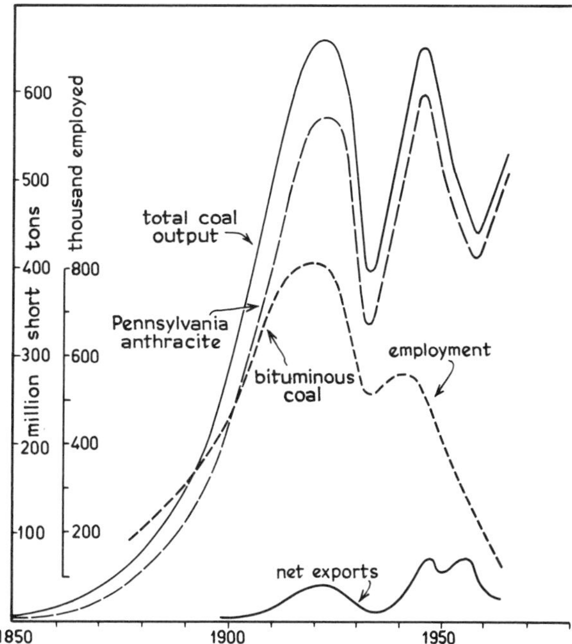

FIG. 8:1 Coal in the U.S.A.: production and employment, generalized.

of the Pittsburgh country. These three fields contributed principally to the increase of bituminous coal production from less than ten million short tons/yr in 1850 to more than 200m tons/yr in 1900 (Fig. 8:1). During this fifty-year span the geometric rate of increase in output remained sensibly constant; the arithmetic rate of increase accelerated. From 1900 to the early 1920s it was the arithmetic rate of increase which held steady, taking total production swiftly upward to more than 550m tons/yr. Mining by this time was widely developed in fields additional to those of the Appalachians – notably in the East Central Field of the interior, reaching from Illinois through Indiana into Kentucky. By this time, too, the anthracite field of eastern Pennsylvania had been running for some years at an output of about 90m tons/yr, raising total annual production above 650m tons.

Then ensued the Great Depression, cutting total production down swiftly to 400m tons/yr. A recovery, considerably slower than the fall, and associated in its later part with the industrial demands of World War II, succeeded in raising production of bituminous coal to record levels – about 600m tons/yr – in the mid-1940s. The new peak, however, was

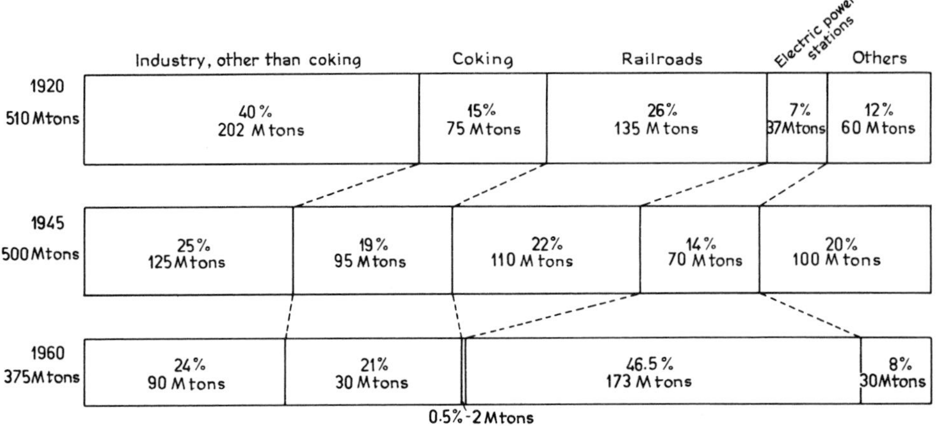

FIG. 8:2 Disposal of coal in the U.S.A.

not long held. Demand fell rapidly away towards 1960, when output was of the same order as that of the depression years. The net fall in coal production from 1920 to 1960, about 135m tons/yr, is almost precisely accounted for by the changing demands of the railways, which between 1945 and 1960 completed for all practical purposes their conversion from steam to diesel operation. Among other groups of consumers, the strength of the demand for coal has changed in definable ways. Industrial plants (including coke ovens) during the forty-year period reduced their percentage call on coal output from 55 per cent to 45 per cent of the total, and their absolute demand from 277m to 170m tons a year. The export trade, perceptible in the 1920s when some 40m tons were shipped each year, was brought very low during the Great Depression, and has failed to maintain the expansion recorded in the late 1940s and the earlier part of the 1950s (Fig. 8:1). Retail deliveries, which account for most of the class of Other Users in Fig. 8:2, were back in 1960 to half the demand of 1920, after a spell of expansion in the mid-1940s. Reduced demand for coal exports reflects the post-war restoration of a number of foreign economies, plus the conversion in a number of countries to alternative sources of power. The reduced retail demand reflects, among other things, the progressive use of oil and natural gas for domestic heating – a trend which has seriously reduced activity on the eastern Pennsylvania anthracite field. The reduction in demand for coking coal between 1945 and 1960 results from improved techniques of metallurgy, and especially from the transfer of pig-iron in liquid form direct from iron furnace to steel smelter. Reduced demand for coal by industries other than the smelting industry in part reflects increased efficiency, but mainly stems from the growing use of oil, natural gas, and electricity. As Fig. 8:2 shows, the one division in which demand for coal has increased – by 43m tons/yr between 1920 and 1945, and by more than 100m tons/yr between 1945 and 1960 – is the thermal generation of electric power. It is this division that chiefly explains the rise in total demand after 1960.

Changes in relative demand and in total demand for coal have set in, long before there is any threat that this resource may become exhausted. Indeed, it is not easy for anyone living in a country short of mineral fuels to comprehend in full the situation where the U.S.A. and Canada both have easily workable coalfields either partly withdrawn from use, or as yet little developed, or even not developed at all. The rank and quality of coal in North America decline in a general way westwards from the highlands of the east towards the Cordilleran edge. Mining has made no great progress in the bituminous coalfields of the western interior, in relation to the available reserves, and has made little or none in the extensive lignite fields of the Plains.

Mining employment in the U.S.A. reached its peak in about 1920, when the collieries employed four-fifths of a million workers (Fig. 8:1). Employment fell away with production during the Great Depression, but failed subsequently to make more than a minor recovery. The explanation is simple enough – progressive mechanization of mining operations. Since about 1945 the trend of employ-

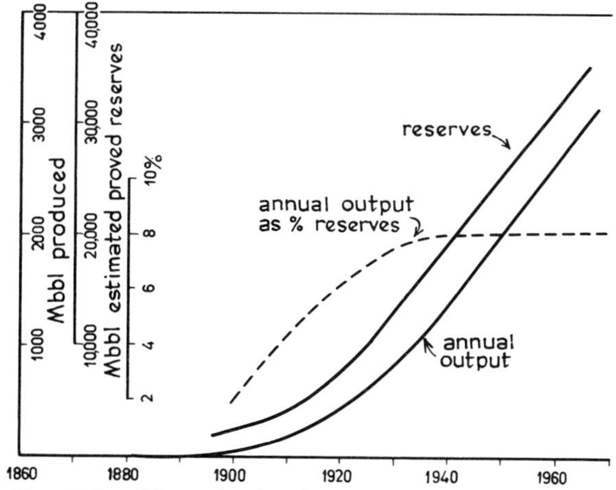

FIG. 8:3 Oil production in the U.S.A.: generalized.

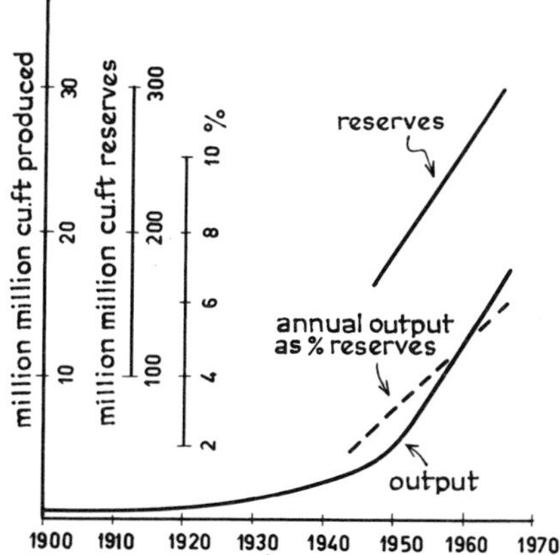

FIG. 8:4 Natural gas production in the U.S.A.: generalized.

ment in coal mining has been consistently, and strongly, downward; the mining workforce of today is less than that of a century ago, when the expansion of mining was still in its early beginnings. The West Virginia coalfield, exclusively dependent on external deliveries and offering very little alternative employment, has suffered particularly badly in human and social terms.

Mineral Fuels: Oil and Natural Gas

Canada and the continental U.S.A. are both rich in resources of oil and of natural gas. The first well drilled in a deliberate search for oil, Drake's 1859 well in Pennsylvania, is justly famous. However, the occurrence of petroleum had been known long before this date – in parts of the Old World, for centuries before. Oil seepages in Pennsylvania were familiar to the Indians who, however misguidedly, used oil for medicinal purposes; and these same seepages were recorded by Europeans as early as 1750. French exploiters of the North American interior, commanding in their day the western part of what is now the State of Pennsylvania, dug catch-wells to collect medicinal oil. Oil was detected elsewhere also before its possibilities were understood. A drill for salt in Kentucky was abandoned in the early 1800s, when it penetrated oil-bearing rocks and was flooded with petroleum. Oil in Texas was struck by accident in a bore for water, in the year 1890. But between Drake's Pennsylvania sinking of 1859 and the Texas drilling of 1890, the internal-combustion engine had been invented. The market for mineral oil, limited at first to so-called health purposes and then to lighting and heating, was to expand beyond the limits of imagination.

A generally similar history is on record for natural gas. Like oil seepages, burning gas vents have been known for hundreds of years. Seeping gas was brought into small-scale domestic use in Ohio, by very crude methods, in the mid-nineteenth century, and was being commercially exploited in the 1860s. Its industrial applications, even more revolutionary in some ways than the use of petroleum, have until fairly recently been slow to develop.

The exploitation both of oil and of natural gas has some of the characteristics of a race against time. Fig. 8:3 shows how the annual output of oil in the U.S.A., after increasing rapidly from small beginnings, assumed in about 1930 a steady arithmetic rate of increase. Simultaneously, oil prospecting has provided an equally steady increase in the amount of estimated proved reserves. But whereas the known reserves of 1900 were sufficient to last for fifty years at the then prevailing rate of consumption, those of 1930 onwards are only enough for about twelve years, and annual consumption in the mid-1960s equalled the whole of the known reserves of 1900. Matters are somewhat similar with natural gas (Fig. 8:4). Output began a course of rapid arithmetic increase in about 1950. Data on reserves, although available for but a short interval of years, suggest that output tends to amount to an increasing percentage of proved resources. Thus, in the mid-1940s, annual production came to 2 per cent of known reserves, giving the known gasfields a life of fifty years at the then-

8. A geologist interpreting air photographs – a preliminary stage in the search for oil.

9. Seismic sounding during offshore oil exploration in the Gulf of Mexico. The dynamite charge going overboard will be detonated from a distance; the shock waves, automatically recorded, help to indicate geological structures beneath the sea bed.

obtaining rate of output. By the mid-1960s output was up to 6 per cent of reserves, and showing no signs of decreasing its proportionate value. Known resources are now enough for about fifteen years at current rates of consumption (Plates 8, 9).

The take-off point for oil production in Canada came in about 1940 (Fig. 8:5), that for natural gas production in about 1955. Exploitation of each resource has been accompanied by the construction of enormously long pipelines, including the 718 miles of Trans-Mountain oil pipeline from Edmonton to Vancouver, with extensions into the State of Washington, the nearly 2000 miles of Interprovincial Pipeline which delivers Prairie oil to eastern Canada, and the more than 2000 miles of Trans-Canada gas pipeline which takes Prairie gas to Montreal.

Energy Resources in General

Figure 8:6 summarises the exploitation of energy resources in the U.S.A. from 1850 onwards. The marked increases in the absolute use of energy, from about 1900 to about 1920, and again from about 1940 onwards, correspond to bursts of industrial expansion. The second half of the nineteenth century, influenced by the spread of railways and the development of coal mining and of industry in general, saw wood fuel superseded by coal, and coal approach a peak of relative importance which it was shortly to pass. Coal in 1910 supplied more than three-quarters of the total energy generated in the country. Ten years later, the absolute demand for coal was already experiencing the preliminary effects of competition from oil. By about 1940, coal accounted for only half of the energy generated: within five years, it had been surpassed as a power source by petroleum products. During the 1950s, petroleum alone, and then natural gas alone, came to exceed coal as a source of energy. Strikingly enough, hydro-electricity in the U.S.A. still ranks

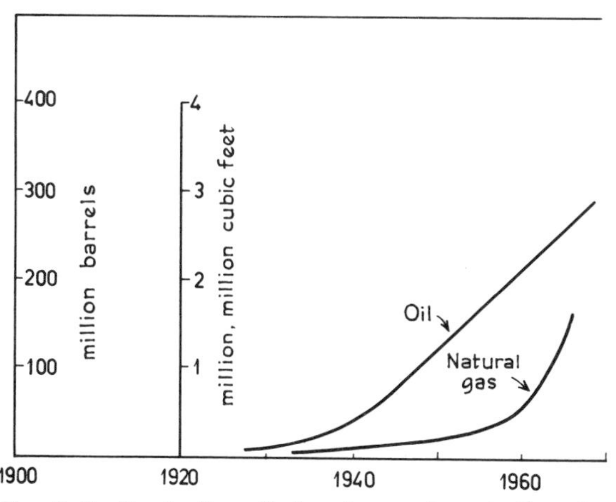

FIG. 8:5 Production of oil and natural gas in Canada: generalized.

low as a supplier of energy, both in relative and in absolute terms. Nuclear energy is as yet of minor relative significance in North America (Plate 10).

Metallic Minerals in Canada

Canada's role as a supplier of metallic minerals is sufficiently well known to require no general emphasis. Canada ranks first in nickel production, with about 60 per cent of world production (Mainland China excluded). In copper production Canada takes fifth place after the U.S.A., Chile, the U.S.S.R., and Rhodesia, in that order, with an out-

10. Nuclear power station at Morris, Illinois, producing electricity for commercial users in the northern part of the State, including Chicago.

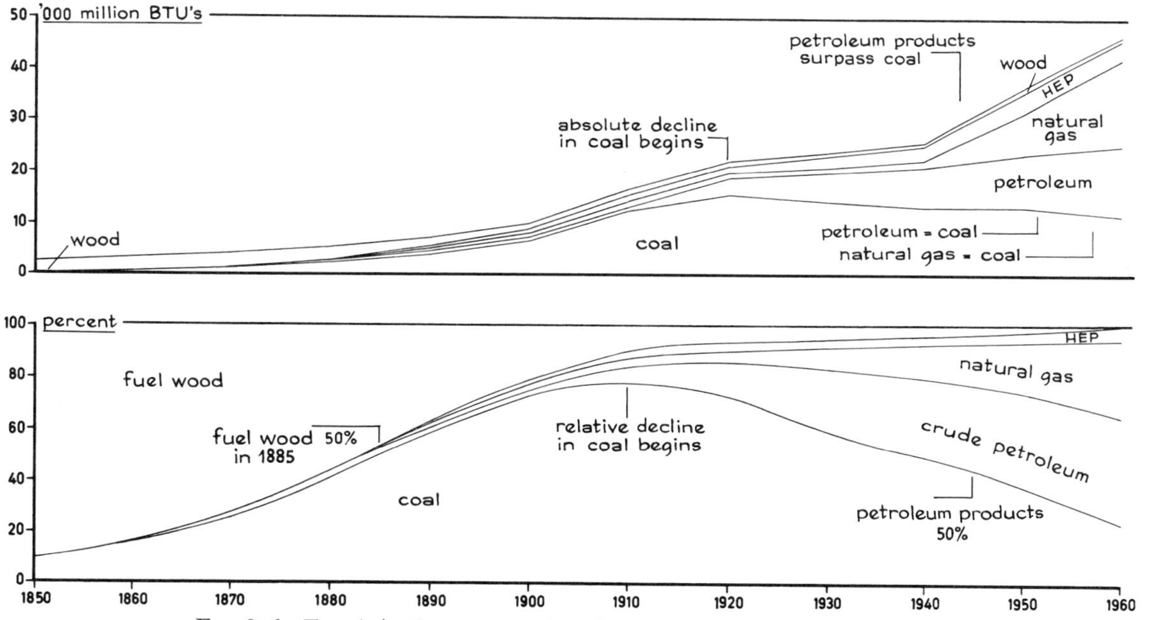

FIG. 8:6 Trends in the consumption of energy in the U.S.A.: generalized.

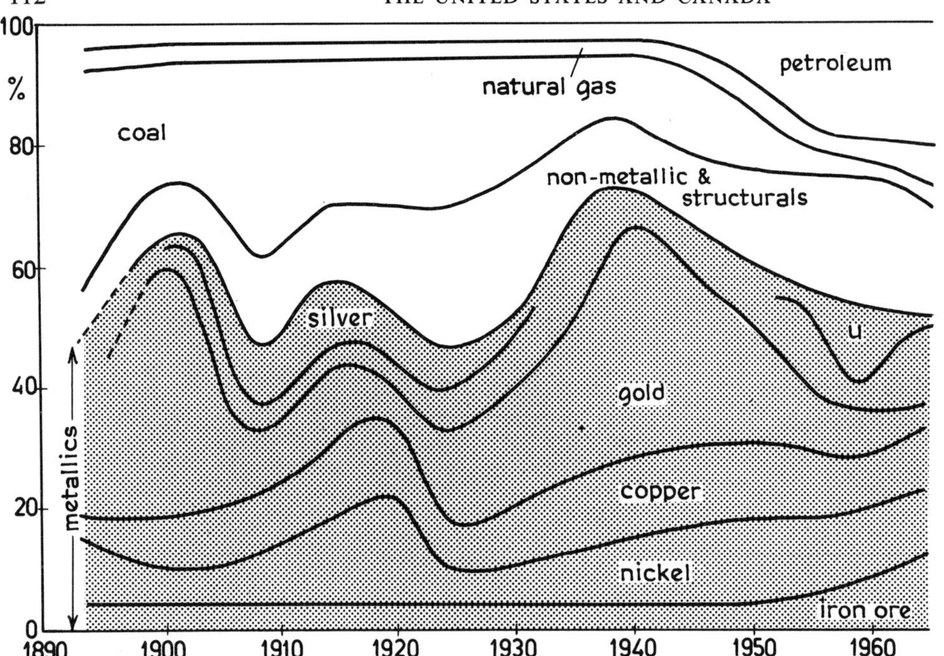

FIG. 8:7 Proportionate trends in Canadian mineral production, by value: generalized.

put about one-third that of the U.S.A. As a producer of iron ore Canada comes third after the U.S.S.R. and the U.S.A., and has distinct prospects of moving into second place. Nickel, copper, and iron ore account together for about a third of the total value of mineral production in Canada, with nickel usually ranking above copper but with iron ore fast overtaking both. In respect of zinc output Canada occupies second place, coming not far short of the U.S.A. and not far ahead of the U.S.S.R. Australia is the world's leading producer of lead, closely followed by the U.S.S.R.; then, after a gap, come the U.S.A., Canada, Mexico, and Peru, closely grouped in that order. Canada's output of lead is about half that of Australia.

Canada is prominent as a supplier of the industrial metals uranium, platinum, cadmium, cobalt, magnesium, and tungsten. It also ranks high with regard to gold and silver. Among the list of countries for which returns are available – a list which excludes the U.S.S.R. and Mainland China – Canada ranks second as a gold producer, with about one-sixth of the output of South Africa, and fourth as a silver producer after Mexico, the U.S.A., and Peru, with an output about one-seventh that of Mexico.

Thus, in the extraction of ferrous ores, nonferrous metal ores, and the ores of the precious metals, Canada stands high in the world economy. But the relative importance of metallic minerals as a group, and of individual minerals within this group, can undergo violent fluctuations.

Certain of the recorded fluctuations are generalized in Fig. 8:7. As this diagram indicates, metallics have supplied at least 50 per cent of the total value of Canadian mineral output during most of the recorded period, and at times have contributed 60 per cent or more; but the proportionate share of individual metals has varied widely. The years about 1900 were those of the last gold-rushes, when alluvial gold was taken from the Yukon Valley on both sides of the Alaskan border: on the Canadian side, the chief mining centre was the Klondike. The sharp peak in gold production was, however, rapidly passed. Exhaustion of the richest and most accessible placers on the Yukon was chiefly responsible for cutting back national gold output by more than half in less than ten years. The industrial demands of World War I (1914–18), plus the expansion of silver mining, briefly permitted metallics to claim nearly 60 per cent of the total value of minerals raised, but their relative importance declined once again in the 1920s.

Subsequent trends in the working of the two precious metals express the interplay of market conditions and politico-economic decisions. Silver has for a good many years been contributing little, either to the total value of mineral production in Canada (about 1 per cent) or to the value of the metallic group (about 2 per cent). One main reason is that rising working expenses, rising prices of silver on a free market, and inflation generally push the metal value of silver coinage above its monetary value. Accordingly, mints reduce the silver content of their coins, or turn to alternative metals. Silver in Canada is now little more than a by-product of lead–zinc mining.

Gold mining, after a series of distinctly slack years, expanded through the 1920s and 1930s, mainly in response to changes in the world currency situation, and increased very fast during World War II (1939–45) when the U.K. especially needed gold for the settlement of international transactions. Since about 1950, however, gold has fallen rapidly away in relative importance, for reasons not altogether unlike those which earlier depressed the working of silver. Gold, as the currency basis of the Western world, has its bullion price rigidly fixed: the U.S. government, for instance, maintains a set rate of exchange between the gold and the dollar. The fixed-exchange-rate system, provided that it can be made to work, has profound advantages in promoting stability of currencies and of international finance. However, the demand for gold as a medium of exchange, the continued rise in costs of production, and the increase in the value of gold on a theoretically open market all combine to make gold mining progressively uneconomic.

Copper is notoriously liable to price fluctuations; and, since the great expansion of copper mining in Canada during the 1920s, which resulted from the rapid development of electrical industry, copper has to some extent felt the challenge of substitute materials. However, copper in Canada typically occurs in mixed ores, especially those of copper–nickel: the term *nickel* is itself taken from the German *kupfernickel*, the devil's copper from which this metal could not formerly be extracted. Copper output is then in part a function of the output of, and demand for, nickel; and this demand in turn reflects in large part the demand for alloy steel and stainless steel, and thus reflects industrial growth. The future of copper and nickel production in Canada is heavily dependent on the U.S. market, and so upon the state of the U.S. economy. Other customers, such as Japan, may turn increasingly to Australia, where extensive nickel strikes were made in the late 1960s.

Lead, zinc, and silver occur in Canada, as in most other producing countries, in the form of mixed sulphide ores. The reduced status of silver as a mineral has already been noticed. About one-third of the lead extracted goes into storage batteries, while zinc is used chiefly in galvanizing and in the making of alloys in the bronze–brass range. Like the market for copper, the markets for lead and zinc are subject to wide variations of price. Increased demand and rising price intensify activity at existing mines, and stimulate the opening of new mines or the reopening of old ones. But the subsequent fall in price, typically occurring after but a few years, leaves base-metal mining geared to high output levels, so that production for a time outruns demand and further exaggerates the usual price fluctuation. Nevertheless, the long-term demand for lead and zinc is likely to persist and to increase, given some degree of expansion on the part of industry in the U.S.A.

A generally similar case is that of uranium, which in the years about 1960 was in strong demand for the supply of nuclear power-stations and atomic weaponry: the uranium boom – perhaps the first of a series – lasted but for ten years or so, before it was damped-out by over-supply (Fig. 8:7).

Prospects among metallic minerals in Canada are perhaps brightest of all for iron ore. The U.S.A., with its ever-rising demand and failing home supplies, has for some considerable time been looking to external sources of iron-ore supply. Canada has very extensive proved reserves of ore which, with a 50 per cent or greater content of metallic iron, can bear the cost of transport in the raw state, although concentration is fairly usual. There are, in addition, little-known but undoubtedly vast reserves of lower-grade ore which could be economically transported after beneficiation.

Despite Canada's long-standing reputation as a mineral producer, and especially as a producer of metallic minerals, the real take-off point in Canadian mining came somewhere in the 1940s (Fig. 8:8). Although price is a somewhat crude guide to volume of output, the value graph from 1950 onwards corresponds, in fact, quite closely to trends in the index of output volume. The *per capita* value of Canadian mineral production is rising almost as

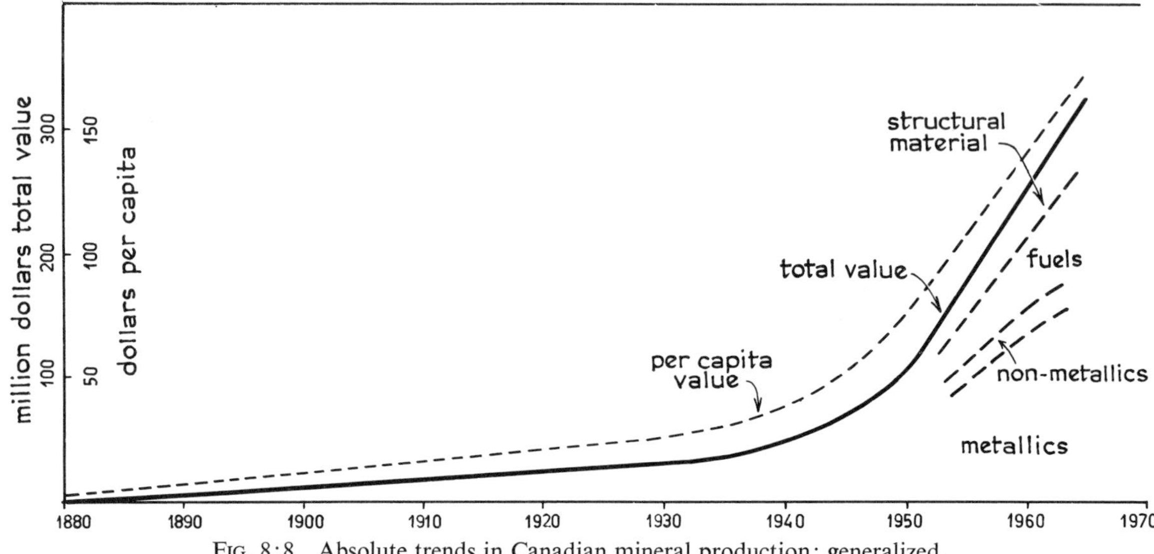

FIG. 8:8 Absolute trends in Canadian mineral production: generalized.

fast as total value, while the sub-graph for metallics, although ascending less steeply, is still strongly inclined upward. Minerals – other than gold, the movement of which is a financial rather than an industrial matter – tend in the long term to take an increasing share in Canada's export trade, rising from less than 5 per cent by value of this trade in the late nineteenth century to 30 per cent in the 1960s.

Resources of metallic minerals in Canada still remain incompletely known. There is no reason to envisage any close threat of exhausted reserves, whether on the Shield or in the mineralized parts of the Cordillera. In both areas, metallic minerals other than iron are associated with intrusions, and mainly with granitic batholiths. The Shield division is currently supreme, producing about 93 per cent of Canadian iron ore, dominantly of sedimentary origin, 85 per cent of Canadian copper, 97 per cent of Canadian gold, and 99 per cent of Canadian nickel.

Furs and Fish

The fur trade and the trapping of wild fur-bearing animals which supported it rose to early prominence in the economy of colonial North America. Despite some three-and-a-half centuries of completely unregulated operation, trapping has proved on balance less destructive than might have been expected. Of the leading species trapped in Canada – beaver, mink, muskrat, lynx, squirrel, and otter, in that order – beaver and muskrat still persist in settled areas. The other types, apart from retreating before advancing settlement, have, like beavers and muskrats, maintained their numbers well. The escape from destruction, however, has in places been narrow indeed. In Nova Scotia the beaver was at one time almost extinct: twenty successive years of complete protection were necessary to preserve it in New Brunswick; and in Saskatchewan, trapping was so determined up to 1945 that alternate seasons had to be closed in order to allow the beaver and muskrat populations to maintain themselves.

It is only since about 1900 that any measures have been taken to conserve the wild fur resource, and only since about 1925 that any effective measures have been in operation. Practice varies from province to province. However, it is reasonable to say as a generalization that the emergency device of closed seasons, and the more flexible device of open seasons of variable length, are being partly superseded by the effect of the registration of traplines. Under registration, a particular trapping area is assigned to an individual trapper, whose own interest it becomes to conserve the fur-bearers. In addition, the annual renewal of registration can be made conditional on methods of operation which act to conserve species and to sustain yields. Largely in consequence of the register system, what could be called fur mining is being replaced by fur harvesting. For Canada as a whole, the take of wild pelts in the mid-1960s ran at about four million a year, with catches of beaver, otter, and lynx the highest since records began in 1919. In addition, the value of establishing reserves where conservation is strictly enforced has been amply demonstrated – for instance, in Quebec – and considerable success has been achieved in transplanting – e.g., in Ontario, where beaver populations have been restored by this means.

Fur farming started in Canada in about 1890, when fox farms began on Prince Edward Island. The fur trade in general is subject to fluctuations of demand as fashions change; and fur farming is the most vulnerable of all. By 1950 the demand for black and silver fox fur was so low that prices fell below production costs. Meantime, mink farming, begun in about 1910, expanded vigorously. Since about 1950 mink has been the leading fur on the world market, and Canada in the mid-1960s was producing about $1\frac{1}{2}$ million pelts from its mink farms. So successful has fur farming proved that it now accounts for about two-thirds of the total value of Canadian fur production. Among its side-effects is the growth in Newfoundland of a wild mink population descended from animals escaping from the farms: Newfoundland was able to declare a mink-trapping season in 1958.

Conservation of fisheries is more complex than that of wildlife on land, partly because of the long history in commercial fishery of completely unregulated operation. A contributing factor here is the unpredictable variability, sometimes from year to year, in the amount of catch. Since the advent of canning, it has been possible to make good seasons offset bad seasons and simultaneously to escape the worst effects of glut, at an increased risk however of over-fishing. Even when measures of conservation are laid down, they are by no means easy to enforce; and conservation of deep-sea fisheries needs international agreement and control. Fish populations, once reduced to dangerously low levels, are not easy to restore. Competition for water use in inland and inshore fisheries comes from towns and industrial plants, which unless prevented employ rivers, lakes, and inlets as dumping-grounds for toxic wastes. Complications of a special kind arise in the case of salmon, which need unobstructed passages along the rivers which they enter at spawning time.

To their great credit, Canada and the U.S.A. have led the way in international measures of fishery conservation. Two early agreements concerned the halibut and salmon fisheries of the Pacific, involving the regulation and limitation of catches, and, in the second of the two, the construction and maintenance of salmon fishways by which the salmon bypass artificial dams: it is claimed that the fry, passing through the turbines of power plants on their way to the sea, undergo no slaughterous rate of killing. One of the earliest of all international agreements of maritime conservation was that of 1911 by the U.S.A., Canada, Japan, and Russia to prevent the Pribiloff Island seals from being wiped out. Both the U.S.A. and Canada adhere to the Northwest Atlantic Fisheries Convention, an investigating and advisory body, and to the Convention for the High Seas Fisheries of the North Pacific, the signatories of which undertake to encourage conservation practice. The two countries have also set up a fisheries convention for the Great Lakes.

The halibut and salmon fisheries of the Pacific have been saved, with catches nowadays running higher than ever. Not all dangers, however, were taken in time. The lobster fishery of the Pacific coast has been destroyed by over-fishing, and attempts to transplant lobsters from the Atlantic have not yet been successful. On the Atlantic side itself, the lobster fishery of New Brunswick could be wiped out by a single uncontrolled season. Parts of the Great Lakes system, and numbers of the inlets on the Middle Atlantic coast, experience serious pollution from industries and towns – pollution made all the more noxious by the liberal outflow of liquid detergents. But in total, the fish take in North America is currently running higher than ever before – about 5000m lb/yr in the U.S.A., and about 2000m lb/yr in Canada.

Fishery conservation has produced a development somewhat similar to fur farming – namely, the establishment of fish hatcheries, where younglings are produced for purposes of restocking (Plate 11). As yet, hatcheries are intended primarily to sustain sport fishing, which in North America lacks the class associations which it carries in Britain, and which commands a great following. To name examples, Nova Scotia has hatcheries for salmon, while trout hatcheries occur in Quebec, Ontario, Manitoba, Saskatchewan, and Alberta. The close

11. A Canadian fish hatchery: yearlings are being packed alive, 500 at a time, into special containers for distribution.

attention to sport fishery as a facet of tourism is well exemplified from the Ruby Mountains of Nevada, where the tarns are annually restocked from the air.

Forests

Lumbermen in the U.S.A. cut about ten thousand million cubic feet of timber a year; the corresponding figure for Canada is four thousand million cubic feet.

Lumber production in the U.S.A. reached its record output in the early 1900s. Output subsequently, running at less than peak levels, has remained fairly constant in the long term except during the Great Depression. In consequence, the trends in Fig. 8:9, which shows percentage contribution by areas to total U.S. lumber production, represent real trends in absolute output. The decade 1930–40 imposed no more than a temporary check on changes, some of which were already well in evidence by 1900. Lumbering in the New England and mid-Atlantic States was already of minor importance at the turn of the century, although the main period of decline was to continue until 1920. Decline of lumbering in the Lake and Central States was somewhat longer drawn-out, although a sharp falling-off can be distinguished for the Lakes area up to 1910. Output in the Southern States, increasing rapidly after the Civil War, held steady from 1900 to 1930, making this the chief lumber-producing area up to the mid-1920s when it was overtaken by the West Coast. The relative and absolute reductions in Southern lumber production have alike accelerated since 1940. By 1950, half the total output came from the Rockies and the West Coast combined, and by 1960, half came from the West Coast alone. These various effects represent the progressive consumption of particular resources, and the progressive switch of attack to alternatives. The one exceptional case is that of the Southern Atlantic States, where since about 1930 relative output has been slowly increasing, and where absolute output is on the rise. Forestry in this part of the continent is encouraged by the rapid growth of softwoods – including trees meant for pulping, since processes have been worked out for making paper from the Southern Pine. It is particularly in the South Atlantic parts of the U.S.A. that tree nurseries operate.

Canadian authorities, and Canadian citizens at large, are possibly more acutely conscious than those of the U.S.A. of the needs and possibilities of forest conservation. Rapacious demands for lumber, pulp, and newsprint from Canada's populous neighbour constitute potential threats to forests on which a significant part of the nation's export trade relies. Nevertheless, some widespread customs of lumbering practice caused extensive damage before they were understood or could be checked. Among these were clear felling, whereby whole forests were completely removed, leaving none of the cover which

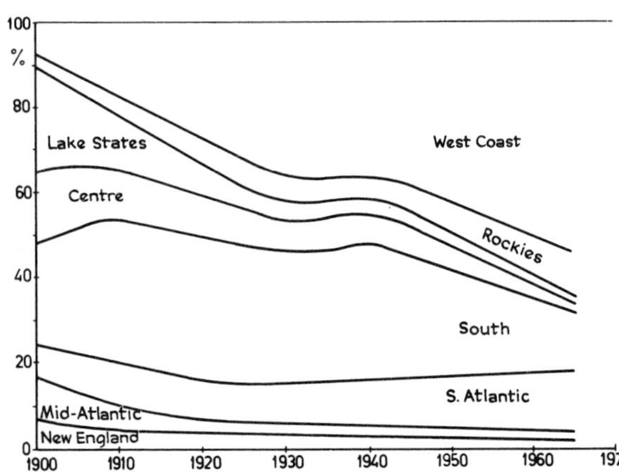

FIG. 8:9 Proportionate trends in U.S. lumber production: generalized.

12. Forest conservation in Canada: a demonstration of the water-bombing technique used in fighting fires.

seedlings need if the forest is to regenerate; the strewing of cutover areas with slash, the unwanted branches of the felled trees and the gravest of fire dangers (Plate 12); and methods of transport in which logs, dragged forcibly through the forest, tore up the ground and destroyed all seedling trees in their path.

By contrast with those in the U.S.A., lumbermen in Canada could not move readily towards new forests in next westward regions. Lumbering on the Shield was certain to increase its costs as the uncut edge moved steadily northward, as transport lines lengthened, and as costs accordingly increased. It is natural enough in the circumstances that nursery planting and the eco-biological study of forests are highly developed in Canada. However, the exploitation and management of Canadian forests, in addition to including deliberate measures to renew the forest resource, also exhibits characteristics of a kind usually associated with non-renewable resources. The reserve of timber has been reclassified, partly on account of techniques – especially techniques of pulp production – which permit formerly unwanted kinds of timber to be used, partly on account of the economies of scale attained in logging operations, and only in part on account of fire defence and of replanting. Fig. 8:10 shows that the net rate of forest depletion has been reversed. At the same time, estimated total and estimated accessible reserves have been reassessed, with the result that reserves appear good for about two hundred years at the present rate of depletion. This is surely time enough for deliberate renewal.

Parklands and Reserves

Probably the best-known measures of conservation in North America are those concerned with the establishment and management of national parks. The use of the term *park* in North America differs from that in Britain. Whereas in the latter the word calls to mind a privately-owned enclosure surrounding a mansion, or a municipally-owned open space in a town, in North America it usually means a tract of countryside owned and managed by a govern-

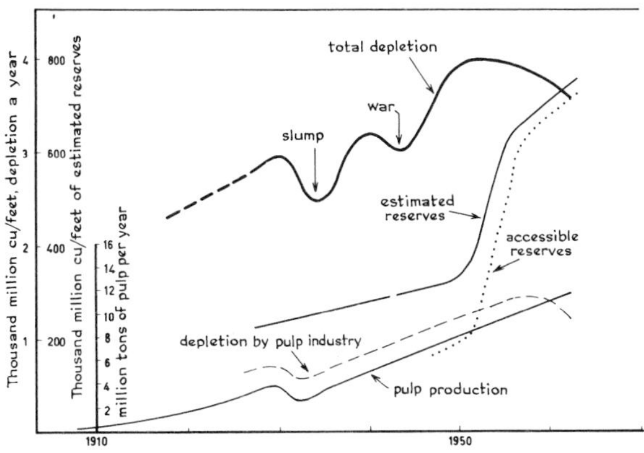

FIG. 8:10 Trends in forest depletion and assessment of forest reserves in Canada: generalized.

ment agency, and accessible to the public. Again, the typical private park of Britain has been landscaped, possessing trees and clumps ornamentally planted, and not infrequently containing an artificial lake; town parks follow much the same model. But the public parklands of North America preserve scenery in its natural state.

Several factors contribute to the contrast of concept, ownership, purpose, and use. On the political side comes the fact that, when the two federal governments of North America came into being, considerable areas had not been taken into private occupation. The U.S. government, for instance, acquired some 400,000 square miles of country by State cessions in the period 1781–1802, and double this amount again by the Louisiana Purchase of 1803. It had the opportunity and the power to forestall private occupation, especially in the West. The first reservation, at Hot Springs, Arkansas, was set aside in 1832. However, the U.S. National Park system as it now exists post-dates the formation of the Department of the Interior in 1849, the first National Park, that of Yellowstone, being established in 1872. Canada was swift to follow, the federal government in 1885 establishing a reserve of ten square miles enclosing the hot springs of Sulphur Mountain at Banff, Alberta. By the mid-1960s there were some twenty national parks in Canada and some thirty in the U.S.A., ranging in size up to the 3500 square miles of Yellowstone National Park and the 17,300 square miles of Wood Buffalo National Park which overlaps from Alberta into the Northwest Territories.

From the outset, the aim of establishing national parks was to combine the preservation of scenic areas with the provision of public access. Not surprisingly, a great deal of national parkland lies in the Cordillera – for instance, Yellowstone, Rocky Mountain, Grand Canyon, and Yosemite National Parks in the U.S.A., or Banff, Glacier, and Mount Revelstoke National Parks in Canada. However, there are also well known and popular parks on the eastern side of the continent, such as Terra Nova National Park in Newfoundland and the Great Smoky Mountains National Park in North Carolina–Tennessee. Throughout the two systems, it is the rule for the parks to be staffed by rangers or wardens, and for the operating agencies to provide camp-grounds, picnic areas, roads, and trails. Motels, hotels, and lodges operate privately under lease. Recreational facilities vary from park to park. Prince Albert National Park in central Saskatchewan offers fishing, swimming, and boating on the intricate waterways of the Shield, while Banff National Park is particularly noted for ski-ing, Some parks, for instance Jasper National Park in Alberta, are notable as wildlife sanctuaries, while others function specifically to preserve forms threatened with extinction: among this latter group is Wood Buffalo National Park, which contains the largest surviving herds of plains and wood bison.

From five million visitors a year in the mid-1920s, the National Parks of the U.S.A. have increased their record to 100 million in the mid-1960s. The corresponding total for Canada is ten million. In addition, the National Forests and State Parks in the U.S.A., and the Provincial Parks in Canada, attracted more than three times as many visitors as the National Parks. Like so much else in North America, access to the public parks depends heavily on the automobile, and on the deliberate encouragement of car travel by the provision of wayside tables, picnic grounds in remote places, and motels at the ends of roads constructed solely for tourist use. But the demand for access may well relate in part to the frontier tradition, which is also reflected in the shooting of game; an air-conditioned lodge deep in a western forest, alongside a canyon, or overlooking a lake can be taken – unconsciously, perhaps – as the twentieth-century representative of the log-cabin of the pioneer.

Whatever the drives behind the parkland movement, its results are praiseworthy in the extreme. Although some parks, or some parts of them, do constitute reserves of plants or sanctuaries for wildlife, it seems worth re-emphasizing that the general purpose is recreational use. Some of the best scenic areas of the continent have been secured for public benefit and enjoyment, and have been deliberately opened up. The policy contrasts powerfully with the idea of conservation as mere preservation, a principle which could discourage rather than promote public access. Parkland management is in general of a very high standard indeed. National parks, for instance, are completely free of any threat of commercial vulgarization: none contains advertisement hoardings, which elsewhere in North America are undoubtedly the largest and the most visually obtrusive in the world. Moreover, other operators than the parkland authorities are coming to see the benefit of development but unspoiled scenery. Meteor Crater, Arizona, is a well-known tourist attraction: it also happens to be privately owned, but has nevertheless escaped vulgarization. The State of Florida maintains sixty miles of highway from the capital, Tallahassee, to the shore of the Gulf, where hoardings are absent and where the road is bordered by very broad strips of mown grass dotted here and there with trees. At another remove again, the thirty-five miles of road from Tallahassee to Monticello has been planted along both verges with alternating dark cypresses and climbing roses. It could be that not all effects of the commercially-run and State-encouraged tourist trade will be forever hideous.

Soil Erosion and Soil Conservation

Soil erosion in North America presents one of the most appalling instances of wasteful exploitation in the whole of history. It has fallen far more heavily on the U.S.A. than on Canada, but only because the more southerly country is by nature the more vulnerable. Estimates in the 1930s gave more than a million acres of eroded land in the U.S.A., equivalent to the total extent of farmland; and although erosion was by no means confined to farms, it was reckoned that well over half of all cropland had suffered grave damage by soil erosion, with another quarter under serious threat.

A variety of circumstances combined to activate accelerated erosion; and the combination varied somewhat from region to region. In the south of the U.S.A., as has been pointed out, cotton planting developed into shifting cultivation, chiefly because cotton, in common with several lesser commercial crops of the area, made heavy demands on the nutrients of the easily exhausted latosols, and because cropping left the fields bare after the harvest. Erosion became most acute on the southern Piedmont, where gullies could easily trench through the soil and into the deeply weathered bedrock, and in the hilly country which encloses the southern Appalachians on the south and west. In all this area, more than three-quarters of the topsoil was lost.

On the farms intended originally for family holdings in the Midwest, pioneers cleared the forest and put the land to the plough. They and their successors planted whole fields with row crops, not understanding that they were inviting disaster. Whereas many of the farmland soils of Europe will resist to some extent dislodgement by raindrops, those of the Midwest are in general less cohesive; and they are also liable to be exposed to more intense rainfall than is usual in most parts of Europe. Row cropping exposes whole fields to violent rainbeat, to sheetwash across the entire surface when rain is heavy, and to gullying whereever the water collects itself into defined channels (Plate 13, *upper*). Thousands of corn-raising farms in the Ohio Valley, and in the most highly cultivated Midwestern portions of the Mississippi and Missouri Valleys, lost as much as three-quarters of their topsoil.

Once it was understood that the eastern Prairies could be brought under the plough, grain-growing reached westward through Oklahoma, Kansas, and parts of Nebraska, and westward in Canada from near Winnipeg towards the Rockies. But something had been left out of account – the fact that, in addition to its variability from year to year, climate is subject to spells of extreme conditions. The westward spread of grain-farming took place during years of average to above-average rainfall with recessing during droughts. The years 1934, 1935, and 1936 were unusually dry on the Southern Plains. Strong winds lifted the topsoil wholesale, at the rate of up to 200 million tons per storm. Parts of it fell locally, thickly enough to bury farmsteads. Some was carried over the Gulf or the Atlantic, to be lost for ever (Plate 14).

The many thousands of long, hard lives spent in clearing boulders from the farmlands of New England, or in draining the countless swamps of the great spread of glacial till left by the last ice-sheet south of the Great Lakes, count for little in the total reckoning against the acceleration of erosion on much of the farmland of the U.S.A. and on the Prairie farms of Canada. Man-activated erosion works up to 10,000 times as fast as erosion in natural conditions. Beyond the limits of farming, equally severe accelerated erosion is recorded from steep slopes where forests have been cut. Contingent damage results also in the drainage net, where channels can be choked and the liability to flooding increased by the acceleration in the supply of sediment-load to rivers.

13. Upper: a deep gully extending itself headward across grazing land. Lower: the same gully, two years later, after regrading and turfing.

The federal governments in both countries, faced with the threat of the very means of existence for their peoples, were impelled to react, in the first instance by setting up advisory services. Advice rather than compulsion was required by the traditional North American resentment of direction and suspicion of central government agencies. Processes of persuasion are inevitably slow, especially among farmers, usually a notably conservative section of the community. However, a majority of farmers both in the U.S.A. and on the Canadian Prairies are now sympathetic and co-operative with the intentions of the official agencies of soil conservation. Conservation districts in the U.S.A., for instance, total some 2000 million acres, where the federal government meets about half the cost of measures of protection against erosion, improvement of productivity, and conservation of water.

Where land is classified as suitable for cultivation, the principal need is to control the downslope flow of water. The simplest practice is that of contour ploughing, which avoids the opening of furrows with a downslope component. Contour ploughing may however be an insufficient protection where soils are readily erodible or where slopes exceed a certain degree of steepness. The next most elaborate measure is that of strip cropping, where row crops (e.g. corn) and cover crops (e.g. alfalfa) are planted in alternate strips of 50 to 200 ft wide, once again with the plough taken along the contour. A more expensive but still more effective method is to terrace; with terraces, water may be altogether retained, or may be fed into watercourses only at the ends of terraces (Plate 15). In this way, direct downslope run-off can be eliminated. Fig. 8:11 gives a generalized example of the effectiveness of the various forms of conservation. Contour ploughing can alone reduce the loss of topsoil to not much more than half that expectable when no protective measures are employed, while strip cropping brings the loss down to something like a quarter. This practice is extensive in the Midwest, where in views from the air it reveals the form of the ground in striking detail.

14. Erosion and deposition by wind: farmyard on the Southern Plains occupied by a sand dune.

A particular advantage of strip cropping is that it is likely to involve crops which are not harvested simultaneously. A corn-small grain-hay rotation will usually produce some fields with strips of small grains and corn, and others with strips of corn and hay or small grains and hay. The phasing of the various harvesting seasons means that the fields become available for pasture in turn.

Gully control has two aspects: prevention of gullying in the first place, and the checking and stabilization of existing gullies. The conservation measures already described are effective in preventing gully formation, provided that they are properly adapted to local conditions of slope and rainfall-intensity, except that steep slopes may need to be taken out of cultivation altogether and planted with grass or trees. Since watercourses remain necessary to take surface run off, it is not practicable to eliminate them altogether. But gullies, unless in some way controlled, will continue to spread. In the worst-attacked areas they have taken over completely; but where something remains to be saved, it is a matter of preventing their further growth. Widening, and in part extension, can be reduced or

15. Strip cropping, alternately of corn and hay, on a farm in Wisconsin. The lower slope in the foreground has been terraced.

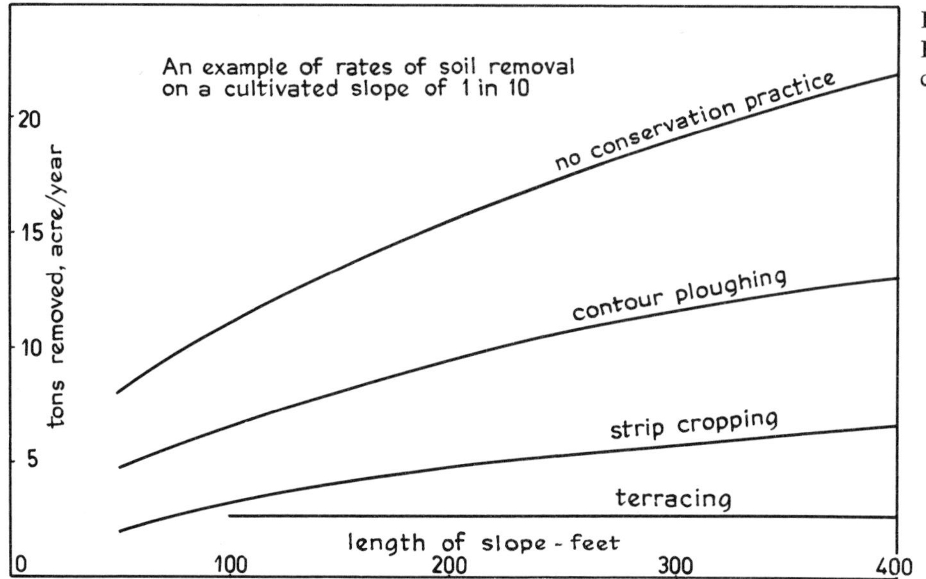

FIG. 8:11 Effects of soil conservation measures.

altogether eliminated by any conservation practice which powerfully reduces the intensity of surface run off; for a widely operating process of extension is piping, whereby copious rainwater percolates through the topsoil, heavily charges an erodible subsoil, and washes this out at the edge of an existing gully, causing the topsoil to collapse and so extending the surface watercourse. Deepening of gullies, which brings widening and headward extension with it, can be brought to a stop if the beds and banks of gullies can be stabilized. One obvious measure is fencing-off and planting – the use of grass in smaller gullies, as in the watercourses designed for use with terrace systems, and grass plus trees in the larger (Plate 13, *lower*). In addition, chains of check-dams can be inserted to convert the gully profile from a continuous downward slope to a series of steps where the velocity of run-off water is reduced and where soil can be trapped. Alternatively, larger structures can convert a gully into a series of small reservoirs, which act to conserve water for farm use. In favourable cases a gully can be largely filled in and the fill sodded-over.

The types of plants used in gully control and in erosion control generally vary, naturally enough, from area to area. One which has proved over-successful is the kudzu vine, widely employed in the South to cover gully-heads and the sides of road cuttings. Escaping from the planted areas into the forests, this tenacious plant is now engaged in covering trees and, by its weight and strength, pulling them down.

Wind erosion is perhaps the most difficult of all to check. It particularly affects cropland on the Great Plains from Texas to the Canadian Prairies, where ploughing leaves the land bare, and where the rotation may well include a year of fallow designed to conserve moisture, but bringing with it the need to clear weeds. Next to the west, wind erosion is also a grave danger in the ranching country, wherever overstocking occurs. One corrective is to withdraw land from grazing or from tillage, as the case may be: a 1955 estimate gave fourteen million acres of the U.S. Great Plains as under crops, although suited only to use as range. Conservation practice includes the planting of erosion-resistant crops, such as sorghum on the Southern Plains; use of improved rotations; establishment of windbreaks; retention of crop residues on or in the soil in tilled fields; wind-strip cropping, wherein wind-resistant crops are planted alternatively with grain at right-angles to the usual direction of spring winds; and the provision, in grazing areas, of enough watering-places to allow the grassland to be used efficiently and with minimum danger of erosion.

Although soil erosion and soil conservation have been hitherto discussed as if they were self-contained topics, this in fact is not so. In soil conservation, more than in conservation of any other kind, the problem, the need, and the implications are ramifying and complex. This circumstance is well illustrated by the conservation, control, and development measures undertaken in the Tennessee Valley by the Tennessee Valley Authority, usually known by its initials T.V.A.

The upper catchment of the Tennessee River lies in the southern Appalachians, where pioneer farmers cleared the land by cutting and burning. They and their descendants planted cash crops – corn, tobacco, and cotton. The minor part accorded to livestock in the farm economy meant a manure supply far too small to offset the heavy demands of these crops on soil nutrients: there was no commercial fertilizer industry. Then, all these main cash crops are annuals; land planted to them lies bare during the winter. They are also row crops. Perhaps for ease in working, the farmers ploughed, and planted, up and down the slope of the land. Inevitably, erosion set in. As the farmed ground lost its soil by washing and then by gullying, ploughing and planting spread farther and farther out, on to slopes of increasing steepness where erosion was still more rapid and still more savage. And even on flat areas, progressive soil exhaustion meant progressively falling yields. Not surprisingly, tuberculosis spread. So did typhoid, carried especially in floodwater; and so did malaria, transmitted by mosquitoes from the increasingly choked, increasingly swampy channels of the stream network. And when the streams rose, flooding of their valleys was far more serious than in the first pioneering days.

In 1933 the federal government passed the Tennessee Valley Authority Act. Its declared purposes were to promote flood control on the Tennessee system, to improve navigation, to establish hydro-electric power-stations, and to achieve proper use of marginal lands. Two measures basic to the whole scheme are the halting of soil erosion and the installation of twenty-seven dams on the Tennessee and its tributaries. Erosion is being combatted by the buying-up and reforesting of some areas, by campaigns to persuade farmers to make check-dams in gullies, by the spread of strip cropping, and by the grassing-down of some slopes to clover, a perennial cover. All these things reduce the charge of sediment into stream channels. They also tend to even out run off, and so to minimize the risk of flash floods on the lesser streams.

Large streams do not experience flash floods, but they are liable to slower-rising peaks and to extensive inundation of their valley-bottoms. Reduction of the sediment supply, combined with the building of dams, has done much to mitigate the flood danger on the trunk rivers. In addition, the nine dams on the Tennessee itself have deepened the water in formerly shoal reaches sufficiently to make the river navigable to Knoxville, 650 miles above the confluence with the Ohio. The upper catchment is now linked by water with the Mississippi navigation.

From the outset, the damming programme was multi-purpose: it included hydro-electric generation. This especially has had profound effects on the life of the valley. Nearly all farms are now electrified. Industry has come in – the processing of aluminium, the production of calcium carbide, and, as new-planted forests began to yield, lumbering and woodworking. Phosphate fertilizer produced at Muscle Shoals, Alabama, is with ground limestone applied to farmland. Farmbound industries include grain milling, cheese making, and the production of frozen foods. Industry generally has done so well that it has outrun the supply of hydro-electric power; coal comes by barge, along the improved waterway, to thermal stations.

The cheese industry is significant: it belongs with the restriction of ploughland and with grassing-down to clover, which in turn relate to a marked expansion of dairying and beef-raising. Farming in the Tennessee Valley has been restructured. Simultaneously, with the aid of fertilizers and lime, and of hybrid strains, it has increased its per-acre yield of corn by 600 per cent. Finally, the chains of reservoirs have promoted a recreation industry with one of its main emphases on boating.

A West European might expect that the T.V.A. project would be admired throughout the U.S.A. Not so, however. The Tennessee catchment embraces parts of seven States, for which reason the project was for years assailed as encroaching on States' rights. It is still sometimes attacked on this count, even today. A second consideration is that the project was established under the presidency of Franklin D. Roosevelt, when the country had yet to emerge from the Great Depression. To many of those whom unrestrained capitalism had served so badly, Roosevelt appeared a far-out socialist. The T.V.A. scheme was lumped with his public works projects in general, as being alien to the country's political nature.

Here is one of the central problems of conservation – the interrelationship of Federal, State, and local authorities. The lowest-ranking administrative unit is the county, or some corresponding division, which can be quite small, for example with a population of no more than 50,000. County officers, however, can exert much control and still more influence, particularly over the application of money which is raised in, or matched by, the county itself. Since many administrative offices at all levels – county, State, Federal – are political appointments, it is possible for a county to find itself in determined and effective opposition to State or Federal policy, or to both at once, just as a State governor and/or a State government can oppose the Federal administration. Since conservation policies are evolved, and partly at least financed, at the Federal level, whereas they are practised at the State and county levels, they need to rely heavily on campaigns of education and persuasion. And in so far as they rely on the actions of individual farmers, they need to convert these farmers to a change of practice, often on a wholly voluntary basis. In educational campaigns, the U.S. Bureau of Agriculture has been conspicuous, and conspicuously successful.

Water: Use, Need, and Competition

The water need of soil has been previously encountered in the discussion of the seasonal variation of North American climates. It can be met by irrigation, provided that irrigation water is available. But the water need of soil is likely to be most severe precisely where surface water is chronically deficient. Something like a third of the farm acreage of the U.S.A. is irrigated, although the intensity of irrigation and the degree of dependence on it vary greatly from region to region. Three-quarters or more of water use in States east of the Mississippi is accounted for by industry; west of the river, irrigation claims a similar fraction. The Cordilleran belt and the nearer parts of the Plains contain some 90 per cent of the nation's irrigated farmland: California alone has about a quarter. Similarly, irrigation in Canada is concentrated chiefly on Prairie farms.

Fig. 8:12 shows how irrigation between 1900 and 1950 exerted half the total demand on the national water-supply in the U.S.A.; and although the relative demands of industry and thermal power-stations are expected to increase, a considerable rise in the absolute demand by irrigators is still in prospect. There can of course be no question of irrigating all the potentially irrigable land: there is simply not enough water to go round. Already, groundwater reservoirs in the extreme southwest of the U.S.A. are suffering progressive depletion. Irrigation in some areas has turned the soil uselessly alkaline; in others, it has caused waterlogging. On balance, however, farmland irrigation in the dry regions has done well enough to guarantee its persistence and to enlist the aid of the central governments. The Canadian federal government is involved with irrigation projects on the St Mary, Belly, and Waterton Rivers in Alberta, and on the South Saskatchewan River in Saskatchewan Province (Plate 16). Work on the Assiniboine in Manitoba, also federally aided, is intended mainly for flood control and reclamation.

In their functions as producers of power, hydro-electric stations are non-competitive users of water. The resource is in no way depleted by its passage through the turbines. Perhaps this circumstance helps to explain the lengthy attention often given to hydro-electric power in presentations of North American geography – attention altogether disproportionate to their ranking on the scale of generation. As has already been seen, hydro-electric power accounts for but a minor fraction of the total power generated in the U.S.A. (Fig. 8:6). In Canada, similarly, water power supplies only about 7 per cent of all energy produced. On the other hand, the large dams, power-houses, and lakes of great hydro-electric stations are undoubtedly impressive as engineering works (Plate 17). Many of them illustrate with remarkable directness the influence of environmental locating factors; and the Canadian stations especially are vital to the country's economy, generating about four-fifths of the national output of electric power.

The economics of hydro-electric power generation can be subtle and complex. Like irrigation alone, hydro-electric power generation alone may not be a paying proposition. The multi-purpose character of the installation in the Tennessee Valley has been summarized above. Similarly, the South

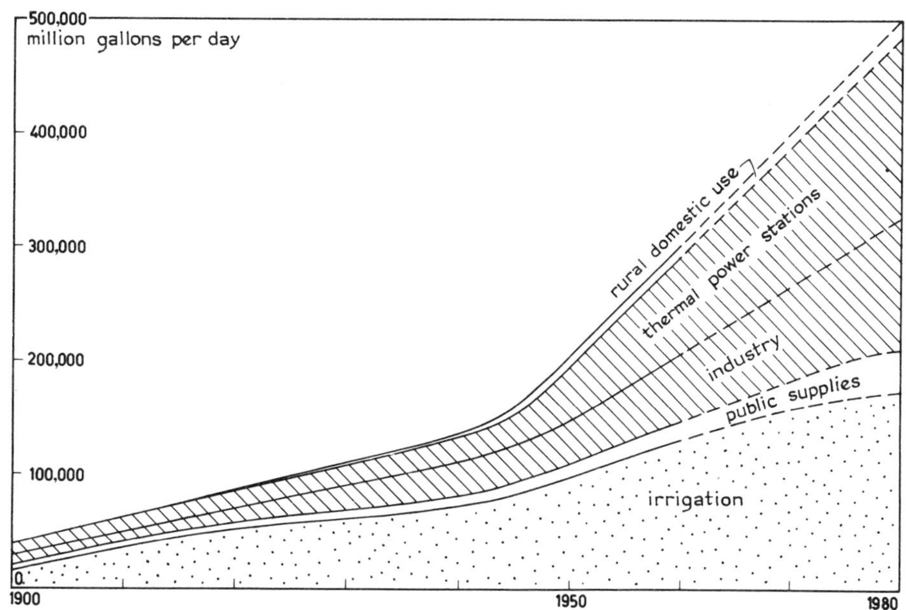

FIG. 8:12 Recorded and projected demands for water in the U.S.A.: generalized.

Saskatchewan Project is designed to provide water for irrigation and for town use, and to improve river control, in addition to developing hydro-electric power – and, incidentally, improving recreational facilities. It follows that the development of hydro-electric power may have the immediate side-effects of increasing demand for water, as on the part of irrigators with their newly-possible supply, and on the part of industries with their newly-available power.

One basic need presses on all hydro-electric schemes: that for copious surface water. The most advantageously-placed areas of the North American continent in this respect are settled eastern Canada, New England, the Appalachians, and the Cordillera in the northern half of its U.S. extent and

16. Irrigation dam and distributary canal system on the St Mary's River in southern Alberta.

17. The Moses–Saunders power dam on the St Lawrence Seaway. Installations include sixteen turbine generators with a total capacity of nearly 2 million kilowatts. The U.S.A.–Canadian border crosses the centre of the dam: the two countries take equal shares in the flow of water.

in the southern portion of British Columbia. Settled eastern Canada and New England are, in respect of regimes of climate and river discharge, best placed of all: for their average rainfall is evenly spread throughout the year, and their average stream discharges are the least variable from season to season. These characteristics are more significant than the broken relief which provides convenient sites for dams and hydro-electric stations, although the descent of east Canadian rivers from the Shield undoubtedly has its great value in practice. About one-third of the hydro-electric power potential in the Appalachian–New England belt has already been developed. On the basis of availability at ordinary minimum flow, turbine capacity in Quebec is almost equal to potential; on the basis of ordinary six-month flow, about half the potential has been developed. Development in Ontario has gone farther still. However, the degree of development quoted for these two provinces cannot be compared with those listed for regions of the U.S.A.; the U.S. figures relate to assessments of all potential, those for Canada to the possibilities of sites which have actually been investigated with a view to development. The hitherto unstudied potential of the eastern Shield cannot fail to be enormous.

Hydro-electric potential in the northern U.S. section of the Cordillera is also great. As yet, no more than 20 per cent has been developed, and the U.S. Cordillera as a whole contains two-thirds of the nation's undeveloped resources. Federally sponsored dams on the Columbia system include the Grand Coulee, Dulles, Chief Joseph, and McNary dams. British Columbia is similarly provided. Its installed turbine capacity equals only 20 per cent of power known to be available at investigated sites. Snow storage among other factors ensures that in British Columbia ordinary minimum flow is almost as great as ordinary six-month flow. The development of power at Kitimat is well known. Among the most recent works are those on the Peace River at Portage Mountain, where the plant is meant for full operational use by 1979.

Competition for water by industrial plants and thermal power-stations is at its most severe in the manufacturing belt. Relatively speaking, these users draw very lightly on public supplies, themselves providing well over 90 per cent of their consumption. Nevertheless, they take about one-third of the water available from utility companies, and in consequence compete against town use. The huge demands of factories and cooling towers would be far greater still were it not for recycling;

and the forecast demands (Fig. 8:12) are frighteningly high. Locations on the Great Lakes seem likely to prove increasingly attractive to heavy industry and to coal-fired power plants. The extent of the danger to town users was well illustrated in the mid-1960s when New York, in consequence of a prolonged sequence of unusually low rainfall, was forced to impose severe restrictions on consumption of public water.

Pollution is also most serious in the manufacturing belt. It affects all the estuaries and lower rivers of the mid-Atlantic coast, but is possibly at its most grave in the Great Lakes. Erie, the shallowest and the most polluted, saw its catch of blue pike practically vanish in the decade 1955–65: the catches of other desirable fish – walleye, whitefish, and lake herring among them – also fell sharply away. The chief pollutants are the phenols and ammonia discharged as industrial waste, which are toxic to fish. Algae, thriving in polluted waters, and above all in those polluted by sewage, deplete the oxygen supply of lake waters and make purification difficult or impossible. The southern end of Lake Michigan is also seriously polluted. Unless conservation is undertaken in time, Lakes Erie, Michigan, and Ontario in that order could readily become unusable as sources of public supply of water; and even as things stand now, they are threatened with the extinction of their best fish.

In western States, and above all in the southern Cordillera, the main competition is that between use of water for irrigation and use in towns and industries. The situation is affected by the political division of the U.S. Cordilleran belt into separate States, none of which is likely to favour the diversion of water outward across its boundaries, and also by the strength of the idea of a drainage-basin as a natural unit. Few early comprehensive plans for the conservation of water and for the development of power and irrigation went beyond the limits of the catchment. Inter-basin transfers are now made, as from Pacific drainage and the Great Basin into the Great Valley of California, or from the Great Basin into the Los Angeles region. But transfers across State boundaries were still unknown as late as 1968. When they do come, as they must, they will probably take the form of reciprocal exchange of water.

Things may be easier on the international level, where there is ample precedent for agreement. Canada and the U.S.A. in 1961 signed the Columbia River Treaty, whereby Canada is to receive half the worth of benefits produced on the U.S. side of the border – benefits of power supply and flood-damage prevention – by the damming of the Columbia on the Canadian side. Although proposals for large-scale international transfer of water meet strong opposition in Canada, this opposition is not universal. One highly ambitious scheme calls for the impounding of rivers throughout the Cordillera in British Columbia, the storage of water in the Rocky Mountain Trench, and its delivery as far south as the border of Mexico and even beyond. Critics generally regard this particular scheme as most unlikely to be realized; but long-distance supply and inter-basin transfer appear certain to increase in the western States, where they are already prominent.

An alternative prospect is that of desalting. Small desalting plants have been successfully producing potable supplies from sea-water for a good many years, but their technical processes are uneconomic in the sense that desalting is more expensive than normal methods of public supply. Intensive research has been going on for some time in the U.S.A., with the aim of bringing the cost of large supplies of desalted water down to near the cost of normal supplies. Nuclear reaction is generally taken as the appropriate power source for desalting. If the process can be made economic in current terms, or alternatively if users of water are prepared to raise their rate of payment sufficiently, the U.S. Southwest will be transformed.

*Air Pollution**

The devastating effects on plant life of fumes emitted by certain smelters have long been recognized: in the main, these are smelters which treat sulphide ores, and which emit fumes of sulphur dioxide and perhaps also of arsenious oxides among their waste gases. Smelting of arsenious copper ores in the Copper Basin of southeast Tennessee completely denuded about forty square miles of country. The Trail smelter in British Columbia, processing lead–zinc sulphides, caused damage in

* This section owes much to the paper by Leighton cited in the Bibliography.

the adjoining State of Washington, where the fumes were carried in the nocturnally-draining cold air of the Columbia Valley. Remedial and control measures applied here included the recovery of sulphur from the waste gases, and control on the timing of gas discharge. In other places, where international issues are not raised, remedy and control have proved less effective or have been absent altogether.

A more general case is that of the large town. Many towns coat their buildings – and their inhabitants – with grime, wherever coal is freely used in industry and in domestic heating. London is a case in point; but its smokeless-fuel regulations, progressively applied to one area after another, rapidly demonstrated that pollution could be much reduced with little difficulty. Pittsburgh, Pennsylvania, before the days of the local clean-air programme, endured what was surely one of the filthiest town atmospheres of the world. Both of these towns exemplify the circumstances which strongly promote pollution of urban air: combustion of smoky fuels, temperature inversion, and pooling.

Temperature inversion – a reversal of the tendency for temperature to decrease with height – inhibits vertical air movement. It prevents polluted air from rising, and thus from being diluted. Inversions can be produced either aloft or near the ground. Those produced aloft are usually associated either with the subsidence of air in a stagnant high-pressure system, or with the overrunning of cold air by warm. Inversions at low levels, which are the more germane to the topic of pollution, are produced by radiational cooling at the surface, as on long winter nights when the sky is clear. Radiational inversions can be strengthened by cold-air drainage, as into the lower parts of the London Basin or the incised valleys of the Monongahela–Allegheny system in the Pittsburgh district. Furthermore, the effects of either type of inversion can be increased, in suitable topographic conditions, by the virtual trapping of air by surrounding high ground. If pooling occurs, and daily outward drainage of air fails to take place, then the effects of pollution can cumulate.

The latest type of pollution to be widely recognized is photochemical pollution. It is most widely known, and most serious, in the U.S.A. – not surprisingly, since it results directly from the emission of noxious substances by motor vehicles and petroleum-processing works. It is an affliction of the automotive age. Photochemical pollutants include nitric oxide, nitrogen dioxide, and hydrocarbons: exposed to sunlight, they undergo chemical changes which produce minute particles capable of reducing visibility, of damaging plants, and of irritating eyes.

Photochemical pollution is popularly called smog, a word probably compounded from smoke and fog. The term seems to have been coined in the Los Angeles Basin, where a reduction of visibility in smog conditions was recorded as early as 1920. Ten years later, the size of locally-grown oranges had seriously diminished: plant damage, the next more serious result of photochemical pollution, had set in, although another ten years elapsed before widespread plant damage was recognized. The third stage of pollution, eye irritation, was reported in 1945. But the nature and origin of smog remained in doubt until 1952, when the main producer of pollutants and irritants was identified as the automobile – the machine to which Los Angeles has made over much of its city structure and practically all of its social movement.

Because automobiles are used principally near to where their owners live – namely, for the most part in great towns – it follows that a large fraction of the population will be exposed to photochemical pollution wherever this occurs. About three-quarters of the people of California live within the range of eye irritation. The whole of the Los Angeles Basin and the San Francisco Bay area lie within the range of plant damage. Reduction of visibility affects about half the State of California. Travellers arriving by air frequently see the smog pouring through passes in the hills into the Great Valley, just as those arriving at New York frequently cross Long Island without being able to see it through the persistent smog blanket.

In this, as in so many other ways, town growth is throwing up unforeseen and urgent difficulties. Although some kind of relief can be expected from controls on the quality of exhaust emissions, it seems unlikely at present that damage to visibility, plant life, and human comfort and health will not continue to increase.

CHAPTER NINE

MANUFACTURING INDUSTRY: CHARACTERISTICS AND LOCATION

Manufacturing takes about a quarter of all workers in paid employment, both in Canada and in the U.S.A. The proportion is slightly the higher in the latter country, where about four people in ten of the manufacturing workforce are employed in metal processing or in the making of products consisting chiefly of metal–machinery, vehicles, aircraft, and instruments (Fig. 9:1). The metals–machinery–vehicles–aircraft groups occupy a similarly dominant position in respect of value added during manufacture and of factory sales value. When petroleum processing, chemical manufacture, paper-making, printing and publishing, the making of textiles and clothing, and the processing of foodstuffs are added, more than 80 per cent of the U.S. manufacturing workforce, total value added during manufacture, and factory sales value is accounted for. The pattern is that of a highly industrialized, highly mechanized, and high-consuming society. If living standard is judged by output and consumption of factory products – as to a considerable extent it is, in Western countries – then this standard in the U.S.A. runs at a high average.

Canadian industry (Fig. 9:2) contains proportionately more primary processing than does that of the U.S.A.; but even so, the metals–machinery–transport equipment groups take a quarter of the total industrial workforce, account for a quarter of the value added by manufacture, and provide a quarter of total sales value. The addition of textile and clothing manufacture and of foodstuffs processing brings the ratio in each case up to about half

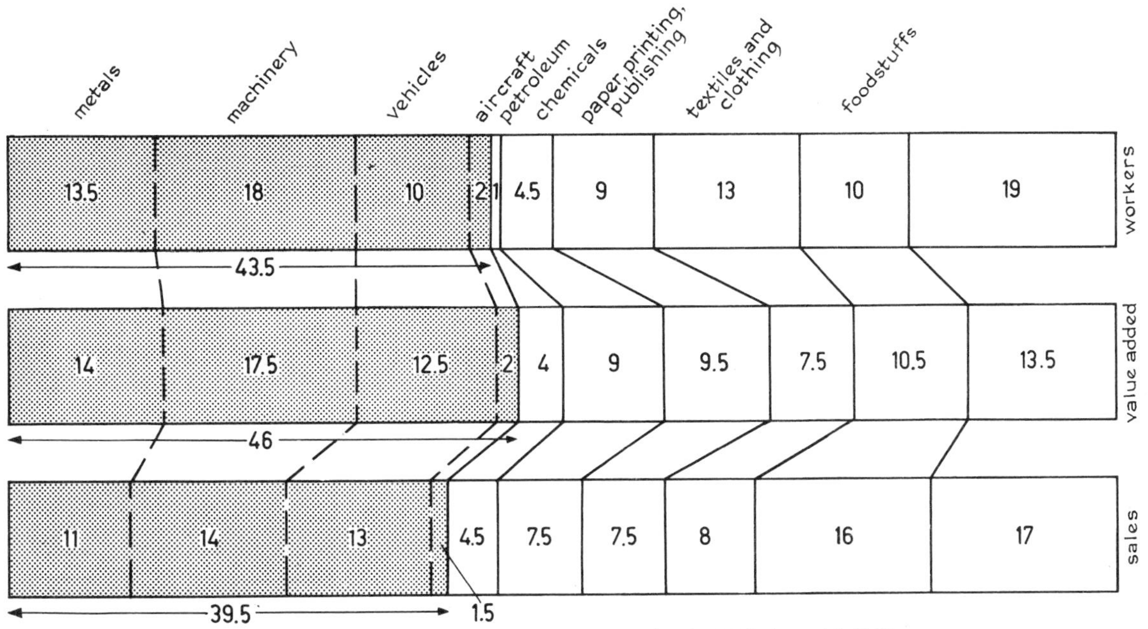

FIG. 9:1 Manufacturing employment in the U.S.A., mid-1960s.

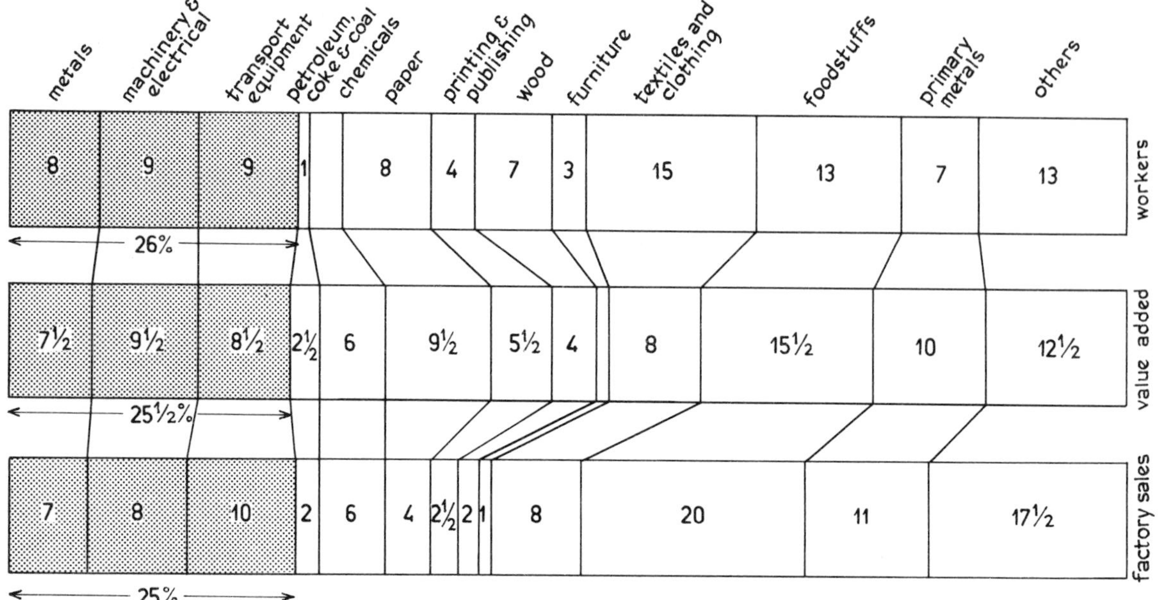

FIG. 9:2 Manufacturing employment in Canada, mid-1960s.

of all manufacturing activity. Furthermore, Canada is the leading single external market for U.S. factory products, paying about one-quarter of the combined export price of machinery, automobiles, textiles, and fabricated iron and steel. In Canada, as in the U.S.A., the consumption of factory-made goods runs at a high level.

Geographers of an altogether different generation, many of them raised in the tradition of determinism, were accustomed – not without wistfulness – to stress the natural advantages which some parts of North America offer to manufacturing industry. The basic assumption was that such industry is materials oriented: that is, that manufactures tend to locate where raw materials are immediately at hand, or at least readily accessible. Such was certainly the situation at Pittsburgh, where the original favourable combination of coal, iron ore, limestone, water-supply, and ease of mining is not to be gainsaid. North American folk-legendry, however, is apt to lay emphasis less on the environment than on the acumen and drive of the entrepreneurs who could perceive and exploit natural advantages – as, in the case of Pittsburgh, Andrew Carnegie. But there is far more to industrial location than raw materials and individual enterprise. A number of additional locating factors have been recognized for a long time.

Market-oriented industries find it more profitable to locate close to their customers than close to their raw materials: an obvious example is the production of office machinery. Labour-oriented industries, such as a great deal of garment manufacture or the conveyor-belt production of light electrical goods, depend heavily on a labour pool. Power-oriented industries, of which aluminium processing is the leading contemporary instance, are controlled in their locational decisions by questions of energy supply.

In the local context, location can readily be affected by transport facilities and the physical properties of factory sites. Waterways, railways, and trunk roads already in existence can attract new industrial plants. Big modern factories, typically requiring a large horizontal spread, need flat open ground at low cost; their preferred locations resemble those of North American suburban shopping centres, which although inevitably market oriented have similar physical requirements of site. Finally, government action at all levels from local to federal can prove either attractive or repulsive to industry.

Even the identification and measurement of this whole series of locating factors is not enough. Decisions to locate, relocate, expand, or contract can also result from the policies and structures developed in a given industrial sector. We come here to a kind of self-correcting (or, at times, self-defeating) mechanism in the industrial economy which is particularly well exemplified in the U.S.A. The notions of private enterprise and free competition, subsumed nowadays under the title *free enterprise*, involve the principles that individual entrepreneurs are at liberty to launch enterprises at their own will, at the risk of themselves and their subscribers, and that competition on the open market will eliminate the least worthy but ensure the survival of the fittest – that is, the most efficient. It is very doubtful, however, that free and open competition of this simple kind ever had a prospect of operating on the processes of natural selection in the industrial context. Where enterprises succeed remarkably well, they are likely to come into actual or potential collision with other equally vigorous concerns. The logical outcome is merger to protect common interests, or, short of merger, agreement on division of the market. Small competitors risk being absorbed or crushed as large corporations expand. At the extreme, however, the government intervenes to prevent the establishment of monopolies: it has done so repeatedly in the U.S.A. under the Anti-Trust Laws. In consequence, the structure of U.S. industry stops short of monopoly, tending strongly, however, towards a state of oligopoly wherein a particular branch of manufacturing is effectively controlled by a few great corporations. Thus, at least 50 per cent and in some cases more than 75 per cent of manufacturing employment and of value of manufacturing output in the respective divisions belong to the four leading U.S. corporations in iron and steel manufacture, aircraft production, tyre manufacture, the making of telephone equipment, computers, and synthetic fibres, and the processing of tobacco. Three companies alone dominate automobile manufacture, where costs of capital investment are such that successful new competitors are scarcely thinkable. As will be seen below, when specific industries are examined, the policy of an oligopoly can strongly influence decisions of manufacturing location and relocation, exemplifying at times the process of industrial inertia, and of inertia deliberately sustained.

Canadian industry is less centrally organized, although it too is increasingly dominated by corporations. These provide more than 90 per cent of total manufacturing employment in the country as a whole, and at least 80 per cent in any given industrial group. Similarly, 2 per cent of Canadian manufacturing establishments by number supply half the total factory sales value of Canadian industry. However, Canadian manufacturing has not yet produced many huge single factories: the largest works average only about 3000 workers each.

The contrast between the two industrial structures in respect of their place in the national societies is well demonstrated by the fact that, whereas the U.S.A. has for many years been implementing anti-trust legislation, the Canadian government as late as 1963 set up the Department of Industry to foster the establishment, growth, efficiency, and improvement of manufacturing. Defence contracts and tariff policy aside, the U.S.A. mainly limits its encouragement to private enterprise to its Small Business Administration, which has helped to reduce the rate of business failure expectable from unregulated competition and from the forcible suppression of minor operators. From 1875, when records begin, until about 1916 the annual failure rate in the U.S.A. varied around 1 per cent of all enterprises. Reduced during World War I, this rate rose to $1\frac{1}{2}$ per cent during the Great Depression, when numbers of large concerns were involved; but since the mid-1950s the rate has stabilized itself at about half the earlier running value. Simultaneously, many large concerns have reacted to anti-trust legislation by effecting mergers with other concerns in quite different lines of business. Attempts to control a particular industry are being supplemented by attempts to control an increasing share of manufacturing production of whatever kind.

Although the notably high average living-standard of North America results in considerable part from the success of manufacturing industry, and although this industry has a long operational history, it is still easy to overlook the fact that the greatest expansion of North American manufacturing is a quite recent development, occurring mainly since the end of World War II. As is shown in a highly generalized manner in Fig. 9:3, the index of industrial production in the U.S.A. was distinctly on the upturn in the late 1920s, but was cut severely back in the depressed early 1930s. Its subsequent

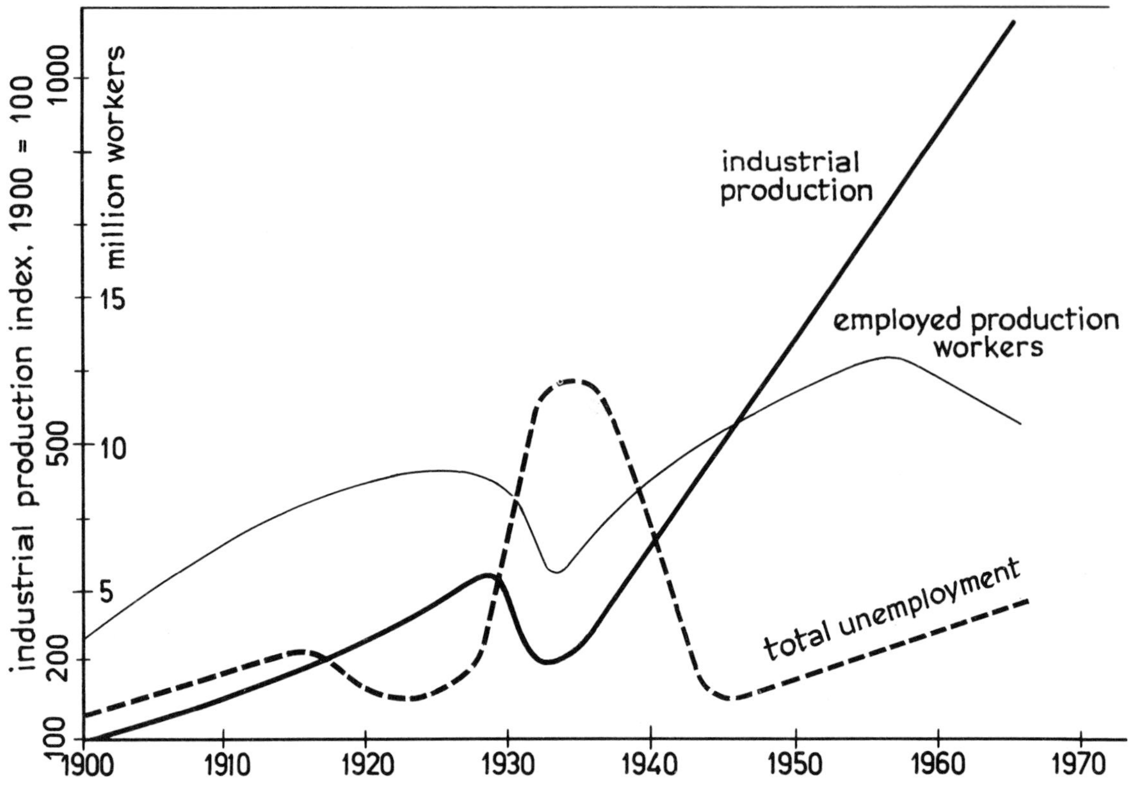

FIG. 9:3 Trends in industrial production, production employment, and unemployment in the U.S.A.: generalized.

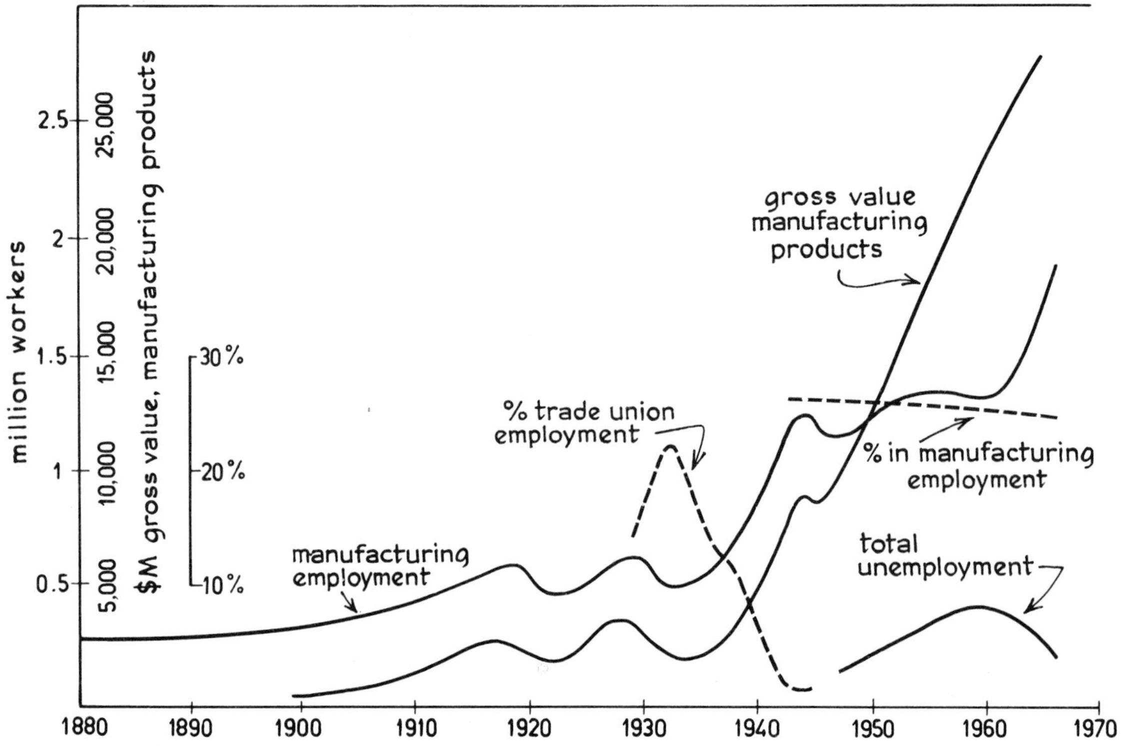

FIG. 9:4 Trends in manufacturing output, manufacturing employment, and unemployment in Canada: generalized.

recovery meant that the earlier peak of output was passed by about 1940, since when a fivefold increase has taken place. And although the criteria available for the measurement of Canadian industrial activity are somewhat different from those available for the U.S.A., it is clear that in Canada too the existing industrial pattern results from the operation of trends closely similar to those observable in the U.S.A. In Canada also, the industrial take-off point, judged by gross value of manufacturing products, came in the mid-1930s, during the economic recovery from the Great Depression; and in Canada, as in the U.S.A., manufacturing output now runs at about five times its level of the late 1920s and late 1930s.

Manufacturing employment, however, has not risen as fast as manufacturing output. Indeed, the absolute total of production workers in the U.S.A. has been on the decline since the mid-1950s (Fig. 9:3). In both countries the ratio of manufacturing employment to manufacturing output has fallen strongly away since the mid-1940s (Figs. 9:3, 9:4). Total unemployment in both countries was very high in the depressed early 1930s, and in the U.S.A. has increased steadily since the mid-1940s. There is no reason to suppose that Canada will escape the effects of ever-increasing mechanization and automation of manufacturing, such as are making themselves progressively felt in the U.S.A., even though for the time being its industrial demands for labour runs high and its level of total unemployment is low. It is ironical that industrial success, secured by mechanized efficiency, should produce increasing volumes of goods while at the same time reducing job opportunities. The situation wherein output can rise while employment falls is well illustrated by Fig. 9:5; this diagram shows how productivity per production worker in the U.S.A., varying little between 1900 and 1920 and cut back during the depression when large numbers were under-employed and when investment and re-equipping were halted, rose powerfully between 1935 and 1955, and then launched into a further interval of still more rapid increase. As with agriculture, so with industry – techniques of production tend wherever possible to eliminate human beings in favour of machines.

The general comments about industrial location which have been offered above will now be amplified with respect to particular industries.

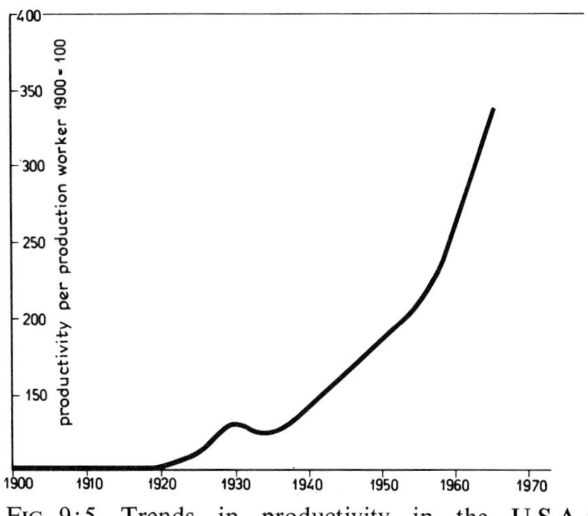

FIG. 9:5 Trends in productivity in the U.S.A.: generalized.

Cotton Textile Manufacture in the U.S.A.

As it first developed, cotton textile manufacture in the U.S.A. was in considerable part power oriented. It located itself in New England, where the first spinning mill was built in 1790; the multiplying factories used the water-power of the dependable New England streams, being located at some or other of the numerous breaks of profile on the low plateau which backs the coast. In the beginning the domestic industry faced strong competition from the British mills in Lancashire, but the war of 1812, interrupting foreign trade, secured for the New England mills high prices for finished cloth while prices of raw cotton from the U.S. South remained low. It would be unjust to neglect the influence of New England entrepreneurs, who appreciated and realized the possibilities of the industrial situation; but it would be equally improper to overlook the protective and encouraging effect of the cotton tariff measures of 1816, which did much to promote the growth of the U.S. textile industry and to prevent the recapture of the market by British makers.

From about 1800 to about 1880 the total of spindles in cotton mills in the U.S.A. doubled every seven years. At the beginning of this period there were 3000: at the end there were eight million. Three-quarters of the two million spindles of the early 1860s were in New England, where mass-

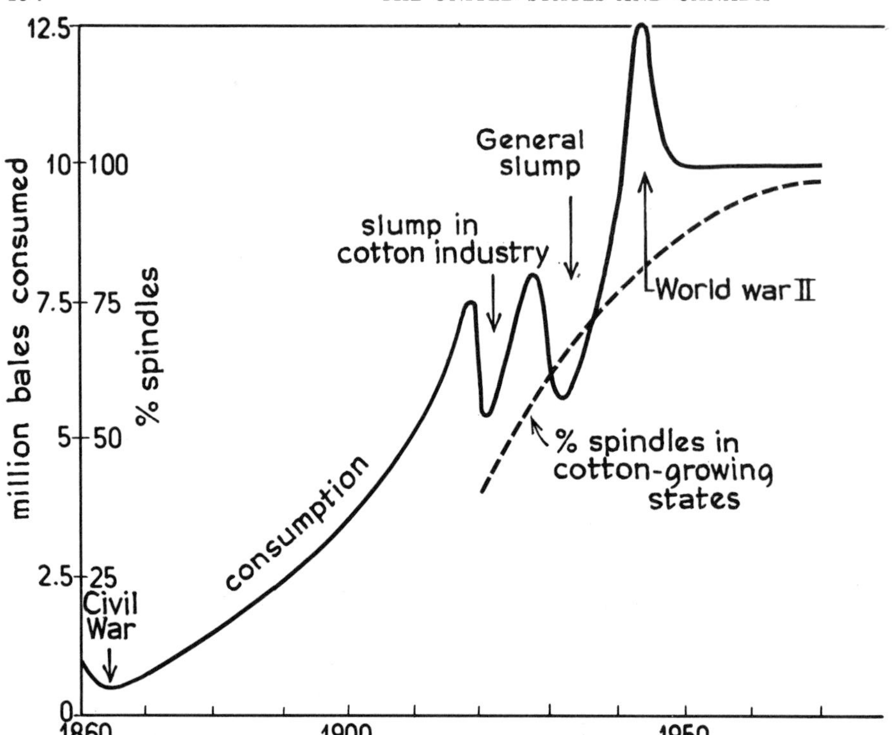

FIG. 9:6
Trends in the U.S. cotton textile industry: generalized.

production of standardized goods was already in progress, and where integration of spinning and weaving, already begun, was to be effectively completed by the end of the century. However, the New England mills were already open to, even if they did not perceive, the threat of competition of milling in the cotton-growing States. The tally of spindles in the South outran that of New England in the 1920s, and almost all spinning today is located in the Southern States (Fig. 9:6). This major industrial relocation is less a matter of reorientation to raw materials from power, capital, and enterprise than a shift from a high-wage to a low-wage area – even though the wage disparity is partly offset by a differential of productivity – and a shift to areas where labour legislation, tax rates, industrial promotion, and eventually power supply (from the T.V.A. and the Fall Zone) are more encouraging than they are in New England. The New England cotton industry has in addition been criticized for its undue conservatism, which at times has stood it in bad stead on the competitive market.

Finishing trades in the cotton textile industry still remain concentrated in New England and the mid-Atlantic coastland, while the great markets for cotton cloth are still held by New York City and Boston. This situation may well persist, since the industry requires large centralized outlets but remains less concentrated than most in respect of manufacturing location.

The output trend of the cotton textile industry has proved partly responsive to manufacturing trends in general, and partly independent. Thus (Fig. 9:6), this industry produced a slump of its own in 1920, in advance of the Great Depression of the early 1930s; and it expanded markedly, in common with most other industries, during World War II, before attaining what promises to be a state of absolute stability. That is to say, in comparison with expansive industries, it is relatively on the decline.

The Iron and Steel Industry

Iron and steel production give a rough index of total industrial output; the best single indicator is possibly the production of crude steel. Iron was replaced by steel as an industrial material fairly early in the history of modern technology. Most of the pig-iron produced today is intended for steel furnaces, while the casting of pig can be effectively by-passed by the use of steel scrap, and actually by-passed by the direct conversion into steel of blast-furnace melt (Plates 18, 19, 20, 21).

Steel production in the U.S.A. was of the order of ten million tons a year in 1900 (Fig. 9:7). Up to that time it had been increasing, but not especially fast. At about the turn of the century, however, a very marked rise in output set in, taking production to about fifty million tons a year in the late 1950s. Two changes in emphasis had occurred by about 1910: steel output had overtaken the output of pig-iron, in response to the falling demand for finished iron goods and to the increasing use of scrap; and open-hearth furnaces – in which the use of scrap offers few problems – had overtaken the output of Bessemer converters.

The Great Depression cut steel production back. Its slow recovery needed ten years to regain the earlier peak of output. But the demands of World War II and of the post-war years of re-equipping and restoration promoted a new rise, steeper than anything previously recorded. Interrupted briefly by a sharp but short-lived depression in the 1950s, this rise is once again under way. Steel production in the U.S.A. is now well over ten times as great as it was in 1900 when the rapid increase began.

In the U.S.A., as in Britain, a heavy demand was exerted on the steel industry in its early days by the expanding railways: in fact, the demand in the U.S.A. was especially heavy, since steel instead of wood was widely used there in the making of rolling-stock. The steel-consuming railways, opening up the potential grainfields of the Plains, and making possible the commercialization of mid-Western farming, contributed eventually to the demand for harvesting machinery with its own call on the products of steelworks. Today, however, the great steel consumers are, in order, the automobile industry (discussed separately below), construction, the container industry, and the machinery and appliance industries, which among them take 60 per cent of domestic shipments of steel in the U.S.A., even when no allowance is made for the eventual destination of the 17 per cent which goes to warehouses and distributors.

Until about 1950 the U.S. steel industry depended negligibly upon imported ore. The local ores of the Pittsburgh district, characteristically being exhausted far in advance of the associated coal seams,

18. Opencast mining of iron ore at Steep Rock, Ontario.

19. Grab taking 15-ton bites at iron ore in transit: Gary, Indiana.

20. Blast furnaces at the River Rouge automobile plant, Dearborn, Michigan: storage bins for coal and limestone in the foreground.

21. Pouring molten steel into ingot moulds.

were supplanted by hematite from the Superior iron-fields which for a long time provided 80 per cent or more of total domestic ore production. The ore occurs in long outcrops pinched down into the southern margin of the Shield. Open-cast working, and an iron content averaging 60 per cent or more, kept production costs down. In consequence, the established smelters of the Pittsburgh district could afford to ship ore along the Lakes and to rail it from ports on Lake Erie such as Cleveland and Toledo. Lake steamers of tanker-like build came, like bulk grainships, into service. Return cargoes of coal and coke aided the rise of ferrous-metal industry along the traffic route, notably at Gary: Detroit, on the same route, is a special case, as will be seen presently.

Ore reserves are not however inexhaustible. Continuing exploitation has so depleted the reserves of hematite in the Superior fields that most workings have passed their peak output, and production from these fields as a group is on the decline (Fig. 9:7). Hematite ore grades at depth into taconite, a mineral with an iron content of about 25 per cent and with a pronounced content of silica. This ore is unsuitable for blasting in the natural state. It can be made suitable by pulverising, concentration, and

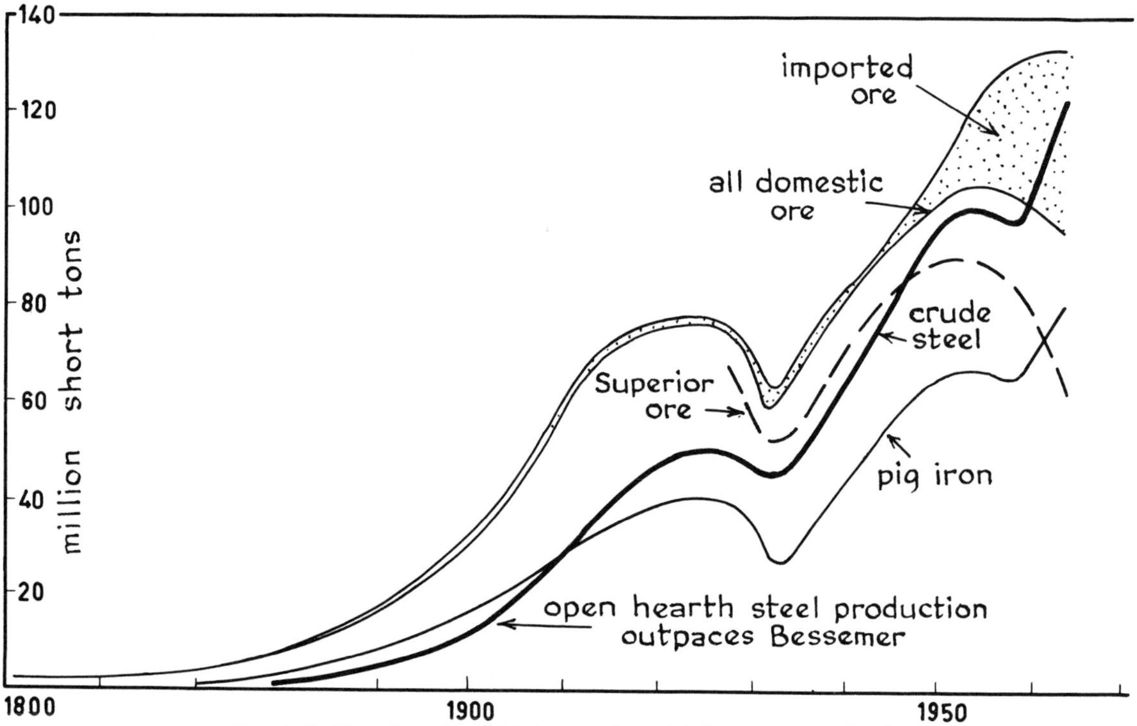

140
120
100
80
60
40
20
million short tons
imported ore
all domestic ore
crude steel
Superior ore
pig iron
open hearth steel production outpaces Bessemer
1800
1900
1950

FIG. 9:7 Trends in the U.S. iron and steel industry: generalized.

agglomeration, but the capital costs of these processes are high. Taconite processing has in actuality been established, but seems unlikely altogether to offset the decline in ore production by the Superior fields. The U.S. consumers have turned progressively to external suppliers: imports now provide a third or more of all ore consumed. The chief suppliers are Canada and South American countries with high-grade reserves in Shield areas, comparable geologically to the hematites of the Superior fields. Canadian reserves appear adequate for the predictable future. If the U.S.A. needs to look still farther abroad, it will presumably turn to Australia, where ores also occur abundantly in a Shield setting, although it would need to compete for this source of supply with smelters in Japan.

The steel industry of the U.S.A. was highly competitive until the very end of the nineteenth century, when in three brief years there occurred a rapid movement of concentration. The U.S. Steel Corporation, formed in 1901, controlled at the time two-thirds of the nation's capacity of steel production. It was able to assume price leadership over the whole industry. One of its fundamental practices, and one which cannot have failed to influence the location of steel-making, was the establishment of basing-point pricing. Such pricing ensures uniform delivery price to a consumer, regardless of where the steel is actually produced. Up to 1924 the single basing point was Pittsburgh; accordingly, Pittsburgh steel could compete anywhere in the country on equal monetary terms with steel from any other producing centre. When the single basing-point system was proscribed by the government in 1924, a multiple basing-point point system was substituted, delivery prices being regulated by the costs relevant to the nearest basing point. The effects of the basing-point system were two: to conserve the interests of established major producers – Pittsburgh to begin with, and then also Chicago and Baltimore – and to concentrate consumers near basing points while newly-entering producers were dispersed into poor locations. The multiple basing-point system was banned in 1948, but price leadership continues. Price stability, achieved by price leadership, is criticized by some as meaning price rigidity; and it cannot be denied that steel prices have risen steadily, regardless of general economic trends.

The U.S. Steel Corporation won a legal fight against dissolution as a monopoly in 1920. Since that time it has tended to take a progressively smaller proportionate share in total steel production, although this Corporation and Bethlehem Steel between them controlled in the 1960s about half of all pig-iron capacity, more than 40 per cent of total steel ingot capacity, and more than 40 per cent also of hot-rolled steel capacity. The twelve largest companies in the industry controlled 80 per cent or more of the industry's capacity for producing pig-iron, ingots, and hot-rolled steel; they also owned more than 80 per cent of domestic iron ore reserves. Some of them have been strongly criticized for conservatism and lack of efficiency: their challengers claim that the corporations are simply too big and too centralized to work at their best. Meanwhile, they are tending to increase their degree of vertical integration. The horizontal integration which produced the great smelting and milling corporations is being followed by vertical integration of steel producers into fabrication, and of steel consumers into steel producers. Significantly in this connection, steel companies are increasingly committed by supply contracts for automobile manufacturers.

The iron and steel industry of the U.S.A. cannot then be treated in isolation, quite apart from its general connection with economic advance. And its location cannot be wholly interpreted in terms of locational factors, since locational decisions – including above all those of the great corporations – also come into play. The greatest single concentration of steel manufacturing is in Chicago–Gary, with about a fifth of the total national capacity: markets and cheap transport can be regarded as more influential than immediate access to raw materials. Birmingham, Alabama, is superlatively well placed with regard to raw materials, but its modest role in U.S. steel production demonstrates that far more is involved than materials orientation: parallel but lesser examples are the steelworks of Geneva, Utah, and Pueblo, Colorado, which depend on local ore. About 10 per cent of the national total of steel capacity is located on the Atlantic seaboard, mainly at Baltimore. About a third is located on the Great Lakes, mainly in Chicago–Gary; and it can be argued that a powerful locating factor for this group is water-supply. Another third remains in the Pittsburgh district, where disinvestment costs and corporation policy have combined to promote and to enforce the processes of industrial inertia, in ways partly outlined above.

Steel-making in Canada is concentrated on the Lakeside, where Hamilton and Sault St Marie produce more than 80 per cent of the pig-iron and crude steel made in the whole country. In terms of location, these two places are comparable respectively with Cleveland and Detroit.

Automobile Manufacture

Although road vehicles powered by steam, petrol, or diesel oil were first developed in Europe, they have become more highly significant to North American economy and society than to the economy and society of any other part of the world. The history of automobile manufacturing in the U.S.A. contains events which epitomize the development of the national manufacturing economy. Private enterprise, hugely successful when judged in terms of industrial growth and productivity, has been combined at times with management–labour relations of the worst sort. The few great corporations which control almost the whole industry rely on mass-production and on rapid wastage of their products in the hands of the consumers. Strenuous and continuous efforts are made by the producers to expand the total market, and to secure for themselves increased individual shares. On the social side must be recognized not only the fact that the private car has long been an essential means of transport in the U.S.A., but also the additional fact that it has strong associations both of prestige and of emotion. To what extent its emotive associations result from successful advertising or from a general enthusiasm for machinery would be difficult to judge.

European automobiles were being imported into the U.S.A. by 1893. Domestic experimenters and inventors, vigorously competing one with the other, enjoyed a rapidly expanding market in the decade 1900–10. The unsuccessful were many: failure rate was high in the incipient automobile industry, which being operated on an assembly basis could be readily entered with little capital. An early attempt at monopoly control in 1903 excluded Henry Ford, who, partly in reaction but also with impressive foresight, set out to create and control a mass market by means of the single and justly famous Model T. When General Motors was formed in 1909, with the aim of protecting its individual members from the worst blows of a still-insecure industry, Ford was able to resist takeover. By 1914 he had conveyor-belt assembly in operation. Mass-production and interchangeable parts allowed him to reduce the price of the Model T by about two-thirds in seven years, and by 1921 he had captured half the national market.

The General Motors Corporation meanwhile had been running into difficulties, spreading itself too far and too fast under unwise leadership. Restored to stability under the guidance of a member of the du Pont family, it emerged in the 1920s first as a serious competitor with Fords and then as the leader of the industry. Fords, responding to the growing competition, introduced in the late 1920s the Model A; but 1930 was the last year in which Ford was the leading producer. By this time, too, another strong contender was in the field – the Chrysler Corporation, founded in 1925, which despite the introduction by Ford of a third standardized vehicle, the V8 of 1932, was able briefly to capture second place in the industry in the late 1930s. Currently the shares of the market taken by the three corporations are 45 to 50 per cent for General Motors, about 25 per cent for Fords, and 10 to 15 per cent for Chrysler.

Fig. 9:8 presents in generalized form some of the recorded trends of the U.S. automobile industry as a whole. The vertical scale of numbers of vehicles is made logarithmic in order to bring out the tendencies towards a steady rate of increase which factory sales and vehicle registrations have been exhibiting since about 1930. The greatest *proportionate* rates of increase in output and ownership operated before the mid-1920s, bringing factory sales rapidly upward to some four million vehicles a year, and registrations up to twenty million. The ratio of cars to population simultaneously rose, from about 1 car to 200 people in 1910 to 1 car to 10 people in 1920, and 1 car to 5 people in 1930. By the mid-1960s there were two private cars running for every five people in the country, regardless of age. Current output is of the order of eight million cars and one million other road vehicles a year, while more than seventy million cars are registered. As shown in the diagram, the number of registra-

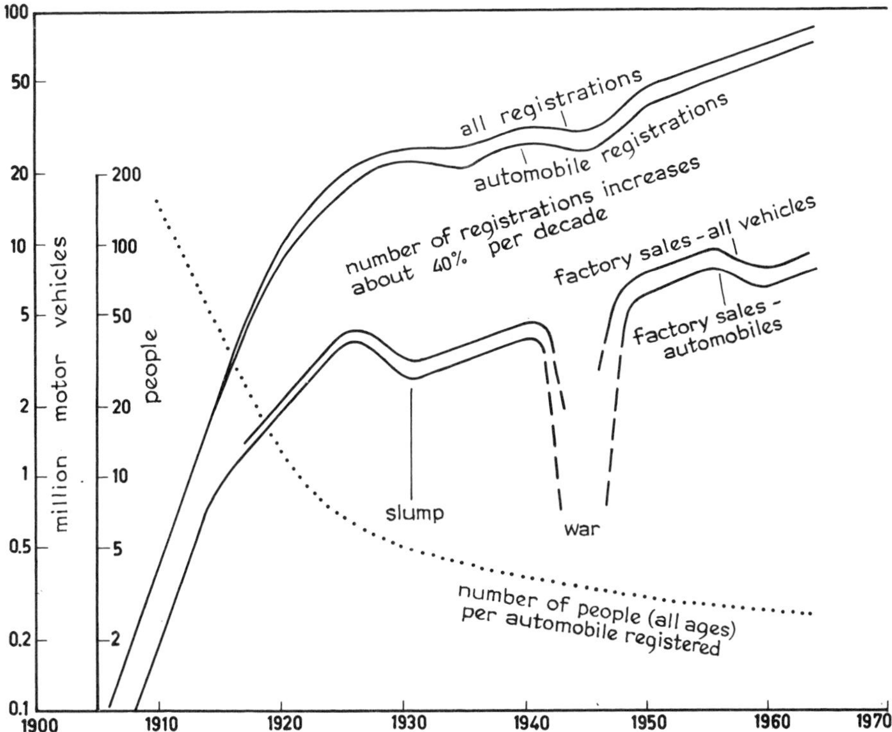

FIG. 9:8 Trends in automobile production and use in the U.S.A.: generalized.

tions tends to increase about 40 per cent per decade: it is this increase which, on certain conditions, promises the automobile industry an equally expanding market.

Among these conditions, the chief is that the useful life of a car should be limited – limited less by wear than by a change of fashion. The U.S. automobile industry in its marketing campaigns relies heavily on changes in styling. Price competition within an individual class (e.g. medium-priced family car) is negligible. Much depends on external appearances. But since a marked change in fashion of styling is apt to spread rapidly through the whole industry, the competition of style is to a considerable extent that of a later model against an earlier model of the same make. The dealer and trade-in systems make it economical for some owners to take a new car every year. In addition, the industry has been highly successful in promoting the idea that two or more cars per family are necessaries – as to many families they have come to be. The average working life of cars has, however, not changed greatly since about 1930. As the diagram shows, the number of cars registered is about nine times the number annually produced, giving a mean working life of nine years. Future development of the industry may then depend on increase of population and increase of multiple ownership, rather than on more intensified use of single vehicles. Similar but slightly less pronounced effects may be observed in Canada, where, with two cars registered for every seven people, the average working life is ten years.

Trade-in and resale increase the advantages of already popular makes, since these are easy to place on the used-car market and will normally fetch better prices, year for year, than similar models from a different manufacturer. In this respect the absence of price competition among new models is offset. Chevrolet, General Motors' best-seller of all North American cars, does notably well in this regard. However, to the extent that they involve the establishment and operation of very large plants, very high sales of particular models or brands of car have attracted criticism from a number of economists. Some of these estimate the best efficient size for an automobile plant at a capacity of 300,000 to 600,000 vehicles a year. While this capacity, representing for a new entrant to the automobile industry an investment of anything from

$500m to $1000m, is large enough to discourage almost all competition with the Big Three corporations, it is much smaller than the capacity of the largest existing plants. Outstanding among these is the Ford Company's River Rouge works in Detroit, the largest single factory in the continent, where processes are fully integrated from smelting to finished production. Perhaps it is the diseconomies of over-large scale which are now producing some dispersion of the automobile industry.

Until about 1950, automobile manufacture was largely concentrated in Detroit. The town has great economic advantages in the cheap water transport of coal, coke, ore, and limestone; it is fairly centrally situated in the manufacturing belt, and has proved capable of attracting the necessary labour force. But the fundamental locating factor for the Detroit industry appears to have been the personal decision of Henry Ford, whose nearest town Detroit was. The subsequent establishment in the same place of General Motors and Chrysler illustrates the agglomerative propensity of manufacturing industry: there are economic advantages in locating close to one's competitors. Since the mid-century, however, a movement of decentralization has made itself felt in the autombile industry. One of the earlier-founded outposts is Flint, Michigan, about sixty miles from Detroit; but Los Angeles, Kansas City, St Louis, Milwaukee, Chicago, Gary, Cleveland, Buffalo, New York, and Philadelphia have all now developed as considerable manufacturers of motor vehicles. The State of Michigan provides less than half the nation's employment in the automobile industry, and suppliers of machinery and parts are scattered throughout the manufacturing belt.

As noted in the foregoing section, the automobile industry is the leading consumer of steel in the U.S.A. It takes about a fifth of all domestic steel shipments. Since about 1920, except when the production of cars was almost brought to a stop during World War II, there has been a close connection between output of automobiles and output of crude steel (Fig. 9:9), making it possible to regard the condition and output level of the automobile industry as indicators of the state of manufacturing in general. But the automobile industry is probably more sensitive than most to market demand, which is far more flexible here than it is in general. Annual changes of styling mean that

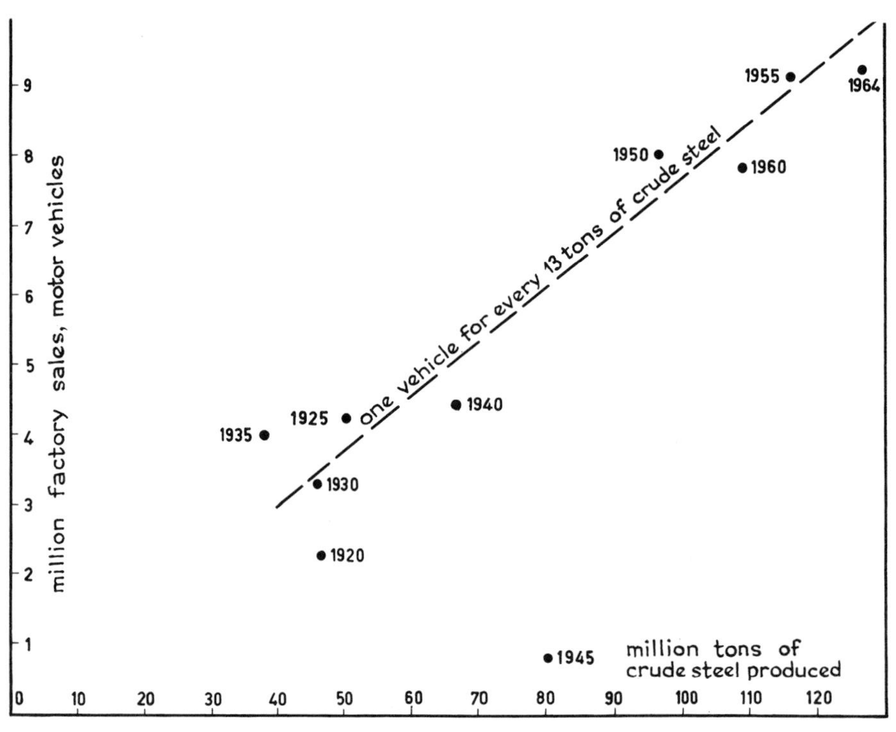

FIG. 9:9
Comparison of auto production and steel production in the U.S.A.

demand and production must be forecast annually, and the retooling must be undertaken and risks renewed on an annual basis. Partly by way of response to the persistent uncertainty of the domestic market situation, and partly in the normal sequence of expansion to which they are committed, the big automobile corporations have followed their export campaigns by the establishment of works abroad, and then by the takeover of foreign manufacturers on their home ground. Takeovers in Britain have been especially remarkable in the 1960s, while parts of the automobile industry of Canada, Australia, France, and West Germany are also controlled from the U.S.A. Almost all the Canadian production of automobiles comes from the province of Ontario, where Windsor, Hamilton, and the lesser towns of Oshawa, Brampton, and Oakville contain subsidiary plants of U.S. firms, either founded by the parent companies or absorbed by them.

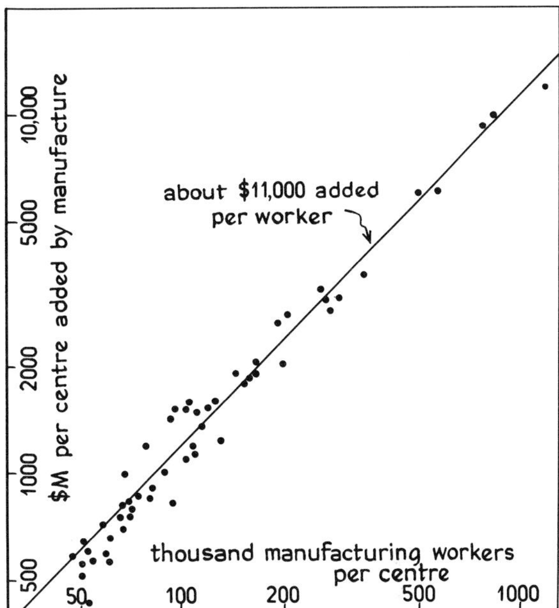

FIG. 9:10 Relationship of value added by manufacture to manufacturing employment: U.S.A., mid-1960s.

The Manufacturing Belt

This is not the place for a discussion of the shortcomings of the now old-fashioned regional names – Corn Belt, Cotton Belt, Ranching Belt, and the like. It might seem at first sight that the use of *Manufacturing Belt* is equally defective: but analyses of manufacturing capacity and activity do in fact confirm the validity of the concept involved, to the extent that capacity and activity are strongly concentrated in an area stretching from Boston–New York–Baltimore in the east to Milwaukee and St Louis in the west (Fig. 9:11). As traditionally defined, and as redefined by specific research, the northern boundary of the Manufacturing Belt encloses the Mohawk Valley, includes Toronto and Hamilton on the Canadian side of Lake Erie, and takes in Detroit and Grand Rapids in Michigan. The southern boundary is sometimes made to leave Baltimore outside the Belt, but includes Cincinnati. Rather than a line, the boundary is in the usual way a threshold across which characteristics change: in this instance, intensity of manufacturing activity falls rapidly away in the outward direction.

Three obvious criteria are available for the measurement of manufacturing: volume of manufacturing employment, value added by manufacture, and value of factory shipments. Of these, the first two are the most commonly used. They can, in fact, be taken for the present purpose as essentially interchangeable, despite the effects produced by automation: as Fig. 9:10 shows, there is a close connection between the two sets of data for the range of manufacturing centres which, in the mid-1960s, had 50,000 or more production workers and where the value added by manufacture ran at $500m a year or more. The graph is plotted on a double-logarithmic scale, merely in order to spread the cloud of points at the lower end: as is indicated, the relationship between employment and value added tends strongly to be linear, throughout the range illustrated.

Fig. 9:11 uses the combined criteria of manufacturing employment and of value added by manufacture to identify and locate the chief manufacturing centres: these, fifty-four in number, carry on 60 per cent of all manufacturing in the two countries combined. The activity actually mapped for the Manufacturing Belt amounts to half of the recorded total: when lesser centres are also allowed for, the Manufacturing Belt claims more than two-thirds of all manufacturing.

This is, however, not an integral region: and the particular concentrations of industry within it can be viewed in a number of ways. For instance, New England conducts about 10 per cent of all manufacturing activity, while New York, Philadelphia, Baltimore, and their neighbours conduct 25 per cent, giving the Atlantic seaboard about a third of the combined Canadian–U.S. total. The New York metropolitan area alone has 10 per cent; an additional 5 per cent share goes to seaboard towns in New Jersey, giving 15 per cent to the New York–New Jersey metropolitan complex. This fraction is closely similar to that commanded by the axial group of steel and automobile producers which extends from Pittsburgh to Grand Rapids and includes Cleveland and Detroit. The metropolitan areas of Chicago and of East Chicago–Hammond–Gary claim a 10 per cent share, equal to that of New York. Centres with Lakeside situations, from Milwaukee in the west to Toronto and Buffalo in the east, combine to account for 25 per cent of all manufacturing activity. Although this series includes Detroit, Toledo, and Cleveland, which have already figured in another grouping, and although it cannot be regarded as constituting a single array, its proportionate significance in North American industry is nevertheless striking. The Lakeside belt is equal in manufacturing importance to the mid-Atlantic seaboard.

It would be simple enough to summarize the growth of industry for each of the various grouping of centres which can be recognized within the Manufacturing Belt: partial accounts have already been given for cotton manufacturing in New England, and for the production of steel and automobiles. The immediate intention at this juncture, however, is to stress the self-sustaining and self-generating qualities of manufacturing industry. Economic and technical considerations which cause industry to be agglomerative have been mentioned earlier. But industrial agglomerations mean high densities of population, and it is a truism that the level of manufacturing activity in a large town or in an area is usually closely related to size of population. Factories provide employment, people supply the workforce: and factories and people join in providing the custom on which factory sales depend. As a market area, the Manufacturing Belt exerts a very powerful total demand for factory-made goods, conducting as it does two-thirds of all manufacturing activity, and containing between one-third and one-half of the combined national populations of Canada and the U.S.A.

Fig. 9:11 indicates accessibility to the combined national markets, in terms of comparison with New York City, the assumed centre. On a percentage scale, the accessibility of New York itself is 100. Areas of low accessibility rank on this scale at sixty or below, i.e., 40 per cent or more below New York. Areas of intermediate accessibility range between 60 per cent and 75 per cent, while the area of high accessibility is everywhere at least 75 per cent as accessible to the market as New York itself. On the northern side, the limit of high accessibility coincides almost precisely with the limit of the Manufacturing Belt: on the southern side, the two follow generally similar east–west trends at a distance apart of 50 to 100 miles. The broad resemblance between the high-accessibility area and the Manufacturing Belt is impressive.

No account is being taken here of the passage through the Manufacturing Belt of part of the international boundary. Some complications are bound to arise from this circumstance: but on the grounds that the two industrial economies have developed similarly on the two sides, and that they are linked in respect of functions and markets, the omission is perhaps not serious. It could nevertheless be argued that the single-focus model, with New York at the centre of accessibility, is too simple. Particularly is this so, since the centre of national population for the conterminous U.S.A. is not far from St Louis. The concept of a centre of population may be a little abstruse, and is certainly of limited geographical value. However, it is at least interesting to observe that the shift of this centre has traced a line very close to the southern limit of the Manufacturing Belt. In 1800 the centre of population was close to Baltimore; a movement almost due westward brought it by 1880 to the outskirts of Cincinnati, and it is now not far from St Louis which lies almost directly in the path of movement. It can be assumed, accordingly, that the Manufacturing Belt, with the partial exception of New England, has throughout its industrial development commanded ready access to the market, in so far as this is defined simply by numbers and location of people.

The information supplied in Fig. 9:11 serves to re-emphasize the inadequacy of treating industrial location primarily in terms of materials orientation. Birmingham, Alabama, placed as well as Pittsburgh in respect of physical environment and natural resources, remains well down the ranking scale of steel producers: it is even surpassed in respect of total manufacturing activity by Atlanta, Georgia, whose main advantage seems to be a rapidly increasing metropolitan population. This is not to say that materials-oriented industries do not exist. Meat packing is concentrated mainly on the edge of the Plains and in the U.S. Midwest, being located with reference not to other industries but to the supply of fat livestock. Flour milling is located mainly on the Plains, in the Twin Cities and St Louis areas, and along the grain routes of the lower Lakes and the St Lawrence. Leather working and furniture making are in part conducted well outside the Manufacturing Belt. Lumber milling and the production of pulp and paper in Canada are considerably dispersed, being controlled in their location by the combination of supply of raw materials and supply of power. It is as it were accidental that some of the activities of the relevant industries are carried on within the Manufacturing Belt. All these materials-oriented industries, however, are wholly or largely concerned with primary processing. In secondary manufacture the Manufacturing Belt remains supreme, despite the shift of the cotton textile industry and the incipient dispersion of the automobile industry. The Belt takes a very large share indeed in the production of machinery of all kinds, including that of electrical machinery, machine tools, office machinery, and household appliances. The numerous factories concerned with the production of machines are invariably accompanied by hosts of ancillary suppliers.

Possibly the gravest defect in the identification of the Manufacturing Belt in the Northeast is that it relegates west-coast industries to remoteness from the national market. In actuality, the west coast is on the way to developing an independent market of its own, and in some respects is a continental leader. Vancouver, not yet great enough industrially to appear in Fig. 9:11, is nevertheless the fourth-ranking industrial town of Canada. Portland, Seattle, San Francisco, San José, and San Diego are

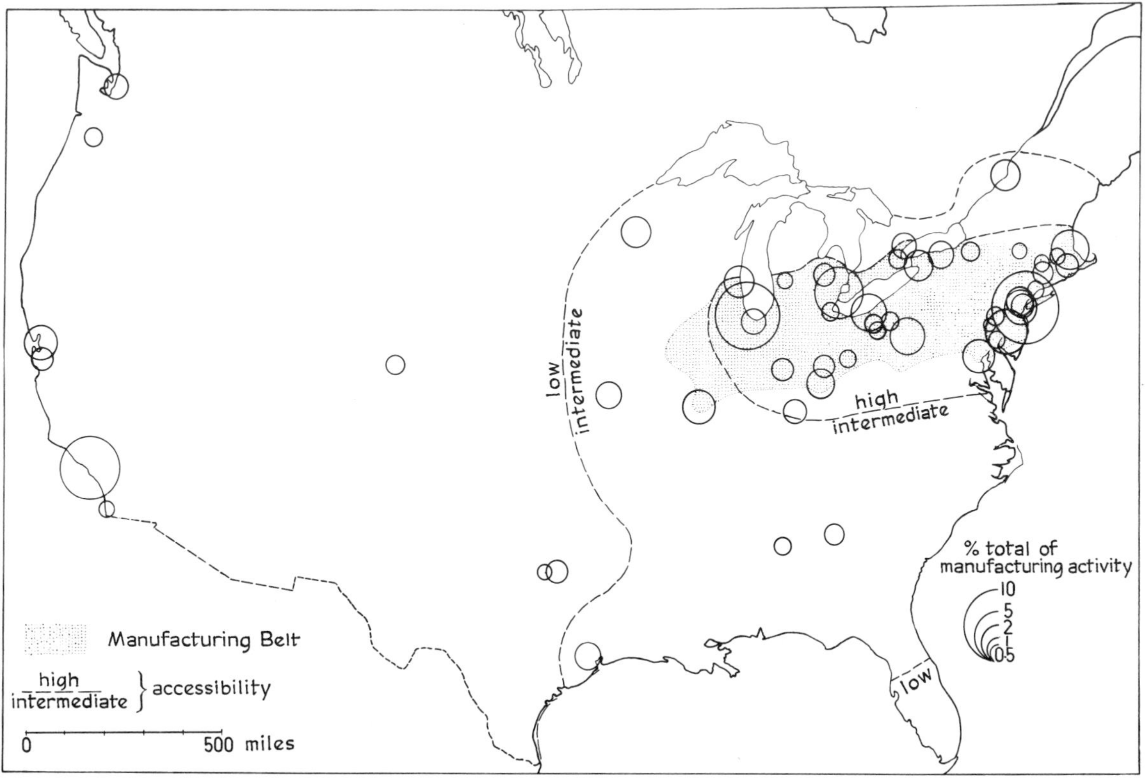

FIG. 9:11 Distribution of manufacturing activity, expressed as percentage of combined U.S.–Canadian total. Manufacturing belt and accessibility limits adapted from Harris and Pred.

all far exceeded as manufacturing centres by the Los Angeles–Long Beach metropolitan area, which with 8 per cent of all manufacturing activity ranks third in the list after metropolitan New York and Chicago–Gary. The west-coast towns as a group conduct between 10 and 15 per cent of all manufacturing activity, being comparable in this regard to the Pittsburgh–Cleveland–Detroit series, or to New York–New Jersey. Los Angeles–Long Beach, with considerable commitments also in the automobile and machinery industries, is the leading centre in the continent for the production of aircraft and aircraft parts. Unlike the manufacture of aero-engines and electronic equipment, which remains substantially within the Manufacturing Belt, the work of aircraft assembly is in the main semi-skilled. Labour supply, if labour is to be had at all, accordingly presents no great problem. The locating factor for aircraft production, respectively at Los Angeles and Seattle, was the interest and success of Douglas and Boeing. The rising demand for aircraft during World War II and during the continuing increase in air passenger travel since 1945 are responsible for the size of the aircraft industry as a whole; and wartime demands, in spite of the deliberate establishment of producers in inland centres, undoubtedly helped to strengthen the location of the industry on the west coast. In the final analysis, however, we are once again obliged, as with the automobile industry, to take great account in discussing industrial location of the effect of entrepreneurship.

TABLE 9:1
United States Domestic Production

	Million short tons				Million bbl crude	Million cu. ft.
	Iron ore	(Superior ore)	Pig-iron	Crude steel	petroleum	natural gas
1860	3·2		0·9		0·5	
1870	4·8		1·9	0·8	5·2	
1880	8·0		3·0	1·4	26·3	
1890	18·0		10·3	4·8	45·8	
1900	30·5		15·4	11·5	63·6	0·1
1910	64·0		29·9	29·2	209·6	0·5
1920	75·5		40·0	47·0	442·9	0·8
1930	65·0	(55·0)	33·5	45·5	898·0	2·0
1940	82·5	(69·0)	47·0	67·0	1353·2	2·7
1950	110·0	(89·0)	64·6	96·8	1973·6	6·3
1960	99·0	(80·0)	66·5	99·3	2574·9	12·8
1964	94·0	(70·0)	85·6	127·1	2805·1	15·5
1965	98·2	(74·5)	88·2	131·5	2848·5	16·0
1966	100·1	(76·8)	91·5	134·1		

CHAPTER TEN

PASSENGER TRAVEL AND FREIGHT SHIPMENT

Canada and the U.S.A. differ considerably from European countries in their relationship between the timing of settlement, the locating of towns, and industrialization on the one hand, and the development of routeways on the other. The long historical processes of the Old World were foreshortened in the New, above all in the interior and the West, where the opening of routes, the establishment of farms, the building of towns and the opening of factories were closely linked both in time and in practice. Nevertheless, as will appear in the following selective review of transport development and transport competition, certain strongly marked trends in the passenger and freight movement of North America, whether internal or external, now closely resemble those observed in other occidental lands.

Railways and their Competitors

Railway development in Canada was for about a hundred years out of phase with that in the U.S.A. The latter country had twenty-three miles of track in 1823, was operating successful steam locomotives in the early 1830s, and by 1850 had laid nearly 10,000 miles of first main track. Work began on Canada's first line in 1835, but total mileage was little more than sixty at the mid-century. Canada in 1900 was approaching 20,000 miles of first main track, but the U.S. companies had then laid nearly 200,000 miles. The U.S. system was virtually complete by 1910 at about a quarter of a million miles, whereas the Canadian system continued to grow. Admittedly, its growth was slow after about 1920, but peak mileage was not reached until about 1960; and it is still being extended where lines are driven into the Northland, even though the total gains are more than offset by closures. Only since 1945 have both systems undergone synchronous changes of identical kinds, forced on them by competition from other carriers. Railways both in Canada and the U.S.A. have lost more than half the passenger traffic of their best years. Far from claiming a consistent share in the increase in goods transport, they seem at times to be hard pressed to maintain their freight traffic in absolute terms. The most recent developments in this connection are however reasonably hopeful, with shipments on the upturn.

This kind of situation is familiar enough in numbers of other countries of the Western world. Competition from other carriers is merely one manifestation of technological change, and the inability of railways to meet it can be looked on as resulting from the inherent inflexibility of railway operation. However, additional factors have also been at work.

In North America, as in Britain, railway building was the task of the entrepreneur and the private company. Its history displays both the best and the worst facets of unregulated competition. On the one hand, the U.S. companies in some single years laid more than 10,000 miles of track; and the lands of the deep interior, both in the U.S.A. and in Canada, could scarcely have been brought under commercial farming without the railways. On the other hand, none of the earlier projects produced more than short lines, meant as feeders or links. Diversities of gauge, completely unimportant in the early stage, constituted serious problems as something like a network began to develop. At one time the standard (4 ft $8\frac{1}{2}$ in) gauge, the 4 ft 9 in gauge, and the 5 ft gauge were all in widespread use, the last throughout much of the U.S. South. Competition between companies produced needless duplication of lines. Most serious of all were the typical

22. Railway traversing a canyon near Canyon City, Colorado. The suspension bridge for road, above, is claimed to be the highest in the world.

financial aspects of railway promotion and railway operation. More than one of the large U.S. companies which eventually emerged was, like many a small company also, permanently handicapped by over-capitalization, the outcome of unscrupulous stock-market transactions by its directors. Thus, while railway ownership could supply colossal personal fortunes such as those of the Vanderbilts, railway management could not provide adequately for wages or for modernization. Worse still, the constant need for income was translated in the light of free-competition principles to the practice of charging the utmost that traffic could bear.

Among the leading differences between North American and British railway experience, three deserve special notice. First, the spread of North American railways began not long after the first successful canals had come into use. Railways, instead of superseding canals, entered into direct competition with them; and the canal-plus-river net is still in a competitive condition. Secondly, much of the new North American construction from 1860 onwards took place towards, or even beyond, an advancing frontier of settlement and farming. Thirdly, western routes towards the Pacific attracted land grants from the governments.

Much is made in railway mythology of the trans-Cordilleran routes, with their engaging wood-burning locomotives and the battles with Indians. More strictly, attention usually concentrates on the Plains sections of these routes, for it was here that law had to be enforced among cattlemen at the point of a gun, and here also that the Indians were mainly threatened by the slaughter of bison. Much is made, too, of the engineering feats of driving lines through the mountains (Plate 22), and of the speed of certain major projects of construction. The first transcontinental link, that of the Union Pacific–Central Pacific, admittedly involved the building of nearly 1800 miles of new main track between Omaha, Nebraska, and Sacramento, California; and it is true that the work was completed in three years, 1866–69, only seven years after the passing of the enabling legislation. It is also a fact that the organization of the enormous work-gangs was highly impressive; so, too, was their recruitment in a labour-hungry country. The Union Pacific solved its labour problem by taking immigrants and time-served convicts wherever it could get them, while the Central Pacific imported Chinese. Rapidity of construction was favoured in plainland sections by low gradients, and everywhere by single-track layout and by the use of spikes instead of shoes for fixing the rails. But it was obtained also at the expense of standards. The Union Pacific section from Omaha to Salt Lake was distinctly shoddy, subsequently needing extensive repair and rebuilding.

In the decade between 1883 and 1893, the Northern Pacific line from Duluth and Minneapolis reached Portland, Oregon, via Spokane and the existing Oregon lines; the Southern Pacific connected San Francisco and Los Angeles to El Paso, Texas, and thence to New Orleans; the Canadian Pacific arrived at Vancouver; and the Great Northern, notable for its soundness of construction and finance, ran from the Twin Cities to Seattle via Spokane. Cross-connections included that between the Union Pacific in southwest Wyoming with

Portland and the Oregon net; that between Denver and the Union Pacific at Ogden, Utah; and that of the Santa Fé between Kansas City and Albuquerque, extended by 1888 to Chicago at one end and Los Angeles at the other. The final additions to the list of transcontinental railways came in 1913–15, when by way of Yellowhead Pass the Canadian Northern reached Vancouver and the Grand Trunk reached Prince Rupert. These two lines, ambitiously projected as any, later merged into the government-operated Canadian National Railway.

To claim that the railways opened up the West is over-simple. The nearly 300,000 square miles of land grant accorded to the transcontinental lines in the U.S.A. acted for some time as a hindrance to settlement, wherever homesteading was delayed by the reluctance of the railway companies to complete the complex process of selection and land registration. However, in the later part of the nineteenth century the companies were sufficiently interested in promoting settlement to pursue vigorous campaigns of advertising and land sale among migrants. The westward shift of cropping after the Civil War became increasingly a shift and intensification of commercial cropping, as trunk lines pushed westward, threw out feeders, and in some areas enmeshed themselves in reasonably integrated networks. In the drier areas the railways made possible the large-scale expansion of commercial ranching. Millions of longhorn cattle were railed in the 1870s from places such as Abilene and Dodge City, which transformed themselves from decrepit cow-towns to flourishing stockyard centres; and refrigerator cars next made possible the rise of slaughterhouses, meatworks, and packing plants. But the widespread practice of charging the maximum freight rates which could be borne was a handicap both to the spread of farming and to its progressive commercialization. In this respect the midwestern States proved exceptional, quite early developing legislation to protect their farmers. Rate wars between companies brought little help to cultivators, while rebates and allied concessions worked solely in favour of bulk shippers such as oil companies. Not until the early twentieth century were freight rates in the U.S.A. regulated at the Federal level; and by that time, no more than a generation of prosperity remained for the railways.

From 1850 to the 1920s, the U.S. railways could expect to handle progressively increasing shipments of coal. From about 1880 they dealt increasingly with traffic in finished manufactured products, while the Canadian railways became simultaneously involved with the rise of wheat and mineral traffic. The various networks equipped themselves with automatic couplers and with Westinghouse brakes, aids alike to safety and efficiency, and with the powerful coal-burning locomotives required to pull the weights made possible by large loading-gauges. But signs of competition were already appearing. The peak number of passengers on the U.S. railways, more than 1250 million, was recorded in 1920. Demand for passenger services fell by nearly half during the next ten years, mainly because of the switch to private cars. Time-tables were already being reduced on some of the less profitable and less optimistic lines, when the depression sharply cut back business of all kinds. Railway passenger traffic did not subsequently recover, except to a modest extent during World War II. Private cars now account for 90 per cent of intercity passenger travel. Of the remainder, airlines take about half and railways and commercial road services about a quarter each.

Freight traffic on the U.S. railways broke all previous records during World War II, but subsequently declined, both absolutely, and still more strongly relative to the traffic of other carriers. It would however be unsafe to forecast a further decline, since the latest records indicate that the trend has been reversed – if only for the time being. The changes are due in part to the previously mentioned competition from other carriers – in this instance, pipeline and trucking companies – and in part to the declining demand for coal. Trucks account for the serious loss of traffic dispatched in less than carload lots: the railways have been progressively forced into the role initially envisaged for them, that of bulk carriers. To this end, both in the U.S.A. and in Canada, they have converted to diesel operation, or to electric power on some lines, running freight trains a mile or more in length; in the course of conversion they inevitably reduced their own coal traffic and stimulated the spread of oil pipelines.

It is only since the mid-1950s that Canadian railways have felt serious competition (Fig. 10:2). This comes chiefly from roads and waterways,

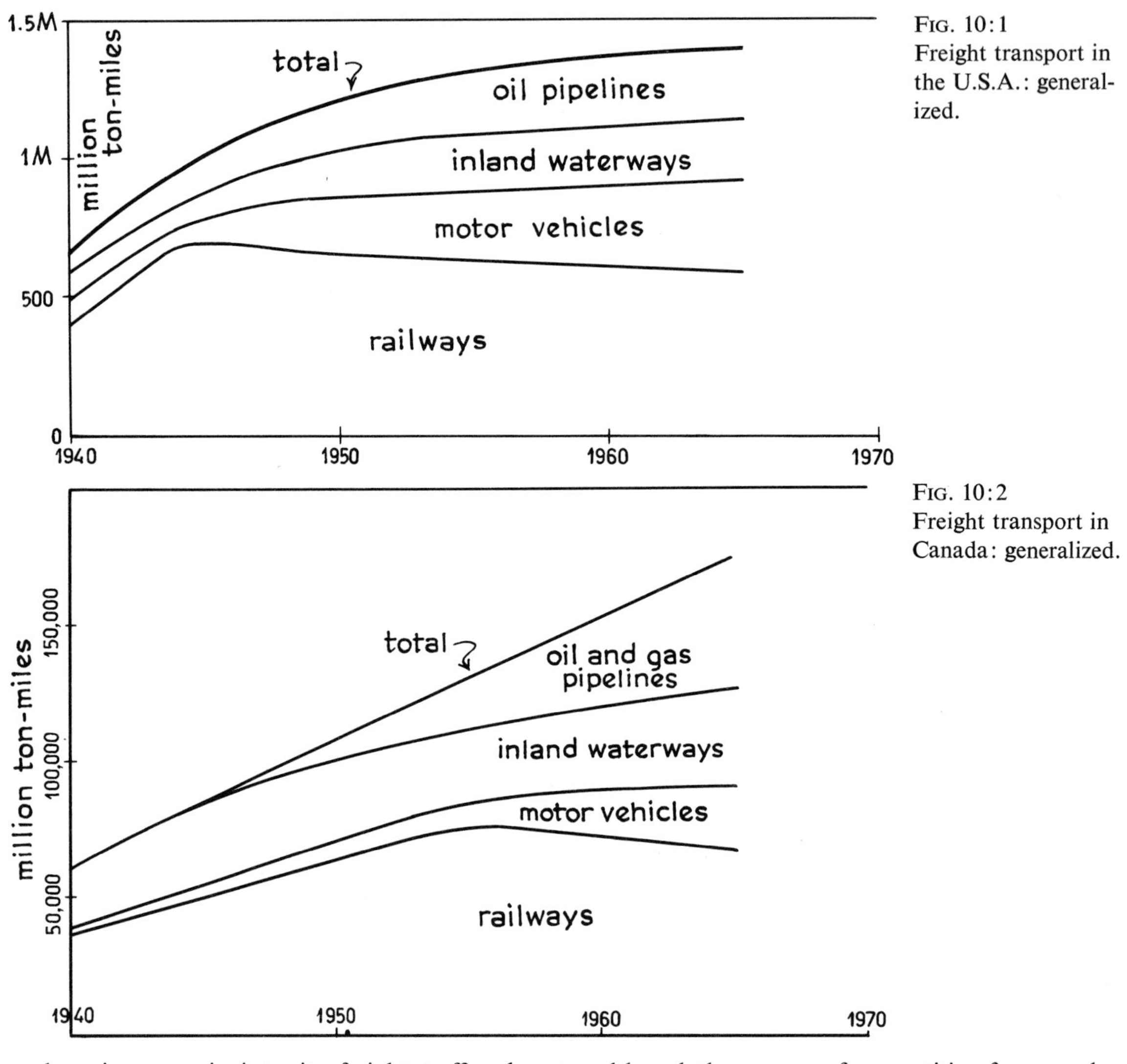

FIG. 10:1 Freight transport in the U.S.A.: generalized.

FIG. 10:2 Freight transport in Canada: generalized.

where increases in intercity freight traffic almost precisely offsets the decrease on the railways. Simultaneously, the development of oil and natural gas in Canada has been accompanied by the construction of pipelines which take almost the whole of the traffic in the two items. If existing trends continue, pipelines could before very long surpass railways, in terms of total freight carried. But railways in Canada seem likely to keep their hold on traffic in minerals other than oil and natural gas, which accounts for about 40 per cent of the tonnage hauled, with ores and concentrates alone providing 20 per cent. Similarly, the traffic in wheat and in forest products, each about 10 per cent of tonnage hauled, should also be maintained. Furthermore, Canadian railways have fared better than those of the U.S.A. in retaining their passenger traffic, although the menace of competition from road and air travel is still with them and unlikely to abate.

Provision and Use of Roads

Turnpike companies in the U.S.A. sprang up by their hundreds during the early part of the nineteenth century; few, however, achieved financial success. As passenger routes they were swifter than waterways, but far from comfortable. As freight routes they possessed none of the advantages in bulk carriage which rivers, canals, and railways could offer; and railways also competed, as fast as they spread, for the passenger trade. Nevertheless, roads were necessary; by 1900 the country had some 300 million miles of road, chiefly rural (= outside towns) and chiefly unsurfaced (Fig. 10:3). Surfac-

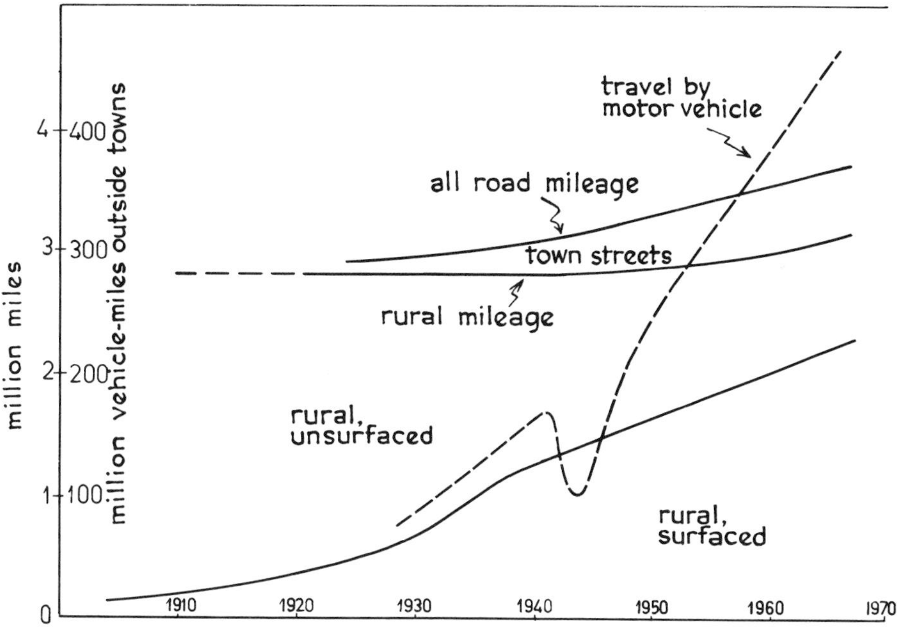

FIG. 10:3
Road mileage and road travel in the U.S.A.: generalized.

23. Part of an urban freeway system, with entry and exit ramps. Time exposure in a night photograph makes the images of headlamps trace out the movements of traffic.

24. The Chesapeake Bay Bridge, one of several elevated roadways across the long but shallow inlets of the U.S. eastern and southern shorelines.

25. A motel – now a necessary item in the North American social system. This one lies near the rocket-launching site at Cape Kennedy, which has become a tourist attraction.

26. Drive-in payment of local government charges.

ing in the 1930s was widely undertaken as a form of relief work during the depression, but has since continued as a response to the growing demand for motor transport and motor-vehicle carriage of goods. Motor travel, measured on a vehicle–mile basis, recovered smartly from the petrol rationing and lack of output of private cars in World War II, increasing far more rapidly than road mileage could. However, road capacity has itself risen faster than mileage. The U.S.A. has led the world in the provision of multi-lane limited-access highways designed for high-speed travel, being the first country to accommodate itself to the changes produced in the technical situation by the automobile (Plates 22, 23, 24, 25, 26). Federal legislation in the 1940s and 1950s provided for the construction or improvement of extensive highway systems meant in part for the routine purposes of peacetime and in

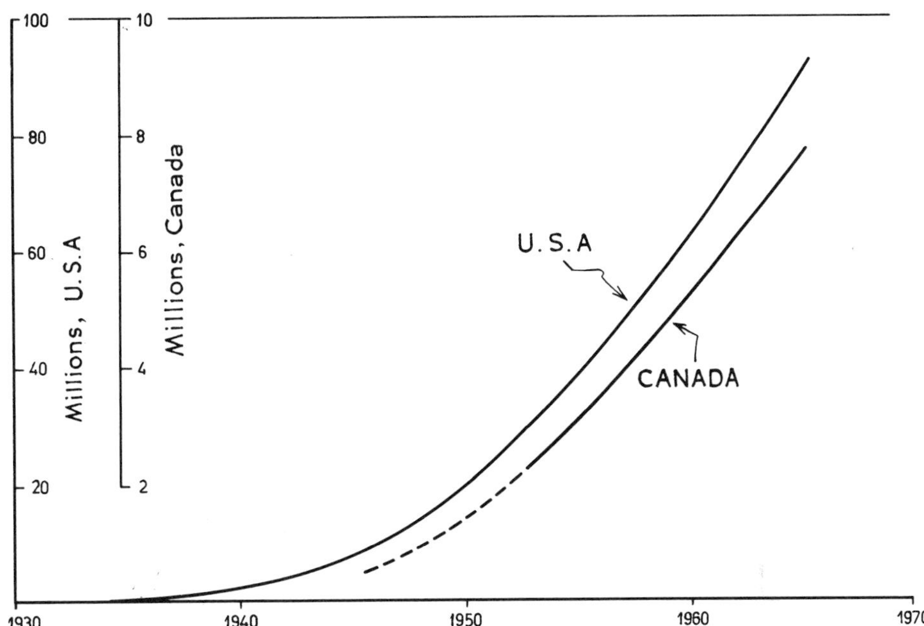

FIG. 10:4
Air passenger travel.

part for strategic ends in times of war. The net of interstate highways has been complemented, and to some extent superseded, by a net of superhighways. With the improvement and extension of the highway net has gone a steady increase in intercity truck transport, which surpassed waterway carriage of freight in the late 1950s and could well surpass railway carriage also. Public transport systems in all large towns have been checked in their growth, cut back, or even extinguished by the use of private cars in commuter travel.

Canada is somewhat differently situated. It is not far from being as highly automotive as the U.S.A., in respect of numbers of vehicles in proportion to population, and in respect also of its social dependence on car travel. However, it has felt less need for road construction and improvement. Of the 450,000 miles of rural road in Canada in the mid-1960s, two-thirds of the total was surfaced, but only about one-tenth was surfaced with rigid pavement. However, in Canada as in the U.S.A. the federal government is deeply concerned with road travel and transport and with road construction, having legislated in 1949 for the 4860-mile Trans-Canada Highway which was opened in 1962. In addition, the federal government is contributing a two-fifths share to the building and extension of roads into the Canadian North, quite apart from its massive assistance to mine-access and mine-development roads.

Airlines

Canada and the U.S.A. are very similar indeed in respect of their proportionate development of air travel (Fig. 10:4). The graphs in the diagram are not strictly comparable, since the Canadian data exclude passengers in transit across the country: it is reasonable to infer that total air passenger traffic in Canada is about one-tenth that in the U.S.A., in keeping with the relative sizes of national populations. The pattern or increase in air travel is practically identical in the two countries. Already, the number of passengers carried by air is approaching half the number carried by rail, despite the use of railways in commuter journeys. The tally of international traffic by air from the U.S.A. is about equal to that of international sea travel, and is rising by far the more rapidly.

Technical problems in air travel include those of transit between city terminals and airports, provision of landing facilities for increasingly fast and increasingly large aircraft, congestion of the skyways, and allocation of routes. Although air transport in North America has been developed mainly by private enterprise, it is necessarily subject to strict control for the sake of safety. Thus, competition for business is to a large extent competition for operating rights: especially is this so in international flying, where international control is exercised. Increases in the speed and size of aircraft mean increased lengths of runway, and in consequence tend to concentrate long-distance flying on particular airports.

In one respect Canada is more dependent on flying than is the U.S.A.; aircraft, including some specially developed for the purpose, have done and continue to do a great deal to extend and maintain communications in the Northland, where they are also widely used in mapping and in the exploration of mineral and forest resources.

Waterborne Freight: The St Lawrence–Great Lakes System

In the early days of French settlement in Canada, the lower St Lawrence provided more than a means of ingress and egress, and more than a powerful locating factor: it stood as a sign of hope that a continuous water route might exist from the Atlantic side to the little-known ocean far to the west. The idea of a round world, incorporated in the planning of Columbus and embedded in the application of *Indies* to the island of the Caribbean and of *Indians* to the native peoples of both Americas, was of strictly practical significance in relation to the spice and silk trade with the Orient. The circumnavigation of the globe by Magellan's expedition (1519–22) gave the first actual demonstration that the Orient could be reached by way of Cape Horn instead of the Cape of Good Hope. A complete lack of knowledge of the deep interior and the remote west combined with rumours of vast inland waters to sustain the prospect of an open passage to the Far East of the Old World.

Cartier, probing the St Lawrence route, reached in 1535 the Lachine Rapids upstream of the site of present-day Montreal. These, as will appear, long proved a serious obstacle to the development of navigation on the St Lawrence–Great Lakes system as a whole. For the time being, it was clear that penetration westward along the St Lawrence would not be easy. Drake's voyage of circumnavigation (1577–80), repeating and confirming Magellan's experiment, stimulated attempts to by-pass the North American landmass along some high latitude. Of the various attempts to discover a northwest passage, Hudson's (1610–11) was the most tragic and is the best remembered. Shortly afterwards, Champlain in 1615 reached Georgian Bay on Lake Huron after journeying up the Ottawa, subsequently crossing the isthmus at the south end of Georgian Bay and coming to Lake Ontario. Lake Erie was not brought on to the map until Joliet's expedition of 1669. In the later years of the seventeenth century, La Salle crossed the low divide between the Great Lakes and the Mississippi, continuing down this river to arrive at New Orleans.

By this time the notion of a through-way to the Pacific was losing its attraction and force. Subsequent voyages of Pacific discovery were to be independent of exploration of the North American landmass, as is shown by the activities of Bering, Bougainville, and Cook in the interval 1741–78. Meantime, the French in North America had identified routes to and through the interior, along which moved supplies for military garrisons and furs for export: it had become clear that the new lands were worth exploiting for their own sake. It was equally clear, at least to some, that the natural facilities of the St Lawrence–Great Lakes system could bear improvement.

Low narrow divides typical of former spillways offered little obstacle to portage, whether on the St Lawrence–Great Lakes system or in the connections between the Lakes and the Mississippi. Many of these divides could actually be crossed by the flat-bottomed five-tonners built by the French to work on the Lakes. Nevertheless, portage, whether of the lake boats or of canoes, meant unloading, reloading, and delay. A still more serious problem was that of rapids.

Whereas the Lakes themselves are deep, and eminently navigable in the ice-free season, their interconnections in the natural state were hampered by rapids and waterfalls. Lake Ontario, 246 feet above sea-level, was separated from the head of the St Lawrence estuary by a number of difficult reaches, including those of the Lachine Rapids and International Rapids. The main descent from Lake Erie (571 feet) to Lake Ontario occurs at Niagara Falls. Farther upstream in the system the obstacles are less serious, for Lakes Huron and Michigan at 581 feet are but 10 feet higher than Lake Erie, while Lake Superior at 602 feet is but 21 feet higher than Lake Huron. Some rapids could be traversed in the upstream direction by means of haulage; the alternative to portages in the downstream direction was the risky practice of rapid-shooting, in which the lake boats proved remarkably stable but highly vulnerable to destruction if they struck rocks. Losses were at times considerable. It was not surprising that projects to make canals should be advanced: indeed, an abortive plan to open a cut by the Lachine Rapids was implemented as early as 1700. In the event, working locks in this reach were not completed until 1780. The first Lachine Canal, with its modest controlling depth of 5 feet, opened to navigation in 1825.

In the same year, the Erie Canal from Buffalo to Albany, with a controlling depth of 7 feet, was also opened. Meantime, steamships had been plying upon the Lakes since 1809. There followed a century and a half during which development of the interior produced an export trade in wheat, the establishment of the metal manufacture of western Pennsylvania, and the exploitation of the Superior hematite ores. With the huge increase of traffic on the Lakes went an increase in the size of lake-ships. Although improvements were made at various points of the system, there was but spasmodic effort to open the Lakes to ocean-going vessels. The Welland Canal, circumventing Niagara Falls, was constructed in 1824–32, and various works were undertaken between Montreal and Lake Ontario in the following decade, so that by about 1850 an ocean-going ship of 8-foot draught could reach Lake Superior. The 9-foot canal route was completed, far too late to be of real value.

The next distinguishable episode of canal-making involved plans to provide a minimum water depth of 14 feet, either by enlarging existing cuts or by opening new ones alongside. Deepening of the Welland system was finished in 1877, that of the Lachine system not until 1903. Already before this, the St Lawrence channel between Montreal and Quebec and the Michigan–Huron–Erie links had been deepened to a minimum of 20 feet. The size of lake-ships, constantly tending to exceed the capacity of the inter-lake waterways, still further exceeded that of the Welland canals between Erie and Ontario and of the cuts on the Ontario–St Lawrence section.

A number of issues were involved. After about 1850 the railways entered strongly into competition for the transport of wheat. Plans for improved or additional canals gathered and lost force according to the condition of the wheat trade, and in particular according to the short-term economics of wheat transport. Apart from wheat, a great deal of the cargo transported on the Lakes originated at, and was destined to, Lake ports between the eastern end of Lake Erie and the western end of Lake Superior: thus, the development of Lake transport proper had but minor impact on proposals relating to Lake Ontario and the upper St Lawrence River. As seems typical of the history of canal-building in an entrepreneurial society, the full record of projects and of actual works on the St Lawrence–Great Lakes system is complex, and in a fully detailed form distinctly tedious. Among the significant events of the early twentieth century were the deepening of the Erie Canal to 12 feet in the 1920s, the construction of 22-foot canals at Sault St Marie between Lakes Superior and Huron (1914–19), and the opening of a new Welland Canal with a 25-foot depth in 1932. The great ore-ships and grain-ships could now travel throughout the Lakes system as far as transhipment points on the St Lawrence, but the shallow canals of the Lachine section still constrained access to and from the ocean.

As the cost of increasingly large works became greater, the responsibility for finance and control passed progressively to governments both in Canada and in the U.S.A., eventually at the Federal rather than at the State level; and it was the two national governments which at last combined in the St Lawrence Seaway and Power Project. Fifty-nine years elapsed between the appointment of the Joint Deep Waterways Commission in 1895 and the final formal agreement of 1954. To the complicating factors already listed as affecting canal projects were added, in the governmental context, alternations of enthusiasm for the scheme on the two sides, checks during times of economic setback, postponements in time of war, and powerfully organized opposition from interested groups in the U.S.A. Understandably enough, the railway companies feared loss of freight and of revenue, while coal companies were prepared to oppose any developments of hydro-electric power which would reduce their markets. However, the early 1950s brought serious power shortages to New York State and Ontario, revealing serious deficiencies in generating

27. Part of the St Lawrence Seaway. Left, the 27-foot channel, with locks. Centre and right foreground, power dams.

capacity which could most readily be made good by the installation of new hydro-electric stations on the St Lawrence. Simultaneously, the alarmingly low estimates of ore reserves in the Superior fields joined with the cost and the strategic risks of ore import from overseas, and with the recent proving of vast reserves in Quebec–Labrador, to bring the navigational part of the St Lawrence scheme into strong official favour on the U.S. side. After the signing of the necessary agreement, five years only were needed to complete the new canals: they opened, with a minimum 27-foot depth throughout, in the spring of 1959 (Plates 17, 27).

Cargoes carried on the Lakes–Seaway system remain in very great part bulk cargoes, and lake steamers are easily the chief carriers. Iron ore, oil, coal, wheat, corn, and barley are prominent in the list of commodities shipped along the Seaway. Traffic on the Welland Canal section between Lakes Ontario and Erie is still heavier than that between the St Lawrence and Lake Erie, chiefly concerning iron ore, grain, and coal. In common with the Sault St Marie canals, these two sections record an excess of downbound over upbound freight: the imbalance would be far greater without the shipments of iron ore from the lower St Lawrence to consumers in the U.S.A.

Waterborne Freight: The Mississippi and its Connections

Easy canoe portages between the Great Lakes and tributaries of the Mississippi have been noticed in a previous chapter, in connection with the fur trade of early colonial times. The Allegheny–Ohio, reached through one or other of the Appalachian passes, supplied a route for settlers when occupation of the Midwest gathered real force. By about 1850, when the settlement frontier was moving west of the Mississippi, canals had been dug along the former portage routes from Chicago, Toledo, Cleveland, and Erie to connect the Lakes with the navigable Illinois and Ohio Rivers and so with the Mississippi system. However, the boom of prosperity and expansion which New Orleans might

28. A diesel-powered barge tow on the Ohio River.

have expected, in its function as gateway to the Mississippi, was not to be. The canal links with the Lakes were rapidly superseded by railways; and railways diverted traffic from north–south to east–west lines – that is, to and from the towns of the emergent industrial belt of the Northeast, and to and from the great ports of the mid-Atlantic coast.

Nevertheless, traffic on the Mississippi persisted. If it was slow, it was also remarkably cheap after the introduction of steamboats; and the broad inner valley from Memphis southward itself generated much cargo in the form of raw cotton. Navigation, however, was not everywhere easy. Numerous feeders, like the lower Mississippi itself, possess meandering channels; and these, like meandering channels everywhere, contain riffles at the inflections between their bends, where water is shallow at the best of times and can be dangerously shallow in the low-flow season. The Mississippi traders overcame the obstacle of alternating riffles by developing the stern-wheeler, as engaging an object as the wood-burning locomotive of the early railways; vessels of the stern-wheeler type, remarkably shallow in draught, were able to penetrate the bayous of the delta and the lowermost valley, effectively extending the system of navigable ways.

However, the capacity of stern-wheelers remained limited by small controlling depths of water in the worst reaches. It remained for the U.S. federal government to undertake a long programme of dredging, improvement, and control, which has converted the unsatisfactory natural streams into a branching waterway of great total length and great areal extent, and with a controlling depth of 12 feet. The Mississippi is navigable up to the Twin Cities, while the Illinois River plus canal connection to Chicago has been improved and elaborated. The Missouri is navigable from its confluence with the Mississippi at St Louis to Sioux City, Iowa. Navigation on the Ohio system extends well upstream of Pittsburgh, with feeder routes coming in on the south. Improvements on the Tennessee, navigable as far as Knoxville, are discussed elsewhere in the context of T.V.A. Throughout the system as it now

29. Control and improvement of inland navigation: model studies of flood walls, levees, channel improvement, and channel management, at the U.S. Waterways Experiment Station, Vicksburg, Miss.

exists, bulk cargoes are the rule. They are shipped in dumb-barges, which are assembled into rafts and propelled by a motor vessel attached at the rear. Since barges may be taken singly from a particular tow, and since they are not always identical in size and shape, planning of an assembly can offer its problems. But the system is an undoubted success: one tow can be equivalent in capacity to a 20,000-ton ocean-going carrier (Plates 28, 29). Total traffic on the Mississippi system, measured in ton–miles, is three-quarters as heavy as that on the Great Lakes, and in simple terms of total tonnage handled exceeds the combined traffic of U.S. ports on the Lakes system. Most of it is interior traffic.

A kind of extension to the Mississippi navigation is the Gulf Intracoastal Waterway. This runs from the Mexican border in the west, through the delta of the Mississippi and New Orleans, to Apalachee Bay in the Florida panhandle. A canal now under construction across the Florida peninsula will eventually link the Waterway with the Atlantic Waterway and coastwise routes. In some reaches, the Gulf Waterway takes advantage of the long lagoons enclosed behind coastal barriers; elsewhere, it has been dredged through the swamplands, or in the shallow near-shore waters of the open sea where a very gently shelving bottom reduces wave height to a foot or so. Conceived in part as a safeguard against submarine attack during World War II, the Waterway has fully proved its economic value in subsequent years, providing a coastal outlet for the salt, potash, and oil of Texas, and by way of the improved Warrior River an economically navigable route to the Birmingham district of Alabama.

External Trade

Differences in the presentation of trade statistics for the two countries prevent the making of identical forms of analysis. However, a general breakdown is simple enough in each case.

Fig. 10:5 compares the import and export trades

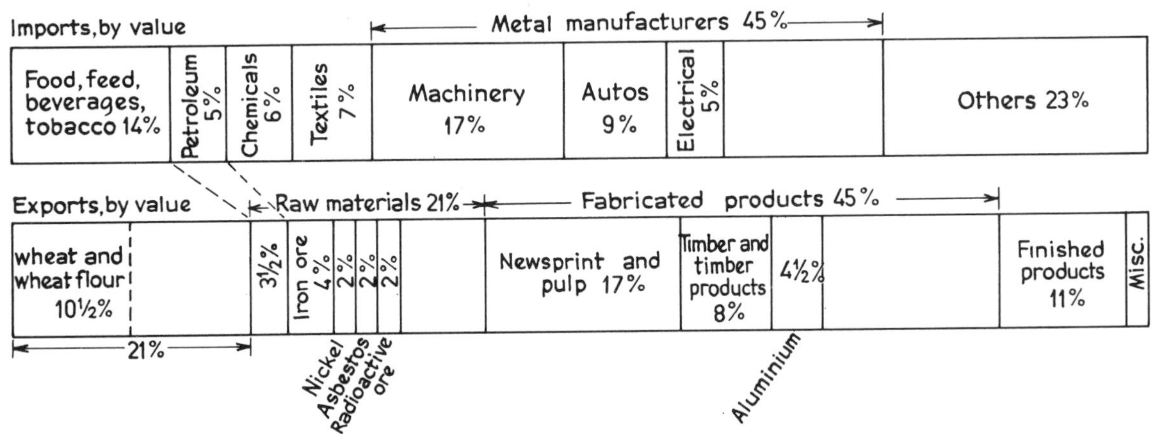

FIG. 10:5 Import and export trade of Canada, mid-1960s.

of Canada in the mid-1960s. Metal manufactures approach half the total value of imports; and among these manufactures, machinery, automobiles, and electrical apparatus fall not far short of a third of all import value. The export graph shows how heavily Canada depends on its external trade on primary and processed materials: wheat and wheat flour account for half the export value in the food, feed, beverages, and tobacco group, and for about a tenth of all exports. Forest products, chiefly in the form of newsprint, pulp, and sawn timber come to a quarter of the whole. Iron ore, nickel, and radioactive minerals combine with asbestos to account for another 10 per cent. Additional ores bulk largely in the remainder of the raw materials group.

The U.S.A., with a national economy more complex than that of Canada, conducts a more complex external trade, particularly in respect of semi-manufactures and finished manufactures. These two classes in combination claim well over half of all import trade by value (Fig. 10:6), with paper and pulp (7 per cent) and textiles (6 per cent) the most prominent items. In the export trade of the U.S.A., semi-manufactures and finished manufactures are even more outstanding, commanding about three-quarters of the whole: machinery alone takes one-quarter.

This pattern is not in the least surprising: a highly industrialized country can be expected to offer a wide market for imported manufactured goods. Nevertheless, the pattern as it now exists has not been long developed. In the mid-nineteenth century the U.S.A. functioned in relation to external trade as a primary producer, with 90 per cent of its

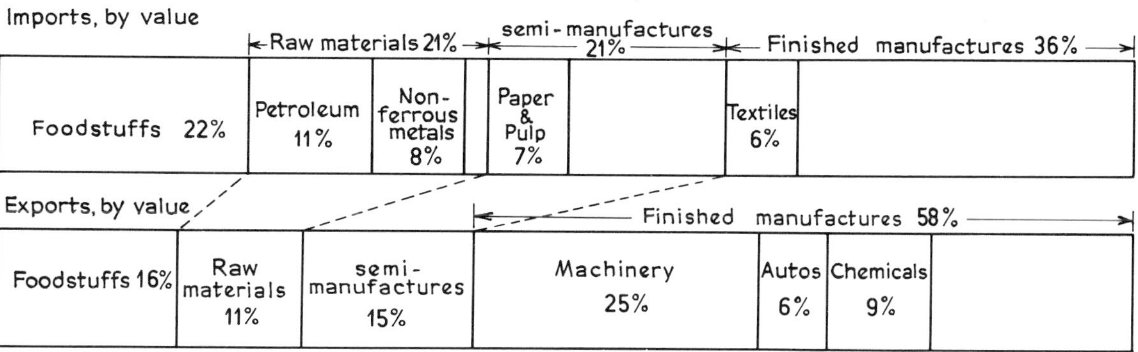

FIG. 10:6 Import and export trade of the U.S.A., mid-1960s.

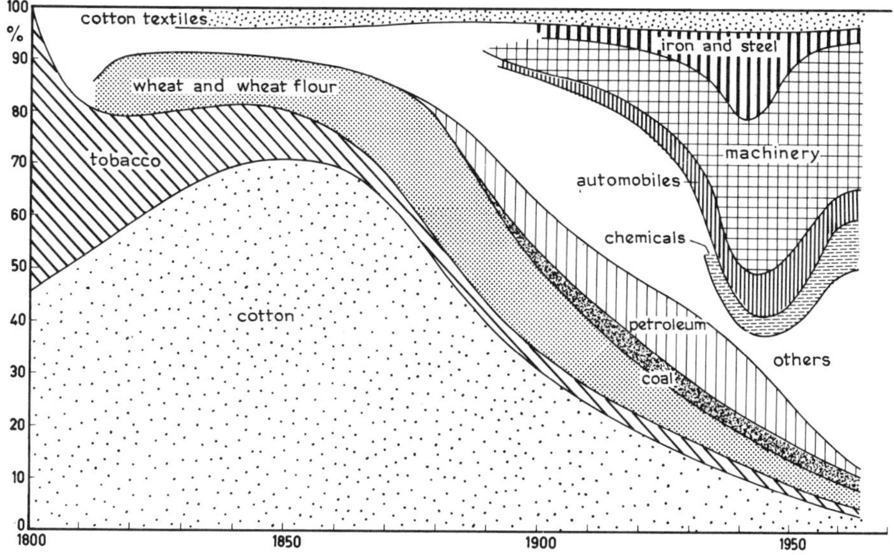

FIG. 10:7 Trends in the export trade of the U.S.A., by value: generalized.

exports provided by cotton, tobacco, wheat, and wheat flour (Fig. 10:7). Despite the decline in exports of tobacco and cotton, the three commodity groups were still supplying half the exports of 1900; and these three plus coal and petroleum still made up half the export trade of 1920. But between 1900 and 1920 the production for export of metal manufactures – and especially of machinery – increased rapidly. During World War II, iron and steel exports also increased. Although these have since reverted to their former minor status, the export of machinery and of automobiles has remained high, while export of chemicals has considerably expanded. For about fifty years – roughly, between 1840 and 1890 – the external trade balance of the U.S.A. was generally unfavourable. The situation had altered greatly by 1920, when exports brought in half as much again as imports cost. It was between 1890 and 1920 that the first really great expansion of manufacturing industry was accomplished; and although, as has been seen, the U.S.A. at the end of this period was still chiefly an exporter of primary products, the rising export of manufactured goods contributed powerfully to establish a favourable trade balance. Volume of trade fell away drastically during the depression, and the balance came near to equality, only to swing rapidly upwards again in the years of economic recovery and during World War II. Since the mid-1950s, export value has been running at about 20 per cent greater than import cost. However, the real balance is less favourable than the raw data might suggest, since total export value includes the price realized for bullion; and bullion exports indicate runs on the dollar, such as in 1968 produced an international financial crisis and placed the U.S.A. in an unsatisfactory position with respect to its balance of payments.

Canada's export trade expectably proves very sensitive to the requirements of external markets. Demand for manufactures though not of minerals increased sharply during World War I: demand for both increased during World War II (Fig. 10:8). Over the approximate century of record, the combined minerals–manufactures group has increased its share in total export value from about 10 per cent to about 50 per cent in peacetime conditions; forest products, their exports greatly restricted in time of war, hold steady in peacetime at about 25 per cent of all export value. The great proportionate reduction has been in agricultural, animal, and fish products, which provided 50 per cent or more of all export value up to the mid-1930s, but are now reduced to about 20 per cent.

The U.S.A. is more complex than Canada in the direction of its external trade: so much is apparent from Figs. 10:9 and 10:10, even though the bases of these two graphs are not comparable. Both in its import and in its export trade, Canada is dominated by the U.S.A., on which it relies for two-thirds of its

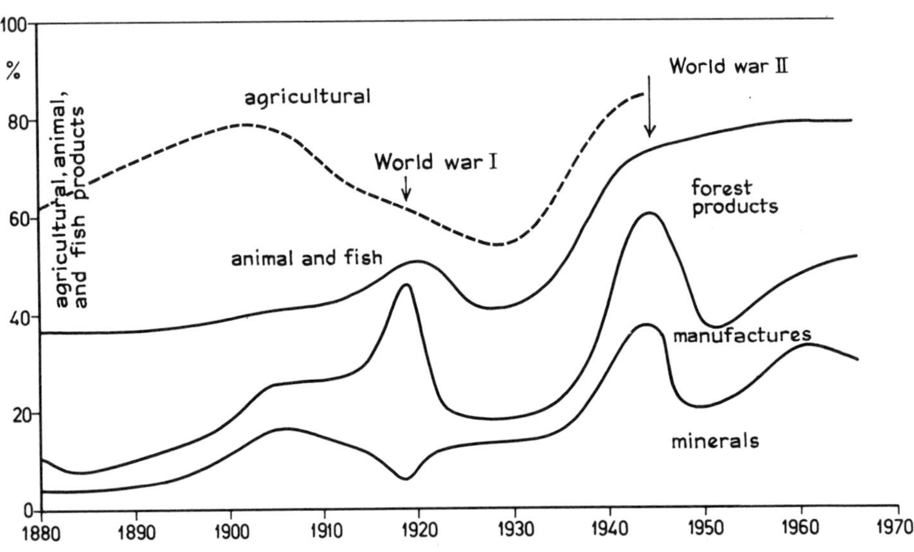

FIG. 10:8
Trends in the export trade of Canada, by value: generalized.

imports and for more than half of its export market. Britain is the next ranking customer and supplier. The U.S.A. and Britain combined supply three-quarters of Canada's imports and take more than two-thirds of Canada's exports.

Apart from the oil trade, Canada is the leading trading partner of the U.S.A., with a one-quarter share in total dry cargo traffic, and roughly equals the combined Caribbean, Mexican, and South American area as a supplier of imports. Among Canadian imports into the U.S.A., forest products and metal ores are prominent. It is clear that U.S. exporters have done far better in northwestern Europe than northwestern European exporters have in the U.S.A. An even greater contrast appears for Japan and the Mediterranean area, which offer considerable export markets but supply little by way of imports. Tanker traffic is essentially traffic in oil, with a great preponderance of imports over exports, and with three-quarters of the imports coming from Latin America and the Caribbean.

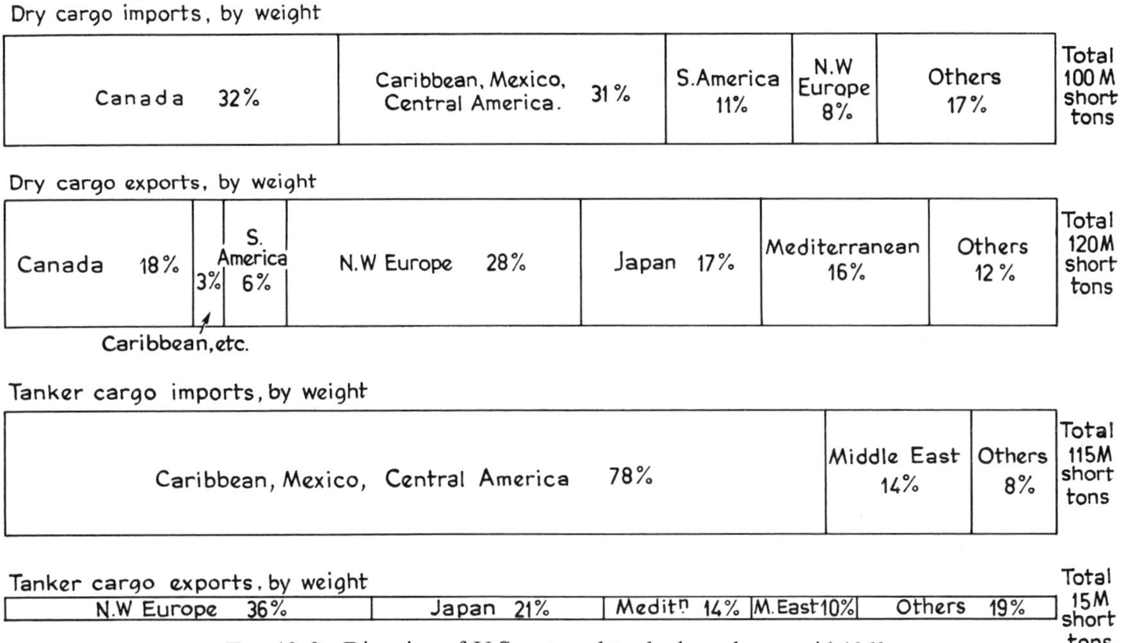

FIG. 10:9 Direction of U.S. external trade, by volume, mid-1960s.

FIG. 10:10 Direction of Canadian external trade, by volume, mid-1960s.

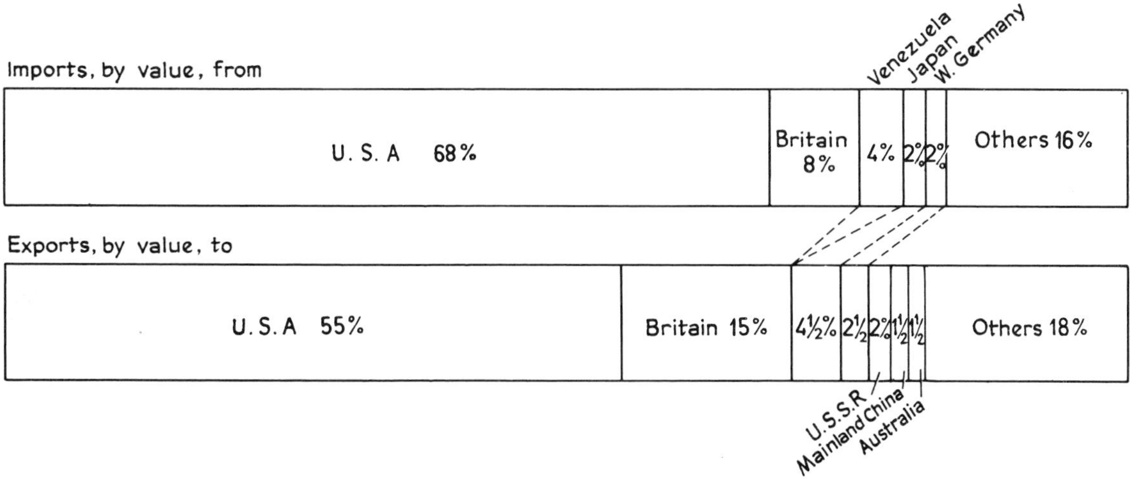

Ports

Table 10:1 summarizes the trade volume of the forty-one ports in Canada and the continental U.S.A. which, in the mid-1960s, were each handling at least five million short tons of cargo a year. The data are illustrated in Figs. 10:11 to 10:17.

Functions of individual ports can be discussed in more than one aspect – in terms of volume or value of traffic, character of goods handled, direction of trade, size and character of hinterland or of distant supply and market areas, comparative volumes of external and of coastwise shipments, and comparative value or volume of exports and imports. This last aspect traditionally commands a good deal of attention in accounts of port trade in North America, wherein it may be stated (or at least implied) that an imbalance between incoming and outgoing volume is regrettable. In one sense this is so: ships carrying general cargo can operate most cheaply when their holds are full both on outward and on inward voyages. In other senses, however, the idea is not relevant, or is only partly relevant, to the real situation. It needs to be qualified by reference to specialized ports which are dominantly exporters or dominantly importers, and to the fact that, as a group, the general ports of North America record a marked excess of import volume over export.

The topic of export–import balance in North America is usually discussed in relation to New England ports, and especially in relation to Boston. As is generally known, the hinterlands of the New England ports have long failed to provide much in the way of bulky return cargoes. The extinction of the former New England whale fishery inflicted its own damage on port activity in general, while New York has proved so successful a competitor that it is the principal outlet for Boston itself.

Fig. 10:11 shows how the forty-one ports under consideration rate in respect of comparative import–export volume. The dominantly exporting series, Port Cartier to Baton Rouge, is concerned primar-

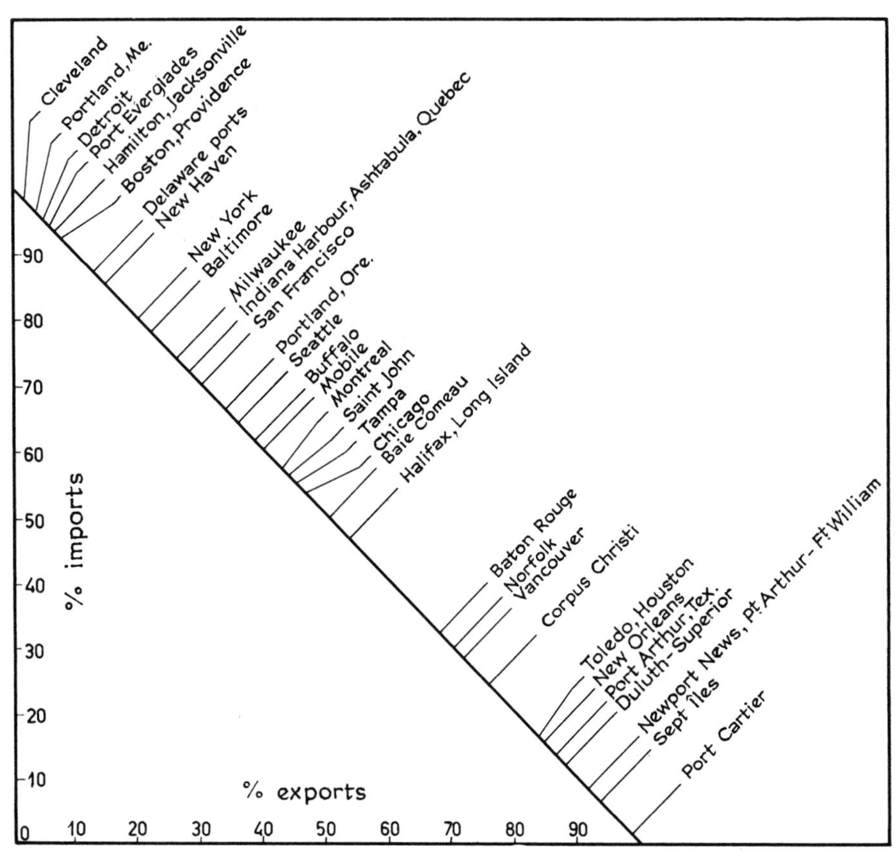

FIG. 10:11 Import/export ratio at leading ports, by volume, mid-1960s.

ily with the dispatch of bulk commodities – iron ore, coal, wheat, salt, oil, gypsum, and potash. At some ports in this series, a single commodity provides almost the whole of the traffic. The second and larger series, which includes all the general ports and the great importing centres on the Great Lakes system, ranges with little sign of a break from 46 per cent imports at Halifax and Long Beach to 98 per cent imports at Cleveland. The only port where imports and exports precisely balance is Baie Comeau, a highly specialized handler of wheat. The import percentage is 78 at Baltimore, 80 at New York, and 87 at the Delaware ports. Thus, the import percentage of 85 at New Haven, 92 at Boston and Providence, and 96 at Portland (Me.) might at first sight be taken as nothing more than somewhat extreme expressions of a general trend.

The matter can however be taken further when allowance is made for comparative amounts of total trade. In Fig. 10:12 total trade is plotted against port ranking order, on a double logarithmic scale, for the nineteen centres which can be classed as ocean ports engaged in general trade. As shown, the plotted points arrange themselves in a distinctly orderly fashion, permitting the scatter to be generalized by a straight line.* The rank–size graph can now be used in an elementary analysis of the relationship of comparative import–export volume to total volume.

As has been observed, import percentage run high at the high-ranking ports of New York, the Delaware ports, and Baltimore – respectively, numbers 1, 2, and 3 in the list of nineteen general ocean ports – and low at Halifax and Long Beach, which rank tenth and eleventh respectively; St John, ranking seventeenth, records 56 per cent imports. There seems to be a suggestion that import percentage tends to increase as total volume increases, at least among part of the group. Boston, Portland (Me.), Providence, New Haven, Jacksonville, Quebec, and Port Everglades provide exceptions. For the remainder, it can be shown that the tendency for import percentage to increase with increasing total volume is significant,* and that this relationship accounts for half the variation in comparative import–export volumes. The bottom scale in the diagram is so drawn that the graphed line represents a mathematical fit of import percentage to ranking order.

Among the seven ports named as exceptional, import percentage averages 89, or 92 if Quebec is left out, regardless of total volume of trade. If they conformed strictly to the pattern defined by the graph, then Boston would record about 63 per cent

* This line can be described by a simple mathematical expression of a kind familiar in rank–size studies.

* The probability that the increase is due to chance alone is about one in a hundred.

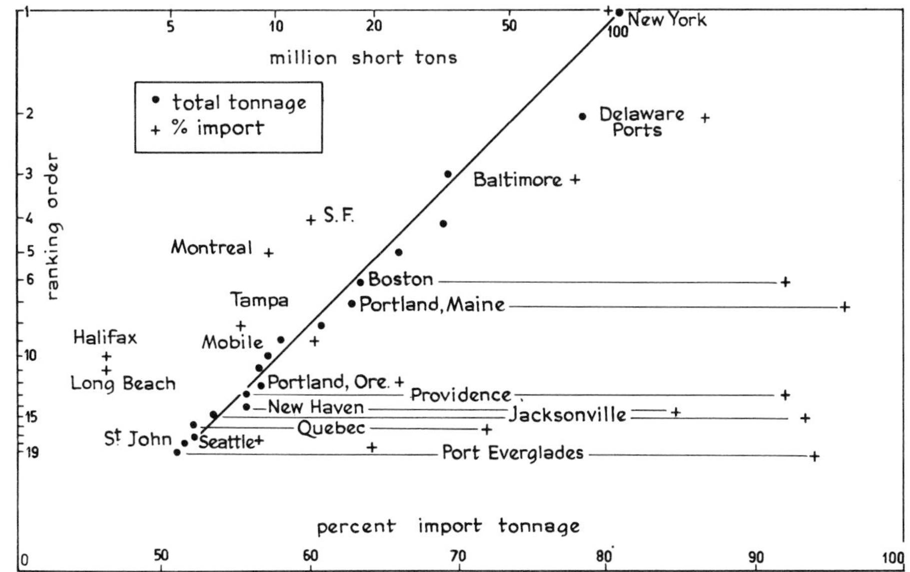

FIG. 10:12
Total trade, ranking order, and import percentage for selected ports, mid-1960s.

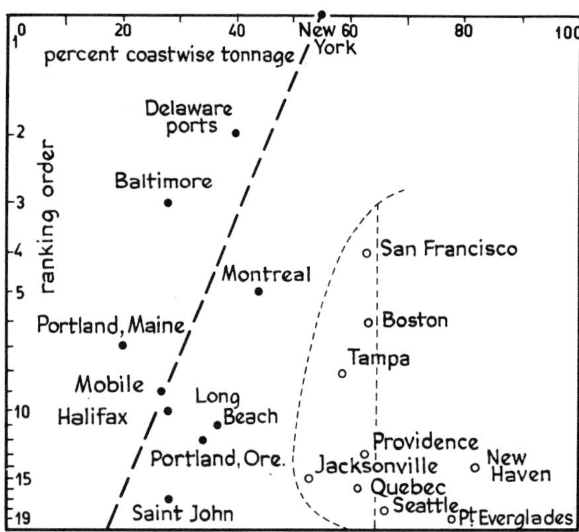

FIG. 10:13 Ranking order and percent coastwise trade for selected ports.

imports against the actual 92 per cent, Providence and New Haven about 55 per cent, against 92 and 85 respectively, and Port Everglades about 51 per cent instead of the recorded 94 per cent. Even Quebec, the least disparate of the group, would have 52 per cent imports as against the current 72 per cent. There can be no doubt that Quebec, the two Florida ports, and the four New England ports are truly anomalous in recording very large import percentages *in comparison with total trade volume.* Import percentages are also somewhat on the high side at the Delaware ports, but not at Baltimore where the difference between the recorded 78 per cent, as against the 70 per cent predicted by the graph, is within reasonable limits of variation.

The rank–size classification can be further employed in an elementary analysis of comparative coastwise and external trade volume. In Fig. 10:13, ranking order on a logarithmic scale is plotted against values on a plain scale of the percentage contribution of coastwise trade to total trade. As before, the nineteen ports separate themselves into two series. In one series, New York to St John, the coastwise percentage tends to increase as total trade increases, although the tendency is less well-marked than that which connects import percentage with total trade. New York, the highest-ranking port in the series, records the highest percentage, while St John, the lowest-ranking, has one of the lowest coastwise percentages. The second series includes nine ports, San Francisco to Port Everglades, where the coastwise percentage averages about 65, regardless of total volume. Six of the ports involved here – Boston, Providence, New Haven, Jacksonville, Quebec, and Port Everglades – have already appeared in the list of ports where the import–export ratio is anomalously high. Accordingly, they can be regarded both as deficient in providing return cargoes, and as among the least successful in general overseas trade, account being taken of their total trade volumes.

In respect of specialized ports which ship huge quantities of a single commodity, or at the most of a very few commodities, the economies implied by the notion of balanced volume have been overtaken by developments in production, demand, and the technique of transport. There is, for instance, simply no market on the Canadian Prairies which could fill the holds of returning wheat-ships or ore-ships; equally, there is no market on the eastern Shield which could use cargoes capable of filling the ore-carriers returning to ports on the lower St Lawrence. Here, as elsewhere, the economies effected are economies of scale – the use of huge vessels and of mechanized port equipment. It is true that wheat-carriers and ore-carriers can be used for alternative cargoes, as they are upon the Lakes; but some types of bulk carrier – tankers in particular – are specialized upon cargoes for which alternatives are in practice most unlikely. Although the movements of a particular tanker are likely to be more complex than, say, a full run from the Middle East to the U.S.A. and an empty return trip, the costing of the construction and operation of giant tankers assumes considerable travel in ballast.

Figs. 10:14 to 10:17 illustrate the volume and character of port trade, area by area. The square symbols are proportional in area to total trade volume, while internal subdivision show the relative proportions of inward and outward movement. In addition, coastwise volume is separated from external volume, except for Lake ports in the U.S.A.

The huge port complexes of New York and the Delaware (principally, Philadelphia and Wilmington) are chiefly importers, in respect of external and coastwise traffic alike (Fig. 10:14). Baltimore is generally similar, except for a lesser emphasis on coastwise imports. As has been indicated, high import and coastwise percentages are expectable in view of the high volume of total traffic. Within the

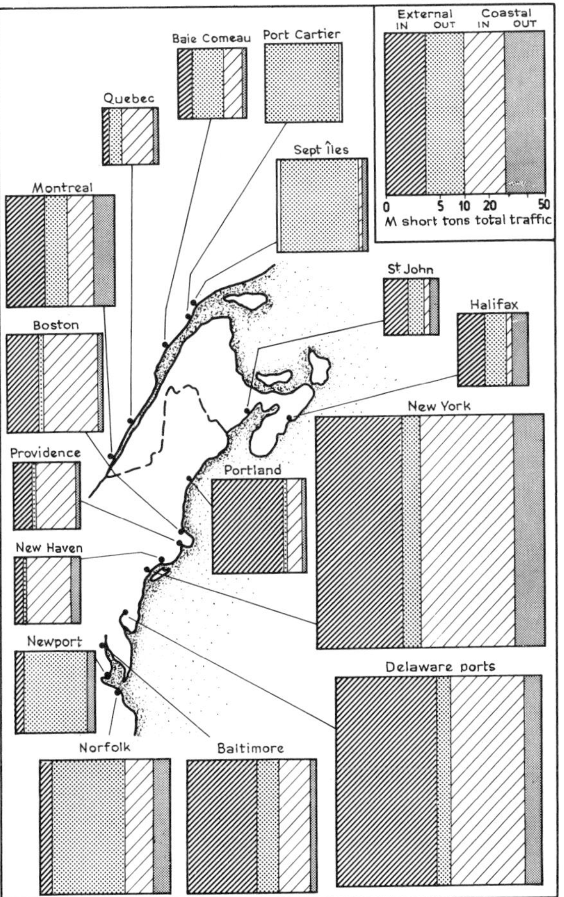

FIG. 10:14. Trade at ports in the Northeast, mid-1960s.

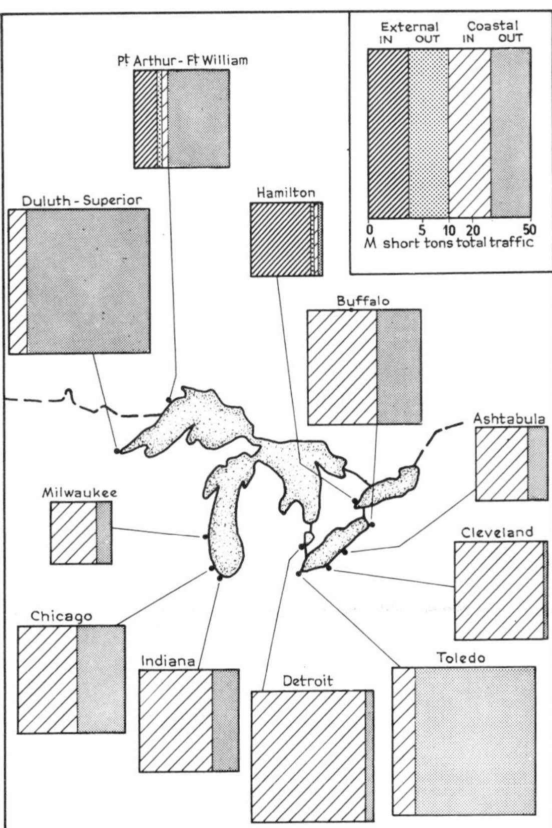

FIG. 10:15 Trade at Lakes ports, mid-1960s: external and coastwise trade not separated for ports in the U.S.A

New York complex, the growing practice of transporting non-bulk goods in containers of uniform size has displaced much traffic from the Manhattan piers to the New Jersey side of the Hudson, where the necessary handling equipment has been installed.

The New England ports have already been discussed. Boston, like its neighbours Providence and New Haven, functions today mainly as a coastwise importer. Portland (Me.), more remote than the others from New York, is dominantly a direct overseas importer; Halifax and St John are broadly similar.

Port operations at Norfolk and Newport News on Chesapeake Bay are concerned largely with the export of coal, while those at Sept-Îles and Port Cartier on the lower St Lawrence are still more exclusively concerned with the shipments of iron ore. These four ports are essentially unifunctional, their equipment designed to handle a single type of outward-moving cargo. Baie Comeau, despite its neat balance between inward and outward volumes, belongs in the same group, since it was built to serve as a transhipment point in the wheat-export trade. Movement at Montreal is not far from evenly balanced, and indeed this port records a higher import percentage than might be expected from its total trade volume. Quebec on the other hand is tending strongly to assume the role of coastwise importer: its similarity in this respect to the southern New England ports has already been observed.

As could be expected, the Lake ports (Fig. 10:15) are, as a group, very highly specialized indeed in respect of direction and character of trade. The two exceptions are Buffalo and Chicago, at each of which out-movement is of the same order as in-movement. Buffalo especially functions as a transhipment point between waterborne and railborne traffic. Exports of wheat and of iron ore figure very largely in the returns for Port Arthur–Fort William and Duluth–Superior, most of the wheat being destined eventually for export but the ore going to furnaces at Lakeside towns or in the Pittsburgh district. Milwaukee, Indiana Harbour, Cleveland, and Ashtabula are dominantly importers, with their import trade in turn dominated by iron ore; limestone from the Michigan peninsula, particularly suitable as a furnace flux, is also noteworthy. Detroit is almost exclusively an importer, taking in ore, coal, and limestone for its automobile industry. Hamilton's trading characteristics, reflecting its heavy metal industry, are similar to those of Detroit. The one prominent exporting port on the lower Lakes is Toledo, which dispatches coal and coke from West Pennsylvania.

Shipborne trade of the Great Lakes has rightly commanded frequent and close notice in geographical writing, although it has at times been misrepresented. As Fig. 10:10 shows, and as has been outlined above, most of the leading ports concerned are essentially engaged in one-way traffic. The great economic advantage of the Lakes – and even then, one not fully realized until the system was improved by canals – is that of bulk carriage by water, between areas supplying and areas consuming or dispatching wheat, ore, coal, coke, and limestone. This is not a matter of simple exchange of ore for coal. The phenomenal exception to the general rule is provided by Detroit, where the up-Lake movement of coal and coke meets the down-Lake movement of ore, and where both streams have been tapped.

Specialization on particular types of cargo, and in particular commodities, is well illustrated by an outline comparison of ports in Lakeside and eastern Canada. Sept-Îles and Port Cartier function almost exclusively as dispatchers of iron ore to the U.S.A.; Port Arthur–Fort William ships iron ore as 70 per cent of external exports and wheat as 80 per cent of coastal exports. Baie Comeau ranges between 60 per cent and 80 per cent wheat in its incoming coastal and outgoing external trade. Iron ore accounts for 50 per cent of the volume of imports at Hamilton, and coal for another 40 per cent. Coastal imports here are 50 per cent fuel oil, a commodity noteworthy throughout the ports of the Canadian Lakes, the lower St Lawrence, and the Atlantic coast of Canada: Montreal, for instance, loading wheat as 50 per cent of its external cargoes and receiving wheat as 65 per cent of its incoming coastwise cargoes, also unloads large quantities of petroleum and fuel oil from abroad and dispatches fuel oil coastwise. Eighty per cent of St John's external imports are provided by fuel oil. Halifax loads gypsum for export (50 per cent of external export tonnage) and receives 80 per cent of incoming external tonnage as petroleum, while fuel oil makes up 65 per cent of its coastwise shipments. At Quebec, wheat provides 35 per cent of external shipments, fuel oil 67 per cent of external receipts. Among coastwise unloadings here, pulpwood accounts for 30 per cent, wheat for 20 per cent, petroleum for 14 per cent, and fuel oil for 20 per cent.

Ports on the Gulf of Mexico and in Florida sort themselves into three groups, respectively in Florida, on the Texas coast, and on the Mississippi or near by (Fig. 10:16). Among the Florida ports, Jacksonville functions as an importer. The comparative advantage of carriage by sea, as opposed to carriage by rail from the north, is here great enough to promote port activity. It appears significant that Jacksonville is the first port south of Norfolk to appear in the list in Table 10:1; whatever their prominence in earlier times, Wilmington, in North Carolina, Charleston in South Carolina, and Savannah in Georgia have as ports undergone both absolute and still greater relative decline. Tampa and Port Everglades are both on balance coastwise importers, despite their interest in the export of phosphate. The three Texan ports shown in Fig. 10:16 are by contrast mainly coastwise exporters – of oil, salt, gypsum, or potash. Among the third group, Mobile has long been commended as the natural outlet for the metallurgical works of Birmingham, Alabama: but it is difficult to specify what the expression *natural outlet* is supposed to mean, especially since Mobile remains chiefly an importer of general cargoes. New Orleans functions powerfully as an outlet, both externally and coastwise, for the products of the Mississippi Valley, but its import trade is minor. Bâton Rouge is concerned primarily with shipments of oil.

Nothing so far has been said about the siting of ports. It is obvious enough that many are located upon inlets of some kind or other. Houston, now comparable to New Orleans in volume of total trade, is a wholly artificial port, connected to the sea by its ship canal. It is natural enough that founders of settlements, and port engineers coming after them, should have sought to maximize the advantages of a natural setting: but trade is a fact of economics, not of the physical background. The leading physical difference between the Lakes area, the lower St Lawrence, and the northern Atlantic coast on the one hand, and the southern Atlantic coast and the Gulf on the other, is that the former group offered a wide choice of port locations, while the latter group, physically handicapped by lack of inlets, is in its natural character more restrictive.

The Pacific coast is by nature more restrictive still, with great stretches of unbroken coastline where few natural inlets occur. Ports on this coast handle far less tonnage, as a group, than do those on the Lakes, on the north Atlantic coast, or in Florida and on the Gulf, despite their access to Atlantic trade by way of the Panama Canal; and although the potential outlets are few in number, the low total volume of seaborne trade on this coast ensures that port activities generally are on the modest side (Fig. 10:17). Vancouver resembles a number of Gulf coast ports in being chiefly an exporter, although differing from them in being committed to external trade: wheat provides 40 per cent of its external exports, pulpwood about 45 per cent of coastwise exports, and sand and gravel – like cement, in high demand for twentieth-century construction – about 45 per cent of coastwise imports. Seattle and Portland (Ore.) are .chiefly coastwise importers, although less markedly so than the New England ports on the far side of the continent: they too lack the means to provide bulky export cargoes. San Francisco, the greatest port and the chief general port of this coastline, is also deficient – although not seriously so – in exports; it is, however, worthy of notice for the high proportion contributed to its total trade volume by coastwise movement (Fig. 10:17). Long Beach, with oilfields in its hinterland, is alone with Halifax among the general ocean ports in recording an excess of export over import tonnage.

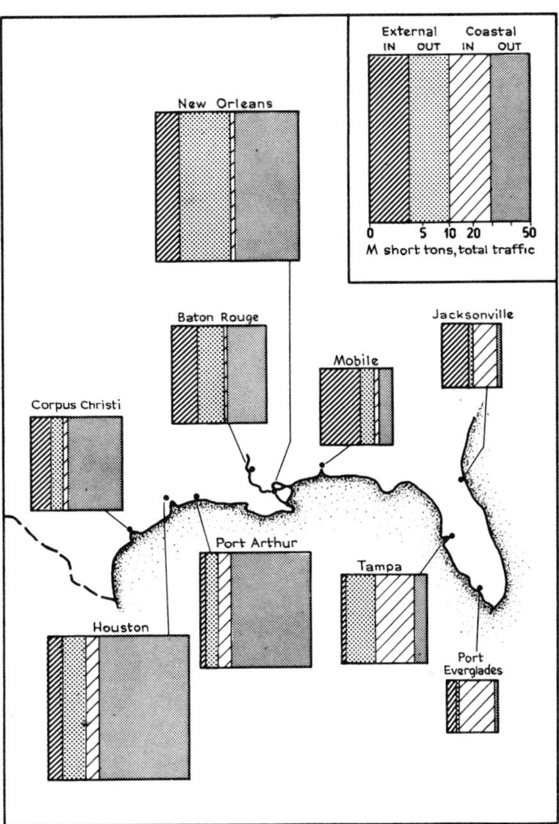

FIG. 10:16 Trade at ports in the South, mid-1960s.

FIG. 10:17 Trade at Pacific Coast ports, mid-1960s.

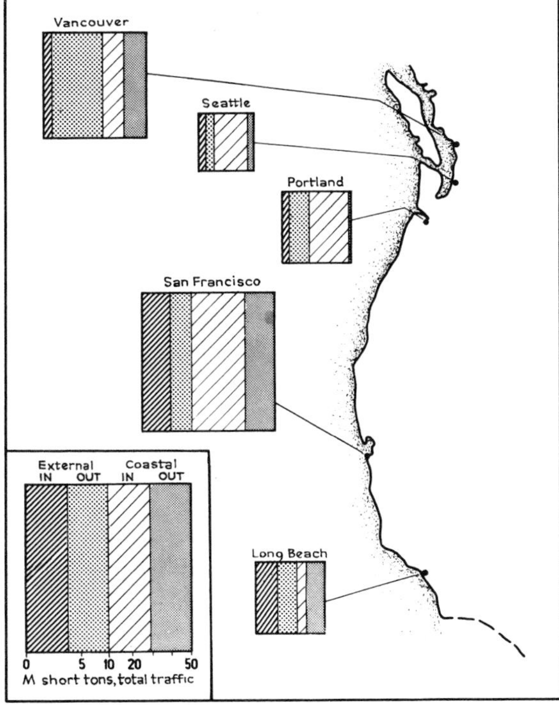

CHAPTER ELEVEN

PEOPLE

Reference has been made at several junctures to population – totals, immigration, internal migration, population-growth, and structure of employment. The themes involved have appeared in connection with processes of settlement and of economic change. It is now time to review the record of total numbers and of rates of increase for their own sake, and also to outline the composition of national populations.

Figure 11:1 generalizes trends in total populations through some three centuries. In order to bring out rates of increase, and changes in these rates, the graph is semi-logarithmic: time is marked on a plain scale but totals lie along a logarithmic scale. Where the graph ascends steadily, the percentage rate of increase is steady. A constant percentage increase is, of course, something different from a constant numerical increase. A 20 per cent increase in a ten-year period would raise a population of 100,000 by 20,000, whereas a starting population of a million would gain 200,000. Rates of increase show population trends, and changes in these trends. If a graph becomes less steep, the rate of increase is falling off.

FIG. 11:1 Population trends: semi-logarithmic.

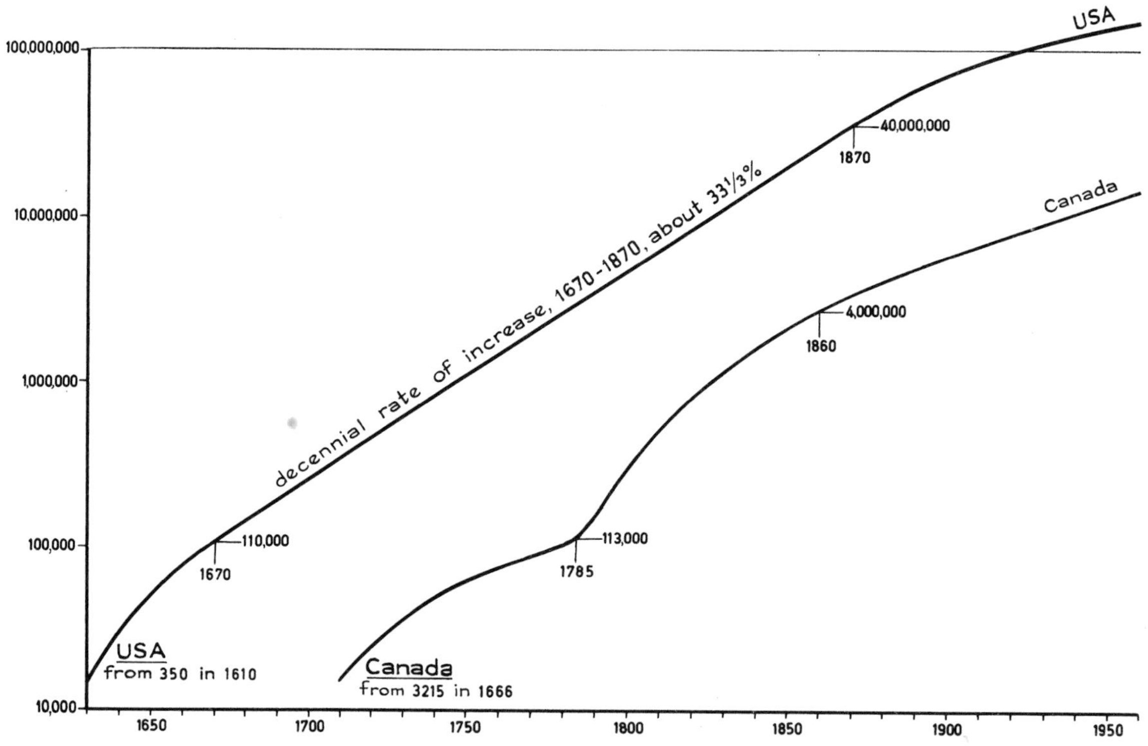

Swift Early Growth

A very rapid rate of increase took the population of what is now the U.S.A. from about 350 in the year 1610 to 110,000 in 1670. Little more than half a century had produced eventual success in the planting of new settlements. The combined total of immigration and births far exceeded the opposing combined total of departures and deaths. By the late 1600s a number of self-maintaining and expansive communities were in existence, and parts of the seaboard had been brought under firm and lasting control. Then began a remarkable two centuries during which the population maintained a steady increase at the rate of about one-third per decade. The sustained course of this increase and its end result are alike impressive. Beginning with a total resembling that of a modest twentieth-century town, the population rose by 1870 to a mark well above the marks of many twentieth-century nations.

Fall of the Birth-rate

In the last years of the nineteenth century the rate of increase began to decline, although the numerical total went on growing. In the first half of the twentieth century the rate of increase was only about half of what it had been between 1670 and 1870. Such a decline in the rate of increase characterizes Western countries generally. It has been deliberately brought about. It reflects millions of individual decisions to limit family size.

A whole complex of reasons underlies what amounts to a mass custom. One reason seems to be that the risk of dying has been reduced by advance in medicine: it is no longer necessary, as it once was, to produce large numbers of children in order to offset numerous child deaths. Another factor, which is not without its ironical side, is the increase of real wealth and its connected rise in standard of living. Parents who are at least reasonably well-to-do, tend, as a group, to spend heavily on their children, especially for education. They may judge it impossible to support a large family at what they consider a reasonable level. A more generalized and more obscure factor is that people in large towns tend to have fewer children than do people elsewhere. At one time, large families among farmers were undoubtedly favoured by the custom, and the need, of using family help on the land; but comparative studies (e.g. in the British Isles) make it clear that much more than labour supply is involved in the contrast between rural and urban birth-rates. The decline in the rate of increase of population in the U.S.A. set in almost precisely when the change began from chiefly rural to chiefly urban location of people.

This shift belongs with the expansion of town-based industry. It also goes in the temporal sense with progressive mechanization of industry: but it would be indefensibly crude to suggest that declining urban birth-rates mean a direct response to the replacement of men by machines. Hand workers, and unskilled workers in particular, are with the unemployed among the least likely to produce small families. The lack of long-term connection between family size and condition of the labour market is well demonstrated by Australia; this country in the 1960s recorded a chronic shortage of workers of all kinds, but its rate of natural increase remained low. Significantly, perhaps, Australia is very highly urbanized indeed.

At the same time, it is important to discriminate between long-term demographic trends and short-term responses to unusual situations. The depression years of the early and mid-1930s markedly reduced the birth-rate throughout the U.S.A. as a whole.

Another circumstance influencing rates of population-growth is the altered social and economic position of women. In one sense this circumstance is a demographic factor; in another it is an economic effect. If women in Western societies choose, or if they have no alternative, they can now be self-supporting. This also means that wives can go out to paid work. Many wives do so – in many cases, specifically to add to the family income and thus to achieve some particular standard of living. The net effect is to reduce the number of births per marriage, and also to shorten the average span between the first and the last child. The mid-nineteenth century prospect of ten or twenty years of child-bearing has been destroyed.

Indeed, when the effect of immigration into the U.S.A. is discounted, it can readily be shown that the rate of natural increase (excess of births over deaths) was already slackening as early as 1850; by 1870 it was down to about 20 per cent per decade, and by the early 1900s had fallen to 10 per cent or less. Although in 1940–60 it recovered to about 15 per cent per decade, it still remained only half what it had been in the early 1800s. The new prosperity which farming settlement, town growth, and immigration itself brought to so many people in the U.S.A. proved the opposite of encouragement to have large families. What some commentators regard as the mother-myth in the social life of the U.S.A. is little bar to restrictions on motherhood.

Trends in Canada

Canada, with a history of occupance about as long as that of the present U.S.A., has fared differently in respect of population-total, and in part differently in respect of trends. Even with its halved rate of natural increase, the population of the U.S.A. rose from 40 million in 1870 to nearly 180 million in 1960. Canada, attaining 4 million by 1860, reached 18 million a century later.

Canada's high rate of increase in the early 1700s is typically early-colonial. It involves but a small absolute figure – about ten thousand at the beginning of the century. The rate of increase fell rapidly away towards the mid-1700s, in response to the policy of exploiting rather than of developing the holdings in the French-held or French-controlled territory of the time (Chapter Five). The end of the Seven Years War in 1763 produced no immediate effects on demographic trends in Canada, but the War of Independence was at once followed by a burst of increase. Loyalists moving north into Canada across the new border contributed something to the renewal of rapid growth: migrants from Britain, choosing a British colony rather than a newly-independent foreign country, supplied the rest. By 1825 the Canadian population-total had increased ninefold, from little more than 110,000 in 1785 to a round million. Although the rate of increase was already on the decline at the end of this period, it was still roughly equal to the one-third per decade of the contemporary U.S.A. However, by the time that a total of 4 million was reached in 1860, the rate of increase was already well down. For about half a century afterwards, Canada was unable to match the attractions offered to migrants to the U.S.A. When the Canadian Prairies were opened up, and when large towns grew in the St Lawrence Valley, Canada was already under the influence of social and demographic trends identical to those noticed for the U.S.A., although the 15 per cent rate of natural increase per decade, recorded in Canada between 1940 and 1960, is somewhat above the corresponding rate in the U.S.A.

Like the U.S.A., Canada is becoming progressively urbanized; and its people aim at living-standards equal to those sought on the other side of the border. But, unlike the U.S.A., Canada finds difficulty in retaining its immigrants. During the late nineteenth century it was on balance losing people by external migration, and in the fifty years from 1891 to 1941 the net gain from external migration was less than 650,000, only 10 per cent of the actual increase in population-total.

When national totals and national trends are broken down, marked contrasts between area and area become apparent, especially in respect of the rate and the timing of population-increase. Fig. 11:2 presents semi-logarithmic graphs for selected areas of Canada. The Maritime Provinces, markedly rural and experiencing persistent out-movement for generations, record a very slow rise in total population since 1875. The increase in numbers between that year and the mid-twentieth century was but about 40 per cent of the starting total. Ontario, long settled and possessing all the necessary foundations of urban development, has recorded a persistent rise in numbers of people, unbroken except in the early 1900s, and a steady rate of growth which has multiplied its population fourfold in a century. Alberta in the Prairies, and British Columbia on the west coast, both exhibit that rapid early rate of increase which, combined with low absolute numbers, has already been described as typically early-colonial. In this context, however, the term early-colonial needs to be taken in the demographic rather than in the political sense. British Columbia started its first drive of expansion rather earlier than Alberta. Both provinces lost impetus, Alberta the more obviously, in the interval 1920–50, but both have embarked on a surge of renewed increase which has taken their individual totals above the combined population of the Maritime Provinces. At the current rates of growth they have no chance of surpassing Ontario until well into the twenty-first century; but their trends are nevertheless well worthy of notice, Alberta's as representing the impact of the petroleum and allied industries on a one-time agricultural society, and British

Columbia's as corresponding to the west-coast development which is so pronounced in California.

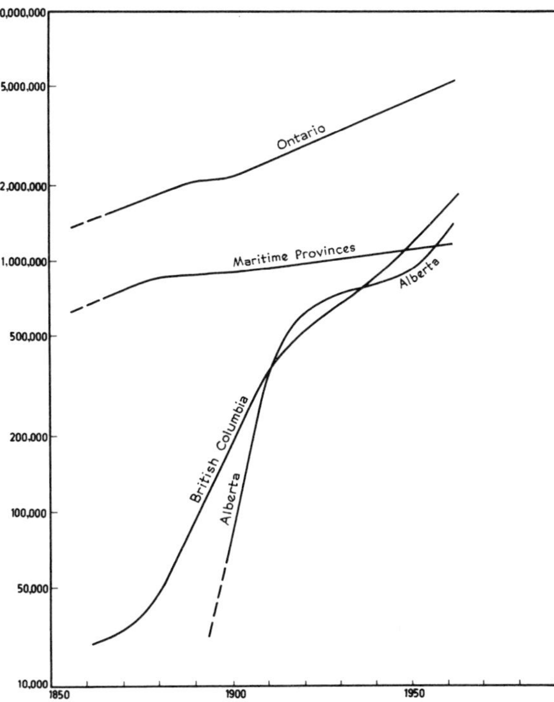

FIG. 11:2 Population-trends for selected parts of Canada: semi-logarithmic.

Distribution in the U.S.A.

A generalized summary of the proportionate distribution of people in the U.S.A. is given by Fig. 11:3. The marked changes in the comparative populations of the three divisions, between 1800 and 1900, were due largely to the internal migration previously discussed in connection with farming settlement. Whereas the Atlantic seaboard states contained more than 90 per cent of the country's people in 1800, their share had fallen to 50 per cent at the time of the Civil War, and to 40 per cent by the end of the century. Proportionate increase in States between the seaboard and the Mississippi occurred mainly between 1800 and 1850, that in areas west of the Mississippi between 1850 and 1900. Changes since the end of the century have been slight by comparison, with the western States recording faint proportionate gains at the expense of the two other divisions. However, the west coast embarked during World War II on a renewed surge of increase which continued and strengthened in the post-war

FIG. 11:3 Trends in the proportionate distribution of people in the U.S.A.

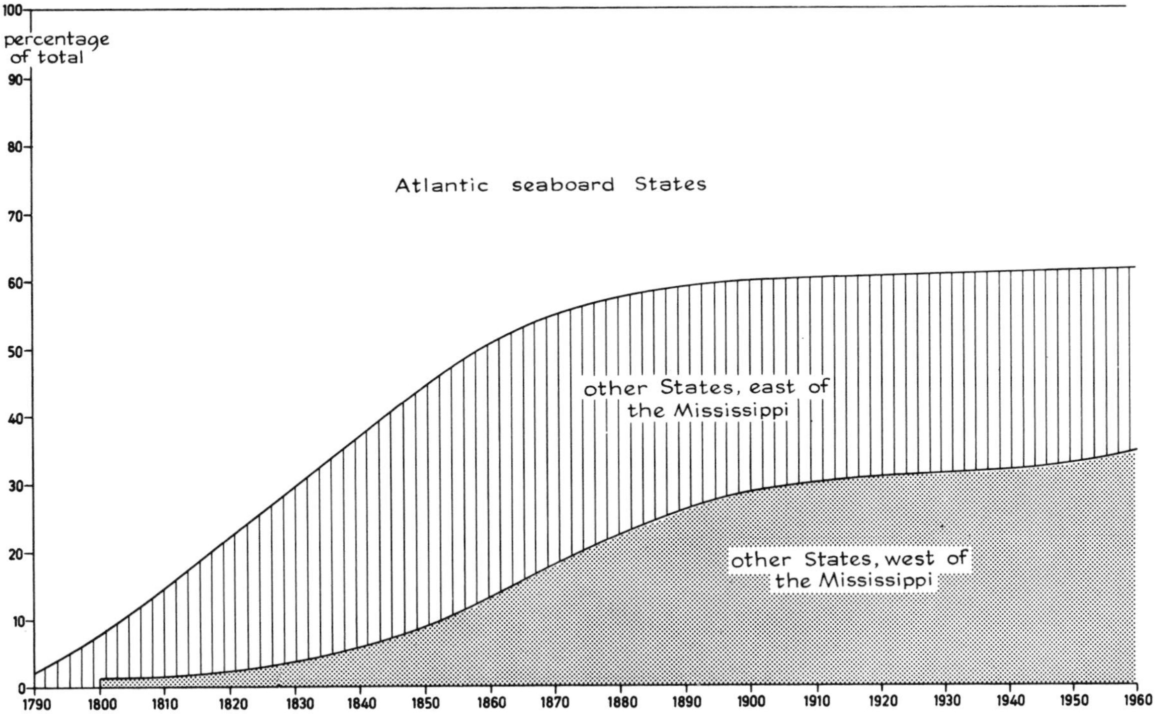

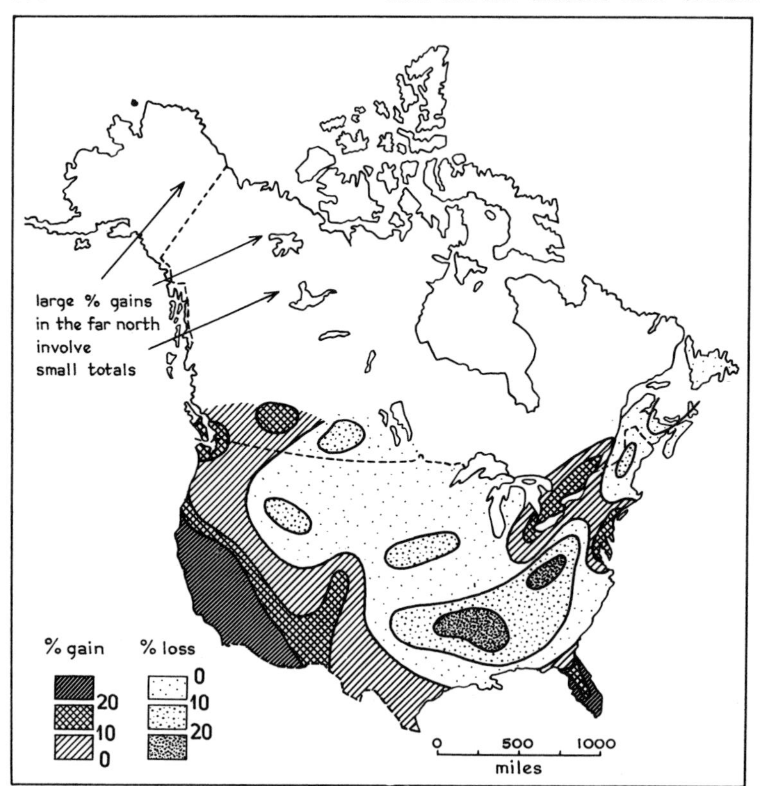

FIG. 11:4
Net gains or losses by migration in the decade 1950–1960 (U.S.A.) or 1951–1961 (Canada), as percentage of population at the earlier census: generalized.

FIG. 11:5 Proportional distribution of the national populations between rural and urban: generalized.

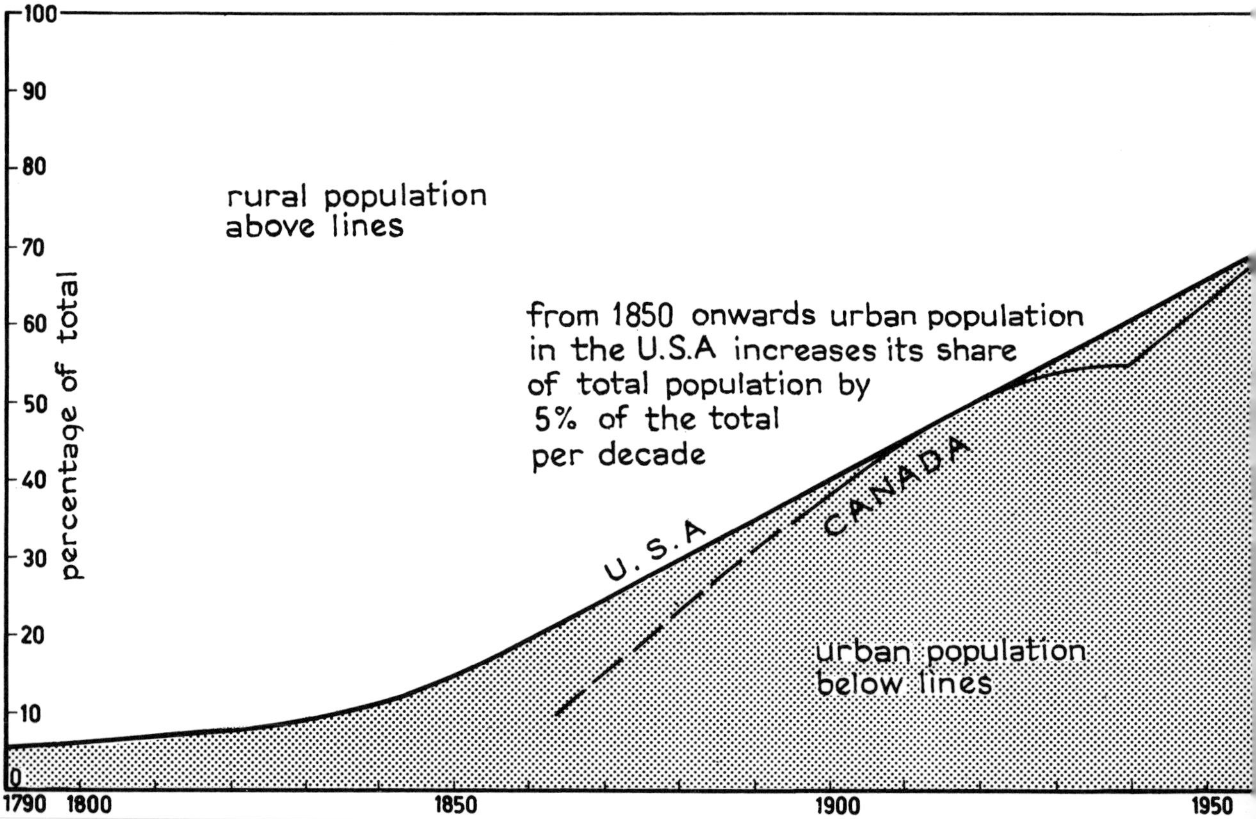

period. Its effects, experienced chiefly in California, are not merely of demographic significance. Because voting strength in presidential elections and in the federal House of Representatives is distributed according to State totals of population, the west-coast trends have great political significance.

Internal Migration

These trends involve powerful internal migration. The short-term effects of this process, for the intercensal period 1950–60, are summarily presented in Fig. 11:4. Areas with especially high rate of gain include the Lower Lakes–St Lawrence country, the Atlantic coastland from New York to Washington, D.C., and parts of the territory intervening. There is another concentration in greater Chicago, which is however obscured in the records by the disparity between administrative boundaries and effective town limits, and which is omitted from Fig. 11:4 because of the small scale employed. Gains in Alberta relate more or less directly to the development there of petroleum resources, while those in the Vancouver–Puget Sound country belong to early-stage growth. The most marked of all percentage rates of increase occur on the west coast in California and in the southeast in Florida. In both of these States the principal increases in numbers are taking place on or close to the actual coastland. California, assisted both by its climate and by industries established during World War II and subsequently retained and expanded, exerts a strong pull on actual and potential migrants from other parts of the U.S.A. Florida, long having promoted its claims to the winter resort trade, is now also attracting permanent migrants. Some of these are retired businessmen who can afford to escape the harsh winters of the industrial northeast, but others are well within working age. It remains to be seen whether or not Florida will match the industrial expansion of California, and if so, how effectively manufacturing industry can be combined with tourism. But whatever developments are to occur in the future, Florida is exceptional demographically, as in many other ways, among the Southern States.

The highest rates of migratory loss, 20 per cent or more of the starting population, are recorded for a large block of the U.S. South and for parts of the Appalachians. Out-movement from the Appalachian belt results chiefly from depressed economic–social conditions in the West Virginia coalfield. The whole of the agricultural interior of the continent records net losses, which also appear in parts of the Cordillera, in New England, in the Maritime Provinces of Canada, and in Newfoundland. Southern Saskatchewan, Indiana–Nebraska, and a huge extent of the U.S. South run at more than a 10 per cent rate of net loss by migration. Moreover, out-movement from some of these areas has persisted through a whole run of decades.

Whereas a great attraction of North America in the pioneering days was freely available farmland, internal and external migrants of the twentieth century tend to make for towns. Both in Canada and in the U.S.A., the number of town-dwellers came to equal the number of country-dwellers in about 1920 (Fig. 11:5). The change from mainly rural to mainly urban residence is better documented for the U.S.A. than for Canada. A slow previous increase in the proportion of townspeople to total population was converted in the U.S.A., in the mid-nineteenth century, to a swift and sustained increase, which altered the urban percentage from about 15 per cent in 1850 to about 70 per cent in 1960, with the changeover still inexorably in progress. In part, the shift reflects the growth of towns in areas which were originally settled by farmers; but much of it results from country-to-town migration. Developments in Canada in this context have been generally similar to those in the U.S.A. The townward movement gathered force in Canada about twenty years later than in the U.S.A., but has proved the swifter. A check in the 1930s has been followed in Canada by a strongly renewed townward drive, with Canadians in 1940–60 being absorbed by towns, or relocating in towns, even more rapidly than citizens of the neighbour country.

Country-to-town migration is familiar in westernized societies generally. It inevitably accompanies developments in manufacturing industry, and the increase of employment in tertiary occupations. On the negative side it goes with the mechanization of farming. The effects of this mechanization in reducing the need for farm workers has already been examined. Of the 45 per cent of the U.S.A., population classed as rural residents in 1910, about eight in ten actually lived on farms, amounting to

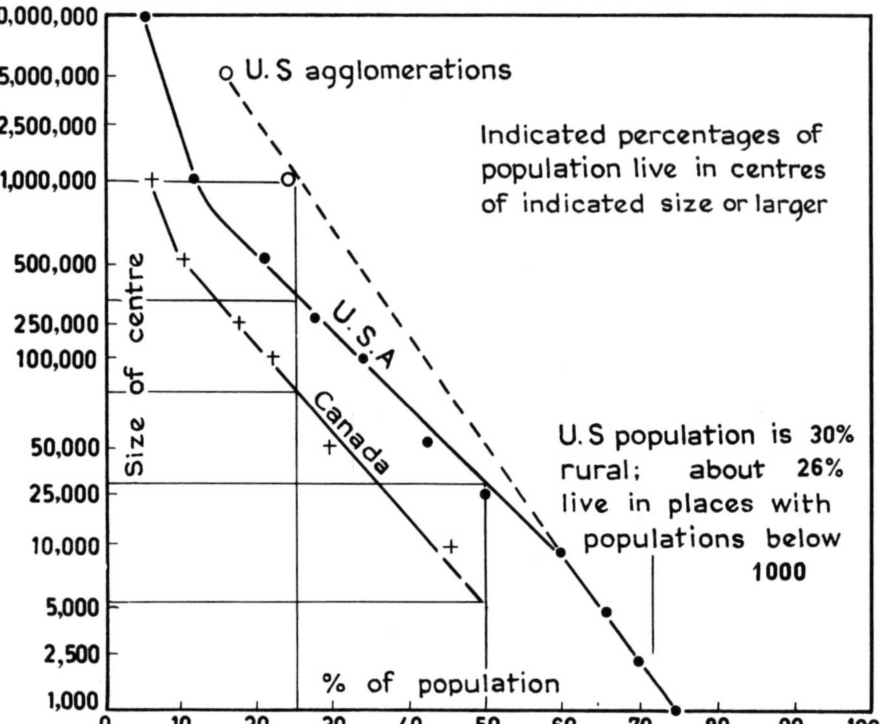

FIG. 11:6 Cumulative distribution of urban populations.

32 million people and more than a third of the population of the whole country. Fifty years later the number of farm-dwellers was down by half, representing well below 10 per cent of the country's people and only about a quarter of those classified as living outside towns. Out-migration from farms in the U.S.A., in the interval 1940–60 amounted to no less than 17 million people.

Town Sizes and Town Rankings

Although in comparisons of urban with rural populations something depends on definition, the slight uncertainty involved in choice of criteria does not seriously affect the general statements offered in Fig. 11:5. Comparisons among towns are another matter. Population-totals listed for administrative units can differ strongly from the larger totals of effective urban concentrations. Commuter linkages, retail trading, and spread of masonry have no necessary connection with governmental limits.

Nevertheless, when towns are ranked by reported size of population, they arrange themselves in orderly fashion (Fig. 11:6). As this diagram shows, half of Canada's people in 1961 lived in places with 5000 inhabitants or fewer, while places with half a million people or more accounted but for 10 per cent of the national total. By contrast, a quarter of the people of the U.S.A. in 1960 lived in centres with at least a million inhabitants.

The potential difference between administrative and effective size, to which attention has just been directed, suggests that the relationship between town size and cumulative percentage of population in the U.S.A. may be best indicated by the pecked line in the diagram. If so, then half the inhabitants of the U.S.A., in 1960 lived in towns with 50,000 people or more. About a quarter lived in places with 1000 or fewer.

Corresponding diagrams for selected distinct areas point up contrasts in degree of urbanization and in urban ranking (Fig. 11:7). The graph for the industrial northeast resembles that for the U.S.A. as a whole, except that it shows a still higher concentration of people in towns, with huge agglomerations at the head of the list of ranking. On the northeastern seaboard, New York has merged physically with its administrative neighbours, and these in turn have joined their own outer neighbours, to produce urbanization on a regional scale and to attract the invented name *megalopolis*. The

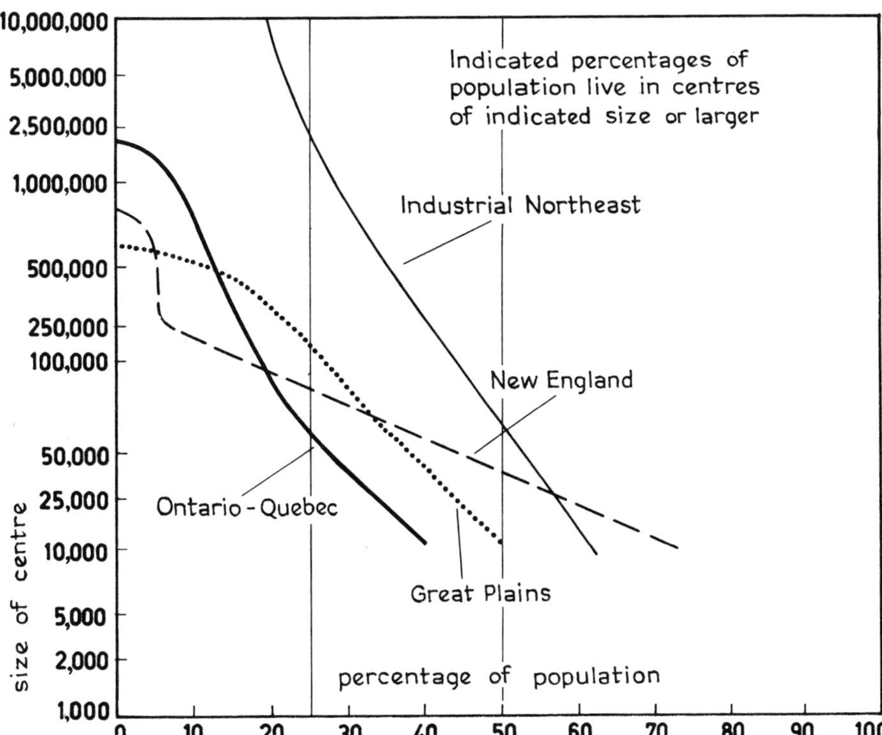

FIG. 11:7 Cumulative distribution of urban populations for selected areas.

graph for Ontario–Quebec in turn resembles the graph for Canada as a whole, except that concentration of people into towns begins, in these two provinces, at about the 50,000 mark. On the provincial scale, a town with 50,000 inhabitants is likely to be a fast-growing concern, whereas the main contrast on the national scale occurs between towns with more than, or fewer than, half a million people.

The Great Plains are more highly urban than Ontario–Quebec up to this mark of half a million people per town, but have not as yet produced million-cities. But since the urban drive in the Plains is well under way, the emergence of large towns on the Plains can be expected to produce a smoothed-out ranking scale similar to that of the whole country. Similarly, Ontario–Quebec can be expected to develop towns with as many as 5 million people, and to achieve a distribution of their inhabitants through the ranking scale like that recorded for the industrial northeast. New England differs strongly from these other areas. In respect of the ratio of urban to rural population it is the most highly urbanized of all; but its people live chiefly in towns ranging between 10,000 and 250,000 in population. Above the quarter-million mark comes a pronounced break, with no New England towns in the range between 250,000 and 500,000 people. The number of towns in New England is remarkably high in proportion to the total of inhabitants, but many are of modest size, and most have been recording low growth-rates for a long time.

Negroes in the U.S.A.

A theme which combines migration from one part of the country to another with the rural–urban shift, and also with the expansion of towns and their internal changes, is that of the Negro element in the U.S. population. At one time this element was very largely Southern; the South was largely Negro, and the Southern Negro was largely rural. The South is still more highly rural than most other divisions of comparable size, with two-fifths of its people living outside towns; but at the 1960 census nearly half the country's total of Negroes were living outside the South, and three-quarters of them, 14 of some 19 million, were town-dwellers. Of this 14 million, nearly 4 million were located in the northern towns of New York, Newark, Baltimore, Chicago–Gary, and the border town of Washington, D.C. New

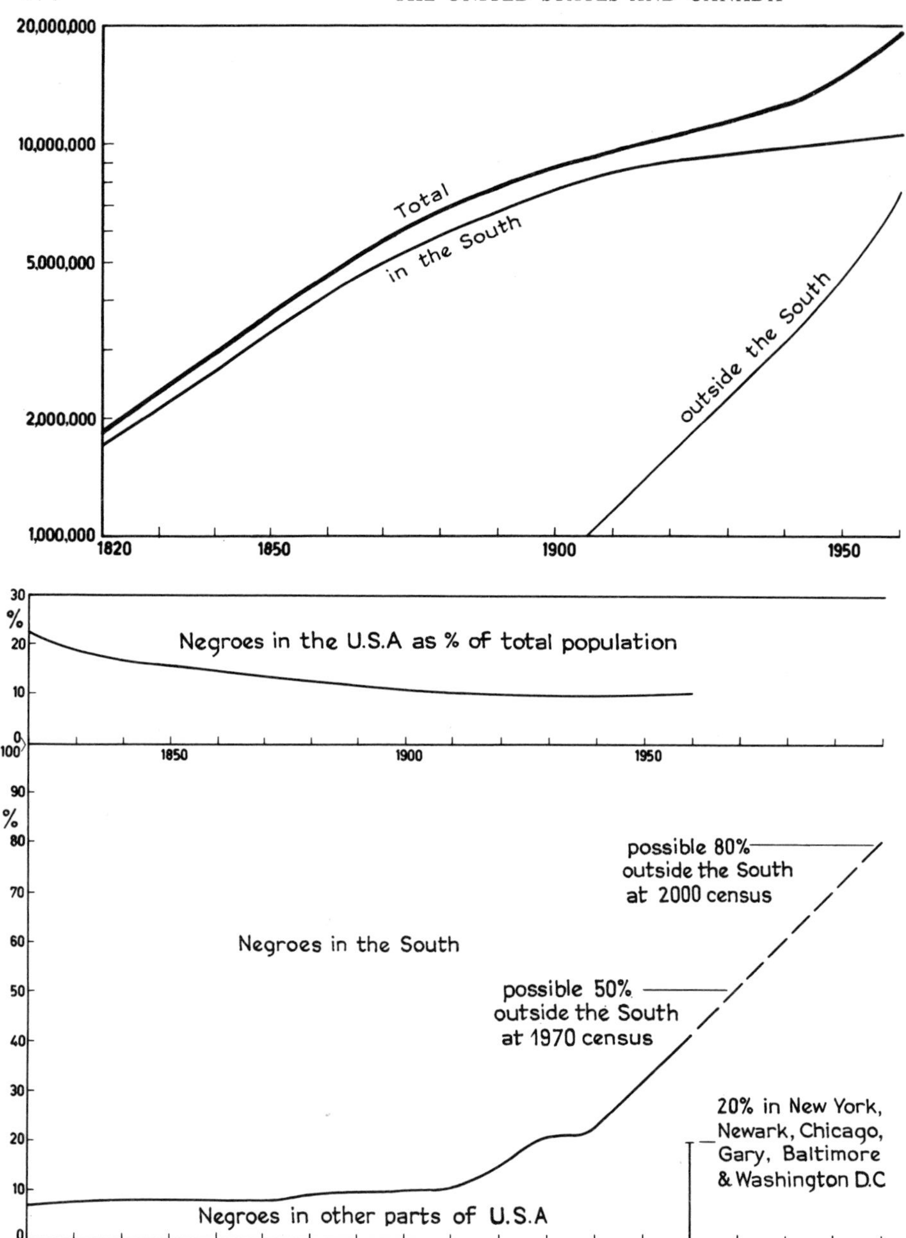

FIG. 11:8
Trends of the Negro population of the U.S.A.: generalized, semilogarithmic.

FIG. 11:9
Negroes in the U.S.A. as percentage of total population; proportionate distribution of Negroes inside and outside the South: generalized.

York excepted, all these towns recorded populations more than 30 per cent Negro. Another $1\frac{1}{4}$ million Negroes lived in large Southern towns with an equally high fraction of Negro inhabitants – New Orleans, Atlanta, Memphis, and Birmingham being prominent in the list. The tally of Negro inhabitants already reached in ten towns is equal to the national total of rural-dwelling Negroes.

Taken together, Figs. 11:8 and 11:9 show how the shift of Negroes from the South has gathered force. More than 90 per cent of the Negro people in the U.S.A. lived in the South prior to the Civil War. For about a decade after this war there took place a slight out-movement from the Southern States, but 90 per cent of Negroes were still located there by the end of the nineteenth century. Then, at about the time when the national demand for farm workers reached and passed its peak, the shift began. Like many other changes it was checked by the slump, but it resumed during World War II as strongly as before. By the 1960 census it had concentrated 40 per cent of the country's Negroes in areas outside the South. If it continues unchanged, one in every two Negroes will be living outside the Southern States by 1970, and three-quarters will be elsewhere by the year 2000.

Extrapolation of trends through nearly half a century is admittedly speculative; but the current out-movement of Negroes from the South is a recorded fact. Up to 1960 it failed to offset the natural rate of increase among the Negro population there (Fig. 11:8), but if the existing trends continue to strengthen themselves, it is likely to do so in the future. That is to say, there is a prospect that Negro emigration from the South will more than offset the excess of births over deaths, leading to an absolute decline in numbers.

The graph of Negro population, plotted on a semi-logarithmic base, bears comparison with the earlier graph (Fig. 11:1) of the national total of people. From Civil War days to about 1900 the rate of Negro increase fell persistently away, stabilizing in about 1900 at a value somewhat below that recorded for the country in general. Indeed, in the early part of the twentieth century the contribution of Negroes to the national total of population became progressively less (Fig. 11:9). A fraction of the percentage decline is probably due to racial admixture sufficient to allow some people of mixed ancestry to cross the social barrier between coloured and white; an undoubtedly larger fraction results from the abolition of the slave-trade and the subsequent restriction of immigration mainly to whites. But, in addition, the reduced rate of natural increase among Negroes parallels that recorded for the whole country.

The one exceptional fact is the rise in the rate of Negro increase from about 1945 onwards. This rise, greater than that recorded for the white element of the population, has accompanied the accelerated move away from the South. If the rate is maintained, it will produce 40 million Negroes by the year 2000. If the shift from South to North persists, so that 80 per cent of these potential 40 million live in the North, then the South by the year 2000 will contain but 8 million Negroes, distinctly fewer than the 11 million and more at the 1960 census. As always in the projection of demographic trends, these forecasts are little better than guesswork: but there is at least a distinct possibility that the Southern Negro population will become stabilized, with out-migration concentrating increases in other parts of the nation.

Grave social problems result from the migration already on record. Like all migrant groups who are generally poor, the Negro immigrants to large U.S. towns tend to locate in run-down inner districts. They have no choice. Rents and prices in the outer suburbs are impossibly high, quite apart from questions of deliberate exclusion by whatever means. The depreciated condition of property in many inner districts tends to keep rents down to some extent, and a further effective reduction can be had at the expense of overcrowding. Conditions of this type are common enough throughout the world, but they may perhaps be more severe in the U.S.A. than in some other countries. In the first place, some inner residential districts in that country include numerous frame houses which, once repair work is neglected, deteriorate very rapidly. Secondly, the customary out-movement of people from inner districts to the suburbs is complicated in the U.S.A. by the establishment of suburban supermarkets and retailing complexes. These great outlets, first developed in the U.S.A., but rapidly imitated by some other countries, rely on techniques and processes which are typically (although by no means exclusively) North American – mass-production, mass-marketing, and travel by private car. In achieving their own pronounced success, the suburban stores have destroyed much of the retail function of the older, inner, parts of their towns. Thirdly, heavy reliance on private cars has damaged many city transit systems, or at least has prevented them from expanding. Residents of the inner districts are in consequence less mobile than they could otherwise be.

The type of demographic effect produced in these various connections is well illustrated by Washington, D.C. As administratively defined, the national capital excludes the commuter settlements in adjacent parts of Virginia and Maryland, which are however effective working parts of the town. The formal boundaries included at the 1960 census a population which was more than half Negro. But Washington's Negro total of 400,000 was far outdistanced by the 800,000 in Chicago, and still farther by the 2,225,000 Negroes in New York, which held 12 per cent of all the Negroes in the country.

It might have been thought that the migration of Negroes from Southern farms to Northern factories would relieve some of the social and economic pressures and tensions which had so long operated on Negroes in the South. In actuality, the outcome has at times been open discord. Its causes are presumably linked with the long and troubled campaign to secure for Negroes political rights and educational advantages equal to those of other citizens; but it would be erroneous to regard the problem merely as one of colour. Equally serious troubles are on record, both in the U.S.A. and in countries abroad, wherever particular groups have identified themselves as minorities surrounded by majorities who are at best indifferent but more usually hostile. Relationships are not always good, for instance, between Puerto Rican groups in New York and the New Yorker natives of the mainland. Similarly, serious disorders in the past have involved migrants from Europe. At the same time, the very fact of colour readily distinguishes Negroes from whites; if it does nothing else, it serves to encourage the concentration of Negroes in distinct areas, and to promote the retention and development of a kind of subculture. In this respect the U.S.A. faces a social task without parallel as yet in the occidental world.

Other Ethnic Groups in the U.S.A.

Ethnic minorities other than Negro have fared better, possibly in part because they are far smaller. Chinese communities, prominent in New York and San Francisco, are in any event not given to turbulence. Their group behaviour may be influenced by their close-knit and effective family structures, and also by their deep involvement with retailing and the restaurant trades or with market gardening in country districts. To a considerable extent, the quarter million Chinese in the U.S.A. are capitalists operating in a capitalist economy.

Filipinos, rather less numerous than Chinese, and Japanese, numbering about half a million, live mainly in the west, particularly in California. Representative occupations of these two groups include those listed for the Chinese, plus domestic service: numbers of young male Filipinos and Japanese work as houseboys. The half million Indians of the U.S.A. live partly on reservations – e.g., in Arizona–New Mexico, Oklahoma, and Florida where their traditions are to some extent preserved. These traditions are more varied than would be guessed from the stereotype Indian of the Plains. Neither in the Painted Desert of the Southwest nor in the swamplands of Florida did Indians hunt bison or live in teepees. The Hopi, Navajo, and Seminole tribes are all sessile, inhabiting permanent dwellings. To varying extents they are involved in production for the tourist trade, their handcrafts becoming somewhat debased in consequence; but the Hopi and Navajo, for instance, still produce excellent hand-woven goods, pottery, and silverware.

Ethnic Groups in Canada

Canada has something over 200,000 Indians. The total is increasing. Three-quarters of this minority group live on reservations, mainly on the Shield or in the Cordillera; and some of their settlements are characterized by teepees. Eskimos are far fewer, numbering about 14,000. Their economy, carefully adjusted over many centuries to one of the most rigorous human habitats of all, was almost overthrown by culture-contacts with white Canadians, partly because of the changes in methods and results of hunting effected by the introduced rifle. Nowadays, however, the rapid spread of co-operatives in the Far North is ensuring for the Eskimo peoples trading outlets and levels of production which were formerly impossible.

Among Canadians of European descent, ancestry at immigration is less than half British – specifically, 44 per cent, against 53 per cent of other European nationalities. However, the term *at immigration* can refer back a long way. For many of the $5\frac{1}{2}$ million French-Canadians, who constitute 30 per cent of the country's total population, it refers back to 1763 or earlier. In that year there were 70,000 inhabitants in French Canada. The preservation of the French language and its accompanying social traditions, during more than three centuries during which the number of French-Canadians has multiplied eighty times, impressively demonstrates cultural continuity and persistence. About three-quarters of the group live in Quebec Province, which contains $4\frac{1}{2}$ million of them; the next highest provincial total is recorded by New Brunswick, with half a million.

Although the French-Canadians are frequently regarded as a minority group, on the ground that they are outnumbered by English-speaking Canadians, it is possible to argue that they form the largest individual fraction of the Canadian people. Although 44 per cent of Canadians are British by descent, only 23 per cent are English. It is not surprising that the French-Canadians, strongly concentrated as to location and closely bound by their own social practices, are able to feel different from other inhabitants of Canada. They have registered strong protests at the entry into Quebec of industrial concerns run by English speakers, and have protested against involvement in the Boer War and in World Wars I and II – chiefly, be it said, in principle, for they have accepted their full responsibility for the actual fighting. At the extreme, some French-Canadians propagate ideas of separatism, the complete removal of French Canada from the Canadian federation.

Supplies of Immigrants

Attitudes taken in the U.S.A. to the ancestry of its whites are not altogether identical with those taken in Canada. The most readily available data are those on foreign white stock – inhabitants with one or both parents foreign born. In 1960 this group totalled 33 million, the contributions coming chiefly from Italy, Germany, Canada, the U.K., Poland, and the U.S.S.R., in that order. Canada identifies its immigrants by country of birth. Whereas the British Isles normally ranks very high in the list, it does not always lead. Italy, the U.S.A., Germany, and Poland are often prominent among suppliers of migrants to Canada.

Both countries face problems of assimilation. Although the U.S.A. has long pursued an official policy of obliging applicants for naturalization to learn the English language, the principles of the Constitution, and the rudiments of national history, recent studies suggest that immigrants tend to agglomerate, retaining and even strengthening their imported cultures. There is no prospect that the French-Canadians will surrender their Gallicism. Situations of this kind are without strict parallel in Europe, where ethnic conflicts have for centuries been resolved or suppressed by military means. Accordingly, they are not to be judged in European terms.

TABLE 11:1

Population (millions)

U.S.A.		Canada	
1790	3·9	1791	0·275 (approx.)
1800	5·3		
1810	7·2		
1820	9·6		
1830	12·9		
1840	17·1		
1850	23·2	1851	2·4
1860	31·4	1861	3·2
1870	39·8	1871	3·7
1880	50·2	1881	4·3
1890	62·9	1891	5·0
1900	76·0	1901	5·4*
1910	92·0	1911	7·2*
1920	105·7	1921	8·8*
1930	122·8	1931	10·7
1940	131·7	1941	11·5*
1950	150·7	1951	14·0
1960	178·5	1961	18·2
1965	191·9	1965	19·6
1966	193·8		

*Excludes Newfoundland.

PART TWO

CHAPTER TWELVE

THE NORTHEAST

We propose to give, for each of the macro-regions distinguished in this and the subsequent chapters, an introductory summary of area, population, urban centres, land use, and numbers of livestock. We do not claim precise accuracy for the data listed, particularly since these are expressed in round numbers. However, the values given do represent the outcome of a fairly complex process of partition, distribution, and transfer, which we have at least partly controlled by reference to detailed locational maps, to data for states, provinces, and territories wholly contained within a given region, to the divisional breakdowns of official returns, and to national totals. The use of round numbers inevitably produces some discrepancy, which however is not greater than 5 per cent in gross livestock numbers – probably a tolerable error, in view of the year-to-year fluctuations involved – and is far less than 1 per cent in respect of area, population, farm acreage, and acreage of cropland. We consider that some regional differences may have been somewhat understated, and that the differences apparent in the regional summaries and in the general maps which illustrate these are real differences (Figs. 12:1–12:7).

The northeastern division of the continent extends over some 500,000 square miles: its total population is about 80 million. That is to say, not much below half the combined populations of Canada and the U.S.A. live in this area. It is the most highly urbanized part of the continent, with four in every five of the largest towns. No fewer than 65 of the 100 leading industrial firms, as measured by sales volume, have their headquarters here; and the industrial output of the area is well over half the joint total of the two countries (Figs. 9:11, 12:8, 12:9).

In numbers of ways, this can be regarded as the core area of the continent. In addition to having concentrations of people, towns, and factories, it conducts vigorous international commerce in New York, Philadelphia, Boston, Montreal, and Quebec. International diplomacy has its bases at Washington, Lake Success, and Ottawa. At the same time, some districts carry very strong historical and emotional associations. Reminders of the continent's more than three centuries of development stud the landscape in the placid valleys of New England and the Appalachians. Ghost farms and misfit settlements recall the days of the Pilgrim Fathers and the Acadian pioneers who first introduced European ways and adapted these to the new environment. Valley Forge and Gettysburg belong with the struggles resulting from the independence of spirit fostered in the new homeland. It was in this area that contact with Indians made crops known which were to have profound effects on the agriculture, not only of North America but of Europe and indeed of the world. Chief among these was maize, still called in North America by an abbreviated form of the name Indian corn.

Place-names signalize the origins of early settlers: Manchester, Chatham, Portland, Berlin, Montpelier, Notre Dame, and Bonavista record transatlantic migration. Many peoples were involved. And although the Anglo-Saxon element has risen to dominance, the continuing possession by France of Miguelon off Newfoundland, and the existence of numerous French speakers in Quebec, remain to demonstrate that cultural and political linkages have been complex indeed.

As treated in this chapter, the area under discussion does not coincide with the Manufacturing Belt previously identified. It does, however, correspond to what is customarily spoken of in North America

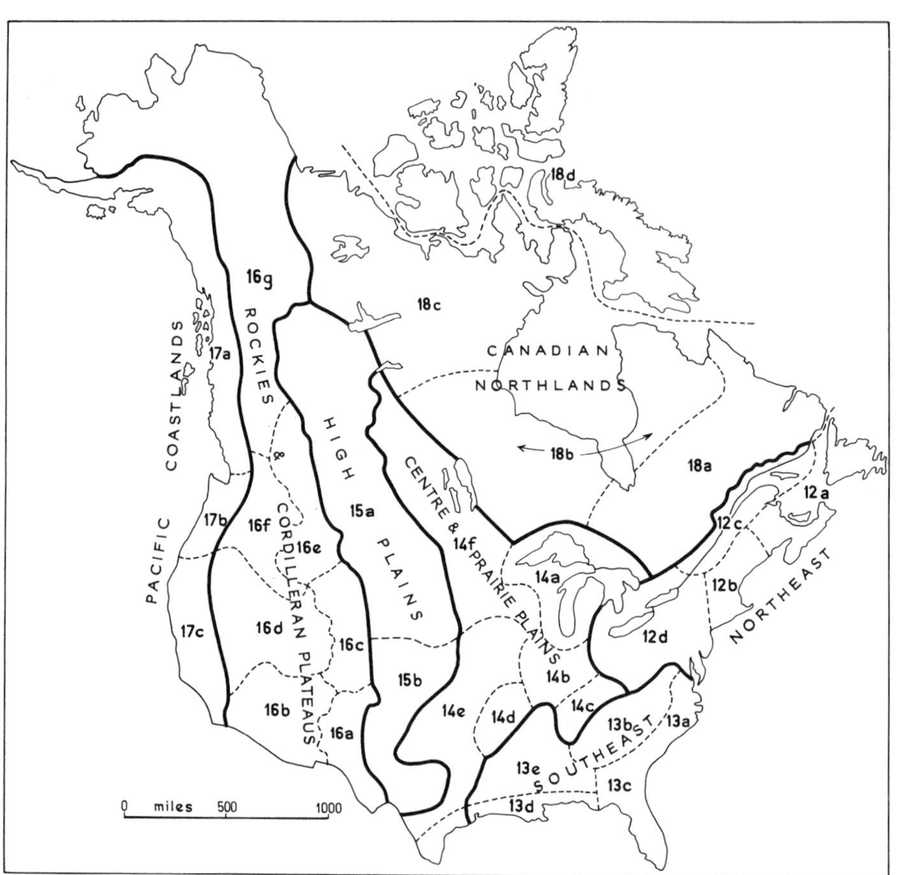

FIG. 12:1 The regional breakdown.

Key to FIG. 12:1. Numbering corresponds to position in the text.

The Northeast
- 12a: The Maritime Provinces of Canada
- 12b: The New England Region
- 12c: The St Lawrence Valley
- 12d: The Industrial Northeast

The Southeast
- 13a: The South Atlantic Seaboard
- 13b: The Piedmont and Southern Appalachians
- 13c: The Extreme Southeast
- 13d: The Gulf South
- 13e: The Southern Lowlands of the Mississippi

The Centre and the Prairie Plains
- 14a: The Western Great Lakes Region
- 14b: The Central Agricultural Lowlands
- 14c: The Kentucky–Tennessee Hills
- 14d: The Ozark and Ouachita Massifs
- 14e: The Central and Southern Low Plains
- 14f: The Northern Low Plains

The High Plains
- 15a: The Northern High Plains
- 15b: The Central and Southern High Plains

The Rockies and the Cordilleran Plateaus
- 16a: The Southern Rockies
- 16b: The Interior Southwest
- 16c: The Central Rockies
- 16d: The Great Basin
- 16e: The Northern U.S. and Southern Canadian Rockies
- 16f: The Northern U.S. Cordilleran Plateaus
- 16g: The Northern Inland Cordillera

The Pacific Coastlands
- 17a: Coastal Alaska and British Columbia
- 17b: The Coastlands of the Pacific Northwest
- 17c: The Pacific Southwest

The Canadian Northland
- 18a: The Eastern Uplands
- 18b: The Canadian Lakes Plain
- 18c: The Far Northern Mainland of Canada
- 18d: The Arctic Archipelago

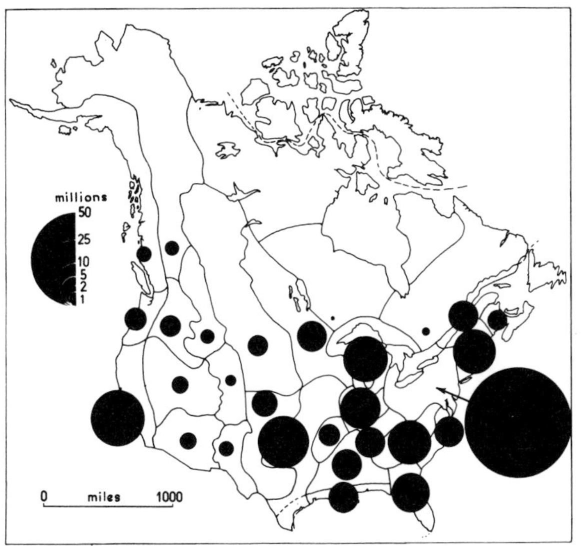

FIG. 12:2 Population, by regions.

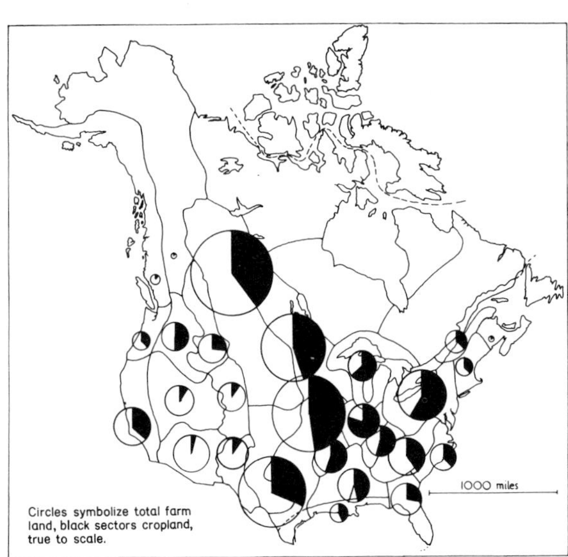

FIG. 12:3 Summary land use, by regions.

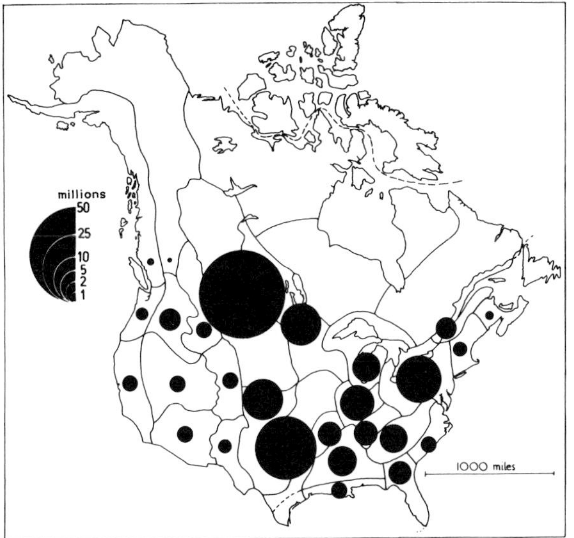

FIG. 12:4 Cattle, by regions.

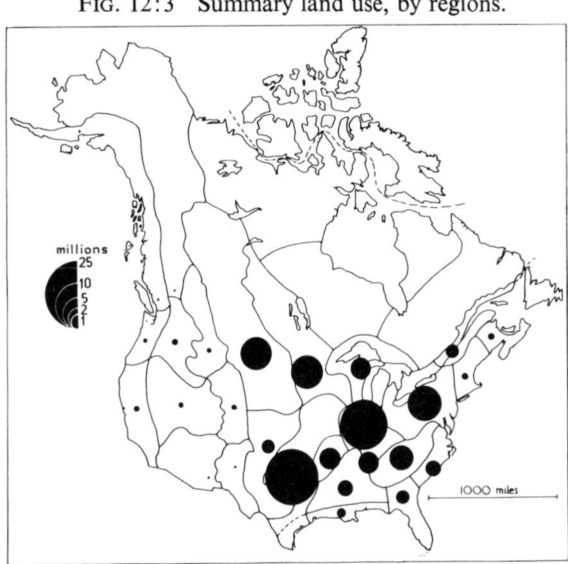

FIG. 12:5 Pigs, by regions.

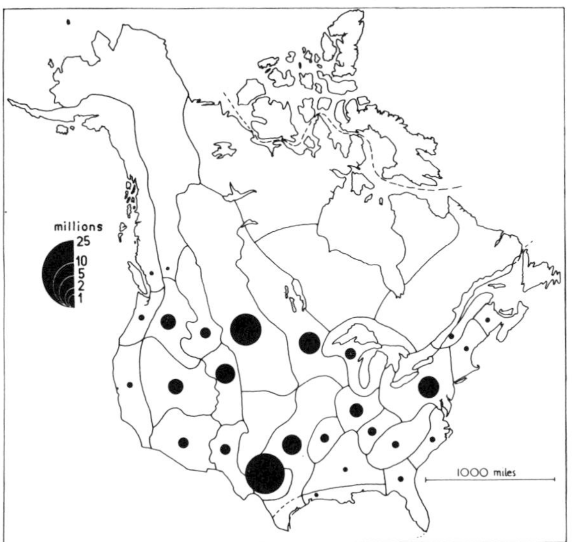

FIG. 12:6 Sheep, by regions.

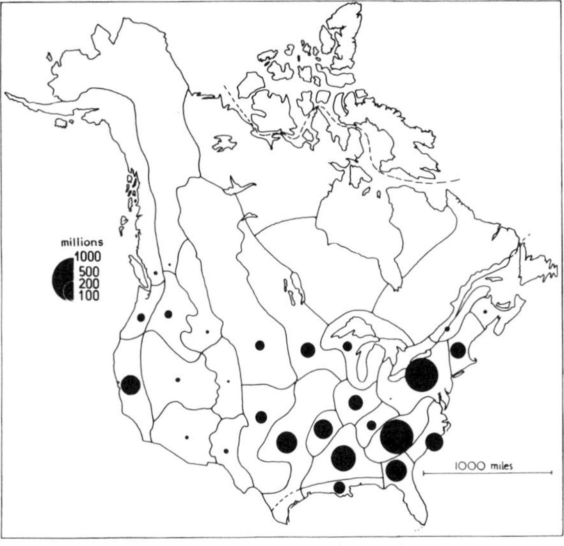

FIG. 12:7 Poultry, by regions.

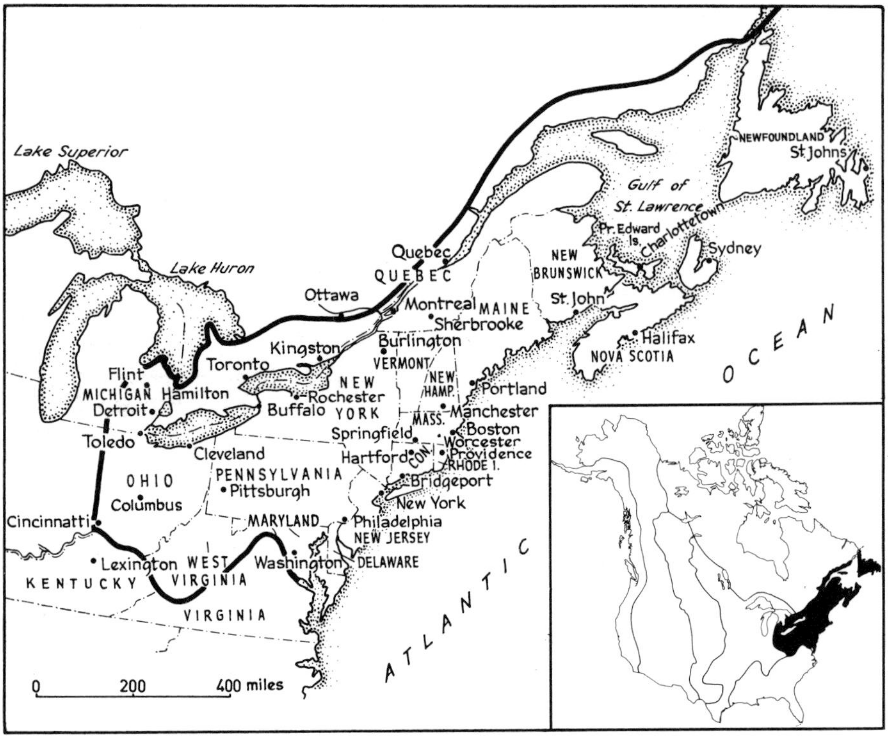

FIG. 12:8
The Northeast.

as The East. It includes the Maritime Provinces of Canada, New England, the St Lawrence Valley, the Industrial Northeast, and the Near-West. That is to say, it takes in all the northern part of the Appalachian system, the continuation of upland country through the Acadian belt into Newfoundland, the middle and northern Atlantic seaboard, and what is often distinguished as the Lower Lakes–St Lawrence country. Despite the concentrations of people and industry, some districts which are readily accessible from the large towns still appear remote. There is, as would be expected, a high level of tourist and recreational activity.

12a: The Maritime Provinces of Canada

Area: about 95,000 square miles.

Population: about 2 million.

Cities* with at least 25,000 people: populations of some metropolitan areas given in brackets:

Halifax, N.S., 92,500 (184,000)
St John's, Nfld., 63,500 (91,000)
Saint John, N.B., 55,000 (95,500)
Dartmouth, N.S., 47,000
Moncton, N.B., 44,000
Sydney, N.S., 34,000
Corner Brook, Nfld., 25,000

Population density outside the largest cities and metropolitan areas: about 15 per square mile.

Rather more than half the population of this region is classed as rural, and distinctly less than half live in places with more than 10,000 inhabitants. Well below 10 per cent of this region is in farmland, of which cropland takes less than a quarter and farm woodland nearly three-quarters. Forests, including farm woodland, cover more than three-quarters of the region.

Numbers of livestock: cattle, about 425,000, of which 155,000 are milk cows; sheep, 100,000; pigs, 155,000; poultry, 4 million.

The Maritime Provinces are traditionally made to include New Brunswick, Nova Scotia, and Prince Edward Island. However, now that Newfoundland

* The term *city* in the U.S.A. connotes an incorporated settlement with town status; it has nothing to do with the city charters of the U.K. Accordingly, and especially since much of the literature about the geography of towns in North America goes under the style of city studies, we shall generally prefer the use of *city* to the use of *town* in this chapter and those following.

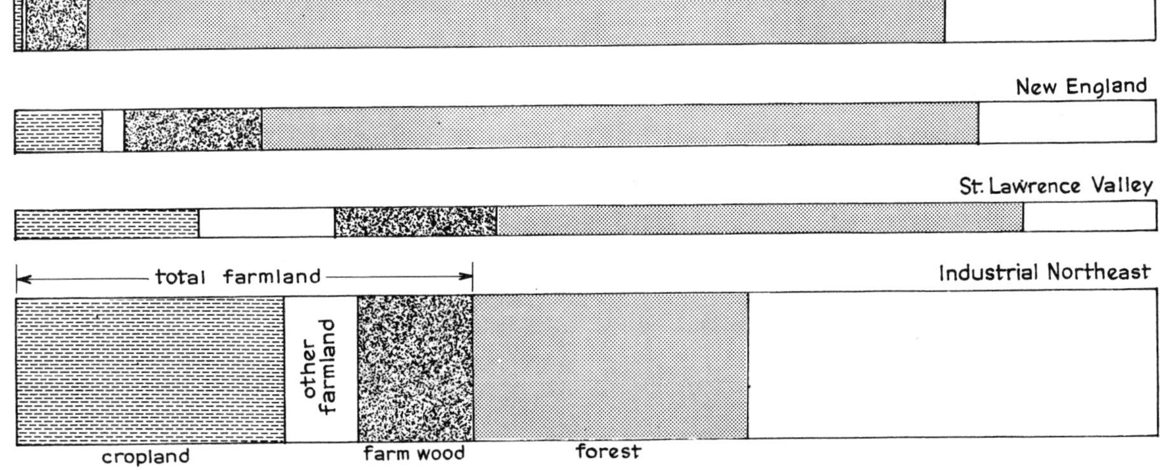

FIG. 12:9 Land use in the Northeast, by regions.

is fully integrated into Canada's political structure, it seems reasonable to extend the title to the island of Newfoundland, although not to Labrador which is part of Newfoundland Province. The region as thus defined belongs to the folded belt of Palaeozoic rocks which borders the southern edge of the Laurentian Shield. These rocks, now strongly compressed and in some parts metamorphosed, originated as sediments in a shallow marginal geosyncline. The earth-movements that closed the geosynclinal trough have produced a marked N.N.E.–S.S.W. grain, expressed in patterns of ridge and valley. There is no very high country: no hills rise as far as 3000 feet above sea-level. Nevertheless, relief in detail is varied. Its variety has been increased by Pleistocene glaciation, which roughened some parts of the landscape and left others mantled with till. Valley mouths have been drowned by the rising sea-level of deglacial times, as in the Bay of Fundy, St Mary's Bay, and Bras d'Or in Nova Scotia, producing a coastal pattern not unlike that of southwestern Ireland. Where material exists on which soils can form, the uneven glaciated terrain of crystalline outcrops, boulder fields, and till patches has developed podsols. Quality of parent material, the brief time available since deglaciation for soil formation, and a harsh climate ensure that, in the natural state, the podsols are unpromising to agriculture. There is much forest – the spruce and balsam fir which colonized the region as the last ice-sheet melted back, and the beech, hemlock, basswood, and maple in the moister valleys; and the forests support a thriving lumber industry.

Apart from the exploitation of wild berry barrens – a practice representative of gathering economy – agriculture in this region is concentrated where maritime influences on the climate ameliorate to some extent the general harshness. The most favourable agricultural soils are those developed on outcrops of Triassic limestones and marls, on the alluvial deposits of the larger rivers, such as the St John, or on the lacustrine silts which fill the basins of former glacial lakes. Field crops are limited to the hardy – buckwheat, hay, oats, potatoes; buckwheat, for instance, grows well along the Chaleur Bay coast. Exceptionally, there is one outstanding commercial crop; the Annapolis Valley produces half the total Canadian crop of apples. There is some commercial dairying and poultry-meat production for the national market, but the region is handicapped in this respect by large distances and high transport costs.

Part of the economy of the region depends on the fur farming discussed in an earlier chapter. Although production is only about 6 per cent by value of all Canadian furs, and only about 7 per cent by value of all ranch furs, fur farming is economically of considerable significance, especially in Nova Scotia and Newfoundland.

Mineral resources are limited. A downfold of coal-bearing rocks of Carboniferous age includes six small coalfields, between Sydney on the Bras d'Or of Cap Breton Island, and Picton and Stellarton. The 12,000 feet of coal-bearing strata dip northeastward under the ocean; early workings, extending as far as two miles beyond the shore, have been abandoned on account of flooding. The upper and most accessible horizons of the coal measures, however, contain bituminous coal of good coking quality, which supplies metallurgical coke to the steel industry at Sydney and New Glasgow. Iron ore comes from near-by Wabana on Bell Island, which is well placed as an exporter; in the form of concentrate, the Wabana ore can bear the cost of shipment to the U.S.A. and to Europe.

Non-ferrous metal ores are patchily distributed, occurring mainly in association with batholithic intrusions. They include lead, zinc, and copper, along with small quantities of gold, silver, and the rarer metals. Alloy materials for the steel industry, such as tungsten, antimony, and manganese, are worked.

It is fair to state that the terrestrial resources of the Maritime Provinces offer but a weak base for economic development. This has long been known as a region of difficulty and persistent out-migration, lying somewhat apart from the rest of the country. On the maritime side, however, it is far better provided. Numerous fishing grounds lie off-

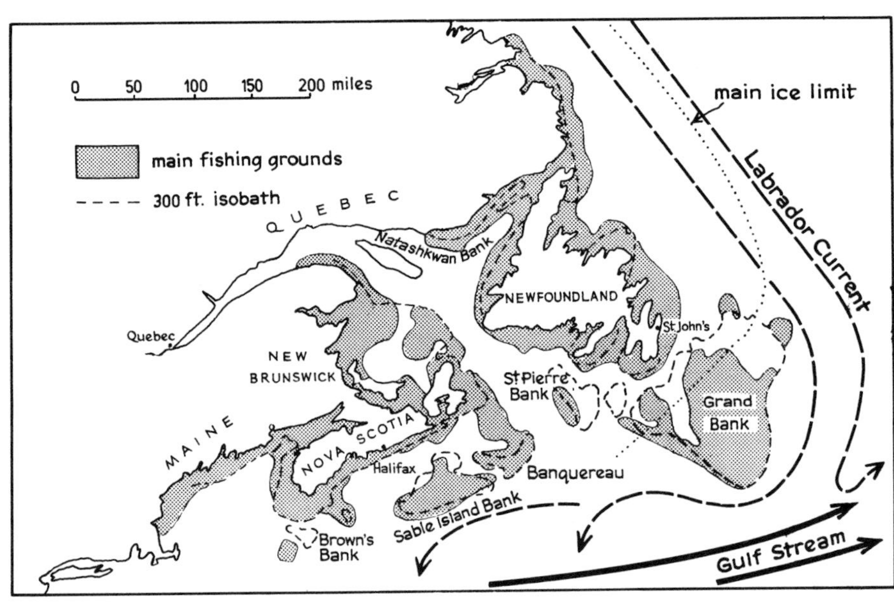

FIG. 12:10 Fishing grounds off Newfoundland and New England.

30. Dipping for cod in trapnets, Newfoundland.

shore, from Newfoundland to New England, many of them being of international importance (Fig. 12:10). The continental shelf here is unusually broad; and it carries extensive banks, probably the morainic deposits of the continental ice-sheet, where the waters are shallow. The Grand Banks of Newfoundland extend over 400,000 square miles, equivalent to the land area of the region. Other fishing grounds include Green, St Pierre, Banquereau, Sable Island, La Have, Brown's, and St George's Banks. All these record depths of less than 300 feet, in a part of the ocean where warm northward-moving waters of the Gulf Stream system adjoin the colder, denser southward-moving waters of the Labrador Current near the coast. Plankton, both plant and animal, flourishes, providing the first link in a chain of prolific fish life. Most of the commercial fish of the open waters, such as cod and halibut, belong to the boreal group; they make winter migrations to the southernmost Banks (Plate 30). The main fishery lasts from March to September, when the closing season is menaced by drifting icebergs and advection fogs. Herring, lobster, and inshore fish are also taken during the summer. Halifax and Lunenberg are chief among the many fishing harbours from which schooners and modern diesel trawlers put out to the Banks.

Lobster is the most valuable species, being worth about a quarter of the total catch. Lobster fishing depends, however, on the cod fishery for the supply of heads with which the lobster traps are baited. Canneries dot the coast from the Gaspé peninsula to the international border, and beyond that as far south as Cape Cod: lobster farming, in pounds formed in rocky inlets, has developed in Maine. The second most valuable species is cod, also worth something like a quarter of the total catch; this fish, like halibut and flounder, is taken by trawl. Haddock and scallops come next on the list. Herring, mackerel, and shad, all schooling fish, are taken by purse-seine nets. Malpeques oysters, systematically farmed in Richmond Bay, Prince Edward Island, are widely sold on national and international markets.

12b: The New England Region

Area: about 66,500 square miles.

Population: about 10½ million.

Cities with at least 100,000 people in the metropolitan area, plus Manchester, N.H.: population of metropolitan areas in brackets:

- Boston, Mass., 697,000 (2,600,000)
- Providence, R.I., 207,500 (815,000: includes Pawtucket and suburbs)
- Worcester, Mass., 186,000 (323,000)
- Springfield, Mass., 174,500 (475,000: includes Chicopee, Holyoke, and suburbs)
- Bridgeport, Conn., 157,000 (334,500)
- New Haven, Conn., 152,000 (312,000)
- Hartford, Conn., 162,000 (525,000)
- Lawrence–Haverhill, Mass., 117,000 (188,000)
- Waterbury, Conn., 107,000 (180,000)
- New Bedford, Mass., 102,500 (143,000)
- Fall River, Mass., 100,000 (138,000)
- Stamford, Conn., 93,000 (175,000)
- Lowell, Mass., 92,000 (158,000)
- Manchester, N.H., 88,000 (95,500)
- New Britain, Conn., 82,000 (130,000)
- Pawtucket, Mass., 81,000 (see note on Providence)
- New London–Groton–Norwich, Conn., 72,500 (157,000)
- Portland, Me., 72,500 (120,000)

Population density outside the largest metropolitan areas: about 55 per square mile.

Less than a quarter of this region is in farmland: about a third of the farm acreage is cropland, rather more than half is woodland; grassland pasture takes about 10 per cent of the farm acreage. Forests, including farm woodland, cover three-quarters of the region.

Numbers of livestock: cattle, 1 million, of which about 600,000 are milk cows; sheep, 80,000; pigs, 180,000; poultry, 150 million.

The New England region includes the states of the northern U.S. Atlantic seaboard: Connecticut, Rhode Island, Massachusetts, Maine, New Hampshire, and Vermont. Of the 10½ million inhabitants, the great majority live in the south near the Atlantic coast. Connecticut and Massachusetts contain three-quarters of the total population; densities decline rapidly towards the north and in the inland direction from the coast.

Apart from French Canada, New England is the only region of the North American continent where colonial history is more than a thin veneer. It has developed a distinctive architectural style of undeniable handsomeness. Thus, quite apart from the settings on the rocky, ocean-swept coast, or against backdrops of forested mountains, the small settlements of New England are visually attractive in themselves (Plate 5). Scenery and buildings contribute alike to the tourist and recreational trades. Coastal resorts in summer double their populations by their intake of holidaymakers, while inland districts capitalize on forested mountains, on rivers and on lakes, on the annual display in the forests of autumn colours, and on the 100 inches of winter snowfall which supports the operation of alpine playgrounds.

Travel and tourism are easy enough to understand, given the scenic and recreational attractions of New England, its historical associations, and the general affluence which makes travel and touring widely possible. But the deliberate promotion of the resort trades in New England also represents a response to an environment which is little less forbidding than that of the Maritime Provinces. Like the Maritimes, the New England region suffers by being glaciated. Its high country, rising above 6000 feet in the White Mountains of New Hampshire, has been heavily scoured by ice. Glaciation accentuated the already-existing trends of major relief, which, although the region belongs to the N.E.–S.W. belt of Palaeozoic rocks, are determined mainly by faults and shatter-belts with north–south lines; accordingly, overland travel in the east–west direction is hampered. At its maximum extent, the ice-sheet reached beyond the present coastline. When it decayed, the till and outwash which it discharged into the New England valleys proved to be coarse; and between the valleys, as on the low coastal platforms, the melting ice revealed uneven ground from which the waste mantle had been widely stripped. This was unpromising territory for agriculture, and indeed for settlement of any kind. The earliest farms, set on uneven ground, littered with boulders and interrupted by bogs in glaciated hollows, were cleared and brought into cultivation only at the expense of great labour. Winters are long, stormy, and cold. Mineral resources are sadly deficient: coal is absent altogether. Yet it was here that the first individual settlers, as opposed to highly financed colonists and planters, chose to establish themselves: and it was here that, despite the gross deficiencies of the resource base, concentrated industry was first developed in North America.

Neither the settlement pattern nor the economic development of New England can be understood without reference to religion. The Pilgrim Fathers were dissenters from the established church in England, where by 1600 Protestantism had, as events were to prove, at last gained supremacy over Roman Catholicism. But the Protestant–Catholic struggle, entangled as it was with the political relationships between England and Spain and the English throne and the Stuarts, left the Protestant powers with no disposition to countenance division within the Protestant range. Thus it came about that the Pilgrim Fathers set sail for a new land where they could hope to follow their own beliefs. The south Atlantic coast was already being taken over by colonists and planters; the mid-Atlantic was held by Indians, the St Lawrence by France. The New England coastline remained; and it was here that the Fathers and their successors came. New England contained half the white population of the Atlantic colonies in 1640, and 40 per cent in 1700. By 1770, when settlers were over the Appalachians, it still had a quarter of the inhabitants of what were shortly to become the United States, and had increased its population fortyfold since 1640 to more than half a million.

In accounting for the firm establishment of settlement in New England, much allowance must undoubtedly be made for the social and religious attitudes of the settlers, even though the effect of these attitudes is not susceptible to measurement. Expectation and acceptance of austerity, shortage, and hardship were basic to the dissenting faiths of the age. In most of its aspects, religion in New England was, to say the least, puritanical; on the positive side, it encouraged thrift, determination, and hardihood. There can be no denying that it helped the New England colonists to bear the poverty and the winter cold of their environment: indeed, poverty itself could be regarded as a virtue. At the same time, religious freedom did not mean religious harmony. Dissenting groups, having split off from a major creed, are still liable to division within themselves; and the determination necessary to deal with the New England colonial environment was apt to translate itself into obstinacy in religious dispute. In consequence, numbers of the earliest settlements threw out new villages, where the original process of migration in a religious cause was repeated on the local scale. This kind of thing, just as much as the detailed variation in the relief of New England, accounts for the large numbers of separate towns and villages in the region.

New England's commerce developed powerfully and soon. Although the aim of settlement was religious and political freedom, and although the settlers deliberately set to work to establish a self-supporting subsistence economy, the potential of external trade was not long in being realized. Boston, on the great circle route which linked England to the southern colonies and the Caribbean, became deeply involved in the traffic in sugar, rum, turpentine, tobacco, English manufactures, and African slaves. During the eighteenth century, the New England ports developed as exporters, first of timber for naval construction, and then of ships. New York and the New England ports shared among them during this century between a quarter and a third of the overseas commerce of the Atlantic colonies; and it was not until the 1760s, shortly before the War of Independence, that the growing external commerce of New York overtook that of the New England ports as a group. In this group Boston was supreme, functioning both as a general port and as an entrepôt. Smaller ports tended to be more specialized than Boston, New Bedford and Nantucket, for example, becoming deeply implicated with the New England whale fishery, which in 1775 had a hundred and fifty whaling ships based on Nantucket alone.

Industrialization in New England grew in part from the domestic crafts of the colonials. Beyond the established commercial links with England, it had at the outset few advantages: but these included the high level of effectiveness of the New Englanders as members of an industrial workforce, the obduracy of the local entrepreneurs, and widely distributed supplies of potential power. In respect of water power, the climate and the glacial history of the New England region are powerful assets. The climatic regime ensures not only copious run-off, but also a minimal difference between discharge respectively at the high-flow and the low-flow seasons. The break of relief between the coastland and the low plateau which backs it joins with the accidented topography of sheet glaciation to produce numerous waterfalls, where mills could be established. Power potential was developed, among other places, at Fall River, Providence, Pawtucket, New Bedford, Lowell, Lawrence, Manchester, and Holyoke. The first wave of industrialization, that of the nineteenth century, was dominated by the cotton industry: New England was capable of providing the necessary power for cotton mills, and of supplying the required capital and workforce, in a way that the cotton-growing States could not match. The rise of the cotton industry was accompanied by that of other manufactures – woollen textiles, leather goods, and metal products which, their manufacture developing to a considerable extent out of domestic craft, involved high costs per unit bulk, great skill in production, and marked specialization in small districts.

The shift of much of the cotton industry to the cotton-producing States has been traced in an earlier chapter: it represents in part a response to New England conservatism, in part a purely economic movement towards the source of the raw material, and in part an exchange of the cheaper labour in the South against the dearer labour of the Northeast. A comparison of the original location of cotton milling in New England with its contemporary location in Lancashire is obviously indicated. While both regions possessed definable physical advantages for cotton textile manufacture, and while both lay on the transatlantic trade route, it was entrepreneurs who made the locational decisions. The fact that both areas have now lost much of their former industry shows that physical advantages and trading connections are not enough for industrial survival.

In the event, New England surrendered sooner than did Lancashire its commitment to cotton manufacture; and part of the accompanying woollen industry has also gone. Residuary skills and the control of machinery patents enable New England to retain the finer variations of textile working. The region's industry today is dominated by the factory production of metal, mechanical, and electrical goods (Plate 31). Like the metal products of the craft industries from which the existing industries in part derive, the items produced by the modern factories have high cost/bulk ratios – firearms, aero engines, missile guidance systems, office machinery,

31. Eighteen-thousand-ton machine-press in an aircraft manufacturing plant at Worcester, Mass.

machine tools, precision instruments, computers, and electrical and electronic equipment of all kinds. Among the older-established industries, the production of silverware and of high-quality cigars persist. The pulping industry has relocated itself within the region. Many early plants were located at rapids on upland streams; but the economies of scale induced by cheap electric power and by the use of giant Fourdrinier-machine mills have relocated pulping at tidewater sites in Connecticut.

Like the settlements which contain it, and like the power sites with which many of these settlements are associated, manufacturing industry in New England is rather scattered. Lawrence, Lowell, Worcester, Providence, Pawtucket, and Fall River form a rough half-circle at a distance of forty or fifty miles from Boston: Manchester, Concord, and Springfield are more remote. And although the three southernmost New England States are as highly urbanized the group formed by New York, New Jersey, and Pennsylvania, none of their towns except Boston is large by North American standards, and even Boston has fewer than three-quarters of a million people. Providence, the next largest, is but a third the size of Boston.

Farming in New England tends to be specialized, in much the same manner as industry and for much the same reason – transport costs. Many of the pioneer farms now lie abandoned, overtaken by secondary forest. However, the cranberries and blueberries of the New England berry bogs, the potatoes and canned corn of Maine, and the beans and tobacco of Massachusetts all command national markets. The success of these crops owes something to climate, much to successful marketing policies, and little to soils; for, as in the Maritime Provinces, the soils of the New England region are in the main poor. Here again, it is on strips of Trias, on river terraces, and on lacustrine silts that farming is mainly practised. There is a signal difference between the farming of the three northern States and that of the three southern. In the former group, the average farm size is very close indeed to the 160 acres of the quarter-section, whereas the latter group contains numerous small but highly intensive holdings: nearly 20 per cent of its farms are under ten acres in area, but the average farm value in the south is four times that in the north. The difference is in part that between dairying and horticulture, for the southern coastland of New England belongs to the belt of fruit and truck farms which reaches from the outskirts of Boston to the federal capital. However, the north of the region also has its specialisms – potatoes on the heavily fertilized glacial loams of the Aroostock Valley of northeastern Maine, pome fruits which are tolerant of acidic soils, and turkeys – while dairying for the liquid milk market has increased markedly in the south.

Of its former maritime activity, New England has lost much of its external commerce to New York; its shipbuilding declined with the progressive phasing-out of wooden ships, being represented nowadays by the making of pleasure craft. Whaling has gone, but other fisheries continue, as was mentioned above in the account of the Banks. The New

England region has 20,000 fishermen and 12,500 fishing craft, which bring in something under 20 per cent by value of the national catch. Haddock, ocean perch, herring, cod, and flounder are chief among the deep-sea species taken, while inshore fisheries produce lobsters and shellfish roughly equal in total value to the deep-sea catch. Boston, Gloucester, New Bedford, Portland (Me.), and Rockland are the region's leading fishing ports.

12c: The St Lawrence Valley

Area: about 52,000 square miles.

Population: about 5 million.

Cities with more than 50,000 people: populations of some metropolitan areas given in brackets:

Montreal, Que., 1,191,000 (2,110,000)
Ottawa, Ont., 268,000 (430,000)
Quebec, Que., 172,000 (360,000)
Verdun, Que., 78,000
Sherbrooke, Que., 67,000
Hull, Que., 57,000
Kingston, Ont., 53,500
Three River, Que., 53,500

Population density outside the largest cities and metropolitan areas: about 30 per square mile.

About two-fifths of this region is in farmland, of which cropland and farm woodland each take about a third. Forests, including farm woodland, cover nearly two-thirds of the region.

Numbers of livestock: cattle, 2 million, of which half are milk cows; sheep, 150,000; pigs, 1 million; poultry, 12 million.

The St Lawrence Valley is narrowly confined by the Notre Dame and Shickshock Mountains on the southeast and by the abrupt edge of the Shield on the northwest. Within it lie strips of low terrace, the products of lacustrine and estuarine sedimentation during glacial times, and of the post-glacial isostatic uplift of the crust. It was on the terraces that French immigrant farmers settled: it was along the river that explorers and fur traders penetrated inland. The pattern of farm holdings is still typically that of the first colonists – long narrow strips running back from frontages on the river. The St Lawrence itself is more important than ever in the past as a transport route. The valley has developed industries of a distinctive kind, and in Montreal has produced the largest town of Canada and the sixth most populous of the whole continent.

Agriculture, originally designed in this region for subsistence, has long been commercial. The most widespread specialism is dairying, which relies on the excellent hay growth and on the harvesting of corn for green fodder. Cattle must be barn-fed throughout the long winter. Ayrshire and Holstein cattle, noted for their high yields of milk, supply the cheese-making industry, while Jerseys and Guernseys, whose milk has a very high fat content, are kept for butter production. Clovers and grasses are cultivated in this region for seed; oats and potatoes are the main tillage crops on the poorer soils. Maple syrup is produced throughout the southern forest areas. Montreal, Quebec, and Ottawa have all generated market-gardening activity in their near neighbourhoods; and Canada's chief tobacco-growing areas, lying east of Montreal, produce burley and flue-cured types of tobacco which are processed in Montreal and Quebec.

Farmland however is limited in extent, and the place of farming in the regional economy is a modest one. Industry has arisen from the forest, water, and mineral resources of the Shield. Once the most accessible forests had been cut over, the emphasis of forest exploitation changed from the production of lumber to that of pulpwood; and it is rafts of timber for pulping that now float in the summer down the rivers leading to the St Lawrence. Pulp- and paper-mills, with their associated hydro-electric stations, are typically set where these rivers fall over the edge of the Shield into the St Lawrence Valley; their total demand for electric power is equal to half that generated in the region. In order to protect the national milling industry, the Canadian government enforces an embargo on the export of pulpwood; and paper-milling, especially for newsprint, has developed strongly in connection with pulping. The main paper-making centres are Ottawa, Three Rivers, East Angus, Kenog, and the eastern townships of Sherbrooke and St Hyacinthe.

The Saguenay River falls 300 feet in its last thirty miles before entering the St Lawrence. On this lower reach are the Shipshaw Dam and generating plant, which supply electricity to the aluminium works at Arvida. The St Maurice River is dammed at Shawinigan Falls, twenty miles northeast of Three Rivers; the works there supply power

32. Montreal, Quebec: part of the Bonsecours Market area, an older part of the commercial city.

to Montreal, in addition to the aluminium industry. Raw materials for this industry are brought in along the St Lawrence – bauxite from Guyana and Surinam, cryolite from Greenland; while exports of aluminium pig are shipped downstream to the U.S.A. and Europe.

Hydro-electric power plants are located also on the Ottawa, Richelieu, and St Francis Rivers, and on the St Lawrence at Lachine. The most recent installations are those on the St Lawrence Seaway, e.g. at Moses–Saunders and Beauharnois (Plate 17). The demand for power within transmission distance of this region is great; part of the supply is taken by industrial consumers in upper New York State. Within the region, town-based consumers include the rolling-stock, meat-packing, leather and fur working, paper-milling, and chemical and electrical industries of Montreal; the shipbuilding and armament production of Sorel; the aircraft manufacture of Longeuil; the electro-metallurgy of Beauharnois; the newsprint, leather, textile, tobacco, and meat-processing factories of Three Rivers; and the shipbuilding of Lauzon on the far bank. Montreal is also served by the gas pipeline from the Prairies.

Although this region at present lies outside the Manufacturing Belt as this is usually defined (Fig. 9:11), the St Lawrence Seaway may bring it within. Navigation on the Great Lakes–St Lawrence system has been previously discussed. At this juncture, it remains to emphasize that the Seaway works permit ocean-going ships to reach Duluth, 2225 miles from the seaboard, and that vessels of 9000 gross registered tons can now enter the Great Lakes harbours, which are thus accessible to some 80 per cent of the world's freighters. Seaway locks at Ste Catherine, Beauharnois, Snell, Eisenhower, and Iroquois provide water depths of 26 feet, greater than the depths at many ocean ports; and the St Lawrence Ship Channel, running from Montreal to forty miles beyond Quebec, has been correspondingly improved along the necessary 130 miles of its 200-mile length. Indeed, the opening of this channel preceded the construction of the Seaway, converting Montreal into a deepwater port before bulk transport farther inland was made easy. Stress was laid in the earlier chapter on the hindrances to navigation offered on the International Rapids section of the St Lawrence; and it was these hindrances which for so long

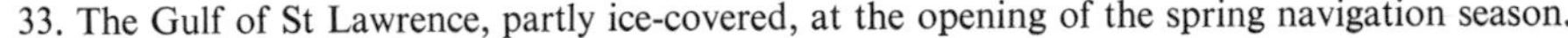

33. The Gulf of St Lawrence, partly ice-covered, at the opening of the spring navigation season.

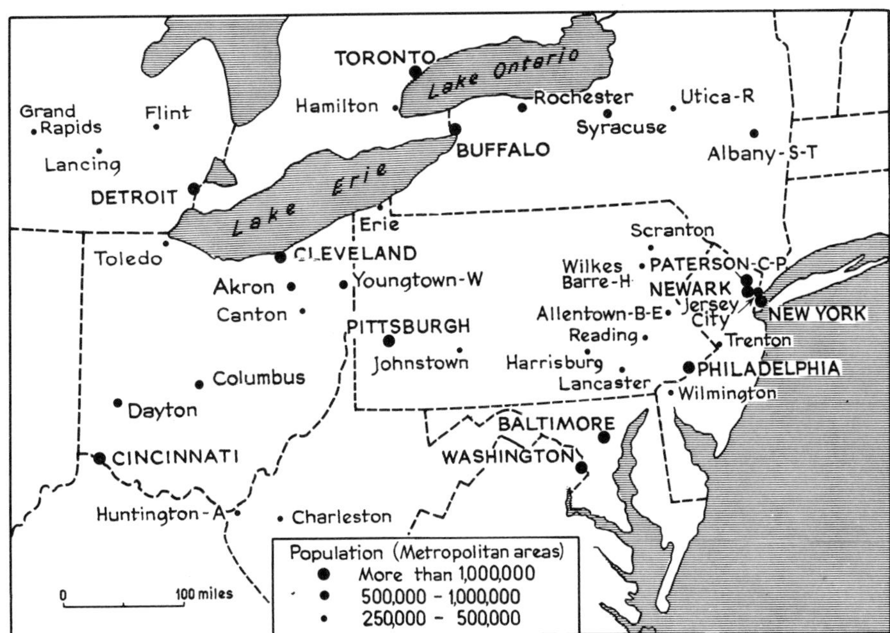

FIG. 12:11 Location map, The Industrial Northeast.

kept Montreal as the effective head of ocean transport on the St Lawrence (Plate 32). The same handicaps appear to have kept the St Lawrence Valley somewhat detached from the remainder of Canada – a region on its own, with defective transport links to the west.

On the other hand, Montreal's competitive position as a port was obviously great, so long as it remained the main ocean terminal. A comparison of this town with Quebec shows that to be an old-established provincial capital is not enough to ensure growth; and now that it has passed the million mark, Montreal is presumably assured of still further expansion.

The one handicap, and that unavoidable, is the seasonal closure of navigation by ice. The ocean waters off the St Lawrence estuary are kept chilled by the Labrador Current; the river and the Lakes are repeatedly overspread every winter by the cAK air generated over the northern part of the continent. Ice closes the Seaway for about 120 days each year, and the St Lawrence Ship Channel for 100 to 110 days, in each case between some time in December and some time in April (Plate 33).

12d: The Industrial Northeast

Area: about 250,000 square miles.
Population: more than 60 million.

Cities with at least a quarter of a million people in the metropolitan area: populations of metropolitan areas in brackets:

New York, N.Y., 7,800,000 (10,700,000)
Philadelphia, Pa.–N.J., 2,000,000 (4,350,000)
Detroit, Mich., 1,675,000 (3,750,000)
Baltimore, Md., 940,000 (1,725,000)
Cleveland, Ohio, 876,000 (1,800,000)
Washington, D.C., 765,000 (2,000,000)
Toronto, Ont., 672,000 (1,825,000)
Pittsburgh, Pa., 600,000 (2,400,000)
Buffalo, N.Y., 533,000 (1,300,000)
Cincinnati, Ohio, 502,500 (1,072,000)
Columbus, Ohio, 470,000 (680,000)
Newark, N.J., 405,000 (1,700,000)
Rochester, N.Y., 320,000 (585,000)
Toledo, Ohio, 318,000 (455,000)
Akron, Ohio, 290,000 (515,000)
Paterson–Clifton–Passaic, N.J., 280,000 (1,190,000)
Albany–Schenectady–Troy, N.Y., 280,000 (657,000)
Jersey City, N.J., 276,000 (610,000)
Hamilton, Ont., 274,000 (395,000)
Dayton, Ohio, 262,500 (695,000)
Youngstown–Warren, Ohio, 226,000 (500,000)
Syracuse, N.Y., 216,000 (560,000)

Allentown–Bethlehem–Easton, Pa.–N.J., 216,000 (490,000)
Flint, Mich., 197,000 (375,000)
Grand Rapids, Mich., 177,500 (363,000)
Utica–Rome, N.Y., 152,000 (330,000)
Erie, Pa., 138,500 (250,000)
Huntingdon–Ashland, W.Va.–Ky.–Ohio, 115,000 (255,000)
Trenton, N.J., 114,000 (265,000)
Canton, Ohio, 113,000 (340,000)
Scranton, Pa., 111,500 (235,000)
Lansing, Mich., 108,000 (299,000)
Reading, Pa., 98,000 (275,500)
Wilmington, Del.–N.J., 96,000 (365,000)
Wilkes Barre-Hazleton, Pa., 96,000 (345,000)
Charleston, W.Va., 86,000 (253,000)
Harrisburg, Pa., 80,000 (345,000)
Lancaster, Pa., 61,000 (280,000)
Johnstown, Pa., 54,000 (280,000)

Population density outside the largest metropolitan areas: about 65 per square mile.

About two-fifths of the region is in farmland; more than half the farm acreage is cropland, about one-quarter is farm woodland, and about one-fifth is pasture other than woodland pasture. Forests, including farm woodland, cover about a third of the region.

Numbers of livestock: cattle, 9 million, of which nearly half are milk cows; sheep, $1\frac{3}{4}$ million; pigs, 4 million; poultry, 500 million.

Regional identity and distinction from adjoining macro-regions are primarily economic. As an expanse of terrain, the Industrial Northeast (Fig. 12:11) includes the mid-Atlantic seaboard of the U.S.A., a narrow northeastward extension of the Piedmont, and the northern part of the Folded Appalachians; in its western portion, the Appalachian Plateaus descend towards the lowlands which flank Lakes Ontario and Erie. However, it would be wrong to claim that responses to the environment have not occurred. The Hudson–Champlain trough, the westernmost of the north–south structures noticed for New England, lies at that region's boundary; both it and the perpendicular Mohawk trench lead right through the mountains, respectively to the St Lawrence and Lake Ontario, at altitudes of less than 600 feet. Although the port of New York is man-made, the deepwater harbour is a product of nature. South of New York, where Long Island represents a duplex outermost moraine of the continental ice-cap, the mid-Atlantic seaboard is unglaciated. Here, the deglacial rise of sea-level has drowned Delaware and Chesapeake Bays; Philadelphia today stands at the head of the one, Baltimore near the head of the other. Behind this piece of coast the fronting Blue Ridge of the Appalachians cuts out; explorers, pioneers, settlers, and traders penetrated the Appalachians by way of valleys belonging to the Delaware, Susquehanna, and Potomac systems, marking out lines now followed by road and rail. Drainage on the far side of the divide is collected mainly by the Ohio, which provided a long-used route into the interior.

The northern Appalachians belong to a mountain system different from that of New England. In northwest Europe, the ancient Caledonoid structures of Scandinavia and Scotland converge westward on the less ancient Altaid structures which loop across the mainland. In South Wales the two belts touch: in North America they cross, with New England and the Piedmont corresponding to the Caledonoid belt and the Folded Appalachians and the Appalachian Plateaus corresponding to the Altaides. On both sides of the Atlantic the older groups of rocks are poor in minerals and totally lacking in coal. But the Altaides of Europe and the Appalachians of North America were constructed on the site of a geosyncline where, during the Carboniferous period, swamp-forests accumulated the peat layers which now form coal. So thick did the succession of coal-bearing rocks of North America become that they are divided into two systems, the Mississippian and the Pennsylvanian, which are jointly equivalent to the Carboniferous of Europe. In the northern Appalachians, as in South Wales, the tightest folding drove off volatiles and raised coal to the rank of anthracite, which occurs in eastern Pennsylvania. In western Pennsylvania on the other hand the coal-bearing rocks are flat-lying; dissection of the plateau makes the seams readily accessible from the valleys incised through the coalfield. It was in Pennsylvania that mineral oil was first produced from a deliberately-sunk bore, Drake's famous well of 1859; both oil and natural gas contributed to the rise of industry in western Pennsylvania.

The two lower Lakes provide water for industry

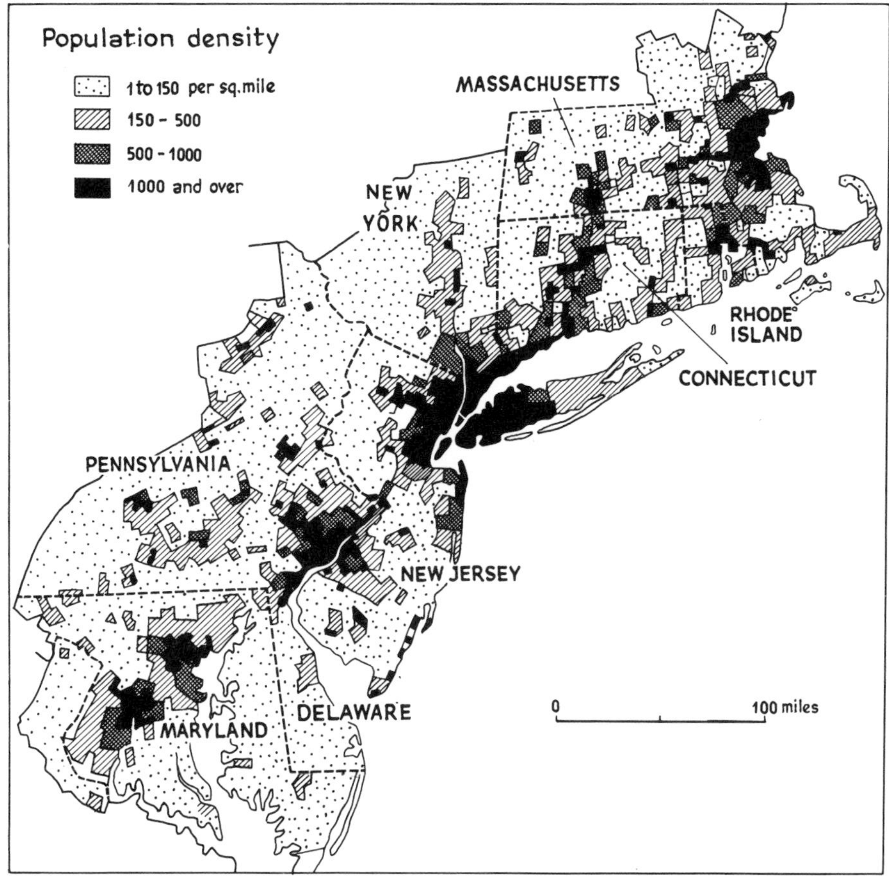

FIG. 12:12 Population on the northeast coast.

and routes for bulk transport. Their summer heat storage and winter heat supply significantly ameliorate the climate of the Lakes Peninsula: the amelioration is reflected in agriculture. Niagara Falls, where the river plunges over the outcrop of Niagara limestone, is the location of noteworthy hydro-electric power plants.

Apart from its winter climate, which invariably includes troublesome storms and snow, this region is then physically favoured. It is highly populous, with a quarter of all the people in the U.S.A. and Canada combined. The towns listed at the head of this chapter alone contain 10 per cent of this combined total, while the metropolitan areas contain 20 per cent – 40 million people living in built-up agglomerations each with at least a quarter of a million inhabitants (cf. Fig. 12:12). There is too much here for a block description: accordingly, this macro-region will be broken down into regions, as follows:

12d 1. The New York Metropolitan Region.
12d 2. The Hudson–Mohawk Lowlands.
12d 3. The Coastal Lowlands.
12d 4. The Uplands.
12d 5. The Pittsburgh-Lake Erie Region.
12d 6. The Detroit Region.
12d 7. Industrial Southern Canada.
12d 8. The Near-West.

12d 1: The New York Metropolitan Region

This region has at least 15 million inhabitants, a total of the same general order as the national populations of Colombia, Peru, the Netherlands, South Africa, Australia, or Canada; metropolitan New York alone has more people than Austria, Belgium, or Sweden. It is more than an urban agglomeration or a conurbation: it is an agglomeration of conurbations, containing not far below 10 per cent of all the people of the U.S.A.

34. The tourist's New York: skyscrapers by night, seen from Governor's Island.

Its centre is Manhattan Island. Here, on a site traded from the Indians in the most one-sided land sale in the history of man, has arisen New York City. The firm bedrock of Manhattan made possible, as the limited area made necessary, the vertical growth of buildings; here it was that skyscrapers first developed their form and received their name. Manhattan has two groups, one at the southern tip in the financial quarter of Wall Street, and one in Midtown in the retailing and entertainment quarter. Skyscrapers have for a long time now passed the stage of being responses to limitations of site, and are symbols of prestige, imitated throughout the westernized world; Midtown Manhattan's Empire State Building is a notable tourist attraction (Plates 34, 35, 36).

Wall Street is the financial centre of the country, Midtown Manhattan the national shopping and entertainment centre. Theatres on Broadway make or break the reputations of the stage; the great stores of Fifth Avenue do much to shape national taste in dress. Madison Avenue in its Midtown part has become the location of, and the symbol for, the contrived and expensive advertising required by manufacturing committed to continued expansion.

Between Midtown Manhattan and Wall Street buildings are lower, less pretentious, less dignified, and less well kept. Here are located, sometimes in

35. The garment-worker's New York: hand trucks, laden with finished clothing, in the vicinity of 14th Street.

36. The New York of the artist or writer: Washington Mews, former stables converted into studios and flats, in Greenwich Village.

quite concentrated form, industries which rely on a large metropolitan market near at hand. Food processing, clothing manufacture, footwear manufacturing, the production of jewellery, cosmetics, and pharmaceutical products, the manufacture of refrigerators, and the furniture and furnishings trades all belong in this group. But some of these industries are also labour oriented, having relied in their early days on the employment of women either as factory hands or as outworkers. The garment trades earned a bad reputation for the sweating of their women workers; and the formation of trade unions has not altogether counteracted over-intense employment. In the same part of New York are industrial enclaves, surviving from earlier days, where prestige manufactures are made such as high-grade fashion wear, furs, silver, and expensive jewellery. It is normal for the second group of industries to maintain close contact with outlets in Midtown Manhattan. For a considerable time, rising ground rents and other costs have been driving industry out of inner Manhattan into the suburbs, except when some maintain token workshops in the original area.

A third group of industries comprises those of New York as a port. These in general require tide-water sites, room to spread, and connections with railroads and freight yards. They include petroleum refining, copper refining, heavy chemical manufacture, base-metal refining, automotive assembly for export, soap-making, and paint manufacture. Some of the factories are located on the east bank of East River, but most are in New Jersey. Shipbuilding at Bayonne belongs in this group. Glass manufacture at Glassboro., N.J., uses local sands to supply the metropolitan region with hollow-ware and bottles; but, in the main, industry in New Jersey away from the waterfront conforms to a fairly undifferentiated metropolitan pattern. The region as a whole is very diversified in its industrial structure.

The large waterfront factories have large payrolls; but the great total extent of manufacturing activity in the metropolitan region is elsewhere chiefly a matter of large numbers of small establishments. In New York State, the average workforce is about fifty per factory. This region is however undoubtedly a manufacturing region, with some 30 per cent of its workforce in manufacturing employment. Next in ranking order is wholesale and retail trading, and then service occupations. These three classes in the New York region provide well over 10 per cent of all paid employment in the country.

Large numbers of workers in New York travel

daily back and forth from their homes to their workplaces. Car travel is aided by freeway systems, although neither the freeways nor the cross-river bridges can cope adequately with the ever-increasing flow. Manhattan is served by subways, which run north and south with few interconnections, having been constructed as independent and rival systems by private enterprise; driverless trains on the subways illustrate how far mechanization can go.

Ferries on the Hudson, and suburban railroads on land, work to capacity. The growth of manufacturing, trading, and business activity in New York, and the growth of population supported by these activities, have promoted a colossal urban spread, with the metropolis progressively invading the surrounding country. Extension of the metropolis has been accompanied by continuing internal differentiation, whereby Harlem has become a Negro quarter, the West Side has been colonized by Puerto Ricans, and Brooklyn has developed an accent, even if not a folk-culture, all of its own. Parts of Long Island, of Connecticut, and of the rural areas of New Jersey act as dormitories for the wealthier commuters to Manhattan.

So heavily is the coastal part of the region built-up, that it seems surprising to have land available for cultivation. Nevertheless, there is room on eastern Long Island and in coastal New Jersey for market-gardening and poultry-farming of the most intensive kind: the potentialities and the demands of the markets are overriding.

12d 2: The Hudson–Mohawk Lowlands

This industrialized corridor runs northward from metropolitan New York up the Hudson Valley, and then westward along the Mohawk adjoining the noted resort area of the Adirondacks, wherein a fragment of the Shield stands south of the St Lawrence. In the metropolitan areas of Buffalo, Rochester, Albany–Schenectady–Troy, Syracuse, and Utica–Rome, it contains 1 in 20 of the inhabitants of the U.S.A. Physically, the corridor is by far the easiest route from New York into the interior. Industrially, it has profited first by the Erie Canal (now the New York State Barge Canal), then by railroads using the corridor, and then by roads. Among its towns and manufacturing centres, Buffalo is one of the two Lakes Ports (the other being Chicago) where import and export cargoes roughly balance. Buffalo became a great bulk-of-break point for the Canadian wheat trade, since this trade took advantage of the permanently ice-free condition of New York as opposed to the seasonal closure of the St Lawrence. Milling of flour and of vegetable oils at Buffalo are accompanied by meat-packing, timber processing, oil refining, copper refining, steel-making, electro-chemical manufacture, aircraft manufacture, and shipbuilding, industries all located with reference to the Lakes–Mohawk–Hudson system of transport routes. What readjustments will result from the St Lawrence Seaway remain for the future to show.

The other leading manufacturing towns of this region are involved mainly with the production of goods with high cost/bulk ratios, such as machinery, electrical equipment, and instruments. Some have developed specialisms: thus, Rochester is known for cameras and optical goods, Albany–Schenectady–Troy for heavy electrical machinery and heat-resistant glass and enamelware, and for shirts and fine linen cloths. A rather dispersed and contrasted type of industry is the fruit and vegetable canning on the southern side of Lake Ontario.

This last industry relates to the fruit and vegetable farming of the drumlin belt south of the Lake, where the onset of winter is somewhat deferred by the release of heat stored in the Lake waters. Elsewhere in the region, farming is strongly oriented towards the great urban markets, with dairying widespread.

12d 3: The Coastal Lowlands

Southwestward from the limits of the New York Metropolitan Region, the Atlantic Coastal Plain widens rapidly in a series of peninsulas. The inlets of Delaware Bay, Chesapeake Bay, and the lower Potomac which branches off the latter, run inland to the Fall Zone at the edge of the Piedmont. On the Fall Zone stand Philadelphia, Baltimore, Washington, and Wilmington, respectively the 2nd, 4th, 6th, and 27th towns of the Industrial Northeast.

Philadelphia rose as the capital of William Penn's Quaker State. Its early history of craft industry resembles that of southern New England towns. However, Philadelphia developed into one of the leading inlets for immigrants, and into one of the leading ports of the continent; and, like New York, it engages in heavy industry on the waterfront and in highly diversified manufacture elsewhere. Its textile production, which includes carpet weaving, owes something to the Quaker tradition; wool is imported from Australia and synthetic fibre from Japan. The metal trades are strongly represented by fabrication and the making of machinery, automobiles, and aircraft. Philadelphia's twin town of Camden, on the opposite side of the Delaware River, specializes in the production of canned soup; both Camden and Chester, lower down the Delaware, have shipbuilding yards, while Chester is also a centre of paper-making. Trenton, upstream of Philadelphia, is a leading centre for pottery and ceramics, and has rubber factories using either imported latex or locally-produced synthetic material. Wilmington is another of the number of paper-manufacturing centres on this coast. Its tanneries represent an evolved industry originally based on local supplies of hickory and oak tanbark. However, Wilmington's industrial reputation is overwhelmingly that of a chemical and pharmaceutical manufacturer: here are the headquarters of the giant du Pont corporation, which dominates this type of industry in the U.S.A.

Baltimore, also a great port, became an outlet for west Pennsylvanian coal and for wheat for the interior, with the aid of the Baltimore and Ohio Railroad which runs up the Susquehanna Valley, across the divide, and to Pittsburgh and beyond. Industries linked to the port have developed on a large scale – sugar refining, fertilizer manufacture, and copper refining which uses Chilean concentrate. Shipbuilding is carried on at near-by Sparrow's Point, a notable centre of smelting and steel-making where ore is imported from Scandinavia, Chile, and Venezuela; manganese comes from India and the U.S.S.R. Baltimore's chemical industry takes in nitrates from Chile, potash from Germany, and phosphates from Oceania and Florida. Among outgoing cargoes, nowadays far less bulky in total than those incoming, are iron and steel manufactures, machinery, and farm products destined for Europe and Latin America. In addition to its port-bound industry, Baltimore has metal and engineering manufactures generally similar to those indicated for Philadelphia.

Fishing ports from the Hudson to Chesapeake Bay operate a fishing industry which is apt to be overshadowed, or cast altogether into oblivion, by the manufacturing and commercial activities of the great east-coast cities. In fact, however, the take of this group is strictly comparable with that of New England, even indeed if not somewhat greater, at about 20 per cent by value of the national catch.

Allentown and its neighbours in the upper Lehigh Valley are dominated by heavy industry. Bethlehem, the home of the great Bethlehem Steel Corporation, originally used local ore which has been since exhausted, and local limestone which remains available both for blasting and for cement manufacture. Lancaster stands in a district where live numerous descendants of settlers who were religious dissidents – Mennonites, Amish, Moravians, and others. The social system of the dissident settlers relied on farming: it also included an attempt to opt out of the cash economy, so that, with personal spending reduced to a minimum or even abolished altogether, capital accumulated and farms improved. This is, in any case, some of the best farming land in the whole country. Lancaster County and neighbouring parts of the Delmarva Peninsula between Delaware and Chesapeake Bays raise fruit and vegetable crops by intensive methods; Lancaster has a highly-developed canning and freezing industry, while the peninsula is noted for the production of broiler fowl. Truck farms are also set densely along the immediate coast, many of them on the muck soils of empoldered and reclaimed tidal saltings, raising berry fruits and vegetables for metropolitan markets. Although freezer plants absorb the fluctuations of production and demand, market accessibility for fresh produce still counts for much: accordingly, the intensity of working rises towards the great towns, being greatest of all in New Jersey. About fifty miles southwest of Washington, D.C., where market accessibility cuts off rather sharply, the coastal belt of specialized and intensive farming comes to its end, as also does the concentration of dairy farms which borders and interpenetrates the truck-farming belt along its landward edge.

Washington, D.C., is a special case among the region's cities. Founded after the successful War of Independence, and situated on the Maryland–Virginia boundary where the North and South abutted on one another, the national capital has far outspread what seemed initially to be the generous

37. New suburban housing in Virginia, on the outskirts of the Washington, D.C., metropolitan area.

38. Suburban shopping centre on the outskirts of the Washington, D.C., metropolitan area; designed solely for visits by car, it serves the residents in housing developments like those in Plate 37.

Fig. 12:13 Coalfields in the Northeast.

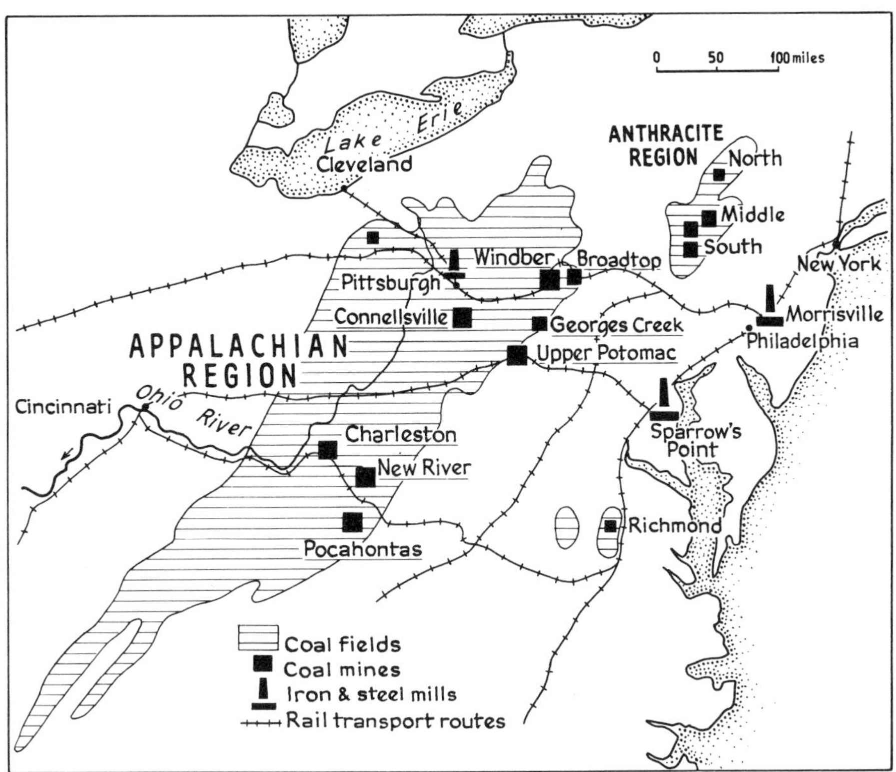

limits of the District of Columbia. The two million people of the metropolitan area include more than half a million federal employees, about a quarter of this occupational class in the U.S.A. Built to the plan of the Frenchman l'Enfant, inner Washington possesses a gridiron pattern of streets and squares on which is superimposed a radial net of main roads centred on the White House; its chief buildings are low by North American metropolitan standards, although many are handsome in a successful classical style, and manufacturing industry is but slightly developed. Central Washington, housing numberless government offices, generates a huge commuter traffic which relies almost wholly on automobiles. Its inner residential districts have as a group run down, except for the picturesque pre-revolutionary settlement of Georgetown; and the resident population of the District proper is more than 50 per cent Negro. Beyond the administrative limits of the District of Columbia, the metropolis merges into extensive dormitory settlements such as Arlington, Virginia, and Bethesda, Maryland, where houses and expanding community centres are progressively taking over the farmland of the Piedmont (Plates 37, 38).

12d 4: The Uplands

Parts of the upland country of the Industrial Northeast are inevitably incorporated in regions distinguished by the criteria of mining and manufacturing economy. However, sufficient remains outside the chief mining and manufacturing regions to warrant some discussion. Harrisburg, Johnstown, and the smaller Altoona and Williamsport lie somewhat apart from the principal manufacturing complexes of the Northeast. Their industries range from pottery and glassware manufacture, using piped-in gas and local clays or glass sands, to locomotive-building and woodworking; this last is a development from the early exploitation of the Appalachian forests. Harrisburg has undoubtedly profited by the nodality of a position where routes converge in one direction down the valleys of the Susquehanna and its tributaries, and in the other across the Coastal Lowlands, towards the gap cut by the river through the Folded Appalachians.

39. An exception to the general lack of industrialization on the West Virginia Coalfield: a coal-hydrogenation plant, taking chemicals direct from coal, at Institute.

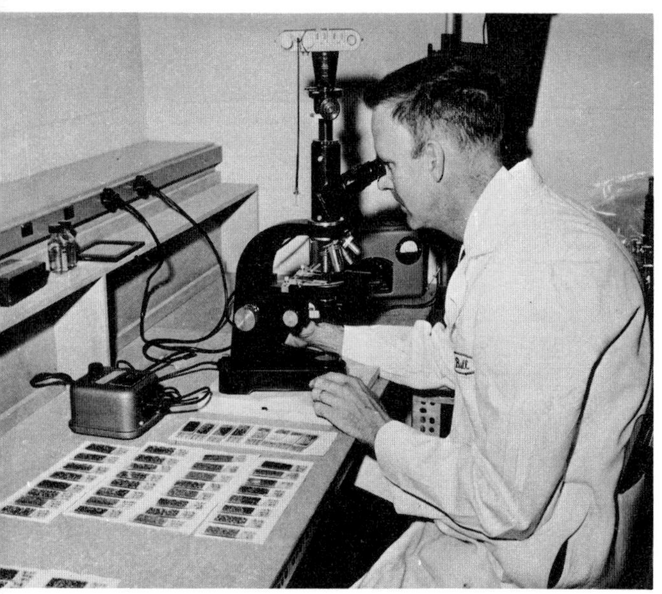

40. Microscopic analysis of coal to determine its behaviour in the coke oven.

The non-industrialized parts of the Uplands are widely tree-covered: forests occupy about half the area of the State of Pennsylvania. Although lumbering is far reduced below its one-time importance, nearly all this forest is commercially managed. Needless to say, the Uplands are heavily drawn on for water-supply. As already noticed for the Adirondacks, they provide resort and recreational areas; the Finger Lakes of upper New York State, where Pleistocene ice converted river valleys into lake-basins, and the Catskill Mountains, are especially well known. The States of New York and Pennsylvania between them operate some three hundred State parks, visited by six million people a year.

What is frequently called the Anthracite Region of eastern Pennsylvania developed its manufacturing activity in association with the exploitation of the anthracite field. The great customers for anthracite were the great towns of the coast, where the fuel used to be in heavy demand for internal heating. Competition from oil and electricity, plus rising costs of mining, have greatly reduced anthracite production below the levels of this region's most prosperous days, and the local economy is in consequence chronically depressed. However, Scranton, Wilkesbarre, and Hazleton are considerable manufacturing towns, making a wide range of metal goods which includes locomotives, forgings, and wire ropes. Silk and other textile industries, plus garment manufacture, developed early as labour-complementary industries to mining and metal-working; these also continue to operate.

In contrast to eastern Pennsylvania, West Virginia raises bituminous coal – about 35 per cent of this grade consumed in the whole U.S.A. – from fields straddling the Kanawha Valley in the Charleston, New River, and Pocahontas districts, and from the upper Potomac field in the north of the State (Fig. 12:13). This last-named field produces high-grade coal suited to the making of metallurgical coke; this coal goes direct by rail to the steelworks at Sparrow's Point (Baltimore) and Morrisville (Philadelphia), but coal from the Kanawha Valley is more economically transported by rail to Norfolk, Va., and thence by sea. Much of the West Virginian coal and coke moving towards Lakeside manufacturers passes through Toledo.

The coal-mining districts of West Virginia have not undergone marked industrialization: persisting in their role of primary production, they have suffered grave social damage in consequence of advancing mechanization and of the associated decline in the demand for labour (Plate 39). The State of West Virginia, anomalously for the macro-region, actually suffered a slight decline in population in the decade 1950–60, and seems at present barely attractive enough in the economic sense to hold its total population steady. Charleston, at the confluence of the Elk and Kanawha Rivers, has manufactures of chemicals, glass, mining machinery, furniture, and hardwood veneers, and functions as a dispatching centre for coal and Appalachian hardwoods. Huntingdon, with the neighbouring Ashland, on the Ohio River, is a rail-to-water transhipment point, and the centre of a quite thriving agricultural district which raises pome fruits (especially apples), tobacco, and livestock.

12d 5: The Pittsburgh–Lake Erie Region

Pittsburgh can be regarded as exemplifying the effect of locational forces at their simplest and most direct. The actual site, at the confluence of the Alleghany and Monongahela Rivers, was selected by the French for the construction of one of their principal forts in the interior – Fort Duquesne. Captured eventually by the British, the post subsequently operated under the name of Fort Pitt. It rose to town status, and changed its name from the frontier style, when it became a staging-post on the migrant route down the Ohio system.

Already in earlier contexts it has been necessary to mention most of the physical advantages which Pittsburgh and its surroundings offered to manufacturing industry – flat-bedded coal, accessible in thick seams by means of adits driven into valley-sides, and highly suitable in part for the manufacture of coke; iron ore occurring in association with the coal; locally available limestone; water-supply and transport routes provided by the rivers; and local reserves, available with unusual ease, of petroleum and natural gas. The necessary entrepreneurs, chief of them Andrew Carnegie, succeeded brilliantly in realizing the industrial potentialities of Pittsburgh. Markets for heavy and iron steel goods opened even wider during the nineteenth century, whether in the interior farmlands with their emergent towns, or in the older but far larger and rapidly expanding coastal centres of the East.

In addition to the effects of locational forces, the Pittsburgh district illustrates those of comparative economics and industrial inertia. An earlier chapter has already mentioned the persistence and continued growth of metal-working at Pittsburgh after the exhaustion of the district's own iron ores; and attention has also been drawn to the management

41. A coking plant in western Pennsylvania: fresh coke from the ovens at right is being quenched.

practices of the steel industry, whereby relocation of the industry in other areas was to some extent discouraged. The Pittsburgh district, then, is still a principal area of heavy metal manufacture, importing ore from the Superior fields – or, increasingly nowadays, from the Canadian Shield – and producing coke from the Connellsville coal-seams (Plates 40, 41). About three-quarters of the industrial employment in the Pittsburgh metropolitan area is provided by the metal trades, and about half of this share by primary metal-processing. Smelting, steel-making, steel fabrication, and electro-mechanical engineering are all prominent, whereas the production of office machinery, motor vehicles and parts, and of aircraft parts is distinctly modest in scale. Industries other than metallurgical in the Pittsburgh district include plate-glass manufacture, which depends on local supplies of glass sands. The magnesite and chrome refractory bricks needed in the steel industry are made in eastern Ohio, where

42. City Hall, Toronto: an example of the ebullient architecture of urban Canada in the 1960s.

a thriving porcelain industry is also conducted. Pittsburgh itself is developing some light industry, for example in the form of light textile manufacture; but it, like Youngstown and Canton, remains dominated by heavy metallurgy. Akron is closely linked to the automobile industries of the Detroit region by its production of rubber tires.

In their retention and continued development of ferrous metal-working, Pittsburgh, Youngstown, Canton and their smaller neighbours depended, and still depend, on the transport routes of the Great Lakes. However, the Lakeside ports have even greater advantages than the coalfield towns in respect of incoming movements of ore, and are also well placed in respect of coal and coke shipments which constitute much of the bulk of the return traffic. The iron and steel industry is firmly established at Cleveland, Toledo, and Erie, which among them sustain about as many people as the Pittsburgh metropolitan area; they too are engaged in heavy metal-working, fabrication, and the manufacture of machinery. Cleveland also has electrical manufactures wherein conveyor-belt assembly recruits female workers. Toledo ships coal and coke both from western Pennsylvania and from West Virginia. Lorain, Lima, and Marion, all on the shores of Lake Erie, are noted for the manufacture of heavy constructional machinery of the type required by modern large-scale civil engineering. The first of these in fact has a considerable steel capacity, greater than that of either Toledo or Erie. With the opening of the St Lawrence Seaway, and with the steadily increasing significance of water-supply in the metal industries, it seems entirely possible that the Lakeside towns as a group will come to surpass the Pittsburgh district in heavy steel manufacture.

12d 6: The Detroit Region

Detroit and its satellites take a stage further the

43. Hydrocarbon polymer storage installations at Sarnia, Ontario, where synthetic-rubber production is one form of petrochemical industry.

industrial shift illustrated by the comparative locations of the metal industries and Pittsburgh on the one hand and the Erie towns on the other. Detroit is not a transhipment point; but, between Lakes Erie and Huron, the downflow of ores on the Lakes route meets the upflow of coal and coke. Detroit then has ready access to the raw materials of the ferrous metal industry, and it is not surprising that this industry has developed there. However, as was discussed in a previous chapter, manufacturing in the Detroit region is highly specialized on the production of automobiles. The chief locational decision in automobile manufacture was that of Henry Ford, whose success fixed much of the automobile industry, until fairly recent times, in Detroit and its satellites.

In addition to the works in the Detroit metropolitan area, which includes the Ford plant at River Rouge, there are automobile factories at near-by Pontiac, Mount Clemens, Royal Oak, Ferndale, Grosse Pointe Park, and Dearborn. The industry has spread to towns in the Michigan peninsula – Flint, Saginaw, Grand Rapids, Lansing, and South Bend at the root of the peninsula in Indiana; and Windsor on the Canadian side of the Detroit River, the smaller twin of Detroit, is also involved.

The full range of industrial processes is represented at Detroit, from blasting to final assembly of finished products (Plate 20). However, the Detroit complex is not self-sufficient in fabricated steel, for which it draws partly on suppliers outside the region, or in machinery and parts, for the supply of which southern New England is prominent. Again, it is more economic to ship cars in the knocked-down rather than the whole form; and distribution from Detroit has promoted the rise of assembly and reassembly plants in all the main market areas. The assembly side of the industry typically draws on a wide range of suppliers, who may or may not be members of the corporation which operates the assembly plants; in consequence, assembly at places outside the Detroit region is helping to promote that partial relocation of the automobile industry which was described earlier. Apart from automobile production, the Detroit region manufactures fabricated steel, industrial machinery, household machinery, machine tools, hand tools, aircraft parts, and – at River Rouge – ships; thus, the relocation of some automobile manufacture is tending to convert the region into one typified by a somewhat generalized range of engineering activity.

If this conversion should occur, the regional boundaries which we are here using would have to be redrawn. Indeed, it is already a somewhat arbitrary line that separates Toledo from Detroit, since for a number of industrial purposes Toledo belongs in the region of concentrated automotive industry. Similarly, the reaching-out of this industry from Detroit to South Bend brings it within seventy-five miles of the manufacturing towns at the head of Lake Michigan, which belong firmly in the Mid-west.

12d 7: Industrial Southern Canada

The shores of upper Lake Ontario and the Lakes Peninsula between Erie and Huron are included in the Industrial Northeast; here lie Toronto and Hamilton on the lakeside, Windsor on the Detroit River, London, Brantford, and Kitchener in the Lakes Peninsula, and a whole string of smaller industrial towns along the Welland Canal.

Toronto, the provincial capital of Ontario, stands where Canadian railways along the Great Lakes are joined by lines coming round the northeastern side of Superior and Huron (Plate 42). Its industries are highly diverse – meat-packing, food-processing, garment making, metal-working, and the production of machinery and electrical goods, developed with regard to markets rather than to raw materials. An oil refinery at Port Credit, near Toronto, is fed with Prairie crude oil by the Interprovincial Pipeline, which also serves the refining industry of Sarnia at the head of Lake Huron (Plate 43).

Hamilton is the outstanding centre of ferrous-metal manufacture in Canada. Ore comes either by way of Port Arthur–Fort William from the Steep Rock field north of Lake Superior, which corresponds in its geological setting to the Superior iron-fields of the U.S.A., or – increasingly – from Quebec–Labrador. Coking coal arrives from the Appalachian fields via the outlet ports of Lake Erie. Scrap metal is also brought in by Lakes shipping. Lake Ontario is drawn on for the copious water-supply needed by the heavy metallurgical industry, and limestone for fluxing is taken from the Niagara escarpment. Not only heavy metal processing, but also heavy steel manufacture is concentrated in Hamilton, except that shipbuilding is centred in Toronto, Collingwood, and Midland. Moreover, Hamilton is proving increasingly attractive to the automobile industry, which is partly relocating itself near the sources of steel supply.

Windsor, the region's third largest town, has already been noticed as an automobile producer. In this role, Windsor belongs in the Detroit region. However, although as a settlement Windsor is a smaller complement of Detroit, and although it is a kind of industrial offshoot of the larger town, the international boundary along the Detroit River marks a separation of two market areas. In terms of organization and management control, the Windsor automobile industry is a subsidiary of the Detroit industry; but it receives tariff protection from the Canadian government, enabling it to compete with the import of automobiles from manufacturers in the U.S.A.

Among industries in this region which use non-ferrous ores from the Shield are the nickel refining at Port Colbourne, which is well linked by rail to the producing area of Sudbury, and the radium refining of Port Hope. A contrasted industry with a local base in the canning and freezing of fruit and vegetables in the Lakes Peninsula, where, thanks to the heat storage of the Lakes, the horticultural growing season is distinctly longer than in any other part of eastern Canada, and where fruit, vegetables, grapes for wine-making, tobacco, and corn are intensively cultivated. Coincidentally, the climatic northern limit of the farming, horticultural, and orchard areas closely resembles the limit of glacial deposition as opposed to glacial erosion: the most favoured lands are underlain by outwash, end-moraines, and drumlins, as against the scraped and gouged bedrock surface of the Shield.

12d 8: The Near-West

To locate in the macro-region called the Industrial Northeast a region distinguished by the name Near-West may at first sight seem anomalous. The circumstances serves, perhaps, to exemplify the general difficulty of selecting regional titles which are at the same time specific and brief. However, this is still part of the Manufacturing Belt (Fig. 9:11), with a total population, south of the great Lakeside cities and west of the inland centres of eastern Ohio, of some 3½ million; and of these, 2½ million live in the metropolitan areas of Cincinnati, Dayton, and Columbus. It is true that much of the region consists of till plains, physiographically similar to and contiguous with those of the country next to the east. It is also true that the three-quarter share which cropland takes of the region, and the half share taken by cropland, indicate strong land-use similarities with the Central Agricultural Lowlands – similarities which include a high development of commercial farming, and a prominent place for pigs in the farm economy. On the other hand, the farming systems of the Near-West depend far less strongly on corn than do those of the country next to the west, in the Central Agricultural Lowlands and the central Low Plains. There is a rough kind of westward transition across the region, from dairying through mixed farming to the corn-based working typical of the central interior; similarly, the region effects a transition from the very highly urbanized, very highly industrialized East to distinctly less urbanized and less industrialized parts. Among its most populous metropolitan areas, Columbus and Dayton reached the quarter-million mark more than half a century ago, and have subsequently maintained a growth rate of about 25 per cent per decade; The Cincinnati metropolitan area, with half a million people at the turn of the century, and now with well over one million, has been increasing its population less rapidly; but the agglomeration is indisputably a very large one, with its steady growth by no means yet ended.

Cincinnati, despite its Italianate name, developed in part as the urban focus for German settlers who came into the Ohio Valley mainly after 1840: they introduced viticulture, eventually developing one of the best grape-growing and wine-making districts of the country; the brewing industry of Cincinnati has a related origin. By 1827, Cincinnati was linked with Lake Erie by way of the Miami Canal; and it rose early as a river port on the Ohio. It still ships coal, lumber, steel, and salt; and it has profited by affording a railway crossing of the river. Among its manufactures are meat-packing, especially the packing of pork; the brewing already mentioned, which relies on barley produced in the region and on the lime-charged waters of the local streams; tobacco processing; and a fairly complex range of metal and machinery production, particularly of machine tools. It is, however, probably best described as a general-purpose city, and a distinctly large one of its kind.

Columbus and Dayton, which have closely similar populations in their metropolitan areas, and Springfield, which is of a significantly smaller order, also discharge central-place functions. Meat-packing at Columbus is referable to a location intermediate between the producing farms to the west and the big urban markets of the East. This has been the Ohio state capital since 1812, acquiring a fine art gallery, several universities, and many colleges; in addition to unspecialized industries, it has developed a specialism of the manufacture of high-grade paper of book-making quality. Dayton, on the Miami River, has historical associations with the early days of flying: it was the home of the Wright brothers. It is today a thriving centre of aviation and of aeronautical research and engineering, concentrating on engines rather than on airframes. Skills in precision engineering count for much in its manufacturing – the making of automobile parts, cash registers, air-conditioning equipment, and precise measuring devices: a highly specialized activity here is government printing for security purposes, requiring the making of dies. Springfield, on its own scale, well exemplifies the admixture of industries of the general-purpose type with industries related more or less closely to the specific products and needs of the region: alongside its engineering and truck factories stand those producing incubators and farm generators.

CHAPTER THIRTEEN

THE SOUTHEAST

This portion of North America extends in its eastern part from the Potomac to Florida; it extends westward to the low-lying inner valley of the Mississippi and to the western coastland of the Gulf of Mexico (Figs. 13:1, 13:2). Its total area is about 450,000 square miles, very close to that of the Northeastern division; but its population, at about 32 million, is less than half the Northeast's total. Furthermore, the Southeast is not urban but rural, with less than one-third of its people living in towns. Here at once is a marked contrast with the Northeast, which is matched by an equal contrast in

Fig. 13:1
The Southeast.

the level of industrialization. With more than 8 million Negroes disseminated through it, the area exhibits all the characteristics of a deeply-divided plural society. It is a region of large families, low standards of literacy, and outmoded farming systems; it is the only large portion of the Western world where hookworm, insect-borne encephalitis, and the deficiency disease pellagra are endemic. It is also an area where the aristocratic traditions of Western Europe took root and flourished; where Indians made their most successful efforts to opt out of Western culture; where French colonization is recorded by the creole people of the Mississippi Delta, and where some poverty-stricken whites constitute a poor-white social class despised by the Negroes. It is an area where cultures collide; alongside the traits inherited from the plantation system are the commercial operations of tourism in Florida and the oil-based industry of the Texas coastland. However, as will be seen, Florida and the Gulf section of Texas stand somewhat apart from the remainder: they have been shaped by historical and geographical processes of their own.

The Southeast is certainly special. It possesses a distinctive accent of speech, presumably derived from a blending of the North American accent in general with aristocratic imports from England and, above all, with the sounds produced by Negro mammies who cared for the children of the cotton-planters in the days before the Civil War. Feeling between North and South is still strong. A Southerner can be identified at once by his speech – and not infrequently also by his social attitudes. Southern accents debarred Southern actors from the talking films of Hollywood, except perhaps as clowns or villains; accordingly, the image of North America presented to the outside world on the cinema screen has very seldom dealt faithfully with this part of the country. The South, however, has produced its own school of literature, where a main concern is the singularity of life and conduct among fictional great Southern families. The authors concerned have contributed to produce a popular image of the South, which, as has been said, is created half out of dreams and half out of slander.

But despite its persistent social troubles, the Southeast possesses an economy which works – not by any means smoothly, and not at all lucratively for most of the inhabitants, but profitably at least for some, and well enough to sustain many. Crops are of prime importance – cotton, tobacco, vegetable oils, and the softwoods of managed forests, plus the specialized fruit and vegetable crops which depend for their profit level on long growing seasons, early ripening, and rapid transport to urban markets. Livestock farming is as highly favoured as cropping by the length of growing season and the relative mildness of winter conditions. Oil, natural gas, sulphur, salt, phosphate, bauxite, iron ore, and coal are all to be had within the area; and part of

FIG. 13:2 Land use in the Southeast, by regions.

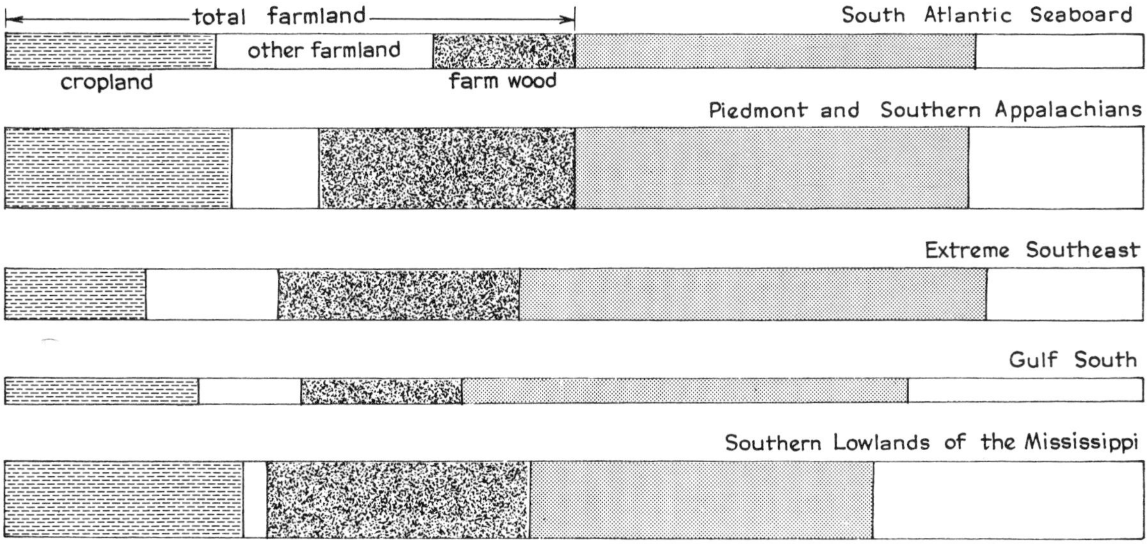

total farmland
South Atlantic Seaboard
other farmland
cropland
farm wood
Piedmont and Southern Appalachians
Extreme Southeast
Gulf South
Southern Lowlands of the Mississippi

the Southeast has proved capable of wresting much of the cotton textile industry from New England. Economic progress is undoubtedly under way; but in the Southeast it seems to be inordinately slow. At least one Southern State opposes industrialization as a matter of set policy. Elsewhere, industrial development (except in Texas) often proves a matter of stimulus from Northern companies who perceive advantages in Southern supplies of pulpwood, raw materials for the chemical industry, alumina, cheap power, and above all cheap labour. Labour in the South is less highly unionized than that in the North, especially where the workers involved are Negroes or poor whites; for some industries, almost completely uneducated workers are suited to the necessary simple routine tasks, or can be made suitable by on-the-job training. The one great industrial handicap for the Southeast is that it fails to provide much itself in the way of urban markets for manufactured goods, and that it is not very readily accessible to the towns of the Manufacturing Belt where most urban consumers are concentrated (Fig. 9:11). Unless the Southeast produces great towns of its own – as it is starting to do at Atlanta, Georgia – it seems likely to continue to lag, comparatively speaking, in its industrial development.

The Southeast is susceptible of division into macro-regions, as follows:

13a. The South Atlantic Seaboard.
13b. The Piedmont and the Southern Appalachians.
13c. The Extreme Southeast.
13d. The Gulf South.
13e. The Southern Lowlands of the Mississippi.

As the list suggests, the main basis of subdivision is physiographic: but attention will also be drawn to distinctions of other kinds.

13a: The South Atlantic Seaboard

Area: about 62,000 square miles.

Population: about 5½ million.

Cities with at least 150,000 people in the metropolitan area: populations of metropolitan areas given in brackets:

Norfolk, Va., 306,000 (578,500: includes Portsmouth and suburbs)
Richmond, Va., 220,000 (408,500)
Newport News, Va., 113,500 (224,500: includes Hampton and suburbs)
Charleston, S.C., 66,000 (216,500)
Savannah, Ga., on the regional boundary, with 188,000 people in the metropolitan area, is treated in the later section on the Extreme Southeast.

Population density outside the largest metropolitan areas: about 45 per square mile.

Half of the region is in farmland; about two-fifths of the farm acreage is cropland, another two-fifths woodland. Forest, including farm woodland, covers about half the region.

Numbers of livestock: cattle, 1½ million, of which one-third million are milk cows; sheep, 165,000; pigs 1¼ million; poultry, 200 million.

The South Atlantic Seaboard extends from the Potomac River and Chesapeake Bay to the Savannah River, and from the Atlantic to the Fall Zone, which however is so ill-marked in some sections that the western limit of Cretaceous or younger rocks provides a more convenient boundary. The coast is dominantly one of submergence, where shallow seaward gradients have enabled post-glacial drowning to produce shallow but highly ramified inlets in the north, but where wave-action has constructed offshore barriers in the south, sealing off some estuaries and converted them into swamps, and making access from the sea difficult throughout. There is no good natural harbour of any great size south of Chesapeake Bay. The sounds and inlets behind the barrier systems have been partly converted into an Intercoastal Waterway similar to that of the Gulf, but work is still far from complete: the limiting depth of 8 feet in some sections is small enough to keep out most freighters, and one leading current function of the Waterway is to carry pleasure craft to and from Florida. Under the name of Sea Islands, the barriers themselves had at one time a high reputation for long-staple cotton.

The outer, eastern, part of the Seaboard rises little above sea-level. Its clays and silts descend into marshes and coastal saltings, requiring much work to render them suitable for cultivation. The inner western portion is underlain by gravel and sand sheets of Tertiary to Pleistocene age, which readily transmit percolating water and can often promote physiographical drought in plants, even though the evenly distributed rainfall, averaging 40 to 80 inches a year, would seem adequate for most farming purposes. Throughout the region, soils in the natural state are impoverished by deep and vigorous leaching: to be used successfully for commercial agriculture, they need heavy applications of fertilizer.

Tenant farming and share-cropping increase progressively through the Atlantic seaboard in the southward direction. Whereas only 3 or 4 per cent of New England farms are held under tenancy, with share-cropping virtually unknown, the combined percentage of the two kinds of tenure is 28 in Virginia, 64 in North Carolina, and 86 in South Carolina. The two systems in this region are not stages on the road to eventual ownership: they are permanent institutions. They go with farming practices which sometimes belong to a subsistence economy, or to something like the cottage farming of western Ireland: small acreages of tobacco and small pine woodlots may provide the only cash income, the remainder of the produce being consumed on the farm.

The strong subsistence element in the farming of this region is partly a direct outcome of the breakdown of the plantation system, and partly a reflection of physical and economic handicaps. Except on the Sea Islands, cotton-growing was never particularly successful, for autumns are too wet to promote the best conditions for it. Of the chief commercial crops of the former plantations, indigo, was eliminated by the substitution of aniline dyes derived from coal tar, while the rice of the Carolina swamplands could not withstand the competition of mechanized rice-farming in Texas, Louisiana, Arkansas, and California. Corn is scarcely a commercial proposition on a typical eighty-acre farm. Tobacco-growing, however, continues. It extends along a belt of fine, sandy soils from North Carolina into Virginia and Maryland. North Carolina raises half the U.S. tobacco crop, but its per-acre yields are generally low on account of rather poor farming practices: management is better, and yields higher, on the tobacco farms of the other two States named. Such farms are everywhere family concerns, with seldom more than five acres under the crop at any one time. When quality is poor, auction prices run low, increasing the scarcity of credit to the farmers and further hindering prospects of farm improvement.

Despite its early springs and the light warm soils of some districts, the region is not especially well placed for the raising of truck and industrial crops. Working expenses of intensive cropping would run high: and the climatic advantage is not enough to offset the differential in transport costs between the South Atlantic and the mid-Atlantic coastlands. Florida and the extreme Southeast in general do much better, for their crops, coming on very early indeed, command premium prices which absorb the costs of transport. The South Atlantic Seaboard has all the disadvantage of a cost–distance handicap, without a countervailing spell of high-volume production at high average prices.

Limited then in its possibilities of commercial farming, the region has proved tardy and restricted in its mechanization of agriculture, even on the commercial tobacco plots which are mainly worked by hand. An exception to the general picture is provided by groundnuts, a successful crop grown on the sands of inland districts for the vegetable-oil industry. The coarseness and permeability of the sands increase towards the Piedmont, promoting the growth of pine barrens. These have been exploited for turpentine and naval stores, ever since they were reached by the early colonists; and they yield some pulpwood for use in the rayon industry as a source of cellulose. Pines are grown on some farms as a cash crop.

In the coastal waters from Delaware to the Carolinas there are marine fisheries which yield about 10 per cent by value of the total U.S. catch. Oysters are taken from the muddy estuaries. The leading sea fish is the inedible menhaden, which, available each season in huge shoals, serves industrial oil-extraction plants and fish-meal plants dotted along the shore; the meal is a protein-rich component in animal feedstuffs.

There is nothing in any of this which is capable of stimulating strong urban development, any more than there was under the plantation system. The tier of colonies from Delaware to South Carolina contained between 40 and 50 per cent of the population of the whole seaboard from New England to the Savannah River, throughout the period from 1630 up to the Civil War; but an increasing fraction consisted of the rural Negro element. Negroes in this set of colonies increased from 5 per cent of the population in the mid-1600s to 25 per cent soon after 1700 and to nearly 40 per cent by 1750. Towns were required merely for the not particularly demanding tasks of colonial administration, as importers of slaves and manufactured goods, and as exporters of plantation produce. The States of Delaware and Maryland have subsequently become largely incorporated in the Industrial Northeast. Charleston in South Carolina, Wilmington in North Carolina, and Norfolk in Virginia developed as the chief ports farther south. But the early shift of cotton-growing away from the Atlantic coastland and the southern Piedmont eliminated an essential and still unreplaced export function of Charleston and Wilmington, although these have attracted some modern industry in the form of fertilizer manufacture and of oil refining. Richmond also was, in former times, a port of much significance, at the original head of navigation on the James River, but its functions today are chiefly those of a State capital and of a retail distributor of no more than medium size.

The ports of Hampton Roads, at the entrance to Chesapeake Bay, have fared otherwise. Norfolk is the maritime outlet for the West Virginia coalfield, complexly equipped with sorting yards and loading berths; the railway between the coalfield and the port is the only one in the U.S.A. to retain steam locomotives for haulage – an indication of its dependence on the coal traffic. Among other cargoes handled in the Hampton Roads ports are tobacco, petroleum, wood pulp from Canada and Scandinavia, raw materials for fertilizer manufacture, and raw sugar. Portsmouth and Newport News contain naval dockyards and the headquarters of the U.S. Atlantic Fleet. Warships are built and dry-docked here; and Newport News is the centre for construction of atomic-reactor engines and nuclear-powered submarines.

13b: The Piedmont and Southern Appalachian Region

Area: about 140,000 square miles.

Population: about 11 million.

Cities with at least 150,000 people in the metropolitan area: populations of metropolitan areas given in brackets:

Atlanta, Ga., 487,500 (1,017,000)
Birmingham, Ala., 341,000 (635,000)
Charlotte, N.C., 201,500 (272,000)
Greensboro–High Point, N.C., 181,500 (246,500)
Montgomery, Ala., 134,500 (169,000)
Chattanooga, Tenn.–Ga., 130,000 (283,000)
Columbus, Ga.–Ala., 117,000 (218,000)
Knoxville, Tenn., 112,000 (368,000)
Winston–Salem, N.C., 111,000 (189,500)
Roanoke, Va., 97,000 (159,000)
Raleigh, N.C., 94,000 (169,000)
Columbia, S.C., 97,500 (261,000)
Augusta, Ga., S.C., 70,500 (217,000)
Macon, Ga., 70,000 (180,500)
Greensville, S.C., 66,000 (210,000)

Population density outside the largest metropolitan areas: about 45 per square mile.

Half of the region is in farmland: about two-fifths of the farm acreage is cropland, another two-fifths woodland. Forest, including farm woodland, covers rather more than half the region.

Numbers of livestock: cattle, 4 million, of which nearly one million are milk cows; sheep, 250,000; pigs, 3 million; poultry, 550 million.

The major physical elements of this region are the Piedmont, the Blue Ridge, the Folded Appalachians, and the Southern Appalachian Plateaus. The Piedmont block, of Precambrian granites, gneisses, and schists, forms a low undulating plateau. Having been extensively planated, the block was submerged in early Mesozoic times and mantled by Triassic sediments; but renewed upheaval has permitted these to be largely stripped, and the metamorphic rocks of the Piedmont to be subjected to deep weathering and the formation of latosols. A few resistant outcrops rise above the general low level, as in the steep exfoliation domes of granodiorite near Atlanta; but for the most part the Piedmont is very subdued, shallowly but intricately dissected by the dense net of streams nourished by abundant rainfall. The Blue Ridge rises abruptly from the Piedmont through a range of at least 800 feet, and in some places of far more: in Mount Mitchell, N.C., it reaches 6684 feet above sea-level. Its name is due to the blue haze exuded from the forests rooted in its shallow, stony mountain soils or in crevices in the sandstones and quartzites; the name of the Great Smoky Mountains on the Tennessee–North Caroline border has a similar origin. There is only one reasonably easy passage through the Blue Ridge in this region – that provided by the

44. Dairy farm on the Georgia Piedmont: the cows are of the Jersey breed.

cross-cutting valley of the Roanoke River, which is either antecedent to the last uplift of the Appalachians, or else has been superimposed from a vanished cover of Triassic or Cretaceous sediments. Next to the Blue Ridge comes the Great Appalachian Valley, cut in tightly folded limestones and shales, and drained northeastward by the Shenandoah and southwestward by the Tennessee system, whose erosion in the Folded Appalachians generally has developed ridge-and-valley terrain with a markedly trellised pattern of drainage. In its southern part the Great Valley is the most widely opened, containing broad plains draining to the Tennessee and the Coosa, where road construction is freed from the complications of pattern forced upon it by the zigzag plan of the terrain to the northeast.

Next west again lie the Cumberland Plateau and its southward extension in the Cumberland Mountains, rising from the Folded Appalachians in the steep east-facing scarp of the Cumberland Front. In much of its extent, this scarp is cut in coal-bearing rocks; and no fewer than six trunk railroads extended themselves along the Valley to compete for coal haulage and potential industrial traffic.

Agriculture in this region enjoys distinct climatic advantages, but in many parts is handicapped by soil quality. The latosols of the Piedmont, subjected to frequent intense rainstorms, have been much gullied, especially where high elevations induce winter freezing of the ground: they are, however, used for bright-leaf tobacco cultivation in southern Virginia and North Carolina: Winston–Salem and Durham take most of the Piedmont bright-leaf, and make about 70 per cent of the nation's output of cigarettes. Limestone outcrops on the Virginia Piedmont include phosphates, which encourage mixed farming in which the cropping of corn, potatoes, groundnuts, and fodder sorghum are integrated with animal husbandry including sheep for wool and cattle and pigs for meat (Plate 44). Leached soils in the upland districts support only the most tolerant of deciduous trees, although in the Blue Ridge country, the Great Smokies, and the southern Appalachians generally they can be used for orchard cropping which supplies high-grade apples to northern markets. There is a dense concentration of meat-producing poultry farms in the north of Georgia and Alabama, lying athwart the Piedmont/Appalachian boundary (Plate 45). But farming in the least accessible parts of the uplands country is restricted both in extent and in aims, having a partially subsistence character; corn

45. Egg production line on a mechanized poultry farm near Atlanta, Georgia.

is the main field crop, butter and cheese are leading products. Commercial forestry merges into camouflage for moonshining, the operation of illicit distilleries. Loamy soils in the Great Valley are well suited to a wide range of commercial crops – bush fruit, peaches, primeur vegetables, and apples as a standby on slopes with poorer soils but with a southern aspect. The reclamation and transformation of the Tennessee Valley have been outlined in Chapter Eight.

Cotton-growing in the Piedmont south of Winston–Salem relies heavily on continuous fertilization. Cotton is also grown in the Great Valley, especially on limestone soils: sands carry tobacco as their leading crop. The southern Piedmont between Atlanta and Macon is noteworthy for its peach orchards, which however suffer in some years by late cold waves which can destroy the early spring flowers of the peach trees; here too are grown pecans, nuts very similar in form and taste to walnuts, which command a national market. Pig-raising pays well throughout the region; the pig strains carry heavy infusions of the semi-domesticated razor-back pig, which is well adapted to foraging in forests of oak and hickory without a great deal of attention. Horses and mules are bred for use as draft animals in the Mississippi Lowlands, where cotton-growing is neither prosperous enough nor mechanized enough to pass generally beyond animal traction.

Brightest in the regional economy is the development of industry, especially in the Piedmont. In its rural aspects, the region lacks job opportunities: but these are increasingly provided by manufacturing towns. Although these are few in number and modest in size compared with the industrial centres of the Northeast, they do at least exist. Cotton textile mills and rayon plants, using Southern cotton and wood pulp, are scattered throughout the Piedmont division (Plate 46). Steep river gradients at the Fall Zone combine with heavy rainfall to favour the development of hydro-electric power, which has been complemented in massive fashion by the works in the Tennessee Valley; potential in the Carolinas and Georgia is 40 per cent developed (Figs. 13:3, 13:4). Both the even seasonal regime of rainfall and the brevity of winter frost help hydro-electric stations on the Piedmont to supply cheap base-load power throughout almost the whole year; and hydro-electric power can be supplemented by thermal power generated on the Appalachian coalfields.

Early developments in the Piedmont textile industry comprised the manufacture of coarse cloths and towelling materials; but the relocation of cotton manufacture from New England has given the Piedmont not only finer cotton manufacture but also the milling of synthetic and mixed fibres, and a two-thirds share in the national output of cottons. Some leading causes of the shift from New England

46. A pulpwood train in the southern Piedmont.

– cheap labour, power, land, and local taxes – have been mentioned earlier: to these can be added low-cost service industries, plus favourable rail freight rates whereby finished goods bear only the charge appropriate to raw materials. By contrast, the garment trades are but slightly developed. Pulp and paper production have minor significance by national standards, but the furniture-making industry is prominent.

Ferrous-metal processing, metal fabrication, and engineering are largely restricted to the Birmingham district. Metallurgy in the region, after making small beginnings at Sheffield, Alabama, was placed on a modern footing by the opening of the U.S. Steel plant at Birmingham in 1907; the plants at Gadsden in Alabama and Atlanta in Georgia can be regarded as outliers of the Birmingham industry. Birmingham profits by the seams of the Warrior coalfield, which include excellent coking coals, and by the self-fluxing calcareous hematites of Red

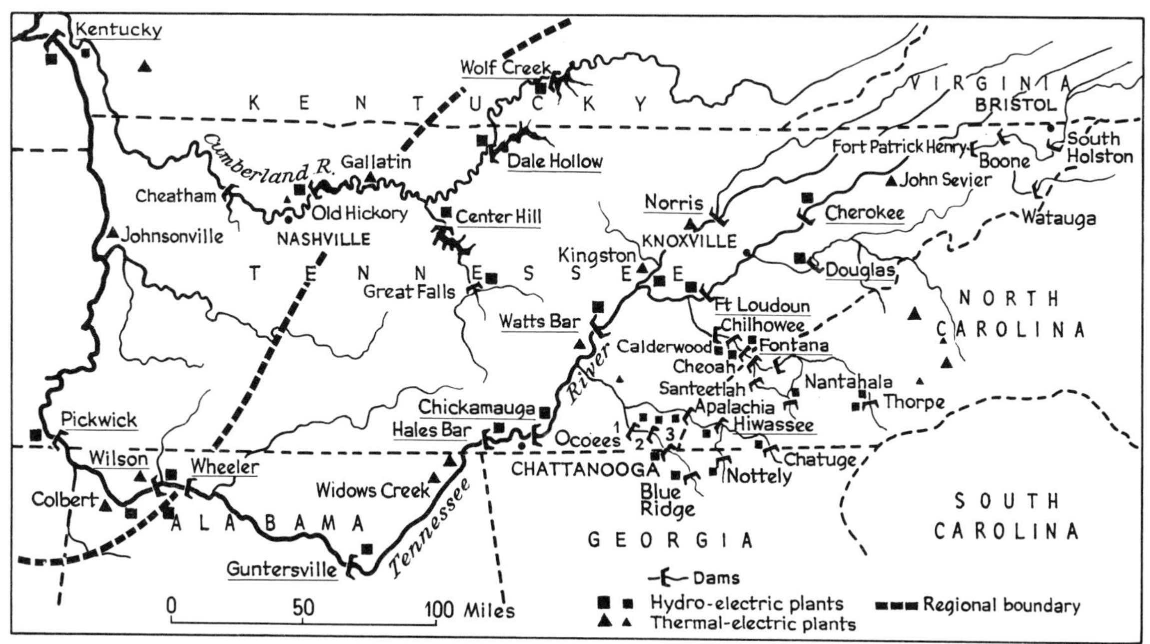

FIG. 13:3 Dams and reservoirs on part of the southern Piedmont.

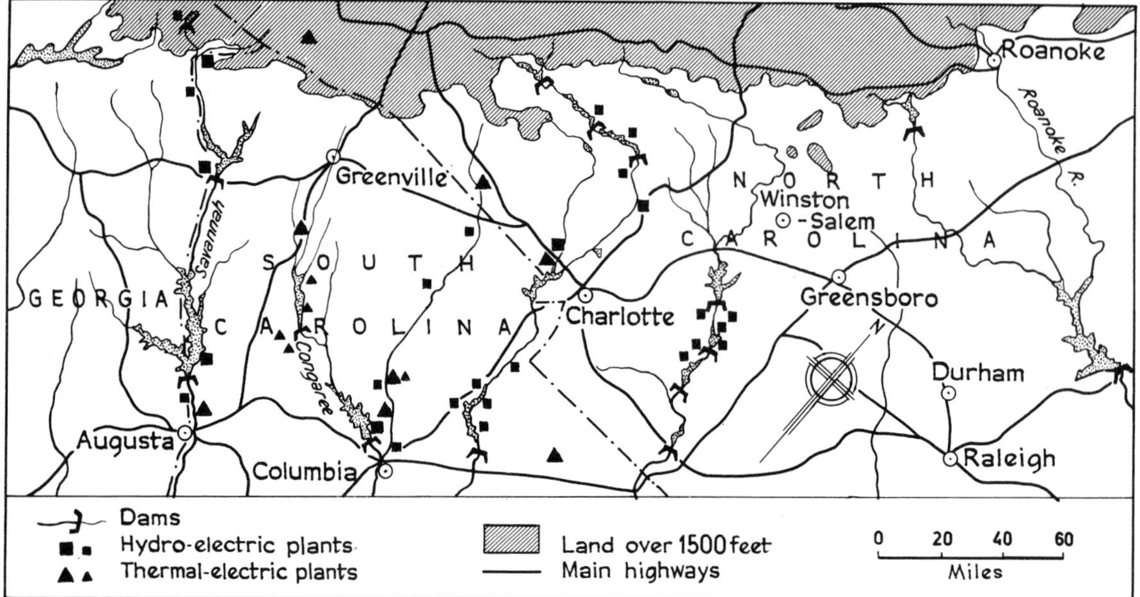

FIG. 13:4 Dams and reservoirs on another part of the southern Piedmont.

Mountain, with their iron content not far below 40 per cent, and the by-product slag is useful to the local cement industry.

However, Birmingham lies far from the centralized markets of the main Manufacturing Belt (Fig. 9:11); its industrial development has been slower than could have been expected, were ready access to raw materials the prime consideration, and has not hitherto included a great deal of sophisticated engineering or machinery production.

Finally, the region conducts a range of minor industries with bases in mineral resources other than coal and iron. Kaolin, a deep-weathering product extracted in South Carolina and Georgia, is used in the ceramic industry and as a weighting additive in paper-making. North Carolina mines about 60 per cent of the nation's mica requirements, principally for use in electrical manufacture.

Chief among the settlements in or very close to the Fall Zone are, in order of location, Roanoke, Raleigh, Columbia, Augusta, Macon, and Columbus. None has yet grown very large; their population, combined with that of the smaller Tuscaloosa and that of Montgomery, amounts to about 1½ million. Montgomery lies about twenty miles south of the Fall Zone on the Alabama River, the commercial centre for a district of cotton-growing where soils benefit by outcropping limestone, and the State capital of Alabama. All but one of the cities of the southern Piedmont are also small to medium in size: Greensboro–High Point, Winston–Salem, Charlotte, Greensville, and Atlanta contain some 2 million people in their metropolitan areas, more than half of them in the Atlanta metropolitan area. Although Birmingham belongs geologically to the Appalachians, it could be added to this urban series by virtue of its location in low plateau country which, fringing the mountains, resembles the Piedmont physiographically; the addition would bring the sub-total of population above the 2½-million mark.

Chattanooga and Knoxville, deep in the Appalachians, are both readily accessible river ports in consequence of the works of the T.V.A. They discharge the normal central-place functions for cities of their size; Knoxville has tobacco factories, and cement works which use the local 'marble' limestone; Chattanooga has a metal industry which includes the production of farm machinery, and also makes textiles and furniture.

Reasons for the scarcity of large cities include a generally low level of demand for urban services, the dispersion of the textile and furniture industries through a number of localities, none with outstanding advantages in manufacture over the others, and the further dispersion of these industries into smaller places than the largest cities. Birmingham, the leading centre of heavy industry in the region, has already been discussed. Atlanta, five or more times as populous as the generality of cities in the region, and growing very fast, demonstrates that forces other than those of manufacturing industry can promote vigorous town growth. It is an excellent example of the central place – a flourishing centre of retail distribution, a State capital, the possessor of an international airport, and fast becoming, by deliberate effort, a conference centre: to this end it has constructed whole blocks of multi-storey motels, of the most luxurious and up-to-date sort, and in competition with other noted conference centres can offer climate far more genial than that of Chicago and accessibility superior to that of Miami. In Atlanta's programme of modernization and expansion is a system of urban freeways, much already constructed. It would be interesting, however, to ascertain how much of its indisputable urban force results from the financial injections of the Coca-Cola fortunes, which among other effects have produced the city's well-endowed Emory University.

13c: The Extreme Southeast

Area: about 87,500 square miles.

Population: about 7 million.

Cities with at least 150,000 people in the metropolitan area: populations of metropolitan areas given in brackets:

- Tampa–St Petersburg, Fla., 456,000 (772,500)
- Miami, Fla., 292,000 (935,000)
- Jacksonville, Fla., 201,000 (455,500)
- Savannah, Ga., 149,000 (188,000)
- Fort Lauderdale–Hollywood, Fla., 119,000 (334,000)
- Orlando, Fla., 88,000 (318,500)
- West Palm Beach, Fla., 56,000 (228,000)

Population density outside the largest metropolitan areas: about 45 per square mile.

Rather less than half the region is in farmland; about one-quarter of the farm acreage is cropland, and about one-half is woodland. Forest, including farm woodland, covers nearly two-thirds of the region.

Numbers of livestock: cattle, $2\frac{1}{2}$ million, of which one-third million are milk cows; sheep, 15,000; pigs, 1 million; poultry, 250 million.

Peninsular Florida, the Florida Panhandle, and the coastal plain in Georgia are distinctive in landscapes as they are in economic activities. South of Jacksonville the Peninsula is based principally on limestone with thin veneers of unconsolidated marine sediments. Solution underground and collapse at near-surface levels have pocked much of the surface with shallow and roughly circular karstic depressions, some occupied by lakes but most by swamps. Straddling the Georgia border, the Okefenokee swamp occupies a very extensive hollow of little depth, due perhaps to horizontal solution of the Tertiary limestone rocks; and the equally extensive and equally shallow depression of the Everglades, in the south of the Peninsula, may have a similar origin. Between the limestone sinks the ground rises in low plains and subdued undulating hills, merging along the Atlantic coast into sandy barriers which obstruct almost every inlet, on the west coast of the Peninsula into very gently-shelving inlets, and along the Gulf coast into dunes and swamps.

Although the region is liable to cold waves in winter, these are uncommon. The northern part can be classed climatically as subtropical, the southern part, latitude notwithstanding, as tropical. Mangroves and coconuts grow round the fringes of the Peninsula south of the Tampa–Cape Kennedy line, with summers of very high humidity and frequent thunder–rain dominated by mTW air off the Gulf or the Gulf Stream, and seasonal temperatures averaging 80°F or more. Winter conditions are less debilitating, with average temperatures around the 64°F mark and rainfall at its least. Spanish moss drapes the trees of all but the most northern forests; magnolias are common; and azaleas, camellias, and dogwood figure as ornamental plants in town streets. White cedar, southern pine, palmetto palms, and swamp cypress grow in the forests: water hyacinths deck, and also choke, the peat-blackened bayous. Alligators, snakes, bear, and deer inhabit the forests and the swamps.

Florida has capitalized on its climate, its coastline, its subtropical to tropical vegetation, and on its karstic drainage system to develop a vigorous resort trade. Its winter climate is as genial to visiting northerners as the summer is oppressive to the locals. Aided by vigorous promotion of tourism and by equally vigorous real-estate salesmanship, Miami has raised itself in fifty years from the status of a Seminole Indian trading-post to that of a pre-eminent riviera resort. Seminole villages still exist in the Everglades; the refusal of the Seminoles to change their ways – except for some attention to the tourist trade – was rewarded in 1967, when the federal government decided that the original purchase by whites of tribal lands was transacted at a totally unscrupulous price, and decided to pay millions of dollars in compensation. The whole coast from West Palm Beach to the Florida Keys is made over to the resort trade or to high-grade residential settlement. Organized game-fishing and pleasure sailing and boating are highly developed, with links and outposts in the near-by British-controlled Bahamas. In the inland areas of the east coast, Silver Springs, Sarasota Springs, Rainbow Springs, Waukulla Springs, and other centres use the fish-stocked waters of limestone resurgences as the basis of tourist activity. But the climate is not without its drawbacks. Florida in summer is within reach of tropical cyclones generated in the Caribbean or over the warm waters off the Antilles. Prostrate and regrown trees throughout the peninsula record the hurricanes of earlier days; the Keys railway, leading to a train ferry terminal for services to Havana, was destroyed by the hurricane of 1935, never to be rebuilt. In winter, northern Florida can be reached by cold waves, at times severe enough to promote frost.

Generally mild winters, early springs, and soils formed either on warm superficial sands or on the peaty muck of coastal swamps, provide a highly encouraging setting for specialized crop farming, with an emphasis on the cropping of primeur vegetables. Salad crops, peas, string beans, and early soft fruits such as strawberries reach the north-eastern urban markets from the Extreme Southeast as early as January. The products are moved by express refrigerated rail cars. However, each group of growing districts from Florida northward experiences a short period of market ascendancy when production reaches its peak, and unseasonal stimulation of plant growth can lead to short-term glutting of the market. On this account, numerous canneries, freezing plants, and juice extraction works have located themselves on the Atlantic Seaboard from Georgia to New Jersey, taking advantage of persistent local production and of temporary situations of over-supply. Risks of seasonal weather, imperfect market forecasts, and the constant need for intensive fertilization and working can render specialized market-farming very hazardous: strawberry production, for instance, runs in its worst years at 25 per cent of the level of glut years. Farmers in these circumstances tend to buffer themselves by diversifying, extending their acreages, or by marketing under contract to processing plants or through producers' exchanges. The main areas for the production of early vegetables in this region occur just south of Tampa, round Lake Okeechobee, and in a narrow strip along the east Florida and Georgia coast. The earliest of early crops are grown on sandy soils which warm up quickly in the spring, in advance of the loams and silt-loams of pedologically richer but more tardy districts.

Citrus groves, predominantly of grapefruit, kumquats, and Valencia oranges occur in a belt between Tampa and Jacksonville (Plate 47). They are sited on sand-mantled hills where cold-air drainage mitigates the worst effects of nocturnal cooling and its attendant frost. At the same time, the groves of northern Florida are sufficiently open to frost damage that citrus production has shifted steadily southward; in addition, Florida growers find it difficult to compete with superior but dearer fruit from California and the Rio Grande, and accordingly have shifted their market emphasis towards juicing and canning works. The frost danger, referable to incursions of cPK or even cAK air in winter cold waves, is partly mitigated by the use of smoke-pots which reduce out-radiation and of blowers which churn up the air at very low levels.

Peaches are grown chiefly on the slopes of the Appalachian Valley in westernmost Georgia, south-west of Macon, and around Spartenburg, S.C. Their cultivation has replaced that of cotton in some Piedmont areas, but it too is liable to suffer from frosts, the danger being greatest at the higher levels. Southern Georgia and northern Florida grow a great deal of tobacco of the types needed for flue-curing for the medium-grade cigars manufactured in Jacksonville. Cessation of imports of Havana leaf from Cuba, in consequence of the political dispute between that country and the U.S.A., has terminated the customary means of supply for the high-grade cigar manufacture of Tampa; but

47. Citrus groves in the inner part of the Florida peninsula.

this town's cigar industry is, understandably, trying to maintain its reputation while using available sources.

Manufacturing in the Extreme Southeast is but slightly developed. Tampa ships phosphate rock in quantity from pebble deposits in western Florida to fertilizer plants on the Atlantic and elsewhere on the Gulf, and also manufactures fertilizers, lumber, and cement for export. Jacksonville, on the harbour of St John's River, twenty-eight miles inland from the Atlantic, exports lumber, naval stores, and agricultural produce. But these two ports, like the smaller Port Everglades, are hard pressed to provide export cargoes except for phosphate, while the region as a whole has no more than low to intermediate accessibility to the main national market. Savannah, Ga., contains derelict cotton sheds and wharves, testimonies to its former but now extinct trade. It has, however, experienced some industrial development, with oil refineries processing crude petroleum from the Gulf, fertilizer works using Chile nitrate, potash from Germany, and Florida phosphate, and paper and paper-board mills. The inner city, although partly stagnant, is indisputably charming. Orlando, the largest inland city of

48. Scene at Fort Lauderdale, Fla.: powered sport-fishing boats, with resort hotel beyond.

Florida, is a centre of fruit packing and of juicing; near at hand lies a great strategic air base, operationally connected to the missile-launching sites of Cape Kennedy.

The region's greatest economic asset is probably its remarkably swift rate of population increase. Miami, Fort Lauderdale–Hollywood, Pensacola, and West Palm Beach are all resort centres and centres of winter (or permanent) residence for the rich; and in recent times there has been a strong movement of in-migration by the less rich (Plate 48). The Atlantic beaches run with few breaks along the ocean side of the coastal barriers; the Gulf shore of the Florida peninsula, protected from wave-action by the very gentle shelving of the sea-bed, is highly indented and irregular, with few resorts of noticeable size. Long curving beaches come in again on the coast of the Florida Panhandle, where the winter resort trade and game-fishing in summer appear likely to develop strongly – that is, to invade the eastern portion of the Gulf South region; these activities already have a strong advance post in Panama City.

13d: The Gulf South

Area: about 37,500 square miles.

Population: about $4\frac{1}{2}$ million.

Cities with at least 50,000 people in the central area: populations of metropolitan areas given in brackets:

Houston, Tex., 940,000 (1,245,000)
New Orleans, La., 627,500 (868,000)
Mobile, Ala., 203,000 (314,000)
Beaumont–Port Arthur, Tex., 186,000 (306,000)
Baton Rouge, La., 152,000 (230,000)
Galveston–Texas City, Tex., 100,000 (140,000)
Lake Charles, La., 63,000 (145,000)
Pensacola, Fla., 57,000 (204,000)

Population density outside the largest metropolitan areas: about 25 per square mile.

About two-fifths of the region is in farmland: rather less than half the farm acreage is cropland, about one-third is woodland. Forest, including farm woodland, covers about half the region.

Numbers of livestock: cattle, $1\frac{1}{4}$ million of which 200,000 are milk cows; sheep, 40,000; pigs, one-third million; poultry, 60 million.

A convenient northern boundary for the Gulf South region is the zero isochrym, the line of nil frost. Fortuitously, this line somewhat resembles the line of the 10-inch autumn isohyet which marks the southern limit of cotton-growing. This is not cotton country: farm crops are sugar, rice, mangoes, water-melons, and the like, distinctly tropical or near-tropical in character.

Rainfall exceeds 60 inches annually, rising in some districts to more than 80 inches, and coming in part in the form of savage summer downpours. It fills the lakes, lagoons, and bayous of the coastland and nourishes the swamps. All these features suffer the disadvantages of impeded drainage, and harbour snakes and mosquitoes: and the swamplands are also reputed to offer a hideaway for criminals. Wild vegetation in the many ill-drained areas is of swamp cypress, white cedar, and live oaks, festooned throughout with the epiphyte Spanish moss. Podsolized sands on higher ground tend to be pine-covered. Scattered patches of better soils occur where small limestone outcrops with their subterranean drainage induce prairie grassland as the natural cover; and it is such soils, along the coasts of Texas and eastern Louisiana, that have been put to mechanized rice-farming integrated with the grazing on the rice stubble of Brahmin (zebu) or Brahmin-cross cattle. These breeds are immune to tick fever. On account of their hydrological characteristics, the prairie lands of the Gulf are liable to physiographical drought, despite the high rainfall of the region, and consequently need irrigation from deep bores or, where possible, from bayous.

Sugar-cane is extensively grown where the water-table is high. Before the opening of the dispute between the U.S.A. and Cuba, the Gulf coast produced about 5 per cent of the national requirement of sugar, but the fraction is now considerably higher. Most of the cane mills are located within forty miles west of New Orleans. Frost danger in the northern-most sugar-producing districts, which lie north of the zero isochrym, reduces the cropping season to nine or ten months, and encourages the cutting of immature cane which is low in sucrose content. A useful by-product of the sugar-mills is bagasse, the fibrous part of the cane which is converted into hardboard.

Pulp- and paper-milling take advantage of the regional warmth and humidity, which make it profitable to plant forests of longleaf, yellow, and black pines. Since paper-mills in the region depend primarily on northern and overseas markets, they are located on tidewater; apart from newsprint, the production of which from Southern timber was at one time technically impossible, they make kraft papers.

The region's second city is New Orleans, located – despite its name – by Spanish founders, between the Mississippi and Lake Pontchartrain. The site is unpromising – below river-level at many stages, protected in the natural state only by natural and breakable levees, and episodically subjected in the early days of the city to flooding and to epidemic disease. Nevertheless, it offered deep water close inshore, on the outer bank of a meander; and it controlled traffic on the Mississippi system of waterways. The vieux carré, the innermost city, is a district of narrow streets and enclosed patios which is famous for its decorative ironwork, high-grade restaurants, cabarets, and jazz musicians; and the city has something of a local subculture among the cajuns, descendants of French migrants from Acadia who intermarried with Indians and Negroes. The broad Canal Street of New Orleans is filled each year by the processions of the mardi gras festival, an event resembling the fiestas of Spain and Latin America.

As a trading centre and port, New Orleans encounters competition from the inlets of the mid-Atlantic coast, which were able to draw traffic away from the Mississippi after their railway connections with the interior were established, and which not only provide markets in themselves, but are easily accessible to the rest of the Manufacturing Belt. Its principal exports are cotton, lumber, petroleum, and petroleum products; it takes in Santos coffee, bananas from Central America, vegetable oils for its soap and oleo (margarine) industries, and bauxite, the ore of aluminium, from Surinam and Guyana. As a manufacturing centre the city is also handicapped by distance: it does not figure in the series of leading manufacturing towns plotted in Fig. 9:11. Baton Rouge, at the head of ocean navigation on the Mississippi, has large oil refineries and petrochemical works, and links pipelines to the coastal tankers plying on the Inter-

49. Oil-drilling crew inserting drill pipes into the well bore.

50. Near-shore oilfield, Gulf Coast of Texas.

51. Gas pipeline, transmitting from a processing plant in southern Louisiana.

52. Offshore sulphur mine, coast of Louisiana.

53. Terminus, including turning basin, of the Houston Ship Canal.

coastal Waterway.

Industry in the Gulf South west of the Mississippi Delta relates largely to mineral resources – oil, natural gas, salt, and sulphur (Plates 49–52). Oil and gas are piped to the Northeast, while oil also moves by sea, both in the crude and in the refined state. Offshore drilling has been highly successful along the Texas coast, where oil-bearing structures continue on to the continental shelf. Houston, Beaumont, and Lake Charles are important refining centres, with a great range of petrochemical manufacture; and sulphur, mined by the low-cost Frasch process, joins with deposits of rock salt in sustaining the heavy chemical industry in general. Houston, fifty miles upstream from the Gulf on the San Jacinto River, has long overshadowed Galveston as a port (Plate 53), although Galveston still ships wheat and sulphur. With the aid of mineral raw materials, mineral fuels, and of the ship canal opened in 1914, Houston has become the largest manufacturing centre and the most populous city of the region.

The imported mineral bauxite is processed at Mobile, and in factories located on the Mississippi from Baton Rouge to New Orleans. Unlike the separation of aluminium from alumina, an electrolytic process, the extraction of alumina from bauxite is a matter of crushing, baking, and chemical treatment. Alumina mills are accordingly not limited by questions of power supply. They stand by the waterside, where bauxite from Jamaica, Guyana, and Surinam can come in direct. New Orleans alone, using thermally-generated power, produces aluminium.

The only two large cities in the region east of the delta are Mobile and Pensacola; each stands on an inlet, where a breach in the coastal barrier system gives access to a river valley and to routes inland. Each is involved with industries based on local resources – lumber milling, cement manufacture and export, and the processing of turpentine and resin, while Mobile, already mentioned as a processer of bauxite, uses steel from Birmingham in its shipbuilding.

13e: The South Mississippi Lowlands

Area: about 125,000 square miles.

Population: about 4½ million.

Cities with at least 50,000 people in the central

area: populations of metropolitan areas given in brackets:

Memphis, Tenn., 500,000 (627,000)
Little Rock, Ark., 166,000 (243,000)
Shreveport, La., 164,000 (280,000)
Jackson, Miss., 144,000 (187,000)
Monroe, La., 52,000 (102,000)

Population density outside the largest metropolitan areas: about 30 per square mile.

Rather less than half the region is in farmland; rather less than half the farm acreage is cropland, rather more than half is woodland; cotton takes about a fifth of the cropland acreage. Forest, including farm woodland, covers about half the region.

Numbers of livestock: cattle, $4\frac{1}{2}$ million, of which more than three-quarter million are milk cows; sheep, 125,000; pigs, $1\frac{1}{4}$ millions; poultry, 350 million.

The title *South Mississippi Lowlands* is meant to be taken in a very broad sense, for this region is made to include the lowland catchments of the Alabama–Tombigbee system in the southern half of Alabama State. On the west, it takes in the subdued plains drained by the lower Arkansas and Red Rivers. Its southern boundary has already been fixed by the demarcation of the Gulf South region; on the northeast it abuts against the Piedmont and the southwestern Appalachian plateaus; on the northwest it adjoins the Ozarks. The western boundary runs approximately where cotton-growing falls off sharply in the westward direction; and here also there is something of a physical break in the landscape. The whole region belongs structurally to the Mississippi Embayment, a crustal feature marked by persistent down-sagging and shallow-water sedimentation.

In many contexts the Mississippi Delta is understood not as the district where the river subdivides itself into distributaries on its approach to the sea, but as the whole of the alluvial flats of the lower valley from Cairo southwards, which average eighty miles in width and are 550 miles from end to end. The Delta in this sense is the alluvial fill of a trench, cut during glacial episodes of low sea-level, and infilled during deglacials when sea-level rose. Alluvium is still coming down the Mississippi, borne on water sufficient to promote flows of one million cubic feet per second at the bankfull stage; and it lodges temporarily as point bar and levee deposits on the broad floodplain. Soils formed on it are in some places sandy or gravelly, but most fall into the clay or silt grades, in which a heavy charge of organic matter makes the soils black. The easily ploughed black soils of the bottomlands make the best cotton lands; they are covered with a dense pattern of one-mule farms. Although cotton has been losing importance in this region for a perceptible period of time, it still remains the main economic base of numerous districts.

Like all soils of the Southeast, the black soils of the cotton-farming districts of the Mississippi Lowlands are subject to intense chemical weathering; and cotton is in any event an exhausting crop. Depletion of soil nutrients is therefore rapid. Past neglect has only been overcome where owner-farmers, as opposed to share-croppers, have made heavy application of industrial fertilizers; and soil depletion, with the associated damage of soil erosion wherever the ground is sloping, is serious in this region – especially in the poorer parts where low yields induce poor husbandry. Ravages of the boll weevil and the pink worm have been widely checked by eradication programmes using industrially produced chemical insecticides, but not before some localities found it profitable to convert from cotton to other crops.

When this region, with the southern Piedmont, could be defined by contemporary geographers as the Cotton Belt, much attention was paid to its northern limit. The southern limit, as already stated, is set by the wetness of the Gulf coast. A fair approximation to the northern limit was fixed by the isochrym of 200 frost-free days; in practice, the bounds of commercial cotton-growing lie where a profitable crop can be expected in four years out of five. Frost and the length of the growing season are the controls; and the boundary encircles the southern margins of the Ozarks–Ouachitas and the Appalachians, bending north along the low ground of the innermost Mississippi Valley.

Perhaps the most serious difficulties of the region concern human relationships and socio-economics. Cotton prices trend downwards in response to oversupply of the markets. Slavery after the Civil War was widely converted into share-cropping, with its corollaries of small-sized holdings, permanent indebtedness, and lack of farm capital. Cotton farms in this region are small by national standards, and also by national standards inefficient: their production costs are high compared with those of the mechanized farms of California, Arizona, and Texas, where large sizes of holdings and mechanized working have effected noteworthy economies of scale.

Social strain here is regional. Although slavery was abolished by the Civil War, social division was not. The whites as a group succeeded in enforcing the segregation of workplaces, dwelling areas, schools, and churches; in addition, they contrived for many years to keep coloured people from voting in elections. One reaction has been migration of Negroes to the North: but this provides no complete solution, for the migrants and their descendants concentrate in particular districts of the great northern cities – districts which, inevitably, are the most run-down, for the educational standards of the migrants is in general low, and their earning-powers are correspondingly small.

Rural population-densities are not high in comparison with the national average; nevertheless, they can be regarded as maintained at undesirably high levels, in view of the general level of farm productivity. Problems of land tenure, a partial approach to monoculture, and a low living-standard in the countryside all militate against agricultural improvement, and specifically against mechanization and heavy expenditure on fertilizers. Standards might be improved if the share-cropping system were broken up, and if holdings were consolidated. Consolidation could introduce economies of scale; and share-cropping encourages exploitation, rather than management, conservation, and improvement. On the one hand lies the need for employment: on the other lie the diseconomy of the hand-picking of cotton, the domination of the farming year by the cotton crop during its long season of cultivation from March to November, and the existing situation of a labour-intensive system of farming. Cotton plantations, technically defined as farms greater than 260 acres in area and under single management control, could be viable: but their historical antecedents are against them. Whereas a good plantation owner employs Negroes in generous conditions, his regard for their welfare is paternalistic; and racism and social feeling in the South are highly ambivalent in their reaction to paternalism. Among the less successful farmers, self-management can easily seem more important than good management.

Diversification of agriculture has met patchy success with the aid of small grains, corn, groundnuts, soybeans, and crops related to the feedlot production of beef cattle. Industry in some sectors has done distinctly better than farming; its fastest-growing divisions are petro-chemical manufacture, electro-metallurgy, paper-milling, and plywood making, and fertilizer production which uses Louisiana sulphur. All the industries concerned here are capital-intense rather than labour-intense, and thus do not provide ranges of job opportunities comparable with those of the Piedmont. There is scant chance to absorb any workforce which might be released or displaced by a reorganization of agriculture.

In a triangle incorporating western Louisiana and eastern Texas, and with an apex on the Kansas–Nebraska line, occur the continent's greatest oil- and gasfields, grouped under the title Mid-Continental. Extensive pipeline networks link these fields to the Manufacturing Belt and to tanker terminals on the Gulf. Monroe, Shreveport, and Little Rock are centres of oil processing and of oil and gas distribution. Little Rock is the State Capital of Arkansas, sited on the boundary of the Lowlands with the Ozark–Ouachita country, and with access to the latter along the Arkansas River; it ships cotton and hard winter wheat. Shreveport is at the head of navigation for bulky shipments on the Red River; among its industrial activities is the making of cotton textiles. Jackson, the State capital of Mississippi, is a collecting and dispatching centre for cotton, with cotton-seed and textile mills. Memphis, a route focus where the Mississippi is bridged, carries on a vigorous waterborne trade, marketing and shipping cotton, hardwoods, grain, livestock, and oil.

CHAPTER FOURTEEN

THE CENTRE AND THE PRAIRIE PLAINS

In total area, this division approaches one million square miles; its population is not far short of 45 million. It is pre-eminent in commercial farming, containing 40 per cent of the total combined cropland of the U.S.A. and Canada: this category of land use takes a third of the mega-region. Grain-growing is prominent, as also are stock-fattening and dairying: the division has a third of all cattle in the two North American countries, and two-thirds of all pigs (Figs. 14:1, 14:2, 12:4, 12:5). Resources of coal, iron ore, oil, and natural gas sustain heavy manufacturing; and manufacturing industry in general is highly developed, employing 60 per cent of all workers. Thus, on the mega-regional scale, the economy is better balanced than that of any of the other divisions, even though industrial activity is by no means uniformly distributed throughout it. This is the one mega-region of North America which could attain a significant degree of autarky.

The northern limit is drawn to take in the upper Lakes, in view of the linkages established by Lake and rail transport. The eastern boundary excludes the regions discussed in the Lower Lakes–Appalachian division, while the southern boundary cuts off the regions allocated to the Southeast. The zone of demarcation on the west is jointly physiographic and demographic: population-densities and the degree of urbanization fall rapidly away in the westward direction, once the edge of the High Plains has been passed.

On the other hand, the limit of the Plains does not everywhere coincide with a rapid change in land use. The concentration of winter-wheat production in western Kansas, western Oklahoma, and the Texas panhandle overlaps from the Prairie Plains on to the High Plains, where at present most of it lies. The concentration of spring-wheat production, mainly in North Dakota and Saskatchewan, straddles the physiographic boundary between the Prairie Plains and the High Plains, curving widely across the latter. A further complication arises from the distribution of soils: from close to

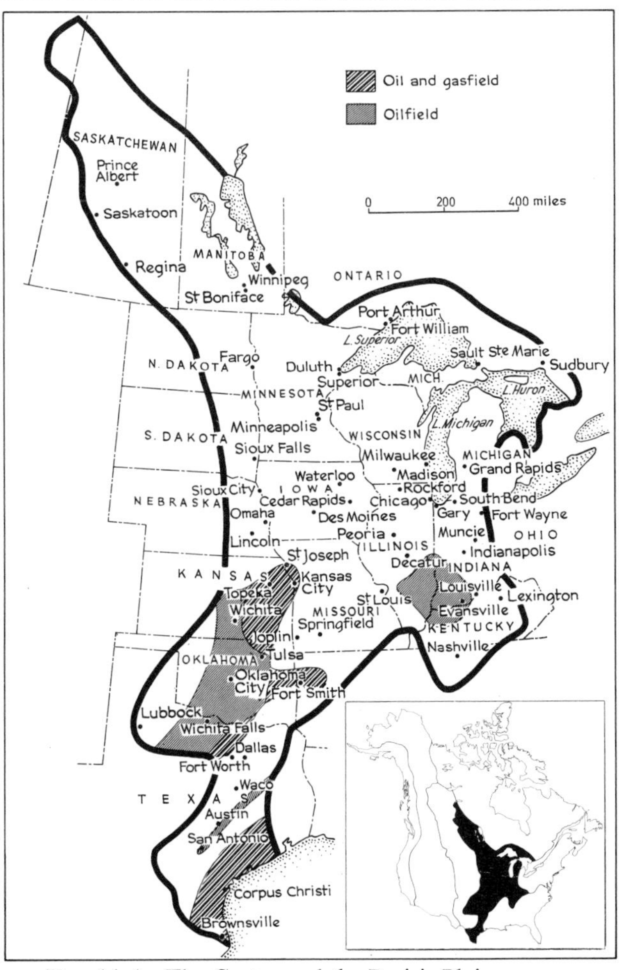

FIG. 14:1 The Centre and the Prairie Plains.

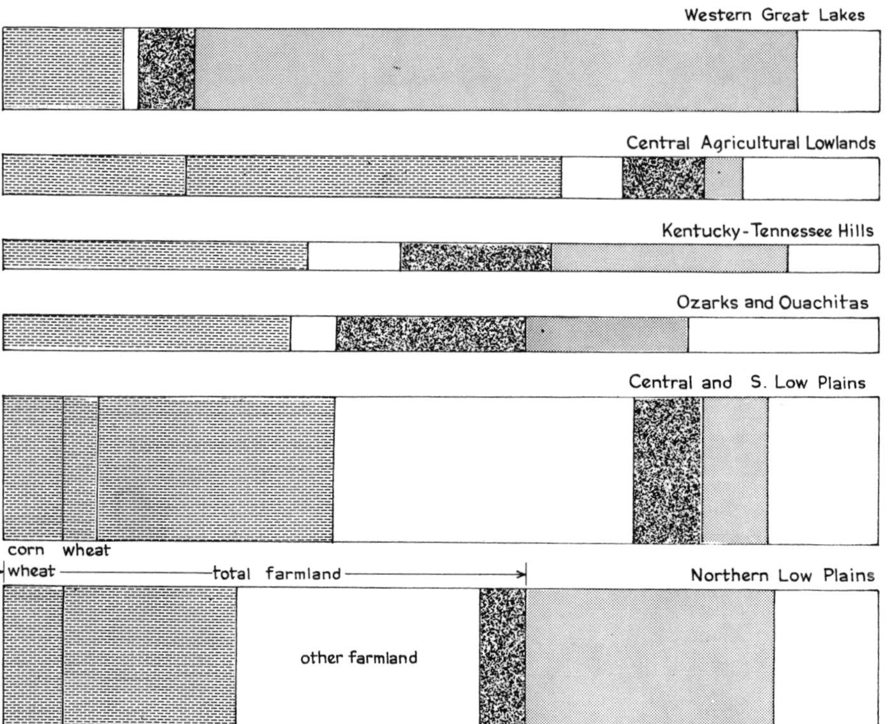

FIG. 14:2
Land use in the Centre and the Prairie Plains, by regions.

the Rockies in southern Alberta, the chernozem belt loops across the High Plains on to the Prairie Plains, passing well out upon the lower ground, before swinging southward once more to encroach – obliquely this time – on the High Plains. The concentration of spring-wheat growing overlaps widely from the chernozem belt on to the chestnut soils next to the west, while the southwesternmost winter-wheat farms are on latosols.

It would be artificial to break up the two concentrations of wheat-growing, each into two parts, assigning each part to a different region. Accordingly, spring-wheat production will be dealt with in the present chapter, while winter-wheat growing will appear in the following chapter where the High Plains are discussed.

The history of this division is distinctive. It owes little, if indeed anything, to the motives which prompted settlement on the Atlantic seaboard; and it certainly owes nothing to the former plantation economy of the South. Equally, it has been largely independent of certain streams of migration. Immigrant Irishmen and Italians of the nineteenth century tended to lodge in the great cities of the east, or alternatively to enlist in railroad construction: the Midwest–Prairie division was settled largely by Germans, British, and Scandinavians, plus internal migrants from New England. Because the process of settlement was guided by the principle of establishing family farms, and because the 160-acre quarter-section is a viable proposition in much of this division, the existing patterns of tenure, location of settlements, and roadways have a certain uniformity throughout. The eventual commitment to commercial farming served to promote much identity of interest; and it has been claimed that the U.S. Midwest acted for a long period as an electoral pendulum, throwing out the serving President, and his party, whenever presidential elections came at times of agricultural difficulty and depression. It was in the Midwest, too, that isolationism in American politics reached its greatest strength. In some ways, then, this division has become inward-looking, focussing its attention less on the world beyond than on its own economic affairs and on its great urban centre of Chicago.

In so far as they rely on physical criteria, the subdivision of most of this area into macro-regions and internal differentiation within macro-regions are concerned as much with soils and with the pattern of terrain as they are with the gross distribution of relief. It is true that the Ozarks, the Ouachitas, and the highest ground embracing the head of Lake Superior all rise to more than 1500 feet above sea-level, but relief in the remainder of the division is mainly low and subdued. At its most extensive, the continental ice of Pleistocene glaciation reached as far south as the Ohio and the Missouri, depositing sheets of till when it decayed. These are extensively covered with loess, which came from the silt-charged outwash channels of late-glacial times. Now the ice in the last major advance failed to reach as far south as it had done in earlier advances. The youngest till sheet is highly irregular in detail, with countless little hollows where drainage can be trapped, and in Minnesota with numberless kettle-holes, some of great size and many occupied by lakes. South of the youngest till, older tills are exposed; and there has been enough time since they were deposited for natural drainage to organize itself. South again, beyond the extreme ice-limits, the soils have not been enriched by the glacial importation of mineral matter. In addition to the north–south variation in the parent material of soils, there is an east–west variation of profile characteristics related to the influence of climate and vegetation. The north–south range is from the podsols of the upper Lakes through the grey-brown and brown podsolics of the Ohio Valley: the east–west range is from grey-brown podsolics through prairie soils to the black chernozems which fall within this division in the U.S.A. and loop round the northern fringe of the cultivated Prairies in Canada.

14a: The Western Great Lakes Region

Area (excluding the Lakes): about 175,000 square miles.

Population: about $10\frac{1}{2}$ million.

Cities with at least 200,000 people in the metropolitan area, plus Port Arthur–Fort William and Sudbury: populations of metropolitan areas given in brackets:

- Chicago, Ill., 3,550,000 (6,220,000)
- Milwaukee, Wis., 741,500 (1,200,000)
- Gary–Hammond–East Chicago, Ind., 348,000 (573,500)
- Duluth–Superior, Minn.–Wis., 140,500 (277,000)
- South Bend, Indiana, 132,500 (240,000)
- Madison, Wis. (on the boundary), 127,000 (222,000)
- Rockford, Ill. (on the boundary), 127,000 (210,000)
- Port Arthur–Fort William, Ont., 90,500
- Sudbury, Ont., 80,000

Population density outside the largest metropolitan areas: about 10 per square mile; however, densities are far less in the north of the region than in the south.

About a fifth of the land area is in farms; cropland takes more than half the farm acreage, farm woodland about one-quarter, and grassland pasture about one-tenth. Forests, including farm woodland, cover about three-quarters of the land area.

Numbers of livestock: cattle, 4 million, of which $1\frac{3}{4}$ million are dairy cows; sheep, $\frac{1}{2}$ million; pigs, $2\frac{1}{4}$ million; poultry, 40 million.

The Canadian section of this region is sometimes called New Ontario, to distinguish it from the older-settled parts of Ontario province. Railways here preceded the establishing of settlements, which are still scarce; but the railways and the Lakes routes combine to bring the regional economy within the ambit of the macro-regional economy with which this chapter deals. So severe are the winters, with temperatures averaging between 0° F and 10° F, that dispersed settlement is scarcely possible: the small consolidated towns characteristically use district heating, with pipes reticulating from central generators. Farming settlement on the U.S. side has retreated somewhat from its former limits, allowing cleared land to be recovered by the forests. Lumbering here has diminished, in consequence of the heavy felling of past years, so that some parts of the region seem now to be exempted from the course of geographical change. On the other hand, the region's resources of iron ore have been fundamental to the continent's industrial development; commercial dairying is very well established indeed in southern districts: and at the head of Lake Michigan lies Chicago, a great manufacturing city by any standards.

Agriculture in the northern part of the region is handicapped by a very short growing season, with an average of about seventy-five days a year free of killing frosts. Moreover, rainfall is concentrated in the interval midsummer to August, ensuring maximum interference with harvesting and minimum opportunity to prepare the ground against the oncoming of spring. In any event, workable farmland in the north is uncommon: the best of it is provided by the heavy clays of former glacial lakes. Neither the Canadian side of the boundary, nor the U.S. side in North Michigan, most of the northern half of Minnesota, nor the northern quarter of Wisconsin is at all closely integrated with the economy of commercial farming; the farm products which move from ports on the head of Lake Superior are commodities in transit. The dairy farms which supply Milwaukee and Chicago constitute another kind of proposition, as also do the fruit and vegetable farms on a narrow strip of the east coast of Lake Michigan: here, as along the southern shores of Ontario and Erie, and in the Lakes Peninsula, summer heat storage by the water is a great practical benefit to specialized cropping.

Lumbering on the Canadian side exploits stands of white pine, white spruce, and jack pine, or black spruce on belts of glacio-lacustrine clays, to supply pulp-mills at Smooth Rock, Marathon, Terence Bay, and Nipigon, or integrated pulp- and paper-mills at Iroquois Falls, Sault Ste Marie, Kapuskasing, Port Arthur, Fort William, Fort Frances, and Kenora; paper other than newsprint is produced at Sturgeon Falls, Espanola, Kapuskasing, Red Rock, Port Arthur, and Dryden. Sawmills, about fifty times as numerous as pulp-mills, are widely scattered.

The western end of Lake Superior is enclosed by rocks belonging geologically to the Laurentian Shield. On the U.S. side, these rocks contained what was, before its exploitation, one of the largest groups of iron-ore reserves in the world. Beneath a mantle of glacial drift, the Superior ores of the U.S.A. occurred as hematite–magnetite in six belts of hills: The Vermilion, Mesabi, and Cuyuna Ranges for which rail-linked outlets were constructed at Duluth, Superior, and Two Harbours; the Gogebic Range, which ships through Ashland; and the Marquette and Menominee Ranges with ports at Marquette and Escanaba. On these ores depended the great expansion of ferrous-metal manufacture in the U.S.A.; over the years, some 2500 million tons of ore have been taken out. Working is mechanized and opencast. The largest single cut, that of Hall-Rust at Hibbing, Minnesota, is $2\frac{1}{2}$ miles long by one mile wide, and 350 feet below surface level at its deepest point; the excavation here is equivalent to that required for the Panama Canal. About 100 million tons of freight, mainly iron ore and coal, pass annually in Lake vessels through the Soo (Sault Ste Marie) Canals. Some 80 million tons is supplied by ore, about two-thirds of it from the Mesabi Ranges; and the ore goes by water to Chicago–Gary, Detroit, Hamilton, the Erie towns in the U.S.A., and the Pittsburgh district, after a rail transit of only twenty-five to ninety miles. But the ore traffic is now faced by prospects of decline, little more than a century after its effective beginning with the opening of the first Soo Canal in 1855: intensive working has seriously depleted reserves, especially in the Mesabi Ranges; and although resources of the siliceous ore taconite are available, the Superior fields now have to compete in the eastern markets with ore supplies from the eastern Shield or from other continents. Corresponding deposits occur in the Steep Rock district of Canada, about 100 miles west of Fort William (Plate 18). A geological survey of 1897 suggested that iron ore might underlie some 400 feet of glacial deposits beneath the floor of Steep Rock Lake. Exploration in the 1930s proved the existence of a large ore-body of high grade and low phosphorus content. By 1938 the Seine River had been diverted, and the lake pumped dry to allow access to the ore, which is now worked for the supply of the furnaces at Hamilton and the Lakeside steel centres of the U.S.A. Low-grade sideritic ore is worked in the Michipicoten district, being concentrated and sintered before shipment, mainly to Sault Ste Marie.

Apart from iron ore, the chief mineral resources of this region are ores of non-ferrous metals. The Keweenaw Peninsula of North Michigan has a long-established copper-mining industry, modest in total scale and in part no longer active: the surviving mines extract native copper from the shales through which, in very low proportion, it is disseminated.

The southern borders of the Shield possess non-ferrous ores in great quantity, associated largely with the emplacement of batholiths, enabling this region to account for half of Canada's mineral production. Uranium ores are mined at Blind River. Nickel, occupying the first rank, is worked in the Sudbury district where there is a nickel–copper–platinum ore body; metallic ore production here averages 10 million tons annually. The ore body was discovered in 1883 during the construction of the Canadian Pacific Railway. Nickel is refined today at Port Colborne, and copper at the electrolytic works at Copper Cliff. All facilities – mines, refineries, and the associated hydro-electric plants at High Falls, Big Eddy, Wabageshik, and Nairn Falls – are owned by the International Nickel Company of Canada. This company also has a refinery and several rolling mills in Britain. A second company, Falconbridge Nickel Mines Limited, concentrates nickel–copper and ships the product to Kristiansand in Norway, which uses cheap hydro-electric power for refining.

Industry in the north of the region relies on hydro-electric power, or on oil piped in from the Prairies. Large hydro-electric plants are situated at Tunnel on the Missiagi River, near Sudbury; at Sault Ste Marie; and on the Spanish and Vermilion Rivers. Plants which cater both for industrial and for urban supplies of power are at Nipigon on the Cameron Falls, Pine Portage, and Alexander. The low divide between Lakes and Hudson Bay drainage makes it possible and economic to tap north-flowing rivers for water.

Industrial activity is however concentrated primarily in the south, where Chicago, Gary, and their industrial neighbours, plus Milwaukee, belong in the westernmost extension of the Manufacturing Belt. Although industry in this part inevitably displays characteristics common to all great urban clusters, it has developed in some respects along lines drawn by the requirements of the region and of the adjacent agricultural country next to the south again. Chicago's industrial rise belongs with the commercialization and mechanization of farms in the interior (Fig. 14:3). Its stockyards, meat-packing works, flour-mills, and grain auctions depend on supplies from close at hand. Its mechanical engineering developed to a considerable extent in relation to demand for farm machinery and tractors: the International Harvester concern provided some huge personal fortunes to members of the McCormack family, one of whom, Colonel Robert, did much to shape regional opinion through his ownership of the widely-read *Chicago Tribune* and of a leading radio station in the city. Chicago

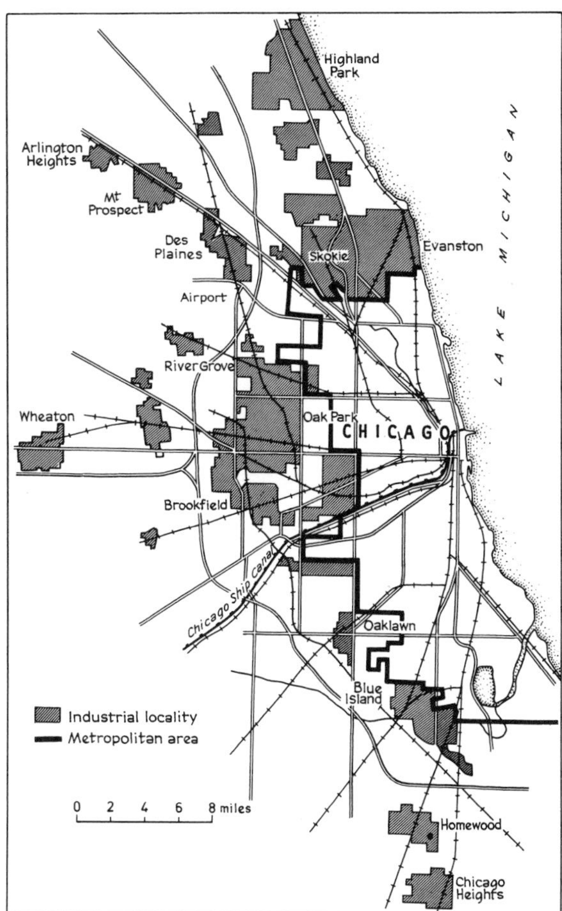

FIG. 14:3 The Chicago metropolitan area.

is also a centre of printing, oil refining, and steel-making, although heavy metallurgy is concentrated more highly in the Gary complex than in the Chicago metropolitan area. The manufacture of mechanical equipment, electrical machinery, and mining machinery is carried on both in Chicago and in Milwaukee; and Milwaukee is famous for its huge breweries.

Chicago has a vast commercial hinterland, exploited, for example, by mail-order retailers, of which the leader is Sears Roebuck. When railways came, it developed as a terminus. Through-running of the declining passenger services have reduced the city's nodality, but to no damaging extent, for it remains a focus of freight traffic (Plate 54) and of passenger traffic by road and air. Its rail yards at Proviso can sort and assemble a 100-car train in two hours. Originally, the location of Chicago was

54. The Corinth Yards of the Santa Fé Railroad at Chicago. The installations include a 32-track automatic retarder yard with a capacity for 1800 cars, a transfer yard with a capacity of 1350 cars, holding and local yards, freight sheds, locomotive shop, loading facilities, and offices.

55. The port of Superior, Wisconsin: grain elevators in the background, shipbuilding yards and dry-dock installations in the foreground.

determined by the Lake Checagau portage beween the Great Lakes and the Mississippi, on a route now followed by the Illinois River–Des Plaines Canal; but siting in this subdued landscape is less important than situation, at a point where routeways bunch round the southern extremity of Lake Michigan, where industrial raw materials are readily accessible by means of Lakes transport, and where agricultural products come in quantity from the surrounding countryside.

Steel-making at Gary, Haute Terre, Hammond, Joliet, Aurora, Evanston, Milwaukee, Racine, and Kenosha rely for part of their power supply on the low-grade bituminous coals of Illinois and Indiana. These coals are contained in synclinal structures, where working depths in some areas are so slight as to promote open-cast extraction. Coking coal moves cheaply in, as back-loads to iron ore, from the Pennsylvania fields. At South Bend, as has been noted elsewhere, manufacturing belongs in part to the automobile production of the Detroit district. Madison, closely surrounded by dairy farms, has machinery and equipment industries associated mainly with commercial agriculture. Rockford well exemplifies the moderate-sized general-purpose city of the central interior, while Duluth–Superior and Port Arthur–Fort William have previously been noticed as the products of the Lakes traffic in wheat and iron ore (Plate 55).

14b: The Central Agricultural Lowlands

Area: about 93,000 square miles.

Population: about 7¾ million.

Cities with at least 100,000 people in the metropolitan area: population of metropolitan areas given in brackets:

St Louis, Mo.–Ill. (on the boundary), 750,000 (2,000,000)
Indianapolis, Ind., 467,500 (700,000)
Fort Wayne, Ind., 162,000 (232,000)
Evansville, Ind.–Ky. (on the boundary), 141,500 (200,000)
Peoria, Ill., 103,250 (290,000)
Springfield, Ill., 83,275 (146,500)
Decatur, Ill., 78,000 (118,250)
Muncie., Ind., 69,000 (111,000)

Population density outside the largest metropolitan areas: about 40 per square mile.

Four-fifths of this region is in farms; cropland takes four-fifths of the farm acreage, and about two-thirds of the region; corn for grain occupies about a third of all cropland. Less than a tenth of the farm acreage is in woodland. Forests, including farm woodland, cover about an eighth of the region.

Numbers of livestock: cattle, 6¼ million, of which one million are dairy cows; sheep, 1 million; pigs, 13 million; poultry, 125 million.

Commercial farming in this region is highly and successfully developed. Its main basis is the corn crop, grown where average annual rainfall exceeds 30 inches, where average summer temperatures are in the range 70° F–80° F, and where the average length of season without killing frosts varies about 120 to 150 days. Conversion to hybrid corn has brought yields up to 60 bushels per acre; the region grows a fifth of all the corn of the U.S.A. However, corn is emphatically not the only crop; it takes no more than two-fifths of the region's harvested cropland. Soybeans, grown mainly for beans, are also extensive, supplying about a third of all national production. Spring wheat and oats are cultivated in the north of the region, winter wheat (both hard and soft) and alfalfa and other legumes in the south. Hay, the third-ranking crop by value after corn and soybeans, is grown throughout.

Rotations and crop-combinations vary considerably from district to district; in any event, cropping in this region is very closely integrated with livestock farming. Although corn is the main single foodstuff of the U.S.A., only 10 per cent is consumed directly as grain or as primary grain products: the main bulk of 90 per cent is taken as meat or as additives to processed food. Much of the conversion of corn feed into animal protein occurs in this region, where it reduces transport and marketing costs: it is as meat that most corn and soybeans, plus some of the small grain output, reach the consumer. At the present day, the farm income in this region from cash crops is somewhat less than the income from livestock.

Over the years, farming practices have undergone a certain reorientation. At one time, the main supply of cattle for fattening came from the High Plains, but improved techniques of grass-fattening there, plus the rise of breeding and rearing in the Central Lowlands, have made this region its own main deliverer of stores. It has always produced its own pigs, which, as the summary shows, are about twice as numerous as cattle: and the corn–pig combination developed as distinctive to the region.

The challenge to the traditional classification of North America into agricultural regions developed with specific reference to the Corn Belt, where, as has been said, crop-combinations and crop–livestock combinations represent something far different from monoculture. Nevertheless, the so-called Corn Belt States had sufficient identity of interest to lobby powerfully, and successfully, for price-support programmes capable of enabling farmers to absorb ever-rising costs. But the market prices both of home supplies and of exports has risen so high, at the same time that productivity has remarkably increased, that neither the internal nor the external market can be expanded on terms of free competition. The government has intervened, establishing storage facilities for surpluses of grain, and organizing sales and gifts abroad.

The region proved well suited to the quarter-section, 160-acre farm of the original pioneer settlement, and its layout remains distinctly rectangular today. However, farms do tend to be somewhat larger in the west than in the east, doubtless in response to the gradation of climate, with its westward decrease of moistness. The earlier system of family farms has been largely supplanted by one of salaried farm management; and the former close-knit family and small-community life has been considerably modified by the automobile, extensions of the road net, radio, and television.

Their flatness enables the region's till plains to approach closely to the uniformity postulated in the models of central-place theory; and numerous studies of central places and of urban hierarchies have been conducted here. Apart from the inner Ohio Valley, where the river has for more than two centuries provided an axial routeway, it is easy enough to characterize city sites, but less easy to distinguish between one situation and another, except in terms of distance between pairs of cities. Here, as markedly as anywhere on earth, the towns have arisen to serve the countryside.

Chicago, the primate city, is identified above as belonging in the Western Lakes region. However, it exerts an influence on much of the Central Lowlands, for which it provides a huge urban focus. St Louis ranks second only to Chicago, not only in respect of this region but also in respect of the U.S. interior as a whole; but its industrial development has probably been handicapped by the superior market accessibility of cities farther to the east: St Louis lies as the very westernmost extremity of the Manufacturing Belt. It began as a trading-post for the fur and forest products shipped down the Mississippi system in the days when the interior was held by the French: it lies just downstream of the confluence of the Missouri with the Mississippi, and is easily reached from Lake Michigan by way of the Illinois River Valley. As settlers filled the Midwest, St Louis expanded as a service centre for traders, pioneers, and rail and river transportation. Its industries today have local agricultural or mineral bases – e.g., meat packing, flour-milling, leather manufacture, oil refining, and the brewing which relates to a tradition of Germanic settlement – or else are highly diverse and unspecialized.

Indianapolis is a railway node, located roughly in the centre of its State where lines cross the White River; it packs meat, and manufactures machinery, automobile parts, and hosiery. Fort Wayne, placed where the Maumee River drains from a gap in a massive frontal moraine, produces electrical goods, petrol bowsers, and automobile components. These two cities have obvious links with Detroit, specifically representing the diffusion of the automobile industry, and also exemplifying the westward extension of manufacturing into the once dominantly rural Midwest. Evansville, with a specialism of aluminium milling, serves as a marketing and distributing centre for a district which includes the tobacco-growing lands of Kentucky and Tennessee. Factories in Peoria produce tractors and earth-moving equipment; the former line is a direct response to the mechanization of the region's agriculture, the latter an extension of engineering manufacture. Muncie is distinguished for its making of glass.

Coalfields in the Central Lowlands are not industrialized: instead, they supply fuel to industrial centres elsewhere, particularly to those on the Lake Michigan shore. Nearly a third of the U.S. national total of coal production comes from the Central Lowlands, if the producing field in the extreme west of Kentucky, south of the Ohio River, is included: other producing districts are in Indiana, about sixty miles southwest of Indianapolis, in Illinois about half-way between Indianapolis and St Louis, and, also in Illinois, in the Illinois River Valley rather closer to St Louis than to Chicago. These districts belong to the eastern division of the Mid-Continental bituminous coalfields; their production, of 150 million short tons a year, amounts to nearly one-third of the national output. Oil and natural gas wells, scattered through the southeastern half of the region, are less significant, yielding but some 3 to 4 per cent and some 1 per cent respectively of U.S. production. The coal is worked at the margins of shallow synclines, wherever possible by stripping. In some places it has an undesirably high content of sulphur; but reserves are great, and it seems likely that this branch of mining activity has a dependable future. Apart from coal, the mineral resources of the Central Lowlands are mainly non-industrial: central Indiana, for instance, produces a large fraction of the country's building limestone.

If the coal-producing districts can be said to have principal urban foci, these are Springfield and Decatur. Both stand on the Sangamon River: both exemplify the interdigitation of manufacturing with corn-based farming. Springfield, for example, makes corn starch, corn meal, and brand-named livestock feedstuffs.

14c: The Kentucky–Tennessee Hills

Area: about 62,500 square miles.

Population: nearly 5 million.

Cities with at least 100,000 people in the metropolitan area: metropolitan area population given in brackets:

Louisville, Ky., 390,500 (725,000)
Nashville, Tenn., 171,000 (400,000
Lexington, Ky., 63,000 (132,000)

Population density outside the largest metropolitan areas: about 55 per square mile.

Nearly two-thirds of this region is in farmland, and about one-third is cropland. Farm woodland takes less than a fifth of the farm acreage. Forest, including farm woodland, covers about two-fifths of the region.

Numbers of livestock: Cattle, $3\frac{1}{2}$ million, of which something less than a million are milk cows; sheep, 1/3 million; pigs, 2 million; poultry, 50 million.

Low dissected plateaus lead in this region from the Appalachians down towards the Ohio River. It might perhaps have been expected that the Ohio routeway could have brought the region firmly within the ambit of commercial farming, especially since its winters are at least no more severe than those of the most prosperous midwestern areas of corn-based farms. In actuality, this is something of an agricultural and economic backwater; subsistence farming and rural poverty are widespread. The former national purpose of establishing independent family farms has here proved a sad failure.

Reasons are easy enough to suggest, but difficult to verify. The podsolic soils of the northern part of the region are – at least in their gross characteristics – not inferior to those of other districts where commercial farming has succeeded very well indeed. The latosols of the south are equally comparable to those of many areas of profitable cotton-planting. However, the Hill Belt appears to be too far south, too warm, too humid, and too greatly handicapped in its seasonal regime of rainfall for commercial corn-growing or corn-based farming to pay well; and at the same time it is too far north, and too liable to frost, to grow cotton. In addition, the complex slopes of an intricately dissected surface promote soil erosion: and this has proved disastrous on many a hoe-tilled hillside.

Subsistence farming provides a diet, the staples of which are hominy and pork. The subsistence economy and the culture which it has produced are Oriental rather than Western. Small in-breeding communities, each in its own little valley, have but minor contact with the outside world.

The one signal exception to this general rule is the commercial production of tobacco. In the Lexington area of Kentucky and in northwestern Tennessee, soils derived from limestones prove well suited to tobacco farming, which produces about 40 per cent of the U.S. crop; there is an outlier of such farming around Owensboro, on the Ohio.

Burley tobacco, developed in 1864, is grown on the phosphatic limestone soils of the blue grass country around Lexington. Here, a large dome structure brings weak rocks towards the surface, and erosion of the central parts has caused relief to be inverted; Lexington thus stands on a scarp-girt, limestone-floored plain. Burley tobacco is air-cured. By contrast, the Clarksville–Paducah district produces fire-cured tobacco: drying is effected by means of open fires lit on the floors of the tobacco barns. The surroundings of Owensboro and Bowling Green used to be noted for the dark air-cured tobacco sold for chewing or for snuff manufacture, but decline in the demand has led to a substitution of varieties.

Tobacco yields about 800 lb/acre, requiring 400 man-hours of labour. Nearly all the cultivation is carried out by hand: consequently, tobacco plots tend to run small – from 1 to 5 acres only. The balance of the small family-farm area is typically in fodder crops, grazing, or woodlots.

The blue grass district has developed sheep-farming, fat lamb production, and baby-beef raising, using corn as a supplement to forage grass. The Nashville district, a second area of doming and of inversion of relief, is the one part of the region where general commercial farming – producing corn, sheep, cattle, and pigs – is really well established.

Lexington has not developed manufacturing specialisms of note; Nashville's industries are generally diverse, although textile and leather working indicate a general resemblance to the cities of the Piedmont–Southern Appalachians region. In respect of its furniture making, general-purpose metal fabrication, and somewhat limited machinery industries, Louisville also fails to be distinctive. It is however, a noteworthy centre of distilling – specifically, the production of bourbon whisky. No definable locating factors can be perceived, for the local corn supply is inadequate to cater for the distilleries, while the repeated claim about the virtues of the local water has yet to be substantiated. The fact remains that Kentucky bourbon has a firm grip on the national market. Its advertising is frequently associated with the racehorses, for the breeding of which Kentucky is also famous.

14d: The Ozark and Ouachita Massifs

Area: about 76,500 square miles.
Population: rather more than $2\frac{1}{2}$ million.
Largest cities:

Springfield, Mo., 96,000 (126,250 in the metropolitan area)
Fort Smith, Arkansas, 53,000
Joplin, Mo., 40,000

Population density in the remainder of the region: about 20 per square mile. About three-fifths of the region is in farmland; cropland takes rather more than half the farm acreage, farm woodland rather less than a quarter. Forest, including farm woodland, covers about two-fifths of the region.

Numbers of livestock: cattle, 3 million, of which more than half a million are milk cows; sheep, one-third million; pigs, $2\frac{1}{2}$ million; poultry, 225 million.

Too far north, and too elevated, to be incorporated in the cotton-growing economy of the adjacent Southeast, and too far south, and too uneven, to belong to the concentration of corn-based farms in the Midwest, this region is partly detached from commercial farming. It was avoided by the main streams of pioneer settlers, who passed by – chiefly on the northern side – its expanses of closely dissected low plateaus. The Ozarks rise gently southward across tilted sedimentary formations of Palaeozoic age, merging along their southern rim into the higher and more uneven Boston Mountains. The upland is traversed along a belt of structural weakness and depression by the Arkansas River, before once again rising in the sharply folded Ouachitas.

The region escaped continental glaciation during the Pleistocene. Its soils, accordingly, are the products of prolonged weathering and pedogenesis, which have brought them into the latosol group. Weathering is generally deep, but leaching is correspondingly severe; in consequence, the soils in the natural state are deficient in nutrients, in addition to being highly erodible. Rainfall of about 40 inches a year, and July temperatures averaging about 75°F, are however sufficient to offer some encouragement to farming, which has displaced part of the original hardwood forest.

Grass-fat cattle move from the Ozarks to the stockyards and packing factories of Kansas City and Oklahoma City; young beasts are shipped out to the Plains as stores. Most of the region's farms keep poultry for meat-production; dairying is concentrated around Springfield. In the remoter areas farming becomes essentially a subsistence activity, relying on corn and winter wheat as grain crops, and chiefly on dairying among the branches of animal husbandry. There is a summer tourist trade, with groups of cabins especially around Lake Taneycoma and the Lake of the Ozarks. The combination of moderate to moderately heavy rainfall with the dissection of the landscape into capacious incised valleys has encouraged widespread damming of streams and the development of hydro-electric power.

Little, however, operates to encourage urban growth. The forests sustain a modest furniture industry. Bituminous coal at Pittsburg, Kansas, and along the northern flanks of the Ouachitas near Fort Smith is worked opencast. Zinc-complex ores contained in sedimentary rocks are raised in the Tri–State district in the Spring River Valley, where Joplin and Galena are situated, and lead-complex ores are exploited near Fredericktown, Mo., on the northeastern flanks of the Ozarks near St Louis. The galena goes for refining to Alton, Illinois. Zinc and lead reserves in this region make up a substantial fraction of the U.S. total, although they are generally of low grade and only marginally economic. Bauxite is mined and processed into alumina, and aluminium is extracted from the alumina, in the Arkadelphia district in the south-east.

The population-totals of Springfield and Joplin, the leading commercial cities inside the region, show how slight is the demand for urban services.

14e: The Central and Southern Low Plains

Area: about 320,000 square miles.

Population: about 15 million.

Cities with at least 100,000 people in the metropolitan area, plus St Joseph, Mo.: populations of metropolitan areas given in brackets:

- Dallas, Tex. (on the boundary), 680,000 (1,100,000)
- Kansas City, Mo.–Kans. (on the boundary), 475,000 (1,050,000)
- San Antonio, Tex. (on the boundary), 590,000 (690,000)
- Fort Worth, Tex. (on the boundary), 356,000 (573,250)
- Oklahoma City, Okla., 324,500 (512,000)
- Omaha, Neb. (on the boundary), 302,000 (458,000)
- Tulsa, Okla., 262,000 (420,000)
- Wichita, Kans., 255,000 (343,500)
- Des Moines, Iowa, 210,000 (270,000)
- Austin, Tex. (on the boundary), 187,000 (212,500)
- Corpus Christi, Tex., 170,000 (222,000)
- Lubbock, Tex. (on the boundary), 129,000 (156,500)
- Lincoln, Neb. (on the boundary), 129,000 (155,500)
- Topeka, Kans., 120,000 (141,500)
- Brownsville–Harlingen–San Bernito, Tex., 106,000 (151,000)
- Wichita Falls, Tex., 102,000 (130,000)
- Waco, Tex. (on the boundary), 100,000 (150,000)
- Sioux City, Iowa (on the boundary), 90,000 (110,000)
- St Joseph, Mo., 80,000 (91,000)
- Waterloo, Iowa, 72,000 (122,500)

Population density outside the largest metropolitan areas: about 25 per square mile.

More than four-fifths of this region is in farmland. Cropland takes not much less than half the farm acreage, grazing other than woodland grazing about one-fifth. One-fifth of the cropland is under corn (mainly in the north), one-tenth under wheat, and one-twelfth under cotton (in the south). Farm woodland and other woodland, which are about equally extensive, cover an eighth of the region.

Numbers of livestock: cattle, 22 million, of which only two million are milk cows; sheep, 2 million; pigs (mainly in the north), 16 million; poultry, 130 million.

More probably than any other, this region exemplifies the complexities of defining boundaries, even on the macro-regional scale. In the south it merges into the Gulf coastland, where the exploitation of oil and natural gas ally it in one sense with the Gulf South; on the other hand, the westward reduction of rainfall in this same part takes it out of the ambit of tropical maritime cultivation. Between the Ozarks and the High Plains the region is distinctive enough – far more developed agriculturally than the one, far more populous and urbanized than the other. In the north, the western boundary runs along the edge of the Nebraskan sandhill belt; but the central Low Plains in northern Missouri, eastern Nebraska and in Iowa have distinct agricultural affinities with the Central Lowlands. Indeed, they are not infrequently grouped with Illinois, Indiana, and most of Ohio as the Midwest.

The central Low Plains are agriculturally phenomenal. In cash farm income, Iowa is second only to California; in numbers of cattle, it is second only to Texas; and it leads all States in income from livestock, production of corn, and pig population. Its farm economy resembles that described for the Central Lowlands, except that it also possesses numbers of small feedlot farms. These neither rear animals nor raise feed; instead, they buy in stock and feed alike, concentrating solely on intensive fattening.

Singularly enough, the farming potential of this section remained for a good many years unappreciated by the settlers who had filled, and partly cleared, the forest country next to the east. West of the Mississippi and north of the Ozarks, the subdued plains of till and loess were, in the natural state, extensively under grass; and grassland was believed to be useless for cultivation. Corn-growing did not sweep across them until very late in the nineteenth century. The original difference is still recorded in the soils, which are mainly prairie soils between the Mississippi and the Missouri, and chernozems west of the latter.

Southward into Kansas and Oklahoma, increased summer temperatures – for instance, July means of 80°F as against 70°F on the central Low Plains –

serve to increase evaporation; furthermore, the westward gradient of increasing dryness steepens sharply. Corn becomes supplanted as the leading grain by winter wheat. However, as was said earlier, winter-wheat growing spreads broadly on to the High Plains, under which head it will be discussed in the following chapter. Animal husbandry mainly takes the form of beef-cattle raising, which is widespread throughout the southern Low Plains, but not everywhere particularly intensive.

South of the Canadian River, partly on the Low Plains but overlapping on to the High Plains, occurs a concentration of cotton-growing farms which grow perhaps 15 per cent of the national cotton crop. It was here, beyond the limits of the Old South, of the plantation system and of its successors, that mechanized cultivation and harvesting of cotton was developed. The original advantages were several. The growing season attains the necessary length for cotton: winter frosts, however severe the cold waves which bring them, do not affect cropping, except beneficially by helping to keep down pests. A mean annual rainfall of about 25 inches is on the light side for cotton, but is on the other hand concentrated mainly in the early and middle parts of the growing season, precisely when it is needed. At the outset, the Texas cotton farms were beyond the range of the boll weevil that was already well established in the Old South. Generally flat terrain made mechanized working as easy as, in the absence of a Negro workforce, it was necessary; and the soils (mainly latosols) of the new cotton-growing districts were at least no worse than many of those of the older plantation areas. The myth that cotton could not be grown without a large force of hand pickers persisted long after machines were successfully at work on the Plains. Yields admittedly run low – at about two-thirds of the national average – but this is partly on account of the somewhat extensive character of the farming involved. The State of Texas is able to produce a quarter of all the cotton grown in the U.S.A.

In Des Moines and Waterloo, Iowa, the Manufacturing Belt has two of its most westerly members, even though not highly industrialized ones. The central Low Plains contain the principal extent of the Mid-Continent coalfield's western division, but the seams are as yet little exploited: annual output from this part of the region is a million or so tons a year. Oil and natural gas either do not occur, or have not yet been proved in economic quantities. The largest cities are typically located where the former trails took off from the rivers – Sioux City on the Missouri, and the confluence of the Big Sioux and Floyd Rivers, Omaha near the junction of the Missouri and the Platte, and Kansas City at the elbow of the Missouri where the Kansas River comes in. These were all, in their time, bases for movement towards the west, just as were Minneapolis–St Paul on the northern Low Plains: that movement needed bases of assembly, equipping, and supply, for it characteristically involved the wagon-trains in which pioneers set out to cross, rather than to occupy, the High Plains.

Sioux City, Omaha, and Kansas City belong to a series of plainland cities, all of them extensively engaged in the packing of beef and pork, and most also in flour-milling (Plate 56). To this series, in addition to the three named, belong Winnipeg and Minneapolis–St Paul on the northern plains, and St Joseph, Topeka, Wichita, Oklahoma City, and Wichita Falls. Milling is less evenly spread than is packing, being partly concentrated in Winnipeg, the Twin Cities, and Kansas City; it is one of the lesser industrial activities in Omaha, while Sioux City and Wichita Falls do not rank as prominent milling centres. St Joseph ranks in the packing trade with Chicago, developing strongly in this respect as the production of beef lost some of its original dependence on the corn-based farms of the centre.

Metal manufacture and engineering in the cities of the central and southern Low Plains are either slightly developed, or else are specialized. Lincoln, the state capital of Nebraska, is a commercial rather than an industrial centre. Sioux City makes farm machinery, while Topeka has railway workshops, plus the smelting of lead–zinc ores and the founding of brass and bronze; it was at one time a way-station on the Oregon Trail. Oklahoma City produces clothing, furniture, pottery, electrical equipment, and batteries. Wichita Falls is the centre of a dairying district where the Lake Kemp reservoir supplies irrigation water for lucerne. The Kansas City metropolitan area is the one elaborately industrialized agglomeration, with steel-mills and machinery production. In common with the other right-bank cities of the Missouri in this

56. Rail-served livestock markets and meat-packing plants at Omaha, Nebraska.

region, its Kansas side possesses large rail marshalling yards.

There are also oil refineries. A complex of oil and gasfields runs broadly through the region, beginning in the north roughly on the line of the Kansas River, and passing on to the High Plains along a 100-mile front from Fort Worth westwards. Some other cities of the Low Plains, additional to Kansas City, are also engaged in oil refining and related activities – Wichita, Oklahoma City, and above all Tulsa. This last is the leading financial and transport centre for the Mid-Continent oilfields; both it and Wichita manufacture machinery and drilling equipment for the oil industry.

Two other groups of oil and gasfields occur farther to the south. One, more than fifty miles wide, overlaps from the immediate coastland on to the floor of the Gulf: this is the continuation of the fields already encountered in the Gulf South. The second group lies 100 to 150 miles inland. The significance of oil and gas production in the several parts of the High Plains, Low Plains, and Gulf South regions which are here in question is readily shown by summary figures: Texas, Oklahoma, and Kansas in combination produce nearly two-thirds of the national output of natural gas, Texas alone producing half. They are responsible for half the national output of oil, Texas alone producing a third. It is on oil and gas that industry here depends – and, for that matter, the processing of oil and gas with which a great deal of industry is concerned. Coal from the Mid-Continent coalfield's southern extension is a very minor interest by comparison, with an output of some 2 million tons a year.

Another type of industrial activity on the Southern Plains is the manufacture of aircraft and aircraft parts, which was deliberately stimulated here during World War II on defence grounds. It has persisted subsequently. Its works are located in Wichita and Tulsa, among the cities already named, and also in Dallas and Fort Worth. These last two are within industrial reach of cotton-growing, with textile industries which, at Fort Worth, include the making of military uniforms, and with sufficient manufacturing output to bring them into the series of industrial cities mapped in Fig. 9:11.

Fort Worth belongs to a series of towns with a single type of distinctive location – precisely on the margin between the Low Plains and the High: the largest other members of this series are Lubbock, Waco, Austin, and San Antonio. Lubbock is the urban focus of the cotton-growing districts of the Plains. Waco, on the Brazos River, conducts a port trade; among its manufactures are leather goods and cotton textiles. Both Austin and San Antonio pack meat; the former processes cotton-seed feedstuffs and cans Mexican-style food, while the latter has oil refining, brewing, clothing manufacture, wool processing, and pecan shelling.

Corpus Christi and Brownsville–Harlingen–San Bernito, the two remaining of the region's largest agglomerations, lie in the coastal belt of oil and gasfields: they have oil refineries and petrochemical manufacture. In addition, Corpus Christi is a cargo port of some note, and also a fishing port landing Gulf prawn and oysters. One of its industries is highly unusual – the extraction of magnesia from sea-water, established during World War II and persisting since. After the magnesia has been precipitated, it is electrically smelted in a nitrogen atmosphere to yield the metal magnesium, an alloying material widely used in the aircraft industry. Brownsville, Harlingen, and San Bernito, on or near the lowermost Rio Grande, are centres of irrigated districts which produce cotton, vegetables, and citrus; prominent industries are vegetable canning and the manufacture of cotton-seed oil. A leading item in the list of citrus shipped through these centres is the 'pink' grapefruit, in which the locality specializes.

14f: The Northern Low Plains

Area: about 320,000 square miles.

Population: about 4½ million.

Cities with at least 50,000 people: population of some metropolitan areas given in brackets:

Minneapolis–St Paul, Minn.–Wis., 800,000 (1,500,000)
Winnipeg, Man., 265,000 (500,000)
Regina, Sask. (on the boundary), 112,250
Saskatoon, Sask., 95,500
Fargo–Moorhead, N. Dak.–Minn., 70,000 (106,000)
Sioux Falls, N.D., 65,500

The following have between 25,000 and 50,000 people:

Brandon, Man.; Grand Forks, N.D.; and Prince Albert, Sask.

Population density outside the largest towns and metropolitan areas: about 7 per square mile.

Nearly three-fifths of the region is in farmland, about two-fifths in forest; farm woodland is not extensive. Cropland takes less than half of the farm acreage, wheat (concentrated in the northwest) about one-tenth of this acreage and one-quarter of all cropland; about one-fiftieth of the cropland is irrigated. Summer fallow is widespread.

Numbers of livestock: cattle, 10 million, of which three million (mainly in the southeast) are milk cows; sheep, 2½ million; pigs, (mainly in the southeast) 5¾ million; poultry (mainly in the southeast) 100 million.

The Pleistocene ice-sheets at their maximum extent covered much of this plainland region: but whereas in the Central Lowlands their till obliterated much of the pre-glacial topography, on the northern Low Plains they failed to mask the physical breaks which, located at outcrop boundaries, separate the region from the one next to the west and provide the means for internal physiographic differentiation. The Canadian part of the region includes the well-defined First and Second Prairie Steps.

The First Prairie Step is the Manitoba lowland, about 1200 feet above sea-level, parts of it occupied by Lakes Winnipeg, Winnipegosis, and Manitoba; these are relicts of Glacier Lake Agassiz, a huge water-body which, formerly hemmed in by ice on the north, took in much of the catchment of the present Red River in Minnesota and North Dakota, spilling southwards across a very low divide into the basin of the Mississippi. Disappearance of the ice and attendant reorganization of surface drainage have left much of the floor of Lake Agassiz as an almost dead-flat expanse of clayland. East of the lake site in Minnesota occurs a vast extent of gravelly outwash, pitted by innumerable kettles where melting blocks of varied ice caused the overlying loose deposits to collapse. In western Wisconsin the terrain merges into the till plains of the central interior: but the low dissected plateau of the Driftless Area, ice-free at least during the later glacial maxima, rise above the depositional plains through heights of a few hundred feet.

The Second Prairie Step is, fortuitously, typical of Saskatchewan rather than of Manitoba. The Manitoba Scarp, rising from the First to the Second Step, takes the level of the land up to about 2000 feet above sea-level; gentle upward slopes towards the west produce altitudes of about 2500 feet,

57. Combine harvesters reaping spring wheat on the Northern Plains. Despite the long daylight hours of summer, the harvest season is so hasty that the machines work night shifts.

before the next scarp, the Missouri Coteau – coinciding in part with the ice-limit – introduces the Third Prairie Step of the Alberta High Plains, and marks the macro-regional boundary. This scarp is also identifiable southward through the Dakotas.

Farm economies contrast strongly with those of the Central Lowlands. As indicated in the regional summary, wheat takes a quarter of all cropland: it is the supreme grain and the supreme crop; and it is spring wheat, grown on farms where the winter frost is too severe for autumn planting. Its great commercial advantage is that it is hard, and in consequence suited to the contemporary demands of millers. Although by no means all the concentration of spring-wheat farming belongs in this region, as physiographically defined, this is an appropriate juncture at which to notice the significance of the three Prairie Provinces in Canadian wheat production: in combination, they have more than 95 per cent of the national wheat acreage, and yield about 95 per cent of the national crop. Their yield rate is not especially high – about 20 bushels/acre – but tends to rise, chiefly in response to improvement in the strains of seed. Wheat is less pre-eminent in the Dakotas, where it takes only about 15 per cent of harvested cropland, and is not in all parts the leading cash crop: nevertheless, the U.S. part of the region has about a third as much wheatland as the Canadian part, and, thanks to per-acre yields which approach 30 bushels on many farms, a greater proportionate output.

Despite its eventual success, wheat-farming on the northern Low Plains is not without its hazards. Its development to its modern form has, in addition, involved some reshaping of the farm economy and also a certain degree of relocation. For instance, when Minneapolis–St Paul developed their flour-milling industry during the nineteenth century, they were located amid the spring-wheat producers of the time; now, the main concentration of spring wheat begins 200 miles west of the Twin Cities. On the Canadian Prairies, the original plan of settlement was one involving 160-acre farms: today, the median farm size in Manitoba is about twice as great, and in Saskatchewan three times as great. In addition, the family-farm concept has long been superseded by commercial cropping and by heavy dependence on farm machines (Plate 57).

The wheat-growers have had to come to terms with a highly variable climate, in which a mean annual rainfall of 20 inches or less need bear little relationship to what actually falls in a given year. Similarly, the mean concentration of 40 per cent of the annual fall into the short warm summer months, with their long hours of daylight, is favourable to cereal growing: but it does not preclude serious droughts in the growing season, or even in several growing seasons in a row. This summer precipitation, being largely convectional as befits a deep continental interior, can take the form of destructive hail. Both on the agricultural and the social sides, the region has to cope with mean January temperatures of zero Fahrenheit or below, and with a frost-free season of 80 days or less: all depends on the events of the brief summer. Furthermore, although spring wheat is by far the most promising of cash crops, it is none too easy to integrate into a rotational system – a fact which partly explains why, on the Canadian Prairies, oats and barley are only about one-sixth each as extensive as wheat.

Wheat-growing itself could not have attained its actual measure of success, had it not been for the selective use of suitable strains. Red Fife hard wheat was the first successful variety to be introduced into the environment of prolonged cold, moisture deficiency, and short growing season. Marquis, an earlier-ripening kind, followed, allowing wheat-growing to spread westward. Garnet and Reward wheat, ripening earlier still, permitted an extension northward. Most serious of the diseases attacking the wheat crop is the fungus affliction rust: its appearance and spread caused Marquis wheat to be replaced on western farms by the more resistant Thatcher, Apex, and Renown strains.

Dry-farming techniques, involving the introduction into the rotation of summer fallow, are widely employed; the inevitable weed crop is ploughed in. In the Prairie Provinces of Canada, about 60 per cent of the improved farmland is reported as under crops: but, at the same time, a third is listed as in summer fallow. Statistics for the U.S. portion of the region are differently reported: cropland not harvested or used only for pasture is there nearly half as extensive as cropland actually harvested.

Dairying and pig-farming have been introduced in some districts, particularly on the chernozem belt, in an effort to lessen the dependence on wheat. Soils with high lime contents, in the neighbourhood of Lakes Winnipegosis and Manitoba, prove excellent for barley, for seed alfalfa, and for mixed farming; and mixed farming borders the concentration of wheat-growing all along its northern edge, before in turn giving way to pioneering on the fringe of the boreal forest.

In the southwestern part of the region, mainly in Wisconsin, occurs a powerful concentration of commercial dairying, which overlaps the regional boundary into the Western Lakes Region west of Lake Michigan. Pig and poultry farming are here something of appendages to dairying, rather than main interests as they are elsewhere. Wisconsin and Minnesota were originally settled mainly by immigrants from Scandinavia, whose immediate descendants took readily to the opportunities provided by commercial dairying. Except within the near neighbourhood of Chicago and Milwaukee, the dairy farms lie outside the economic limits of liquid-milk supply. Wisconsin produces about two-thirds of the cheese made in the U.S.A., using milk from high-yielding cows: milk solids content is a basic consideration, butter fat not. A large fraction of the cheese is of a plain Cheddar-like kind, but the demand for more specialized varieties of the sorts familiar in Europe exists, and is growing. Farther west, cattle which give milk high in butter fat are the basis for creamery butter production. Throughout the cheese- and butter-producing districts, skimmed milk is fed to calves and pigs: since they never become over-fat, the pigs make good baconers.

This commercial dairying is labour-intense but also highly mechanized. Capital costs are high, since silos are needed to store feed, and barns to house the herds during the protracted winters: nevertheless, owner-operation is more characteristic than not. Some of the fodder must be brought from outside, since local supplies of hay and of green-cut corn are insufficient.

Labour-intense working in the dairying districts means that the average figure cited for population-density outside the largest metropolitan areas needs a brief comment: this density is far greater in the southeast than in the northwest, where rural settlement is distinctly sparse. The southeast, in addition to its dairy farms, has produced a number of minor service centres, including those of the now-defunct lead–zinc minefields of the Driftless Area of Wisconsin: this district, geologically similar to but much smaller than the Ozarks, contains a whole series of little stagnant towns, part of whose function was taken away by the failure of the mines. Urban development in the region is generally slight: apart from Minneapolis–St Paul and Winnipeg, cities are limited mainly to the discharge of central-place functions on a modest scale, except for

Regina which is the provincial capital of Saskatchewan.

Winnipeg has grown from the Hudson's Bay Company's post of Fort Rouge, at the confluence of the Assiniboine and Red Rivers. It functions for the Canadian Prairie lands as Chicago and Minneapolis–St Paul do for much of the U.S. interior. Like Chicago, Winnipeg is a rail focus; also like Chicago, it has stockyards, abattoirs, meat-packing plants, and mail-order houses. But its marshalling yards are intended to serve the grain trade rather than the cattle trade. As in Minneapolis–St Paul, there are in Winnipeg grain elevators and flour-mills. A certain degree of industrial diversification has added engineering works, lumber-milling, furniture-making, and the processing of dairy produce.

Minneapolis and St Paul face one another across the Mississippi, where the Falls of St Anthony impose a check on navigation and offer a source of power: and the power was developed early, in the original flour mill dependent on the pelton wheel. The Twin Cities became prominently established in the milling industry at a time when they were surrounded by wheatlands. Wheat-growing has subsequently moved westwards, the nearer edge of its main concentration being 200 miles distant; but the milling industry has persisted and expanded. Production of linseed oil and cattle cake, the processing of dairy produce, meat-packing, the manufacture of milling machinery, paint and varnish manufacture, and a somewhat limited range of general-purpose industry help flour milling to make the Twin City agglomeration one of the two greatest manufacturing centres of the whole Low Plains. The relationship between Minneapolis and St Paul involves an element of rivalry, but in actuality they are complementary if not indeed symbiotic: many people live in one and work in the other.

CHAPTER FIFTEEN

THE HIGH PLAINS

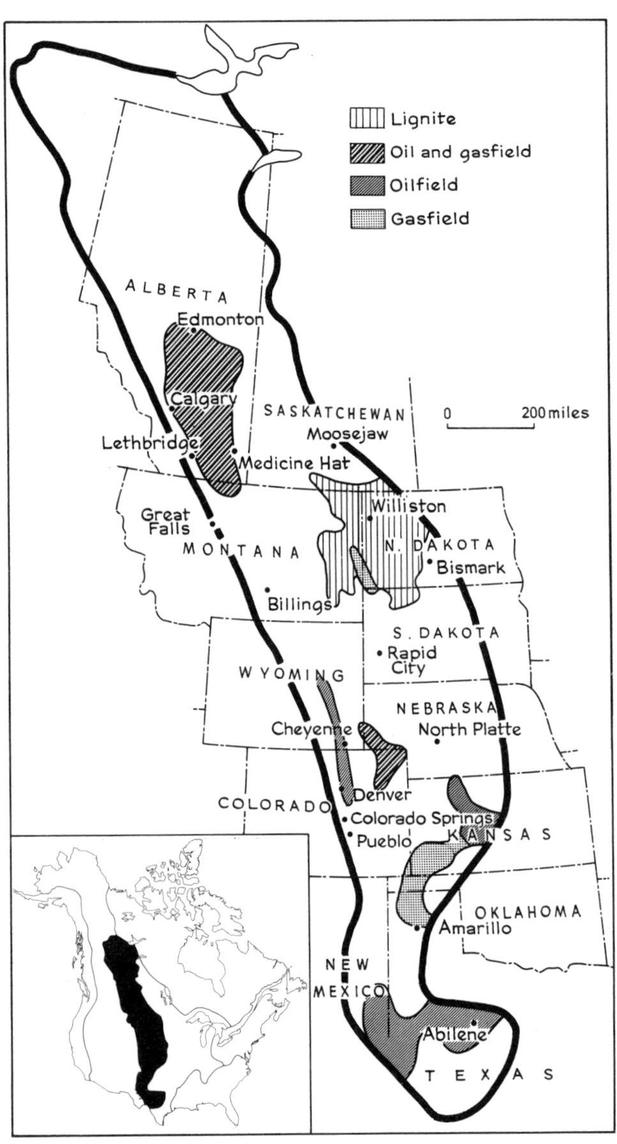

FIG. 15:1 The High Plains.

Stretching between the western edge of the Low Plains and the eastern limit of the Cordillera, and extending from the north of Alberta to the Rio Grande, the Great Plains mega-region encompasses an area approaching a million square miles (Figs. 15:1, 15:2). It is not far from being equal in size to the Centre and Prairie division; but it is far less populous than the latter, with only one-ninth as many people. Its climates are at the best subhumid, degenerating widely into subarid. Its natural cover was short-grass prairie, degenerating in the south into steppe: and it was this southern part of the region, not the truly arid portions of the inner southern Cordillera, which earned the name Great American Desert.

This was formerly the joint habitat of the bison and the Plains Indians – the Blackfoot, Sioux, Cheyenne, and the Crow, Ute, and Kiowa tribes – who followed the bison in the northward summer migrations, taking them for food, clothing, and the means of shelter. Pemmican, the cake of dried meat pounded up with melted fat, helped to sustain life through the winter. Bison hides became leather for clothing and for teepees; and clothes and tents alike were sewn with bison sinews. The bison even supplied fuel; for their dried dung was far more abundant on the Plains than was natural timber, except in the belts of trees along the river valleys.

As mentioned earlier (Chapter Six), all but a very few of the bison were wiped out by 1885 – shot for their skins. With them went the economy of the Plains Indians – and also many of the Indians themselves; for these, in any event aggressive by tradition, could join battle in mounted war-parties. Their pinto (= painted, piebald) ponies were descended from escaped Spanish-owned stock. A second group of escapes, this time cattle, developed into

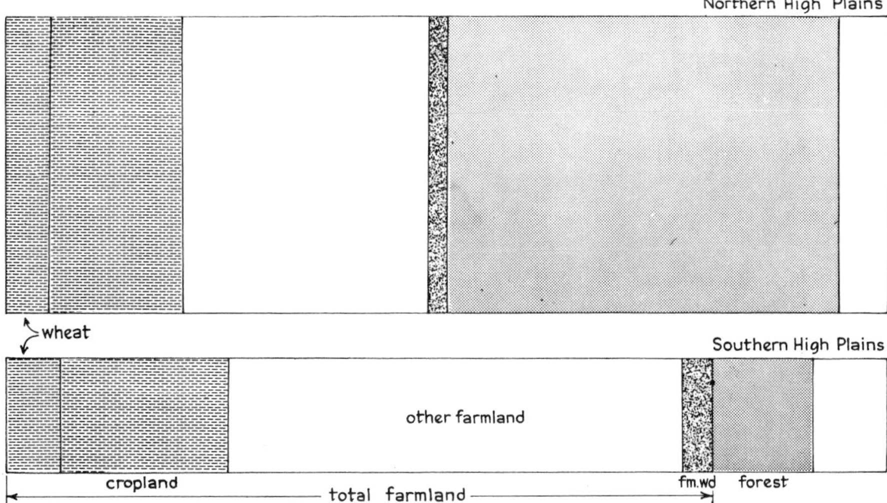

FIG. 15:2 Land use in the High Plains, by regions.

the Texas longhorn breed, which provided an early basis of beef production. It is unnecessary to repeat here the outline previously given (also in Chapter Six) of the three-way conflict which developed on the southern High Plains among cattlemen, sheepmen, and homesteaders, or to recount the ruin by the Great Blizzard of the early cattle empires. Equally, it is unnecessary to do more than recall the significance of the railways in the commercial opening-up of the whole division, or the early fluctuations of grain farming. Suffice it to say that, ranching and oil production apart, the economy of the division achieves at best a somewhat uneasy balance. The great bulk of the land has admittedly been taken into farms; and many but by no means all of these are devoted principally to cattle-raising. Ranches here are enclosed: the open rangelands belong in the Cordillera, where cattle are far less numerous than on the High Plains.

Population-densities are low throughout: great cities are few. To a considerable degree, this is a mega-region where natural resources other than the land itself either await development, or have only in recent times been exploited on a large scale. Although spatial variation certainly occurs, it is broader and less complex than that of the other mega-regions discussed hitherto: in addition, the description of the High Plains involves some overlap with what has gone before. Accordingly, this chapter will be brief.

15a: The Northern High Plains

Area: about 650,000 square miles.

Population: about $2\frac{1}{4}$ million.

Cities with at least 50,000 people: populations of some metropolitan areas given in brackets:

Edmonton, Alta., 280,000 (340,000)
Calgary, Alta., 250,000 (280,000)
Great Falls, Montana, 58,000
Billings, Montana, 55,000

The following have between 25,000 and 50,000 people:

Bismarck, N.D.; Cheyenne, Wyo.; Casper, Wyo.; Grand Island, Neb.; Jasper Place, Alta.; Lethbridge, Alta.; Medicine Hat, Alta.; Minot, N.D. (on the boundary); Moose Jaw, Sask.; and Rapid City, N.D.

Population density outside these places: about 2 per square mile.

About half the region is in farmland, rather less than half in forest: farm woodland is scarce. Cropland takes about one-third of the farm acreage, and roughly one-fifth of the region. About one-fiftieth of the cropland is irrigated; one-quarter is under wheat. Improved grassland takes about one-fifth of all farmland.

Numbers of livestock: cattle, 45 million, of which only one million are milk cows; sheep and pigs, each nearly 5 million; poultry, 45 million.

Winters are severe throughout the northern High

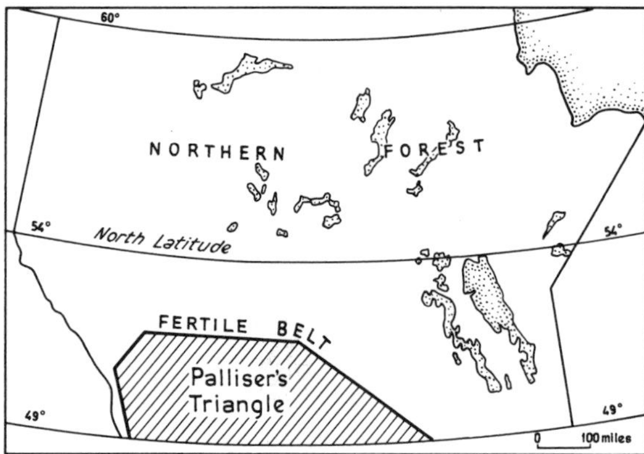

FIG. 15:3 Palliser's Triangle.

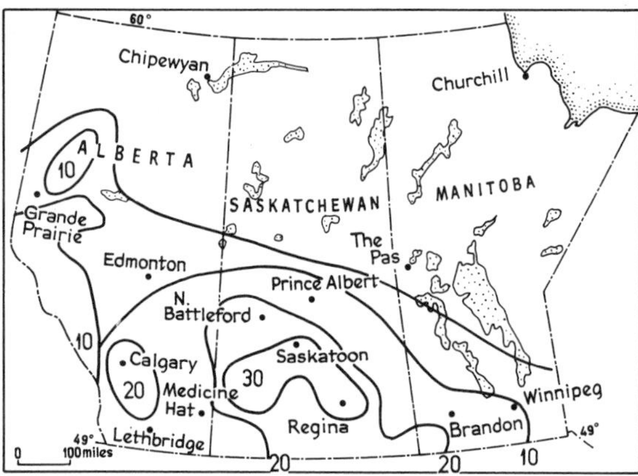

FIG. 15:4 Palliser's Triangle (continued). Year to year Variability of Rainfall (% of Mean Rainfall)

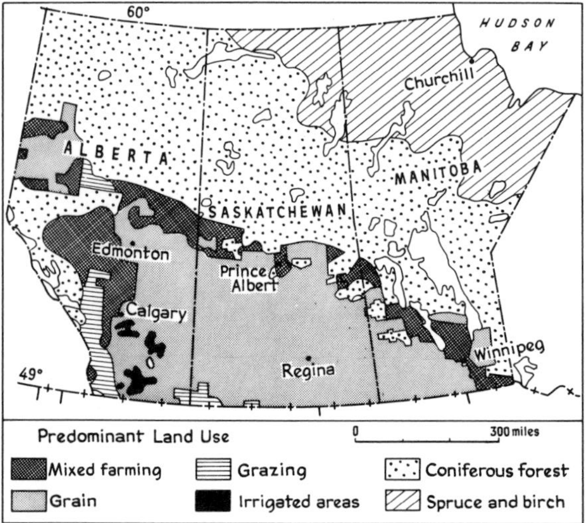

FIG. 15:5 Palliser's Triangle (continued).

Plains, being dominated by cAK air. They bring January mean temperatures down to 10° below zero Fahrenheit in the extreme north – i.e., to the mean level of some 40° F of frost – and rise but to about +15° F in the extreme south, still well below freezing-point. July means range in the same direction from about 60° F to 70° F. There is no room in the climatic regime for spring or autumn: the onsets of winter and summer are equally abrupt. Precipitation, ranging from 10 to 20 inches a year, has its average maximum in the spring: it is however unreliable. The northernmost part of the region – roughly speaking, that with January mean temperatures of zero Fahrenheit or below, and with an average frost-free season of eighty days or less – lies beyond the limits of farming. Like the northernmost Low Plains in Saskatchewan, the northernmost High Plains in Alberta and the extreme northeast of British Columbia are extensively forested with black spruce, tamarack, and jack pine. A concentration of saw-mills, some fifty miles in width, extends roughly east–west across Alberta into the middle basin of the Peace River, with a curvilinear offshoot whose inner edge lies at about 100 miles distant from Edmonton. On the High Plains, as on the Low Plains, the forest fringe has been partly invaded by pioneer farming, which gives way southward to better-established mixed farming, and that in turn to farmland dominated by spring-wheat production (Plate 58). This is located not on the chernozem belt, which is too exposed to the danger of frost, but chiefly on the chestnut soils next to the south. Southwards again, the drought risk becomes severe; and the brown soils of southern Alberta and southeast Saskatchewan are widely given over to ranching. This is the area of Palliser's triangle, so called from the low assessment of its potential made by that explorer in the mid-nineteenth century (Plate 59 and Figs. 15:3–15:5).

In eastern Montana, easternmost Wyoming, the western parts of the Dakotas, and most of Nebraska, ranching and grain-cropping are also widespread. As previously explained, spring-wheat production overlaps in this southern part of the region from the Low Plains on to the High. Soils lie mainly in the range from chestnut to prairie soils, for the chernozem belt has swung eastward on to the Low Plains. Here the progression

58. Railside grain elevators in Alberta. Overhead, a cumulonimbus threatening to discharge intense rain or hail.

of soil and climate leads from east to west, in response to the rapid eastward increase in dryness; and western districts generally are committed to the management of ranch cattle. Ranching extends farther westward still, in the Wyoming Basin, into the Cordillera. In the region as a whole, farm income from crops is less than four-fifths as great as that from livestock.

Wheat-growing is dependent on weather patterns – even more so here than on the Low Plains. Snow retained on the over-winter stubble can be very light, dissipating quickly as soon as the warm weather comes on. Moisture stress at the time of germination is all too common: unless the wheat can form an adequate root system, in sufficient conditions of soil moisture and soil warmth, the crop will fail. A second critical period occurs in summer, when drought can prevent the grain from swelling. Nevertheless, wheat remains the most likely profitable crop. Once the soil has lost its

59. Range cattle crossing the Milk River, Alberta, on the way to summer pasture.

winter frost to a depth of eight inches, seeding can begin. As in all parts of the North American grainlands, working is highly mechanized; but the pressure of seasonal weather is especially great here, and working days both during sowing and during the harvest tend to be inordinately long.

The emphasis which is being laid on the wheat crop is not meant to imply monoculture. Three-quarters of the region's cropland carries plants other than wheat. These, apart from the hay crop – which is both extensive and valuable – include rye, flax, oats, barley, sweet clover, sugar beet, and potatoes.

Farm sizes are on average well above the 160-acre mark, although there is considerable local variety according to purpose of working and potentiality of the soil. Data for complete states or provinces serve to illustrate something of the dimensions involved. Thus, Alberta and Nebraska, at the two ends of the region, record a median farm size of about 320 acres, twice as great as that of the land-grant holding. In the Dakotas and Wyoming the median size rises toward, or above, 500 acres, while in Montana it exceeds 1000 acres. Increase in size has perforce been made to compensate for low capacities of crop yield or stock-carrying.

In view of the fact that the regional soils are generally lime-rich, cultivation could doubtless extend profitably, much more widely than it has already done, if only irrigation water were to be had. However, irrigation on the High Plains tends to be economically marginal at the best. To begin with, the variable character of rain during a given year means that large-scale works are essential; and although the characteristically incised valleys of the streams which traverse the region offer useful sites for storage (Plate 16), the need remains to raise the water from the valleys to the general plain surface. Huge impounded lakes already exist, especially on the Missouri River, where the Fort Peck Reservoir in Montana has an axial length of a 100 miles, the Garrison Reservoir in North Dakota one of 150 miles, and where the Fort Randall, Big Bend, and Oahe Reservoirs occupy some 250 miles of valley-bottom in North and South Dakota. The Platte is dammed to form Lake McConaughty in Nebraska, while parts of southernmost Alberta between Lethbridge and Medicine Hat are irrigated from dams on the South Saskatchewan River. Irrigation farming can perhaps be looked on to introduce specialized cropping. It should, in any case, render farming practices more highly intensive in the irrigated areas. The significance of these is understated in the regional summary (above): Montana, for instance, has one-quarter of its cropland under irrigation.

Metallic minerals are exploited in the Black Hills, on the South Dakota–Wyoming boundary, where a metalliferous structural dome injects a far-outlying portion of the Cordillera into the High Plains. Dissection of the dome by radial streams has opened routeways into the margins and centre: it has also revealed ores of silver–lead–zinc, mercury, and gold. Settlements in the Black Hills – Spearfish, Sturgis, Lead, Deadwood, and Custer – have none of them grown large: the biggest of all, Rapid City, has fewer than 50,000 people. Base-metal mining is far less vigorous than it once was; but the Homestake Mine at Lead, first opened in 1876, is currently the leading U.S. gold producer, with 40 per cent of the national gold output.

Reserves of mineral fuels are great, but their exploitation is as uneven as it has proved tardy. Coal of bituminous to sub-bituminous grade occurs widely: the reserves of Alberta alone, mainly of the sub-bituminous rank, are estimated at 48,000 million tons, with 20,000 capable of being mined. However, demand is slight: output is a mere 3 million tons or so a year, while only about 2½ million tons a year are raised from the lignite deposits of North Dakota. Oil and natural gas are different propositions. Output of the latter from the region is at present less than 10 per cent of the combined production of Canada and the U.S.A., although the Albertan gasfields account for some three-quarters of all gas raised in Canada; oil output comes to 20 per cent of the combined Canada–U.S. total, about two-fifths of it from Alberta which takes a major share – again one of about three-quarters – of production in Canada.

A striking feature of the working of oil and natural gas in this region is its late development. For instance, the oil deposits of the Williston Basin of North Dakota were discovered as late as 1951, and have been producing only since 1956. The exploitation of petroleum on the Canadian High Plains is largely a matter of the years since 1945, and that of natural gas in the same area

60. Oil refinery and storage tanks at Edmonton, Alberta.

almost wholly so. Multiplying its oil production tenfold between 1950 and 1965 – chiefly by means of wells on the Albertan High Plains – Canada has become one of the top ten oil-producing countries of the world (Plate 60).

Oil and natural gas occur quite widely in Alberta; and the rapidly-shifting development of the main fields makes generalization difficult. It can however be said that the Leduc and Redwater fields, close to Edmonton, and the Pembina field about a hundred miles west of that town, are leading producers. The Peace River field, which lies mainly across the border in British Columbia, is a fourth. Oil is piped southwestwards to Vancouver and into the Pacific Northwest; gas goes as far as San Francisco. In the eastward direction pipelines lead as far as industrial eastern Canada. Within Alberta, oil refining is complemented by petrochemical industries deliberately fostered by the government.

Deposits related geologically to oil and natural gas are those of bitumen in the bituminous sands of northern Alberta. Reserves are immense; working is so far confined to the McMurray District, where the bitumen content of the sands is 15 per cent or above.

The contrast of size between the largest and the next largest cities is at least as great on the Northern High Plains as it is upon the adjacent Northern Low Plains. The generality of service, administrative, and (in the Black Hills) metal-mining centres run uniformly small.

Edmonton and Calgary are both active in oil-refining and the distribution of oil and gas. The former has some coal-mining. It functions as a centre for part of the wheat trade, and also for trade in furs – a reminder of its origin as a fort, stockade, and trading-post of the Hudson's Bay Company. Calgary, with elevators, flour-mills, and packing works, serves the wheat-growing and the ranching districts alike; in addition, it has commercial links with minefields in the Rockies.

15b: The Central and Southern High Plains

Area: about 250,000 square miles.

Population: about $3\frac{1}{2}$ million.

Cities with at least 75,000 people in the metropolitan area: populations of metropolitan areas given in brackets:

- Denver, Colo., 500,000 (930,000)
- Amarillo, Tex., 140,000 (150,000)
- Pueblo, Colo., 91,250 (119,000)

61. Drought on the Southern High Plains: cattle grazing as best they can on sorghum stubble.

Abilene, Tex., 90,500 (120,500)
Colorado Springs, Colo., 70,250 (143,750)

Population density outside the largest metropolitan areas: about 8 per square mile.

More than four-fifths of this region is in farmland; about half the total is in pasture other than woodland pasture. Cropland takes rather more than a quarter of the farm acreage, wheat about a quarter of the cropland. Forest – including farm woodland, which is not extensive – covers about an eighth of the region.

Numbers of livestock: cattle, 9 million, of which only half a million are milk cows; sheep, 8 million; pigs, less than a million; poultry, 65 million.

Liable to hot summers and with light and unreliable rainfall, the central and southern Great Plains have suffered badly from over-exploitation.

62. Shelter belts of trees enclosing fields on the Southern High Plains.

Cropping, as will be seen, has more than once been pushed much too far west for safety. Over-stocking and over-grazing of the ranchlands has in many districts denuded the vegetal cover. Both the plough and the trampling of cattle disturb the topsoil – everywhere shallow in this region, and underlain by infertile lower horizons. Wind erosion has proved severe: it remains a constant threat (Plates 14, 61).

It is in this region that some of the main efforts of the Bureau of Reclamation have been required. On the other hand, the soils in their natural state are rich in plant nutrients, including lime; and the bunch and tussock grasses, the sagebrush and other xerophytes of the drier parts, are all suitable as forage. Where irrigation is practised, it can be agriculturally effective and economically sound; and the general danger from strong winds can be mitigated by the planting of shelter belts (Plate 62). Furthermore, price support measures can tide cultivation and ranching alike through the inevitable spells of adversity.

Winter wheat is extensively cultivated in western Kansas, western Oklahoma, and the Texas panhandle. Concentrated patches of wheat-growing farms began to appear here in the later years of the nineteenth century; in the early 1900s they spread and consolidated themselves over a very large piece of country, partly on the Low Plains and partly on the High. The northern limit of the main wheat-growing districts settled itself at about the average of 140 days for the frost-free season, where January mean temperatures are about 25° F and July means about 75° F. The southern limit came to correspond roughly to the 200-day frost-free season, beyond which cotton becomes a prospective crop, and one more attractive than wheat. On the eastern side the choice of principal cash grain lay between wheat and corn; and corn proved the more profitable of the two, at about the line of the 30-inch isohyet. Crude though these annual values are as indicators of what actually affects the growing wheat, they serve to illustrate the fact that, for all its extensiveness, wheat in this part of the region is by way of being a compromise crop.

The western boundary of the wheat-growing districts is a highly mobile one, useless for the definition of an agricultural region. It approximates only very roughly to the zone where ranching becomes more profitable than cropping; for it is impossible to forecast, when the wheat is sown, what will be the weather of the growing season. Wheat farms have repeatedly spread westward in wet years, only to be ruined by droughts; moreover, drought can on occasion inflict itself on a very large fraction of the whole wheat-growing area. In consequence, production fluctuates wildly, sometimes from one year to the next. It is possible to generalize the combined record of wheat production for Kansas and Oklahoma to give a steady upward trend in the long term – one which involves an increase in production by 100 million bushels in every twenty-five years; but the output of individual years can be half as great, or half as great again, as the value indicated by the long-term trend (Fig. 15:6).

Every grave setback to the wheat crop drives farmers off the land. The most disastrous on record so far was that of the 1930s, when for some years on end the crop was only half the trend value. Soil erosion – already serious enough, mainly in the form of gullying and washing in eastern districts, and of blowing in the west – abruptly increased in force: the ploughed topsoil, lacking all protection, lifted into the air and moved cloudily downwind. Conditions improved into the 1940s, but the 1950s brought another scatter of very bad years. As at comparable times in the past, the ruin and departure of some farmers was accompanied by the extension of company holdings. For a long time, the wheat-growing districts have been recording a progressive increase in farm size – a sensible response to the hazards of climate, but also in practice the supplanting of family farms by managed, and larger, concerns. For many years, too, the wheat-farming has been very highly mechanized; and mechanized working lends itself readily to large-scale operation. Furthermore, companies can afford to plant wheat essentially as a catch crop, whereas individual farmers cannot. It is not surprising that the rate of tenancy runs at about 40 per cent of all farms: in terms of farm acreage, it is higher than this.

Sheep farming is concentrated on the High Plains in Texas, which carry something like 1 in 10 of all the sheep in North America. Angora goats are also kept here, for the production of mohair. This part of the region benefits from lime-rich soils

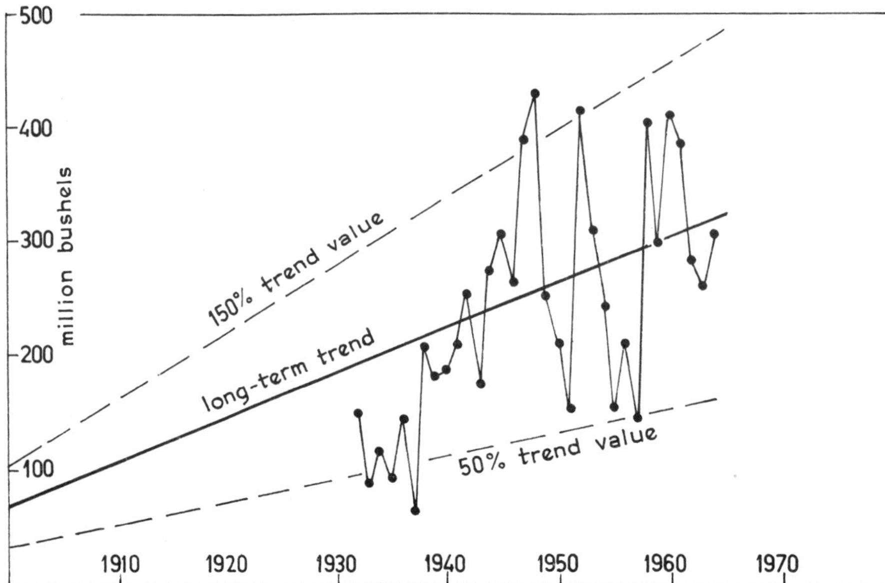

FIG. 15:6
Trends in wheat production on part of the High Plains.

and from high elevations which do something to mitigate the regional dryness. Sheep and goat ranching are associated with the growing of grain sorghum, a crop capable of supporting heat and drought where wheat or corn would die – e.g., an annual rainfall of 10 inches with July mean temperatures of 80° F. Sorghum not only provides a substitute for corn as stockfeed: it also has industrial uses, for instance, in the manufacture of wallboard and of the drilling mud required by the oil industry. On the farther, northern, side of the wheat-farming districts, cultivation on the High Plains relies chiefly on irrigation, producing alfalfa, hay, and sugar beet.

Beet sugar is economically handicapped in competition with imported cane sugar, but is protected by import quotas. Its costs relate in part to the low comparative yield of sucrose from beets, and the low comparative tonnage raised per acre/year. Planting, topping, and lifting have been mechanized, but seasonal hand labour is still needed for thinning and for cultivation within the rows: it is scarce and dear.

Grazing depends on high-protein forage. It also depends increasingly on irrigated fodder-cropping, which contributes strongly to the production of grass-fat cattle; these go directly to the packers, without an intervening spell on corn-based farms. Most ranches today raise some fodder crops; but they cease to become classified as ranches if the crop acreage reaches one-tenth of the combined acreage of permanent grazing and rotation grass. Carrying capacities run low – from 17 to 25 acres per head of beef cattle: that is, 25,000 acres could be needed for a herd of a thousand beasts. Herefords and Black Angus are the main preferred breeds.

Considerable changes have come about in the ranchlands since the end of World War II, giving the most modern ranches some aspects of an industrial production line. Investments in fencing, barns, shelter-sheds, wind-pumps, irrigation, stock improvement, and veterinary services have all left their mark; and investment in ranching generally by organized companies has favoured an increase in ranch size, plus the separation of management from risk-taking. Increased efficiency has increased the density of stocking, in which better use of fodder – both range fodder and supplemental protein – plays a considerable part. Production programmes are designed to put young cattle on the market, instead of the former six- or seven-year-old animals. Beef production per acre has risen fourfold. Increased efficiency is moreover to some extent a forced response to the withdrawal of grazing leases from federal lands where erosion is serious: the buffer of open range for emergency use is being removed. Marketing of store cattle is now concentrated where the more arid districts have ready access to railway transport; the animals go for fattening to the Flint Hills of Kansas, the Ozarks, or the Central Lowlands.

Feedlot farming which produces baby beef is carried on where irrigation crops or cheap fodder of other kinds makes it profitable; the lean baby-beef cattle yield lean cuts, greatly favoured by the consumer market and well adapted to mass packaging and mass marketing. Waste pulp from beet-sugar mills is among the commercial feedstuff used.

Mineral production on the central and southern High Plains includes oil and some natural gas from the southwestern end of the complex of fields that reaches from Kansas City, on the Low Plains, to west Texas; natural gas and oil are also taken from an area overlapping from the Texas panhandle through the Oklahoma panhandle into Kansas, and from small scattered fields near the Rocky Mountain front or about 100 miles out on the Plains. Reserves of bituminous to sub-bituminous coal, also scattered in their occurrence, are considerable in total: current output from strip mines is of the order of 2 million tons a year. Near the regional boundary lies Carlsbad, N.M. (25,500), the centre of a potash-mining district exploiting some of the 70,000 square miles of potash-bearing beds: production is rising steadily, in response to the demands of the fertilizer industry.

Except at Denver, urban growth in the region has so far proved limited. Abilene and Amarillo are the only two of the largest cities to stand well out on the Plains. Both refine oil. Part of the industry of Abilene is related to cotton-growing, and especially to the processing of cotton-seed – the refining of cotton-seed oil and the manufacture of feedstuff concentrates. Amarillo contains a government-run helium plant; it ships grain, packs meat, and has zinc-smelting and founding works.

Denver, Colorado Springs, and Pueblo are the chief members of a whole string of towns along the Rocky Mountain piedmont in Colorado. They developed originally as camptown bases for the orefields of the adjacent highland. Thus, Colorado Springs was the base for gold-mining at Cripple Creek. Denver, during one episode of its gold-mining activity, was known as *Auraria;* the dome of its capitol building, plated over with gold, shines elegantly against the dry clear skies. Subsequently, Colorado Springs became a health resort greatly favoured by sufferers from tuberculosis, and has still later emerged as a general-purpose resort and recreation centre. Pueblo, too, is accessible to ore-fields – those of the uppermost Arkansas catchment. Near-by coal favoured the establishment here, under government stimulus during World War II, of integrated iron and steel manufacture and of machinery production. The city is the focus for a stretch of irrigated farmland. In addition, it conducts a vigorous resort trade of its own, wherein hunting (i.e., shooting) and fishing are prominent.

63. Denver, Colorado, with the Rocky Mountain Front in the distance.

Denver dominates the urban array of the central and southern High Plains even more markedly than Dallas dominates that of the southern Low Plains. Fairly centrally located on the mine-connected piedmont, it has become a considerable manufacturing city (cf. Fig. 9:11) with a complex range of industry – the making of mining machinery, precision apparatus, and rubber products, and the refining of beet sugar – and is a principal regional base of federal government agencies (Plate 63).

CHAPTER SIXTEEN

THE ROCKIES AND THE CORDILLERAN PLATEAUS

In this division are comprised two of the three major parts of the North American Cordillera: the high mountains of the eastern border, and the lofty enclosed plateaus of the centre (Figs. 16:1, 16:2). Of the total area of nearly $1\frac{1}{2}$ million square miles, rather more than two-thirds lies in the U.S.A. Total population is about $4\frac{1}{2}$ million: it is clear at once that economic opportunities are limited, although, as will appear, some parts are highly significant to the two national economies.

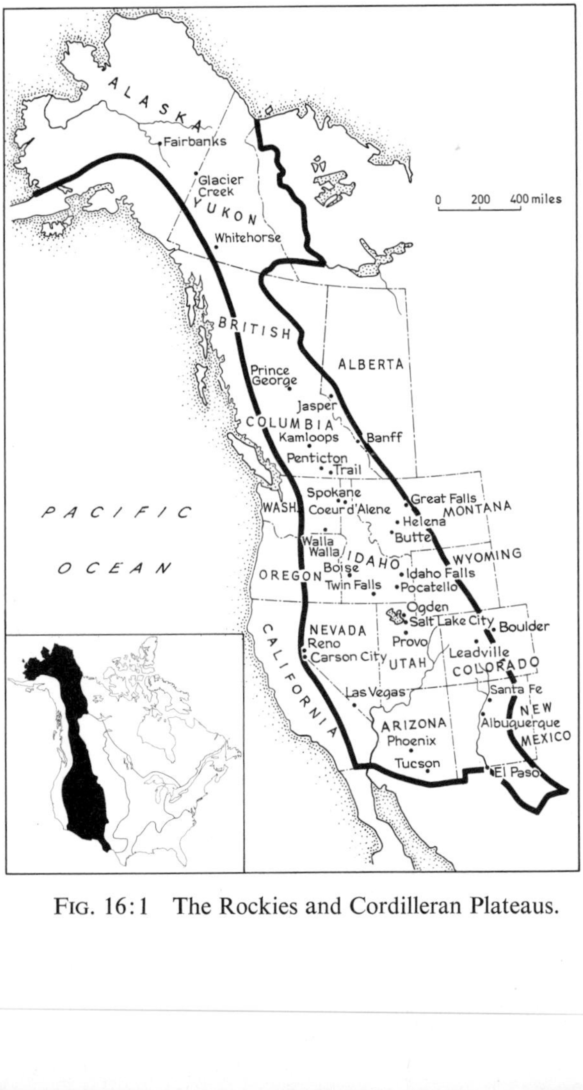

FIG. 16:1 The Rockies and Cordilleran Plateaus.

Here are found some of the highest points of the continent, and also the lowest point. Death Valley, California, descends to nearly 280 feet below sea-level. Peaks in the Canadian Rockies exceed 12,000 feet, some of those in the U.S.A. are above 14,000 feet; and a widespread similarity of maximum elevation allows peaks exceeding 10,000 feet to be numbered in their hundreds. In Nevada, Utah, and Colorado the division reaches its maximum breadth of about 800 miles, constituting a formidable barrier between the interior and the Pacific coast: and this barrier is made all the more difficult by climate, for the plateaus throughout most of their extent are shut off from moisture by the enclosing belts of mountain. Ruggedness of the eastern mountains increases northward on account of increasingly severe Pleistocene glaciation: the Wasatch and Uinta Ranges, for instance, are deeply scalloped by cirques, but the Columbia, Selkirk, and Stikine Ranges of British Columbia are gouged through by huge glacier troughs. Snowfall was sufficient during glacial maximum to fill the Canadian plateau section with ice, although the Alaskan plateau remained dry and unglaciated.

The first Europeans to penetrate the Cordilleran country were the Spanish who, as in Latin America, came at first in search of mineral wealth. They made contact with the native Indians, who unlike the nomadic Indians of the Plains had developed sedentary communities where domestic crafts could be pursued (Plate 64). Among the tribes were the Apache, the Hualpai, the Unte, the Zuni, the Hopi, the Papago, and the Navajo; the craft of potting was well developed in some districts, while the Navajo, in particular, were skilled in making

FIG. 16:2 Land use in the Rockies and Cordilleran Plateaus, by regions.

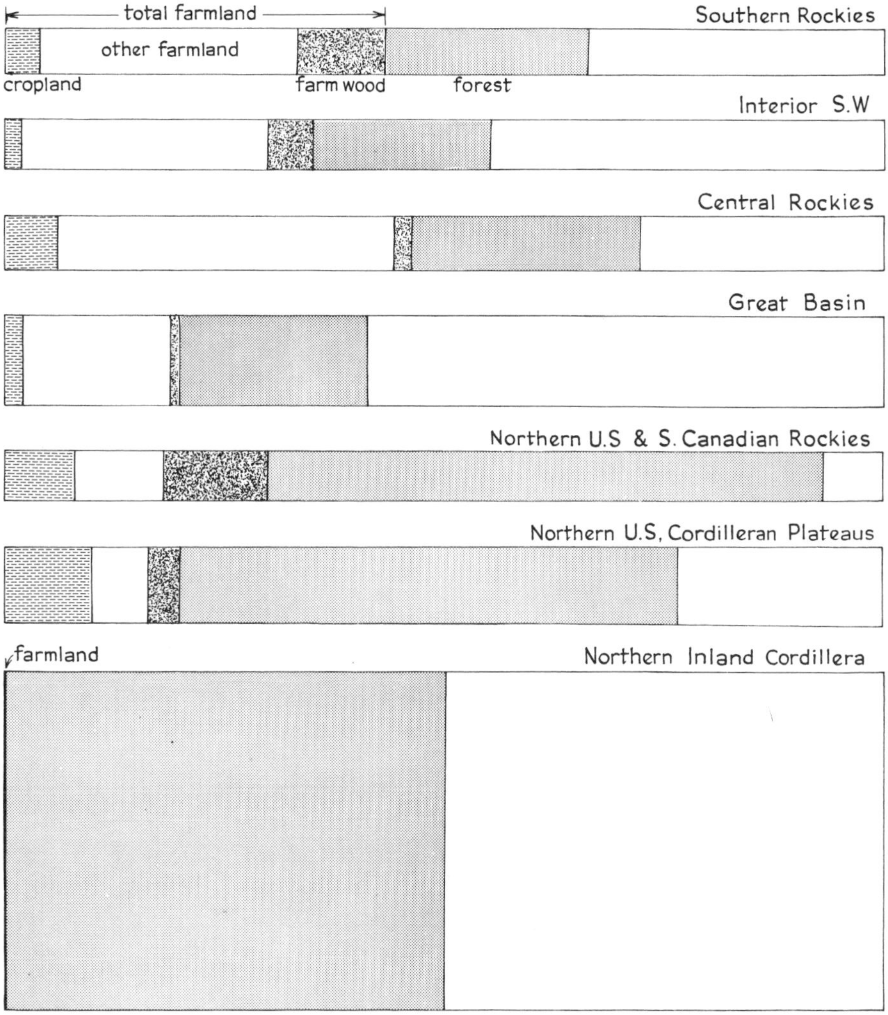

total farmland
Southern Rockies
other farmland
cropland
farm wood
forest
Interior S.W
Central Rockies
Great Basin
Northern U.S & S. Canadian Rockies
Northern U.S, Cordilleran Plateaus
farmland
Northern Inland Cordillera

64. Pueblo Bonito, New Mexico: the ruins of a prehistoric Indian settlement in Chaco Canyon.

jewellery – Navajo ornaments of silver and turquoise are still widely produced and sold today. It was clear to the Spanish explorers that the Cordillera had rich mineral resources; and repeated expeditions set out in search of these, as, for instance, under the leadership of Francisco Coronado. Generally speaking, however, the Spanish were unsuccessful; and they certainly failed to locate the mythical El Dorado. Nevertheless, they have left their mark in the demotic speech of New Mexico, and in the names bestowed by them on some main blocks of mountain – the San Andreas, Sacramento, San Juan, Guadalupe, and Santiago Ranges, among others, and the Sangre de Cristo Mountains named for the blood-red hues of its majestic arêtes. Elsewhere, the older Indian names persist, as with the Wasatch and Uinta Mountains and the peaks of Sawatch and Uncompahgre.

Apart from the Spanish settlements in the south, the whole of this division remained unoccupied, unsettled, and largely unwanted – except by the Indians – up to the mid-nineteenth century. Spanish rule became Mexican rule in 1821; the independent Republic of Texas was established in 1837, and joined the Union in 1845, precipitating the war of 1846–47 by which Mexico lost not only Texas but also New Mexico, Arizona, Colorado, Utah, Nevada, and California. The whole of the Cordillera lay open to penetration from the east. It attracted explorers, such as Clark and Lewis and the members of governmental parties of military and geological surveyors; it attracted prospectors; and, as reports of mountain pastures and water for irrigation filtered back, it began also to attract farmers who looked with disfavour on the potential of the subarid Plains. Among the settlers were the Mormons, a dissident religious group led by Brigham Young, who deliberately selected a site in the remote Great Basin. Here, on the edge of the Great Salt Lake, a shallow remnant of pluvial Lake Bonneville, the Mormons founded Salt Lake City, and with the aid of streams from the snowy Wasatch Mountains developed irrigation farming. Prospectors located gold, silver, lead, zinc, and copper. As is typical of the working of non-ferrous ores, some deposits were rapidly exhausted, while others have grown progressively uneconomic: among the abandoned settlements left by mining, refining, and smelting is Jerome, in the centre of Arizona, which proclaims itself the largest ghost town in the world.

Transport routes are inescapably guided by relief, with railways and roads winding up river valleys and through the passes. As described in Chapter Ten, the railways had a great deal to do with the opening-up of the central and eastern Cordillera; feeder lines of narrow gauge served the minefields, and intra-regional hauls are involved today in the upward shift of flocks and herds for summer grazing on high pastures.

Aside from grazing, which is general throughout the division from southern British Columbia to the bounds of the driest and unused lands of the extreme Southwest, farming activities are localized. They depend heavily on irrigation. The earning power of lumbering is limited by depletion of the forest reserve, and also by the fact that the lower treeline rises high in the Southern Rockies, in response to a combination of low precipitation with high temperatures. Mining remains a leading form of economic activity.

In what follows, the regions will be taken in pairs, one mountainous and one of plateau. The first pair takes in the rather broken southern end of the mountains, chiefly on the eastern side of the upper Rio Grande, with a large block of plateau country next on the west, drained by the middle and lower Colorado and the Gila systems.

16a: The Southern Rockies

Area: about 105,000 square miles.

Population: about $1\frac{1}{4}$ million.

Largest cities: totals in brackets are for metropolitan areas:

El Paso, Tex., 277,000 (315,000)
Albuquerque, N. Mex., 201,000 (262,250)
The next largest city is Santa Fe, N. Mex., (35,000)

Population density outside the largest metropolitan areas: about 3 per square mile.

About two-fifths of this region is classed as farmland, but grazing land takes about three-quarters of the farm acreage and one-third of the region: there is also extensive open range. About one-twentyfifth of the region is in cropland, about one-quarter of it irrigated. Forest, including farm woodland, covers about one-third of the total area.

Numbers of livestock: cattle, 800,000, of which

only about 20,000 are milk cows; sheep, ½ million; pigs, 15,000; poultry, 9 million.

16b: The Interior Southwest

Area: about 115,000 square miles.

Population: about 1½ million.

Largest cities: population of metropolitan areas given in brackets:

Phoenix, Ariz., 440,000 (665,000)
Tucson, Ariz., 213,000 (266,000)
The next largest city is Mesa, Ariz. (35,000)

Population density outside the largest metropolitan areas: about 4 per square mile.

Half this region is classed as farmland, but grazing land takes about four-fifths of the farm acreage and two-fifths of the region: much of it is open range. About one-fiftieth of the region is cropland, about one-quarter in forest. More than half the cropland is irrigated.

Numbers of livestock: cattle, 1¼ million, of which only about 50,000 are milk cows; sheep, ½ million; pigs, 30,000; poultry, 3½ million.

Rainfall exceeds 20 inches a year only in restricted areas of the highest mountains; it is extensively below 10 inches. Summer temperatures both on the mountains and on much of the plateaus are, however, kept down by altitudes in excess of 5000 feet, running below an average of 70° F in July. The two regions are able to conduct a summer tourist trade, which benefits from the abundant, reliable sunshine, and from the remarkable scenery. The larger streams of the open drainage-net have cut deeply into the land, sawing through great thicknesses of colourful sandstones and producing sharp-edged canyons; the greatest of all, the Grand Canyon of the Colorado, attracts more than 1½ million visitors a year to Grand Canyon National Park (Plates 2, 22).

The two regions together contain two-thirds of the tribal Indian land of the U.S.A.; such land amounts to nearly a fifth of their combined area (Plates 65, 66). The Indian population, about 150,000 strong, is more than a quarter of the national total. To a considerable extent the economy of the Indian groups is integrated into tourism, for numbers of trading-posts offer hand-made pottery, jewellery, rugs, and blankets. Regrettably, some craft production has debased itself into manufacture for the junk trade, but the best items, representative of long and elaborate traditions, are outstandingly good. Another type of economic opportunity is offered to the Indians by farmers who recruit them for seasonal work – on the cotton farms to the south, or on the potato fields of Idaho.

65. Hopi Indian cultivation in the Painted Desert, Arizona: seepage moisture from the valley sides aids the cropping of corn.

In the Southern Rockies and on the adjoining eastern parts of the interior plateaus live numerous people of Mexican–Spanish descent. Well into the twentieth century, New Mexico remained largely Spanish-speaking. Spanish still ranks with English as an official language. And even today, when immigrants from other parts of the States have considerably reduced the proportion of those with Spanish or Mexican ancestry, this group still amounts to a third of the whole population, developing in its rural sector a patois of its own.

Grazing is extensive in both regions, with sheep in the Southern Rockies more numerous than cattle, and 75,000 angora goats in the plateaus. But although no more than a small fraction of each region is in cropland, farm income from crops is about four times as great as that from livestock. The chief crop is irrigated cotton, which takes about a third of all cropland, and accounts for more than 10 per cent of U.S. cotton production. Yields run well above the national average. Cotton farms are strung along the Rio Grande upstream and downstream of El Paso, along the Gila River downstream

66. A Navajo-Indian girl herding in Arizona. The rocks in the background owe their sculptured forms not to sand-blasting but to cavernous weathering.

of Coolidge Dam, along the Salt River downstream of Roosevelt Dam, and along the Colorado downstream of Parker Dam. Principal irrigation crops other than cotton are hay, sorghum, barley, citrus, and vegetables (Plate 67).

Run-off regimes are highly uneven: the Little Colorado, for instance, with a drainage net confined to the plateaus, is waterless for most of the time. The sole means of guaranteeing water-supply is to dam the canyons of rivers leading from rainy ground. In addition to those already mentioned, large works occur at Elephant Butte Reservoir on the Rio Grande, and at Hoover Dam (formerly Boulder Dam) on the Colorado itself. Hoover Dam, 726 feet in height, impounds the 115-mile-long Lake Mead, in which the water load is great enough to depress or compact the earth's crust by a matter of inches. Some engineers have their eyes on the Grand Canyon as a likely reservoir site.

Except for the extraction of natural gas from the San Juan field of northwestern New Mexico, mining in both regions is concerned largely with the quarrying of structural materials and with the exploitation of non-ferrous metal ores. The Interior Southwest alone produces about half the U.S. total of copper, while the two regions together account for not far short of two-thirds of national output. Lead and zinc are also worked; gold and silver are obtained as by-products of copper processing; and the Southern Rockies possess two-thirds of the U.S. national reserves of uranium ore. In total value, mineral production is roughly equal to the production of crops, although in the Interior Southwest minerals bring in more than do all farm products.

The main open-cut working for copper ore is located at Morenci, Arizona, but some twenty additional sites are also exploited, either in southern Arizona or in southwestern New Mexico. Ore grade is typically low, at 1 per cent copper or less, but large-scale mechanized working and the recovery of other metals from the mixed sulphide ores make the undertakings economic. Copper smelting is as widespread as copper mining, although not identically located, while refining is carried on at Inspiration, Ariz., Hurley, N. Mex., and El Paso in Texas. The chief mining area with a custom smelter, which charges a tonnage fee to mineral companies for its services, is at Ambrosia Lake, near Grants, New Mexico.

El Paso stands on the Rio Grande, opposite the Mexican city of Ciudad Juarez, acting as a centre for railway transhipment and for wholesale and retail trade. Its service area is principally that of the valley-bottom, where water from Elephant Butte Reservoir irrigates peaches, apricots, avoca-

67. Applying irrigation water to cropland in southern Arizona: the pipes siphon water from a distributary canal.

does, lima beans, peppers, and cotton. Cotton-cropping benefits from early maturing and from the high yields of fine cotton from Egyptian strains. Mineral exploitation in the region is reflected at El Paso in oil refining, copper smelting, and the refining of silver.

Albuquerque, also on the Rio Grande more than 250 miles upstream of El Paso, was successively a Spanish military post (presidio), a Mexican military post, and then for some time after the Mexican War a post of the U.S. forces. Like El Paso it is the centre of irrigated farmland which produces fruit and vegetables; part of the crop goes to the city's canneries. Here again are oil refineries. A distinctive manufacture is that of woollen textiles, with linkages to the regional grazing, Indian and Mexican craft production, and the tourist trade.

Phoenix, located on the Salt River in southern Arizona, is chief among a group of settlements in the general area of the Salt–Gila confluence, where, as around El Paso, long-staple cotton is grown under irrigation: the Verde, Salt, and Gila Rivers are all impounded. Among other leading irrigated crops are lucerne, fruit (citrus, olives, melons, grapes), and vegetables – especially lettuce. Industries in Phoenix have in the main an agricultural base – brewing, cotton-ginning, and flour-milling. Tucson, although again a centre for irrigation farming, is concerned also with the handling of range-grazed livestock.

Next northward of the Southern Rockies and the Interior Southwest come the Central Rockies and the Great Basin. The Great Basin, contained principally in Nevada and the western half of Utah, is typified by interior drainage and by the sheaves of uptilted, sub-parallel fault-blocks of its regional structure. The term *Central Rockies* is meant to be taken in a broad sense, for the region includes not only the Rockies proper, but also the Wasatch and adjoining mountains to the west of the Green River.

16c: The Central Rockies

Area: about 125,000 square miles.

Population: about half a million.

There are no large cities: the largest settlement is Casper, Wyo. (40,000). Population density outside Casper: about 3 per square mile.

About two-fifths of this region is classed as farmland, but grazing land takes well over half the farm acreage and about a quarter of the region: there is

68. Separation of sulphide ores by the flotation process: the pulverized ore, floating on the oily skin of the bubbles, can be skimmed off from worthless rock, and then itself be separated according to type.

also extensive open range. About one-fifteenth of the region is in cropland, about one-quarter of it irrigated. Forest, including farm woodland, covers about one-quarter of the total area.

Numbers of livestock: cattle, 1¼ million, of which only about 50,000 are milk cows; sheep, 2 million; pigs, 60,000; poultry, 1½ million.

16d: The Great Basin

Area: about 200,000 square miles.

Population: about 1½ million.

Largest cities: populations of metropolitan areas given in brackets:

Salt Lake City, Utah, 190,000 (385,000)
Ogden, Utah, 70,250 (111,000)
Las Vegas, Nev., 65,000 (127,000)
Provo–Orem, Utah, 55,000 (107,000)
Reno, Nev., 51,500 (85,000)

Population density outside the largest metropolitan areas: about 2½ per square mile.

About one-fifth of this region is classed as farmland, but grazing land takes well over three-quarters of the farm acreage and about a third of the region: there is also extensive open range. About one-fiftieth of the region is cropland, about half of it irrigated. Forest, including farm woodland, covers about one-fifth of total area.

Numbers of livestock: cattle, 1¼ million, of which only a tenth are milk cows; sheep, 1½ million; pigs, 75,000; poultry, 9 million.

Pike's Peak in the Central Rockies, rising to more than 14,000 feet and overtopping the general level, is visible for many miles to the east. It served as an aiming-point to the squadrons of prairie schooners moving across the High Plains on their way to the Pacific coast: and *Pike's Peak or bust* became a common slogan among the migrant groups. But the Central Rockies, almost as continuous as the Rockies in Canada, were too difficult to cross; the wagon-trains were forced to round them at one end or other. They became a magnet in themselves when gold was discovered in 1858, and when a gold-rush occurred in 1859. Thousands of inexperienced prospectors flooded across the High Plains. Most in the event were disappointed; but a few, such as John Gregory who located a gold-bearing quartz vein near the present-day Central City, struck it really rich. After the working of gold followed the longer-term and more stable exploitation of the sulphide ores of lead, zinc, silver, and copper (Plate 68). Cripple Creek, Colorado, has been reduced from a noteworthy centre of gold-mining to a tourist resort, but the uppermost Arkansas River Valley contains the lead-producing centres of Leadville, Buena Vista, and Salida. Climax, Colorado, possesses the world's greatest molybdenum mine.

A second metalliferous belt occurs on the western edge of the mountain section, while further deposits are found in the Great Basin. Copper is again prominent. The two regions between them produce nearly one-quarter of the U.S. output of this metal. Mining and concentrating are carried on at Magna in Utah and Ely in Nevada, smelting is done at McGill, and smelting and refining are both conducted at Garfield. Bisbee and Bingham Canyons give access to the low-grade ores, which pass by gravity feed to the crushing and concentrating plants. Geneva, in Utah, uses local iron ores in the furnaces which feed its steelworks.

Mineral potential apart from iron and copper is great, but under present conditions of price remains largely uneconomic and thus unrealized. The Wind River, Green River, and Big Horn tectonic basins of Wyoming contain coals, mainly of sub-bituminous rank, for which immediate prospects of working are poor – especially since the conversion of railways to diesel working, which has caused numbers of mines to close. There are, however, limited reserves of anthracite in the headwater catchment of the Arkansas River. Prospects for the more distant future depend on the demand for thermal power raised on the coalfields, on the long-distance supply of gas, and on the requirements of that sector of the chemical industry which uses coal as a raw material. Huge reserves exist of oil shale, mainly in the Green River fields of southwestern Wyoming and the Uinta fields of nearby Utah and Colorado; but although the physical conditions of extraction are highly favourable, with vast open-cut quarries directly supplying retorts and distillation plants, and although the extraction process is the simple one of thermal distillation, maximum yields are only about 80 gallons per ton of shale treated, and a high ash content makes the chief product, kerosene, only marginally competitive with the products of oil refineries. Even the extraction of mineral oil in liquid form is handicapped in this region by distance and costs, although on the other hand the high quality of crude warrants deep drilling in some

69. Measuring the winter-charged reservoir of the snowfields which supply irrigation water in summer.

districts. Mineral extraction of a totally different kind is practised in the Great Basin, where the evaporite deposits of former Lake Bonneville are worked for common salt, magnesium chloride, sulphates, and borax.

In total, mineral production in the two regions brings in more than twice as much as does farming. Opportunities for cultivation are confined to irrigable farmland, while open-range grazing is both extensive and, perforce, extensively exploited. One of its specific effects is the establishment in the Great Basin of a group of Basque sheep-farmers: these, coming in as shepherds, have saved enough to settle on their own land. Although their dwellings are remote, and lacking in the amenities which tend to be taken for granted on most North American commercial farms, it seems likely that the development of geothermal power will at least provide them with an electricity supply.

Cultivation is concentrated chiefly along the foot of the Wasatch Mountains on either side of Salt Lake City, where snowmelt proves the means of irrigation and a string of settlements constitutes a noteworthy local market (Plate 69). The leading crops, except for market-garden produce, are hay, sugar beet, potatoes, barley, and alfalfa grown for seed. Elsewhere, throughout most of the two regions, the existing small patches of irrigation farming could perhaps be characterized as jackpot agriculture: they depend on the vagaries of the seasons and the weather – the incidence and intensity of storms, flash floods, dry spells, and droughts.

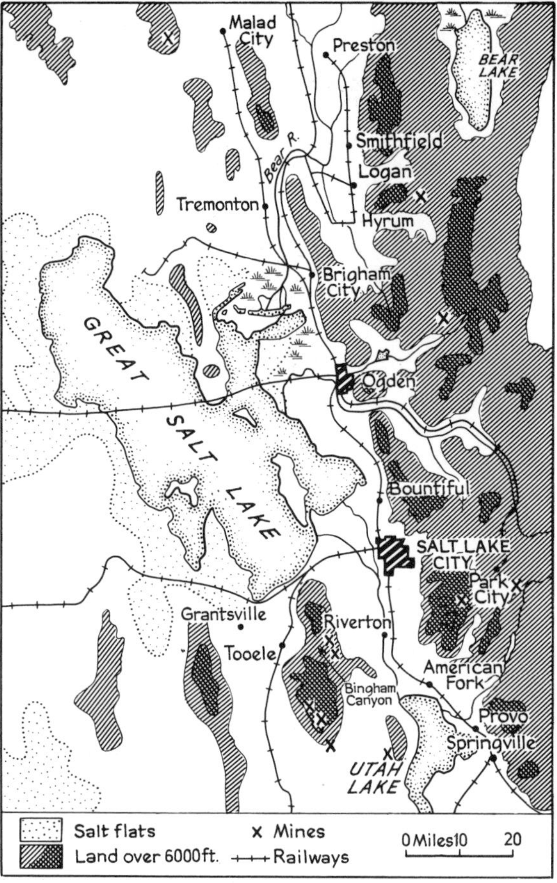

FIG. 16:3 The Wasatch Piedmont.

Some of the irrigation practices of the Great Basin are distinctly crude: streams are dammed where they emerge from the fault-blocks on to alluvial fans, being made to flood sideways from their channels and so to wet the slopes below the dams. In this way, grass can be kept green and vigorous for much of the year. The climate-tolerant lucerne, itself grown under irrigation, also serves the livestock sector. Contrasting and far more favourable conditions are found in the Central Rockies, where good grazing country invades the mountain belt in the Wyoming Basin.

Salt Lake City, Ogden, and Provo–Orem are the three first-ranking agglomerations in a chain of settlements more than 200 miles in length, occupying the valleys of the Bear, Provo, and Sevier Rivers and the shores of the Great Salt Lake (Fig. 16:3). Immediately on the east rises the steep linear fault-scarp of the Wasatch Mountains. All three centres are Mormon foundations. In 1849, two years after its establishment, Salt Lake City had already become a significant outfitting post for expeditions to the Californian goldfields. Both in their Piedmont location and in their connections with ore-mining, these three cities are comparable with Denver and its neighbours beneath the edge of the Rockies. All pack meat, mill flour, and can vegetables; the canning industry of Orem is highly specialized on tomatoes and on products with a tomato-pulp base. Beet sugar is refined at Salt Lake City and Ogden. The latter functions as a tourist centre, similar in a number of respects to Colorado Springs. Salt Lake City is, like Denver, industrially complex. Apart from its involvement with the processing of agricultural produce and of non-ferrous metals, it possesses an oil refinery and an iron and steel plant – once again, a plant established in wartime for strategic reasons; a second integrated iron and steel plant occurs at Provo. Highly complex manufacturing is represented at Salt Lake City by a radio and electronics industry; and there are also textile mills, plus printing and publishing devoted in considerable part to Mormon literature.

Only two settlements of any size lie elsewhere in the Great Basin or on its margins – Las Vegas in the extreme south, and Reno on the very boundary with the Sierra Nevada on the west (Plate 70). Both have attained notoriety, the one as a centre of organized, State-licensed, and State-controlled gambling, the other as a dispenser of quickie divorces. Faced with the blank circumstances of sparse population, totally inadequate water-supply, and severely restricted agricultural opportunities, Nevada has solved its financial problems by capitalizing on its dry climate and by legalizing – and taxing – gambling of many kinds. Although the reaction to the environment is direct enough, it is ironical that the Great Basin should have given rise to the laxity of Nevada on one side of it, and to the high level of social decorum and restraint in Utah on the other.

In another sense, the gambling trade can be regarded as part of tourism. Las Vegas is only 250 airline miles from Los Angeles, Reno only 200 miles from San Francisco. But the few small settlements in the interior of the Great Basin are neither particularly accessible nor with distinctive claims to scenic attraction, unless one counts the mirages of the Great Salt Lake Desert along the road west from Salt Lake City. Utah, with ski-lodges in the Wasatch Mountains, and with the spectacular rainwashed natural pillars of the canyons in Zion and Bryce Canyon National Parks, is better suited than Nevada to tourism of the conventional kind.

North of the Central Rockies and the Great Basin come the northern U.S. Rockies, continued by the southern Rockies of Canada. The Cordilleran belt as a whole is considerably narrower here than it is farther to the south, being only 500 miles wide at the U.S.–Canadian border, as against 1000 miles between Denver and San Francisco. The entire difference is absorbed by a constriction of the plateau segment; for the Rockies (in the broad sense) are still 400 miles wide in Idaho–Montana, while the southern Canadian Rockies are followed immediately westward by the almost equally high ground of the Columbia and Selkirk Mountains, which pinches-in the northern U.S. Cordilleran plateaus as a separate topographic unit.

70. Las Vegas, Nevada: even more than New York's entertainment district, Las Vegas is designed to display itself principally by night.

16e: The Northern U.S. and Southern Canadian Rockies

Area: about 100,000 square miles.

Population: about $\frac{3}{4}$ million.

There are no large cities: the largest settlements are:

Missoula, Mont., 28,000
Butte, Mont., 27,500
Helena, Mont., 22,000
Kamloops–North Kamloops, B.C., 17,000
Penticton, B.C., 13,000
Trail, B.C., 11,500

Population density outside these places: about 5 per square mile.

About one-fifth of this region is in farmland; cropland takes about a quarter of the farm acreage, and grassland pasture another quarter. Forest, including farm woodland, covers about three-quarters of the region.

Numbers of livestock: cattle, $1\frac{1}{4}$ million, of which fewer than 100,000 are milk cows; sheep, $\frac{1}{2}$ million; pigs, 85,000; poultry, $2\frac{1}{2}$ million.

16f: The Northern U.S. Cordilleran Plateaus

Area: about 170,000 square miles.

Population: about $2\frac{1}{2}$ million.

Largest cities: populations of some metropolitan areas given in brackets:

Spokane, Wash., 182,000 (280,000)
Boise, Idaho, 35,000 (75,000)
Idaho Falls, Idaho, 35,000
Pocatello, Idaho, 30,000
Walla Walla, Wash., 26,000
Twin Falls, Idaho, 20,000

Population density outside the largest towns and metropolitan areas: about 5 per square mile.

About one-fifth of this region is in farmland; about half the farm acreage is cropland, and rather less than half is in grassland pasture; there is also open-range pasture. Forest, about one-tenth of it farm woodland, covers two-fifths of the region.

Numbers of livestock: cattle, $2\frac{1}{2}$ million, of which about 1 in 10 is a milk cow; sheep, $1\frac{1}{4}$ million; pigs, $\frac{1}{4}$ million; poultry, 30 million.

The alpine scenery of the northern U.S.A. and

the southern Canadian Rockies can be called nothing less than grandiose. Here, in the northwest of Wyoming, lie Grand Teton and Yellowstone National Parks, where expanses of mountain grassland lead from the upper treeline towards the glacially-fretted peaks. Yellowstone has its own special attraction in its famous geysers. Waterton–Glacier International Peace Park lies athwart the international boundary. Kootenay, Mount Jasper, and Banff National Parks in the Canadian Rockies all possess mineral hot springs; resort facilities at Lake Louise, in the last of these three, are highly developed. Yoho National Park in the Canadian Rockies, and Glacier and Mount Revelstoke National Parks in the Selkirks, complete the series. Its total area exceeds 14,000 square miles; more than 12 million visitors come each year. Warm-season tourism has produced dude ranches, which offer every possible domestic comfort, but rely on trail-riding rather than on the automobile to introduce their customers to the wilderness. Winter sports flourish, not only in the Parks but also in commercial centres such as those of Sun Valley, Idaho.

Grazing in the southern part of this mountain region does well. Sagebrush plains in the enclosed valleys and basins, and the grasslands of the mountain slopes, provide excellent natural forage. Rates of evapotranspiration are lower here than they are farther south, and the regime of soil moisture is favourable to forage plants. Irrigation can be used for supplemental rather than essential purposes, reducing the costs of producing fodder crops and beef. Cattle are commonly maintained on small ranches in the valleys, moving in summer to mountain pastures after the snow has melted. In the winter season, animals that have not been sold away are stall-fed under cover. Hay comes from the harvesting of the wild plant cover, or – on the best farms – lucerne crops grown under irrigation, supplemented by irrigated small grains. Grazing in the national forests is restricted by law, although some rights of access are still granted on the basis of the amount of land owned privately by the applicants. This arrangement, obviously favouring the large-scale rancher, has been condemned as adverse to the national interest. Whether small-scale ranchers are notably conscious of their responsibility for conservation has not been determined; but the Northern Rockies, where small ranches are typical, certainly has a better record than most parts of the continent in its adjustment of intensity of working and stocking to the capabilities of the land.

Sheep grazing for the production of greasy wool and lamb is confined principally to the poorer sections of the sagebrush country, involving long shifts towards the north in the summer and towards the south in the winter. Each flock is in the charge of a shepherd, much of whose life is distinctly solitary. Spring grazing in the lambing season is supplied by the alpine meadows of the mountain flanks, where pastures become very rich in the moist conditions which follow snowmelt. In some districts the price-cost differential between cattle and sheep is so small that there can be frequent changes from one type of stocking to the other. On the other hand, although sales of lambs and wool provide fairly regular incomes, falling wool prices, the semi-nomadic life of shepherding, the prejudice of the North American consumer market against lamb in favour of beef, and the increasing use of supplemental feeding of cattle which irrigation makes possible, all combine to encourage the ranching of cattle rather than of sheep.

Agricultural development owes not a little to the demands of mining communities; but the unpredictable life of many of these, like the progressive invasion of the regional market by mass-produced foodstuffs, somewhat mitigates the local advantages. A notable exception to this general circumstance concerns the growing of orchard fruit, particularly of apples, which are produced in quantity, both in eastern Washington and in British Columbia alongside Lake Okanagan. The Okanagan orchards are located on irrigable terraces formed of reworked volcanic ash: their economic base is the demand of the Prairies, their social base soldier settlement after World War I. Cold-air drainage off the orchards and the heat-storage of the Lake ensure a suitable climatic environment, although the economies of production are not far from marginal. Southward, in response to increasing temperatures, the apple orchards are replaced by cherries, plums, and peaches. Generally speaking, planting represents a compromise between the frost danger to particular types of tree, and the effectiveness of frost in destroying specific fruit pests (Plates 3, 71).

This section of the Rockies and the interior mountain knot of southernmost British Columbia are again concerned with ore-mining; and once again the ores are principally mixed sulphide ores of copper and silver–lead–zinc. The U.S. portion produces about 10 per cent of the national output of copper, about 20 per cent of the zinc, more than 20 per cent of the lead, and half the national total of silver. Silver-mining is, however, strongly affected by government policy and by international trends in the status of currencies: the U.S. Silver Purchase Act encouraged overproduction which had to be absorbed by stockpiling, but the financial events of the late 1960s may well stimulate further working. Mixed silver ores are mined at Coeur d'Alene and Wallace in Idaho, copper ores at Butte, Helena, and Anaconda in Montana. Copper concentrating is carried on at Butte, smelting at Anaconda, and refining at Great Falls. On the Canadian side, British Columbia produces by value about 10 per cent of Canadian copper, more than 15 per cent of the silver, 40 per cent of the zinc, and 75 per cent of the national total of lead. The chief mining area is in the south of the province around Kimberley; smelting and refining are carried on at Trail.

71. Orchard land in the Willamette Valley, Oregon: the leading crop in this particular section is, in actuality, not fruit but nuts. Sloping ground to the left of the view promotes cold-air drainage away from the trees.

Mining and mineral processing dominate the urban activities of Missoula, Helena, Trail, and Butte; the last-named contains the famous Montana School of Mines, which – unusually for such an establishment in the Western world – is coeducational. Kamloops, with linkages to copper–gold orefields, is yet another mining centre; but its functions are more varied than might be expected from the city's population, including as they do the canning of fruit, and the provision of services for grazing districts on the interior plateaus to the

72. Freight train on the Canadian Pacific, alongside Box River and below Storm Mountain in the Rockies.

73. Concrete siphon, twenty-five feet in diameter, delivering enough water to irrigate more than a million acres of the farmland of Washington State. In the distance, dissected basalt plateaus.

northward. Furthermore, Kamloops is a notable railway junction: Canada's two main transcontinental lines converge on it from the east, respectively via Calgary and Kicking Horse Pass, and via Edmonton and Yellowhead Pass, before running down the lower Thompson and Fraser Valleys to Vancouver (Plate 72). Penticton, smaller still than Kamloops, acts as collector and distributor for the fruit-farms of Lake Okanagan.

The Northern U.S. Cordilleran Plateaus, drained by the Snake–Columbia system, contrast strongly with adjoining regions. They are distinctly lower than the enclosing Cordilleran Mountains – 5000 feet above sea-level and downwards as against 10,000 feet upwards. Like all the plateaus of the entire Cordilleran system, they are strongly rain-shadowed by the mountains to their west, with annual average precipitation ranging from 20 inches down to 10 inches and even below. On the other hand, they possess great through-going rivers, which the Great Basin lacks. Their average frost-free period ranges between 140 and 200 days over extensive tracts of the lower ground, as opposed to 100 days or so in the next-northern plateau section in British Columbia: and mean January temperatures, as high as 32° F in contrast to 15° F or below, differ similarly.

Physiographically, too, this plateau region is distinctive. It has been the site of basalt floods, which before they began to be dissected covered 100,000 and possibly as much as 200,000 square miles of country. Basalt-derived soils, whether formed directly on the sheets of lava or upon basaltic alluvium, are mineral-rich and moisture-retentive. Irrigation is of course necessary; but irrigation water is available (Plate 73), ultimately from snowfall on the Northern Rockies, while useful basins for impounding it are provided by the canyons and their tributary coulees. These last features are the product of erosion by glacial melt-water, some of it flowing in huge occasional bursts as an impounded lake was suddenly released.

Cultivation in the region is much specialized on grain and fruit. The leading crop is apples, grown along the north–south reach of the middle Columbia River and in the valley of the confluent Yakima. Wheat (mainly spring wheat) is the chief grain, but barley and oats are increasingly cultivated. This region is far less liable than the Southern Plains to wild fluctuations in its wheat output, although the total crop is by no means constant from year to year; it produces the bulk of the combined wheat crop of Washington, Oregon, and Idaho, which varied around some 80 million bushels a year from 1900 to the early 1930s, and then rose to a running average of 130–140 million bushels. Part of the rise reflects improved farming practices and the progressive use of higher-yielding strains, but another part results from the immigration during the 1930s of farmer refugees from the dust of the Southern Plains. A persistent handicap to wheat production, for all its extensiveness, is the great distance between the producing farms and markets in the east: but the Pacific Southwest, much more readily accessible than the east coast, exerts a steadily-growing demand. The potato crop, by contrast, has long held a firm grip on a nationwide market. The chief potato-producing areas lie on the Snake River Plains of Idaho, which alone grow something like a fifth of the national crop: the term *Idaho potatoes* is frequently used in the sense of a brand-name.

Irrigation farming developed to some extent independently of, and indeed in advance of, the installation of multi-purpose works supported by the federal government; and these, in respect of their generation of hydro-electric power, have implications far beyond the bounds of the region. The greatest works are on the Columbia itself, where the Chief Joseph and Grand Coulee Dams convert some 200 miles of river into reservoirs; but these two sets of installations are two among many.

A number of the region's towns have histories as fortified bases during the wars with the Indians. All today are implicated in one way or another with the agriculture of their surroundings. Thus, Idaho Falls, Pocatello, and Twin Falls, on or near the Snake River, are service centres for districts of potato, sugar beet, and wheat production; Pocatello has a reputation for cheese-making, while Twin Falls processes fruit and vegetables. Boise, towards the downstream end of the Snake River Plains, has canneries and packing works, and creameries which take the yield of spray-irrigated pastures. It contains the headquarters of the Columbia River Reclamation Scheme. Walla Walla processes lumber – chiefly Ponderosa pine – mills flour, and cans fruit, including that raised on farms of the Columbia County Veteran Settlement.

Spokane, very much larger than any of the others, is outstandingly the prime regional city. Alongside its general central-place functions, it discharges those of resort trade and tourist base. Industry is represented not only by the milling of lumber and flour, but also by railway workshop production; Spokane, like Kamloops, is an important railway focus, but with links to two west-coast ports – Portland and Seattle.

16g: The Northern Inland Cordillera

Area: about 750,000 square miles.

Population: about $\frac{1}{4}$ million.

There are no large cities: the largest settlements are:

Prince George, B.C., 15,000
Fairbanks, Alaska, 13,500
Whitehorse, Yukon Territory, 5000

Population density outside these places: about 1 per 5 square miles.

Only about one-tenth of 1 per cent of this region is in farmland, and less than a fifth of the farm acreage is in cropland – about 1750 square miles of farmland, and 300 square miles of cropland. Perhaps a half of the region is under forest.

Numbers of livestock: cattle, 125,000, of which 1 in 5 is a milk cow; sheep, 25,000; pigs, 10,000; poultry, $1\frac{1}{2}$ million.

The Northern Inland Cordillera extends the series of mountain-girt basins, mountain knots, and mountain ranges which have so far been traced from the Mexican to the Canadian borders. The total area involved is great; and although physiographic subdivision is easily possible, the minuscule total of population and the low or zero level of economic development throughout most parts justify its treatment, for present purposes, under a single head. Manufacturing activity, even at the level of processing, is limited essentially to the area on and south of line between Prince George and Prince Rupert; and even in the south it is distinctly patchy. Lumber mills are strung near the railway to Prince Rupert; mixed farming is practised in somewhat marginal conditions in the same general area; and farms relying on livestock combinations occur in the middle Fraser Basin. However, as the regional statistics show, farming makes but a very small demand on the land available: local markets are tiny, extra-regional markets are remote and unpromising.

The southern plateau section (c.f. Fig. 3:7) is traversed by a railway which, using in part the Fraser Valley, links Vancouver through Quesnel to Prince George. Quesnel, a former centre of placer-gold mining, proved in a brief three-year episode of prospecting highly attractive, but has since been converted to the hydraulic mining of low-grade deposits of gold, tungsten, platinum, and tin. Prince George is as yet the northernmost railway node of the Cordilleran plateaus, where the Canadian National Railway between Edmonton and Prince Rupert crosses the line looping northward from Vancouver through the Peace River catchment. Land communications farther to the north are limited chiefly to the 1500-mile Alaska Highway, built in 1942 for military purposes, which links Dawson Creek, B.C., with Fairbanks in Alaska, and to the rail lines which connect Whitehorse to Skagway and Fairbanks to Anchorage. Both Fairbanks and Whitehorse were bases for alluvial mining in the short-lived times of prospector operation; both retain some of their significance as centres for alluvial working, and Whitehorse channels the traffic of the chief Canadian silver-producing mines which, 200 miles away to the north, raise silver–lead–zinc ores. A certain unity, or at least centrality of dependence, in the economy of this northern region is perhaps indicated by the processing of these various ores at Trail.

Mineral resources additional to metals appear potentially great: oil, already proved in northern British Columbia, could well emerge as a principal mining interest. It can be expected that exploration and exploitation will shift progressively northward and northwestward. Meantime, the economy of the farthest northwest remains in the hands of native Indians and Eskimos. The deliberate introduction of reindeer, although not providing an external market for produce, has done a great deal to improve the local level of food supply. There are some 40,000 reindeer in Alaska, of which about one-third are in Indian hands on Nunivak Island, the remainder being grazed by individual Eskimo herders on the mainland, either in the Mackenzie Delta or on the low-lying, lake-studded Arctic Coastal Plain.

CHAPTER SEVENTEEN

THE PACIFIC COASTLANDS

A total area of more than a third of a million square miles makes this division broadly comparable in size with the southern Low Plains macroregion; and the two population-totals are something of the same order. But the great latitudinal extent of the Coastlands makes averages even less meaningful than usual: there is scope, as will be seen, for a markedly uneven distribution of people, which leaves some parts with no settlement at all, and others with great urban clusters of people, commerce, business, and industry (Figs. 17:1, 17:2).

The tripartite arrangement of seaward mountains, landward mountains, and central axial basins includes a number of major structures which are still active. The San Andreas Fault, running obliquely out to sea near the Golden Gate, is on the move: it produced the San Francisco Earthquake of 1906. Alaska experienced a violent series of shocks in 1964, which caused considerable damage: the tilting of Kodiak Island drowned many fishing harbours. While the shapely volcanic cones of Mount Whitney in the southern Sierra Nevada, Mount Shasta in the southern Cascades, Mount Rainier in the northern Cascades, and Mount McKinley in the Alaska Ranges were produced by vulcanism which ceased in the Miocene, the Lassen Peak volcano at the north end of the Sierra Nevada has displayed slight activity during the present century, and really active volcanoes occur in Alaska and the Aleutian Islands.

Climate varies greatly from one end of this division to the other. Whereas the coasts of Alaska, British Columbia, and the Pacific Northwest are dominated by maritime air ranging from arctic to polar, much of California is affected by the summer dryness of stable tropical air.. All the basins are strongly affected by rain-shadow; part of the Great Valley of California, and the Salton Sea depression, experience desert climates. In general, the landward belt of mountains is higher than the seaward – in California, for instance, little of the Coast Ranges lies above 6000 feet, whereas much of the Sierra Nevada is above 10,000; and a less pronounced but still marked contrast occurs between the Coast Ranges and the Cascades of the Pacific Northwest. In consequence, the landward moun-

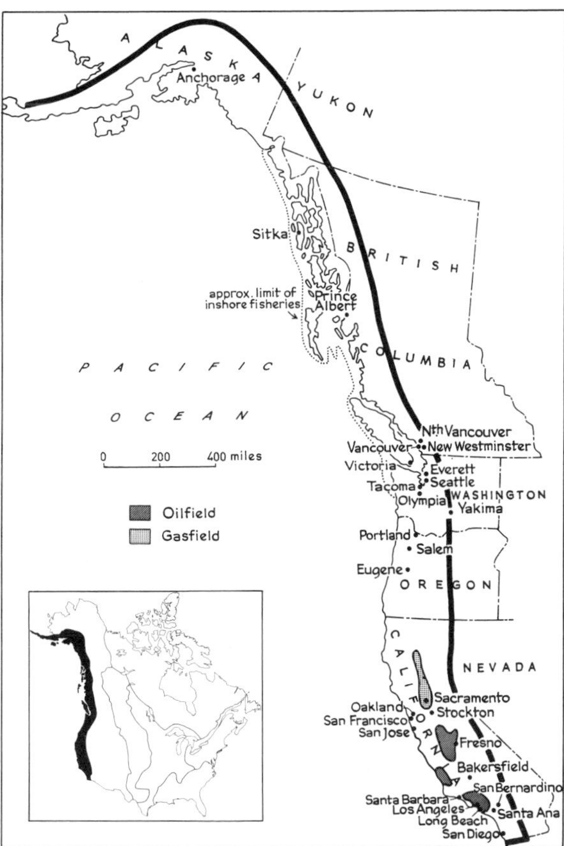

FIG. 17:1 The Pacific Coastlands.

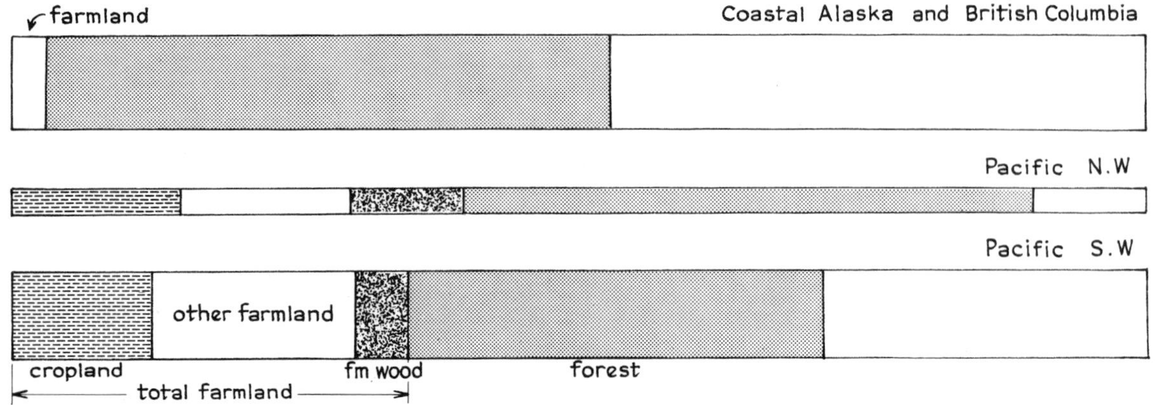

FIG. 17:2 Land use in the Pacific Coastlands, by regions.

tains can promote rainfall and snowfall in the lifting air-streams which have already passed over the first belt of high ground. Snow storage in the Sierra Nevada is basic to irrigation in the Great Valley.

In Los Angeles and San Francisco, the division possesses two of the earliest of the Spanish foundations in the West. In Alaska, it contains the latest of the U.S. States on the mainland: from 1867, when it was bought from Russia, Alaska held territory status for nearly a century, being admitted to Statehood in 1959, forty-seven years after 1912 when New Mexico and Arizona, the last of the conterminous States, were formed. The lag in economic and political progress is due largely to climate: for agricultural possibilities north of the Fraser Delta are severely restricted, and the only local markets are mining and logging camps, sawmills, and fishing bases. Urbanization is patchy round the Straits of Georgia and in the Puget Sound–Willamette Valley lowland, but it does include modern industry in the form of aircraft manufacture at Seattle. The shores of the Golden Gate are heavily built-up, in San Francisco, Oakland, and their neighbours. The greatest urban development of all is in the south, at Los Angeles–Long Beach, which have merged with a whole series of smaller towns. The economic development of the Los Angeles Basin is, in its present form, largely a matter of the twentieth century. Its motion-picture industry, one of the greatest single stimuli to its growth, benefits from the wide range of scenery available within short distances, and from the long hours of hard bright sunshine; the industry is also alleged by some to have profited by an early location near the Mexican border, across which film-makers could be safe from the law. Oil refining, the use of oil, natural gas, and hydroelectric power in the industries of the Los Angeles complex and of San Diego, plus the industrial emphasis on aircraft and machinery, belong like the movie industry to recent and current times.

17a: Coastal Alaska and British Columbia

Area: 170,000 square miles.

Population: about $1\frac{1}{4}$ million.

Largest cities: Populations of two metropolitan areas given in brackets:

Vancouver, B.C., 400,000 (800,000)
Victoria, B.C., 55,000 (175,000)
Anchorage, Alaska, 45,000

Population density outside these centres: less than 2 per square mile; large areas are however unpeopled.

Only about 3 per cent of the region is used for farming; cropland and farm pasture each take about one-half of 1 per cent of the total area. About half the region is under commercial forest, although by no means all of this is at present exploited. Cultivation and the keeping of stock are almost entirely concentrated in the extreme south.

Numbers of livestock: cattle, $\frac{1}{4}$ million, of which 50,000 are milk cows; sheep, 60,000; pigs, 20,000; poultry, 4 million.

Many U.S. citizens disapproved strongly of the Alaska purchase, dubbing the territory *Seward's Icebox*, after the Secretary of the Interior who negotiated the deal. But the fishery resources in Alaskan waters, commercially exploited since 1878, have alone proved the Purchase an outstanding bargain. Each year, the take of salmon, halibut, herring, the giant Pacific crab, other commercial fish, and Pribiloff Islands fur seals returns far more than the price of $7\frac{1}{2}$ million dollars paid for Alaska. Even when full allowance is made for reduction in the value of the dollar, Alaska has emphatically proved worth its price.

Fjords and skerry channels of British Columbia also abound in fish (Plate 74); the harbours of this province land about 40 per cent by value of the entire Canadian catch. Alaska and British Columbia, taken together, claim a 20 per cent share by value of all landings in the two countries. Of the British Columbian landings more than two-thirds of the value is provided by salmon, and pink salmon – the cheapest variety – alone supplies about one-third. The next most valuable species are, in order, sockeye salmon, coho salmon, halibut, and herring; crabs, oysters, and clams appear in the list of shellfish. Canneries and freezing works are scattered along the coast. Alaska alone has 120 canneries, which are, however, in some danger from the serious depletion of the valuable sockeye. Populations of the canning centres are almost wholly transient, coming only for the fishing season. Canned fish from Alaska is shipped to Seattle for distribution. The main landing port for halibut is Prince Rupert, where the fish is sliced into fillets and dispatched in the frozen state.

Forest resources are great, although those of Alaska are as yet little exploited (Plates 75, 76). Mature hemlock, Sitka spruce, Engelmann spruce, western red cedar, and Douglas fir are widely taken from the British Columbian forests for the timber-milling industry, while the younger spruces and hemlock of regrowth are felled for pulpwood. Alaskan reserves include Alaska cedar, which is eminently suited to the production of lumber. Most Alaskan timber comes from the Tongass and Chugach National Forests under a system of controlled silvicultural management. In British Columbia the western mountains yield nearly one-quarter by value of all the timber cut in Canada. Three-quarters of the land area of this province is under forest – not all of it under mature trees, for areas recently cut or burned, and immature stands,

74. Repairing fishing nets at Port Renfrew, B.C.

75. Fur auction at the February Fur Rendezvous at Anchorage, Alaska. Gemstones, particularly jade, are also put up for sale.

76. Sawmill in the foreground, sulphite plant in the middle distance, at Port Alberni on Vancouver Island.

are included in the data; but British Columbia still possesses 60 per cent of the entire national reserve of standing timber. It cuts two-fifths by value of all Canadian timber, and produces 70 per cent of all lumber shipments and of saw-mill products generally.

Saw-mills are even more scattered than fish-processing plants, since numbers of them are located inland. The initial exploitation of forests in British Columbia was strictly coastal: trees were felled on the slopes leading down to the fiords, and rafted in huge booms to tidewater mills. But as more and more of the most accessible forests were depleted, logging perforce moved inland, adopting the use of movable mills, and delivering timber to the coast in the cut state. Less than two-thirds of the province's cut now comes from the coastal mountains, and a series of mills line the valleys of the Skeena, Nechako, and upper Fraser Rivers, where the railway connects them with Vancouver or Prince Rupert. The greatest inland concentrations of mills are around Prince George, Kamloops, and Nelson, while Vancouver, Victoria, and the west coast of Vancouver Island have mills on tidewater sites. The milling industry is classed as primary processing. It has however undergone some elaboration, producing plywood and allied materials, and dispatching part of its output in the manufactured state. Pulping, increasing with the ever-rising demand for newsprint (and also capitalizing on the increasing supply of small timber from second-growth forests), is located mainly on the coast, much of it on the shores of the Straits of Georgia.

Mining throughout the region is far less vigorous today than it has been in the past, although copper ores are worked near Vancouver and on Vancouver Island, and also – sporadically – in the general neighbourhood of Prince Rupert. The chief mineral-based industry is aluminium smelting at Kitimat. This uses hydro-electric power generated at Kemano, fifty miles away; the power head of more than 2500 feet is secured by the damming of the Nechako River, and the diversion of the impounded waters through a ten-mile tunnel beneath the divide. Kitimat is placed at the head of the deep Douglas Channel, accessible to the ocean-going freighters which bring in Jamaican bauxite. Of the current annual production of 200,000 tons of aluminium most goes for export; export demands are expected to absorb the planned future increase to 500,000 tons a year.

Farming in almost all parts depends on markets immediately at hand, for the distances to other markets are great indeed, and the climatic disadvantage is also large. Nevertheless, the building of the Alaska Railroad from Anchorage into the interior, and the development of Anchorage as a large military base during World War II, succeeded in promoting farming in the Matanuska Valley, which conducts dairy farming, maintains fodder production – in part from rotation pastures – and grows potatoes and hardy green vegetables. Poultry-farming for fresh eggs is also known, and there is some pig-keeping which uses farm waste in addition to fodder crops. Farther south, the one great urban market is Vancouver. The delta of the Fraser is noted for its market gardens, many of them operated by Chinese; and fruit and vegetable crops are also raised on the rain-shadowed eastern side of Vancouver Island.

Vancouver is by far the most populous city in the region, and the only large one: it has more than four times as many inhabitants in its metropolitan area than has Victoria, the next in rank. Its more southerly location has obviously given it an advantage over Prince Rupert, the second terminal of transcontinental railways in the region; Prince Rupert, with but 12,000 people, records a rate of growth far slower than that of Vancouver. The latter city has, of course, undoubtedly profited by the channelling of Canadian traffic by the international boundary. Oil is pumped into Vancouver through the transcordilleran pipeline from Edmonton; a feeder line increases the flow with oil from the Peace River District, which is also linked to Vancouver by a gas pipeline. Vancouver's industries are dominated by primary processing – lumber-milling, pulp- and paper-making, and oil refining; the city also has numbers of food-processing works and fish canneries. Its port, on Burrard Inlet, ships the products of these various industries, plus Prairie wheat.

Victoria, on Vancouver Island, is the State capital. It too is a port, although a minor one, with a fine harbour on the Strait of Juan de Fuca; its port activities are handicapped by separation from the mainland. Anchorage, at the head of Cook

Inlet in Alaska, has rail links with the former gold-mining Fairbanks district in the interior, and with Seward on the open coast: it functions as a military base. As in a number of U.S. States, as also in British Columbia, the State capital in Alaska is one of the smaller towns – here, Juneau (7000), sheltered amid the fiord passages of the Panhandle.

17b: The Coastlands of the Pacific Northwest

Area: about 35,500 square miles.

Population: about 3 million.

Cities with at least 50,000 inhabitants: population of some metropolitan areas given in brackets:

Seattle, Wash., 557,000 (1,110,000)
Portland, Ore., 373,000 (822,000)
Tacoma, Wash., 148,000 (322,000)
Eugene, Ore., 70,000
Salem, Ore., 63,000
Everett, Wash., 51,000

Population density outside the largest cities and metropolitan areas: about 15 per square mile.

About two-fifths of the region is in farmland, of which cropland and grassland each take about one-third, the remainder being chiefly in farm woodland. Forest, including farm woodland, covers nearly two-thirds of the region.

Numbers of livestock: cattle, $1\frac{1}{2}$ million, of which more than half a million are milk cows; sheep, 575,000; pigs, 150,000; poultry, 25 million.

Fishing and forestry contribute strongly to the economy of this region, as also does tourism, which is more highly developed here than in the coastlands of British Columbia and Alaska. But the region also contains sizeable extents of commercial farmland, and possesses highly-developed manufacturing industries.

Forest exploitation has gone farther here than it has in British Columbia, leaving extensive areas covered by second-growth timber. Western hemlock and western red cedar have been widely stripped from the Olympic Mountains and the Coast Ranges of Oregon, the latter species now remaining only in the remotest districts. The natural cover of the western faces of the Cascades includes Douglas fir and Sitka spruce, with stands of noble and silver fir. Douglas fir is the most useful of all constructional softwoods, being remarkably knot-free and resistant to rot: accordingly, it is the most heavily exploited. If second-growth forest is allowed to reclaim the cutover areas, it will frequently fail to include the best of the species which have been removed: particularly is this so in the case of the Douglas fir, which is threatened with extinction unless logging is adequately controlled. Tree farming and scientific forest management have, however, already somewhat restored the timber resources and the lumbering activities of the region as a whole (Plate 77). Some completely cutover tracts, where water-tables are high, have been converted to grasslands used for grazing and dairying, or even semi-subsistence farming. The so-called stump farms, taxed at the low rates applicable to forests, can provide an income for the retired; they have helped to maintain the production of cedar shingles, which, although expensive, are popular for use as roofing and cladding materials for weekend and holiday dwellings.

77. Reforestation by seeding from the air, Pacific Northwest.

Saw-mills, pulp-mills, paper-mills, and plywood factories line the inner Willamette Valley and extend along the fifty miles of the south–north course of the lower Columbia; another series is located on Puget Sound, a third and lesser series on and near Grays Harbour; and furniture manufacture is carried on, mainly at Portland.

Fishing ports in Washington and Oregon share in the fisheries like those of British Columbia, landing something less than 10 per cent by value of the total U.S. catch: here also, the fish is destined for canning or freezing.

Mining activity is in the main small. Scattered reserves of coal exist, chiefly of sub-bituminous grade, but are exploited only in the most minor fashion. Crude oil and gas from Canada, and hydro-electric power developed within the region, produce the energy demanded by industry and by rail transport. Gold is mined in the Chelan district, and is also a by-product of copper and zinc mining in the Holden and Index fields.

The Puget Sound–Willamette Valley Lowland has done well with the cultivation of fruits and other special crops, which are raised on the silty to sandy soils of glacial and terrace deposits. Berry fruits – raspberries, strawberries, blackberries, and loganberries – sell widely across the nation in canned or frozen form. Nut groves mainly produce walnuts; plums, prunes, and cherries are sold from the orchards of the Umpqua and Rogue River Valleys, while Dutch-descended nurserymen in the Skagit and Puyallup Valleys raise bulbs of daffodil, narcissus, and tulip. Field crops include blue barley and hops, which are shipped to breweries at Olympia and Milwaukee. Peas, corn, and beans are grown both for the towns of the region and for the canning and freezing industries. Dairying, relatively more prominent on the Pacific coast than in the axial basin, caters for the regional liquid-milk market, and supplies the raw material for export butter. Cranberries and blueberries are cultivated on acidic bog soils in the coastal strip.

Manufacturing in the Pacific Northwest relies for its energy supply on hydro-electric power – generated mainly in the adjacent plateau country – and on natural gas piped in from Alberta. Although less than one-third of the power potential of Washington and Oregon has so far been developed, the best sites have already been used: additional development would be less attractive in cost–benefit terms. If transmission systems could be sufficiently improved, hydro-electric power might be imported from Alaska: this possibility is perhaps nearer realization than those highly ambitious proposals of water-supply which involve huge extents of the central and western Cordillera. Already at present, however, the power available is sufficiently ample and sufficiently cheap to support aluminium manufacture at a number of works in Washington and northern Oregon: a leading market is the aircraft industry of Seattle.

Seattle at one time entertained high hopes of becoming a main outlet on the Pacific; at the terminus of the old Yellowstone overland trail, it attracted four transcontinental railways, but in nationwide traffic has been far outstripped by San Francisco and Los Angeles. In addition to its aircraft industry, it has specialized timber-milling which cuts layers for plywood manufacture; flour-milling which takes Columbia grain; shipbuilding; electrolytic steel-making wherein scrap-metal is the raw material; and the manufacture of cans for the fish, fruit, and vegetable trades. Its harbour on Puget Sound has been developed for industrial sites by means of reclamation.

Portland, on the Columbia River at the confluence of the Willamette, is accessible by navigable water, although navigation is handicapped by the sinuosity of the downstream channel. Its chief industries are closely related to the agricultural activities of its surroundings – flour-milling, freezing, and butter- and cheese-making. Tacoma, a third seaport, virtually at the head of navigation on Puget Sound, uses hydro-electricity and natural gas in the treatment of copper and copper ores, and in milling wood for constructional timber. Its milling is however suffering from the increasing distance to the sources of timber, and there has been some relocation of it on the Columbia River.

Everett, about as far distant from Seattle on the north as Tacoma is on the south, conducts a port trade largely connected with its timber-milling. The mills here are fully integrated: nearly all parts of the logs are used, the bark, for instance, being made into soil-conditioner and scrap wood compressed into artificial billets. There are also salmon and crabmeat canneries, but these are affected by a decline in supplies for which over-fishing in the past, plus the pollution of streams by industrial waste – principally, decaying effluent from timber-mills – are responsible.

Salem is the local service centre for the middle Willamette Valley, Eugene for the upper valley. Salem, the State capital, processes fruit and vegetable products, makes linen, collects and ships hops, and produces high-grade cellulose for chemical papers. Eugene's industries – e.g. the making of light farm implements – are as a group meant to serve its own surrounding district, although there still remain vestiges of the early gold- and silver-mining which promoted the founding of the town in 1851.

17c: The Pacific Southwest

Area: about 160,000 square miles.

Population: about 17 million.

Cities with at least 150,000 people in the metropolitan area: population of metropolitan areas given in brackets:

- Los Angeles–Long Beach, Cal., 2,850,000 (6,750,000)
- San Francisco–Oakland, Cal., 1,110,000 (2,785,000)
- San Diego, Cal., 575,000 (1,000,000)
- San Bernadino–Riverside–Ontario, Cal., 223,000 (810,000)
- San Jose, Cal., 205,000 (650,000)
- Sacramento, Cal., 192,000 (500,000)
- Fresno, Cal., 134,000 (365,000)
- Santa Ana, Cal., 100,500 (150,000)
- Stockton, Cal., 86,500 (250,000)
- Santa Barbara, Cal., 60,000 (170,000)
- Bakersfield, Cal., 57,000 (292,000)

Population density outside the largest metropolitan areas: about 22 per square mile.

About one-third of this region is in farmland; rather more than one-third of the farm acreage is cropland, rather less than half is grazing other than woodland; farm woodland takes about 10 per cent of the total farm acreage. Forest, including farm woodland, covers about two-fifths of the region.

Numbers of livestock: cattle, $1\frac{1}{2}$ million, of which about 1 in 10 is a dairy cow; sheep, 200,000; pigs, 150,000; poultry, 200 million.

This region is constituted essentially by the State of California, which, although a political entity, is frequently discussed on its own in regional treatments of North America. The northern and central parts of the State, as defined by the political boundary, do in fact correspond quite well to a section of the orogenic belt adjoining the Pacific. South of Death Valley and inland of the San Bernadino Mountains, an area amounting to something like a fifth of the State lies east of the mountains of the coastland division; but since this is scarcely peopled – taking in, as it does, the Mojave Desert – it usually receives little attention in accounts of land use, settlement, and industry.

Little more than a century ago, California, which is now the most populous State in the Union, had very few people. In 1850, it exceeded in population, of the States east of the Mississippi, only the remote and chilly Vermont and New Hampshire, the tiny Rhode Island, the mountainous West Virginia, and the scarcely penetrated Florida. Already by 1850, however, its invasion had begun; and in the ten years to 1860 its population rose fourfold. In 1869 San Francisco became the Pacific terminus of a transcontinental railway: seven years later, Los Angeles followed. Oil was discovered in California in 1894. By 1900, when there were nearly $1\frac{1}{2}$ million people in California, the State had risen more than half-way up the ranking list; by 1940 it was almost identical in total population to Ohio, coming effectively third after New York and Pennsylvania, and a decade later was alone in second place. It has sustained a most remarkable rate of decennial increase in population – not far below 50 per cent – for more than a hundred years. The fact that California is larger in area than most other States of the Union must influence the view taken of its absolute total of population: but it does not affect the political implications of this total, since seats in the House of Representatives are allocated on a population basis. California, accordingly, has emerged as a strong force in the nation's internal politics.

The first influx, that of 1848–49, was dramatic: it had a single cause – gold fever. When gold was first struck at Sutter's Creek in 1848, a major rush began as the word rapidly spread. Every gulch leading up into the Sierra Nevada from the Great Valley contained at least minor shows of gold. All were earnestly explored. Mining towns sprang up in numbers. They remain today as ghost towns such as Grizzly Flats and Angel's Lamp; for most of the placers have long been worked out, the alluvial prospectors are long since dead, and only a few dredges operate in working over river gravels,

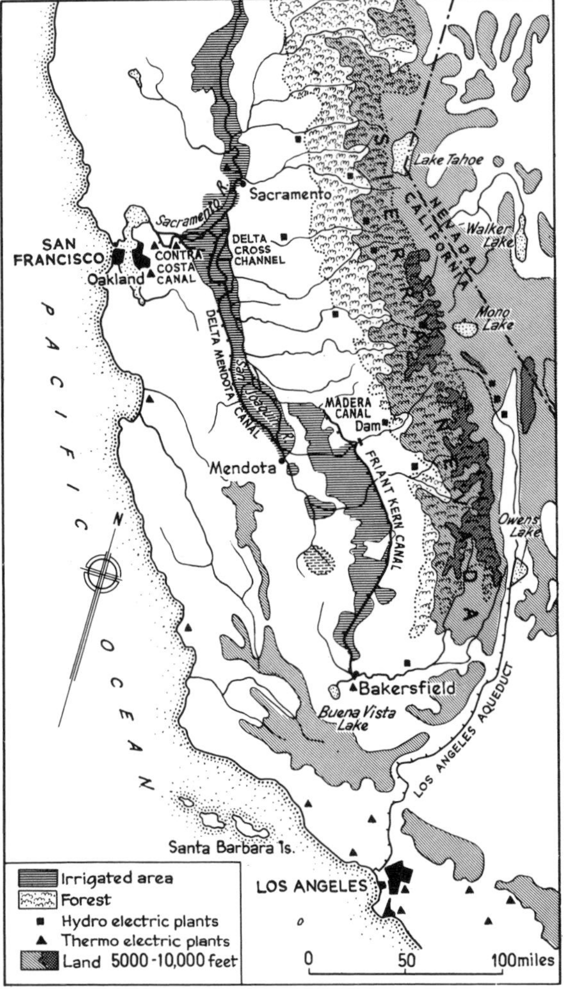

FIG. 17:3 The Great Valley of California.

while a few sluices process mine tailings. Deep mining of the primary lodes at Keystone, Lone Star, Argonaut, and elsewhere is also depressed. But the gold-rushes established San Francisco, whose middlemen and swindlers took into their hands much of the riches won from the minefields.

Ever since then, California has proved strongly attractive to migrants, and above all to internal migrants. Ten million people moved in between the mid-nineteenth and the mid-twentieth century. In one form or another, it has consistently appeared as the land of opportunity. In some ways it has proved to be just this, with scope for prosperity in commercial farming, oil and gas mining, the movie industry, and in manufacturing. Its social structure and social demands are noticeably less rigid than those of the east, while the frequently sunny and normally genial climate of most inhabited areas favours outdoor living.

Tourist attractions are numerous. The Sierra Nevada, for instance, contains the Lassen Volcanic National Park, Sequoia National Park in which lies Mount Whitney, and the spectacular glaciated scenery of Yosemite National Park; Yosemite alone is visited by two million people a year. But nowadays the greatest attraction of all is probably that of sea and sun combined. The central Californian coast is handicapped in this respect by the cold, southward-moving Californian Current close inshore, which keeps the waters chill until late in the year, and which promotes the fogs sucked in through the Golden Gate; but the beaches of southern California, with warmer waters, draw people powerfully to them. Since about 1960, large caravan parks have arisen, partly to serve the needs of motoring tourists, and partly to act as more or less permanent residential districts: the large modern trailer, luxuriously equipped, and possessing TV and up-to-date plumbing, is increasingly prominent in the lives of foot-loose workers and of the retired.

Agriculture is highly productive: the Great Valley of California (Fig. 17:3) is possibly the most intensively farmed region in the world, with a value of farm output greater than that of the corn-based farmland of the Midwest. Drained by the Sacramento River in the north and the San Joaquin in the south, deeply filled by sediment brought down from the bordering mountains, bordered by chains of alluvial fans, and endowed with a sunny summer-dry climate, the Valley is excellently adapted to the cultivation of a whole range of fruit crops – adapted, that is to say, in all respects but that of water-supply.

Grapes are probably the most widely known and also, in one form or another, the most widely sold of the Californian fruits. Fruit-drying establishments, concentrated to some extent in the San Joaquin Valley around Fresno, use the powerful sun to convert grapes into raisins, sultanas, and currants. All growers belong to the non-profit Sun-Maid Raisin Organization, which receives, records, grades, and packs the crops of individual growers and is responsible for advertising and marketing: members share in the total income on the basis of their annual deliveries. About a quarter of the State's grape crop goes for drying, but the continued increase in output has threatened to outrun market demand; accordingly, emphasis is shifting somewhat to the growing of grapes for wine-making. Wineries have in any event been operating in California for many years, being most successful in the making of white wines. Processes in the wine industry are large-scale and mechanized, so that the Californian wineries make no attempt to identify vintages such as characterize French wines: on the other hand, their products, simply because they are standardized, are of fixed quality. Conversion from grape-growing for the dried fruit industry to growing for wineries or for the table grape market means a change of variety of stock. The Thompson's Seedless, very popular among the fruit-growers, is far less suitable for the wine industry than are the Alicante Bouschet and the Grenache, while table grapes come largely from the Almeria, Ribier, and Cardinale varieties. If a vineyard is replanted at a single time, it will cease to be a source of income until the new wines reach maturity. That is to say, grape-growing carries with it a risk of disrupted returns.

Similar risks attend the growing of figs and of stone fruit – peaches, apricots, and nectarines. The decline of that part of fruit-drying which uses these, in favour first of canning and then of quick freezing, has led to a substitution of varieties. The Muir and Lovell peaches have been displaced by the Elberta, while the Colimyrna drying-fig has given way to the green Kadota which is canned in syrup.

Other tree crops of the Great Valley include the olive, which has proved highly successful with the aid of careful selection of strains, and of the carefully-controlled application of irrigation water to what is normally a dry-climate crop. Vegetables for canning and for direct supply to urban markets, with tomatoes prominent among them, are also raised in the Valley; and southern districts are so mild and sunny that they can profit by cool-season cropping of grain, potatoes, and salad vegetables. Similarly, 'spring' lamb fattened either on winter-grown alfalfa or on the saltings of the Sacramento can be delivered to northern and eastern markets in the middle of their coldest season.

The principal field crop is cotton, mainly of the Acala variety. Cotton-growing is confined to patches of irrigated land in the extreme south of the State, and to the San Joaquin Valley where it is most extensive. It would be more widespread than it actually is, were it not for government controls on planting. As matters stand, California produces about one-eighth of the total U.S. crop; its cotton farms are typified by large sizes, an advanced state of mechanization, a low incidence of pest attacks, and high yields – well over twice the national average, and almost exactly twice as high as the yields of the Southeast.

Rice-growing is equally highly mechanized, but also subject to limitations on acreage. It is located in the lower valleys and delta lands of the Sacramento–San Joaquin system, where subsoils are impervious. It risks seasonal inflow of subsurface water from the saline Bay, but drainage works and sea-gates which close on the rising tide have offset the risk and extended the potential extent of the ricefields. Rice is seeded from the air; cultivation and weeding rely on the marsh-buggy with its huge buoyant tires; and harvesting is entirely mechanical.

The Sacramento Valley, cooler and moister than

78. Feedlot farming in the Great Valley of California: forty thousand cattle can be fed simultaneously on 600 acres. Trucks deliver feed to the concrete troughs at the edges of the corrals.

the valley of the San Joaquin – up to 40 inches of rain a year, as opposed to as little as six – is in part given over to dairying, stock-fattening, poultry farming, and the growing of wheat and sugar beet (Plate 78).

Citrus fruit – oranges, lemons, grapefruit, and limes – accounts for about 40 per cent of the value of cultivated crops in California. Its growing is concentrated in the south of the State, on the gritty soils of mountain-foot alluvial fans where cold-air drainage guarantees the absence of frost. Citrus fruits have at times been described as Mediterranean crops. However, although they enter strongly into Mediterranean agriculture, they are natives of the Cfa climate and make heavy demands of water – the equivalent of 30 inches of rainfall a year. Thus the dryness entailed by the very sunny climate of southern California needs to be offset by copious irrigation; and the water employed must have a low alkaline content. Furthermore, the groves need to be sheltered from the hot drying winds draining from cT air-masses generated over the desert. Suitable land for citrus production, which has not already been taken up, is distinctly scarce, and the price of established groves runs high. However, the departure from this form of cultivation of marginal operators has allowed in either real-estate developers, or wealthy retirees for whom a place in the Californian sun, surrounded by however unprofitable an orange-grove, seems idyllic.

Water quality is less of a problem than water quantity. Some 5 million acres – nearly 60 per cent of the Great Valley – are under irrigation. The San Joaquin Valley takes part of the waters of the Sacramento, drawing on the reservoirs impounded by the Shasta and Red Bluff Dams. Artesian water, sub-artesian water, and groundwater generally are heavily exploited throughout the Valley – so heavily that water-tables have seriously fallen in some districts, and that salt-water is invading the aquifers of the infilled coastal valleys. Streams from the Sierra Nevada are copiously tapped; and Los Angeles, going two hundred miles for its water to the Owens River, is on the lookout for additional supplies. Demand for water is overtaking prospective, and indeed conceivable, provision, faster in California than in any other part of the continent. Meantime, serious doubts are arising on the economics of irrigation. In some areas the capital cost of reservoirs and reticulation systems is as high as $10,000 per irrigated acre, involving an annual capital charge of $500 at 5 per cent interest. An individual farmer, with his per-acre income controlled essentially by prices, can only repay as water rates a fraction of the cost incurred. In effect, therefore, irrigation farming must be subsidized by the general taxpayer.

Californian forests, in the Coast Ranges north of the Golden Gate, include stands of the giant redwoods (*Sequoia sempervirens* and *S. gigantea*), which attain great height and bulk during lives up to 3000 years in length. Douglas fir also grows on the northern Coast Ranges, while rain-shadowed slopes in the Sierra Nevada support sugar pine, Ponderosa pine, and white fir. Lumbering has signally reduced the extent of forest cover along all its lower fringes; and the more accessible of the surviving forests are widely used for the grazing of livestock.

Metallic ore-mining in the region is negligible at the present day; minerals other than fuels consist principally of gravel, limestone, clay, and sand for highway building and the construction industry. The mineral fuels are gas from the Great Valley, and oil from fields in the extreme south of the Great Valley around Bakersfield, on the coast at San Luis Obispo Bay, and in the Los Angeles Basin. Pipelines bring in gas from Canada, and gas and oil from Texas and New Mexico. There is a regional oil-refining industry, located mainly in Los Angeles, San Francisco, and Bakersfield. The Californian oilfields have probably in the past suffered more than most from highly competitive extraction, unregulated spacing of wells, and ineffectual pumping programmes; and, in the Los Angeles Basin, housing development forestalled the oilmen in some parts.

California conducts a vigorous fishing industry, which, by contrast with that of the north Pacific coastland, is strongly centralized. The fishing port of San Pedro, part of the Los Angeles–Long Beach complex, alone takes a 20 per cent share by value of all Pacific landings in Canada and the U.S. together, and a 10 per cent share in the U.S. national catch; with San Diego, it dominates the fisheries of tuna, mackerel, and Pacific sardines. Tuna are caught mainly in the ocean waters off

California, but some of the vessels range as far out as Hawaii and American Samoa.

The original climatic and scenic advantages of the film industry were mentioned at the beginning of the chapter. Although these now have but limited relevance, there is no good reason for the industry to relocate, even though more than half the annual footage produced is short films for television companies. Climate also benefits aircraft manufacture in Los Angeles and San Diego, the dryness permitting much outdoor work and storage; and testing is rarely held up by adverse weather. Nevertheless, it would be wrong to underrate the influence of the original Douglas, who opened his first small aircraft factory in Los Angeles in 1923. The city today is the leading producer of aircraft in the whole country, with about one-fifth of all workers in the aircraft industry.

Distilling at San Francisco, the manufacture of tin cans at both San Francisco and Los Angeles, and the canneries scattered through the fruit and vegetable districts, have obvious agricultural bases. The iron and steel industry of California was deliberately fostered by the federal government during World War II, as a safety or insurance measure. San Francisco, Pittsburg near by, and Los Angeles all have steelworks, but the largest group is at Fontana, east of Los Angeles, where the integrated Kaiser plant comprises blast furnaces, open-hearth steel furnaces, and rolling mills. Smelting here has the disadvantage of long hauls for its ore – 164 miles from Eagle Mountain, Utah – and for its coal, some of which comes for more than 800 miles from Oklahoma. The steel goes to industrial consumers in the San Francisco Bay area, in the Los Angeles Basin, and in San Diego; this last has a shipbuilding industry, also greatly stimulated during World War II.

A contrasted and distinctly market-oriented industry is car assembly: in this, Los Angeles ranks second only to Detroit. Its regional market is vast and expansive, much of it located in the Los Angeles Basin itself. Not all effects of prosperity and industrial expansion are good, however: through its liberal use of cars, Los Angeles has significantly changed its climate for the worse by the generation of smog.

Bakersfield, Fresno, Stockton, and Sacramento are the chief central places of the Great Valley, just as San Jose is the local focus for the Coyote Valley draining into San Francisco Bay: some of the industrial and service interests of this group have already been observed. Santa Barbara is a service

79. The Bay Bridge, with Oakland at the far end. Yerba Buena Island anchors the mid-portion of the $8\frac{1}{2}$-mile total span.

80. Another aspect of San Francisco's transport links: the International Airport.

town and centre of commercial fishing seventy-five miles distant from Los Angeles. The San Bernardino–Riverside–Ontario complex has a combined population fast approaching the million mark set by San Diego. A further rapidly-growing urban area near the coast includes Santa Ana; its focus, Anaheim, is one of California's oldest towns. All these, however, are hugely surpassed by the San Francisco and Los Angeles agglomerations. Thanks to the Bay Bridges, San Francisco is physically continuous with Oakland, Berkeley, Richmond, and Alameda on the eastern side of the Bay, while also merging southward along its own shoreline with San Mateo (Plates 79, 80). Los Angeles, in addition to merging with Long Beach, has overrun San Fernando, Glendale, Pasadena, Alhambra, Monrovia, Santa Monica, Inglewood, and Redondo Beach, while Long Beach has fused with San Pedro.

As late as 1880, Los Angeles had not many more than 10,000 people; and as late as 1900, its population was little over 100,000 (Fig. 17:4). Twenty years later it was over the half-million mark and had outstripped San Francisco. Today, with some eight million people, the agglomeration is one of the world's largest. It contains two-fifths of the inhabitants of California, and 1 in 30 of all town-dwellers in the U.S.A.

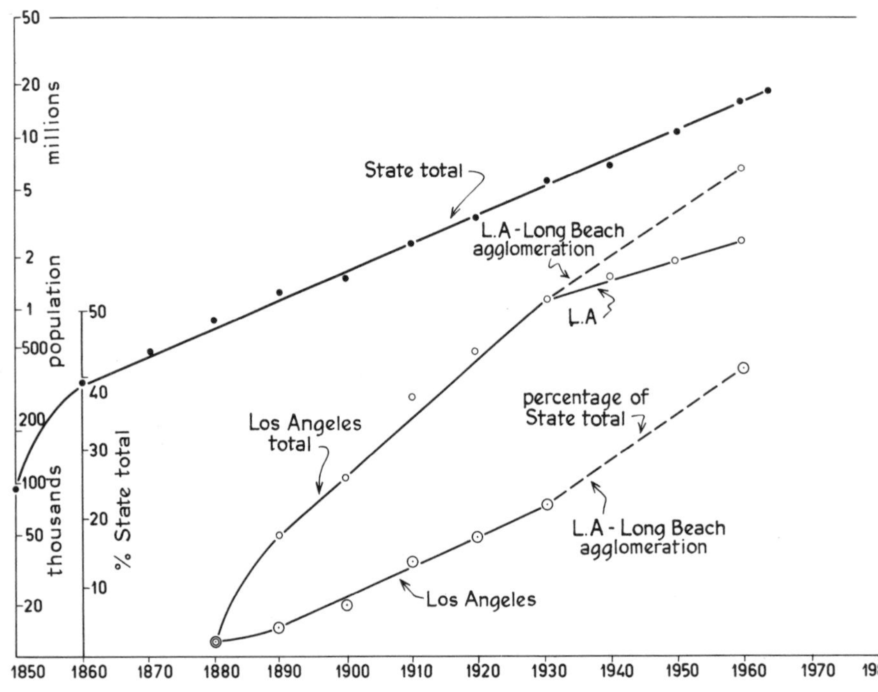

FIG. 17:4 Population trends in California and Los Angeles.

CHAPTER EIGHTEEN

THE CANADIAN NORTHLAND

In this division, fewer than half a million people are located in some two and a half million square miles of country (Fig. 18:1). The average population density of one to every eight square miles has very little meaning, vast areas being uninhabited. In few parts of the world of comparable size is it harder for men to earn a living. Economic activities are very limited in range, taking the form of primary production – trapping, fishing, forestry, and mining. These last two are markedly dominant in terms of wealth produced. There is some subsistence and semi-commercial agriculture, fur-farming, and

Fig. 18:1
The Canadian Northland.

woodlot management, but opportunities are severely limited by demand, accessibility, and above all by climate.

The Northland division contains most of the Shield, some parts of which have, however, already been dealt with under the heads of the Western Lakes and the lower St Lawrence. We are concerned here not with the extreme borders but with the inner and northern portions, where average January temperatures approach zero Fahrenheit, or fall below this mark, and where the boreal forests degenerate rapidly northwards towards the tundra. The southern boundary drawn for the Eastern Uplands and the Lakes Plain regions coincides fairly closely to the northern limit of commercial farming. In the west, the Northland division takes in much of the Mackenzie Valley. In the farthest north, it includes the Arctic Archipelago.

The Shield is one of the world's great rafts of Precambrian crust, repeatedly planated during a history of landform evolution extending through hundreds of millions of years. Its periphery is studded with enormous lakes – Huron, Erie, Winnipeg, Athabaska, Great Slave, and Great Bear. Countless other water-bodies are scattered across the Shield, for the generally subdued surface has been roughened in detail by sheet glaciation: this was the source of the glacial tills deposited on the interior plains to the south and southeast. Drainage is complex, dense, and disorganized. Very little of the Shield rises above 1500 feet, except in Quebec–Labrador where the limiting height is however still not much over 5000 feet. Rocks younger than Precambrian lap gently on to the Shield along the southern shores of Hudson's Bay, but crustal depression here ensures that they rise little above sea-level. The islands of the Arctic Archipelago, also composed of rocks younger than those of the Shield, are also in the main subdued, even though numbers of them rise abruptly from the sea: the chief highlands of the archipelago are those of the far northeast, where parts of Baffin Island and Ellesmere Islands, rising above 3000 feet, carry plateau glaciers.

18a: The Eastern Uplands

Area: about 500,000 square miles.

Population: of the order of $\frac{1}{4}$ million (estimated).

There are no large cities. The most populous settlements are:

Timmins, Ont., 29,000
Rouyn, Que., 18,700
Noranda, Que., 11,500
Val d'Or, Que., 11,000
Roberval, Que., 7750
Amos, Que., 6000
Dolbeau, Que., 6000
Chibougamau, Que., 4750
Cochrane, Ont., 4500

This region is essentially beyond the limits of farming. About $1\frac{1}{2}$ per cent of its area can be classed as agricultural, and more than half of this is grassland or woodland pasture. Open-range pasture takes about half as much again. The natural vegetation cover is mainly needleleaf boreal forest; nearly a quarter of a million square miles of this, covering about 40 per cent of the region, are classed as commercial, although not the whole extent is commercially exploited.

The last of the continental ice-sheets were still extensive enough, only 10,000 years ago, to cover the whole of this region to depths as great as two miles. Accordingly, the landforms of sheet glaciation here are very fresh. Large expanses of the bedrock surface lie completely bare of waste-mantle; others are thinly littered with the generally coarse deposits of recessional moraines. Outwash channels are complex, numerous, and debris-choked. The detailed irregularity of the surface is increased by the effects of glacial plucking and scouring, and of subglacial channelling by melt-water near the decaying ice-front. Surface drainage, entirely deranged by ice-erosion and glacial deposition, is still further complicated by post-glacial isostatic recovery from the ice-load. Enclosed basins, many lake-filled, are abundant in the extreme. Flat ground is limited to the clayey floors of former lakes from which the water has escaped, or to muskeg (peat swamp) where this has succeeded in filling some hollow completely.

On the Labrador coastland, the ice worked on higher ground than elsewhere; pouring out to sea through gaps, it converted the coastal valleys into deep trenches of which post-glacial drowning has made fiords. Where mountains of gneiss, granite, and gabbro protruded through the ice-sheet, they were sculptured and fretted into the horns, arêtes, and cirques of alpine glaciation. Dotted along this coast, typically at fiord mouths, are trading settlements, successors to the factories (trading-posts) of the Hudson Bay Company. Goose Bay, nearly two hundred miles from the open sea at the head of Hamilton Inlet, was for a brief interval a busy staging-post on the transatlantic air routes, similar in this respect to Gander in Newfoundland but superior to Gander in its low incidence of fog. Increases in the flying range of large passenger aircraft have abolished the need for staging-posts on many long-distance routes: one-hop flights between London and New York, or London and

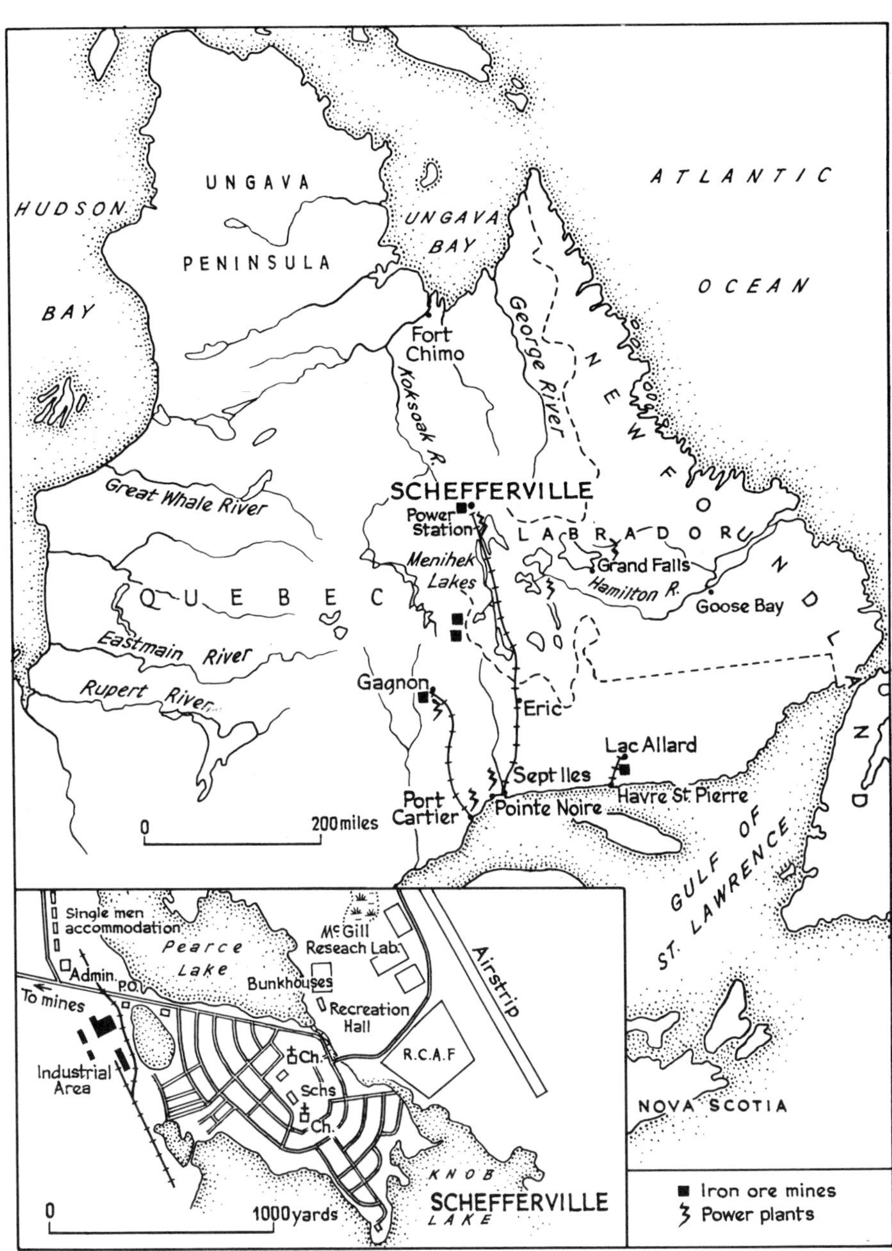

FIG. 18:2
Ironfields of Labrador–Ungava.

Washington, D.C., are for example now the rule. Goose Bay continues in use as an emergency field and as a military base.

West of the mountains, running from Ungava Bay to the headwaters of the Hamilton River, lies the 370-mile long Labrador Trough, wherein surface drainage has developed a partly trellised pattern under the control of the imbricated structures of a shatter-belt. Sedimentary formations outcropping on the valley-sides contain thick beds of iron ore, similar to those of the Gelliväre fields in Sweden. For more than half a century after their discovery, remoteness kept these deposits from being exploited. During World War II, however, it became clear that the Superior iron-fields of the U.S.A. would no longer be able to sustain almost the whole of the nation's steel industry, as they had been doing for so long; and the Quebec–Labrador fields were accordingly opened up. Prospecting parties of the Hollinger Consolidated Gold Mines Organization of Montreal located economic ore-bodies at Ruth Lake, Burnt Creek, and Sawyer Lake. Six major steel companies, and the iron-ore supplying Hannah corporation of Cleveland entered into partnership with Hollinger, forming the Iron Ore Company of Canada, one of the continent's greatest resource development organizations to be controlled by private capital. Construction of 357 miles of railway from Schefferville to Sept-Îles permitted the first ore to be shipped out in 1954. A branch line some thirty miles in length takes off at about 200 miles north of Sept-Îles to Labrador City on Wabush Lake, where another group of orefields has been opened up. Output of ore from the Quebec–Labrador Trough is more than 30 million tons a year, representing 80 per cent of Canadian production. A third group of ironfields occurs in the Gagnon district, which is linked by 193 miles of railway to Port Cartier (Fig. 18:2). Extraction is everywhere very highly mechanized: in consequence, populations of the mining town remain small – Schefferville, for instance, records a summer population of some 3000, while the corresponding figure for Labrador City is, as yet, only about half as great.

Metallic minerals other than iron are worked in a number of districts in the west-centre and west of the region. Ores for the most part are mixed. Thus, the Chibougamau district yields auriferous copper ores; the copper ores of Noranda and Rouyn contain gold, lead, zinc, and silver. Haileybury and Cobalt extract cobalt ores with a useful silver content; however, their long history of ore-mining, which began with the discovery of the reserves in 1904, is now approaching its end, except for brief reprieves promoted by U.S. stockpiling policies. Most of the workable ore has gone, and part of the current output relies on the reworking of mine tailings. The two towns have a combined population of about 5000; they are not expanding. Gold is the leading mineral of the Porcupine–Timmins–Kirkland Lake district, although ironfields near Kirkland Lake are now also being exploited.

Summary data for Quebec, Ontario, and Manitoba readily illustrate the significance of the Shield in the mining economy of Canada; in addition, they come fairly close to indicating the joint significance in mining of the Eastern Uplands and the Lakes Plain, except that the Sudbury district belongs in the Western Lakes region. The three Provinces in combination produce 75 per cent by value of all metallic minerals in Canada; their own metallics are worth 40 per cent of all Canadian mineral production. Copper, nickel, and iron from these three Provinces account for about half their total value of metallic mineral output, and for about a quarter of the corresponding national total.

The populations listed for the largest settlements in the region demonstrate that mining activity fails to promote the growth of large cities. Correspondingly, markets for farm produce are very restricted, quite apart from the fact that the region is generally too limited by climate for farming to develop on any perceptible scale. Cultivation, where it occurs, is practised in frontier conditions. Its growing season is limited to three or four months. On the other hand, the summer temperatures of 68° F or more are screen temperatures, which greatly understate the temperatures in which plants actually grow, near the ground and on favoured sites. Green vegetables, some hardy grains, and root crops can be raised. Sustenance crops are cultivated locally in sheltered valleys, to support mining, forestry, and railway communities. Farm animals are few, and kept principally by individual householders. Stall feeding is usual; the long summer days promote a reasonably good growth of wild hay grasses in forest clearings, the year-round supply of moisture is adequate, and the spring flush of grasses is rapid. At one time the farming prospects of the Clay Belt around Cochrane were optimistically regarded. Here, an extensive patch of drained lake-floor is available for clearing and settlement. However, much of the land that was taken up was made to yield nothing more than the first crop of felled timber, and has reverted to second-growth forest.

Commercial transport linkages are few. Moosonee on James Bay is connected by rail to Cochrane, which in turn has lines running west towards Winnipeg, south to Toronto, and east to Quebec. The orefields on the two sides of the Ontario–Quebec border have developed something of a rail network, while a loop to the north of the Quebec line penetrates the Chibougamau district. Lumbering companies have opened numerous routes of their own – wherever possible, water routes – to allow timber to move southward: the southern boreal forests, unlike the inner taiga, yield excellent woods. A belt some 150 miles wide, bordering the St Lawrence, supplies balsam fir, black spruce, and other quick-growing conifers to the pulping industry of the St Lawrence Lowlands.

18b: The Canadian Lakes Plains

Area: about 300,000 square miles.
Population: of the order of 100,000 (estimated).
Largest settlements:

Flin–Flon, Sask.–Man., 11,000
The Pas, Man., 4750
Thompson, Man., 2250
McMurray, Alta., 1200

Other settlements in this region are below 1000 in population.

This region is essentially beyond the limits of commercial farming. Perhaps 1 per cent of its extent could be classed as agricultural, and about half of this is grassland or woodland pasture. Open-range pasture takes about as much again. Natural vegetation cover ranges from needleleaf boreal forest in the south, through park-tundra, to tundra in the north. Something of the order of half the total area is classed as commercial forest, but exploitation is as yet restricted.

Much of what is said about the physical landscape on the Eastern Uplands could be repeated for the Lakes Plain, except that relief in the latter region is still more subdued than in the former, and that the drainage net is still more extensive, and more highly complicated, in consequence of ice-action.

The regional economy is dominated by fur-trapping, which is widespread throughout, and by mining, which is highly localized. Communication depends heavily on gravel tracks laid across the muskeg and the barrens, on canoes during the summer, and on the aircraft which serve the remote trading and mining settlements. These last are frequently little more than seasonal camps. Radio networks substitute for the mailman. In contrast to the situation in the U.S.S.R., Canada's Arctic drainage is of little use in transport, being heavily encumbered with glacial deposits in the channels. There is a railway linking Regina to Churchill on Hudson Bay, by way of The Pas on the regional boundary; but former hopes that Churchill might become a main seasonal outlet for Prairie wheat had not been fully realized, even before the opening of the St Lawrence Seaway. A chief function of the line today is to tap minefields, such as those of Thompson, where nickel ore is smelted: power for the Thompson plant comes from the hydro-electric station at Grand Rapids on the Nelson River. Built since 1957, Thompson illustrates the rapid type of local development which characterizes non-ferrous metal mining (Plate 81). Similarly, the town of Lynn Lake was established in 1954 to work nickel, copper, and

81. Thompson, Manitoba, 400 miles from Winnipeg amid the boreal forest: nickel smelter in the middle distance.

cobalt ores; in the first stages of construction at Lynn Lake, houses were brought in from the ghost mining town of Sherridon. Lynn Lake is connected by rail with the Churchill–Regina line at The Pas; and the Lynn Lake–The Pas line sends out branches to the orefields of Flin Flon, where copper, zinc, silver, cadmium, and selenium are worked, with gold obtained partly as a by-product, and eastward to the more recently developed zinc-mining district of Snow Lake. McMurray on the Athabaska River has a rail link with Edmonton.

Mining potential is undoubtedly great: much however depends on facilities of access and transport. The eastern half of the region is largely unpenetrated by practicable routes; its mining activity is as yet concerned mainly with gold at small settlements such as Long Lac, Red Lake, and Pickle Crow, all close to the southern boundary.

18c: The Far Northern Mainland of Canada

Area: about 1,250,000 square miles

Population: about 25,000, of whom two-thirds are Indians or Eskimos.

This region is outside the limits of farming: land classed as agricultural, in the broadest sense, amounts only to 150 square miles. The natural vegetation cover is mainly tundra or park-tundra: 2 per cent of the region is classed as commercial forest, but exploitation is negligible.

In Northwestern Quebec, and from Hudson's Bay to the Great Bear and Great Slave Lakes, this region takes in portions of the Shield. In the Mackenzie Basin it is allied structurally to the Great Plains. However, given the generally subdued topography and the ubiquitous evidence and relics of sheet glaciation, climate is more effective than anything else in determining the physical characteristics of the landscape. Most of the region, with mean sea-level temperatures below 60° F in July and under 20° F below zero in winter, is too cold for continuous forest. Except where rail and road penetrate the Mackenzie catchment, routes are non-existent, and settlement is equally absent apart from the mining communities of the southwest and the trading-stations and seasonal Eskimo bases on the coast. Patches of boreal forest exist, especially in western parts around the big lakes and along the Mackenzie Valley: but they are far too remote from markets to offer any prospects of economic exploitation. Farming on the perennially-frozen ground, where only a few inches of topsoil melt during the warmer season, is impossible.

The historic support of this region is the fur trade. Ever since the seventeenth century, when the Hudson's Bay Company was first chartered, the fur resources of Canada have been strongly drawn on. Wild white and red fox, beaver, lynx, marten, mink, muskrat, and ermine all maintain strongholds – for some, the last safe strongholds – in the Far North. But even the fur trade is handicapped by remoteness: this region produces only about 5 per cent by value of the wild furs taken in Canada.

The effects on this region of remoteness and distance are clearly shown in the history of oil production in the Mackenzie Basin. Discovered at Norman Wells as early as 1920, the oil reserves remained very little exploited until World War II, when a pipeline was constructed to the Alaska Highway at Whitehorse. Working has persisted subsequently; the Norman Wells refinery, processing an annual output of crude exceeding half a million barrels, supplies about half the petroleum consumed in the Northwest Territories.

Radium-rich silver ores discovered in 1930 at Echo Bay on Great Bear Lake helped Canada to become the world's leading radium producer, although the workings, and the exporter of Port Radium, now lie abandoned. Uranium City on Lake Athabaska mines silver ores rich in uranium, cobalt, and radium; but its production costs are high, while market demand for radioactive metals fluctuates greatly. Yellowknife (3250 inhabitants) on the Great Slave Lake has been a gold producer since 1938. In this same general section of the western Shield, ores of nickel, copper, lead, and zinc have also been proved, although not yet completely assessed; cobalt, tungsten, uranium, beryllium, and a number of rarer metals are also present. Both in its current activity and in it future prospects, mining is controlled by the possibilities of transport. The Mackenzie River system provides a 1700-mile route from its mouth at Inuvik–Aklavik to the Athabaska and Slave Rivers; an additional 800 miles of summer navigation is available on Lake Athabaska, Great Slave Lake, and Great Bear Lake. A railway was completed in the 1960s, from Roma, in Alberta, to Hay River, 430 miles away near the lead–zinc orefields of Pine Point, while major all-weather roads connect Yellowknife and Fort Smith with the Mackenzie Highway; the latter, taking off from the Alberta net in the upper Peace River Basin, reaches Norman Wells. These land routes can scarcely fail to extend the possibilities of economic mining far beyond those offered by air transport. Nickel ores are known to be present in a belt stretching from Ungava Bay to Hudson's Bay, but their prospects of exploitation seem at present remote: indeed, this whole part of the region can be classed as unused.

Eskimo settlements, occurring on the north coast, are few and small, even in comparison with the size of the Eskimo population. Unlike the North American Indians, the Eskimo do not live in a tribal society. Instead, they hunt and fish in bands composed of two or three families: home territories, defined by custom, are rarely infringed. The traditional Eskimo economy is semi-nomadic; dwellings in the high-sun season are sealskin tents, those in the winter are igloos or sod huts. Winter hunting journeys depend on the dog-sledge, those of summer on sealskin kayaks or larger family canoes. Introduction of the rifle has made seal-hunting far easier than with harpoon or spear, but has also induced a risk of over-exploitation. More recently, whalers and power boats have also been coming into use. However, the ability of this region to generate money capital is as yet small.

So much has been written of the very close and highly specialized adaptation of Eskimos to their environment, that it is easy to forget that the conditions described are those existing at the time of contact with whites. In a tragically familiar way, this contact produced some very bad effects, allowing alcoholism to lay grip on some Eskimo groups, and exposing all these natives of the wastes to virus, respiratory, and pulmonary infections against which they had no immunity whatever. Influenza epidemics among the Eskimo are characteristically savage; tuberculosis was seriously widespread for years, although the government's eradication programme is now succeeding handsomely. More serious still was the reduction of sections of the Eskimo population to a state of semi-dependence on government support. The 14,000 or so Eskimos of Canada are however Canadian citizens, receiving all the benefits of the nation's social welfare schemes, including those specially designed to strengthen Eskimo family and community life. Schools are provided for about 90 per cent of the school-age section; they can lead on to higher education. There are also vocational training classes, and an apprentice training programme which began in 1964. A housing programme dating from 1959 promotes permanent settlement.

An undertaking which has enjoyed much success is the introduced herding of caribou (reindeer). In summer, the sedge-covered Mackenzie Delta (Plate 4) becomes the principal grazing area, while the herds return during the winter to upland areas where they dig out reindeer moss from under the snow. Small reindeer herds, controlled by groups of Eskimos rather than by the government, have increased in number; and in many places, such as in the Horton and Anderson Valleys, native communities have fully integrated herding into their economy. Use of the animal for food and hides has tended to offset the fluctuations in yields from hunting and from furs, especially since the caribou is not subject to the cyclic changes of numbers which affect wild-animal populations. The arctic fox, for example, undergoes a marked short-term change in abundance; and market demands in times of scarcity can promote a rate of killing sufficient to reduce stocks below the recovery level.

18d: The Arctic Archipelago

Area: about 550,000 square miles.

Population: estimated at 6000, mostly Eskimos or Indians.

All the settlements indicated on Fig. 18:1 are seasonal, except for Lake Harbour on Baffin Land. There is no farmland or commercial forest. Outside the permanent icefields and snowfields, the vegetation cover is tundra.

Most of this region is uninhabited: considerable parts have not been explored. All but a portion in the southeast lies north of the Arctic Circle, with permanent polar ice closely adjacent to the coastlines of the northwest. Ellesmere, Axel Heiberg, Melville, Bathurst, and Devon Islands are the largest of the Queen Elizabeth group, almost the whole of it north of 75° latitude. Between the Queen Elizabeth Islands and the mainland is another island group, known collectively as the Franklin District; it comprises Banks and Victoria Islands, numerous lesser islands, and Baffin Land. The following comments apply also to the Melville Peninsula and Southampton Island, at the north-west entrance to Hudson's Bay. Settlements are those of the Eskimo, who depend on the water for their subsistence – the land has very little to offer. Seals are the mainstay, supplemented by arctic char from the sea, and by ciscoes (lake herring) from brackish water. In late summer and autumn, fishing brings people together at the river-mouths of Baffin Island and Frobisher Bay. Occasional catches of white whales are greatly welcomed.

Eskimo co-operatives hold out much promise. Some twenty in all, either in the Archipelago or on the north mainland coast, engage in commercial fishing and in traditional art and craftwork; the West Baffin Eskimo Co-operative has made Cape Dorset a noted centre of art production, while soapstone carvings are sold from a number of bases.

The seasonal settlements are Indian or Eskimo encampments. Some include Royal Canadian Mounted Police patrol posts; the R.C.M.P. officers discharge a complex range of duties, including collection of census data, registration procedures, and local magistracy. Lake Harbour is a permanent R.C.M.P. base.

Permanent settlement of a special kind, although not one involving permanent inhabitants, concerns continental defence and the continuous manning of strategic airfields and of early-warning stations against ballistic missiles. Defence activities, mining, commercial fishing, and art and craftwork for export are bringing the Eskimo groups within the twentieth-century cash economy; and numbers of them nowadays work in the south of Canada.

Although the mineral potential of the Arctic Archipelago remains to be assessed, it seems probable on general grounds that reserves of various kinds will be found to exist – coal, of dubious economic significance in such a geographical setting; iron ore, which could well prove worth exploiting; and oil, for which prospecting is vigorously under way.

CHAPTER NINETEEN

OFFSHORE AMERICA

The various island groups to be dealt with in this chapter are the Hawaiian Islands – since 1959 the 50th State of the American Union – plus the U.S. possessions and dependencies in the Caribbean and the Pacific (Figs. 19:1, 19:2). For the sake of completeness, the Panama Canal Zone will also be mentioned. Although only some 10,000 square miles of land area are involved, with a total population of about three million, some of the larger islands are economically significant in respect of their production of tropical crops, while military bases throughout the whole scatter demonstrate a very high strategic value.

To mention strategy is to introduce the theme of power politics: emotional overtones at once begin to sound, and the words colonialism and imperialism – which nowadays are dirty words – begin to offer themselves for use. This, however, is not the intention here: facts alone are at issue. It is true that the U.S.A. succeeded to parts of the Spanish colonial empire in the Pacific and the Caribbean; but it is also true that Britain, France, Japan, New Zealand, and Australia still have interests, authority, and responsibilities in parts of the Pacific, and that the Netherlands and Germany formerly had. The corresponding list for the West Indies includes Britain, France, and the Netherlands, and formerly included Denmark.

It seems important to distinguish between attitudes to occupation of the mainland on the one side, and those to the taking-over of islands on the other. Many leading U.S. politicians of the first half of the nineteenth century were fond of proclaiming the Union's manifest destiny to take in all the land from the Atlantic coast to the Pacific. Some of the proposals for settling the Canadian and Mexican boundaries were admittedly bellicose; but the Canadian boundary was fixed by negotiation, while the Mexican War, itself by no means welcomed throughout the nation, was followed

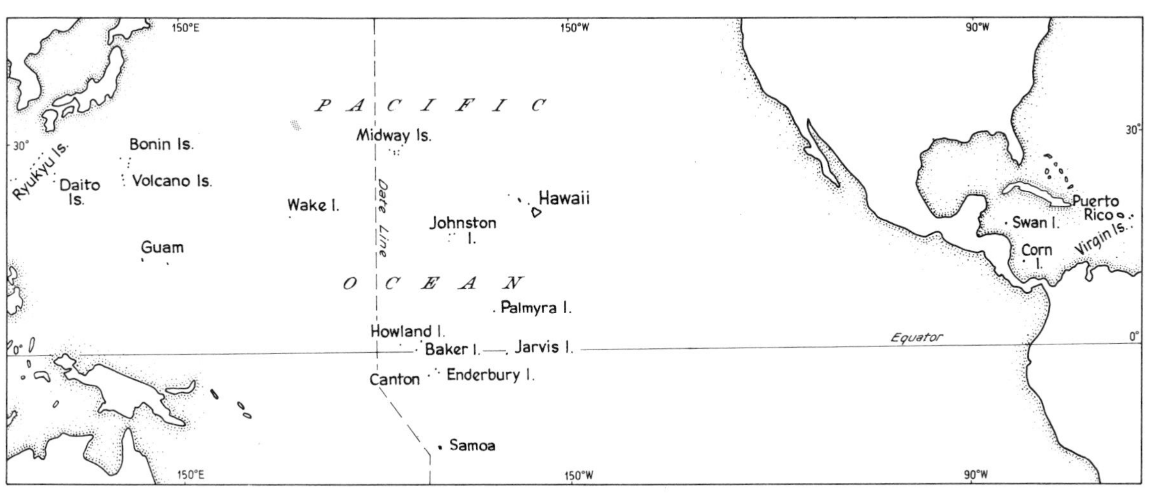

FIG. 19:1 Offshore America.

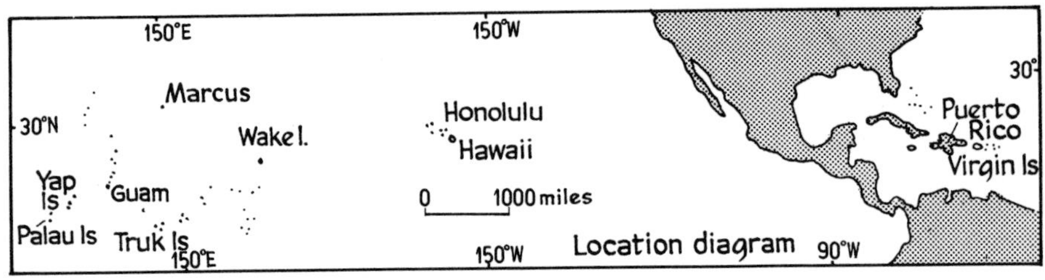

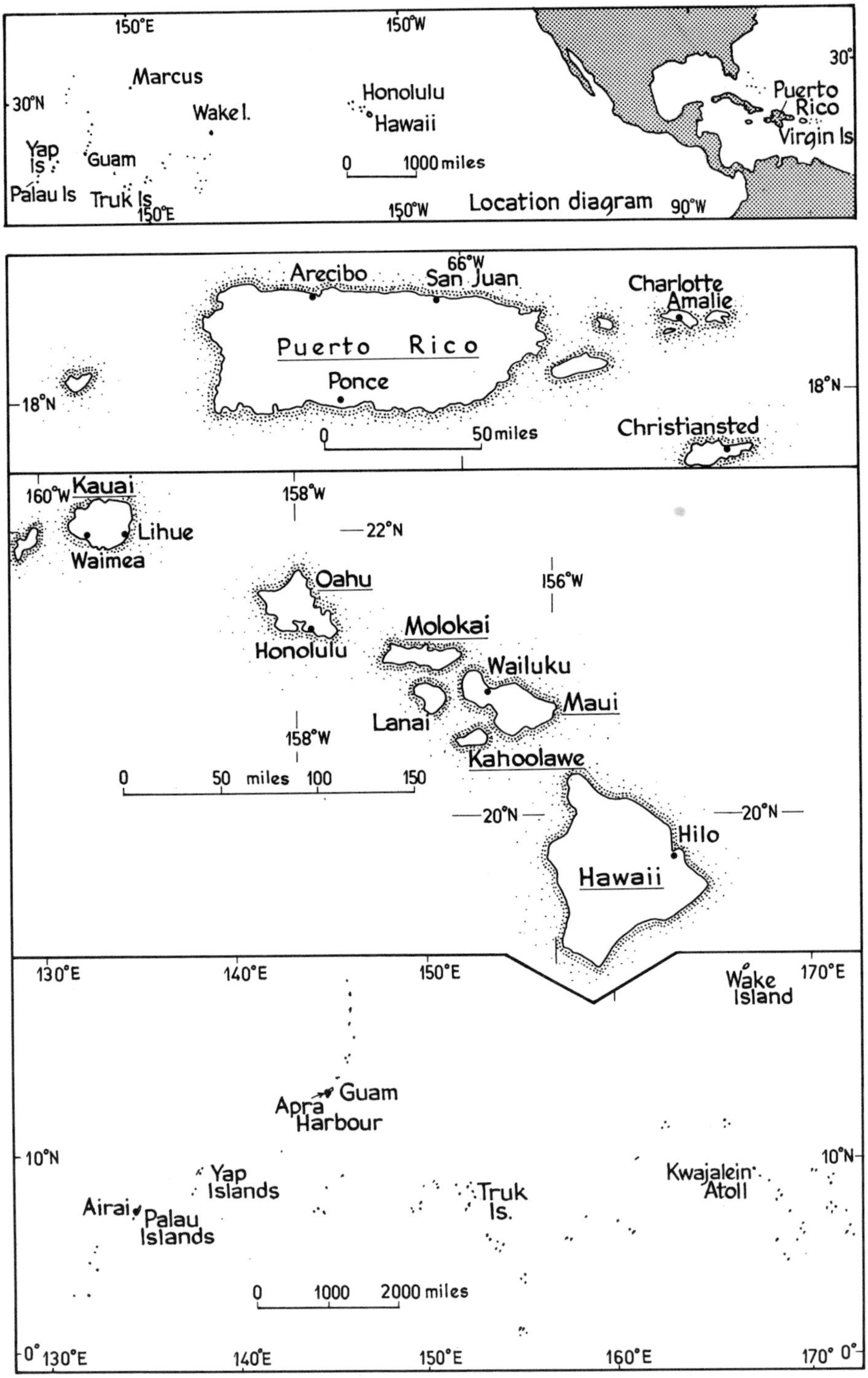

Fig. 19:2 Offshore America (continued).

within a few years by the negotiated Gadsden Purchase. Perry's irruption into the lengthy isolation of Japan, in the same year 1854 wherein the Gadsden Purchase was concluded, was scarcely an act of imperialism. Alaska was bought in 1867; Midway Island, taken by the U.S.A. also in 1867, was unoccupied at the time.

The Spanish–American War of 1898, by contrast with the earlier Mexican War, could be, and was, interpreted in the U.S.A. in the simplest possible fashion – namely, as a struggle against the colonialism of Europe. Although the mainland colonies in South and Central America had broken away from Spain and Portugal early in the century, Spain still retained others in the Caribbean, the greatest of them Cuba and Puerto (then Porto) Rico. A revolt in Cuba gave the U.S.A. the opportunity to supply assistance, and in 1898 to demand the recognition by Spain of Cuban independence, plus removal of Spanish forces from the island. Spain's refusal precipitated a brief war, wherein that country's Atlantic and Pacific fleets were both destroyed. Cuba became independent, effectively for a time under the protection of the U.S.A., and until 1934 under certain inhibitions with regard to its treaty relationships with foreign powers; as events of the mid-twentieth century have proved, the U.S.A. is fully justified in feeling sensitive about the strategic possibilities of the Caribbean in general and of Cuba in particular. Puerto Rico was ceded completely to the U.S.A., as also were the Philippines – eventually to become fully independent in 1946 – and Guam in the Marianas. The U.S.A. possessed bases within 2500 miles of Japan, and well within 1000 miles of China.

It is needless to trace the complex history of the island of Hispaniola, between Cuba and Puerto Rico: suffice it to say that conflicts among Spanish, French, and British figure in its colonial history, and that Haiti in the west became independent in 1804, and the Dominican Republic in the east in 1821. Here, less than 600 miles from the nearest part of the U.S. mainland, is another potential trouble-spot. Both countries were occupied by the U.S.A., the one from 1915 to 1934, the other from 1916 to 1924: the cause of the occupation was strategic – protection of the Panama Canal. The same cause justified the U.S. purchase of the Virgin Islands from Denmark in 1917, and the leasing of options on bases in Nicaragua.

The Canal might at one time have been the Nicaraguan Canal; but the declaration of Panamanian independence of Colombia in 1903 was rapidly followed by a treaty between the U.S.A. and the new republic, providing for the opening and operation of a water link between the two oceans. U.S. engineers, supported by adequate doctoring, succeeded in a task on which the French had laboured for twenty years in face of the overwhelming and finally overpowering attacks of insect-borne disease. The fifty-mile canal, opened in 1914, has proved a signal economic success: its tolls have been held down to the original level, but still amount to $75 million annually from the 12,000 ships which pass through. Strategically, its importance was at once made obvious. It is, however, now too small for the largest vessels, and is being widened from the original limiting width of 300 feet to one of 500 feet. The ten-mile-wide Canal Zone is, by treaty, granted to the U.S.A. in perpetuity for use, occupation, and control; but the treaty is not now fully enforced.

Among the Pacific Island groups, the Hawaiian Islands were taken over by the U.S.A. in 1898, the year of the Spanish–American War: but the annexure had nothing to do with this conflict. When Cook discovered the Islands in 1778 there were four separate kingdoms and a population of 300,000. Diseases introduced by European sailors reduced the population to 50,000, greatly damaged the economy, and weakened the political structure. By the late nineteenth century the single existing Polynesian monarchy was very weak. It was overthrown in 1893 in a revolution led by North Americans; and the annexure of five years later was strongly backed by New England capitalists with investments in sugar planting.

American Samoa passed to the U.S.A. in consequence of treaties with Germany and Britain in 1899–1900, and of cession by the local chiefs. Its people, 20,000 in number, are mainly Polynesians, but are classed as U.S. nationals inhabiting an unincorporated territory. In the Caroline, Marshall, and Mariana Islands (Guam excepted) the U.S.A. acts as United Nations trustee, succeeding Japan, the former League of Nations mandatory power: earlier, before World War I, these islands had been imperial possessions of Germany. The three groups make up Micronesia, comprising more than 2000 islands or atolls – less than 700 square miles of land in 3 million square miles of ocean, and fewer than 100 inhabited. Truk and Yap became battlefields during World War II. After that war, the U.S.A. assumed control also of the Ryukyu Islands, chief among them Okinawa, which had formerly been in Japanese hands. At the end of 1968 the Ryukyus were returned to Japanese administration, with U.S. bases guaranteed by treaty.

19a: The Hawaiian Islands

Area: about 6400 square miles.

Population: 700,000, of whom about 120,500 are military personnel and dependents.

Largest cities:

Honolulu, on Oahu, 295,000 (500,500 in the metropolitan area)

Hilo, on Hawaii, 26,000

Sixty per cent of the land area is in farms.

In the main group there are eight principal islands; the archipelago also includes numerous smaller islands extending northwestwards to Midway. In order from the northwest, the principal islands are Niihau (72 square miles), Kauai (555 square miles), Oahu (604 square miles) on which stands the capital, Honolulu; Molokai (260 square miles), Lanai (141 square miles), Maui (728 square miles), Kohoolawe (45 square miles), and Hawaii (4090 square miles), from which the group takes its name.

The largest islands rise 30,000 feet above the deep ocean floor, and in Mauna Kea on Kauai attain nearly 14,000 feet above sea-level. The whole Hawaiian group is volcanic in origin, constructed in the course of millions of years as volcanic activity has shifted eastwards along a suboceanic crustal fissure. On Kauai, the westernmost of the large islands, eruptions ceased long enough ago to permit the cutting of canyons which incise the lavas to depths of more than half a mile. In contrast, the volcano Kilauea on the island of Hawaii is still distinctly active and frequently in eruption.

The volcanoes of this archipelago are lava domes, formed of fluid basalt. Explosion-craters occur in places, and the volcanic deposits include some dust, but the typical mode of eruption for a very long period has been the extrusion of lava from large vents known as calderas. Moving downslope at each eruption, the lava has constructed great crustal bosses on the ocean bed, forming islands where it rises above the sea. As in the Snake–Columbia Plateau, basalt can sustain steep slopes: but in the Hawaiian Islands the steep slopes belong not to dissected edges of basalt flows but to sea-cliffs or to the precipitous inclined walls of valleys inland. All the older basalt areas are complexly grooved by nets of valleys. Despite the fact that the basalt in bulk is permeable, the climate is warm enough, and in most parts also wet enough, to promote powerful weathering and general sculpture of the ground.

Climatically, Hawaii belongs in the A group of the Köppen classification (see Chapter Four) – specifically, to the Am class of winterless climate with monsoonal, or seasonal, characteristics of rainfall. Temperatures run consistently high at low altitudes; daily and seasonal ranges are alike slight (Fig. 4:8, graph for Honolulu). Moisture comes in on the Northeast Trades. These are great rain-bringers: Mount Waialeale, for instance, averages more than 400 inches a year. Aspect and altitude count for much: rain is typically released from the thick unstable clouds which form on windward slopes, whereas lee slopes at low levels can lie in deep rain-shadows, with average precipitation as low as 10 inches. Temperature, as everywhere, declines with increasing height, here from a sea-level mean of 82° F (28° C). Vegetation ranges upward from tropical rain-forest to tropical grassland and cactus. Parent materials of soil consist chiefly of basic lava, including some fresh and unweathered flows, but also comprise coral limestone, coastal sand, and volcanic loess; these last three kinds underlie 10 per cent of the total area. So extensive is fresh lava, and so ruggedly dissected a great deal of the high ground, that no more than a tenth of the group's land area has fully-formed soils. Apart from bare rock and lithosols, the principal soil cover is latosolic, reddish- to yellowish-brown in colour, acid in reaction, and with little contrast in the profile. Above the limit of cultivation, which varies from 1500 to 5000 feet, the latosols carry rain-forest.

Despite the raininess of many districts, water-supply for agriculture has its problems: the rate of

82. Harvesting pineapples in Hawaii.

soil-moisture depletion is high, and serious deficiencies can occur in the hotter part of the year, which is also the least rainy (Fig. 4:12, graph for Honolulu).

Cultivation looks to the conterminous U.S.A. for a large part of its market. Sugar, grown under the unified control of the Hawaiian Sugar Planters Association, brings in more than half of Hawaii's agricultural income; the annual output from Hawaii's twenty-seven raw sugar-mills, about 1·2 million tons a year, satisfies more than 40 per cent of the U.S. domestic demand. Raw sugar is shipped to Crockett, California, where the H.S.P.A. has a refinery. The main sugar-producing islands are Oahu, Hawaii, Maui, and Kauai; most canefields are located on the windward side of the islands, although the supply of cane from irrigated fields in rain-shadowed districts is increasing. Application of Chilean nitrogenous fertilizer raises yields to more than 9000 lb of sugar per acre. In all, sugar production employs a workforce 50,000 strong. Canefields range from those of company plantations through tenant farms to owner-operated holdings.

Pineapples are processed for canning and juicing by nine companies, who take a considerable share in the field operations of pineapple growing. Production and processing of this fruit absorb a workforce of 25,000. Unlike sugar-cane planting, pineapple growing requires machinery – to grade the fields, open ditches, and to gather the crop. Work-gangs, often Filipinos or Koreans, follow the loading machine, placing the cut pineapples on to its conveyor belt (Plate 82). Filled boxes are carted off by high-standing tractors.

Coffee of the parchment variety is produced in the Kona district of Hawaii, largely by Japanese growers. The archipelago as a whole contains nearly 600 coffee farms. The commercial farms which raise sugar-cane, pineapples, and other tropical fruit number about 3000. In addition, there are some 3500 subsistence farms, and some beef cattle ranches catering for the tourist demand.

Apart from the craft industries associated with the tourist trade, manufacturing in Hawaii is almost wholly in the form of food-processing – sugar and tropical fruits, and tuna canning which takes about 10 million pounds of fish a year. Civilian employment in dockyards and military bases is great; and there is, of course, much employment generated by, although not directly absorbed by, these various installations.

Planters were responsible for introducing indentured labour from China, Japan, the Philippines, and elsewhere: and Chinese came independently to trade. Some of the descendants of the imported plantation workers have moved well up the social and economic scale, so that Hawaiian society is very mixed indeed. In addition to the descendants of the incoming workers and traders, and to the Hawaiians themselves, it includes numbers of North Americans – some permanent residents, others servicemen or dependents: there are also tourists from many countries. Among the population of the archipelago are 210,000 stateside Americans (5000 of them Negroes), about 80,000 native Hawaiians, 203,000 Japanese (of whom 30,000 are foreign born), 69,000 Filipinos, 38,000 Chinese, and less numerous groups who total 102,000 in all. There is some tendency for particular groups to concentrate on particular forms of activities – Filipinos on farm and plantation work, Japanese on market gardening, coffee growing, and poultry keeping, Koreans on fishing, and Chinese on market gardening and retailing.

During World War II, the bombing by Japan of the U.S. fleet in Pearl Harbor provoked the authorities to intern the whole of the Japanese in Hawaii. Only 37,000 of the 157,000 involved were, however, foreign-born; the internment of the remainder led to an outcry of protest. Subsequently, the U.S. authorities were sufficiently reassured of the loyalty of the Hawaiian-born Japanese, not only to release them, but also to recruit from them a battalion for service against the Imperial Japanese forces. It is difficult to imagine a similar event in many parts of this politically straitened world: perhaps the spontaneity and good humour of the Polynesians has contributed something to the ease and stability of a plural society in which intermarriage is frequent and few stresses are apparent.

These attributes certainly assist the tourist trade. Visitors to the islands number well over half a million a year; and about half of them are simply on tour. Others make stop-overs from transPacific flights, have business on the islands, or are connected with governmental or military activities. Visitors to Hawaii spend $265 million annually, placing the tourist industry in the first rank as an income-earner. It is not however the chief provider of income, for the federal wages paid to public servants and servicemen total more than the receipts from sugar production, pineapple growing, and the tourist trade combined.

Hotels or hotel-apartment establishments in the archipelago number more than 15,000; most are on Oahu, which contains the international airport of Honolulu. By the mid-1970s it is forecast that 20,000 or 25,000 establishments will offer tourist accommodation, for the trade is confidently expected to expand when giant jet-liners bring fares down. More than 90 per cent of the visitors who stay for one day or more already come by air; the remainder arrive on the transPacific ocean liners and cruises which interconnect the U.S.A., Hawaii, Tahiti, New Zealand, and Australia. The great majority of visitors, 98 per cent, are from the U.S.A., 54 per cent from West Coast States. Canada takes a 1·3 per cent share, while twenty-five additional countries contribute the other small fraction.

Honolulu has an excellent natural harbour, which contains the Pearl Harbor naval base. The city merges eastward into suburban Waikiki, the main resort location on Oahu. Hilo, the centre of tourism on Hawaii Island, offers access to the active volcanoes of Mauna Kea, Mauna Loa, and Kilauea, in Hawaii National Park.

19b: Puerto Rico and the Virgin Islands

Area: 3435 square miles (Puerto Rico)
133 square miles (Virgin Islands)
Population: 2,660,000 (Puerto Rico)
50,000 (Virgin Islands)

Largest cities: population of some metropolitan areas given in brackets:

San Juan, Puerto Rico, 450,000 (600,000)
Ponce, Puerto Rico, 14,000 (146,000)
Mayaguex, Puerto Rico, 50,000 (84,000)
Arecibo, Puerto Rico, 70,000
Caguas, Puerto Rico, 65,000

The largest settlement in the Virgin Islands is Charlotte Amelie (13,000) on St Thomas.

Population density outside the metropolitan areas or towns listed: in Puerto Rico, 510 per square mile; in the Virgin Islands, 275 per square mile. About half the population of Puerto Rico is rural. Most of the land of Puerto Rico is under cultivation of some kind: sugar-cane takes 15 per cent of the total area.

Puerto Rico is not fully integrated into the U.S.A., although its nationals may pass freely to and from the mainland. Large numbers of them live permanently in New York City's West Side; but since they are not separately classed in published census summaries, their total cannot be given. The island is subject to U.S. conscription but not to U.S. taxes; it sends to Congress an elected Commissioner, who however does not vote. Independence is on offer, but at present seems less probable than Union: the independence party polled less than 3 per cent of the votes cast at the 1964 elections, whereas the statehood party collected 33 per cent – it would doubtless have attracted still more, had it not been committed exclusively to the policy of one of the two mainland parties, and that party moreover the one out of office at the time.

Forming part of the strongly folded Antillean chain, Puerto Rico is distinctly hilly throughout most of its extent. Dissection is deep and complex on the mountain side, which faces the trade winds: these bring rain amounting to 60 inches a year near the coast, rising to well over 100 inches on the high ground of the interior, where the tallest summits exceed 4000 feet above sea-level. The south, perennially rain-shadowed, is much drier, with 35 to 45 inches a year – an inadequate supply for a climate where temperatures average somewhere in the seventies the whole year round. Residual patches of uncultivated cover in the south indicate that the original wild vegetation here was scrub forest: the north, and the high ground of the centre, presumably at one time carried rain-forest, but almost all the ground here is, or has been, under cultivation. Reforestation is going on, in the form of projects encouraged by the U.S. government, but the planted timber is not yet mature enough for cutting.

Areas of permanent cultivation are used intensively for the production of oranges and other citrus fruit, coconuts, coffee, sugar-cane, pineapples, tobacco, and bananas, sustaining a produce export trade to the U.S.A. led by sugar ($\frac{3}{4}$ million tons a year, $125 million), tobacco leaf (7 million lb, $30 million), and rum (3 million gallons, $10 million). Exports of oranges can however find markets closed to them by quarantine regulations, while coffee farms have suffered severely from competitors elsewhere in the Caribbean and in South America. The generally impoverished coffee-growing areas, concentrated mainly on the steep rainy slopes of the west-centre, provide a large fraction of migrants to the U.S.A.; to some extent they are being taken over by pineapple planters, who raise fruit smaller than that of Hawaii but reputedly better in flavour.

Pressure of the increasing population on the available land during the early years of World War II led the U.S. government to set up a Puerto Rican Land Authority, with power to buy from corporations – chiefly, corporations domiciled on the mainland – holding in excess of 500 acres. The 500-acre rule had previously existed for many years, but was widely disregarded: a few sugar companies held almost all the land available for commercial planting, either in growing plantations or for bullock-grazing; and soil erosion had seriously damaged land taken out of cane-growing. The reforms instituted from 1940 onwards enable bought-out land to provide small allotments, with homesteads, for hitherto landless would-be farmers. Somewhat larger family farms are leased to farmers of proven competence. Still other land has been allocated to collective farms by groups. Because of the political connotations of the term *collectives*, these farms are called *proportional profit farms*: they now number more than sixty, most of them producing sugar-cane.

As in the days of company planting, the sugar farms of today, like all farms on the island, are exposed to the risk of occasional hurricanes. These, curving westward and northward along the Antilles, can at their most severe destroy the entire season's crop. A further problem is that much of the work of the cane farms is seasonal; and although the growing season is long, the working year still includes a period of slackness and resulting unemployment.

The sugar industry, with its twenty raw-sugar mills, has profited by the discord between the U.S.A. and Cuba which followed the 1959 overthrow of the former Cuban dictatorship; but the growing or processing of cane do not suffice as the mainstay of the island's economy. Concerned with the sagging of this economy, the U.S. government encourages North American investment in manufacturing industry in Puerto Rico; and revenue from manufacturing now exceeds that from farming and forestry combined. Exports of textile, garments, timber products, and leather goods are worth well over the combined export value of sugar, tobacco, and rum. More than 90 per cent of total trade is with the U.S. mainland.

Puerto Rico offers manufacturers abundant and cheap labour, exemption from company taxes for a period of ten years, and – most importantly – duty-free access to the mainland market. The government assumes the responsibility for selecting and training industrial workers, and also extends help with marketing and transport. As a further means of stimulating the island economy it promotes tourism – for example, financing the construction of the luxury Caribe Hilton Hotel. Visitors, who number more than a million annually, can savour the insular tropics in Puerto Rico at less expense than in Hawaii.

Tourism in the Virgin Islands is also deliberately promoted. This group, formed by St Croix (82 square miles), St Thomas (32 square miles), St John (19 square miles), and some fifty small and mainly untenanted islands, has its production of sugar, rum, cattle, and vegetables; but its great assets are its tropical maritime location, its scenery, its winter climate, and the liberal tax exemptions offered to those prepared to invest in industry or in the tourist trade. Of the total population of 40,000, only about 1000 live on St John; but this island alone can cater for half a million visitors a year and collect $50 million annually in tourist income. Water-supply is a problem: St Thomas operates a desalting plant with a capacity of one million gallons per day. These islands increased their population by 50 per cent between the 1950 and the 1960 census: whatever the ultimate origins of wealth in an industrial society, it is at least clear that access to industrial raw materials is not alone involved.

BIBLIOGRAPHY

Chapters 1 and 2

American Geographical Society (1952): *Readings in the Geography of North America.*

Dominion Bureau of Statistics, Ottawa: *Canada Year Book* (annual).

Dominion Bureau of Statistics, Ottawa: *Canada* (annual handbook).

R. L. Gentilcore (ed.): *Canada's Changing Geography.* Prentice-Hall of Canada, Scarborough, Ontario.

C. M. Green: *American Cities in the Growth of the Nation.* Athlone Press, London.

M. Jensen (ed.): *Regionalism in America.* University of Wisconsin Press.

W. R. Mead and E. H. Brown: *The United States and Canada – A Regional Geography.* Hutchinson, London.

G. J. Miller, A. E. Parkins, and B. Hudgins: *Geography of North America.* John Wiley & Sons, New York.

R. Minshull: *Regional Geography – Theory and Practice.* Hutchinson, London.

J. H. Paterson: *North America – A Regional Geography.* Oxford University Press, London.

D. F. Putnam (ed.): *Canadian Regions – A Geography of Canada.* J. M. Dent & Co., London.

C. S. Tomkins and T. L. Hills: *A Regional Geography of North America.* W. J. Gage Ltd., Toronto.

M. C. Urqhart and K. A. H. Buckley (eds.): *Historical Statistics of Canada.* Macmillan Co. of Canada, Toronto.

U.S. Department of Commerce: *Statistical Abstract of the United States* (annual).

U.S. Department of Commerce: *Historical Statistics of the United States.*

J. Warkentin (ed.): *Canada – A Geographical Interpretation.* Methuen, Toronto.

C. L. White and E. J. Foscue: *Regional Geography of Anglo-America.* Prentice-Hall, Englewood Cliffs, N.J.

W. W. Wood and R. S. Thoman (eds.): *Areas of Economic Stress in Canada.* Industrial Relations Centre, Queen's University, Kingston, Ontario.

Chapters 3 and 4

E. A. Ackerman: 'The Köppen classification of climates in North America.' *Geog. Review*, **31** (1941), 105–11.

W. A. Albrecht: 'Soil fertility and biotic geography.' *Geog. Review*, **47** (1957), 86–105.

W. W. Atwood: *The Physiographic Provinces of North America.* Ginn & Co., Boston.

R. T. Coupland: 'A reconsideration of grassland classification in the Northern Great Plains of North America.' *Journ. Ecology*, **49** (1961), 135–67.

A. Court: 'Temperature extremes in the United States.' *Geog. Review*, **43** (1953), 39–49.

R. F. Flint: *Glacial and Pleistocene Geology.* John Wiley & Sons, New York.

S. Haden-Guest, J. K. Wright, and E. M. Tacleff (eds.): 'A World Geography of Forest Resources.' *Amer. Geog. Soc., Spec. Pubn. No.* **33**, B(1956). Ronald Press Co., New York.

F. K. Hare: 'The boreal conifer zone.' *Geog. Studies*, **1** (1954), 4–18.

C. Hodge and P. C. Duisberg (eds): *Aridity and Man.* American Association for the Advancement of Science, Washington, D. C.

S. S. Holland: 'Landforms of British Columbia – A Physiographic Outline.' *B.C. Dept. Mines & Petr. Resources, Bull.* **48** (1964). Queen's Printer.

P. B. King: *Evolution of North America.* Harvard University Press.

D. B. Lawrence: 'Glacial fluctuation for six centuries in South-Eastern Alaska and its relations to solar activity.' *Geog. Review*, **40** (1950), 191–223.

A. K. Lobeck: *Physiographic Diagram of North America.* C. S. Hammon & Co., Maplewood, N.J.

A. R. Suner: 'Standard deviation of monthly temperature in Anglo-America.' *Geog. Review*, **43** (1953), 50–59.

W. D. Thornbury: *Regional Geomorphology of the United States.* John Wiley & Sons, New York.

C. W. Thornthwaite: 'An approach towards a rational classification of climate.' *Geog. Review*, **38** (1948), 55–94.

S. S. Visher: *Climatic Atlas of the United States.* Harvard University Press.

H. Williams (ed.): *Landscapes of Alaska.* University of California Press.

Chapters 5 and 6

R. A. Billington: *America's Frontier Heritage.* Holt, Rinehart, and Winston, New York.

J. B. Bird: 'Settlement Patterns in maritime Canada, 1687–1786.' *Geog. Review*, **45** (1955), 385–404.

H. E. Bolton and T. M. Marshall: *The Colonization of North America 1492–1783.* Macmillan, New York.

R. H. Brown: *Historical Geography of the U.S.A.* Harcourt, Brace & Co., New York.

D. Creighton: *The Empire of the St Lawrence.* Macmillan Co. of Canada, Toronto.

R. England: *The Colonization of Western Canada – a Study of Contemporary Land Settlement (1896–1934).* P. S. King & Sons, London.

S. E. Forman: *A History of the American People.* Allen & Unwin, London.

J. K. Fornoe: *Norsemen Before Columbus.* Allen & Unwin, London.

H. R. Frus: 'A series of population maps of the Colonies and the United States, 1625–1790.' *Geog. Review*, **30** (1940), 463–79.

R. L. Gentilcore: 'The agricultural background of settlement in eastern Nova Scotia.' *Ann. Assoc. Amer. Geog.*, **46** (1956), 378–404.

R. C. Harris: *The Seigneurial System in Early Canada.* University of Wisconsin Press.

W. T. Jackson: *Wagon Roads West.* University of California Press.

E. C. Kirkland: *A History of American Economic Life.* Appleton, New York.

L. C. A. Knowles: *The Economic Development of the British Overseas Empire – Canada, vol II.* Routledge & Sons, London.

D. W. Meinig: 'Colonization of wheatlands: Some Australian and American comparisons.' *Austr. Geog.*, **7** (1959), 205–13.

R. B. Nye and J. E. Mopurgo: *The Birth of the U.S.A.* (vol. I of *A History of the United States*). Penguin Books, Harmondsworth, Middx.

R. B. Nye and J. E. Mopurgo: *The Growth of the U.S.A.* (vol. II of *A History of the United States*). Penguin Books, Harmondsworth, Middx.

T. J. Oleson: *Early Voyages and the Northern Approaches, 1000–1632.* McClelland and Stewart, Toronto.

C. O. Paullin: *Atlas of the Historical Geography of the U.S.* Carnegie Inst. & Amer. Geog. Soc., Washington and New York.

F. J. Phol: *The Viking Explorers.* Thom. Crowell Co., New York.

R. E. Riegel and R. G. Athearn: *America Moves West.* Holt, Rinehart, and Winston, New York.

R. M. Robbins: *Our Landed Heritage, The Public Domain, 1776–1936.* P. Smith, Gloucester, Mass., and Lincoln, Nebr., University Press.

C. O. Sauer: 'A geographical sketch of early man in America.' *Geog. Review*, **34** (1944), 529–73.

F. Thistlethwaite: *The Great Experiment: An introduction to the History of the American people.* Cambridge University Press, 1955.

J. W. Watson: 'The influence of the frontier on Niagara settlements.' *Geog. Review*, **38** (1948), 113–19.

Chapter 7

C. D. Harris: 'Agricultural production in the United States – the past fifty years and the next.' *Geog. Review*, **47** (1957), 175–93.

L. Haystead and G. C. Fife: *The Agricultural Regions of the United States.* Methuen & Co., London and Oklahoma University Press.

E. Higbee: *American Agriculture – Geography, Resources, Conservation.* John Wiley & Sons, New York.

H. B. Johnson: 'Rational and ecological aspects of the quarter section.' *Geog. Review*, **47** (1957), 330–48.

F. J. Marschner: *Land Use and its Patterns in the United States.* U.S. Dept. of Agriculture (1959).

M. Prunty: 'The renaissance of the Southern plantation.' *Geog. Review*, **45** (1955), 459–91.

U.S. Department of Agriculture: *Land* (1958 Yearbook).

U.S. Department of Agriculture: *Power to Produce* (1960 Yearbook).

B. G. Vanderhill: 'Post-war agricultural settlement in Manitoba.' *Econ. Geog.*, **35** (1959), 259–68.

Chapter 8

H. H. Bennett: *Soil Conservation.* McGraw-Hill Co., New York.

R. A. Bryson and J. E. Kutzbach: *Air Pollution.* Association of American Geographers, Washington, D.C.

I. Burton and R. W. Kates (eds.): *Readings in Resource Management and Conservation.* University of Chicago Press.

R. M. Highsmith, J. G. Jensen, and R. D. Rudd: *Conservation in the United States.* Rand McNally, Chicago.

J. V. Krutilla and O. Eckstein: *Multiple Purpose River Development.* Resources for the Future, Inc., Johns Hopkins Press, Baltimore.

H. H. Landsberg: *Natural Resources for U.S. Growth.* Johns Hopkins Press, Baltimore.

P. A. Leighton: 'Geographical aspects of air pollution.' *Geog. Review*, **56** (1966), 151–74.

P. Meigs: 'Water problems in the United States.' *Geog. Review*, **42** (1952), 346–66.

C. F. Powers and A. Robertson: 'The ageing Great Lakes.' *Scientific American*, **215** (1966), 94–104.

G. H. Smith (ed.): *Conservation of Natural Resources.* John Wiley & Sons, New York.

G. F. White: 'Industrial water use – a review.' *Geog. Review*, **50** (1960), 412–30.

Chapter 9

W. Adams (ed.): *The Structure of American Industry.* Macmillan, New York.

J. W. Alexander: *Economic Geography.* Prentice-Hall, Englewood Cliffs, N.J.

G. Alexandersson: *The Industrial Structure of American Cities.* Allen & Unwin, London.

G. Alexandersson: 'Changes in the location pattern of the Anglo-American steel industry, 1948–1959.' *Econ. Geog.*, **37** (1961), 95–114.

H. Boesch: *A Geography of World Economy*. Van Nostrand, Princeton, N.J.

P. Camu, E. P. Weeks, and Z. W. Lametz: *Economic Geography of Canada*. Macmillan Co., of Canada, Toronto.

R. C. Estall and R. O. Buchanan: *Industrial Activity and Economic Geography*. Hutchinson, London.

C. D. Harris: 'The market as a factor in the localization of industry in the United States.' *Ann. Assoc. Amer. Geog.*, **44** (1954), 315–48.

W. Isard and W. M. Capron: 'The future locational pattern of iron and steel production in the U.S.A.' *Journ. Polit. Econ.*, **17** (1949), 118–33.

G. Manners: *The Geography of Energy*. Hutchinson, London.

E. W. Miller: *A Geography of Manufacturing*. Prentice-Hall, Englewood Cliffs, N.J.

A. K. Philbrick: *This Human World*. John Wiley & Sons, New York.

A. Pred: 'Towards a typology of manufacturing flows.' *Geog. Review*, **54** (1964), 65–84.

H. C. Roepke and T. J. Maresh (eds.): *Readings in Economic Geography*. John Wiley & Sons, New York.

R. S. Thoman: *The Geography of Economic Activity*. McGraw-Hill Co., New York.

C. L. White: 'Water – a neglected factor in the geographical location of iron and steel.' *Geog. Review*, **47** (1957), 463–89.

R. A. Will: 'Federal influences on industrial location.' *Land Economics*, **40** (1964), 49–57.

Chapter 10

L. Chevrier: *The St Lawrence Seaway*. Macmillan Co. of Canada, Toronto.

D. Creighton: *The Empire of the St Lawrence*. Macmillan Co. of Canada, Toronto.

T. L. Hills: *The St Lawrence Seaway*. Methuen, London.

D. P. Locklin: *Economics of Transportation*. Richard D. Irwin, Inc., Homewood, Illinois.

D. J. Patton: 'General cargo hinterlands of New York, Philadelphia, Baltimore and New Orleans.' *Ann. Assoc. Amer. Geog.*, **48** (1958), 436–55.

J. F. Stover: *American Railroads*. Chicago University Press.

R. S. Thoman and E. C. Conkling: *Geography of International Trade*. Prentice-Hall, Englewood Cliffs, N.J.

E. L. Ullman: *American Commodity Flows*. University of Washington Press.

Chapter 11

J. K. Hadden and E. F. Borgatta: *American Cities – Their Social Characteristics*. Rand McNally, Chicago.

P. Haggett: *Locational Analysis in Human Geography*. Edward Arnold, London.

P. Hall: *The World Cities*. Weidenfeld and Nicolson, London.

J. F. Hart: 'Changing distribution of the American negro.' *Ann. Assoc. Amer. Geog.*, **50** (1960), 242–66.

E. Higbee: *The Squeeze – Cities Without Space*. Wm. Morrow & Co., New York.

A. L. Kroeber: *Cultural and Natural Areas of Native North America*. University of California Press, Berkeley.

E. N. Thomas: 'Areal associations between population growth and selected factors in the Chicago urbanised area.' *Econ. Geog.*, **36** (1960), 159–70.

J. Warkentin: 'Mennonite agricultural settlements of southern Manitoba.' *Geog. Review*, **49** (1959), 342–68.

G. Wissler: *Indians of the United States – Four Centuries of Their History and Culture*. Doubleday, New York.

Chapter 12

L. M. Alexander: *The North-Eastern United States*. Van Nostrand, Princeton, N.J.

G. W. Carey: 'The regional interpretation of Manhattan – population and housing patterns through factor analysis.' *Geog. Review*, **56** (1966), 551–69.

G. F. Deasy and P. R. Griess: 'Local and regional differences in long-term bituminous coal production in the eastern United States.' *Ann. Assoc. Amer. Geog.*, **57** (1967), 519–33.

L. Durand: 'The historical and economic geography of dairying in the North Country of New York State.' *Geog. Review*, **57** (1967), 24–47.

R. C. Estall: *New England – A Study in Industrial Adjustment*. Bell, London.

J. C. Gottman: 'Megalopolis, or the urbanisation of the Northeastern Seaboard.' *Econ. Geog.*, **33** (1957), 189–200

J. C. Gottman: *Megalopolis*. Twentieth Century Fund (Plimpton Press), New York.

J. B. Kenyon: 'The industrial structure of the New York garment center.' in R. S. Thoman and D. J. Patton (eds.), *Focus on Geographic Activity*. McGraw-Hill Co., New York, 159–66.

D. Kerr: 'Geography of the Canadian iron and steel industry.' *Econ. Geog.*, **35** (1959), 151–63.

N. M. McArthur: 'Recreational Resources of Ontario's St Lawrence Frontier.' in R. S. Thoman and D. J. Patton (eds.), *Focus on Geographic Activity*. McGraw-Hill Co., New York, 194–99.

E. W. Miller: 'The southern anthracite region.' *Econ. Geog.*, **31** (1955), 331–50.

A. Rodgers: 'The iron and steel industry of the Mahoning and Shenango Valleys.' *Econ. Geog.*, **28** (1952), 331–42.

C. J. Sharer: 'The Philadelphia iron and steel district – its relation to the seaways.' *Econ. Geog.*, **39** (1963), 363–67.

J. O. Wheeler and E. D. Brunn: 'Negro migrations into rural southwestern Michigan.' *Geog. Review*, **58** (1968), 214–30.

Chapter 13

L. Durand: 'Mountain moonshining in East Tennessee.' *Geog. Review*, **46** (1956), 168–86.

J. F. Hart: 'Functions and occupational structure of cities of the American South.' *Ann. Assoc. Amer. Geog.*, **45** (1955), 269–86.

R. E. Lonsdale: 'Two North Carolina commuting patterns.' *Econ. Geog.*, **42** (1966), 114–38.

W. H. Nicholls: 'Human resources and industrial development in the upper East Tennessee Valley, 1900–1950.' *Quart. J. Econ.*, **71** (1957), 289–316.

H. R. Padgett: 'Some physical and biological relationships to the fisheries of the Louisiana coast.' *Ann. Assoc. Amer. Geog.*, **56** (1966), 423–39

J. Parsons: 'Some recent industrial developments in the Gulf South.' *Geog. Review*, **40** (1950), 67–83.

M. Prunty: 'Recent expansions in the Southern pulp-paper industries. *Econ. Geog.*, **32** (1956), 51–57.

G. W. Schesselman: 'The Gulf Coast oyster industry.' *Geog. Review*, **45** (1955), 531–41.

Chapter 14

A. F. Burghardt: 'The location of river towns in the Central Lowlands of the United States.' *Ann. Assoc. Amer. Geog.*, **49** (1959), 305–23.

J. H. Garland (ed.): *The North American Midwest*. John Wiley & Sons, New York, and Chapman & Hall, London.

L. P. Hoag: 'Location determinants for cash-grain farming in the Corn Belt.' *Professional Geographer*, **14** (1962), 1–7.

H. B. Johnson: 'Location of German immigrants in the Middle West.' *Ann. Assoc. Amer. Geog.*, **41** (1951), 1–41.

M. Kaups: 'Finnish place names in Minnesota – a study of cultural transfer.' *Geog. Review*, **56** (1966), 377–97.

T. L. McKnight: 'The distribution of manufacturing in Texas.' *Ann. Assoc. Amer. Geog.*, **47** (1957), 370–78.

C. F. Kohn and R. E. Specht: 'The mining of taconite, Lake Superior iron mining district.' *Geog. Review*, **48** (1958), 528–39.

W. M. Kollmorgen and D. S. Simonett: 'Grazing operations in the Flint Hills bluestem pastures of Chase County, Kansas.' *Ann. Assoc. Amer. Geog.*, **55** (1965), 260–90.

H. M. Mayer: 'Prospects and problems of the port of Chicago.' *Econ. Geog.*, **31** (1955), 95–125.

M. W. Reinemann: 'The pattern and distribution of manufacturing in the Chicago area.' *Econ. Geog.*, **39** (1960, 139–44.

A. Sas: 'Dutch concentrations in rural southwestern Ontario during the post-war decade.' *Ann. Assoc. Amer. Geog.*, **48** (1958), 185–94.

J. C. Weaver: 'Crop-combination regions in the Middle West.' *Geog. Review*, **44** (1954), 175–200.

J. C. Weaver: 'Changing patterns of cropland use in the Middle West.' *Econ. Geog.*, **30** (1954), 1–47.

Chapter 15

M. Clawson: 'An institutional innovation to facilitate land use changes in the Great Plains.' *Land Economics*, **34** (1958), 74–79.

D. F. Doeppers: 'The Globeville neighbourhood in Denver.' *Geog. Review*, **57** (1967), 506–22.

A. H. Doerr and J. W. Morris: 'The Oklahoma Panhandle – a cross-section of the Southern High Plains.' *Econ. Geog.*, **36** (1960), 70–88.

L. Hewes: 'Causes of wheat failure in the dry farming region, Central Great Plains, 1939–1957.' *Econ. Geog.* **41** (1965), 313–30.

A. V. Johnson: 'Relative decline of wheat in the Prairie Provinces of Canada.' *Econ. Geog.*, 24 (1948), 209–16.

W. M. Kollmorgen and G. F. Jenks: 'Sidewalk farming in Toole County, Montana, and Traill County, North Dakota.' *Ann. Assoc. Amer. Geog.*, **48** (1958), 209–31.

G. M. Lewis: 'William Gilpin and the concept of the Great Plains Region.' *Ann. Assoc. Amer. Geog.*, **56** (1966), 33–51.

M. J. Loeffler: 'The population syndromes on the Colorado Piedmont.' *Ann. Assoc. Amer. Geog.*, **55** (1965), 26–66.

W. A. Mackintosh: *Prairie Settlement*. Macmillan Co., of Canada, Toronto.

M. W. Mikesell: 'Comparative studies in frontier history.' *Ann. Assoc. Amer. Geog.*, **50** (1960), 62–74.

E. Rostlund: 'The geographic range of the historic bison in the Southeast.' *Ann. Assoc. Amer. Geog.*, **50** (1960), 395–407.

B. H. Vanderhill: 'The direction of settlement in the Prairie Provinces of Canada.' *Geog. Journ.*, **58** (1959), 325–33.

J. K. Villmore: 'The nature and origin of the Canadian Dry Belt.' *Ann. Assoc. Amer. Geog.*, **46** (1956), 211–32.

Chapter 16

W. G. V. Balchin and N. Pye: 'Recent economic trends in Arizona.' *Geog. Journ.*, **120** (1954), 156–73.

W. Calef: *Private Grazing and Public Lands*. University of Chicago Press.

D. R. Harris: 'Recent plant invasions in the arid and semi-arid Southwest of the United States.' *Ann. Assoc. Amer. Geog.*, **56** (1966), 408–22.

C. H. Holmes: 'Development of the steel industry in intermontane America.' *Geog. Journ.*, **58** (1959), 20–31.

P. D. McGovern: 'British Columbia Natural Resources Conference – an approach to co-ordinated regional development.' *Scot. Geog. Mag.*, **76** (1960), 164–69.

D. W. Meinig: 'The Mormon culture region – strategies and patterns in the geography of the American West.' *Ann. Assoc. Amer. Geog.*, **55** (1965), 191–220.

D. W. Meinig: 'The comparative historical geography of two railnets – Columbia Basin and South Australia.' *Ann. Assoc. Amer. Geog.*, **52** (1962), 394–413.

J. L. Robinson: 'Canada's western Arctic.' *Canadian Geog. Journ.*, **37**(b) (1948), 242–259.

J. E. Vance: 'The Oregon Trail and Union Pacific Railroad – a contrast in purpose.' *Ann. Assoc. Amer. Geog.*, **51** (1961), 357–79.

T. E. Weir: 'Winter feeding period in Southern Interior Plateau of British Columbia.' *Ann. Assoc. Amer. Geog.*, **44** (1954), 194–204.

T. E. Weir: 'Ranching in the Southern Interior Plateau of British Columbia.' *Memoir 4, Geogr. Branch, Mines and Tech. Surveys*, Ottawa.

Chapter 17

G. B. Barbour: 'Kitimat.' *Geog. Journ.*, **125** (1959), 217–22.

G. F. Fielding: 'The Los Angeles milkshed – a study of the political factor in agriculture.' *Geog. Review*, **54** (1964), 1–12.

K. E. Francis: 'Outpost agriculture – the case of Alaska.' *Geog. Review*, **57** (1967), 496–505.

R. L. Gentilcore: 'Missions and mission lands of Alta California.' *Ann. Assoc. Amer. Geog.*, **51** (1961), 46–72.

H. F. Gregor: 'Industrialised drylot farming – an overview.' *Econ. Geog.*, **39** (1963), 299–318.

P. F. Griffin and R. L. Chatham: 'Urban impact on agriculture in Santa Clara County, California.' *Ann. Assoc. Amer. Geog.*, **48** (1958), 195–208.

W. G. Hardwick: 'Port Alberni, British Columbia, Canada – an integrated forest industry in the Pacific Northwest,' in R. S. Thoman and D. J. Patton (eds.), *Focus on Geographic Activity*. McGraw-Hill Co., New York, 60–66.

D. C. Large: 'Cotton in the San Joaquin Valley – a study of government in agriculture.' *Geog. Review*, **47** (1957), 365–80.

J. F. Lounsbury: 'Recent developments in the aluminum industry of the United States.' *Journ. Geog.*, **61** (1962), 97–104.

M. E. Marts and W. R. D. Sewell: 'The conflict between fish and power resources in the Pacific Northwest.' *Ann. Assoc. Amer. Geog.*, **50** (1960), 42–50.

R. S. Mathieson: 'Economic trends in the Alaska salmon industry.' *Austr. Geog.*, **8** (1960), 17–24.

D. W. Meinig: 'Colonization of wheatlands – some Australian and American comparisons.' *Austr. Geog.*, **7** (1959), 145–46.

H. J. Nelson: "Spread of an artificial landscape over southern California.' *Ann. Assoc. Amer. Geog.* (supplement), (1959), 80–99.

E. T. Price: 'Future of California's Southland.' *Ann. Assoc. Amer. Geog.* (supplement), (1959), 101–16.

H. F. Raup: 'Transformation of southern California to cultivated land.' *Ann. Assoc. Amer. Geog.* (supplement), (1959), 58–78.

R. Siddall: 'Seattle – regional capital of Alaska.' *Ann. Assoc. Amer. Geog.*, **47** (1957), 277–84.

R. Steiner: 'Reserved lands and the supply of space for Southern California Metropolis.' *Geog. Review*, **56** (1966), 344–62.

K. Stone: 'Populating Alaska.' *Geog. Review*, **49** (1959), 76–94.

K. Thompson: 'Riparian forests of the Sacramento Valley, California.' *Ann. Assoc. Amer. Geog.*, **51** (1961), 294–315.

R. N. Young and P. C. Griffin: 'Recent landuse changes in the San Francisco Bay area.' *Geog. Review*, **47** (1957), 396–405.

Chapter 18

R. J. E. Brown: 'The Mackenzie River Delta.' *Canadian Geographer*, No. **7** (1956), 21–26.

G. Humphrys: 'Schefferville, Quebec – a new pioneering town.' *Geog. Review*, **48** (1958), 151–66.

T. Lloyd: 'Iron ore production in Quebec – Labrador,' in R. S. Thoman and D. J. Patton (eds.), *Focus on Geographic Activity*. McGraw-Hill Co., New York, 85–92.

G. L. McDermott: 'Frontiers of settlement in the Great Clay Belt, Ontario and Quebec.' *Ann. Assoc. Amer. Geog.*, **51** (1961), 261–73.

E. W. Miller: 'Hudson Bay railway route – a geographical reconnaissance.' *Geog. Journ.*, **57** (1958), 163–73.

E. W. Miller: 'Mineral regionalism of the Canadian Shield.' *Canadian Geographer*, No. **13** (1959), 17–30.

E. W. Morse: 'Voyager's highway – the geography and logistics of the Canadian fur trade.' *Canadian Geog. Journ.*, **62** (1961), 148–61, and **63** (1961), 3–17 and 65–75.

N. L. Nicholson: 'The face of the North.' *Canadian Geog. Journ.*, **57** (1958), 70–75.

N. L. Nicholson: 'The Northwest Territories – geographical aspects.' *Canadian Geog. Journ.*, **57** (1958), 3–27.

J. Sonnenfeld: 'Changes in Eskimo hunting technology. *Ann. Assoc. Amer. Geog.*, **50** (1960), 172–86.

J. Sonnenfeld: 'An Arctic reindeer industry – growth and decline.' *Geog. Review*, **49** (1959), 76–94.

C. R. Twidale: 'Recent and future developments in the Labrador Peninsula.' *Austr. Geog.*, **7** (1959), 103–12.

R. I. Wolfe: 'Transportation and politics – the example of Canada.' *Ann. Assoc. Amer. Geog.*, **51** (1961), 261–73.

Chapter 19

L. Durand: 'The dairy industry of the Hawaiian Islands.' *Econ. Geog.*, **35** (1959), 228–46.

P. F. Griffin: 'Geographic aspects of Californian and Hawaiian sugar industry.' *Journ. Geog.*, **53** (1954), 325–41.

A. W. Lind: *Hawaii's Japanese – an Experiment in Democracy*. Princeton University Press.

J. F. Lounsbury: 'Farmsteads in Puerto Rico and their interpretative value.' *Geog. Review*, **45** (1955), 347–58.

D. D. MacPhail: 'Puerto Rico dairying – a revolution in tropical agriculture.' *Geog. Review*, **53** (1963), 224–46.

INDEX

Entries in italic indicate the main sections on that subject.